Families Across Cultures

Contemporary trends such as the increasing number of one-parent families, high divorce rates, second marriages and homosexual partnerships have all contributed to variations in the traditional family structure. But to what degree has the function of the family changed and how have these changes affected family roles in cultures throughout the world? This book attempts to answer these questions through a psychological study of families in thirty nations, carefully selected to present a diverse cultural mix. The study utilizes both cross-cultural and indigenous perspectives to analyze variables including family networks, family roles, emotional bonds, personality traits, self-construal, and "family portraits" in which the authors address common core themes of the family as they apply to their native countries. From the introductory history of the study of the family to the concluding indigenous psychological analysis of the family, this book is a unique source for students and researchers in psychology, sociology, and anthropology.

JAMES GEORGAS is Professor Emeritus of Psychology at the University of Athens, Greece.

JOHN W. BERRY is Professor Emeritus of Psychology at Queen's University, Ontario, Canada.

FONS J.R. VAN DE VIJVER is Professor of Cross-Cultural Psychology at Tilburg University, the Netherlands, and Extraordinary Professor at North-West University, South Africa.

ÇIĞDEM KAĞITÇIBAŞI is Professor of Psychology at Koç University, Istanbul.

YPE H. POORTINGA is Emeritus Professor of Cross-Cultural Psychology at Tilburg University, the Netherlands, and at the Catholic University of Leuven, Belgium.

Families Across Cultures

A 30-Nation Psychological Study

Edited by

James Georgas, John W. Berry, Fons J. R. van de Vijver, Çiğdem Kağıtçıbaşı, and Ype H. Poortinga

CAMBRIDGE
UNIVERSITY PRESS

CAMBRIDGE UNIVERSITY PRESS
Cambridge, New York, Melbourne, Madrid, Cape Town, Singapore, São Paulo

CAMBRIDGE UNIVERSITY PRESS
The Edinburgh Building, Cambridge CB2 2RU, UK
Published in the United States of America by Cambridge University Press,
New York

www.cambridge.org
Information on this title: www.cambridge.org/9780521529877

© Cambridge University Press 2006

First published 2006

Printed in the United Kingdom at the University Press, Cambridge

A catalogue record for this book is available from the British Library

ISBN-13 978-0-521-82297-8 hardback
ISBN-10 0-521-82297-1 hardback
ISBN-13 978-0-521-52987-7 paperback
ISBN-10 0-521-52987-5 paperback

This book is dedicated to

Στην οικογένεια μου, την Κατερίνα και τον Αλέξανδρο καί, επίσης, σε όλους τους δεκάδες συγγενείς J. G.

All my family, Joan, Heather, Susan, Michael, David, Chris, Janice, Emma, Alex, Nolan, Owen, Graeme, and Charlotte for their strong belief in the importance of family. J. W. B.

Aan onze ouders van wie wij de betekenis van gezin en familie hebben geleerd. F. J. R. v. d. V. and Y. H. P.

Bütün aileme: Oğuz, Elif, Emrah, Ebru, Ece, Rana, Murat, Kitty, Defne onlarin eşleriyle çocuklarina. Ç. K.

Contents

Figures

Tables

Contributors

MUSTAFA M. ACHOUI, Department of Management and Marketing, King Fahd University of Petroleum and Minerals, Dhahran, Saudi Arabia

BOLANLE ADETOUN, CESDEG, Rhosgift, South Africa

ADEBOWALE AKANDE, The Institute of Research and Consultancy, Rhosgift, South Africa

CHARITY AKOTIA, Department of Psychology, University of Ghana, Legon, Accra, Ghana

BENJAMIN AMPONSAH, Department of Psychology, University of Ghana, Legon, Accra, Ghana

BILGE ATACA, Department of Psychology, Bogazici University, Bebek, Istanbul, Turkey

JOHN W. BERRY, Department of Psychology, Queen's University, Kingston, Ontario, Canada

TUYA BUYANTSOGT, Department of Psychology and Pedogogy, Mongolian National University, Ulaanbaatar, Mongolia

KITTY K. C. CHAN, University Health Service, The University of Hong Kong, Pokfulam, Hong Kong, SAR

NEOPHYTOS CHARALAMBOUS, Institute for Personal-Family and Professional Development, Nicosia, Cyprus

SOPHIA CHRISTAKOPOULOU, Chester, United Kingdom

PETER CUYVERS, Den Haag, Netherlands

MARIA AUXILIADORA DESSEN, Colina-UnB, University of Brasilia, Brasilia, Brazil

ROLANDO DIAZ-LOVING, Faculty of Psychology, National Autonomous University of Mexico, Mexico City, Mexico

FRANCISCO DONOSO-MALUF, Department of Psychology, University of La Serena, Coquimbo, Chile

AIKATERINI GARI, Department of Psychology, University of Athens, Athens, Greece

JAMES GEORGAS, Department of Psychology, University of Athens, Athens, Greece

ARTEMIS GIOTSA, Department of Psychology, University of Athens, Athens, Greece

ROBIN GOODWIN, Department of Human Sciences, Brunel University, Uxbridge, United Kingdom

HECTOR GRAD, Department of Social Anthropology, Autonomous University of Madrid, Madrid, Spain

ÇIĞDEM KAĞITÇIBASI, School of Arts and Sciences, Koç University, Istanbul, Turkey

HEIDI KELLER, Department of Developmental Psychology, University of Osnabrück, Osnabrück, Germany

UICHOL KIM, Inha University, Incheon, South Korea

ELENA KRASTEVA, Sofia, Bulgaria

KYUNGHWA KWAK, Department of Psychology, Queen's University, Kingston, Canada

PETER W.H.LEE, Department of Psychiatry, The University of Hong Kong, Hong Kong SAR, China

VELISLAVA MARINOVA-SCHMIDT, Nürnberg, Germany

YUWANNA JENNY MIVANYI, Department of Education, Kaduna Polytechnic, Kaduna, Kaduna State, Nigeria

SHAHRENAZ MORTAZAVI, Department of Education and Psychology, University of Shahid Beheshti, Tehran, Iran

YUKIKO MURAMOTO, Faculty of Business Administration, Yokohama National University, Yokohama, Japan

KOSTAS MYLONAS, Department of Psychology, University of Athens, Athens, Greece

AKINSOLA OLOWU, University of Cape Coast, Ghana

JOHNSTO OSAGIE, FAMU, Rhosgift, South Africa

VICKY PANAGIOTIDOU, Department of Psychology, University of London, London, United Kingdom

PENNY PANAGIOTOPOULOU, Department of Psychology, University of Athens, Athens, Greece

JANAK PANDEY, Department of Psychology, University of Allahabad, Allahabad, India

YOUNG-SHIN PARK, Deptartment of Education, Inha University, Incheon-si, South Korea

VASSILIS PAVLOPOULOS, Department of Psychology, University of Athens, Athens, Greece

GÉRARD PITHON, Department of Psychology, Paul Valery University, Montpellier, France

OLIVIER PRÉVÔT, Social Workers Institute, University of Franche-Comté, France

YPE H. POORTINGA, Department of Psychology, Tilburg University, Tilburg, the Netherlands and the Catholic University of Leuven, Leuven, Belgium

BERNADETTE N. SETIADI, Faculty of Psychology, Atma Jaya University, Jakarta, Indonesia

BASILIA SOFTAS-NALL, Division of Professional Psychology, University of Northern Colorado, Greeley, Colorado, United States of America

SUNITA MAHTANI STEWART, University of Texas Southwestern Medical Center, Dallas, Texas, United States of America

DENIS G. SUKHODOLSKY, Child Study Center, Yale University, New Haven, Connecticut, United States of America

NANA SUMBADZE, Department of Psychology, Tbilisi State University, Tbilisi, Georgia

CLÁUDIO V. TORRES, Department of Social and Work Psychology, University of Brasilia, Brasilia, Brazil

MAGGIE TSERERE, University of Pretoria, Tshwane, South Africa

FONS J. R. VAN DE VIJVER, Department of Psychology, Tilburg University, Tilburg, the Netherlands, and Workwellness, North-West University, South Africa

RIFFAT MOAZAM ZAMAN, Department of Psychiatry, Aga Khan University, Karachi, Pakistan

TAYMIYA RIFFAT ZAMAN, Department of History, University of Michigan, Ann Arbor, Michigan, United States of America

IRINA ZHURAVLIOVA, Athens, Greece

Acknowledgments

There are many people and institutions to thank for their aid in the preparation of this book. The development over the past 20 years of the Family Values Scale, the Emotional Distance Scale, and the Family Roles Scale was accomplished with the help of a number of close colleagues at the University of Athens, once students and now holding positions in universities or working independently as psychologists. We want to thank them for the opportunity that was given to me to be able to work closely with them and for their continual stimulation throughout the years: Aikaterini Gari, Sophia Christakopoulou, Kostas Mylonas, Tsabika Bafiti, Penny Panagiotopoulou, Vassilis Pavlopoulos, Litsa Papademou, and Artemis Giotsa. Many thanks are due to the Research Committee of the University of Athens for their financial support of some of the work on this project, and to the Center for Cross-Cultural Research, University of Athens, and the Center for Family Studies of the Department of Psychology, University of Athens, for their continual aid, encouragement and support. We are grateful to Mel and Carol Ember for their encouragement and comments on Chapter 1.

We would like to thank Sarah Caro, formerly editor at Cambridge University Press, for her support of this project. Many thanks to Andrew Peart, commissioning editor in psychology, and Jackie Warren, production editor, for their advice and continual help in completing this book and the staff of Cambridge University Press for their work in preparing the final manuscript for publication.

James Georgas, Athens, Greece
John W. Berry, Kingston, Canada
Fons van de Vijver, Tilburg, the Netherlands
Çiğdem Kağıtçıbaşı, Istanbul, Turkey
Ype H. Poortinga, Tilburg, the Netherlands

Prologue

This book is about similarities and differences in families across cultures. Family has been studied during the past two centuries by many disciplines, including sociology, cultural anthropology, psychology, education, psychiatry, economics, and historical demography, among other disciplines.

The perspective in this book is the relationships between psychological variables, the ecocultural context of countries, and family variables.

The book centers around three issues. The first examines how families differ in cultures across the world. What are the differences in family networks, family roles, and psychological variables among countries with different ecological and sociopolitical systems?

The second issue examines how families are alike across cultures. That is, to what degree are features of family similar in countries throughout the word?

The third issue involves family changes in societies throughout the world as a result of social changes, such as economic level, education, political systems, the global influence of television, and of communication through telephones, email, and the internet. Changes in family types in the last two centuries, as a result of industrialization and urbanization, have been described as transitions from the extended types of family systems to the nuclear family and more recently to the one-parent family. Understanding the nature of these developments is of scientific interest, but these changes are also important social issues in almost all countries throughout the world; research on the family has influenced government policies in many countries. Some family researchers as well as the media and governments talk about the crisis of the institution of family. Others have predicted the death of the family. Others have described the changes as adaptations to economic and social changes in today's world, and assert that the family is undergoing a transformation, but will continue to be an important social institution.

For some family sociologists, cultural anthropologists, and psychologists, these changes are considered to lead to an inevitable convergence of the types of family structure, function, and psychological relationships in the Majority World toward those characteristics found in North America and Northern Europe. Modernization and globalization theories would predict, as supported by some family experts, the inevitable convergence, sooner or later, of family types, involving changes from the extended family types in non-Western to the nuclear family and the one-person family of Western societies. However, over a hundred years of cultural anthropological studies have documented the diversity of family types in thousands of societies throughout the world and how different family types are embedded in ecological and cultural factors such as means of subsistence, religion, values, and traditions. The question is whether the forces of economic development as embodied in modernization theory and globalization theory will inevitably result in the convergence of family types, or whether cultural factors and psychological factors related to bonding and children are strong enough to maintain diversity in family types, despite changes in the economic and social systems of countries.

This book describes the results of a 30-nation project, in which the countries were chosen so as to represent the different geopolitical zones around the globe: north (Canada, the United States), central (Mexico), and south America (Brazil, Chile); north (the Netherlands, France, Germany, the United Kingdom) and south Europe (Greece, Bulgaria, Turkey, Cyprus, Spain); north (Algeria), east (Saudi Arabia), central (Nigeria, Ghana), and south Africa (South Africa, Botswana); west (Ukraine, Georgia, Iran); south (Pakistan, India), and east Asia (China, Japan, Mongolia, South Korea); and Oceania (Indonesia).

The project was guided by hypotheses stemming from the Ecocultural Framework of Berry (1976, 1979) and the Model of Family Change of Kağıtçıbaşı (1990, 1996a).

The editors are cross-cultural psychologists and the approach is that of cross-cultural psychology. The analysis is from two perspectives: cross-cultural and indigenous. The cross-cultural quantitative analyses are based on data from variables at four hierarchical levels: cultural level ecological and sociopolitical variables; family roles; family networks; and the psychological variables: emotional bonds with members of the nuclear family and kin, personality traits, self-construal, family values, and personal values.

The analyses are directed toward determining similarities and differences among countries in the relationships among the four hierarchical levels. In addition, the findings were not only analyzed between the countries, but between clusters of countries, or "cultural zones" based on ecological and sociopolitical variables of cultures. The similarities among countries may represent psychological universals in family structures and in psychological variables across cultures.

The second perspective was the indigenous approach, which analyzed the common themes across countries, based on descriptions of the relationships between cultural, family and psychological variables in "family portraits" written by the authors in each of the 30 countries. (The quantitative analyses were based on data from 27 of the 30 countries.)

Part 1 consists of eight chapters presenting the theories and findings of family studies, the theory, and methodology of cross-cultural psychology, common themes across the family portraits, the hypotheses of the study, the methodology of the project, the results, and the synthesis.

Chapter 1, Families and family change by James Georgas, reviews the theories and the findings on culture and family, based on the literature from primarily sociological and cultural anthropological studies. The definitions of family are presented and discussed with the goal of seeking a universally applicable definition of family types across cultures. This is followed by discussions of the sociological family theories of the nineteenth century, and the findings of studies of family change and family networks in Western societies. The next section discusses the study of family history and the development of nuclear and extended families in Western countries. The methodological problems related to determining types of families, primarily nuclear and extended, based on demographic data are then discussed. The final section discusses family change in non-Western countries, followed by an examination of the predictions of modernization theory and globalization as possible explanations for family change in these countries and the convergence of family structures and family functioning with those of Western societies.

Chapter 2, Cross-cultural theory and methodology by John W. Berry and Ype H. Poortinga, presents the concepts of cross-cultural theory, culture, and human biology, and discusses three theoretical approaches to how cultural and biological factors are reflected in the course of human psychological development (termed *absolutism, relativism,* and *universalism*). The complementary approaches of the "cultural," the "indigenous," and the "comparative" schools of thinking about cultural and biological influences are then related to these three theoretical

approaches. The Ecocultural Framework of J. W. Berry is one of the
approaches that guides the research reported in this book. From this
perspective, family is considered as an institution that is adapted to its
ecological, cultural, and sociopolitical situation, and in turn provides
the main context for the ontogenetic development from infancy to adulthood. The final section discusses methodological issues in cross-cultural
psychology and their links with the implication of universalism in aspects
of psychological functioning that are common to humans in all cultures.

Chapter 3, Theoretical perspectives on family change by Çiğdem
Kağıtçıbaşı, presents a related conceptual approach to understanding
family dynamics and change from a cross-cultural psychological perspective, with an emphasis on changing global social structural and
ecocultural contexts. The literature on the current Western family,
which has served as a prototype for family research in sociology, is
discussed, followed by the non-Western family, both in the "Majority
World" and also as immigrant communities in the Western countries.
The patterns of change are explained with a comparative orientation
and from an ecocultural perspective. The Model of Family Change
(Kağıtçıbaşı, 1990, 1996a) that has proven useful in understanding
family patterns in relation to different ecocultural contexts is then
presented.

Chapter 4, Family portraits from 30 countries: an overview by Ype
H. Poortinga and James Georgas, is an analysis of the important themes
emerging from the qualitative descriptions of the family portraits in
Part 2 of this book. Each author has presented a family portrait of
the country, from an indigenous perspective, with a standard format so
as to be comparable across the portraits. The chapter summarizes
the common aspects of change in families across the countries, and
functions and roles that have remained much the same.

Chapter 5, Hypotheses by John W. Berry, Çiğdem Kağıtçıbaşı, James
Georgas, Ype H. Poortinga, and Fons J. R. van de Vijver, presents the
hypotheses of the study. The first section presents the hypotheses stemming from Berry's Ecocultural Framework, the second presents the
hypotheses based on Kağıtçıbaşı's Model of Family Change, and the
third presents some specific hypotheses based on the literature from
family studies.

Chapter 6, Methodology of the study by James Georgas, Fons J. R.
van de Vijver, John W. Berry, Çiğdem Kağıtçıbaşı, and Ype
H. Poortinga, describes the methods of analysis. The first section presents an overview of the four levels of analyses: ecocultural, social
structural, family roles, and individual. The second section describes
characteristics of the samples in 27 countries employed in the study and

characteristics of the samples of students in each country (total sample $N = 5,482$). The third section describes the variables and the procedures employed in the study.

Chapter 7, Results: cross-cultural analyses of the family by Fons J. R. van de Vijver, Kostas Mylonas, Vassilis Pavlopoulos, and James Georgas, provides an overview of the cross-cultural data analyses. The first two sections involve the analyses of the psychometric properties of the instruments, that is, they construct equivalence of the variables across countries, and the effects of gender and educational level of the parents of the respondents. The next two sections involve the cross-cultural data analyses and the testing of hypotheses.

Chapter 8, Synthesis: how similar and how different are families across cultures? by James Georgas, John W. Berry, and Çiğdem Kağıtçıbaşı presents a synthesis of the findings of the study. The predictions of the Ecocultural Framework of Berry and the Model of Family change of Kağıtçıbaşı, as well as hypotheses based on the general family literature are discussed. The extent to which families are changing throughout the world, as a result of changes in social, media, information technology, increase in education, reduction of agriculture as the primary means of economic subsistence, and other cultural changes, and the degree to which there are similarities among countries, are discussed and related to the literature on family and family change. The findings are also discussed in terms of modernization and globalization theory.

Part 2 consists of the 30 family portraits and ethnographic descriptions of the participating countries.

Part I

1 Families and family change

James Georgas

INTRODUCTION

The family has been studied within various disciplines, including sociology, cultural anthropology, psychology, education, psychiatry, economics, and demography from the early nineteenth century. This chapter will focus primarily on sociological and cultural anthropological studies of family, with some reference to psychological studies. Chapter 2 by John W. Berry and Ype H. Poortinga will present cross-cultural theory and methodology and its relationship to the study of family. Chapter 3 by Çiğdem Kağıtçıbaşı will present theoretical perspectives on the family, and psychological aspects of the family.

The first section of this Chapter discusses definitions of the family. The definition should be universally applicable across all cultures, account for the variety of types of families, and for recent developments such as the increase of cohabiting, unmarried parents, one-parent families, and homosexual families.

The second section discusses the sociological family theories of the nineteenth century, which presented basic issues related to family change in response to industrialization and urbanization. Family sociology played a major role in the study of family change in the twentieth century, with the theory of Parsons its most seminal influence. Cultural anthropology differed from sociological theories in that it explored the diversity of family structures and functions in thousands of small societies throughout the world, rather than primarily in Western societies, and it continues to influence studies of family and family change.

Family change in Europe, the United States, and Canada is discussed in the next section. Two theories of family change characterize sociological and anthropological thinking in the past 200 years: theories that emphasize family decline and breakdown and theories that emphasize the adaptive elements of family change. Family change in the Majority World, a concept coined by Çiğdem Kağıtçıbaşı, referring to countries outside of the geographical areas of Western societies, is discussed in the next section.

The following section discusses family networks. The findings of research on social support indicate the importance of studying not only the nuclear family but also interrelationships with kin.

The next section presents the study of the history of the family and its analysis of the types of families and family change in societies before the nineteenth century.

The section "Household and family: nuclear and extended families" discusses methodological problems related to determining types of families, primarily nuclear and extended, based on demographic data.

The final section discusses the processes of modernization and globalization as possible explanations of family change in the Majority World, as well as the potential of modernization processes in the convergence of family structures and family functioning with those of Western societies.

DEFINITIONS OF FAMILY

There are numerous definitions of family from different theoretical perspectives, stemming primarily from sociology and anthropology. The term "family" is used by many Western sociologists and psychologists as synonymous with "nuclear family," that is, mother, father, and children. But this perception may reflect to a certain degree cultural values of Western societies about family. In most nations of the rest of the world, grandparents, aunts and uncles, cousins, from both sides of the parents, and even unrelated persons are considered to be "family." That is, as will be discussed in detail further on, in most cultures throughout the world, kinship relations are included in the definition of family.

An acceptable definition of family should assume that family is a universal and necessary institution for human survival in all societies, a statement with which almost all social and behavioral scientists agree. However, as will be discussed later in this chapter, types of families vary across the thousands of societies throughout the world. There are also different family types in most, particularly large, societies. The categorization of the types of families by sociologists and cultural anthropologists enables us to look at family types with similar as well as different structures and functions. Thus, definitions of family, as all definitions, necessarily refer to the minimal criteria for agreement as to what constitutes a family, so that the definition is universally appropriate in all cultures.

One definition of family which served as a point of reference for anthropology for decades was that of Murdock (1949, p. 2): "The family is a social group characterized by common residence, economic cooperation, and reproduction. It includes adults of both sexes, at least two of whom maintain a socially approved sexual relationship, and one or more children, own or adopted, of the sexually cohabiting adults." Murdock's analysis of 250 small societies led him to conclude that the nuclear family was a universal human social grouping, either as the sole prevailing form of the family or as the basic unit from which more complex familial forms are compounded. This minimal definition of family has been challenged by some anthropologists (Bohannan, 1963; Goodenough, 1970; Fortes, 1978, as cited in Yanagisako, 1979) who offer evidence from some societies that the basic core of the family is the mother and her dependent children. Thus, evidence from even a small number of cultures has been used to challenge the definition that the nuclear family is the "building block" of extended families.

Murdock's definition has also been challenged, based on recent changes in the United States, Canada and northern Europe, in relation to the increase in one-parent families, including divorced, adoptive, unmarried, or widowed mothers, and same-sex families. For example, in sociologist Popenoe's (1988) definition, which has influenced the debate about the definition of family, (a) the minimal family composition is one adult and one dependent person, (b) the parents do not have to be of both sexes, (c) the couple does not have to be married.

A second aspect of the definition of family has to do with its functions as a social institution. Murdock defined the functions of the family as sexual, economic, reproductive, and educational. In the study of families in many small societies throughout the world by cultural anthropologists, one finding seemed to be universal: the emphasis on genealogical relationships as a key element in families. Thus, procreation appeared to be a primary function of families in all societies (Bender, 1967; Goody, 1983; Murdock, 1949; Yanagisako, 1979). A second function was socialization of the child, primarily by the mother, but also by other caretakers such as grandmothers, sisters, and aunts. Economic cooperation of the members also appeared to be a key function of the family because subsistence was the means of family survival.

We can come to a tentative conclusion at this point that the issue of the definition of family is controversial at the present time. On the other hand, some (Needham, 1974; Yanagisako, 1979) suggest that words like "family" are useful as descriptive statements but that the concept reflects an inherently complex, multifunctional institution with different cultural principles and meanings. Indeed, some argue that in light of the variety of family types and kinship systems in societies throughout the world, it might be better to talk about "families" rather than attempting to define the irreducible core of "family" as two-person or nuclear. However, in order to provide a standard so that the reader will be able to follow the discussion in this chapter, we will usually use the term "nuclear" or "two-generation" family in referring to a family with mother, father, and child, unless we specifically refer to a one-parent family. The different types of "extended families" will also be referred to as "three-generation" families. In addition, Murdock's paradigm of the extended family as a constellation of nuclear families at different levels of generation is a useful heuristic framework for viewing the relationship between the one-parent, the nuclear, and the extended types of families, and will be employed as a construct guiding the theory and methodology of this study, despite its limitations. We will return to the issue of the definition of family in the section "Family and household".

SOCIOLOGICAL FAMILY THEORIES OF THE NINETEENTH CENTURY

The scientific analysis of the role of the family in society began in France in the nineteenth century with the new science of sociology. Auguste Comte, considered by many to be the father of sociology, viewed changes in the family as a product of the French revolution. That is, the rejection of the hierarchical and autocratic relations between the aristocracy and the common people and the subsequent introduction of the egalitarian climate in the relations between all citizens after the French Revolution also had, according to Comte, a "leveling effect" on the relations between the members of the family which had a negative effect on the patriarchal authority of the family. Thus, Comte analyzed family change in terms of "social change," a concept which developed into the major theme in subsequent sociology and family sociology in the nineteenth century. His idea that social change results in family crisis and family disintegration, disturbing the equilibrium of the traditional extended family system, also became a recurrent theme in family sociology.

Some (Mitterauer and Sieder, 1982; Popenoe, 1988; Segalen, 1996) identify Frédéric Le Play (1855, 1871) as the founder of empirical family sociology. Le Play also perceived family change and the emergence of the nuclear family as a product of the industrial revolution. His theory described the stem family (*famille souche*), consisting of the parents and the eldest son, who inherited the family property, together with his family and the other unmarried children, as the dominant family type in France. The other married sons necessarily left the family home and formed separate nuclear families during the industrial revolution. Le Play also characterized the nuclear family as inherently unstable because it was separated both physically and financially from the stem family.

Le Play's theory of industrialization and the emergence of the nuclear family is considered to be a micro theory rather than a macro theory. The three influential sociological theories of the family in the nineteenth century were more complex and specified in more detail the dynamics between social change and biological evolution and their effects on family.

Evolutionary theory

Darwin's theory of evolution strongly influenced thinking in the nineteenth century. The seminal ideas of biological adaptation to the environment were also applied to theories of the adaptation of the family as a social organism to the physical and social environment. Lewis Henry Morgan (1870) has been identified with evolutionary anthropology and the explanation of the evolutionary development of family through six stages. The first stage was a horde in which promiscuity was the norm, paternity was difficult to establish, and thus the family was basically matriarchal (Popenoe, 1988), and the final stage was the monogamous family. In contrast to Le Play and Comte, that social changes resulted in the progressive decline and fragmentation of the family, Morgan argued, in line with Darwin's theory, that evolution results in the higher development of the species and that social and environmental evolution result in a higher level of development of family. This theory, which reached its epitome in the nineteenth century, was characteristic of the "civilized" nations of Europe and North America, while other "primitive" cultures at "lower" stages of social evolution had lower levels of family structure and function.

Evolutionary theory was also adopted by others, such as Herbert Spencer (1870), another proponent of social Darwinism, to explain how the family evolved from simple to more complex forms and to its present state of high development. However, Spencer was criticized in his view because his explanation was the opposite of theories of family sociologists such as Le Play and Marx and Engels, in which family appeared to devolve from complex extended family systems to simpler nuclear family systems (Popenoe, 1988). Spencer also contributed to family theory with the concept of structural-functionalism, a concept further developed by Durkheim and which formed the basis of Parsons' theory of family change in the nineteenth century, although biological evolutionary theory was not a significant element in Parsons' theory.

The ideas of social evolutionism were unacceptable to many cultural anthropologists in the twentieth century, led by Franz Boas and his students, such as Melville Herskovits, Ruth Benedict, and Margaret

Mead, who argued that evolutionism did not take into account the variations in family types resulting from different cultural contexts throughout the world. They employed the concept *cultural relativism*, that family and other aspects of society should be studied within the context of its culture, and rejected the idea that some cultures were more civilized than others. Although Benedict and Herskovits (as cited in Ember and Ember, 2002) took an extreme position of cultural relativism – that the values of each society were unique and should not be judged by comparison with other cultures – this viewpoint is not shared by all contemporary anthropologists.

Evolutionary theory was criticized at the end of the nineteenth century by Westermarck (1894–1901) and Howard (1904, as cited in Popenoe, 1988). They found no evidence for the stages of early promiscuity and matriarchy in prehistoric families. Evolutionary theory became a moribund theory until it resurfaced in the 1930s in a different form as Ecological Anthropology (Orlove, 1980). The concepts of ecological anthropology were attributed to the work of Julian Steward and Leslie White, students of Boas, and to Daryll Forde. The main features of the theory were the relationship between characteristics of the environment and traits of the culture. The method was comparative, in that similarities – or regularities – in cultural history or in ecological features were sought.

Marx and Engels

A major family theory in the nineteenth century was influenced by Marx ([1867], 1936) and Engels ([1884], 1942). In contrast to the explanatory power of biological determinism in Social Darwinism, Marxist theory employed the concept of economic determinism to explain how economic resources determined social power, which in turn determined class struggle. Employing a historical analysis of the family, and relying partly on the evolutionary model of Morgan, Engels came to a different conclusion as to the status of the family in the nineteenth century. Engels and Marx explained how the patriarchal family, based on the right of private property and the authority and power of the father, resulted in the defeat of the female and the matriarchal system in prehistoric hunting and gathering societies. Industrialization, based on capital and private property, led to the creation of the monogamous bourgeois family in urban centers. The result was that the bourgeois family became an economic unit to be exploited by the capitalistic system and an instrument of class oppression, particularly of women and children, and the dissolution of the family. The solution was, with the dissolution of the capitalist system, the doing away with the bourgeois family, the liberation of the woman and the introduction of collectivist rearing of children. Thus, although Marx and Engels employed a historical analysis of the family, their conclusion was that family change in the nineteenth century was regressive, the antithesis of evolutionary theory which perceived family change in industrialized Europe and North America as progressive (Popenoe, 1988). Marxist family theory has recently had a fairly strong influence in feminist theories of family, particularly regarding gender differences in power.

Structuralism–functionalism

The basic ideas of structuralism–functionalism were attributed to Spencer and further developed by Durkheim (1888, 1892). Functionalism explained the existence and the changes in family structure and function as reflections of changes in society. Family was part of a greater whole, in which other units combined to establish an equilibrium, and in which changes in one part of the system reverberated to other parts. Changes, therefore, could have multiple causes, in contrast with the monocausal biological or economic determinism of Social Darwinism and Marxist theory.

Durkheim also perceived the evolution of family through six stages in societal change, from its primitive form to the village, to the city, to the state. His "law of contraction" proposed that the circle of kin during evolutionary stages contracts from many to smaller numbers of kin, as do the roles of family members. In the last two stages, the paternal family is reduced to the conjugal or nuclear family, in which the relationships between parents and children change from material or economic basis to "personal motives." The focus of the family changed to the conjugal relationship between husband and wife, and one result was the development of more "independent spheres of action" (Popenoe, 1988). According to Durkheim, then, the conjugal family represented the disequilibrium of the family, much in the same manner as Le Play, Comte, Marx and Engels had argued. Indeed, he was concerned that increasing divorce and suicide were harbingers of the decline of the family.

Comments

These grand sociological theories, which shaped the basic parameters and concepts influencing generations of sociologists, psychologists, and anthropologists, were characteristic of the burgeoning scientific theories of the nineteenth century, such as in biology, physics, and chemistry. One characteristic was the diachronic dimension; they attempted to explain family stages on the basis of evolutionary theory or historical periods. They were deterministic in that societal changes were presumed to be the causes and family changes the effect. Economics, and in particular industrialization, generated social change. Another characteristic of this period of generation of theories of family change was the general lack of communication between sociologists, anthropologists, and psychologists. It is true that during the nineteenth century, psychology was identified primarily with experimental psychology and psychoanalysis, the former employing the experimental paradigm to study perception and the senses, for example, and the latter concerned with intrapsychic processes of the individual. Indeed, Durkheim was adamant that psychology had little to offer to the study of family change because of his belief that social processes, and not psychological processes, shaped family change.

Another characteristic of this period was that these sociological theories were products of European sociologists representing European views regarding family as well as the critical issues of European civilization of the nineteenth century, such as science, evolutionary theory, industrialization, urbanization, social unrest, revolution, and the emergence of nation states. Cultures outside northern Europe and North America were perceived as less civilized. The monogamous and nuclear family in northern Europe, the United States, and Canada, with all its problems, was considered to be the historical or evolutionary epitome of social change. Some criticize sociological theory and research in North America and Europe, even today, as employing a white middle-class nuclear family model as the standard with which to compare families, rather than viewing families on their own terms and in a particular sociohistorical context (Ingoldsby and Smith, 1995; Stacey, 1993). Indeed, much of the criticism of this ethnocentric perception of families comes from anthropology, as will be discussed below.

FAMILY SOCIOLOGY IN THE TWENTIETH CENTURY

Family sociology early in the twentieth century, undertook an empirical orientation. During the rise of socialism of this period, family sociologists studied the effects of deleterious economic and social changes on family. Symbolic Interactionism was introduced by Burgess (1926) to study the family as a "unity of interacting personalities." Burgess' approach, considered to have transformed the study of family, was a rejection of the emphasis of the grand sociological theories of the nineteenth century on the focus of social change as a determinant of the structure of the family. Symbolic Interactionism focused on the interacting behavior of family members as a dynamic unit and spawned research such as the systematic observation of group interaction processes leading to the differentiation of instrumental and expressive roles (Bales, 1950; Bales and Slater, 1955). The interactionist school was also strongly influenced by George Herbert Mead (1934). The work of Ralph Linton (1936, 1945) on role theory can also be traced to interactionist theory. Related research on interaction within the family was the study of *power* in family roles (Safilios-Rothschild, 1967), defined as the "legitimate authority" of husbands-fathers to exercise control over wives and children (Blood and Wolfe, 1960; Herbst, 1952).

Talcott Parsons

Talcott Parsons (1943, 1949, 1965) was, perhaps, the most influential sociologist to further develop structuralism–functionalism as a theory for the analysis of family change. Society was viewed in a structural–functional perspective as an organism that strives to resist change and to maintain a state of equilibrium. According to Parsons, family has two main functions: *instrumental*, related to survival, and *expressive*, related to the maintenance of morale and cooperation. The adaptation of the extended family unit to the industrial revolution required a nuclear family structure to carry out societal functions and to satisfy the physical and psychological needs of family members. Parsons argued that the nuclear family was fragmented from its kinship network, leading to psychological isolation. Its reduction in size resulted in loss of its productive, political, and religious functions. The nuclear family becomes primarily a unit of residence and consumption. Its financial and educative functions are dependent upon the state and its major remaining function is the socialization of children and the psychological equilibrium of the parents. The nuclear family parents, who have chosen each other freely based on love, in contradistinction with the extended family system in which marriage choices are based on family interests and not romantic love, are isolated from their kin and share rational and pragmatic values. Social mobility, particularly in the highly mobile North American culture, was made possible by the breaking of family ties.

Parsons' theory of the structure and function has strongly influenced research on family change since the 1940s. In contrast with Durkheim and other nineteenth century family theories, Parsons did not perceive changes from the extended family to the nuclear family system as reflecting the decline of the family, but as a positive adaptation to social change.

The nuclear family, composed of the working father, the housewife mother, and the children, was characterized by an increase in psychological aspects of the companionship between mother and father and greater emphasis on the psychological aspects of the socialization of the children. These changes were partly reflections of the autonomy of the nuclear family from the extended family, owing to their living apart from the extended family, their independent economic activity, and their reliance on the state for education of the children, employment, health, and other provisions granted by the society.

One criticism of Parsons' theory is directed toward his theory of the isolation of the nuclear family from its kin. Historians of the family and anthropologists have antithetical views of Parsons' historical analysis and the presumed lack of kin relationships. Research on social networks in the United States in the 1960s and 70s provided evidence from many studies that the nuclear family is embedded in a network of extended kin who provide social support (Uzoka, 1979). The French sociologist Martine Segalen writes that the dominant ideology of the post-war years, as exemplified by Parsons' analysis of the nuclear family, was that of individualism and freedom. "This has meant that each family cell tended to be seen as unique and independent of cultural influences of economic and historical contingencies" (1986, p. 30). She maintains that many sociologists studying present day families have an a priori assumption that the domestic group is shrinking and that kinship has almost disappeared as a basis of relationships.

A second criticism concerns Parsons' idealization of the nuclear family with gender roles of the working father and the housewife mother. Since the entry of the mother into the workforce and the greater rights of the woman in society, the nuclear family with gender roles described by Parsons has changed in North America and northern Europe, and indeed in many societies throughout the world. We will return to this issue later in this chapter in our discussion of the hypothesized autonomy of the nuclear family and its psychological and financial relationships with kin. However, despite these criticisms, it would be a mistake to underestimate Parsons' contribution to the study of family change.

CULTURAL ANTHROPOLOGY AND THE FAMILY

In contrast with sociology of the family of the nineteenth century, cultural anthropology was more empirically oriented. In addition, cultural anthropology differed from Western sociology in that it studied small societies throughout the world. The result of this methodological and theoretical perspective was a broad spectrum of different family types, role relationships, kin relationships, values, symbols, behaviors, and relationships with their societies based on thousands of research studies. We will begin this section with the discussion of the different family types stemming primarily from myriad anthropological studies.

Family types

The taxonomy of family types can be reduced to two dimensions: two-generation and three-generation families. Structure refers to the number of members of the family and their family positions, e.g., mother, father, son, daughter, grandmother, aunt, etc.

Two-generation families

- The *nuclear* family consists of two generations: the wife/mother, the husband/father, and their children, biological or adopted. Recent developments in Europe and North America would lead to adding homosexual parents with children to this category.
- The *one-parent* family is also a two-generation family. It can be the child and the divorced parent, unmarried parent (usually the mother), or the widow or widower.

Three-generation families

Extended families consist of at least three generations: the maternal and paternal grandparents, the wife/mother, the husband/father, and their children, the aunts, siblings, cousins, nieces, and other kin of the mother and father. The types to be described below are general taxonomies. Each type of extended family varies considerably in different cultures.

In some of the types that follow, extended families can be *polygamous* (multiple wives or husbands) or *monogamous* (one husband and one wife/mother). Polygamous families are further separated into *polygynous* (one father and two or more wives/mothers) and *polyandrous* (one wife/ mother and two or more husbands/fathers). Polygynous families appear to have been the norm in most societies in the past, in 83 percent of small preindustrial societies according to Murdock (1967), in contrast to monogamous families in 16 percent of societies and 0.5 percent polyandrous. Four wives are permitted according to Islam. However, the actual number of polygynous families in Islamic nations today is very small, for example, almost 90 percent of husbands in Qatar, Kuwait, United Arab Emirates, Oman, Bahrain, and Saudi Arabia, have only one wife (see Saudi Arabia portrait). In Pakistan, a man seeking a second wife must obtain permission from an Arbitration Council, which requires a statement of consent from the first wife before granting permission (see Pakistan Portrait). The low percentage of polygynous families at the present time is due to the reluctance of young women in these countries to enter into such a union. The Tiwi, hunter-gatherers of North Australia, had a system of polygyny in which females were usually betrothed before birth. Males married at a relatively late age and attempted to marry as many wives as possible (Robinson, 1997), although the system is rapidly changing to monogamous marriages.

Polyandrous families with one wife and multiple husbands are rare. They are found in Nepal, Tibet, and India, among other countries. Usually the wife/mother marries, and then marries the husband's brothers, most likely because of the lack of women in these societies according to Pasternak, Ember, and Ember (1997).

The main extended family types are as follows:

- The *patrilineal* and *matrilineal*, or in terms of authority structure, the *patriarchal* and *matriarchal* families are at least three-generational. The *monogamous* variation can consist potentially of the grandparents, the married sons, the grandchildren, and also the grandfather's or grandmother's siblings, nieces, grand-nieces, and, in many cases, other kin. The *polygynous* variation consists of the multiple wives and their children. For example, in Africa, the mother's brother raises the children and supports his sister, while the father keeps a distance. The patriarch or matriarch is head of the family, controls the family property and finances, makes the important decisions, and is responsible for the protection and welfare of the entire family.
- The *stem* family consists of the grandparents, the oldest married son, and other unmarried offspring, who live together under the authority of the grandfather-head of the household. The oldest son inherits the family plot and the stem continues through his first son. The other sons and daughters either remain, when they stay unmarried, or leave the household upon marriage. The stem family was found in southern France and central European countries such as Austria and southern Germany. It was also found in Japan, although the patriarch of the family could adopt a son and bequeath the family fortune if he believed his biological son was not worthy.
- The *joint* family is a continuation of the patriarchal family after the death of the grandfather, but differs from the stem family in that all the sons share the inheritance and work together. Joint extended families are characteristic of Europe, India, and East Asia.
- The *fully extended* family, the *zadruga* in the Balkans countries of Croatia, Bosnia, Serbia, Montenegro, Albania, and Bulgaria, has

a structure similar to that of the joint family, but with the difference that cousins and other kin are included as members of the family. The total number of family members might be over 50.

Kinship

Kinship has been the heart and soul of cultural anthropology's study of the family since the nineteenth century and its creation by Morgan (1870). Key figures contributing to its study were, among others, Tylor (1889), Kroeber (1909), Malinowski (1927), Murdock (1949), and Lévi-Strauss ([1949]; 1969). Kinship terminology is a formal and highly complex taxonomic system. Although the study of kinship had declined somewhat during the past few decades, increased interest in feminist anthropology has led to a renewal of kinship studies (Collier and Yanigisako, 1987; Pasternak, Ember and Ember, 1997). According to Peletz (1995), the building blocks of traditional kinships studies were kinship terminology, rules of descent, marriage, and postmarital residence. For a more detailed analysis of these concepts on which the following section is based, the reader might refer to Levinson and Malone (1980) and Ember and Ember (2002).

Rules of descent

Rules of descent refer to relationships with paternal and maternal kin. They are differentiated according to two types of kin. *Consanguineal* kin are those relatives related through blood, while *affinal* kin (in-laws) are related through marriage. *Lineal* relationships are biological relationships such as grandparents, parents, and grandchildren. *Collateral* relationships are those with uncles and aunts, cousins, and nephews and nieces. These are critical concepts in different cultures because they also are related to the types of relationships and obligations toward lineal, collatoral, and affinal kin, to lines of descent, to residence, to inheritance of property, to gender and family roles, economic activities, religious activities, child-rearing practices, and even political behavior.

These aspects of organization center around strict sets of rules with kin, many of them as ritualized behaviors. Societies with specific rules for kin are usually hierarchical in structure and related to how power is distributed between males and females, and across generations.

Ember and Ember (2002) describe three basic rules of descent in lineal societies.

- *Patrilineal* is the most frequent rule across societies; affiliation is with kin of both genders through the men. Each generation belongs to the kin group of the father. However, only the sons transmit the affiliation of the family to their children.

- *Matrilineal* rules of descent are the mirror image of patrilineal; only the daughters transmit the affiliation of the family to their children.
- *Ambilineal* rules of descent are with kin through either the maternal parents or the paternal parents. Some family members may affiliate with kin through their mothers and others through their fathers.

Some societies may have double descent, which is a combination of the above rules. Both patrilineal and matrilineal rules of descent are unilineal in that affiliations with kin are through one sex and have a common ancestor. In addition, this relationship is maintained in the society from generation to generation. Some societies such as the United States, Canada, and many European countries have bilateral kinship in that the mother's and father's relatives are of equal importance, or more aptly, one can chose which kin are of importance and which are to be ignored.

Kinship terminology

Kinship terminology differs across cultures. Two criteria are generally employed to describe kinship systems: (1) identical or different terms for siblings and cousins; (2) identical or similar terms for members of the parental generation such as mother, father, uncles, aunts (Murdock, 1949, 1967).

For example, in Iran (see family portrait) the term in Farsi for the mother's sisters is *khaleh*, and *ammeh* for the father's sisters, with analogous terms for father's brothers. In Pakistan (see family portrait), several cousins may be raised together in the same household. They are referred to in Urdu as *brothers* or *sisters*, with the prefix added, "through-my-maternal-aunt" or "through-my-paternal-uncle." Generic words such as "aunt," "uncle" or even "grandparents," have no equivalent in Urdu, but specific terms related to matrilineal kin, as in Iran, are employed; e.g., *khala* is the mother's sister and *phuphee* the father's sister.

Postmarital residence

Patterns of marital residence, according to Ember and Ember (2002) are as follows:

- *Patrilocal* is residence with or near the husband's patrilineal kinsmen. This is the most prevalent residence pattern throughout the world with approximately 67 percent of societies according to Murdock's World Ethnographic Sample.

- *Matrilocal* is similar to patrilocal, but refers to residence of the wife with or near her matrilineal kinsmen, while the married son leaves and lives with or near the wife's parents (15 percent of all societies).
- *Bilocal* residence is when the son or daughter leaves, but each can live with or near the parents of the husband or the wife (7 percent).
- *Avunculocal* refers to residence with or near the maternal uncle or other male matrilineal kinsmen of the husband (4 percent).
- *Neolocal* means residence apart from the parents or relatives of both spouses. This would be characteristic of nuclear family residence in northern Europe and North America, but accounts for only 5 percent of families worldwide, according to Murdock's World Ethnographic Sample.

Ember and Ember (2002) refer to studies analyzing determinants of different patterns of residence. Few small independent farms are found in most Western societies. The economy is based on wages rather than land ownership. Thus land ownership as a basis of production is not a factor, and small nuclear families with neolocal residence are more functional. In industrial societies, the economic system permits a son or daughter to earn money independently, even before marriage, and to either rent or buy a house. Thus, it appears that with increasing affluence, through either industrialization or other forms of non-agricultural economic activity, neolocal residence increases.

However, it appears that the explanations for patrilocal and matrilocal residences are not necessarily economic, as was assumed in the past. Matrilocal and patrilocal residence has been found to be associated with the type of warfare engaged in by the society (Ember and Ember, 2002). In most small societies throughout the world, neighboring communities engage in warfare. If the communities speak the same language, the term is *internal* warfare, while if they speak different languages, the term is *external*. A potential explanation is that patrilocal residence is functional when the practice is internal warfare, because sons are required to help defend the farm or property. The analogous explanation is that in societies with continual external warfare, the sons might be encouraged to live with the wife's parents so as to aid in defense. Another potential explanation is that when men are frequently absent from the wife because of work, the residence pattern might be matrilocal because her mother can help with the housework and care of children. However, these are only some of the possible interpretations which have been suggested through cross-cultural analysis of residence patterns.

Bilocal residence appears to be characteristic of hunter-gatherers. The subsistence of hunter-gatherers is particularly sensitive to seasonal cycles, temperature, and other ecological features (Spielmann and Eder, 1994). In addition, it appears that in many societies in Africa, South America, and Southeast Asia, hunter-gatherers exchange wild protein foods or other forest-produced products (honey, resins, medicinal herbs, hides) for farmer-produced carbohydrates, which are lacking in their diet, or for technologically produced items such as weapons or cooking utensils. However, hunter-gatherers appear to conform to the organizational and other social demands of farmers rather than the opposite. Hunter-gatherers, then, are often forced to seek close relatives with whom to live in order to survive, even temporarily, so as to seek other forms of work. Thus, bilocal residence in this case would reflect a matter of need for survival rather than free choice.

Marriage

In most societies, marriage is arranged between the families rather than a result of romantic love. Many societies have norms as to whom one is permitted to marry (*endogamy*) and restrictions regarding whom one cannot marry (*exogamy*). In India and Pakistan, endogamy means that marriage is usually restricted to the same caste, the same village, the same religion, the same race. These social norms are not as restrictive in North America and Europe, although marriage to someone of another racial or ethnic group or religion, or with a spouse of a different level of education or social status may meet disapproval in some groups. An example of exogamy is that marriage with a member of the nuclear family, or incest, is a universal taboo in almost all societies. Marriage with someone with the same family name was disapproved in China. In some societies, marriage is not permitted with first cousins, or with the son or daughter of a godparent. In other societies, such as Saudi Arabia, cross-cousin marriage is highly desirable. Marriage to one's cousin, preferably the son or daughter of the paternal brother (uncle) reflected a continuation of the close family bonds and the preservation of the family property. In other societies, if a husband dies, the wife must marry the brother.

In most societies throughout the world, marriages were arranged between the two families, and a verbal or written contract was agreed upon regarding the exchange of property from one family to the other. *Bride wealth* or *bride price* is the gift of money, goods, or property from the potential groom's family to the bride's kin. This is the most widespread kind of exchange of wealth in societies throughout the world (44 percent), and is prevalent in Africa and Asia. These are usually societies in which horticulture is the primary means of subsistence.

The second most prevalent form of premarital economic exchange is *bride service* (19 percent), in which the groom works for the bride's family. This was found in Alaskan Inuit, as well as native North and South American societies. The *dowry* system is the transfer of wealth or property by the bride's family to the bride or the groom, and is found primarily in European societies (8 percent).

The decision of a young couple to marry on the basis of love with or without the consent of the parents occurs in a minority of the world societies, including North America and Europe. One theory is that in societies with neo-local postmarital residence, romantic love as a basis of marriage is more common. It is suggested that marriage based on love and companionship provides a stronger union when the couple must depend on their own economic assets, and not depend on their parents' aid, for survival.

Inheritance of property is an integral part of marriage and lineal descent. Japan and China adapted differently to industrialization in the nineteenth century. Both had an agrarian economy, rapid population growth, and extensive but corrupt and inefficient bureaucracy. In China inheritance was egalitarian, but in Japan a single child inherited the property, which made it possible to accumulate capital. In China loyalty was to the family and nepotism a duty, so every family member could benefit from upward social mobility. In Japan, with a more feudal system, a father could disinherit his son and adopt a young man who seemed more worthy.

Divorce

Divorce is socially disapproved in all societies, and the families usually make great efforts to attempt to keep the couple together. Societies differ in the degree to which divorce is controlled and by which institutions. In some societies, divorce is controlled directly by the family, while in others there is indirect control by social institutions and by the dominant religion. For example, Catholicism does not permit divorce except under highly unusual situations requiring a special dispensation. The Orthodox church permits three marriages. Islamic law, the *sharia*, permits polygamy up to four wives, and also divorce. However, in current Islamic nations, the intent of a husband to take a second wife may lead to the first wife seeking a divorce. Divorce is not an easy matter in Islamic nations because of its legal and social consequences. According to Islamic law the daughter inherits property from the father, half of the sum of the son. The wife retains property in her name after marriage, even gifts from her family, and the husband has no legal claim to it. After divorce, the woman retains her property, and also custody of the children until the age of seven. But the father remains the legal guardian and is responsible for the financial care of the children. Remarriage of a divorced woman is permitted, but the children of the first marriage are subsequently raised by the maternal grandmother.

Subsistence patterns and family types

An important question studied primarily by anthropologists but also by sociologists is how family types are formed in different societies. Subsistence, or means of obtaining food, based on ecological features of the physical environment, for example, climate, flora, fauna, and terrain, appears to be related to different types of family structure and function as well as settlement patterns. Humans originally subsisted through *foraging*, i.e., collection of wild plants, hunting or scavenging, and fishing.

The agricultural revolution approximately 10,000 years ago brought about a different means of subsistence by producing foods rather than gathering. *Horticulture* is the cultivation of crops in fields for brief periods of time. The fields are not permanent, nor are there settlements, and many horticultural societies are nomadic and also live through foraging. *Intensive agriculture* is the cultivation of crops in permanent fields, which is also accompanied by permanent settlements such as villages and cities. *Pastoralism* is the herding of domesticated herds of animals such as sheep or goats. Pastoralists are usually nomads because feeding their herds requires new grasslands. This means of subsistence is also characteristic of intensive agriculturists. Table 1.1 presents characteristics of food collectors and food producers.

Blumberg and Winch (1972) found that the nuclear family is typical in small hunting and gathering societies as well as in urban areas in industrial societies, while the extended family is found in settled, intensive agricultural societies. This is called the *curvilinear* hypothesis. Nimkoff and Middleton (1960) found evidence that highly differentiated social stratification is found in extended families as compared with less stratification in nuclear families, in addition to evidence that is in agreement with the curvilinear hypothesis. In hunting and gathering societies, in which mobility is necessary for subsistence, the small nuclear family appears to be functional. In agricultural societies in which there are permanent settlements and where many hands are necessary for cultivation of the land, the extended family is necessary for subsistence. In modern industrial society, where people are hired to provide services or to work in industries, where money is a means of exchange, and where people live in urban areas and apartments or houses are expensive, the nuclear family is functional.

Table 1.1 *Variation in food-getting and associated features*

	Food collectors	Food producers		
	Foragers	Horticulturalists	Pastoralists	Intensive agriculturalists
Population density	Lowest	Low–moderate	Low	Highest
Maximum community size	Small	Small–moderate	Small	Large (towns and cities)
Nomadism/ permanence of settlements	Generally nomadic or seminomadic	More sedentary: communities may move after several years	Generally nomadic or seminomadic	Permanent communities
Food shortages	Infrequent	Infrequent	Frequent	Frequent
Trade	Minimal	Minimal	Very important	Very important
Full-time craft specialists	None	None or few	Some	Many (high degree of specialization)
Individual differences in wealth	Generally none	Generally minimal	Moderate	Considerable
Political leadership	Informal	Some part-time	Part- and full-time political officials	Many full-time political officials

Source: Reproduced with permission from Ember, C. R. and Ember, M. (2002). *Cultural anthropology* (10th edn.). Upper Saddle River, NJ: Prentice Hall.

Van de Berghe (1979) has made an interesting and plausible comment on the curvilinear hypothesis of the nuclear family system in hunting and gathering societies and in industrial societies by "closing the circle" in terms of an evolutionary path hypothesis. Van de Berghe commented on similarities between the nuclear family in these two vastly different types of societies in that they are both seminomadic (the industrial nuclear family tends to move in order to change jobs or is transferred to another city), and with minimal kinship ties, particularly with collateral relatives. One can add that they both function autonomously from the kin in terms of economic subsistence, education of children, religious education, and care of the household.

It should be emphasized that these generalizations of the relationship of ecological determinants to means of subsistence and family types are based on statistical analyses of a large number of societies and that there are always exceptions to these generalizations. A variety of family types is usually found within all large societies. For example, small family businesses thrive in urban areas in the United States, Canada, and Europe, particularly among recent immigrant families and established ethnic groups. Song (1997) described the ethnic family businesses in Britain as a means of reducing labor costs but also as a means of continuation of the patriarchal family structure and function in an urban setting. The children help the family in the business and this is also a means by which the parents can look after the children while they work. When the children become adults, they have the option of continuing the business. The Chinese in Britain have restaurants and take-away businesses, Greeks, Turks, and Cypriots are involved in catering and manufacturing of clothes, and other ethnic groups such as Indians and Pakistanis are involved in similar or other small businesses. The presence of family-organized small businesses is typical in the United States (Lovell-Troy, 1980) and other countries. Thus, small family-owned businesses are means of autonomous economic activity, in many cases as a replacement for their means of agricultural subsistence in their native country, and are also a means of continuation of a modified extended family structure and function in an urban setting. That is, the attitudes and values related to the autonomy and independence of farmers can be adapted to the operation of a small autonomous family business, as an alternative to the prospect of the loss of autonomy in economic activity as an employee in a large business in urban settings.

A second determinant, in addition to means of subsistence, has been presented by Pasternak, Ember and Ember (1976). They theorize that extended families prevail in societies with *incompatible activity requirements*. These are family requirements that are difficult to fulfill in nuclear families. For example, when the mother works in the fields or gathers food and cannot care for the children and the house, the extended family type is more functional. This is also the case when the father is away from the family for long periods because of his work, and the mother requires help. This may also be the case with low income families, or in ethnic families as suggested above, in the industrial societies of North America and Europe.

FAMILY CHANGE

Up to now, this Chapter has been concerned primarily with three issues: (1) theories of family change, (2) different family types, and (3) rules of descent, marriage, inheritance, and postmarital residence related to different types of kinship relationships in families throughout the world. These issues are related to the structural and functional aspects of family. The major concern of sociologists, anthropologists, psychologists, psychiatrists, and other social scientists has been family change; that is, the types of changes in families, the social determinants of family change, and the social and psychological consequences of family change.

The choice of the term family "change" is deliberate, as its connotation is neutral. As discussed earlier, two viewpoints on family change are characteristic of family studies: (1) the family system is declining, resulting in terms like crisis, breakdown, dissolution, disintegration, marginalization, fragmentation, or (2) changes in family have positive and adaptive elements.

Family change in Western societies

In this section the focus will be mainly on recent family change in Europe and North America, primarily because the bulk of the family studies concerns the effects of industrialization on family change in these Western countries. Family change outside Western countries will be discussed in a later section.

Family decline and breakdown

As discussed above, some family sociologists of the nineteenth century perceived family change as regressive, while others perceived family change as positive. The changes in family types which began during the past two centuries in Western countries as a result of industrialization, have now affected almost all nations throughout the world. The changes in Majority World countries have taken place during the past few decades. Changes have taken place, not only in family types, but also in the cultural and social institutions of the society. Increased industrialization and the concomitant urbanization as a result of abandonment of agriculture as a means of subsistence have resulted in smaller families, the nuclear family, living in urban areas.

One current issue related to changes in the family during the past century is whether children, upon maturation, will continue to live in a structure which is called family. Over 30 years ago Laing (1969) argued that the family is doomed, and the wrong setting to raise children. A second issue is to what degree will these changes in the family result in psychological changes in children and adults? Will children upon reaching adulthood, finding a partner and having children, become independent, isolating themselves psychologically and socially from grandparents and other kin? A third issue is the degree to which changes in the structure of the family presently occurring in the affluent nations of North

America and northern Europe are harbingers of family change in the rest of the world as consequences of modernization and globalization. Will the kin relationships of the extended family system inevitably shrink, leading to nuclear families in the societies throughout the world? Demographic statistics provide a picture of these family changes.

Demographic statistics

A number of changes in family types have occurred during the past 40 years, primarily in Europe, Canada, and the United States. The number of nuclear family households has increased. The greatest increase in families is the single-parent family, primarily unmarried mothers and divorced parents, primarily women. There appears to be a rupture between marriage and cohabitation. Young people increasingly cohabit without marriage, and may choose to marry only if they have children. The age of marriage has increased and the percentage of married couples has decreased. These trends are related partly to the entry of women into the workforce and to their continuing their education for longer periods. The divorce rate has increased. The fertility rate has dropped to a point of nonreplacement. On the other hand, the mortality rate has decreased, resulting in longer lifespan of grandparents.

Demographic statistics for the European family   Demographic statistics for the 15 countries of the European Union for 1999 are presented in the Eurostat-European Community Household Panel (Eurostat, 2001). The average percentage of persons living in house-holds with two adults and one or more dependent children, a nuclear family structure, is 36 percent in the 15 EU countries, a slight decrease from 38 percent in 1988, which can be explained partly by old couples living longer. A surprising finding is that the lowest percentage of nuclear families is in the United Kingdom and Austria (33 percent) followed by Germany and Spain (34 percent), when the expected prediction based on the literature was that the lowest percentages of nuclear families would be found in the countries of southern Europe. The highest per-centages of nuclear families are in France, Ireland, and Luxembourg with (43 percent). The average of households with three or more adults with dependent children, which is a variation of an extended type of family, (sibling of one of the parents or a non-family member) is 11 percent in the 15 EU countries, down from 14 percent in 1988. The lowest are Finland (4 percent) and Denmark (7 percent) and the highest are Spain (21 percent) and Portugal (20 percent). The average of three-generation households, which corresponds to an extended family type with at least one grandparent, one parent, and one child, is 10.8 percent, with Greece 22 percent and Portugal 19 percent having the highest percentages and Finland and Sweden (1.3 percent) the lowest. The single-parent with dependent children family average is 4 percent, up from 3 percent in 1988. The lowest with 2 percent are Greece, Spain, Italy, and Portugal and the highest is the UK (6 percent).

The marriage rate for the 15 members of the European Union decreased from 7.6 percent in 1970–74 to 5.1 per 1,000 population in 1999, while the divorce rate increased from 1.0 to 1.8. The percentage of live births outside marriage increased from 6 percent in 1970 to 27 percent in 1999, an indication of the increase in one-parent families and in the trend among young couples to marry after the birth of a child. Another related statistic is the living arrangements of young people age 16–29, in which 8 percent live in a consensual union and 18 percent are married. The fertility rate decreased from 2.59 in 1960 to 1.45 in 1999, which is below the replacement level. A related statistic is the average household size, which dropped from 2.8 in 1981/82 to 2.4 in 1999. Life expectancy is growing, estimated at 80.8 years for females and 74.5 years for males.

These demographic statistics suggest differences in the types of families in northern Europe and southern Europe. Three-generation families are more prevalent in the south. However, one would not have predicted that the United Kingdom, Austria, and Germany have the *lowest* percentages of nuclear families in Europe, lower than Greece and other southern European countries with a tradition of extended family systems. This finding is relevant to the issue of the "autonomy" of the nuclear family and the importance of investigating kin networks, and will be examined in the section "Household and family: nuclear and extended family."

Demographic statistics for the United States family   Demographic statistics on the family in the United States are reported by Whitehead and Popenoe (2003) with data from the National Marriage Project, and are based on the United States Bureau of the Census (Fields, 2003). A surprising finding was the recent slight increase in the percentage of children in two-married-parent families, from 68 to 69 percent, a recent reversal of a 40-year trend toward a lower number of children, together with a decline in the percentage of births among unwed African-American women, from 70.4 to 68.5 percent. The authors are careful to point out that there is not necessarily a permanent reversal of these trends, but it may be an indication that there is nothing inevitable about the marriage trends of the past 40 years. However, the same trend as in Europe of increasing cohabitation of couples as opposed to marriage was found in the United States, with 439,000 thousand couples in 1960 as compared to 4,746,000 in 2000. In 1960, 9 percent of all children lived in one-parent families as compared to 28 percent in 2002, of which two thirds are African-American children. The percentage of children under age 18 living with two parents is 69 percent in 2002, as compared to 88 percent in 1960. The percentage of three-generation families, with a grandparent living in the household, is 8 percent in 2002.

Men are delaying marriage, preferring cohabitation, having more children out of wedlock, and divorcing more easily. Eighteen percent of males aged 35–44 have never married, as compared to 7 percent in 1970. Women are also delaying marriage, and the number of marriages per 1,000 unmarried women age 15 and older has declined from 73.5 percent in 1960 to 45.6 percent in 2001.[1] The percentage of divorced men and women increased from 1.8 percent in 1960 to 8.1 percent in 2002 for males and from 2.6 percent in 1960 to 10.7 percent for females. At the present time, the probability of a new marriage ending in divorce is approximately 50 percent. The percentage of households with children has dropped from 48.7 percent in 1960 to 32.8 percent in 2000. Also, the percentage of childless women aged 40–4 was 19 percent in 1998 as compared to 10 percent in 1980.

Demographic statistics and the decline of the family

The changes in demographic statistics during the past four decades provide evidence for those who argue for the decline of the family, the crisis of the family, the breakdown of the family. The decrease of the extended family system, the increase in nuclear families, the increase in unmarried one-parent families, the increased divorce rate, the decreasing contact of divorced fathers with their children, the increase in remarriage and families with step-parents and stepbrothers and stepsisters, the gradual replacement of marriage by consensual union, legalization of same-sex marriage, the decrease in the birth rate, all provide strong support to the arguments for the breakdown of the family. The *Journal of Marriage and the Family* (2000) is devoted to examining many of these issues during the previous decade.

The title of Popenoe's book, *Disturbing the nest: Family changes and decline in modern societies* (1988) is illustrative of this viewpoint. However,

---

[1] This statistic is not exactly comparable to the EuroStat measures. Whitehead and Popenoe (2003) point out that this measure of the "number of marriages per 1,000 unmarried women" differs from the usual "crude marriage rate per 1,000 population" to help avoid the problem of compositional changes in the population.

Popenoe makes an interesting differentiation between "decline" and "breakdown" of the family. He argues that although family structures are changing, he does not believe the family system is disintegrating. He views the institution of the family as growing weaker, losing social power and social functions, and becoming less important in life. His book is a study of the Swedish family, but he believes that similar changes are occurring in the European family and in the United States, that these changes are consonant with modernization theory, and that they reflect a global trend in changes in the family. That is, the bourgeois form of family in the past century, in which an institutionally legal, lifelong, sexually exclusive marriage between one man and one woman, with children, where the male is the primary provider and ultimate authority, no longer exists in advanced Western countries. His summary of the changing family conditions for the Swedish family is that the size of the family has decreased, with fewer joint activities and diminished quality contact of parents and children, decreased contact with collateral relatives but increased contact with grandparents, no rich family subculture of norms, symbols, humor, and language, among other changes. Popenoe proposes that the new family system is *postnuclear*.

There is considerable agreement among sociologists that the classic nuclear family model of Parsons of the working father, the housekeeper mother, and the dependent children represents a minority of families in today's Western societies. The primary reason for its reduction is the increasing entry of the mother into the workforce, beginning in the 1960s. Bernardes (1997) reports studies in which the Parsonian nuclear family represents only approximately 14.6 percent of families in the United Kingdom. Gottfried, Gottfried, Bathurst, and Killian (1999) report that the percentage of classical nuclear families in the United States. declined from 61 percent in 1960 to 24 percent in 1990, while nuclear families with both parents in the workforce increased from 36 percent in 1970 to 61 percent in 1990. McLanahan and Teitler (1999) report that during the 1960s, 90 percent of children lived with both biological parents until age 18, while less than half do at the present time. Nearly one third are born to unmarried couples, of which the majority never live together, and another one third are born to married parents who divorce before the child reaches adulthood.

Adaptive elements of the family

An opposite school of thought questions the degree to which many of these changes reflect a "disintegration" of the family. Aerts (1993) argues that children continue to be born and raised by adults in a household. Also, the increase in divorce rates may be one consequence of changes in the economic and social role of women since the 1950s. Thus, divorce represents the opportunity of women or men to leave an unsatisfactory marriage while in the past, when the sanctity of the family was the social norm, the "integrity" of the family often led to pathological relations between the mother and father. Similarly, Skolnick (1993) believes that rising divorce rates do not reflect a flight from marriage so much as rising expectations for satisfaction in marriage.

According to Cuyvers (2000) the decline or breakdown of the family is usually "proved" by summing up demographic statistics, which are similar in western societies. The central issues are replacement of marriage by consensual union, single-parent families and stepfamilies, and same-sex marriages, together with declining birth rates. However, Cuyver argues that in the Netherlands, the other side of the coin is that 85 percent of children do *not* experience change in their family situation. They live with their biological parents until leaving home, and he concludes that in the Netherlands, the "breakdown of family/commitment" has no empirical basis. Muncie and Sapsford (1995) argue that the twentieth-century family is a strengthened version of its predecessors, and that the modern family offers opportunities for greater closeness and intimacy than was possible in pre-industrial societies.

Parsons did not perceive changes from the extended family to the nuclear family system as reflecting the decline of the family, but as a positive change. A legacy of Parsons' influence on conceptualizations of the "family" is its usage by many Western sociologists and psychologists as synonymous with the "nuclear family." The nuclear family has become the dominant ideology of the post-war years (Segalen, 1986) and a standard to compare other forms of new families. This idealization of the nuclear family as the typical family in the United States and the United Kingdom is partly a vestige of the nineteenth-century middle-class ideal of the working man, the glorified housewife and their children which emerged in the eighteenth-century upper-class England. The nineteenth-century Victorian model emphasized order and control and polarized gender roles (Skolnick, 1993). This idealization of the family was also reflected in Morgan's social evolutionary conceptualization of the nineteenth-century nuclear family as the highest level of development in British and North American civilization.

However, a different picture of the London working-class nuclear family at the end of the nineteenth century has been painted by Young and Willmott (1957). Living in poverty with undernourished babies in an overcrowded tenement, the husband took for himself what he should have spent on his family, was callous in sex, harsh with the children, violent when drunk, and often abandoned the family. The burden of maintaining the family fell entirely upon the mother. Men enjoyed the conversation, warmth, and merriment of the pub and took their ease with their "mates."

According to Coontz (2000) comparisons of contemporary families with those of the 1950s are particularly misleading in that the nuclear family of that decade was atypical even for the twentieth century. In the early 1900s many children worked away from parents in mines, mills, and factories. Age of marriage fell sharply. During the 1950s, the baby boom resulted in increasing fertility rates, and the proportion of never-married individuals fell. Values attached to nuclear-family living, such as that grandparents and other kin should not "interfere" in their lives, and the expectation that family life was the main source of personal gratification, were new, as Parsons also described. Coontz observed that this type of nuclear family was only a single and temporary stage in the family cycle of the generations after World War II. Coontz concludes that family is not a dying but a transformed institution. Parents are not declining in their commitment to children, but, antithetically, increasingly committed. Parents coordinate aspects of education, health care, help with home-buying or subsidized boarding in the parental home. In addition, parents bear greater responsibility for grandparents, who in previous generations were unlikely to live long enough to require substantial and prolonged assistance.

Thus, there are conflicting viewpoints in northern Europe and the United States about changes in family types. They center around whether the family is declining or whether these changes in family types represent an adaptation to social and economic changes with some psychological costs, but are not signs of dissolution or crisis or the death of the family. Despite these manifestations by some of family disintegration, there are signs in many of these countries that people agree with the concept of family. In a survey of the 15 EU countries 95.7 percent believe that family is the most important thing in their lives (Eurobarometer no. 39.0/1993).

Family change in the Majority World

In this section we will discuss family change in what Kağıtçıbaşı (1990, 1996a) calls the "Majority World," the 90 percent of the population of the world outside of Western societies. The demographic statistics and studies reported in the previous sections are based on research in Western societies, and represent probably over 90 percent of the literature in family studies during the past 200 years. Family change in the rest of the world is a more recent phenomenon, occurring during the past two or three decades, and reflects recent increases in industrialization, increased trade, tourism, and influences of world wide television and information technology. In addition some family changes, although phenomenologically similar to those in Western societies, seem to have taken a somewhat different course. This section presents a sampling of studies in some countries which describe types of current changes in family structure and function. In addition, the family portraits in this book provide descriptions of family changes and dynamics of intergenerational relationships in these 30 countries from different geographical and cultural zones.

From the extended to the nuclear family system?

Family networks in the urban setting

One development characteristic of most countries throughout the world is related to changes in family types as a result of urbanization and economic development. The traditional means of subsistence in most of the world, agriculture, hunting and gathering, foraging, are being abandoned and people are migrating to the urban areas to seek a better life. Demographic studies in many countries indicate the increase of nuclear family households. However, studies of family networks indicate that the extended family system has not decomposed into isolated nuclear families, but has changed into a modified extended family system in urban areas with close contacts with kin.

D'Cruz and Bharat (2001) state that the long-held view of the changing of the Indian family from joint to nuclear is no longer tenable. They state that the literature indicates that historically a variety of family types existed in India, including joint, nuclear, single parent, dual earner, and adoptive. Despite industrialization, urbanization, education, and employment of women in India, changes have occurred in the structure of the joint family, but not in its functional "jointness." They conclude that the joint family is not changing toward a Western model of the nuclear family, but toward an "adaptive extended family."

Working-class single mothers in Jamaica depend on different types of extended family systems, usually maternal kin, to help care for their children (Lynn Bolles, 1996). These women bring their mothers and kin to Kingston and also send their older children to rural areas to be cared for by kin. She observes that continuing kin relationships for care of children and economic support among working mothers from poor rural households in urban areas is characteristic of other Caribbean and South American families.

Ijo adolescents in Nigeria are the first generation to have experienced a Western type of schooling, which has altered their life expectations and life cycles. However, their extended families, according to Hollos and Leis (1989) are still the buffers between them and society. In addition, Hollos and Leis make an interesting distinction of the adolescents' conceptualization of autonomy and independence which differs from that of Western adolescents. Independence refers to the ability to initiate actions and make decisions by themselves, which is highly valued, while autonomy is the process of dissociation economically, socially, and psychologically from one's family, which is not valued.

One of the determinants of the continuation of close family ties is economic activity. People who migrate to urban areas seek employment in industry or firms. Young people have more opportunities for higher education in urban areas, increasingly including women. But the young person who attends universities in these developing countries requires financial assistance from parents, which may often take the form of the student residing with relatives or even involve a parent or the entire family moving to the urban areas. As discussed above, ethnic groups in Britain (Song, 1997), and the United States (Lovell-Troy, 1980) often establish small businesses in which members of the family, including relatives, take an active part. This indirectly results in continuation of the patriarchal family structure and function in an urban setting. The same phenomenon occurs in urban areas throughout the world. Small businesses, whether restaurants, cleaners, automobile repair shops, taxis, manufacturing clothing for a large corporation, tourist shops, are often run by extended family networks. Many people throughout the world, who had a large degree of independence and autonomy in farming, fishing, or other means of subsistence, find it difficult to give up this autonomy and become transformed to compliant employees in the corporate world. Small businesses composed of family members provide a means of subsistence in the urban setting, and simultaneously sustain the continuation of extended family functioning.

Gender and power in the family

Another characteristic of changes in the Majority World, as in Western societies, is changes in the degree of power of men and women in the family. In most patriarchal families, the male traditionally had jural, social, and economic power. This was also the case with the classic nuclear family in Western societies in which the father was the bread-winner and the mother the housewife and caretaker of the children. Interest in gender differences in power was rekindled among sociologists and anthropologists in the 1960s, after the initial debates on patriarchy and matriarchy by Marx and Engels and Morgan in the nineteenth century (Peletz, 1995). Increases in the power of the women in the family in the United States and Europe were a result of the entry of women into the workforce. The issue of gender and power is a complex issue at different levels of analysis: within the family, at work, political power, etc. (Collier and Yanagisako, 1987; Pasternak, Ember and Ember, 1997) which cannot be dealt with in this volume. This section focuses on changes in power relationships between husband and wife in countries as reflected in changes in extended family values.

Weisner, Bradley, and Kilbride (1997) describe family change in Kenya as characterized by breakdowns of traditional family values and systems, increases in unwed mothers and disrespect of elders. Family relationships are not easily categorized as traditional and modern in that intergenerational contacts among family members appear to be negotiated so as to maintain continuity. In the polygynous family systems in Kenya, women invest in their sons for their personal future security and well-being, while men continue to emphasize the polygynous system in order to maintain labor and services from its many family members.

Seymour (1999) described changes in the patrifocal Indian middle- and upper-class families in Bhubaneswar beginning in the 1960s. The previous segregation of the joint family, sequestering women in the courtyard and separate dining of women, began giving way to a nuclear family household in which husband and wife dined and slept together, and women began leaving the house. Seymour concludes that because traditional values in India differ from Western countries, the prediction is that adaptations to modernization in India will also differ.

A separate residence secured by the nuclear family does not result in dissolving the relationships with the extended family in South Korea. They are transformed by different dynamics (Kim, 1996). The traditional relationships in the traditional Korean stem family, as in other countries, are between the "tyrannical and controlling" mother-in-law and the subservient daughter-in-law. However, in current upper- and middle-class urban families, in which the daughter-in-law is educated and a working mother, the changes in the relationships are described as different from those in Western societies. The daughter-in-law does not have to live in the same household as the in-laws, and the mother-in-law loses her power over her. However, the daughter-in-law still actively respects the traditions of the family and the position of the mother-in-law.

Changes in gender relationships, power, and kin relationships should also be reflected in changes in family values. In studies of traditional values related to family structure and function in Greece (Georgas,

1989, 1999; Georgas, Bafiti, Papademou, and Mylonas, 2004) with samples ranging from 12 to 80 year-olds, factor analyses resulted in three dimensions of family values. The strongest factor that emerged from these studies was hierarchical roles of father and mother, with values related to the traditional roles of the patriarchal extended family, in which the father was the head of the family, authoritarian, controlled the finances, while the mother was submissive, conciliatory, a housewife who cared for the children. While young adolescents and elderly respondents had mean scores of "not certain," all ages in between, as well as females more than males, and urban more than rural residents, strongly rejected these values related to the father having the economic and social power, the strict obedience of children, the dutiful and acquiescent mother, that is, roles consistent with the agricultural extended family in many cultures. In contrast, young people accepted with high mean scores values associated with responsibilities of the parents toward the children and responsibilities of the children toward the family and the relatives. These are values related to responsibilities of children to the family and also to the importance of maintaining ties with kin; that is, traditional values of the Greek and other extended family systems (see Figure 1.1). These findings suggest that the father's power within the family has lessened and the mother's has increased, owing to the increased entry of women into the workforce beginning in the 1980s, the equal proportion of women attending universities, and other developments.

FAMILY NETWORKS: WHAT HAPPENED TO THE KIN?

Most of the current studies reported above focus almost exclusively on changes in family types and associated phenomena such as divorce, consensual union, and one-parent families, employing the nuclear family system as the point of reference. That is, the term "family" is identical with "nuclear family" in the minds of many sociologists and psychologists in Western societies. It appears as if there are no grandparents, nor aunts or uncles or cousins, or that their presence is not of any significant consequence, confirming indirectly Parsons' influence in conceptualizing the nuclear family as isolated from kin. It is useful at this point to refer again to Murdock's (1949) reminder that the nuclear family is a constituent element of all extended families. This conceptualization can be amended in today's world in the sense that even the one-parent family is one family unit within a constellation of nuclear families representing lineal, collateral, and affinal kin, with which one often has psychological, financial, and other forms of ties of different degrees: from none to very close. Demographic studies have shown a wide variety of family types in the

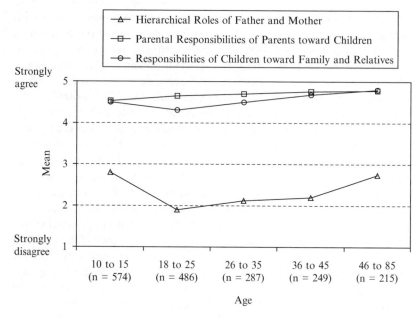

Figure 1.1. Means of hierarchical roles of father and mother, parental responsibilities of parents toward children, and responsiblities of children toward family and relatives according to age groups 10–15, 18–25, 26–35, 36–45, 46–85 in Greece (Georgas, Bafiti, Papademou, and Mylonas, 2004).

United States and Europe. The extended type of family living together on the farm, as in agricultural societies, is almost nonexistent in the United States, Canada, and northern Europe. But three-generation families residing together or residing nearby continue to exist, even in urban areas, among traditional ethnic groups in the United States and Europe, and particularly among recent immigrants, as family network studies show.

Although there has been considerable research during the past 30 years in the United States and northern Europe on kin networks, interest in kinship declined among family researchers in the 1990s (Johnson, 2000). Johnson points to three reasons why family researchers will need to think beyond the nuclear family. One is the increase in one-parent families, either divorced or unmarried. These families often seek social and psychological support from kin. A second is that family diversity is increasing due to recent immigration, and these ethnic groups often continue to live in extended family networks. A third reason is that the lifespan of grandparents has increased, resulting in many nuclear families living with a grandparent or maintaining close contact with grandparents in order to support them financially and in periods of declining health. Muncie and Sapsford (1995) argue that it was rare in 1900 for a young child to reach adulthood with grandparents still surviving, but because of increased life expectancy today, even great-grandparents are not uncommon in families.

Research on social support beginning in the 1960s, played a major role in identifying the members of the immediate family, kin, and friends and associates who ameliorate the deleterious psychological and somatic effects of stress (Ruble, Costanzo, and Oliveri, 1992). Uzoka reviewed a large number of studies, mostly in the United States, in which the nuclear family is embedded in a network of extended kin who provide social support, and he writes of the "myth of the nuclear family . . . as structurally nuclear but functionally atomistic" (1979, p. 1096).

In a study of family interaction Olson et al. (1989) chose a sample of 2,692 traditional families from 31 states. This was not a representative sample of families in the United States, but restricted to white Protestants in central states, of whom 92 percent were Lutherans, and 13 percent lived on farms, 14 percent in rural areas, 27 percent in small towns, 21 percent in small cities, and 24 percent in large cities. A surprising finding was that 36 percent of these families had an extended family member or non-relative living in the household.

Marks and McLanahan (1993) analyzed social support in 5,686 traditional two-parent families and parents and nontraditional two-parent or single-parent families based on national survey data in the United States. In social support relationships, there was little evidence that mothers in nontraditional two-parent families were less likely to be involved in social support relationships with kin, especially with parents. The only exception was mothers with a cohabiting partner, who had reduced contact with parents. Women function as family "kinkeepers" because of their higher levels of interaction with kin. Couples who originate and reside in the same locality are more likely to report close-knit networks and segregated roles relative to couples who reside far from families of origin (Turner, 1967; Gordon and Downing, 1978 as cited in Milardo, 1997). Segregated roles increase with degree of contact with kin (Richard, 1980, as cited in Milardo, 1997), a finding which may be related to the fact that some spouses have close bonds with kin which may result in not developing close marital bonds. Also, wives in kin-centered networks are less likely to discuss personal problems with husbands and are more likely to experience lower levels of marital satisfaction (Blood, 1969, as cited in Milardo, 1997). For husbands, contact with fathers is associated with greater love for partner and lower levels of marital conflict with wives (Burger and Milardo, 1995).

In divorced families, significant changes occur in social networks after divorce. Women report increased interaction with kin after divorce while men are more likely to increase participation with friends (Marks and McLanahan, 1993). Kin, especially parents, were often found to be an important source of support for single parents. Jayakody, Chatters, and Taylor (1993) report that African-American single mothers do not live and function in isolation, but in extended family situations that are comprised of kin and fictive kin, and utilize social and economic resources of the extended family unit to offset the absence of the father. The majority of single mothers lived in close proximity to their families, had daily contact with kin, and reported feelings of closeness to and satisfaction with their families. Besides parents and siblings, however, it appears that friends, and not other kin, are the most significant members of the social support networks of nontraditional families.

Active kin networks in urban areas in France and Britain are cited in Segalen (1986). Grandparents in Paris and Bordeaux provide financial aid and services such as caring for the children of young couples (Michel, 1970, as cited in Segalen 1986). In France Roussel (1976, as cited in Segalen 1986) found that 75 percent of young married couples lived less than 20 kilometers from their parents and Gokalp (1978, as cited in Segalen 1986) found that 63 percent of people with both living parents and married children lived less than 20 kilometers from their parents, 60 percent lived less than 20 kilometers from their parents-in-law, and 51 percent less than 20 kilometers from their married children. When they lived in close proximity or shared a home, 90 percent saw daughter, 86 percent saw mother, 83 percent saw son, and 82 percent saw mother-in-law at least once a week. Cribier (1957, as cited in Segalen 1986) studied retired Parisians, and found more frequent contacts between married children and their parents after retirement. The children often aided their retired parents to keep up a network of friends.

In Bethnal Green, a working-class area of London, a majority of couples lived near the wife's parents, there was high daily level of the exchange of contacts, visits, services, and advice between mother and married daughter (Young and Wilmott, 1957).

A study (Georgas et al., 2001) of family networks across 16 nations indicated differences in means of geographical propinquity, frequency of visits and frequency of telephone calls with grandparents, uncles/aunts, and cousins. Relatives in nations with higher levels of affluence, the United Sates, the Netherlands, Britain, Canada, Hong Kong, and Germany lived further apart from, visited less frequently, and telephoned less frequently relatives than nations with lower affluence, such as Cyprus, Greece, India, Serbia, Turkey, Bulgaria, mainland China,

Ukraine, the Czech Republic' and Mexico. However, the means across countries indicated a similar step-wise pattern, with the closest geographic propinquity and highest frequencies of visits and telephone calls being with siblings, decreasing respectively with grandparents, aunts/uncles, and cousins.

These findings suggest that while contacts between members of the nuclear family and members of the extended family may differ between the more affluent cultures of northern Europe and North America and less affluent cultures, these differences are relative and indicate the presence of family network relationships between members of the nuclear family and kin also in Western societies.

FAMILY HISTORY

As we have emphasized in this chapter, the central and recurring theme of family studies during the past two centuries has been changes in family types as a result of industrialization in Western societies. The theory of the purported "change of the extended family system to the nuclear family system due to the social and economic effects of industrialization" initially put forward by Frédéric Le Play and continued by Marx and Engels, Durkheim, Parsons, and so many others up to the present day, is still evident, with the current addendum being the change from the nuclear family system to the one-parent system. A second recurring theme, and a corollary of the first, is whether these changes have negative consequences – decline, disintegration, etc. – or adaptive consequences on the family. The emphasis of this change has been on family structure, on family function, and family roles.

Such analyses are problematic because family "change" over time is a matter of diachronic analysis, that is, comparison of information about the family "before" and "after," as is the case in much of the current demographic information regarding changes in, e.g., the past four decades. Le Play wrote about the history of the *famille souche* in France. Marx and Engels relied on their historical analysis on the matriarchal household in prehistoric times. Morgan based his theory on evolutionary anthropology, tracing the stages of family development from "savagery" to civilization. In fact there was very little actual data about the stages of family change before the nineteenth century, except for anecdotal accounts from classical literature, such as from the classical period of ancient Greece or the plays of Shakespeare. The empirical work of the cultural anthropologist provided the axe which cut down the underpinnings of this theoretical structure.

Study of the history of family began in the 1960s with the work of Peter Laslett (Laslett, 1971, 1972) and the Cambridge Group for the History of Population and Social Structure. Historical demography, or historical sociology, sought archival data from parish registers, censuses, and other reports. Demographic statistics on family types were compiled, based on records of births, marriages, deaths, and household lists in British towns and cities. Laslett's purpose, based on his demographic research, was to refute the theory that the domestic group was universally an extended family which, during the process of industrialization, resulted in the decline of the tribe and the clan, decay of familial authority, and the reduction of the family to the nuclear family system. He also decried the notion of the industrial nuclear family as a "triumph of individualism." Historical demographic research showed that each domestic group in England and in northern and western Europe in the 1700s consisted of a simple or conjugal family living in its own house. In 1517, for example, the average household in England contained 3.5 members. During the seventeenth and eighteenth centuries, the average size of the household remained at 4.75. Thus, he concluded that the theory of the great households of extended family members was not the case in English history, but the opposite, that the nuclear family was the typical family household.

An excellent comprehensive source of information about the history of the European family, *The European family: Patriarchy to partnership from the middle ages to the present,* has been written by Mitterauer and Sieder (1982); it also contains a rich bibliography of family studies in European countries. They begin with the etymology of the Latin term *familia,* essentially meaning those residing in the house, including servants and slaves and *pater familias,* the master or *despotes* of the household, with absolute authority over the familia. The comparable term for familia in classical Greece was the *oikos.* The manorial household in the feudal system during the Middle Ages in central Europe was a derivative of this large family system in which the aristocracy owned extensive landholdings. The weakening of the feudal system resulted in a number of changes in the great estates. One change was the introduction of a market economy in which cities became the magnet for many leaving the feudal estates and villages. For example, crafts became an important means of economic subsistence in the cities. Also, in the smaller peasant farms, some of which were organized as stem families in which the older son inherited the farm, the other sons either stayed as married servants or had the new option to migrate to the cities looking for work. Among the aristocracy in Austria, as well as among the peasantry, the name of the family was the name of the manor house or castle or simple home. If the property changed hands, the family also changed its name.

It is important to note that in these extended family types, not only in central Europe, but also in most of continental Europe including England, the household did not consist only of members of the family related by blood, but also included servants, or others. And in many cases, the servants were relatives, such as brothers or sisters in stem families in Austria who were called "servants," or nephews or nieces acting as servants or boarders, according to the needs of the family for help with the farm. It was customary in England and even in the American colonies (Coontz, 2000) for nieces and nephews to be sent to work in relatives' families. Thus the terms "household" and "family," as will be discussed in the next section, did not have the current identical meaning of family.

According to Mitterauer and Sieder, the stem family was only one type of three-generational family in Austria and in other parts of central and western Europe, such as Ireland, Switzerland, Norway, and France. The concept of "stipulated retirement rights" was one in which the old master of the house decided to yield his position and authority as head of the house to the middle generation in order to ensure the orderly management of the house and property, in return for regular payments. The old master was usually "retired" to a separate house on the property, not necessary to enjoy his "golden years," but was more likely exiled there in order to avoid the continual bickering and unwanted advice that usually was the consequence of his living in the same house with his heir. In some cases, these beneficiaries of retirement rights agreements and the eventual inheritance of the property were others rather than sons. However, Mitterauer and Sieder emphasize that three-generational families in central and western Europe were rare in preindustrial times. There were a number of reasons for this, primarily low life expectancy and family cycles. The low average life expectancy up to the nineteenth century was a critical factor in the low percentage of three-generational families. With low life expectancy, the duration of a three-generational family might be restricted to a few years.

The age of marriage was relatively high, between 25 and 30, and even somewhat higher for men. This is an interesting statistic in view of the current increase in age of first marriage in Western societies. Coontz (2000) reports that employing the current increase in age of first marriage since the 1950s in Western societies as support for the decline of the family is misleading. That is, during the 1950s, age of marriage decreased, fertility increased, and the proportion of never-married individuals decreased for the first time in 80 years, which was historically an unusual phenomenon.

Returning to pre-19th century central Europe, Mitterauer and Sieder provide a number of household statistics of percentage of family types based on historical demographic sources. Three-generational and joint families of brothers living together predominated in eighteenth century south and central France, up to 40 percent in some areas, while in northern France, between 76 and 81 percent of nuclear families predominated; in some areas with as few as 3 percent of three-generational families. A similar portrait to northern France was found in Belgium and the Netherlands. The picture in eastern Europe was the predominance of three-generation families. High percentages of extended families were found in the Baltics: Estonia in 1683 (41 percent), Lithuania in 1797 (64 percent). A similar picture was in the Rjasan province of Russia in 1814 where 33 percent were one-and two-generation families and 59 percent three-generation, and 7.5 percent four-generation families. Italy shows a diverse picture in types of families according to area. In some rural areas, the percentages of extended families were 9 to 11 percent, while in Tuscany they ranged from 39 to 45 percent in three communities.

Mitterauer and Sieder conclude their analysis, in agreement with Laslett, that the myth of the large preindustrial family transition from large to small family in the course of industrialization can be disproved statistically, at least for certain countries from central and northern Europe, including England.

On the other hand, some historians of the family provide evidence contrary to Laslett's claim that the English family was always nuclear. Anderson's (1971) analysis of the 1851 census in Preston, Lancashire, England suggested that under some conditions, the urban industrial revolution led to the increase in the numbers of parents and married children living together. The working mother in the factories of England in the nineteenth century could not care for her children. In addition chronic poverty or an illness led to the mother seeking help from her nearest relatives, who lived with the nuclear family or resided nearby and helped the family.

A comprehensive analysis of kinship systems in the preindustrial societies of Eurasia (China, India, Tibet, Sri Lanka, Australian aborigines, and Western societies) has been written by Goody (1983). Goody refutes the perception by Western scholars that the women in Eastern societies were completely incorporated into the husband's kinship group. He maintains that married women retained their moral and materials rights and their obligations in respect to their natal families. Married women were not merely pawns of their husbands; because laws protected their rights of inheritance of property, this was a source of power in their relationships with the husband's kin.

Comments

We can conclude, from these analyses of family history based on archival data, that the nuclear family would appear to have been predominant in England, northern and areas of central Europe. On the other hand, southern France, eastern Europe, the Balkans and Mediterranean provided a picture in which the extended family system appeared to predominate, if not in terms of percentage of households, at least with large households. This would suggest that the industrial revolution did not result in the disintegration of the extended, rural family and the emergence of the nuclear family in northern and central Europe, since the nuclear family system existed in previous centuries, but it may have gradually had this effect in southern and eastern Europe during a later period. We will examine this hypothesis in the next section.

A second conclusion is that all these European countries, including England, had all the variety of family types: extended, nuclear, one-parent widowed, and even in some cases, unwed single mothers. The question is one of percentage of these types of families in the population. Another question concerns the determinants of these types of families in the different countries. Agriculture was the primary means of subsistence in Europe before the industrial revolution. In southern, eastern, and in other areas of Europe, peasant families subsisted on relatively small plots of land. It is not certain to what degree this was possible in England, in which the aristocracy owned most of the land and hired people to labor on the estates. Would it be possible for hired help on the estates to have three generations in the household? It seems unlikely, since it was the practice to send children to work in other families, often to relatives, and for children to leave the household to find work and start their own nuclear families when they came of age. Also, in the towns and cities of late medieval England, the wealthy merchants, although living in nuclear family households, had extensive kin relationships with affines and in-laws (Kermode, 1999).

The predictable sequences of family life cycle changes precipitated by family members' biological, social, and psychological needs and development (Smith, 1995) are marriage, the birth of the first child, maturity of the children, and death. The extended family maintains its continuity until the patriarch of the family or one of the brothers of the joint family dies. After death, the extended family changes in composition, with the new generation of nuclear families and independent single adults, but the extended family itself continues through new generations. In the stem family, the scenario is that the father's death leads to the inheritance of the property by the elder son, and the other married sons leave and eventually begin their own extended family. However, the high level of mortality in all countries in the past suggests that the lifetime of a three-generation family was brief. Thus, after the death of the patriarch, the cycle began anew, but now with a small group of nuclear families as well as childless couples and unmarried children. In addition, a high infant and child mortality rate would often result in an only son dying before marriage or before having children. Because of all these contingencies, it was not possible for a society to have a large number of intact three-generation families.

As will be discussed further below, it may be more important to look at the degree and kinds of kin relationships in societies, rather than to count the percentages of types of families, or to characterize countries as predominately extended family or nuclear family societies. Laslett also maintained (Laslett, 1972) that by 1970, historical demographers recognized that the nuclear family predominates in probably all the nations in the world. This claim, of course, echoes Murdock's statement that the nuclear family is present in all societies, either as an independent household or as a constituent part of an extended family. This issue will be discussed in the following section.

HOUSEHOLD AND FAMILY: NUCLEAR AND EXTENDED FAMILIES

The review of the literature on family types, family change, and family history up to now has relied to a great extent on demographic statistics. One issue is how family types are identified in demographic surveys. A second issue is that the definition of family in demographic surveys focuses primarily on the structure of the family, that is those persons who reside in the household, but it does not provide much information about kin relationships or family networks. These issues are related to conclusions in many of the studies above, for example the status of the current family, family change, and family history, and the percentages of nuclear and extended family types in societies.

Demographic definitions of household and family: a paradox

Demographic studies of the family usually employ the term "household" in determining the number of persons residing in a house and their positions. The question in surveys is a variation of, "Which persons reside in this house?" The persons are identified according to family positions: e.g., mother, father, dependent persons, grandparents, siblings, and other residents. The number of persons and the family positions are counted and then categorized as two-generation or nuclear, three-generation or extended, one-parent divorced, etc. The final step is to sum within categories to determine the percentage of types of families in the country.

However, there is a paradox between the concepts of "household" and "family," as employed in demographic studies. An excellent review of this issue is found in Yanagisako (1979). Bender (1967) and Bohannan (1963) clarify that there is a distinction between families and households because they are "logically distinct" and "empirically different." The logical distinction is due to kinship being the referent of family, while common residence or geographical propinquity is the referent of household. Thus Bender observed that families should be defined as kinship relationships and not as common residence. This is because in terms of empirical definitions, co-residents may not be kin members, as in the extended families in most countries, or even in the nuclear families of central Europe or England, as discussed above in the analyses of archival data in family history studies. A second reason is that a series of households may be categorized as nuclear families, for example of the grandparents, the married sons and daughters, but these households may be, in terms of propinquity, in the same apartment building or in adjacent houses or in the neighborhood, and the kin in these different households may visit each other frequently. Grandparents may help the mothers in caring for the children, and also in times of financial need, while the mothers and fathers may care for grandparents in times of ill health or old age. In other words, this constellation of nuclear family households related by kin functions as an extended family in an urban setting, as is described in the family network studies discussed on pp. 33–37. Thus, relying solely on the household as the criterion of whether a family is nuclear or extended neglects the degree of propinquity and more important, the degree of functional interaction with kin.

Indeed, Laslett's work has been criticized by Berkner (1975) for confounding the concepts of family and household. In describing the criteria employed in categorizing types of families in England, Laslett (1972) reported that the actual boundaries of the domestic groups were not clear, and was troubled by what is meant by family and household. If a household contained persons sleeping habitually under the same roof (common residence) and shared a number of activities (functional criteria) but were not related to each other by blood or marriage, was this family? Apparently, because of the problem that archival data was clearest in terms of the members of the household, Laslett most likely chose to employ the criterion of common residence, including servants and boarders. Thus, he described the necessity of excluding as members of the household, children who had left home, as well as kin and affines who lived close by, even if they collaborated in the productive work of the family or frequently took their meals at the family table, and even elderly kin living in a separate house on the property. Employing these rather strict criteria, only common residence in the main house qualified them as members of the household, while other kin functionally related to the family fell short of membership. Laslett's now well-known statistic of 4.75 as the average size of household in preindustrial England, and his statement that the nuclear family was the typical family household, not only in England but throughout the world, are obviously an underestimate and an overgeneralization respectively, and a classic example of the confounding of family and household. What is puzzling is the continued use of this 4.75 average by family researchers, despite Berkner's (1975) and others' criticism of this and other problems in Laslett's work (cited in Yanagisako, 1979).

Categorizing family type in terms of common residence as in demographic surveys, without information on kin relationships or family networks, also leads to errors in estimating the percentage of nuclear or other family types in a country. A common error is the comparison of percentages in nuclear families between countries and conclusions to the effect that higher percentages mean country A is higher than country B in terms of the nuclear family system. A striking example is the finding from the Eurostat (2001) demographic survey of 1999 discussed on pp. 24–25, in which the lowest percentages of nuclear family households in Europe are Britain and Austria with 33 percent, followed by Germany with 34 percent. Greece had a higher percentage, 38 percent, of nuclear families. Should we conclude that Greece has a higher nuclear family *system* than these three countries? Add to this the statistic from the same survey that the average of three-generation households, which corresponds to an extended family type with at least one grandparent, one parent, and one child, is highest with 22 percent in Greece, and we are truly confused. The problem is that kin relationships between nuclear families are rarely examined in these surveys.

In Georgas et al. (2004a), a nationwide Greek survey indicated that kinship relationships of young married nuclear families are very close, both in terms of propinquity and interaction. A potential explanation of the high percentage of nuclear families in Greece is the cultural values in which it is considered the duty of parents to make provision for buying a home for their children when they marry. However, they attempt to buy a home either in the same apartment building or very near. The extended family system in Greece is rapidly changing from patriarchal, in which the father has all the power. People at all ages reject traditional paternal values absolute authority, but maintain traditional values associated with maintaining close contact with relatives, children respecting grandparents, and obligations toward parents (Georgas, 1999).

Although affluence has been increasing in recent years, this suggests that in Greece as well as in other countries (see the country portraits in this volume), the traditional agrarian extended family has not decomposed into isolated nuclear families, but has changed, and that its morphological equivalent is the extended family system in the urban setting with a continuation of contacts with its network of kin. We can infer from this example that the percentage of nuclear families in a country based on demographic surveys may be accurate as such; but without information regarding kinship relationships, such as frequency of interaction and propinquity of residence of the various nuclear family kin, comparisons between countries and subsequent generalizations as to the degree to which a country is characterized by a nuclear family system can be erroneous. It represents a confounding of the nuclear family as two-generation residents in a household and the nuclear family system as autonomous and isolated from its kin; or the confounding between structural and functional elements of family.

An example from family history studies based only on demographic studies is the average family size of the Greek family in the Peloponnese in the eighteenth century, an area in southern Greece. Wagstaff (2001) reexamined the calculations of average family size of 4.0 with 43,366 families reported by Panayotopoulos (1985), based on a census in 1700 by the Venetian governors. One interpretation by Wagstaff is that this finding strengthened historical demographic claims of the universally small size of the family and contradicted "stereotypes" of the large family in anthropological and historical literature on Greece. Can one come to the conclusion from this demographic study that the family in Greece was even smaller and even more "nuclear" than the British family of that period? This again accentuates the problem of equating the concepts of household and family and not having information on propinquity and functional interaction among kin. In any case, Thiersch, an Austrian sojourner in Greece, wrote the following description of the dynamics of the Greek family in 1833:

Because there never was a central government able to control or protect the people, one had to search elsewhere for protection and support. The most natural and secure support was found in the family, whose members, including second cousins, are nowhere so united and so willing to help each other than in Greece. The isolated individual has to ally himself with some group. He becomes a follower, or a leader of a group. In this case, a prominent person has a group of followers dependent on him, who call on him, who ask his advice, who execute his wishes, who protect their common interests, always being careful to be worthy of his esteem and his trust.

The main point of this section is that household refers only to the structural elements of the concept and to common residence in a single household. The major problem of much demographic research on family types is the lack of information on family networks. In addition, some family researchers implicitly adopt the position, a vestige of Parsons' theory, that the nuclear family is functionally independent and autonomous, a position which is supported by the demographic approach of counting the number of persons and family positions in the household. This methodology tends to reinforce the perception of equating "nuclear family" with "family."

MODERNIZATION, GLOBALIZATION, AND FAMILY CHANGE

As discussed above, beginning with the early nineteenth century and continuing to the present day industrialization was identified as the primarily social factor influencing family change. Modernization theory, according to Inkeles (1998), identifies four forces that induce societal change: (1) technological changes, particularly modes of production and distribution characteristic of an industrial and market economy; (2) ecological changes, such as urbanization in which people live in small residential units in high population areas; (3) changes in governance and institutions, such as laws, which may legislate the rights of mothers and children; and (4) changes in norms and values, such as greater individualism.

Modernization theory has another relevant dynamic process: *convergence*. That is, as nations become more "modernized," primarily because of increasing industrialization and affluence, they tend to converge in terms of these types of changes in production and consumption, ecology, social institutions, and values. With increasing economic level and industrialization, countries reject traditional values and traditional culture, and all countries inevitably converge toward a system of "modern" values and increasing individualization. Modernization theory predicts that traditional societies may be presently "underdeveloped" but economic well-being will inevitably result, as discussed above, in changes in its family system to predominantly nuclear with fewer kin relationships, more one-parent families, more divorces, etc. (Goode, 1963). He added that it is highly unlikely that these trends will regress to greater power of the extended families, clans, and lineages, or to increased male authority, growth in percentages of marriages, or increase in multigenerational families. Popenoe (1988) comments that these trends in family change are perhaps some of the "most securely known in the social sciences."

According to Albrow and King (1990), the concept of globalization reflected the assimilation of its tenets into the concepts of modernity, including industrialization, democratization, social networking, television, information technology, the banding together of ecological groups in different countries, and even international grass-root movements such as anti-globalization protests. Thus, globalization is not only a spreading of economic and market processes, but also the general interconnectedness and interdependence of structures and processes throughout the world.

There are also arguments opposing modernization theory. Max Weber's (1904) thesis in *The Protestant ethic and the spirit of capitalism* was that Calvinistic Protestantism after the Reformation changed the religious values of the medieval Catholic church, permitting economic and banking activities of individuals, leading to capitalistic enterprise. For example, the religious beliefs of Calvinistic Protestantism shaped cultural institutions such as the system of government, laws permitting and regulating private enterprise, and the teaching of science in educational systems. In addition, these institutions in Protestant countries in Europe and North America continue to have their influence on all aspects of society and are resistant to change. That is, cultural issues, with religion a central focus, shape societal institutions at all levels and play a significant role in resisting social change or in pointing toward the direction in which the social institutions will be modified.

Harrison (2000) comments that economists have recently been concerned as to why the policies of international institutions, such as the World Bank, have had limited success in underdeveloped countries. He states that an axiom of economists is that the appropriate economic policy will produce the same results in all cultures. He also adds that economists are uncomfortable with concepts such as culture and psychology because they do not fit precisely in mathematical economic models developed in northern Europe and North America.

A recent challenge to modernization theory comes from Huntington (1996), who argues that after the end of the cold war in 1990, cultural values have replaced ideological distinctions and that religion is playing a major role in these changes. Loyalties of nations are shifting back to these cultural zones, indicating the perseverance of identities to long-standing "civilizations." Inglehart and Baker (2000) explored the relationships between modernization theory and religion, employing the dimensions Traditional vs. Secular–Rational values and Survival vs. Self-Expression values. They concluded that although their data supported the type of cultural change predicted by modernization theory, they should also acknowledge the influence of long-established cultural zones described by Huntington's theory in which religion plays a major role. In a cross-cultural study (Georgas, van de Vijver, and Berry, 2004c) of the relationships between economic activity, religious denominations, values, and well-being in a large number of countries, religion and affluence were related to psychological variables in separate and in some ways contrasting ways. Some religions were related to more emphasis on interpersonal aspects, such as power, loyalty, and hierarchy, together with low affluence. Other religions, (particularly Protestantism) and high affluence were associated with more emphasis on intra-personal aspects, such as individualism, utilitarian commitment, and well-being.

Is there only one road leading toward the nuclear and one-parent family structure and function as found in North America and Western Europe, bulldozed by an economic engine, as globalization and modernization theory would predict? Or are there many paths leading to different forms of family structure and function, influenced by economic growth and globalization processes, but also shaped by long standing cultural traditions? The answer is not yet given to these questions, and there are arguments on both sides of convergence and divergence.

Yanagisako (1979, p. 182) cites numerous studies to support her theory that "industrialization, urbanization, and integration into a money economy have not weakened the Balkan extended family but have strengthened it" (Hammel, 1972); "the modernization process is being molded to existing family and kinship institutions and areas of traditional family function" in Latin America (Carlos and Sellers, 1972); "kinship ties endure under conditions of social change and that new functions are assumed by kinship units" (Talmon-Garber, 1970); "in developing nations such as India, it is particularly entrepreneurs and the leaders of modern industry who are members of joint families" (Owens, 1971). Yanagisako concludes that "The above studies provide a necessary corrective to the excessively broad hypothesis that with 'modernization' kinship structures decline."

Interestingly enough, one sociologist who argues that the institution of family has been found to resist the widespread changes predicted by modernization theory in many societies because of cultural patterns and universal psychological needs, is a major theorist of modernization theory, namely Alex Inkeles (1998). He suggests that in some Oriental societies, values of veneration of elders are so strong that they resist breaking kinship ties, even though nuclear families may have separate residences. As discussed in the section above, many societies throughout the world have this pattern, in which extended family relationships are maintained, although modified, even with the married couples living in separate residences. Inkeles also argues that some basic human needs resist some changes in family patterns which are influenced by modernization processes. As an example he presents statistics indicating that the percentage of the population who never marry is remarkably stable, around 10 percent in Europe and somewhat lower in Asia. A third example is family roles. Despite modernization in Western societies, husbands have resisted helping wives with household chores. Inkeles concludes that although modernization research has demonstrated a convergence of similar patterns of family change in Western industrialized societies, family relations appear to be "too complex and subtle to respond uniformly to a uniform set of influences." In addition, he argues that some patterns related to family are constant across countries and over time, suggesting that some human needs are resistive to any change of social organization, and one these is that in which a man and woman are united in a long-term bond called marriage (or other forms of cohabitation).

CONCLUSION

One conclusion that has been drawn by family sociologists and cultural anthropologists from the myriad family studies during the past 200 years is that changes have occurred in the structure of the family in cultures throughout the world. The major determinant of these changes is increasing affluence in societies, primarily as a result of industrialization and urbanization. Demographic studies indicate that with increased affluence and the ability to live in a separate household, the traditional extended structure of three-generation families has changed to two-generation or nuclear family structures, and more recently in Western societies, to one-parent families. However, demographic studies measure primarily structural dimensions of the family, that is, the number of persons and their positions, e.g., mother, father, children, kin in the household. They rarely investigate kin relationships. If the increase of nuclear families in a society is just the increase of separate households because of increased affluence, but with continued kin contact and close bonds, then these changes do not necessarily indicate a change of family systems.

Counting the number of people in the household without taking other factors into consideration often results in erroneous conclusions regarding trends from extended family systems to nuclear and one-parent family systems in a society. This is because there is a confounding of the concepts of household and family. Demographic studies are based on common residence in a household, while the concept of family is based on kinship relationships. Thus, a family in an urban area in a society today may be composed of different nuclear families and may live in separate households, but they may live very close together and share many family functions and have close contact and communication. This is the case in most societies throughout the world, even in ethnic groups and families in Europe and North America, as the thousands of kinship studies in Western societies have demonstrated.

There have been two trends during the past two centuries in characterizing family change. One trend has been that the family system is declining, through crisis, breakdown, dissolution, disintegration, marginalization, fragmentation with increasing individualization of individuals. The opposite trend is that changes in the family have positive and adaptive elements, that is, family structure and function are in the process of transformation but family, as such, is still perceived as very important in people's lives.

Modernization theory and more recently, globalization, have predicted the eventual convergence of family systems in societies throughout the world, from the extended family to the nuclear and one-person family systems, as in North America and Europe. Both concepts are based on economic theory, with little understanding of how cultural factors such as means of subsistence, religion, values, traditions, etc., documented by over 100 years of cultural anthropological studies, are related to family types. In addition, modernization and globalization theories have little understanding of the processes of how psychological variables such personality, values, interaction, communication, and emotional bonds with kin are related to family networks. The question is still open as to whether the influence of economic development and globalization will inevitably result in convergence of family types, or whether cultural factors and psychological needs related to emotional bonds with kin are strong enough to maintain diversity in family types, despite convergence in the economic and social systems of countries.

The study of the relationship between cultural variables, family roles, and psychological variables in this book is an attempt to provide some answers to these questions.

2   Cross-cultural theory and methodology

John W. Berry and Ype H. Poortinga

INTRODUCTION

In a psychological study of family across cultures we should consider how human behavior is related to culture. Cross-cultural psychology attempts to understand similarities and differences in human behavior in their cultural contexts (Berry, Poortinga, Segall, and Dasen, 2002). As such, it takes culture seriously as a factor in the development and display of individual behavior.

The first part of this Chapter introduces cross-cultural theory. We begin outlining by what we mean by culture, taking classical and more recent definitions of "culture" from the discipline of anthropology. Next, we present a relevant set of concepts from the discipline of human biology. Armed with these ideas from our two cognate disciplines, we then consider three broad theoretical approaches to how cultural and biological factors are reflected in the course of human psychological development (termed absolutism, relativism, and universalism). The complementary approaches of the "cultural," the "indigenous," and the "comparative" schools of thinking about cultural and biological influences are then related to these three theoretical approaches. Finally, we elaborate on our own position on these issues, adopting both indigenous and comparative approaches, and situating them within the universalist theoretical perspective.

The second part of the Chapter introduces an Ecocultural Framework that guides the research reported in this book. As cross-cultural psychologists, we examine how human behavior is adaptive to the cultural and biological contexts in which it is nurtured, and how all three domains (behavior, culture, and biological functioning) are adaptive to the broad ecological and sociopolitical contexts in which they are situated. In particular, we examine the issue of how features of group life influence, and become incorporated, during development into individual behavior. The concept of cultural transmission is at the core of this examination; and the role of the family in its functioning is central to understanding the emergence of human behavioral diversity.

This last section sets the general stage for the third part of the Chapter in which we consider the family as an institution that is adapted to its ecological and cultural situation, and in turn provides the main context for the ontogenetic development from infancy to adulthood, and often beyond.

In the fourth and last part of the Chapter we focus on the question of how psychological issues related to the family can be compared cross-culturally. Issues of methodology are linked to theoretical questions. Our choice for universalism implies not only that there are aspects of psychological functioning that are common to humans in all cultures, but also that methods have to be sought to identify and assess such aspects. In this part we will pay particular attention to methodological and psychometric pitfalls of cross-cultural comparison.

CROSS-CULTURAL THEORY

As a discipline, psychology tends to be both culture-bound and culture-blind. By and large, it has ignored the most all-encompassing habitat of human life (a person's culture), and how this relates to behavior. Psychology has also remained mostly an activity of one culture area (the Euro-American), both in terms of its theoretical orientations and its empirical data; its findings by and large have thus been bound to one small part of the world.

Goals of cross-cultural psychology

When we begin to recognize these limitations, and decide to break out of this restricted frame of reference, we need to arm ourselves with concepts and methods that will enable us to achieve our goals. Three goals have been identified by Berry and Dasen (1974): (i) to transport and test our current psychological knowledge and perspectives by using them in other cultures; (ii) to explore and discover new aspects of the phenomena being studied in the local terms of other cultures; and (iii) to integrate what has been learned from these first two approaches in order to generate a more complete knowledge and understanding, one that has a more pan-human validity. The existence of universals in other disciplines (e.g., biology, linguistics, sociology, anthropology) provides some basis for the assumption that we should be able to work our way through to this third goal with some success.

Conceptualizations of culture

From cultural anthropology, we have gained valuable insights into the various meanings of the concept of "culture." Earlier conceptions saw culture as a shared way of life of a group of socially interacting people; and culture as transmitted from generation to generation by the processes of enculturation and socialization. That is, culture was viewed as a "given," which preceded in time the life of any individual member (see Munroe and Munroe, 1997).

This long-standing view of culture continues to have a major influence on thinking in cross-cultural psychology. The main task is to understand how the established cultural context influences the psychological development of individuals, and guides their day-to-day behaviors. In recent years, along with the emergence of more cognitive approaches in many branches of psychology, individuals have come to be viewed, not as mere pawns or victims of their cultures, but as cognizers, appraisers, and interpreters of them. Thus, different individuals are now widely considered to experience different aspects of their culture, and in different ways.

In sharp contrast to this established perspective on the nature of culture is one advanced by those adopting a "social construction" perspective (Gergen and Gergen, 2000; Miller, 1997). From this perspective, culture is not something that is given, but is being interpreted and created daily through interactions between individuals and their social surroundings. This view is one espoused by those identifying with "cultural psychology," which has been defined as "a designation for the comparative study of the way culture and psyche make up each other" (Shweder and Sullivan, 1993, p. 498).

The emphasis on the individual as an active agent who creates and interprets culture may be recent, but the notion of interactive relationships has been part of cross-cultural psychology for a long time. There are numerous examples of interactions between context and person (e.g., feedback relationships in the education of children in the Ecocultural Framework) and of reactions to cultural contact (as one form of adaptation associated with acculturation; e.g., Berry, 1976). The reciprocal relationship between person and culture, leading to modification and creation of new cultural forms as a result of acculturation, has been of long-standing interest in the field (Segall, Dasen, Berry, and Poortinga, 1999).

The importance of human biology

Following the orientation of cultural anthropology and much of psychology in the second half of the twentieth century, cross-cultural research has focused much more on the social than on the biological side of human behavior. As in other fields of psychology there is now a more explicit recognition of the biological basis of manifest behavior (e.g., Keller, 1997, 2002). First and foremost this emerges in the recognition of culture as a multi-faceted faculty of humans. Its phylogenetic origins have been demonstrated in research with groups of chimpanzees, who show local variations in customs related to sexual advances, grooming, and the use of tools. Such customs can be stable across generations, indicating the presence of cultural transmission (Boesch, 1991; Whiten, Goodball, McGrew, et al., 1999). Moreover, remarkable similarities in patterns of behavior have been identified in human ethology and cross-cultural psychology that are difficult to understand except in terms of biological underpinnings. A few examples include "motherese" – the tendency of adults in all cultures on which evidence is available to talk to babies in a higher tone of voice and with more variations in tone (e.g., Fernald, 1992); the presence of gestures such as the shrug (Eibl-Eibesfeldt, 1989); and expressions of politeness (Brown and Levinson, 1987).

Although some researchers tend towards biological determinism (e.g., Tooby and Cosmides, 1992), most take an interactive perspective in which "nature" and "environment" are not seen as separate constituents but as inseparable. For example, Keller (1997, 2002) has postulated pathways of ontogenetic development that differ systematically, because separate cultures enable distinct potentials from an array of biologically given trajectories along which each child potentially can develop. In general, interactive approaches presume genetic mechanisms as capabilities that can be evoked and shaped by specific environmental conditions.

Much of biological thinking centers around the notion of function (Tinbergen, 1963). For the present book this raises the question of what the functions of the family are. From an evolutionary perspective the family, like all arrangements, has to serve the fitness (i.e., the probability of survival and reproduction) of an organism. How does the family serve this purpose? The human child cannot fend for itself for many years after its birth. It needs food and protection and it needs to learn the rules and practices of the larger society in which it is growing up.

Theoretical perspectives

Three broad theoretical perspectives on behavior–culture interaction have been discerned: *absolutism*, *relativism*, and *universalism* (Berry et al., 2002). The absolutist position is one that assumes that human behavior is basically the same (qualitatively) in all cultures: "honesty" is "honesty" and "depression" is "depression," no matter where one observes it. From the absolutist perspective, culture is thought to play a limited role or no role in either the meaning or the display of human characteristics. Assessments of such characteristics are made using standard instruments (perhaps with linguistic translation) and interpretations of differences are straightforward, without alternative culturally based views taken into account. Of course, certain aspects of behavior will show more cross-cultural similarities than other aspects. However, as a general orientation, absolutism amounts to an imposition of a uniform (Euro-American) mold on all of humanity. Following the well-known distinction between etic (culture-general) and emic (culture-specific), this orientation can be said to resemble *an imposed etic* approach (Berry, 1969).

In sharp contrast, the relativist approach assumes that human behavior is culturally defined. This approach seeks to avoid imposition (and ethnocentrism) by trying to understand people "in their own terms." Explanations of human diversity are sought in the cultural context in which people have developed. Assessments are typically carried out employing the values and meanings that a cultural group gives to a phenomenon. Comparisons are judged to be problematic and ethnocentric, and are thus often avoided. Thus, this orientation resembles an *emic* approach.

A third perspective, one that lies somewhere between the first two positions, is that of universalism. Here it is assumed that basic human characteristics are common to all members of the species (i.e., constituting a set of psychological givens), and that culture influences the development and display of them (i.e., culture plays different variations on these underlying themes). Assessments are based on the presumed underlying process, but measures are developed in culturally meaningful versions. Comparisons are made cautiously, employing a wide variety of methodological principles and safeguards, while interpretations of similarities and differences are attempted that take alternative culturally based meanings into account. This orientation can be said to resemble a *derived etic* approach (Berry, 1969).

While few today advocate a strictly absolutist or imposed etic view, we have already referred to distinct approaches that the relativist/emic position has given rise to, such as "indigenous psychology" (see Kim and Berry, 1993), and to some extent "cultural psychology" (Shweder and Sullivan, 1993). And the derived etic view has given rise to a "universalist psychology" (Berry et al., 2002). A mutual compatibility between the emic and derived etic positions has been noted by many: for example, Berry et al. (2002, p. 384) and Berry and Kim (1993) have claimed that indigenous psychologies, while valuable in their own right, serve an equally important function as useful steps on the way to achieving a universal psychology.

For obvious reasons none of these "schools" that address culture–behavior relationships corresponds to absolutism, which, as mentioned, is an a-cultural form of psychology. For some, each culture is viewed as so unique that it cannot be compared with other cultures, without destroying the very meanings that members of a cultural group share. This view is essentially a relativist one, and has taken the name "cultural psychology." Other aspects of this view include the assertion that culture is not independent of or antecedent to, but inherent in human behavior; indeed, their slogan is that "culture and psyche make each other up" (Shweder and Sullivan, 1993).

"Indigenous psychology" is related to this; it also sees human behavior as rooted in unique cultural traditions that need to be fully comprehended as an integral part of psychological research. However, comparisons are not ruled out (Enriquez, 1990); frequently, authors in this tradition are open to a "cross-indigenous" approach, in order to discern what may be culture-specific, and what may be pan-human qualities of human behavior.

The "culture-comparative" approach is related to the universalist conception. It argues that cultural contexts are important factors in human behavioral development and need to be thoroughly examined. However, remaining within a single culture will not allow us to discover what may be human, in its broadest meaning. Thus, the culture-comparative approach is both "cultural" and "cross", generating the term "cross-cultural" that is often employed to refer to this way of thinking about culture–behavior relationships.

THE ECOCULTURAL FRAMEWORK

Historical overview

Over the years, an attempt has been made to incorporate many of the foregoing ideas and issues into a working framework for cross-cultural psychological research (Berry, 1966, 1976; Berry, van de Koppel, Sénéchal, Annis, Bahuchet, Cavalli-Sforza and Witkin, 1986; Mishra, Sinha and Berry, 1996b). This Ecocultural Framework is a kind of map that lays out the categories of variables that need to be examined in studies seeking to understand human behavioral diversity in context.

This ecocultural perspective has evolved through a series of research studies devoted to understanding similarities and differences in cognition and social behavior (Berry, 1976; Berry, Bennett and Denny, 2000; Berry et al., 1986; Mishra, Sinha and Berry, 1996b) to a broad approach to understanding human diversity. The core ideas have a long history

(Jahoda, 1995), and have become assembled into conceptual frameworks (Berry, 1975, 1995) used in empirical research, and in coordinating textbooks in cross-cultural psychology (Berry et al., 2002; Segall et al., 1999). Similar ideas and frameworks have been advanced by both anthropologists (e.g., Feldman, 1975; Whiting, 1974) and psychologists (e.g., Bronfenbrenner, 1979) who share the view that human activity can be understood only within the context in which it develops and takes place.

Basic assumptions

The ecocultural perspective is rooted in two basic assumptions. The first (the "universalist" assumption) is that all human societies exhibit commonalities ("cultural universals") and that basic psychological *processes* are shared, species-common characteristics of all human beings on which culture plays variations during the course of development and daily activity. The second (the "adaptation" assumption) is that *behavior* is differentially developed and expressed in response to ecological and cultural contexts. This view allows for comparisons across cultures (on the basis of the common underlying process) and makes comparison worthwhile (using the surface variation as basic evidence). Not only in life sciences, such as ethology (e.g., Alcock, 1998), but also in the social sciences, such as cultural anthropology (e.g., Murdock, 1975) or sociology (e.g., Aberle, Cohen, Davis, Levy, and Sutton, 1950), there is substantial evidence that groups everywhere possess shared sociocultural attributes. For example, all peoples have language, tools, social structures (e.g., norms, roles), and social institutions (e.g., marriage, justice). It is also evident that such commonalities are expressed by groups in different ways from one time and place to another. Similarly, there is parallel evidence at the psychological level for both underlying similarity and surface variation (Berry, Poortinga, Pandey, Dasen, Saraswathi, Segall, and Kağıtçıbaşı, 1997). For example, all individuals have the competence to develop, learn, and perform speech, technology, role playing, and norm observance. At the same time, there are obviously group and individual differences in the extent and style of expression of these shared underlying processes. This combination of underlying similarity with surface expressive variation has been given the name "universalism" by Berry et al. (2002) to distinguish it from "absolutism," which tends to ignore cultural influence on behavioral development and expression, and from "relativism," which tends to ignore the existence of common underlying psychological processes. Of course, while variations in behavioral expression can be directly observed, underlying commonalities are a theoretical construction and cannot be observed directly (Troadec, 2001). Paradoxically, this search for our common humanity can be pursued only by observing our diversity. And this dual task is the essence of cross-cultural psychology (Berry, 1969, 2000; Bril, 1995).

The following is an outline of our current thinking about how people adapt culturally (as a group) to their long-standing ecological settings. It continues with a proposal about how people develop and perform (as individuals) in adaptation to their ecocultural situation.

Ecological and cultural adaptation

One continuing theme in cultural anthropology is that cultural variations can be understood as adaptations to differing ecological settings or contexts (Boyd and Richerson, 1983). This line of thinking usually known as cultural ecology (Vayda and Rappoport, 1968), ecological anthropology (Moran, 1982; Vayda and McKay, 1975), or the ecosystem approach to anthropology (Moran, 1990) has a long history in the discipline (see Feldman, 1975). Its roots go back to Forde's (1934) classic analysis of relationships between physical habitat and societal features in Africa, and Kroeber's (1939) early demonstration that cultural areas and natural areas co-vary in Aboriginal North America. Unlike earlier simplistic assertions by the school of "environmental determinism" (e.g., Huntington, 1945), the ecological school of thought has ranged from "possiblism" (where the environment provides opportunities and sets some constraints or limits on the range of possible cultural forms that may emerge) to an emphasis on "resource utilization" (where active and interactive relationships between human populations and their habitat are analyzed).

Of particular interest to psychologists was Steward's (1955) use of what was later called the cognized environment; this concept refers to the "selected features of the environment of greatest relevance to a population's subsistence." With this notion, ecological thinking moved simultaneously away from any links to earlier deterministic views and towards the more psychological idea of individuals actively perceiving, appraising, and changing their environments.

The earlier ecological approaches have tended to view cultures as relatively stable (even permanent) adaptations (as a state), largely ignoring adaptation (as a process), or adaptability (as a system characteristic) of cultural populations (Bennett, 1976). However, it is clear that cultures evolve over time, sometimes in response to changing ecological circumstances and sometimes as a result of contact with other cultures. This fact has required the addition of a more dynamic conception of ecological adaptation as a continuous, as well as an interactive process (between ecological, cultural, and psychological variables). It is from the most recent position that we approach the topic. It is a view that is consistent with more recent general changes in anthropology, away from a "museum" orientation to culture (collecting and organizing static artifacts) to one that emphasizes cultures as constantly changing and being concerned with creation, metamorphosis, and recreation.

Over the years ecological thinking has influenced not only anthropology but also psychology. The fields of ecological and environmental psychology have become fully elaborated (see Werner, Brown, and Altman, 1997), with substantial theoretical and empirical foundations. In essence, individual human behavior has come to be seen in its natural setting or habitat, both in terms of its development and its contemporary display. The parallel development of cross-cultural psychology (see Berry et al., 1997) has also "naturalized" the study of human behavior and its development. In this field, individual behavior is accounted for to a large extent by considering the role of cultural influences on it. Ecological as well as cultural influences are considered as operating in tandem, hence the term "ecocultural approach" (Berry, 1976).

Ecocultural approach

The current version of the Ecocultural Framework (see Figure 2.1) proposes to account for human psychological diversity (both individual and group similarities and differences) by taking into account two fundamental sources of influence (ecological and sociopolitical) and two features of human populations that are adapted to them: cultural and biological characteristics. These population variables are transmitted to individuals by various "transmission variables" such as enculturation, socialization, genetics, and acculturation. Our understanding of both cultural and genetic transmission has been greatly advanced by recent work on culture learning (e.g., Tomasello, Kruger, and Ratner, 1993) and on the human genome project. The essence of both these domains is the fundamental similarity of all human beings (at a deep level), combined with variation in the expression of these shared attributes (at the surface level). Work on the process and outcomes of acculturation has also been advancing (e.g., Chun, Balls-Organista, and Marin, 2003; Sam and Berry, 2006), necessitated by the dramatic increase in intercultural contact and change.

To summarize, the Ecocultural Framework considers human diversity (both cultural and psychological) to be a set of collective and individual adaptations to context. Within this general perspective, it views cultures

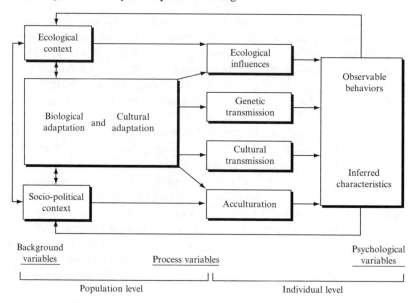

Figure 2.1. Ecocultural Framework.

as evolving adaptations to ecological and sociopolitical influences, and it views individual psychological characteristics in a population as adaptive to their cultural context. It also views (group) culture and (individual) behavior as distinct phenomena at their own levels, which need to be examined independently (see discussion below).

Within psychology, the early ecological research and the findings of the burgeoning field of environmental psychology (Werner, Brown and Altman, 1997), have attempted to specify the links between ecological context and individual human development and behavior. Cross-cultural psychology has tended to view cultures (both one's own, and others one is in contact with) as differential contexts for development, and to view behavior as adaptive to these different contexts.

The ecocultural approach offers a "value neutral" framework for describing and interpreting similarities and differences in human behavior across cultures (Berry, 1994b). As adaptive to context, psychological phenomena can be understood "in their own terms" (as Malinowski insisted), and external evaluations can usually be avoided. This is a critical point, since it allows for the conceptualization, assessment, and interpretation of culture and behavior in non-ethnocentric ways (Dasen, 1993). It explicitly rejects the idea that some cultures or behaviors are more advanced or more developed than others (Berry, Dasen, and Witkin, 1983; Dasen, Berry, and Witkin, 1979). Any argument about cultural or behavioral differences being ordered hierarchically requires the adoption of some absolute (usually external) standard. But who is so bold, or so wise, to assert and verify such a standard?

Finally, the sociopolitical context brings about contact among cultures, so that individuals have to adapt to more than one context. When many cultural contexts are involved (as in situations of culture contact and acculturation), psychological phenomena can be viewed as attempts to deal simultaneously with two (sometimes inconsistent, sometimes conflicting) cultural contexts. This attempt at understanding people in their multiple contexts is an important alternative to the more usual pathologizing of colonized or immigrant cultures and peoples. Of course, these intercultural settings need to be approached with the same non-ethnocentric perspective as cross-cultural ones (Berry, 1985).

Studies using the Ecocultural Framework

Initially (Berry, 1996) the link between ecology, culture, and behavior was elaborated into a framework in order to predict differential development of some perceptual and cognitive abilities between hunting-based and agriculture-based peoples. The first step was to propose that the "ecological demands" for survival that were placed on hunting peoples asked for a high level of these perceptual-cognitive abilities, in contrast with people employing other (particularly agricultural) subsistence strategies. Second, it was proposed that "cultural aids" (such as socialization practices, linguistic differentiation of spatial information, and the use of arts and crafts) would promote the development of these abilities. As predicted, empirical studies of Inuit (then called Eskimo) in the Canadian Arctic and Temne (in Sierra Leone) revealed marked differences in these abilities. Further studies were carried out, and during the course of this empirical work, the ideas became further elaborated into an Ecocultural Framework. In each case, a consideration of ecological and cultural features of the group was taken as a basis for predicting differential psychological outcomes in a variety of domains. For example (Berry, 1967, 1979), differential degrees of reliance on hunting and variations in social stratification (ranging from "loose" to "tight"; Pelto, 1968) and in child socialization practices (ranging from emphases on "assertion" to "compliance"; Barry, Child, and Bacon, 1959) were used to predict variations in the development of these functional abilities. These cultural features are closely linked to the structure and functions of the family, as we shall see later in this Chapter.

Further work on perceptual and cognitive abilities (aligned in part to the theory of psychological differentiation, particularly the cognitive style of field dependence–field independence; Witkin and Berry, 1975) resulted in three volumes (Berry, 1976; Berry et al., 1986; Mishra, Sinha, and Berry, 1996b) reporting results of studies in the Arctic, Africa, Australia, New Guinea, and India. The Ecocultural Framework has also been used to understand sources of variation in perceptual-cognitive development (Dasen, 1975; Nsamenang, 1992). This developmental focus necessarily implicates the structure and function of the family.

While most use of the Ecocultural Framework has been in the study of perception and cognition, it applies equally to the exploration of social behavior. For example, studies of social conformity (Berry, 1967, 1979) have shown that greater conformity to a suggested group norm is likely to occur in cultures that are structurally tight (with high norm obligation). The relationship is robust, whether examined at the level of individuals or by using the group's mean score as the variable related to ecology (see Bond and Smith, 1996, for a review). A further example shows how ecocultural indicators are related to the currently popular concepts of "individualism" and "collectivism" (Berry, 1994a). It is suggested that individualism may be related to differentiation (structural complexity) dimensions, with greater differentiation in a society being predictive of greater personal individualism. However, collectivism is proposed to be related more to integration (structural tightness) dimensions, with greater integration predictive of greater collectivism. It is further suggested that when individualism and collectivism are found to be at opposite ends of one value dimension, it is because data are usually obtained in societies (industrial urban) where the two cultural dimensions (differentiation and integration) are strongly distinguished; if data were to be collected over a broader range, in other types of societies (e.g., hunting or agricultural) where the two dimensions coincide, then opposition may not be observed.

Recent work (Georgas and Berry, 1995; Georgas, van de Vijver, and Berry, 2004) has further extended this interest in social aspects of behavior. A first study sought to discover ecological and social indicators that might allow societies to be clustered according to their similarities and differences on six dimensions: ecology, education, economy, mass communications, population, and religion. The second study further examined ecosocial indicators across cultures, and then sought evidence of their relationships with a number of psychological variables (such as values and subjective well-being). Results showed that many of the indicators came together to form a single economic dimension (termed "Affluence"), and this was distinct from "Religion" in the pattern of relationships with the psychological variables. Specifically, across cultures, a high placement on Affluence (along with Protestant Religion) was associated with more emphasis on individualism, utilitarianism, and personal well-being. In contrast, for other religions, together with low Affluence, there was an emphasis on power relationships, loyalty, and hierarchy values.

THE FAMILY IN ECOCULTURAL PERSPECTIVE

As a cultural institution, the family can be seen as adaptive to ecocultural context and as a vehicle for cultural transmission (Berry, 1976; Georgas, 1988). The family thus occupies a central place in the ecocultural approach, serving to link background contexts to individual behavioral development (see Figure 2.2).

In more detail, it is well established that features of family and marriage are closely related to ecocultural features of a society, especially to settlement pattern, role differentiation, and social stratification. These relationships were already noted in a public lecture by the anthropologist Tylor in the 1880s. He proposed that nomadic societies (mainly hunting and gathering-based peoples) tended to have nuclear families and monogamous marriages, in contrast to sedentary societies (mainly agricultural peoples), who tended to have extended families and polygamous marriages. Tylor suggested that these family and marriage types allowed for efficient economic functioning in their respective habitats: hunters operate best in small units, with symbiotic relationships between two spouses and their direct offspring; agriculturalists require larger working units, facilitated by multiple spouses and a larger network of kin and offspring.

Since these early observations, many empirical studies have demonstrated their validity and have expanded the network of relationships. For example *role differentiation* (the number of specialized tasks that are distinguished within the society) and *social stratification* (the hierarchical arrangement among these roles, leading to variations in status) are now important elements of these complex patterns. Nimkoff and Middleton (1960) divided societies into categories of "great" or "little" social stratification, and into four exploitive patterns; they found that the bulk (76 percent) of the societies classed as "agriculture present," are also classed as "highly stratified," whereas among the societies classed as "hunting or gathering" most (78 percent) were in the "low stratification" category.

The ecology element of the framework proposes that human organisms interact with their physical environments in ways that seek to satisfy their

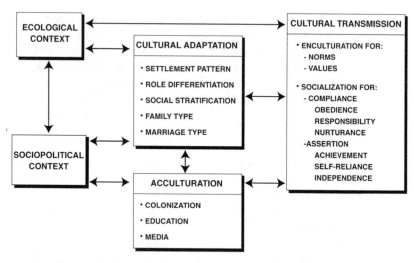

Figure 2.2. Ecocultural context and cultural transmission.

needs. Because of variations in environmental features (e.g., temperature, rainfall, and soil quality), there will emerge variations in economic possibilities.

A well-established dimension of varying economic pursuits is that of "exploitive subsistence pattern" (Murdock, 1969), where preindustrial societies may be classified as gathering, hunting, pastoral, fishing, and varieties of agriculture. Two demographic patterns vary as a function of these economic patterns. For Murdock, "settlement patterns" may be classified as fully nomadic, seminomadic, semisedentary, and fully sedentary; and the size of local population units may range from small camps or settlements up to large towns. Both settlement pattern and population unit size are empirically related to exploitive pattern (Murdock, 1969), hunting and gathering societies being predominantly nomadic or seminomadic with small population units, and agricultural and pastoral societies being predominantly sedentary or semisedentary with much larger population units.

In summary, the evidence for the ecology element of the framework shows that knowledge of physical environmental features allows prediction of the economic opportunities (exploitive pattern and food accumulation), which in turn allows prediction of the demographic distribution (settlement patterns and size of population units). The relationships are all probabilistic or correlational, rather than deterministic. Nevertheless, they are extant and are of sufficient strength to make predictions from ecological factors to the cultural adaptation element of the model.

With respect to *cultural transmission*, a distinction is commonly made between *enculturation* and *socialization*. The first refers to a general, pervasive "enfolding" of developing individuals, leading to their adoption of the norms and values of their society, and their incorporation into the cultural group. The second is a more specific process involving deliberate teaching and reinforcement, so that particular characteristics and skills are acquired by developing individuals. Both these forms of cultural transmission have been proposed as adaptive to ecological context. Specifically, Barry, Child, and Bacon (1959) were able to demonstrate a clear relationship between type of ecological (exploitive) pattern and socialization. Furthermore, training of children for "responsibility" and "obedience" appeared more in agricultural and pastoral societies, whereas training for "achievement," "self-reliance," and "independence" was more frequent in hunting and gathering societies. Thus, we have evidence that an exploitive subsistence pattern is a reasonably good predictor of socialization emphases.

In summary, we can label a broad ecological dimension running from hunting and gathering to agricultural interactions with the environment. Associated with the latter end of the dimension are a sedentary lifestyle, high population density, high sociocultural stratification, polygamy, extended families, and socialization emphases on compliance; associated with the former end of the dimension are a nomadic lifestyle, low population density, low stratification, monogamy, nuclear families, and practices emphasizing assertion. Societies that range along this ecological dimension also vary concomitantly on these other ecological and cultural variables. When this ecological dimension is extended to include contemporary industrial and post-industrial societies, a more complex pattern becomes apparent (Berry, 1994a; Lomax and Berkowitz, 1972). With the increasing high density of cities, we observe a reduction in pressures toward compliance as a result of loss of community cohesion and the increase in anonymity afforded by these large cities. There is also a reduction in the frequency of extended families and a parallel increase in the proportion of nuclear families, which is accompanied by a further reduction in pressures toward compliance. Thus, an increase in stratification, compliance, and conformity from hunting through to agrarian societies changes course to become a decrease in these ecocultural features as societies move from agrarian, to industrial and post-industrial arrangements. In the present study, we examine variations in some of these features, particularly with respect to differences between agrarian, and industrial and post-industrial societies.

In addition to the role of the ecological context, the sociopolitical context has played an important role in shaping both cultural and transmission features of the framework. In particular, the colonization of Asia by Indian and Chinese societies, and of Africa and the Americas by European societies, has brought about societal changes that have altered cultural patterns, including family arrangements and emphases in cultural transmission. Colonization also introduced new religions and forms of education (particularly formal schooling) in most of these societies. And, more recently, the much increased availability of telemedia continues to promote change from outside by portraying alternative lifestyles and consumer goods. Their impact has led to an apparent increase in nuclear families and monogamous marriage in previously polygamous societies with extended families. Associated changes, such as delayed marriage, fewer children, and increased divorce rates, have also been assigned to acculturative influences, mainly emanating from contemporary Western domination of the "Majority World." Sociopolitical impacts on cultural transmission have also been discerned, including increased pressure toward "assertion" and a decline in "compliance" during socialization. The present project also examines variations in cultural, social, and transmission features in relation to the sociopolitical influences.

A systematic view of family in an ecocultural context, which further differentiates the ecological and sociopolitical dimensions, has been proposed by Georgas (1988, 1993). In this view, the developing individual is placed at the core of a set of concentric family and cultural contexts, each nested in the larger setting. The first and most inclusive element, derived from anthropological and sociological research, is the ecology-based *organization and the institutions of society*, such as the subsistence or economic system, the political and judicial system, the educational system, religion, and means of communication. The means of subsistence and the economic system, as discussed above in relation to the Ecocultural Framework, shape the structure and function of the family, family roles, and values. Laws that control aspects of marriage and divorce, care of children, and other aspects of the family are promulgated and enforced by the political and judicial system. Education can be expressed in the form of father or mother teaching family roles and tasks, or in the form of the relationships between the school and the family in the formal education system. Sociopolitical features, such as religion, are related not only to family values but also to shaping other institutions such as laws regulating marriage. Moreover, telemedia and mass communication shape attitudes and values related to the family.

The second element, *bonds with groups in the immediate community*, refers to the degree and quality of contact with significant groups within the community. The family is more than a unit of reproduction. In many cultures, the family is an integral and dynamic unit of the community, with bonds and networks composed of tightly knit extended families and clans, with parallel economic, political, and educational institutions. In these cultures, the community is more important than the national institutions.

The third element, *family*, is a niche within the community, whose function is to provide subsistence, care of children, safety and psychological support, and reproduction of the family. On the other hand, this group connected by biological and psychological bonds must establish ties with the community and the institutions of the society for survival and development.

All three elements are subject to influences from the sociopolitical context. For the first element, these influences include the introduction by an outside (often dominant) culture of formal schooling, telecommunications, and new economic activities, religion, and laws. These interact with, and impact on, the original forms of these institutions, setting the stage for further changes in the other two elements. For the second element, community organizations change, often to resemble those of the outside society. And for the third element, the family type and organization usually change to resemble the monogamous, nuclear form found in industrialized societies.

Thus, the study of family, and of family change, that is guided by the Ecocultural Framework needs to take into account both the ecological bases of the institutions, communities, and families, and the changes introduced by sociopolitical features of their contemporary lives.

CROSS-CULTURAL METHODOLOGY

An essential characteristic of scientific investigation is the explicit validation of results. This implies that scientists try to protect their findings and interpretations against all kinds of pitfalls. In cross-cultural psychology such pitfalls relate particularly to (i) research designs, including the sampling of cultures and individuals, (ii) non-equivalence of measurements, and (iii) aggregation of findings across the levels of individuals and groups.

In culture-comparative research, observed differences in behavior outcomes between two cultural samples are typically interpreted in terms of some antecedent cultural factor. For example, differences in family functions and roles are attributed to antecedent factors such as living arrangements or affluence (Georgas, 1999; Georgas et al., 2001). Psychological outcomes are usually assessed by means of survey or questionnaire instruments administered to individuals. Cross-cultural differences in score distributions are then interpreted in terms of the traits or domains measured by these instruments. Such differences tend to be ascribed to some antecedent condition. However, it is not uncommon that the cultural antecedent is selected post hoc. For example, nowadays many researchers accept that a range of psychological differences between Japan and the United States have to do with the dimension of individualism–collectivism. But reviews of empirical research by Matsumoto (1999) and Takano and Osaka (1999) found the antecedent difference to be questionable.

There are various ways to strengthen the design of cross-cultural studies, such as the inclusion of major alternative antecedent variables and their explicit assessment. In many instances the most important design measure is the extension of research to include a larger number of cultures. There are three levels of sampling in cross-cultural research: populations, groups within a population, and individuals within a group.

First, cultural populations have to be selected. Two strategies can be followed. Cultures can be selected that differ on an antecedent variable of interest; this is called "theory guided" selection. Alternatively, a sample can be drawn from the population (or a subpopulation) of all cultures in the world. Sampling requires that there exists some listing of cultures; in cross-cultural psychology this problem is often preempted by taking countries as separate cultures. Random sampling is approximated when cultural populations are selected with a view to having the various regions of the world represented. The latter strategy has been followed in the project on which we report in this book.

When a complex entity like a country is selected, it may be inappropriate to assume cultural homogeneity, since all contemporary states are culturally diverse. This fact has implications for the selection of a subgroup that is to represent that country. It is almost impossible to find a subgroup that in all respects is representative of a larger cultural population. In the project at hand, the strategy has been to include university students as a section of a national population that has many corresponding features across societies (in terms of age, experience in articulating answers on questionnaires, etc.).

In a representative sample each member of the population of interest has an equal probability of selection. This requires a listing of all individual persons, ways to approach them individually, and the individual administration of research instruments. Such procedures were out of reach for the present project for organizational as well as financial reasons. We had to follow the more common strategy of selecting individuals who happen to be together at the same time and place. Consequently, the instruments were administered to classes of students.

A second pitfall in cross-cultural research is that scores on psychological instruments may not have the same meaning cross-culturally. The scores are then said to be inequivalent or incomparable. Inequivalence can occur for different reasons. It is possible that a certain trait is not part of the behavior repertoire of a cultural population; for example, it has been argued that emotions should be seen as culture-specific (Kitayama and Markus, 1994). Obviously, this logically precludes any comparison; comparing scores obtained in different cultures is like the proverbial comparison of apples and oranges. It is also possible that an instrument does assess the same trait, but on a different scale; this means that quantitative differences in score levels should not be interpreted at face value. Various levels of equivalence have been distinguished and psychometric tests have been developed for each of these levels to examine whether conditions of equivalence are met. Currently the most common distinctions have been formulated by van de Vijver and Leung (1997). They distinguish three levels of equivalence that have been summarized as follows by Poortinga and van de Vijver (2004):

i. Structural or functional equivalence, viz., a test measures the same trait (or set of traits) cross-culturally, but not necessarily on the same quantitative scale (cf. Celsius and Fahrenheit scales).
ii. Metric or measurement unit equivalence, i.e., measurement units of the scales are the same in all cultures, but there is no common scale anchor (origin). A difference between two scores has then the same meaning, independent of the culture in which it was found (cf. Celsius and Kelvin scales).
iii. Scale equivalence or full score comparability, i.e., scores of a given value have in all respects the same meaning cross-culturally and can be interpreted in the same way (cf. Celsius and Celsius).

Most relevant for the present project is the analysis of structural equivalence. This is examined mainly by means of multivariate analyses such as exploratory factor analysis or confirmatory factor analysis. Statistical procedures are available to estimate the degree of factorial similarity in data sets collected in different societies, for example by means of a congruence coefficient usually called Tucker's phi (Tucker, 1951). If factor structures of the items in an instrument show substantial differences across cultures, meaningful comparison is ruled out. If the factor structures are similar, this is taken as an important indication that the same traits are measured. Measurement unit equivalence can be examined by means of analysis of covariance structures (usually confirmatory factor analysis) or by means of comparison of patterns of test scores obtained from repeated measurements. A necessary (but not sufficient) condition for full-score equivalence is the absence of item bias (or differential item functioning) that can be checked with analysis of variance or item response theory (Holland and Wainer, 1993; van de Vijver and Leung, 1997).

A third methodological pitfall has to do with the fact that variables can pertain to individuals or to societies. Individual level measurements, which reflect psychological variables, may acquire a different meaning when they are aggregated to the population level. The same may happen when data collected at population level are disaggregated to individual level. One famous example concerns differences in spatial ability between boys and girls. An individual score can be interpreted in terms of this ability, but when a mean difference is found between two school classes, this may be a matter of differences in proportions of boys and girls attending these classes. It can be argued that aggregation and disaggregation problems do not play a role only when there is equivalence across levels (van de Vijver and Poortinga, 2002). Psychometric tests of equivalence across levels require extensive data sets. However, with fewer data, techniques such as regression analysis or analysis of covariance can be used to eliminate the effects of selected variables (provided they are included in the design of a study) before interpreting cross-cultural differences. Economic affluence and formal education are two such variables.

In summary, cross-cultural research tends to become rather complicated when researchers want to protect their interpretation of observed differences against all kinds of alternatives, including the alternative that such differences are due to artefacts of method. To an important extent competing alternatives can be ruled out by proper design and by analyses for the equivalence of data. When interpreting a complex data set common sense and an open eye for remaining pitfalls will have to complement the methodological toolbox.

CONCLUSION

The ecocultural approach has come to be employed in the study of a variety of domains of human behavior. It has been established that there are systematic relationships between features of the ecosystem in which a population lives, many of the cultural and biological arrangements in a population, and in the distribution over individuals within populations. A critical remaining issue is how these ecological and cultural features of a population become incorporated into the behavioral repertoire of individuals. To answer this question, we will focus in the next Chapter on cultural transmission and the central role of the family in carrying it out.

3   Theoretical perspectives on family change

Çiğdem Kağıtçıbaşı

In this Chapter we will examine family dynamics and change from a cross-cultural psychological perspective. The main focus will be on family change within changing global social structural and ecocultural contexts. Following the previous Chapter, however, we will start by examining the current Western family with a sociological orientation, for it is the Western family that has served as a prototype for family research in sociology. We will then devote most of our attention to the non-Western family, both in the Majority World and also as immigrant in the Western countries, and try to depict patterns of change that can be explained with a comparative orientation and from an ecocultural perspective. There will also be a presentation of a Model of Family Change (Kağıtçıbaşı, 1990, 1996a) that has proven useful in understanding family patterns in relation to different ecocultural contexts and changes in these.

FAMILY RESEARCH AGENDA: THE WESTERN ECOCULTURAL CONTEXT

Even a cursory glance at current scholarship on the family brings forth an interesting, even ironic dilemma. While there is a concern regarding the current state and the future of the Western family, which is claimed to be on the decline, at the same time there is a tacit assumption that the family in the non-Western (Majority) world is shifting toward the Western model. As discussed in Chapter 1, this is the main thesis of modernization theory that permeates social science thinking and everyday parlance, even though it has been questioned ever since its inception in 1960s (Bendix, 1967; Gusfield, 1967). The assumed shift toward the Western nuclear family with urbanization and industrialization is based on the classical Parsonian theory of the nuclear family, central to family sociology (Parsons, 1943, 1949, 1965), and the work of other key theoreticians of family and family change (e.g., Goode, 1963, 1964). Even today there does not seem to be extensive questioning of this assumed shift toward a "failed" ideal, though some social scientists have criticized the dominant ideology of the separate and independent nuclear family as the prototypical Western family (Bronfenbrenner and Weiss, 1983; Keniston, 1985; Mogey, 1991; Segalen, 1986).

In this Chapter several aspects of these rather conflicting perspectives will be discussed and critically appraised. First, some research conducted in Western contexts, particularly in the United States, will be reviewed and then a view from the other side, the Majority World, will be taken up. The term "Western" is used here for lack of a better term to refer mainly to the preponderantly middle-class populations in North American and Western European ecocultural contexts, with the full recognition that there is great diversity in the "West." Similarly, "non-Western" or "Majority World" is utilized to refer to the rest of the world's populations, which again entail great variation. The main reasoning involved in this characterization is that in general the variation between these groups of populations tends to be higher than within each group. However, this is probably the case if social structural factors and ecocultural contexts are held constant, such as in comparisons of urban middle-class populations between the Western and Majority World countries versus urban middle-class populations within each. When urban and rural/agrarian populations come into the picture, however, there tends to be greater difference between them within the Majority World than between the middle-class populations in the West and the Majority World. This is because there are profound differences in ecocultural contexts and lifestyles between urban and peasant groups in the Majority World. Finally, the term "Majority World" is used here, since "developing" world or "developing" countries is a misnomer, as the gap between the "developed" and the so-called "developing" countries seems to be increasing rather than decreasing. The term "third world" is not appropriate, either, after the collapse of the "second world."

Most current scholarship in family sociology is carried out in the North American and Western European ecocultural contexts, particularly the former. The themes often reflect the problems faced by families, especially in the face of changing life circumstances involving economic recession and poverty, unemployment, neighborhood crime and the like, as well as the dynamics of functional and structural changes in the family itself, as an institution. Given the strong problem-oriented approach, the research emphasis is on low income families, particularly the urban poor (e.g., Brooks-Gunn and Duncan, 2000; Burton and Jarrett, 2000; White and Rogers, 2000). However, more generally the changes in families belonging to different socioeconomic strata are also under scrutiny.

This work on the Western, particularly the American, family appears self-contained and turned inward, in terms of theoretical perspectives used and empirical research conducted, such that there is no resorting to the families in diverse global ecocultural contexts, which seem remote and irrelevant. More recently the immigrant family has also been the subject of study, particularly focusing on adaptability to the host society. Here the culture of origin does emerge as relevant; nevertheless, the focus is again on adjustment within the host society rather than on searching for cross-cultural patterns going beyond the Euro-American ecocultural context. Indeed there is not much cross-cultural comparative research on the family in contemporary societies across different regions of the world. Thus, the present volume brings a new perspective to the global study of the family, which fills an important gap in the field.

WHITHER WESTERN FAMILY?

As discussed at some length in Chapter 1, over the last decades there has been a growing concern among family researchers regarding the state of the family in Western society, particularly in the United States. A voluminous body of research has pointed to systematic changes in families, including decreasing family size, increasing family instability with dramatic growth in divorce rates, and marked increases in women's labor-force participation. Concomitant changes in family dynamics, functions, and roles have also been observed, all pointing to significant transformations at demographic, institutional, and cultural levels. Given these substantial changes, which all researchers note, the ensuing debate is on the interpretation, and specifically, whether the family is in decline.

In his highly controversial commentary, entitled "American family decline, 1960–1990," Popenoe (1993, p.527) wrote, "family decline since 1960 has been extraordinarily steep, and its social consequences serious, especially for children." Following up his earlier book, *Disturbing the nest: Family change and decline in modern societies* (1988), Popenoe interprets as alarming the demographic, structural, and functional changes in the family as revealed by data from family research in Sweden and the United States. For quite a while family researchers have indeed noted the historical shrinking of the several family functions down to merely two, namely childrearing and provision of affection and companionship (see Chapter 1). This change has been seen by many as healthy: since having abandoned its peripheral functions such as education and health, and having become more specialized in terms of the two core functions, the family is considered better equipped to perform these functions well. Yet Popenoe claims that even these minimal functions are threatened with the decline of the family, particularly in the

United States. This interpretation is strongly debated by other family researchers as reflecting a conservative ideology that rejects alternative patterns of family composition and functioning (e.g., Cowan, 1993; Glenn, 1993; Stacey, 1993). Giddens, for example (1991, 1992) acclaims what he calls "the global revolution in family and personal life," which entails greater sexual freedom, emotional intimacy, and gender equality. The ongoing debate is elaborated in Chapter 1.

Even those who disagree with Popenoe's claims, however, acknowledge the trends revealed in family statistics, particularly in the United States. These trends can be summarized briefly as follows. Over decades, families in Western societies have become smaller in size and less stable, as people prefer to invest their time and energy in themselves rather than in their families. Numbers of children are decreasing. Some reasons are that many parents want fewer children, with rising costs of childrearing; many women postpone childbearing, and some don't get the number of children they initially desired. Also positive feelings toward motherhood and parenthood have declined, especially as alternative identities become available to women. Therefore, as children comprise a smaller proportion of the population, national concern over children in the United States has shifted to other issues, reflected in inadequate social and economic policies regarding children. Marital roles have changed, with ever increasing labor-force participation of women. With increasing divorce rates, the prevalence of intact nuclear families is declining; stepfamilies and single-parent families are common. Among several causes of divorce, economic factors, changes in gender roles, and higher psychological expectations of the spouses from each other and from the marital union come to the fore. Thus marriage has become a path toward self-fulfillment, "a voluntary relationship that individuals can make and break at will" (Popenoe, 1993, p. 533), rather than entailing moral/religious/social obligations as it had earlier. The increase in non-family living also has to do with the elderly living independently.

Though some of the above changes are not problematic, as they reflect, for example, more egalitarian gender relations and a more democratic family, the net result emerges as a decline of the family, as it has been traditionally defined in the demographic, institutional, and cultural levels. The demographic results are seen in the declining family size, the smaller number of years spent with family members, and the decrease of family households in proportion to all households. The institutional results point to the weakening of the cohesion of the family as an institution, the power it has in society relative to other institutions, and its lower ability to perform its functions. These functions include procreation and socialization of children, provision of affection and companionship, sexual regulation, and economic cooperation. These have weakened with below replacement birthrates, children and adolescents spending less time with the family and more time in childcare and with peers, increasing premarital sexuality, and greater economic independence of the family members.

As indicated above, despite the debate on the meaning of these trends, their existence is not questioned. Clearly these family trends are to a large extent in response to changes in the wider economic, social, and cultural transformations in Western societies, particularly noticeable in the last several decades. Together with the structural and functional modifications noted, alterations in family roles, expectations, values, and ideals – that is, in family culture – are also emerging, which in turn feed back into the patterns of structural and functional changes.

How widespread are these changes in the West? They are noted by many family researchers and are evident in vital statistics, including those regarding marriage and divorce rates, fertility rates, and urban poverty. For example, despite significant differences in social policies between the United States and European social welfare states, there are similarities in the above trends. If we take Sweden as a case in point, as was also done by Popenoe, marriage and family are seen as "eroding institutions" there as well (Liljestrom, 2002), cohabitation being the common pattern rather than marriage, at least until the birth of a child. Combined with increasing age at childbirth (from 24 in 1974 to 29 in 2002), the net result is the smaller number of children, namely 1.5, which is below replacement level. The divorce rate in Sweden is one of the highest in Europe, 64 per cent. It is estimated that 40 to 50 per cent of cohabitations are disrupted within 10 years, 40 per cent of separations involving married couples and 60 per cent unmarried cohabiters. The 1960s marked the rise of the so-called "sexual liberation" in Sweden, with the widespread availability of contraception and the legalization of abortion in 1974. A new foundation was laid for voluntary couple relationships while at the same time dual-earner families greatly increased. The situation is similar in other Nordic countries. These are considered to be important precursors of the present fragile state of the Nordic family (see Liljestrom and Ozdalga, 2002).

It is to be noted again that there are the similarities in the American and the Swedish family trends despite the significant differences in social and family policies in the two countries. The Swedish welfare state supports women's employment and has pronatalist policies providing good quality public childcare when the baby becomes one year old and maternal or paternal paid leave until then. Such substantial family support is apparently still inadequate to strengthen the family and assure its stability.

Family and childcare policies in the United States are inadequate and have been the target of much criticism (e.g., Bogenschneider, 2000; Duncan and Brooks-Gunn, 2000). Urban poverty is also much more marked in the United States than in Sweden. Despite such contrasting social and economic contexts, family outcomes are quite similar and also extend to other Western post-industrial societies. The causes probably lie in some common cultural factors including individualistic outlooks, which will be discussed later. Given this general portrayal of the changes in the Western family, from a global perspective then, how far-reaching are these trends accompanying urbanization and changes in lifestyles, including increasing education and labor-force participation of women and increasing gender equality?

IMMIGRANT AND ETHNIC MINORITY FAMILIES

To address the initial question we started out with – whether the non-Western family is shifting toward the Western family, which is claimed to be on the decline – one needs to study the non-Western family. The natural context for this is the Majority World. Research on the non-Western family, especially from an anthropological perspective, has been going on for a long time. This work has been summarized in Chapter 1. Further coverage will be given later on in this chapter, mainly with a comparative and theoretical perspective. Beyond the Majority World, however, the immigrant family in North American and European countries, with a non-Euro-American background, can serve as another target of study in addressing the above question. It then takes the form of whether the immigrant family is substantially different from the dominant family in the Western host society and whether the former is changing toward the latter.

Immigration, as a worldwide phenomenon of movement of people, usually from less economically developed areas to more technologically advanced societies, has been studied by social scientists from several perspectives. In the last decades psychological work on the topic has addressed acculturation and adjustment problems of families, children, and youth to the host society. A general assumption is that the immigrant family becomes more similar to the host society family with time. Though there is some research substantiating this assumption, there is also much variability. Thus, for example, while some individualistic values are found to increase among Hispanic parents with years spent in the United States, collectivistic values appear to continue, at times with new combinations emerging (e.g., Kwak, 2003; Taylor and Wang, 2000). Not all aspects of individualism emerge with increased contact with Western society. Which aspects emerge and which do not is an empirical issue and has to do with the requirements of the new ecocultural environment. A Model of Family Change to be discussed later on, promises to shed light on this process of change.

There is a concern regarding the loss of status and isolation of the immigrant family, leading to less adaptability than its counterparts in the host society. There is much variability here, also. For example, Kwak (2003) notes that this concern has not been substantiated by research conducted in North America, Australia, and Portugal regarding immigrant families' adaptability and immigrant adolescents' successful school performance and self development. Similarly, Beiser, Hou, Hyman, and Tousignant (2002) point to the good mental health of low-income immigrant children in Canada. On the other hand, problems have been reported in family adaptation and children's school performance among, for example, Turkish and Moroccan immigrants in the Netherlands (Eldering and Leseman, 1999; van Tuijl, Leseman, and Rispens, 2001).

Clearly a myriad of factors play a role in the adaptation of the immigrant family, ranging from general relations with the host society to economic well-being. In any case, where there is healthy adjustment and positive family outcomes, this is often found to be due, at least partially, to support by ethnic family/kin networks and stability of the connected family. These "successful" families are found to be moving not toward individualistic separation/independence but rather toward consolidation and optimal use of their ethnic embeddedness. Thus the intact family structure and the social support provided by extended family and kin appear to be strengths. The modernization assumption of a shift toward the Western family pattern in every respect is not substantiated much by research.

The role of social support networks in contributing to family adaptability is not unique to immigrant families. A good deal of research has stressed the importance of social support, especially in the context of poverty. However, regardless of actual family interdependence, family culture, social values, and expectations (i.e., what is considered normal and desirable) appear to be pertinent factors here. For example, Blair, Blair, and Madamba (1999) found that while the presence of extended kin was related to better school performance of children in African-American households, the opposite was the case in Anglo-American homes. Extended family household might have different meanings in different groups, having more negative connotations, possibly a poorer or a weakened family structure in the Anglo-American context, but a cohesive one in the African-American family culture. Indeed, family/kin support and three generational extended families are more common, thus "normal" in low-income African-American neighborhoods (Slaughter, 1988). In the Anglo-American family, however, where the middle-class ideals of individualistic self-sufficiency and independence are more relevant, it may signify an unwelcome dependency. Indeed, even in situations where intergenerational support is present and functional, ambivalent feelings about it and discomfort have been observed (Cohler and Geyer, 1982).

These considerations point to the importance of social values and expectations, i.e., cultural orientations that provide "meaning." In the context of the immigrant family, with greater connectedness, there tends to be a greater acceptance, even appreciation, of extended family and kin support, which explains the positive family outcomes noted by Kwak (2003) and Beiser et al. (2002), mentioned above.

Regarding adolescent adjustment in immigration contexts, Kwak (2003) notes that studies demonstrate agreement between immigrant adolescents and parents regarding family embeddedness, but disagreement and conflict regarding issues of autonomy. This may be seen as a dilemma when autonomy and embeddedness are considered to be conflictual orientations. Such a consideration is common and is informed particularly by psychoanalytic thinking that claims the necessity of separation for autonomy (Blos, 1979; Kroger, 1998; Steinberg and Silverberg, 1986). As will be discussed below, this may be a culturally biased perspective reflecting an individualistic worldview. Regarding the immigrant adolescent and the family, what seems to happen is that autonomy takes on adaptive value for the adolescent in the new lifestyles of the host society, for example in peer groups or the school. The parents may not recognize this newly emerging need, causing a conflict. However, adolescents who demand greater autonomy appear to be content with their family connectedness and do not want to separate, in agreement with their parents (Kwak, 2003). Thus what we see here is a possible combination of (or aspiration for) both autonomy and embeddedness of the adolescent, not adequately recognized in Western psychology. This situation is in line with views that claim the compatibility of close relations to parents and adolescent autonomy (e.g., Grotevant and Cooper, 1986; Ryan and Deci, 2000; Ryan and Lynch, 1989).

Referring again to the question we started out with in the beginning of this section – i.e., whether the non-Western family is shifting toward the Western family – we can conclude that there does not seem to be a simple answer. Even in immigration context, where intensive culture contact occurs, a direct shift toward the Western pattern is not the rule, even in the orientations of adolescents, the fastest acculturating group. Instead, different aspects of the family culture undergo different degrees of transformation, with changes in some and continuities in the others.

THE FAMILY IN THE MAJORITY WORLD AND MODERNIZATION

As noted in Chapter 1, anthropological work on the non-Western family, particularly in pre-industrial societies, has a long history. It has contributed greatly to our understanding of the diversity of family structures and functions across cultures. However, families in contemporary national societies have not been examined to the same extent. This volume fills that gap. Furthermore, anthropological knowledge has also been produced by Western social scientists. Non-Western Majority World scholarship on the family is limited in scope and volume. Most of it follows in the footsteps of Western anthropological and sociological theory and research, and is therefore not distinguishable from them. Different theoretical perspectives are scarce and far between. Nevertheless, more recently cross-cultural comparative work, conducted in contemporary national societies rather than in isolated pre-industrial human groups, promises to shed light on patterns of family dynamics and functioning in changing ecocultural contexts. This volume is an important contribution to the field with its comparative perspective and extensive coverage of 30 countries.

In contrast to the Western prototype of the conjugal nuclear family, the non-Western prototype has been defined as the extended family. This is commonly seen in sociological scholarship on the family comparing tradition and modernity. Two parallel contrasts are drawn, a spatial one between the Western and non-Western contexts, and a temporal one between premodern and modern within the West. These contrasting parallels underlie the modernization "convergence hypothesis" that with urbanization and modernization there will be a convergence toward the Western pattern. This claim entails two assumptions. The first assumption is a social evolutionist one that whatever is different from the Western pattern is by definition deficient and is bound to change and improve toward the Western end point. This is because only the Western individualistic family/human pattern is claimed to be compatible with economic development. This process of societal progress is labeled modernization. The second assumption is a historical one, which asserts that the Western family was also extended but was transformed into the nuclear family as a necessary outcome of industrialization. Therefore, as non-Western societies industrialize, they also necessarily shift toward the Western nuclear family. This reasoning is the basis of Parsonian family theory.

The first assumption is being seriously challenged today by the examples of great economic advancement in some non-Western societies, such as Japan, Taiwan, Korea, Singapore, and Hong Kong. Indeed, research from various societies shows that despite socioeconomic development, urbanization, and industrialization, the expected shift in family culture is not taking place in the Majority World (for a review, see Kağıtçıbaşı, 1996a). The second assumption is also questioned by historical demographic research conducted in Europe and the United States. It is found that the typical family in Western Europe, particularly in England, was not the traditional extended family for a very long time preceding the industrial revolution, but rather nuclear. Thus, individuation and nucleation of the family was not the *result* of industrialization. For example, MacFarlane (1978, 1986) traces individualistic themes in family history all the way back to the medieval period. Even those who do not accept MacFarlane's thesis note that by the early modern period (sixteenth century) the typical British family was nuclear in structure and not traditional in culture (Lesthaeghe, 1980; Lesthaeghe and Surkyn, 1988; Razi, 1993; Thorton, 1984). This is evidenced for example by church records and other archival material showing that wider ties of kinship were weak, thus villagers relied on institutional support rather than on kin assistance; rural society was highly mobile; children often left home in their teens and spent a few years as living-in servants in other families; women married late, and some never married (see Razi, 1993, for a review). In the United States, also, similar early individualistic patterns predated industrialization (Furstenberg, 1966; Lesthaeghe, 1980; Thorton and Fricke, 1987). Thus, given this historical evidence, if the family individuation and nucleation were not the result of industrialization in the West, it cannot be claimed that it will necessarily occur as a result of industrialization in the Majority World, either.

Indeed, research conducted in different regions of the Majority World provides evidence of diversity as well as common patterns that defy the stereotypic characterizations of the non-Western family as structurally extended. This point was elaborated in Chapter 1, also. For example, D'Cruz and Bharat (2001) note that because joint family in India is the cultural ideal, it has been assumed to be the social reality as well. Yet they point to evidence (Kapadia, 1956; Shah, 1996, 1997, cited in D'Cruz and Bharat, 2001) showing that it was the urban and wealthy higher castes that lived in joint families while the lower castes and the poor had a preponderance of nuclear families. This is mainly because a large family is more expensive to support. Thus jointness symbolized wealth and status and has been the cultural ideal. However, "jointness" may be seen in how families function rather than in how they are structured. Thus, the joint family appears to be changing, though not toward a conjugal nuclear system but toward "adaptive extended family" that functions as a joint family, with closely knit ties, but that is structurally nuclear (Khatri, 1975).

Similarly Timur (1972) in an early national survey in Turkey showed that the majority of the households were nuclear and had always been nuclear despite assumptions to the contrary. She also noted close family/kin ties even in and between nuclear households. Thus there is a need to distinguish the structure of the family from the way it functions. Accordingly, we can differentiate "structurally extended" and "functionally extended" families (Kağıtçıbaşı, 1996a). Whereas the former is more typical in the traditional agrarian context, particularly among the landed and more affluent families and is therefore the cultural ideal, the latter is a nuclear household but is closely connected with other kin also with nuclear households and may carry out family functions such as production, childcare, etc. jointly with them. The latter, functionally extended family, appears to be the more common pattern in many Majority World countries but is often confused with structurally extended family type.

THE VALUE OF CHILDREN STUDY

An ecocultural perspective on family change takes into consideration both the cultural and social structural context and the functional dynamics that enable the family to adapt to changes in this context. Family as an intergenerational system of relationships, as well as family values and child rearing patterns, needs to be considered in an integrated approach. When we understand the contextual/functional dynamics of family from an ecocultural perspective, we can grasp how and why the family changes with socioeconomic change, as well as how families in different eco-sociocultural contexts differ from each other.

A model of family and self, also dealing with family change, has been developed by Kağıtçıbaşı (1990, 1996a) to define and explain some common patterns observed in different socioeconomic and ecocultural contexts. Its empirical basis was the Value of Children (VOC) study carried out in the 1970s (Fawcett, 1983; Hoffman, 1987, 1988; Kağıtçıbaşı, 1982a, 1982b). The VOC study was carried out in nine countries, mainly East and South East Asian but also including Turkey, Germany, and the United States. It examined motivations for childbearing and the values attributed to children by parents. The concept of the value of the child for parents is important in understanding the place of the child in family and society. It also sheds light on intergenerational relations throughout the family life cycle.

The original VOC study pointed to the importance of economic/ utilitarian and psychological values attributed to children by parents. The economic/utilitarian VOC has to do with children providing material benefits to their families while young (working in family business, doing household chores, etc.) and providing "old age security" to their parents when they grow up. The psychological VOC has to do with the love, pride, joy, etc. that children give to their parents. The economic VOC was found to be particularly strong in less developed countries of the Majority World with low levels of affluence and mostly rural/agrarian lifestyles. In these contexts children are expected to be dependent on their parents, that is obedient, while young, this dependence to be reversed later on by the dependence of the elderly parents on their grown-up offspring for their livelihood. The main finding was that with socioeconomic development (comparing countries with higher GNP, urbanization, and higher socioeconomic standing with less developed ones), the economic/utilitarian VOC decreased. However, even though the economic VOC was found to be less in more developed contexts, the overall VOC did not necessarily vary among countries with different economic development levels because psychological VOC did not decrease with increasing affluence and socioeconomic development.

The VOC study has recently been replicated, in part, in a number of different countries, including several from the original study. The findings corroborate the original conceptualization and point to systematic differences over time, reflecting the profound economic and social structural/ecocultural changes over time. Taking up the current findings from Turkey (Kağıtçıbaşı and Ataca, 2005 Ataca, Kağıtçıbaşı, and Diri, 2005) as a case in point, we see that over three decades, profound changes took place in the values attributed to children by parents and in related family values. In particular, a significant increase in psychological VOC and a corresponding decrease in economic/utilitarian VOC were found. Together with other changes in expectations from children, desired qualities in children, actual, desired and ideal numbers of children, and decreased son preference, the findings of variation over time corroborated the earlier findings of variations across countries. They provided empirical evidence for a changing pattern of family interactions, or a "Model of Family Change" to be discussed next.

A MODEL OF FAMILY CHANGE

The realization that the material and psychological VOCs were in fact differentially affected by socioeconomic development led to a focus on the different VOCs and an attempt to differentiate between material and emotional (psychological) interdependencies in the family. This was a conceptual breakthrough that paved the way toward the development of a Model of Family Change. The model (Kağıtçıbaşı, 1990, 1996a) fits with the above VOC study (Figure 3.1). It is a general model that situates the family within cultural and socioeconomic contexts. Socioeconomic and sociohistorical change and its influence on family structure and functioning are dealt with. In this respect it fits in with the more general Ecocultural Framework presented in the previous Chapter. It is, however, more focused on the intra-family dynamics and in particular on socialization values, parenting, and the resultant self.

Deriving from this general model, three different models of family interaction patterns are distinguished (Kağıtçıbaşı, 1990, 1996a), which are the traditional family characterized by overall (material and emotional) interdependence, the individualistic model based on independence, and a dialectical synthesis of the two, involving material independence but emotional/psychological interdependence. These interaction patterns are studied at the intergenerational level.

The family model of total interdependence is prevalent in, though not limited to, less affluent contexts, especially in the traditional rural agrarian society in the Majority World, where intergenerational interdependence is a requisite for family livelihood. The child contributes to the family well-being both while young (for example working in the field and contributing to family economy) and later on in providing old-age security to his/her parents. Thus, in such contexts the child's economic/utilitarian value has salience for parents, and high fertility is implicated, as the economic value of the child (VOC) is cumulative with child numbers (Kağıtçıbaşı, 1982b, 1990). More children contribute more in material terms. In the family model of total interdependence, the independence of the child is not functional and may even be seen as a threat to the family livelihood because independent offspring may look after their own self-interests rather than the interests of the family. Thus obedience orientation is seen in childrearing that leaves no room for autonomy, and intergenerational relations are characterized by hierarchical roles (Fisek, 1995).

A contrasting pattern is seen in the family model of independence, characteristic of the Western middle-class nuclear family, at least in professed ideals. Here intergenerational independence is valued, and

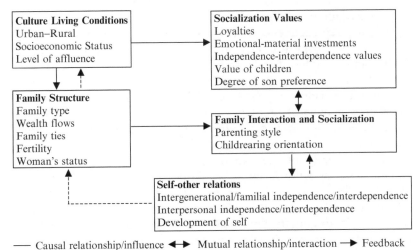

Reprinted with permission from Ç. Kağıtçıbaşı (1996). *Family and human development across cultures: A view from the other side. Hillsdale, NJ: Lawrence Erlbaum.*

Figure 3.1. General family change model.

childrearing is oriented toward engendering self-reliance and autonomy in the child. Individuation-separation is considered a requisite for healthy human development in such a context where objective conditions of social welfare and affluence render family interdependence unnecessary, if not dysfunctional. Old people have their own income, insurance benefits, etc.

As mentioned before, there is a general modernization assumption of a shift from the former model of family interdependence to the latter model of family independence with socioeconomic development. However, recent evidence is questioning this assumption in showing continuities in closely knit interaction patterns despite increased urbanization and industrialization in societies with closely knit human patterns (see Kağıtçıbaşı, 1996a, in press, for reviews; Stewart, Bond, Deeds, and Chung, 1999) or in the context of immigration (Dekovic, Pels, and Model, in press; Koutrelakos, 2004; Phalet and Schonpflug, 2001). What appears to happen is that material interdependencies weaken with increased affluence and urbanization, but psychological interdependencies continue, since they are not incompatible with changing lifestyles. Thus the model involves decreasing material interdependencies but continuing psychological interdependencies with socioeconomic development (particularly urbanization) in societies with collectivistic cultures of interpersonal connectedness.

The emerging pattern is therefore the family model of psychological/ emotional interdependence that is different from the two commonly recognized prototypical models of independence and interdependence. In the family model of independence there is independence in both material and psychological dimensions; in the family model of interdependence there is interdependence in both dimensions. In the synthetic model of psychological interdependence, however, there is independence in the material realm together with interdependence in the psychological realm.

There are important implications of the modifications in family interdependencies for childrearing. In the family model of total interdependence there is intergenerational hierarchy and childrearing is oriented toward obedience, since an obedient child is more likely to grow up to be a loyal offspring. In the family model of independence, autonomy and separateness of the growing child are encouraged, since these characteristics contribute to greater self-reliance and self-sufficiency. In the family model of psychological interdependence, a dialectic synthesis of the other two models is seen in a childrearing orientation that integrates autonomy with relatedness, which may be akin to "authoritative parenting" (Baumrind, 1980). The self that develops in the family model of interdependence is the related self; it is characterized by relatedness and dependency. The self that emerges in the family model of independence is the separate self; it involves autonomy and separateness. The self that develops in the family model of psychological interdependence is the autonomous-related self, manifesting autonomy and relatedness.

IMPLICATIONS OF THE MODEL OF FAMILY CHANGE

In Majority World societies with collectivistic "cultures of relatedness" the model of emotional interdependence explains better than the model of independence the emerging family/human patterns resulting from shifts in lifestyles from rural/traditional to urban. This model also helps to explain the ethnic variations in family/human patterns currently experienced among immigrant groups in Western countries.

There is also some evidence that the model has validity even in Western, especially European, contexts with rising "soft" postmodern values (Inglehart, 1991), replacing the competitive capitalistic individualism/ materialism, as indicated in Chapter 1 (e.g., Fu, Hirkle, and Hanna, 1986 and Mogey, 1991 in the United States; Saal, 1987 and Jansen, 1987 in the Netherlands; and Ekstrand and Ekstrand, 1987 in Sweden). Relatedness is being valued more and competitive achievement is not valued as highly as before.

Indeed, a family/human model that integrates both autonomy and relatedness appears to be more optimal for human development. This is because autonomy and relatedness (intimacy) are considered to be two basic human needs (for a review, see Kağıtçıbaşı, 1996b), and the family model of psychological interdependence recognizes and satisfies both of these basic human needs. In constrast, the family model of independence recognizes and satisfies only the need for autonomy, while ignoring the need for relatedness, and the family model of total interdependence satisfies the need for relatedness at the cost of the need for autonomy. Other thinkers have pointed to the same type of synthesis of autonomy (agency) and merging with others (relatedness), for example, S. R. Sinha (1985) in India; C. F. Yang (1988) and K.-S. Yang (1986) in China; and D. Westen (1985) from a global perspective.

Recent research conducted in a number of Western and non-Western countries and with ethnic minorities in the United States and Europe provides evidence supporting some aspects of the model of psychological/ emotional interdependence and the autonomous-related self. For example, Kim, Butzel, and Ryan (1998) showed a more positive relation between autonomy and relatedness than between autonomy and separateness in both Korean and American samples. Ryan and Lynch (1989), and Ryan, Stiles, and Lynch (1994) in the United States found positive rather than negative links between relatedness to parents and autonomy in adolescents. These findings are notable in pointing to the importance of relatedness together with autonomy, even in individualistic cultural contexts.

Among the more educated and upper-middle SES groups in collectivistic societies relatedness is found to persist while autonomy is also endorsed. Furthermore, this combination is found to be more psychologically healthy. Thus, Lin and Fu (1990) found a combined autonomy and control orientation in Chinese parents. Cha (1994) found both control and encouragement of autonomy in Korean parents. Imamoglu (1987) found low SES Turkish parents to stress material interdependence, but modernized middle-upper SES Turkish parents to value autonomy and closeness to their children. Chou (2000) in Hong Kong and Aydin and Oztutuncu (2001) in Turkey found individuation (separateness) to be associated with depression in adolescents. Stewart, Bond, Deeds, and Chung (1999) in Hong Kong found persistence of family interdependencies together with some individualistic values; family relatedness and parental control were seen even in "modern" families. Stewart, Bond, Ho, Zaman, Oar, and Anwar (2000) in Pakistan and Sunar (2002) in Turkey showed autonomy granting and at the same time close parenting to foster adolescent adjustment.

Even through culture contact in the context of migration to individualistic societies a synthesis of relatedness with autonomy emerges, rather than a shift toward the independence family model. For example, Phalet and Schonpflug (2001) found that among Turkish immigrants in Germany parental autonomy goals do not imply separateness, and achievement values are associated with parental collectivism, not individualism. Finally, Jose, Huntsinger, Huntsinger, and Liaw (2000) found Chinese and Chinese-American parents to endorse both relatedness and autonomy, together with strong control and closeness with their children.

CONCLUSION

It appears that societies upholding individualistic values and reflecting these in their family/childrearing patterns have typically recognized and reinforced the basic human need for autonomy, while ignoring to some extent the basic human need for intimacy/connection. Societies stressing collectivistic values have done the reverse. Recognizing both of these human needs promises to contribute better to human well-being.

The model of psychological interdependence involves such a synthesis. Given its benefits, it may be the future of the family, not only in the Majority World with cultures of relatedness, but also in the West. Recent research evidence seems to point in this direction. For example, in diverse cultures adolescent health and well-being is found to be associated with close ties and attachment with parents rather than with separation and detachment (Chirkov, Kim, Ryan, and Kaplan, 2003). Nevertheless, the established individualistic worldview of the West may still prevail, in line with the modernization prediction, because it is exported by the West to the Majority World as the more advanced model. It takes a great deal of conscious effort to modify this trend toward separation/individuation by showing that this would not be the optimal human condition, given the fact that it does justice to only one of the two basic human needs. An integrative synthesis of the need for both autonomy and relatedness would be a more optimal human condition.

Referring one more time to the question we started out with – whether the Majority World family is shifting toward the Western family pattern – we find that the answer is not affirmative on more than one account. First of all, given the psychological needs and functions the family serves, there does not seem to be a shift toward *psychological* separation/individuation/nucleation of the family globally. Second, the Western family itself is not as separate as is assumed within the Parsonian model, and close psychological ties are associated with greater well-being, particularly during adolescence. With a better recognition of the value of psychological relatedness, it may be expected that there might be an increase in it in the Western context. However, this would require a change in psychological perspectives, particularly as they get transmitted to popular knowledge, toward acknowledging that relatedness is not incompatable with autonomy (Kağıtçıbaşı, 1996b, in press). Indeed, if autonomy and relatedness are two basic human needs, as accepted by many psychologists, then we may have a universal in the autonomous-related self and the family model of psychological interdependence as optimal models for human well-being.

Some of the theoretical perspectives and the Model of Family Change discussed here will be of relevance in the subsequent Chapters in the volume. Several of the common findings in family relations across different societies in our comparative analyses manifest some basic human patterns akin to those presented in this Chapter. Thus, our understanding of family relations and emotional bonds with family and kin, family roles and networks, and self-construals emerging in our comparative study, and in particular how these are influenced by ecocultural contextual factors such as affluence, education, and urban–rural standing, would benefit from the theoretical framework presented in this Chapter.

4   Family portraits from 30 countries: an overview

Ype H. Poortinga and James Georgas

This project has two dimensions. The first is *cross-cultural* and based on the questionnaire data from each country. It is quantitative and comparative with the purpose of determining universals of family and psychological variables among countries, and differences in family and psychological variables between cultural zones. The second dimension is *indigenous* and qualitative. These *family portraits* were structured with a standard format so that the reader could make comparisons between portraits along the same dimensions. The elements of the structure of the portraits are as follows.

1. *A historical description of the country* briefly introduces the reader to some recent changes and elements of the country.
2. *Ecological features* describe the environmental factors (mountains, plains, climate) that can play determining roles in shaping subsistence patterns, types of social institutions, significant in-groups, family types, etc.
3. *Organization and institutions of society* refer to (i) the *economic systems*; (ii) the *political and legal system* and its relationship to the community and the family; (iii) the *educational system* and its relationship to changes in family and gender; and (iv) country *religions* and their relationships to family functioning and their role in shaping laws regulating marriage, divorce, the role of the woman, and other institutions.
4. *Bonds with groups in the immediate community* refer to the types of bonds of the nuclear family with the extended family, networks with clans in the community and their influence on family functioning, means of subsistence, political organization, and the types of relationships with national institutions.
5. *Family* provides descriptions of the different types of families, family roles, marriage, how decisions to marry are made, divorce,

We gratefully acknowledge the help of Els Hoorelbeke in the analyses of the country portraits reported here.

kin relationships, and other aspects of social structure within the country.

6. *Family changes* during the past decades are described in terms of demographic statistics, family values, roles, and other aspects of the family.

The emphasis on social structural aspects was meant to enhance the provision of information from the society's perspective about the history of the country, the ecological bases of the institutions, communities and families, and the changes introduced by sociopolitical features of their contemporary lives.

The common format has imposed some limitations on the portraits. However, the parameters provided were broad, and the restrictions pertained to the order in which various aspects of family life have been reported rather than to what should or should not be reported about structure and functions of the family in the various societies. The most important restriction has been on the length of the reports; here a trade-off between detail and overview was inescapable and a limit of 3,000 words was necessary.

The full text of the portraits has been included in Part 2 of this book to provide the reader with the opportunity to gather firsthand information on the family in all 30 countries. In this introduction we would like to draw attention to some important themes that we see emerging from this material. We look at these from two perspectives, namely (i) widely reported aspects of change in families, and (ii) functions and roles that have remained much the same.

COMMON THEMES ACROSS COUNTRIES

Urbanization, education, and economic development

In most industrialized societies a high proportion of the population is already living in cities. In other countries urbanization is an ongoing process and has increased in recent decades. More than half of the authors refer explicitly to urbanization as a recent process with consequences for the family. It is frequently linked to economic development, which in turn is related to education and reduction of illiteracy. The precise relationships between these variables are not easy to establish (see Chapters 1 and 3). However, all authors refer to these factors, or at least one or two of them. In the various portraits they are related to most of the changes in structures and functions of the family that we shall refer to in this overview. Here we mention the one change that is probably most clearly driven by changes in the societal context, namely nuclearization of the family. The transition from extended family to nuclear family is mentioned by many authors and all of them refer to one or more of the three factors: urbanization, economic development, and education.

Marriage patterns

Most commonly a new family starts with marriage and the majority of the country portraits pay explicit attention to customs of partner choice. The portraits reveal two dominant patterns: individual partner choice and arranged marriages. The latter is the dominant norm and/or the common practice in more than a third of the countries.[1] In Ghana, marriage is said to be between two families rather than between two individuals. It provides links between close relationships, but also between neighbors, friends, and even villages. In the Ghana portrait, Amponsah, Akotia, and Olowu describe how relatives check the credentials of the other family on important matters. They also note that the traditional marriage system is beginning to shift to more nuclear arrangements as a consequence of urbanization and the empowerment of women. In all other countries where arranged marriages are the norm, practices of individual partner choice are mentioned. "Love-based" marriages are increasing; often this trend is limited to certain social categories (educated, urban). However, individual choice does not mean that parental approval should not be sought; in some cases it is still binding (e.g., Indonesia). In all countries with arranged marriages some change is mentioned; this is always in the direction of more individual partner choice.

In the remaining countries, either individual partner choice has been the rule for so long that the issue is not even mentioned (mainly Western countries), or both the traditional and the present practice are described. The latter portraits (mainly in southern Europe) all conclude that arranged marriages belong to the past.

Categorization inescapably leads to some simplification. For example, individual right of choice means that one can go against parental approval of one's marriage partner. However, even in Western countries, a child still likes it when the parents approve of the choice of marriage partner. Moreover, there are additional country-specific formal and informal rules that influence the partner selection process. In the

---

[1] Since the sources of information are provided later in this book, we are giving only approximate trends and largely avoid the tedious listing of country names.

Netherlands, up to a few decades ago, children needed parental permission for marriage until the age of 26. It was rare for parents to withhold this permission, but it did happen if the partner belonged to a different religion, a different social class, or was objectionable as a person. In Greece, where parents often provide financial support for the housing of the newly wed, it is inescapable that this parental support comes with some degree of influence or even control. Nevertheless, the reading of the 30 portraits can lead to only one conclusion, namely that there is a worldwide trend away from arranged marriages and towards individual partner choice.

Residence patterns

Newly-weds have to live somewhere. In more than half of the countries the main pattern is neolocal and nuclear residence. In one-third of the countries the extended family is still the norm, although in all of these latter countries there are tendencies to change towards nuclear households. The distinction is not sharp; in times of economic need youngsters may live with their parents (as mentioned for affluent countries such as Canada and the United States); in other countries the lack of economic affluence makes living together with the parents a more permanent practice. In two-thirds of all the portraits residential patterns are linked explicitly to economic factors; in one-third urbanization is mentioned as a factor in nuclear residence.

As already mentioned in Chapter 1, nuclear residence should not be equated with absence of important family ties and influences. In the country portraits this is confirmed. Half of the authors explicitly refer to childcare or parental care as a function of the family. Moreover, living near the residence of one of the young couple's parents (or both) is common also in Western industrialized countries, unless the couple moves away for occupational reasons.

Rules of exogamy and endogamy

Exogamy rules, which specify persons you cannot marry, are said to apply everywhere to next of kin. Cultural anthropology has established long ago that rules of incest are apparently universal (Murdock, 1949). Differences in exogamy rules between different countries pertain mainly to certain other categories of kin, especially first cousins. Marrying your first cousin is an accepted practice, or even encouraged, in almost a third of the countries in our sample; it is forbidden or frowned upon in another third; and the remaining authors do not mention it as an issue. Cultural variation within some countries (India, Nigeria, Muslim countries) is related to religion. Two authors explicitly mention a decrease in marriages with first cousins (Algeria, Turkey). An interesting shift in practice is reported by Achoui for Saudi Arabia: "Marriage with the sons and daughters of mother's sisters and brothers used to be less frequent than with father's relatives. Now, the trends is in the opposite direction. The main reason is the increasing influence of the mothers on the selection of their sons' wives."

In general, the main reason for the preference of first cousin marriages appears to be economic; it keeps family possessions together.

Endogamy rules restrict the choice of a marriage partner to a certain group, based on such categories as (same) caste, religion, race, or socio-economic status. More than two-thirds of the authors explicitly mention such rules; of these, half refer to contemporary cultural norms. Changes in norms are discussed by a dozen authors; half of them report that the compelling character of religious endogamy at the societal level has disappeared. The absence of norms does not mean that criteria of endogamy are also absent in individual partner selection. Also, in Western countries where there are few pertinent societal norms, most marriages are conducted between partners with similar levels of education and socioeconomic status and with a similar religious background. Of course, one reason for this has to do with the circle in which young unmarried people are moving around; free choice of a marriage partner means that you somehow have to meet your partner. Half a dozen country portraits mention smaller changes in endogamy practices. For example, in India nowadays, more inter-caste marriages do occur, although they are still frowned upon, and in Saudi Arabia traditional norms are less observed in urban and educated population groups. All changes are in the same direction, toward fewer constraints on individual partner choice.

Age of marriage and rates of divorce

At least half of the country portraits mention an increase in the age of marriage. Two factors are widely indicated as reasons: the longer time it takes to complete one's education and start one's profession, and the costs of setting up a family. This should not be taken to imply that changes are driven exclusively by economic factors. For example, Grad (Spain) mentions additional cultural variables: "the importance of family bonds in Catholic and Mediterranean cultures, the tolerance of post-dictatorship parents allowing young people to enjoy their own way of life, and the feelings of comfort by young people at their family homes."

An increase in divorce rates is indicated in half of the portraits, whereas none noted a decrease. We have combined age of marriage and divorce rate, because we see both as a tendency towards a weakening of marriage as a fundamental structure in society. This impression is reinforced by the increasing number of societies where more liberal unions (unmarried couples living together) are not only tolerated but accepted. In most Western countries this appears to be a general trend; when mentioned for non-Western countries it tends to be limited to educated/urbanized sections of society.

Number of children

Most authors mention the number of children per family; in half of the portraits a decrease in number is explicit, in none is an increase in the number of children reported. Economic factors are mentioned by four authors as reasons for the decline. The falling birth rates pertain to quite different initial levels (more than six in Ghana, two in the United Kingdom), but the trend is common. According to Keller (Germany) the typical German family nowadays has 1.3 children; in France (Pithon and Prévôt), and other countries this number is similarly low. It has been noted many times that such numbers are well below the replacement rate, leading to a shrinking and aging population.

The lower number of children is related by two authors to the increasing age at which women tend to get married. At the same time, in Western countries more children are born to unwed mothers, often teenagers. The latter trend, together with the higher rates of divorce, implies that more children in these societies are growing up in one-parent families, usually with the mother. However, one should realize that by tradition unmarried mothers (divorced, or with children born out of wedlock) are not uncommon in some non-Western societies. Such traditions are mentioned by Donoso-Maluf in the portrait on Chile and by Mortazavi on Iran.

Authority and power

An important feature that stands out in the portraits is the traditional autocratic power of the father in the family. Torres and Dessen (Brazil) are explicit in ascribing to the husband/father power that he exerts over his wife and children. Almost all other authors mention patriarchal authority, but attribute influence to the mother in important decisions. This can pertain especially to domestic affairs, or the role of women can be more indirect or hidden. For example, Zaman, Stewart, and Zaman

(Pakistan) point to the considerable power and influence mothers have through their adult children, specially the sons, and how the importance of the mother is reinforced by Muslim conventions.

On the other hand, half of the portrait authors refer, to a varying extent, to changes in the traditional patriarchical hierarchical roles of father and mother, particularly the phenomenon of the waning of male authority. The reduction of the father's autocratic power within the family, and the concomitant increase of the mother's power, has been mentioned frequently, with fathers losing much of their decision-making power within the family.

None of the reports mentions changes in the direction of strengthening of the father's (or general male) authority; all trends are toward more sharing of power between father and mother, although this certainly does not mean that equality has been reached. The most common reason indicated for the changes, mentioned explicitly by one quarter of the authors, is the employment of women outside the home and increasing education, enabling them to make an economic contribution to the family.

In two-thirds of the portraits, reference is made to a dual role of women in contemporary families, related to the increased education of women and their increasing role in the labor force. This has undermined the traditional role of the father; the traditional role distribution with the father as breadwinner and the mother at home with the children is described as being valid today in only four portraits.

The mother as the keystone of the family

From the large majority of the portraits, the mother emerges as the center of the family; in various portraits she is seen as more sensitive to children's needs, as being emotionally closer to the children than the father, and as being more devoted to the children. While the father's role in the family has undergone significant changes in many countries, the traditional role of the mother as the primary caretaker, especially of young children, seems to have been far less subject to change.

This may seem surprising as almost all country portraits refer to an increase in employment of women outside the house. This is linked in various portraits to such factors as, for example, changes in power, decrease in number of children, and higher divorce rates, but not to a lesser significance of the mother's traditional role as caretaker, either in a material or in an emotional sense. As mentioned, reference is made in two-thirds of the portraits to a dual role for today's women, involving working outside the home, while retaining their role in the family. Some facilities, such as daycare for children in Western countries or domestic servants (in Saudi Arabia and Indonesia), alleviate the dual task but only to a limited extent. Moreover, the father's participation in household work is referred to by various authors, but invariably they indicate that his assistance amounts to little in most families. The description of Pithon and Prévôt for France seems appropriate to many other countries: "The sharing of domestic activities remains traditional: men spend a little more time doing odd jobs and shopping while women spend much more time taking care of children, ironing, doing the laundry, housework, cooking, and washing the dishes."

SOME GENERAL TRENDS

Talcott Parsons (1943, 1949, 1965) divided parental roles into *instrumental*, as related to survival, and *expressive*, as related to the maintenance of morale and cooperation. Durkheim (1888, [1892]1921) also perceived the evolution of parental roles of the nuclear family from material or economic basis to "personal motives." The former are assigned to the father, in that it is his task to provide the link with society and material goods by being the breadwinner and family chief. The latter roles are assigned to the mother, in that she is responsible for the emotional equilibrium within the family. Many changes in this traditional role distribution are reported in the country portraits. With the increasing economic independence of women working outside the house, the position, and authority, of the man and father as provider have come increasingly under pressure.

There appears to be a cluster of related changes that show coherence and can all be linked to the shift in economic subsistence from agriculture to industrialization. An ecocultural perspective helps to make sense of this in so far as it points to antecedent conditions in the environment. This shift has opened up new opportunities, particularly for nuclear residence at the cost of traditional extended family residence, higher education, and employment for women outside the home. It is not clear to us whether the diminishing sacrosanct status of marriage should be seen as part of this cluster or as an independent phenomenon with different cultural roots.

Where are less extensive changes to be noted? Here we would like to make two observations. First, the role of the mother as primary caretaker in the family appears to have been subject to change to a far lesser extent than that of the father as authority figure and breadwinner. Second, the breaking up of common residence for the extended family appears to have a limited affect on affective ties and practices of mutual support between parents and children (both at a young age when parents care for children, and at an old age when these roles are reversed).

In a broad perspective Murdock (1949, see also Chapter 1) attributed four functions to the nuclear family: the sexual, the economic, the reproductive, and the educational. All four continue to exist. However, the sexual function is becoming less exclusively tied to marriage and reproduction. The advancement of contraceptive technology since the middle of the twentieth century has led to a separation of sexual expression from reproduction. Probably through this development the importance of sexuality in establishing and affirming affective bonds in couples, whether legally married or not, has become more clearly defined. Perhaps most difficult to interpret are emerging changes in the reproductive function of the family. The number of children born to unmarried women and increasing divorce rates mean that a substantial number of children, particularly in Western societies, do not grow up, at least for part of their childhood, in a nuclear family. Moreover, the decreasing number of children, sometimes already below population replacement levels in affluent societies where parents can easily afford a larger family, is, in our view, difficult to explain from either a sociocultural or a biocultural perspective.

With respect to the two remaining functions, patterns of findings appear to be clearer. The importance of the economic function of the family has been declining; most visibly in Western societies where extensive societal support systems provide the economic security that one could (and in many societies still can) find only with one's own family. The observed shifts in family structure as a consequence of lessening economic constraints, most evident in the less central role of the father, are in line with biocultural perspectives. This also holds for the socialization and caretaking function, which resides mainly with the mother. The upbringing of the new generation emerges from the 30 country portraits as the function of the family that has been most resistant to change, and the mother is the most central figure in this process.

CONCLUSION

Of course, this brief introduction provides only a broad overview of the much richer contents of the 30 country portraits, the integral text of which makes up the second part of this book. We have focused here primarily on common trends across the countries. It is likely that our interpretations have placed undue emphasis on some points and unduly neglected other points. Each portrait is the product of a local researcher, and provides an indigenous viewpoint of family and its changes. Together the portraits provide extensive information on variations in family life and the development of the family. In that respect the portraits are there to speak for themselves.

5   Hypotheses

*John W. Berry, Çiğdem Kağıtçıbaşı, James Georgas,
Ype H. Poortinga, and Fons J. R. van de Vijver*

This project was guided by several basic questions. How are ecological
and sociopolitical features of societies related to the structure and function of families, to family networks, to family roles, and to psychological
variables such as emotional bonds, self-construal, personality, family
values, and personal values? To what extent are the structure and function of the families in societies throughout the world related to increased
economic changes, and how have these changes affected family networks, family roles, personality, and values? To what degree will changes
in family structure, function, and psychological relationships characteristic of North America and Northern Europe also occur in the rest of the
world, as predicted by modernization and globalization theories?

The frameworks used in this study of family differ from the typical
paradigms of sociology and cultural anthropology in their emphasis on
psychological aspects of family. The key concepts that characterize this
study are *culture, social structure, kinship ties, family roles,* and a variety of
psychological variables. An important issue in cross-cultural psychology is
the search for context variables that can aid in the analysis of the
relationships among psychological and cultural variables. This project
attempts to identify both cross-cultural universals and variations in the
relationships among ecological and cultural variables, family roles, kin
networks, and psychological variables.

FAMILY DIVERSITY AND FAMILY CHANGE

In the more than two centuries since Comte and Le Play concluded
that the French Revolution and urbanization resulted in the breakdown
of the traditional stem family in France, the issue of family change has
been examined by sociologists, cultural anthropologists, psychologists,
psychiatrists, and other social scientists. During the nineteenth century,
sociological theories such as evolutionary theory, Marxist theory, and
structuralism-functionalism presented two perspectives regarding family
change. One perspective viewed the family system as in the process of

declining, in crisis, fragmenting from the traditional agricultural extended family to the nuclear family. The second perspective was that changes in family systems have positive and adaptive elements, as described in the influential theory of Talcott Parsons (1949). These theories were a product of primarily European and US sociology and described family and family change in their respective countries. The rapid industrialization and urbanization, revolutions and wars in Europe and North America during the nineteenth and twentieth centuries resulted in sweeping social and political changes, reflected in changes in the family system, from the extended agricultural types of families to the urban nuclear family system

At the end of the nineteenth century, cultural anthropology presented a different method and perspective regarding families. Its focus was not on family change, since the thousands of small societies throughout the world at that time were functioning with their traditional forms of subsistence economy and their traditional cultural systems. One of the most important early contributions of cultural anthropology was the delineation of the diversity of family types and kin relations in these small societies in the rest of the world, rather than examining family change. However, in the past three or four decades, cultural anthropology has greatly contributed to our understanding of the types of family changes taking place in small societies as a result of recent economic and social changes. Psychology and psychiatry entered the sphere of family studies in the twentieth century. Psychiatry, as well as clinical psychology, were involved mainly through family therapy, while general psychology's interest initially took the form of mother–child relationships in the field of developmental psychology.

As outlined in Chapters 2 and 3, we expect there to be both differences and similarities in family structure and function, as well as in many psychological variables. With respect to *differences*, we consider them to be due largely to a society's adaptation to differing ecological contexts, including opportunities and constraints provided by diverse ecosystems. Determining to what extent families change from these adaptive arrangements over time as a consequence of developments that are internal to the cultural context, such as urbanization or innovation, remains an important topic of family research. Our data cannot directly address the issue of change, because a study of family changes would require a pre- and post-test design. Most European and North American nations have been changing economically, politically, socially during the past 200 years, and these changes have brought about changes in family systems. Families in the rest of the world have also been changing in recent decades, owing to cultural, economic, political and social changes, at different rates, in different countries. Hence, with respect to *similarities* in this study, we cannot be certain about the origin of any similarities that we may find in family and psychological variables across these different nations. One possibility is that they have come about as a result of the impact of *sociopolitical* influences (such as education, telemedia, or religion) that emanate mainly from Western nations, as outlined in Chapter 2. Another possibility is that they are a common response to the urbanization and economic changes that are taking place worldwide (termed Affluence in this project).

FAMILY STRUCTURE

Although issues related to family structures and changes from the extended to the nuclear family have been discussed in detail in the previous Chapters, we deliberately did not attempt to determine the family type – nuclear, extended, or other. Family types are studied in terms of various salient aspects, such as family networks and emotional bonds, without attempting to identify which family the respondent states s/he belongs to. The paradox between the concepts of "household" and "family" employed in demographic studies, as discussed in Chapter 1, create problems in determining the actual type of families of respondents. Kinship is a referent of family, while common residence or geographical propinquity is a referent of household. Thus, the percentage of nuclear families in a country based on demographic surveys may be statistically accurate, but information regarding kinship relationships such as frequency of interaction and propinquity of residence of nuclear families is necessary in order to make conclusions regarding the actual type of family. This study is less interested in the percentages of transition in different societies from the extended family systems to the nuclear family system and more interested in the psychological implications of these changes.

Instead of attempting to identify whether the type of family of the respondents is nuclear or extended and then studying the relationships with psychological variables, this study looks at the contacts, communication, geographical propinquity, and psychological variables of respondents with members of the nuclear family and their kin (represented by grandparents, aunts/uncles, and cousins). Some family portraits in this book, together with literature on family networks discussed in Chapters 1 and 3, indicate that in many societies today, nuclear families in urban areas may live in separate households but they often reside near kin, share many family functions, and have close contact and communication.

Conclusions regarding changes from an extended family system to a nuclear family system based on demographic studies often neglect the degree of functional interactions between kin and, most important, their psychological implications. Thus, the basic family unit of this approach is the constellation of nuclear families, to employ Murdock's (1949) concept, in which the individual is embedded and the focus is on the psychological aspects of relationships with nuclear family members and kin.

The conceptual design of the project owes much to the ecological paradigm of Whiting and Child (1953). The project employed an Ecocultural Framework (Berry, 1976, 1979) and the Model of Family Change (Kağıtçıbaşı, 1990, 1996a) within cross-cultural psychology, to study family structure and function as a context for individual development and functioning.

COUNTRIES AND CULTURAL ZONES

Sociologists have often assumed that changes in the family in Western societies will inevitably be reflected in similar changes in the rest of the world, as predicted by modernization theory. This may be a possibility but it may also be an American–Eurocentric assumption regarding families in the "Majority World," which represent approximately 90 percent of the population of the world. The countries in this study are culturally diverse and have different family systems. The countries were selected so as to represent different geographical areas throughout the world. Murdock's (1967) regional classifications were a guideline in these selections: Africa, Circum-Mediterranean, East Eurasia, Insular Pacific, North America, and South America.

The concept of cultural zones was employed in the selection of countries with similar cultures. Many cross-national studies employ large numbers of countries. However, the differences or similarities in psychological scores between nations, or the correlations between the psychological variables are often interpreted by using the name of the country. That is, countries are rated as being high or low on different variables. In this type of study countries are treated as independent units and potential cultural similarities between clusters of countries are not taken into account. One approach is to group nations on the basis of psychological variables. An example is the study of values by Schwartz (1994b) in which nations are grouped into zones on the basis of different value types.

A different approach employs a theory or social structural data to delineate cultural zones and then explores the relationships of these zones with psychological variables. This methodology follows a long-standing approach in ecological anthropology. Kroeber (1939) and Forde (1934) employed the concept of ecological or "natural areas" in anthropology, grouping specific cultural populations into broader "culture areas" and seeking correspondences between them. More recently, Inglehart (1997), and Inglehart and Baker (2000) plotted 65 nations in a two-dimensional space, based on factor scores on a Traditional vs. Secular-Rational dimension and a Survival vs. Self-Expression dimension, and then employed Huntington's (1996) cultural zones as a model in drawing boundaries around groups of countries. Burton, Moore, Whiting, and Romney (1996) employed two classes of social structural variables from 351 societies, resulting in nine cultural regions. Georgas and Berry (1995) argued that cross-cultural studies should employ a theoretical framework to define cultural groups based on potential cultural dimensions – ecocultural variables – rather than beginning with the aggregation of scores on psychological variables and using the inductive method to try to identify potential cultural causal relations. This approach was employed in Georgas, van de Vijver, and Berry (2004c) in exploring relationships between country clusters based on ecosocial indices and psychological variables.

In this study of family, in addition to analyzing the relationships between cultural variables and psychological variables, the analyses will group countries into clusters or zones, based on the ecocultural variables, Affluence, and Religion. Kağıtçıbaşı also employs a Model of Family Change in which countries are grouped into cultural zones. This is based on variations along two underlying determinants. One of these is living conditions (urban–rural, SES, and level of affluence); the other is culture (culture of relatedness–culture of separateness). This aspect of culture used by Kağıtçıbaşı refers to the interpersonal distance dimension or the psychology of relatedness. This is akin to individualism–collectivism but is construed as *relational* individualism–collectivism, not *normative* individualism–collectivism (Kağıtçıbaşı, 1996b).

CULTURAL VARIABLES

Chapter 2 provides a discussion of many aspects of culture. This study could not possibly measure all aspects of culture. It is limited to attempting to measure aspects of family roles, family networks, affluence, religion, education, agriculture, and temperature. Thus, the hypotheses that follow are restricted to these cultural elements.

Many family studies base most of their conclusions on changes in family structure, usually by observing demographic statistics on increase in numbers of nuclear families and concomitant decrease in numbers of extended families in a specific country as discussed in Chapter 1. In the present study, the focus is on psychological changes, rather than on increasing numbers of nuclear families as an indicator of family change. The question is whether the increase in nuclear families in a country results in changes in roles, personality, and values, and in reduction of close bonds among family members and degree of communication and interaction. This study examines the relationships between ecocultural variables, communication and interaction with family and kin, family roles, and psychological variables. However, our primary emphasis is on the psychological variables. In other words, as the younger generation marries and has children, and as increasing affluence permits this new family to live in a home separate from the parents and grandparents, to what degree does this increase of separate nuclear family households result in the loosening of bonds among family members and changes in other psychological variables? This critical question will be investigated by a number of different hypotheses in this study.

HYPOTHESES

This Chapter contains three sets of hypotheses. The first section presents the hypotheses stemming from Berry's Ecocultural Theory (see Chapter 2), the second presents the hypotheses based on Kağıtçıbaşı's Model of Family Change (see Chapter 3), and the third presents some specific hypotheses based on the literature from family studies (see Chapter 1).

Hypotheses based upon the Ecocultural Framework

Ecological variables

In the Ecocultural Framework (see Figures 2.1 and 5.1), ecological variables are those that are internal to the society and serve to link populations to their habitat through economic activity. In this study, these include: percentage engaged in agriculture, highest monthly temperature, and affluence.

Sociopolitical variables

Sociopolitical variables are those that impinge upon a population and its individual members from outside the society. These frequently arrive by way of colonization, evangelization, or telecommunication. In this study,

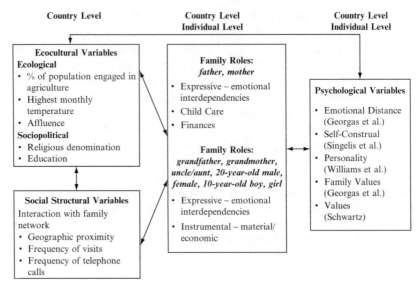

Figure 5.1. Overview of the levels of analyses and the variables employed based on the Ecocultural Framework.

sociopolitical variables include access to formal schooling and religious denomination. These influences may have been introduced historically (and continue to evolve) or may be recent or contemporary.

Both ecological and sociopolitical variables are used to predict three other groups of variables:

1. Social structural variables: family networks – geographic proximity, frequency of visits, and frequency of telephone calls;
2. Family roles: expressive and instrumental (childcare and finances) family roles;
3. Psychological variables: emotional distance, self-construal, personality, family values, and personal values.

The specific hypotheses of the Ecocultural Framework

The specific hypotheses of the Ecocultural Framework in relation to societies, family, and psychological variables are based on Chapter 2.

Greater conformity to a group norm is likely to occur in cultures that are structurally tight, with high norm obligation (Berry, 1967, 1979; Bond and Smith, 1996). Features of family and marriage are closely related to ecocultural features of a society, especially to settlement patterns, role differentiation, and social stratification (Nimkoff and Middleton, 1960).

Training of children for "responsibility" and "obedience" appears more in agricultural and pastoral societies, whereas training for "achievement," "self-reliance," and "independence" is more frequent in hunting and gathering societies (Barry, Child, and Bacon, 1959). Agricultural societies are characterized by sedentary lifestyle, high population density, high sociopolitical stratification, polygamy, extended families, and socialization emphases on compliance. In contemporary industrial and post-industrial societies, increasing high density of cities, reduction in pressures toward compliance as a result of loss of community cohesion, and the increase in anonymity afforded by these large cities, lead to reduction in the frequency of extended families and a parallel increase in proportion of nuclear families. (Berry, 1994a; Lomax and Berkowitz, 1972). Thus, an increase in stratification, compliance, and conformity from hunting through to agrarian societies changes course to become a decrease in these ecocultural features as societies move from agrarian to industrial and post-industrial arrangements.

Increased availability of telemedia continues to promote change from outside by portraying alternative lifestyles and consumer goods, leading to an increase in nuclear families and monogamous marriage in previously polygamous societies with extended families. Sociopolitical impacts on cultural transmission result in increased pressures toward "assertion" and a decline in "compliance" during socialization. In addition high affluence (along with Protestant religion) is associated with more emphasis on individualism, utilitarianism, and personal well-being. In contrast, for other religions, together with low Affluence, there is an emphasis on power relationships, loyalty, and hierarchy values (Georgas, van de Vijver, and Berry, 2004).

Ecological variables

Percentage engaged in agriculture will predict:

- close geographic proximity and frequency of visits;
- high expressive and instrumental childcare;
- close emotional distance, an interdependent self-construal, high agreeableness and conscientiousness, high hierarchy and kin family values, and high hierarchy and embeddedness personal values.

Highest monthly temperature will predict a similar pattern of relationships. *Affluence* will predict an inverse pattern of relationships to these.

Sociopolitical variables

Education will predict:

- distant geographical proximity and fewer visits;
- low expressive and instrumental childcare;
- an independent self-construal, low hierarchy and kin family values, and low embeddedness, hierarchy and harmony personal values.

> *Religious denomination. Catholic, Orthodox, and Muslim adherence will predict:*

- close family networks;
- high expressive and instrumental childcare;
- close emotional distance, and an interdependent self-construal.

There are no predictions for personality, high hierarchy and kin family values, and high hierarchy, embeddedness, and harmony personal values.

Protestant adherence will predict an inverse pattern of relationships to these.

Hypotheses based on Kağıtçıbaşı's Model of Family Change

A general hypothesis is that *the material/economic* and *emotional interdependencies* in families will be distinguished, as reflected in family roles and relationships. Thus, a material/economic and an emotional factor will emerge from analyses of the family roles.

Family patterns

Variations in family patterns will be predicted in line with:

- living conditions (urban–rural, SES, and level of affluence), reflecting socioeconomic development. Here there are many parallels with the predictions of the Ecocultural Framework; and
- culture (culture of relatedness–separateness).

Regarding *living conditions*, affluence, education, and percentage engaged in agriculture will be used as predictors of several indicators of family relationships, as operationalized in terms of family roles, emotional distance, and contact (visits or phone connection). The relevant hypotheses are as follows.

Affluence

Increased affluence will predict:

- greater distance of residence and less frequent contact;
- decreased salience of emotional roles and less emotional closeness (less emotional interdependence);
- decreased salience of material/instrumental roles (less material interdependence);
- less instrumental (material/economic) role of the child;
- less interdependent self;
- less hierarchy and less salience of kin relationships;
- less personal embeddedness.

Education

Education will predict similarly to affluence; percentage engaged in agriculture (rural) will make inverse predictions to affluence. Thus, education is predicted to be associated with the above variables in the same manner as affluence. Percentage engaged in agriculture, however, will show inverse associations with them.

Culture

Regarding culture, three country clusters will be formed by a combination of the affluence and culture of relatedness–separateness variables. The three clusters will be associated with the corresponding three family patterns of Kağıtçıbaşı's (1990, 1996a) Model of Family Change (Chapter 3). The three patterns are expressed in relative terms, in comparison to one another, as follows:

- Cluster 1: Low affluence/High relatedness (Affluence cluster 3). Higher emotional and material interdependencies/bonds (Family model of interdependence).
- Cluster 2: High (increasing) affluence/High relatedness (Affluence cluster 2 + Korea, China, Japan). Korea, China, and Japan are added here, notwithstanding their affluence cluster because they are found in cross-cultural research to be "cultures of relatedness" (collectivistic societies). Relatively higher emotional, weaker material interdependencies/bonds (Family model of emotional interdependence).
- Cluster 3: High affluence/Low relatedness (Affluence cluster 1 minus Korea, China, Japan, given that these three countries are

integrated in Cluster 2). Relatively weaker emotional and material interdependencies/bonds (Family model of independence).

Despite the above differences between clusters, however, emotional bonds may be expected to be important in all family types.

Further hypotheses from the family literature

Hierarchical power

Hierarchical power of the mother has increased in Western societies. The prediction is that females in higher affluent countries have more hierarchical power than in lower affluent countries:

• Father (mother) is the protector of the family.
• When there are arguments or disputes, *father* makes the decision regarding the manner of solution.

Housework

According to Inkeles (1998) fathers in all societies do less housework than mothers. The prediction will be tested here:

• Housework (cleans, cooks, washes).

6   Methodology of the study

James Georgas, Fons J. R. van de Vijver, John W. Berry,
Ype H. Poortinga, and Çiğdem Kağıtçıbaşı

This chapter describes the methods of analysis. The first section presents
an overview of the four levels of analyses: ecocultural, social structural,
family roles, and individual. Some analyses are at the country level and
others at the individual level. The second section describes characteristics of the sample; both the sample of countries employed in the study
and the characteristics of the samples of students in each country. The
third section describes the variables in the study.

A BRIEF OVERVIEW OF THE LEVEL OF ANALYSES AND THE VARIABLES

Ecocultural variables

The ecocultural variables are conceived widely, including economic,
social structural, and sociopolitical variables. They are measured by
archival data at the country level: (1) the ecological variables: percentage
of the population engaged in agriculture; a number of economic indices
labeled affluence, and highest monthly temperature; (2) the sociopolitical variables: education which measures access to education, and
percentage of population per religious denomination.

Social structural variables

The social structural variables are the interaction with family networks.
Three variables are employed: geographic proximity, frequency of visits,
and frequency of telephone calls with members of the nuclear and
extended family.

Family roles

Family roles for nine family positions are as follows: for mother and
father, the three family roles are expressive, childcare, and finances.

For grandfather, grandmother, uncle/aunt, 20-year-old male and female, 10-year-old boy and girl, the two family roles are expressive and instrumental (e.g., Parsons, 1943, 1949). Kağıtçıbaşı (1990, 1996a) employs the terms emotional interdependencies, which is essentially the same as Parsons' expressive role, and material/economic interdependencies, which is the same as instrumental. We will employ both terms in the following chapters.

Psychological variables

The psychological variables at the individual level are: emotional distance (Georgas, Mylonas, Bafiti, et al., 2001), self-construal (Singelis, 1994; Singelis and Brown, 1995; Singelis and Sharkey, 1995), personality (Williams, Satterwhite, and Saiz, 1998), family values (Georgas, 1989, 1991, 1993, 1999), and values (Schwartz, 1992, 1994a).

The arrows of Figure 5.1 symbolize the potential relationships between the four levels. Also, ecocultural variables are analyzed at only the country level, while the other three levels are analyzed at both the country level and the individual level.

SAMPLE OF COUNTRIES AND INDIVIDUALS

Samples consisted of countries and individuals.

Countries

An attempt was made to select countries so as to represent the major geographical and cultural regions of the world: north, central, and south America, north, east, and south Europe, north, central, and south Africa, the Middle East, west and east Asia, and Oceania. The purpose of the selection of countries so as to represent geocultural zones in the world was to attempt to maximize ecocultural variation in presumably family-related variables such as economic measures and religions. The countries were selected so as to represent nations in terms of economic indices, as in Georgas and Berry (1995). The countries are schematically presented in Figure 6.1. Although the project began with 30 countries, data could not be employed for technical reasons from South Africa, Botswana, and Mongolia. Thus, the data analyzed are from 27 countries. However, family portraits of these three countries are included in this volume. Murdock's (1969) regional classifications in his *Ethnographic Atlas*, based on small societies were: Africa, Circum-Mediterranean, East Eurasia, Insular Pacific, North America, and South America. Thus, the countries selected

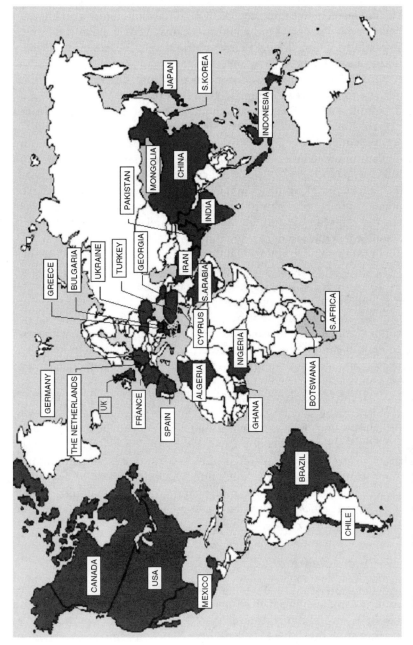

Figure 6.1. Map of participating countries.

113

are from Murdock's regional classifications. However, generalizations from the 27 countries in this sample to the over 200 nations in the world have to be made with caution. One could argue that certain countries, which have not been sampled, might have contributed to the variation in family structure and function.

A second reason for selecting countries from different geocultural zones was to attempt to minimize "Galton's problem" (Naroll, Michik, and Naroll, 1974). The issue is that 27 *countries* in a sample do not necessarily mean 27 *cultures*. If countries are assumed to be independent units, potential cultural similarities between clusters of countries are not taken into account. Cultural features of a country often diffuse to contiguous countries e.g., European culture, Islamic culture, Asian culture. That is, the 27 countries in the sample might well be represented by a smaller group of cultural zones. Thus, Galton's problem arises when the sampling of contiguous/culturally-related societies results in the non-independence of cases (countries).

The traditional solution to Galton's problem has been to select societies for comparison that have some linguistic distance from each other. This solution increases the likelihood that there has been minimal cultural diffusion from one society to another. In the contemporary world, however, this may not be sufficient to establish that one society is culturally independent from another one. This is because, with mass telecommunication mostly distributed in one or two dominant languages, many societies are subject to cultural influence and change from a few sources.

In this study, we have sought to minimize the effect of Galton's problem, first by selecting societies with wide geographical dispersion. Murdock's (1969) regional classifications were a guideline in the selection of the countries. Second, using this dispersion, we have sought to identify clusters of societies (or cultural regions) that allow us to minimize any assumption that any one culture is independent of any other. These cultural clusters, while influencing each other, should provide distinguishable blocks of societies that stand in some independence from each other.

Individuals

The sample consisted of $N = 5,482$ university students from 27 countries. The samples ranged from $n = 65$ from Ukraine to $n = 450$ from Pakistan. A second dimension refers to the characteristics of the sample: university students. These students represent a specific age category of the population and are not representative of other ages. In addition, they represent the most educated group of the population, who probably will not return to the traditional forms of subsistence of their elders. Financial considerations did not permit the collection of representative samples of all ages. This is a characteristic issue in psychological research. However, there is another side to the issue of samples of university students. They often represent the age group and level of education at the cutting edge of cultural changes in terms of attitudes and values. Since this project is interested to a certain degree in the relationship between economic and other cultural changes and family changes, the responses of university students should tend to represent the leading edge of changes in a culture, and not the average level of responses of a representative sample of a culture.

On the other hand, the authors are aware of the dangers of coming to conclusions regarding the possibility that results indicated family change in the different societies. The design of this study is not, strictly speaking, a measure of family changes resulting from increased affluence. That would require a pre- and post-test design. We are not measuring family change, as such, but we *are* examining family patterns that show systematic variations over different ecocultural and social structural factors. We are assuming based on the family literature, that families are changing at different rates throughout the world. But we cannot be certain of the degree to which the findings in our study reflect family change, or, on the other hand, whether they reflect different structures and functions of family, values, and kinship networks as products of different cultures, as have been described by cultural anthropology for over a century. Table 6.1 presents the descriptions of the samples in each country.

Gender and mean age per country

Table 6.2 presents the number of males and females and mean age per country.

Parental education

Table 6.3 presents of number of years of education of father and mother across countries.

VARIABLES

Culture

Culture was analyzed in terms of Berry's Ecocultural Framework and based on the methodological approach described in Georgas and Berry

Table 6.1 *Descriptions of samples in each country*

Country	University	Areas	Ethnic groups
Algiers	Algiers	capital and surrounding areas	Arabs, with 10 to 20 per cent Berbers
Brazil	2 universities	Brazilia region	whites, blacks, and mostly Mestizos
Bulgaria	Sofia, Medical Academy Institute of Technology, School of Economics	Sofia and Varna	Bulgarians
Canada	Queen's	all areas	ethnically diverse
Chile	La Serena	Coquimbo, Metropolitan Region, Valparaíso, northern regions	Chileans
China	Hong Kong	Hong Kong	Chinese
Cyprus	3 universities	Greek Cyprus	Greek Cypriots
France	Belfort, Montpellier	middle eastern	primarily French
Georgia	Tbilisi State, Georgian, Technical, Poti	Tbilisi and Poti	Georgians
Germany	Osnabruck, Dortmund,	all areas	Germans
Ghana		all areas	Ghanians
Greece	universities in Athens	all areas	Greek
India	Allahabad	northwestern	Indians
Indonesia	3 universities	Jakarta, Purwokerto	predominantly Javanese
Iran	Shahid Beheshti	Tehran, Shiraz, other areas	ethnically diverse
Japan	Okayama	cities and towns, Western Japan	Japanese
Mexico	National Autonomous	all areas	Mexicans
The Netherlands	Tilburg	all areas	primarily ethnic Dutch
Nigeria	Ahmadu Bello, Zaria, Kaduna Polytechnic	all areas	all Nigerian ethnic groups
Pakistan	colleges in Lahore	all areas	Punjabi and Urdu speaking
Saudi Arabia	King Fahd University of Petroleum Minerals, Al-Dammam Female College	all areas	Arabs
South Korea	Chung-Ang	all areas	Koreans
Spain	Universidad Autonoma de Madrid, Burgos	all areas	Spanish
Turkey	Bogazici, Marmara	all areas	Turks

Table 6.1. (*cont.*)

Country	University	Areas	Ethnic groups
Ukraine	Sumy State, Kiev State University	all areas	primarily Ukrainian
United Kingdom	Goldsmiths College, London	all areas	primarily English
United States	Hofstra, Northern Colorado	Long Island, New York, Colorado	ethnically diverse

(1995) and Georgas, van de Vijver, and Berry (2004c). Ecocultural variables were collected from archival data from the *World Development Report* of the World Bank (2002), and United Nations Statistics Division (2002a, 2002b).

Ecological variables

Agriculture was measured by percentage of population engaged in agriculture per country indices.

Temperature was the highest monthly temperature per country.

Affluence was measured by economic variables: Gross National Product per capita (in US $), energy use per capita (in kg of oil equivalent), electricity consumption per capita in kilowatt hours, unemployment rate, percentage of population employed in industry, percentage of population employed in services, imports (in US $), exports (in US $).

The indices were factor analyzed and a unifactorial structure was obtained, explaining 57.2 percent of the variance. All indices showed strong positive loadings, with the exception of unemployment rate (with a loading of -.71).[1]

Socopolitical variables

Education was measured by the variables: total adult illiteracy, pupil/teacher ratio education at first level, enrollment ratios at first, second,

---

[1] Affluence scores of the countries: Algeria (−1.06), Brazil (−0.55), Bulgaria (−0.37), Canada (1.62), Chile (−0.40), Cyprus (−0.44), France (0.99), Georgia (−0.74), Germany (1.28), Ghana (−1.34), Greece (0.05), Hong Kong (0.71), India (−1.03), Indonesia (−0.89), Iran (−0.68), Japan (1.08), Mexico (−0.22), Nigeria (−1.36), Pakistan (−0.92), Saudi Arabia (0.04), South Korea (0.32), Spain (0.29), The Netherlands (0.78), Turkey (−0.67), UK (0.78), Ukraine (−0.09), and USA (2.81).

Table 6.2 *Number of participants, gender and mean age across countries*

Country	Gender		Total	Mean age
	Male	Female		
Algeria	41	66	107	20.97
Brazil	52	107	159	21.73
Bulgaria	78	117	195	21.64
Canada	56	159	215	19.24
Chile	103	104	207	21.57
Cyprus	18	114	132	20.49
France	11	86	97	21.19
Georgia	84	116	200	20.17
Germany	40	106	153[a]	22.43
Ghana	54	16	70	27.16
Greece	107	243	350	21.34
Hong Kong	205	218	423	19.00
India	121	98	220[a]	22.02
Indonesia	_[a]	_[a]	239	_[a]
Iran	59	130	189	21.28
Japan	88	97	185	19.52
Mexico	102	124	227[a]	22.73
Nigeria	197	137	337[a]	23.93
Pakistan	212	238	450	19.82
Saudi Arabia	139	59	198	22.22
South Korea	79	120	199	20.85
Spain	26	85	111	19.09
The Netherlands	37	128	165	20.20
Turkey	46	165	211	19.36
UK	32	83	115	20.79
Ukraine	14	50	65[a]	22.26
USA	69	194	263	21.20
Total	2070	3160	5469[a]	21.00

Note:
[a] Total Ns include numbers of individuals with missing data on gender (Germany: 7 cases; Nigeria: 3 cases; India, Mexico, and Ukraine: each 1 case. Information regarding gender and age was not available for Indonesia.

and third levels of education. A first factor explained 63.99 per cent of the variance.

Religion was measured as percentage of adherents in a country declaring a religious sect (Religion Statistics Geography, 2002). Only those major world religions are included for which there is sub-stantial variation of percentages of adherents in the countries in

Table 6.3 *Years of education of father and mother across countries*

	Father				Mother			
Country	0–6 yrs	7–9 yrs	10–12 yrs	>12 yrs	0–6 yrs	7–9 yrs	10–12 ys	>12 yrs
Algeria	63	15	26	1	69	20	14	1
Brazil	49	25	31	52	40	24	36	54
Bulgaria	–	1	57	137	–	1	43	151
Canada	5	2	36	172	1	3	56	154
Chile	26	38	66	76	21	41	79	65
Cyprus	24	21	46	38	26	16	49	38
France	52	24	10	5	46	31	16	–
Georgia	2	31	56	111	3	31	52	114
Germany	6	34	63	48	5	39	68	37
Ghana	11	2	8	40	17	6	10	26
Greece	60	65	88	137	78	43	120	109
Hong Kong	103	110	99	109	121	121	106	73
India	4	8	25	182	26	32	55	106
Indonesia[a]	–	–	–	–	–	–	–	–
Iran	95	22	44	26	125	12	31	19
Japan	–	11	62	110	–	10	88	84
Mexico	56	38	41	86	70	45	60	49
Nigeria	72	49	68	134	98	52	62	101
Pakistan	35	42	153	220	94	70	163	123
Saudi Arabia	55	23	109	7	85	30	71	6
South Korea[a]	–	–	–	–	–	–	–	–
Spain	4	13	29	61	5	19	35	51
The Netherlands	10	43	50	61	15	24	55	69
Turkey	46	23	45	97	75	19	50	65
UK	3	12	45	53	4	11	53	44
Ukraine	–	8	23	33	–	5	21	38
USA	8	13	67	153	13	10	78	138

Note:
[a] No data available for Indonesia and South Korea.
Missing cases listwise: 524 (9.6 percent) for father; and 544 (9.9 percent) for mother.

the current study. The religions were: (1) Christian Catholic, (2) Christian Protestant, (3) Christian Orthodox, (4) Muslim, and (5) Hindu/Buddhist/Traditional Beliefs. The last cluster is so heterogeneous that it is not used in the analyses.

Social structural variables

The social structural variables were based on the social network literature (Georgas, Christakopoulou, Poortinga, Goodwin, Angleitner and
Charalambous, 1997; Georgas et al., 2001). The measures of family
networks were: geographical proximity, frequency of visits, frequency of
telephone calls with father, mother, siblings, grandfather, grandmother,
and uncle/aunt. The same instructions for multiple aunts and uncles or no
aunts and uncles or siblings, as with the family roles questionnaire, were
employed.

Geographical proximity

Geographical proximity from the family positions father, mother, siblings,
grandfather, grandmother, and uncle/aunt was measured by a 6-point
scale: *in the same house, upstairs/downstairs/next flat, opposite house or building, in the same neighborhood, in the same town/city, live far away.*

Frequency of visits

Frequency of visits with family positions father, mother, siblings, grandfather, grandmother, and uncle/aunt was measured by a 6-point scale:
*daily, once or twice a week, every two weeks, once a month, once or twice a
year, rarely.*

Frequency of telephone calls

Frequency of telephone calls with family positions father, mother, siblings, grandfather, grandmother, and uncle/aunt was measured by a 6-
point scale: *daily, once or twice a week, every two weeks, once a month, once
or twice a year, rarely.*

Family roles

The Family roles questionnaire[2] was developed by Georgas, Giotsa,
Mylonas, and Bafiti for this project on the basis of family literature and
questionnaires from countries throughout the world. Because of different roles of family members, i.e., parents, children, grandparents, and
aunts and uncles in different cultures, an attempt was made to determine
roles which were basic to family life, and thus would be found in all
cultures.

---

[2] The questionnaires employed in the study are in the Appendix.

Twenty-two roles were selected based on pilot testing in Greece and discussions with colleagues in the project. The roles are in the following areas: psychological environment and traditions, kinship relations, hierarchical power, housework, school, play, behavior and support of children, finances, babysitting, and helping parents with economic activities. A six-point scale was employed, from *almost always* to *never*.

Nine family positions were chosen: father, mother, grandfather, grandmother, uncle/aunt, 20-year-old male, 20-year-old female, 10-year-old boy, 10-year-old girl. These family positions were chosen so as to have a sampling of: (1) nuclear family members (mother, father, children), with two age levels at the approximate age of the respondents in the study (20 years old) and preadolescents (10-year-olds); (2) three-generation family with grandparents; and (3) collateral relatives (aunts/uncles). These categories are not entirely satisfactory because they do not represent the different types of kinship relationships in extended families throughout the world; for example, the important differentiation in many cultures between maternal and paternal aunts and uncles, matrilineal and patrilineal grandparents, etc., is missing. Pilot testing of additional family positions indicated that the task became too complex for some respondents, resulting in the final selection of the above positions. However, an attempt was made in the directions (see below) to standardize the task for multiple aunts/uncles by asking the respondent to "choose the ones that are closer to you." In order to obtain responses for each family position, avoiding the problem of missing data, the instructions were: "If some members of the family (e.g., grandparents) have passed away, we would ask you to answer as if this person were alive." "If you do NOT have an uncle or aunt, answer in the manner you would most likely respond, if you had one. The same regarding the 10-year-old boy, 10-year-old girl, 20-year-old male, 20-year-old female – that is, refer to yourself at those ages, or if you do not have a brother or sister, answer in the manner they would most likely respond, if you had one."

Table 6.4 presents the categories of the 22 roles for the nine family positions. Some categories have questions for all nine family positions, some have only for the adults, and some do not have questions for mother and father. Because the roles were factor analyzed separately for each position, this is not a problem in itself. But in the factor analyses of some family positions some of the roles will not appear, because the role was inappropriate for some positions, e.g., for the item "When the parents are not home, *x* babysits with *grandchildren*," mother and father are not included.

Table 6.4 *Categories of 22 roles for nine family positions*

Family roles	Family positions[a]								
	Fa	Mo	Gf	Gm	Un/Au	20yM	20yF	10yM	10yF
X[b] provides emotional support to *children*	√[c]	√	√	√	√	√	√	√	√
X keeps the *family* united	√	√	√	√	√	√	√	√	√
X tries to keep a pleasant environment in the family	√	√	√	√	√	√	√	√	√
X conveys traditions, manners and customs (e.g. reads, tells stories) to *children*	√	√	√	√	√	√	√	√	√
X conveys the religious tradition to *children*	√	√	√	√	√	√	√	√	√
X contributes to the preservation of family relations (e.g. family gatherings during the holidays, anniversaries)	√	√	√	√	√	√	√	√	√
X supports (*the grandparents* or *grandchildren or nephews nieces*) when in need (illness, financial problems, etc.)	√	√	√	√	√				
X takes daily care (cooking, shopping) of *grandparents*	√	√	√	√	√				
X is the protector of the family	√	√	√	√	√				
When there are arguments or disputes, X makes the decision regarding the manner of solution	√	√	√	√	√				
X does housework (cleans, cooks, washes)	√	√	√	√	√	√	√	√	√
X does the shopping, pays bills, etc.	√	√	√	√	√	√	√	√	√
X takes the *children* to school	√	√	√	√	√	√	√	√	√
X plays with the *children*	√	√	√	√	√	√	√	√	√
X helps *children* with homework	√	√	√	√	√				
X teaches good behavior to *children*	√	√	√	√	√				
X contributes financially to the *family*	√	√	√	√	√	√	√	√	√
X manages the family finances	√	√	√ - √		√				
X gives pocket money to *children*	√	√	√	√	√				
X supports (at the beginning of their career) *the children*	√	√	√	√	√				

Table 6.4. (*cont.*)

Family roles	Family positions[a]							
	Fa	Mo	Gf	Gm	Un/Au	20yM	20yF	10yM	10yF
When the parents are not home, X babysits with *grandchildren*		√	√	√	√	√	√	√
X helps the *parents* with their work (fields, shop or family occupation)		√	√	√	√	√	√	√

Notes:
[a] Fa: Father; Mo: Mother; Gf: Grandfather; Gm: Grandmother; Un/Au: Uncle/Aunt; 20yM: 20-year-old son; 20yF: 20-year-old daughter; 10yM: 10-year-old son; 10yF: 10-year-old daughter.
[b] In the questionnaire, "X" was replaced by each family position, e.g., *Father* provides emotional support . . ., *Mother* provides emotional support . . ., etc. See Appendix for complete questionnaire.
[c] √ marks which family positions are included for each question.

Psychological variables

Emotional distance

The questionnaire of Georgas et al. (2001) employs scales based on concentric circles, derived from Bogardus' (1925) concept of social distance and the concept of personal space. The central concentric circle represents the subjects themselves (the self). The closer to themselves (the center) they assign a relative, or other social role category, the closer they feel to him/her. The questionnaire refers to 21 persons in society, perceived from the respondent's perspective. A seven-point scale was employed, from *very far* to *very close*. Emotional distance with two categories of people were employed in the analysis: emotional closeness with members of the nuclear family (mother, father, brothers and sisters), and emotional closeness with members of the extended family (grandparents, uncles/aunts, cousins).

Personality traits

A short form (30 questions out of 300) of the Personality Traits Scale (Williams, Satterwhite and Saiz, 1998) was used with items from the five factors: Extraversion, Agreeableness, Conscientiousness, Emotional

Stability, and Openness. A seven-point scale was used from *very much like me* to *not like me at all*.

Self-construal

A short form (18 questions out of 31) of Singelis' Self-Construal Scale was employed. Nine items measure *independent self* and 9 items measure *interdependent self* (Singelis, 1994; Singelis and Brown, 1995; Singelis and Sharkey, 1995). A seven-point scale was used with response categories ranging from *strongly agree* to *strongly disagree*.

Family values

The Family Values questionnaire contained 18 questions. *Hierarchical roles of father and mother* and *Relationships within family and with kin* are traditional values related to extended family roles in agricultural societies, developed in Greece (Georgas, 1989, 1991, 1993, 1999). Deviations from these baseline measures of traditional family values would be a measure of change from traditional values. A seven-point scale was employed, from *strongly agree* to *strongly disagree*.

Values

A short form (21 questions out of 56) of Schwartz's Values Scale (Schwartz, 1992, 1994a) with items from the value types, Hierarchy, Embeddedness, Harmony, Egalitarian Commitment, Intellectual Autonomy, Affective Autonomy, and Mastery. Twenty-four values were originally employed, but because of problems of transmission of the questionnaire to the different associates in countries, Egalitarian Commitment was omitted in a number of countries. Rather than not employing the questionnaire, we proceeded with the six scales instead of seven. A seven-point scale was employed from *very important* to *not important at all*.

PROCEDURE

The English language version of the questionnaire was employed for the translation of the instructions and the items into the home-country language by each research team.

Three types of translation are currently employed in cross-cultural research: *close translation, adaptation,* and *assembly* (van de Vijver and Leung, 1997; cf. also Harkness, van de Vijver and Mohler, 2003).

Close translation is the literal translation into the target country language. However, close translation of the items of a questionnaire may result in different connotations in the target language, so that two different constructs are being measured. The same problem applies in the close translation of the instructions to the subjects in the study. However, close translation may be the best strategy in certain circumstances, e.g., numbers, or symbols, or figures.

Adaptation refers to more culture-sensitive instructions or stimuli while measuring the same underlying construct in all cultures. This most often is accomplished by the method of translation to the target language and translation back to the home language in order to compare for similarity of connotation of the construct or the instructions.

Assembly refers to creating a completely new instrument with different items to measure the same construct. The approach has been employed in indigenous psychology (Sinha, 1997), and aims at maximizing the appropriateness of psychological theories and instruments to local cultures.

Adaptation was the translation method approach employed in this study. Each research team also generated its own suggestions for the addition or elimination of roles in the family roles questionnaires. The items and instructions were translated into the target language by the research teams, each an indigenous member of the home country. The items and instructions were then back-translated into English. The research team compared the back-translated items with the original English version for equivalence in connotation. Items which presented problems in equivalence of meaning were discussed with the first editor and rephrased in the country language until linguistic equivalence was satisfactory.

DATA COLLECTION

The data were gathered by the local research teams. The questionnaire was given in the classroom to university age students in each country. The time for responding to the questionnaire ranged from one to two hours.

Fons J. R. van de Vijver, Kostas Mylonas, Vassilis Pavlopoulos, and James Georgas

This Chapter provides an overview of the cross-cultural data analyses. The Chapter is presented in seven parts. The first two involve the analyses of the psychometric properties of the instruments. "Equivalence and pooled factor Solutions" discusses the equivalence analyses, addressing the question of to what extent the instruments measure the same underlying constructs in each of the 27 countries. Having determined the equivalence (in a few cases leading to the elimination of a few items), we proceed with an analysis of the internal consistencies of the scales in each country in the section on "Internal consistency". The next two sections address the issue of sample differences in the various groups, namely gender (see p. 142) and educational level of the parents (see p. 145). The question is whether any country differences in education and gender need to be controlled prior to the cross-cultural data analyses. The next two sections of the Chapter involve these cross-cultural data analyses. On pp. 147–58 we present an analysis of the size of cross-cultural differences in the various instruments employed. The exploratory nature of the data analyzes changes for a hypothesis-testing perspective on pp. 158–72. The hypotheses of Chapter 5 are tested here. A final section (pp. 172–85) presents an integration of results that are relevant to the hypotheses.

EQUIVALENCE AND POOLED FACTOR SOLUTIONS

A first necessary step in cross-cultural data analyses involves the question of to what extent the same construct(s) has been measured by an instrument in all cultural groups involved. Technically this is known as testing for structural equivalence (van de Vijver and Leung, 1997). We employed exploratory factor analysis to assess the presence of structural equivalence.

The current study involved 27 countries. When only a few countries are compared, it is common to employ pairwise comparison of factors obtained in different groups. However, when 27 countries are compared, the total number of comparisons is $(27*26/2 =) 351$. Finding a pattern-ing in such a large number of comparisons can be quite cumbersome. Problems of integrating pairwise solutions can be avoided by pooling the data. The procedure begins by computing the covariance matrix of the items of the scale to be analyzed per cultural group in the comparison (e.g., 27 covariance analyses in the case of comparison of the national groups). These covariance matrices are then averaged, with the sample size as weights. The overall covariance matrix provides us with a global average. It is our best estimate of the "averaged" covariance matrix. The core of the procedure consists of determining to what extent each country shows a factor structure that is similar to the factor structure in the pooled, global data matrix. The next step is to compare each sample with the global mean. If each group shows a sufficient level of agreement with the global solution, it is concluded that structural equivalence is supported and that a scale measures the same construct (s) in each group. If structural equivalence is not supported, additional analyses are required in order to explore the cause of the deviant factor structure (e.g., psychological constructs might not be identical, one or more items may not work in a particular cultural group, etc.).

The agreement between the factor loadings of items from two differ-ent groups can be expressed via several congruence indices (van de Vijver and Leung, 1997). The proportionality coefficient, also known as Tucker's phi (Tucker, 1951), is an often-used congruence index. This index measures the identity of two factors, up to a positive, multiplying constant. The latter allows for differences in factorial eigenvalues across cultural groups. Unfortunately, the index has an unknown sampling distribution, which makes it impossible to construct confidence inter-vals. Some rules of thumb have been proposed: values higher than .90 are taken to indicate factorial invariance, whereas values lower than .90 (van de Vijver and Leung, 1997) or .85 (Ten Berge, 1986) point to essential incongruities.

It may be noted that in order to compute the factorial agreement for a country, the data of the country were included in the pooled matrix; by including the country itself the value of the factorial agreement may be inflated somewhat. However, with 27 countries the contribution of each country was deemed to be limited.

Family networks

The family network variables were Proximity of Residence, Frequency of Meeting, and Frequency of Phone Calls (Georgas, Mylonas, Bafiti, et al., 2001). Each of the three scales showed a one-factorial solution

Table 7.1 *Factor loadings of geographical proximity, frequency of meeting, and frequency of telephone calls (pooled solution)*

Value and item	Loading
Living distance (47.57 percent)[a]	
Father	.75
Mother	.79
Siblings	.72
Grandfather	.68
Grandmother	.68
Uncles/aunts	.48
Meeting (49.16 percent)	
Father	.72
Mother	.76
Siblings	.70
Grandfather	.72
Grandmother	.73
Uncles/aunts	.55
Making phone calls (55.09 percent)	
Father	.77
Mother	.78
Siblings	.78
Grandfather	.76
Grandmother	.77
Uncles/aunts	.58

Note:
[a] Numbers behind variable names refer to the percentage of variance explained by the factor.

(explaining between 48 percent and 55 percent; see Table 7.1). The factorial agreement was very good, with a few exceptions, notably Hong Kong. Agreement indices of proximity of residence and frequency of meeting did not reach a value of .90. This could be due to the small physical size of Hong Kong, which makes it very unlikely that family members live far from one another and meet each other seldom.

It can be concluded that the analyses supported the structural equivalence of the scales in the 27 countries. The deviances (i.e., low values of Tucker's phi) did not show a particular patterning. It can be concluded that these analyses point to a sound basis for the cross-cultural comparisons of the next Chapter.

Family roles

The Family Roles Scale (Georgas, Giotsa, Mylonas, and Bafiti) was analyzed for the family positions: father, mother, grandfather, grandmother, aunts/uncles, 20-year-old male, 20-year-old female, 10-year-old boy, and 10-year-old girl.

Father

The first five eigenvalues found in the exploratory factor analyses of the 22 items describing the role of the father were as follows: 7.93, 1.49, 1.41, 1.12, and 0.94. A scree plot suggested the extraction of a single factor (or multiple correlated factors), while the extraction of three factors was also defensible. On the other hand, the literature suggests two factors (an expressive and an instrumental role; e.g., Parsons, 1943, 1949). Further analyses revealed that three factors yielded a meaningful clustering of the items (explaining 54.29 percent of the variance). The Varimax rotated loadings are presented in Table 7.2. The first factor corresponds to the expressive role, which is consistent with the literature. Items with high loadings dealt with emotional support provided to the wife, the children, and the grandparents, while items with protection of the family and preserving family relations also showed high loadings. The second factor described the financial role of the father with items such as "father contributes financially," "father manages finances," and "father gives pocket money to children." The third factor involved childcare; items with high loadings dealt with taking the children to school, doing housework, and helping children with homework. Two items had double loadings of about the same size: the item about protecting the family loaded on the first two factors and the item teaching manners to the children showed loadings on the first two factors.

The instrumental role that is usually found in the literature is split in two independent components in our study, namely a financial role and a childcare role. The equivalence of the first factor was fairly good (with a median factorial agreement of .95); the medians of the second and the third were .92 and .85, respectively. The latter values showed that the equivalence of the factors is not perfect. The relatively low values of the second and third factors may be due to the smaller number of items with high loadings on these factors.

Mother

The factor analysis of the roles of the mother yielded largely similar results. Three factors were extracted, explaining 41.10 percent of the

Table 7.2 *Factor loadings of roles of the father and the mother (Georgas et al.) (pooled solution)*

	Father			Mother		
Role	Expressive	Financial	Childcare	Expressive	Financial	Childcare
Emotional support to children	.74	.00	.06	.68	.02	.00
Emotional support to grandparents	.68	−.13	−.03	.61	.00	−.11
Emotional support to wife/husband	.74	.02	−.04	.68	−.05	−.05
Keeps the family united	.74	.19	−.08	.77	.07	−.09
Keeps a pleasant environment	.76	.11	−.02	.75	.05	−.02
Conveys traditions to children	.59	−.07	.22	.42	−.10	.37
Conveys religion to children	.50	−.02	.15	.40	−.19	.27
Preserves family relations	.67	.12	.04	.62	−.05	.17
Supports grandparents	.51	.22	−.06	.53	.15	−.03
Takes care of grandparents	.33	−.08	.32	.29	.01	.18
Protects the family	.53	.44	−.13	.53	.28	−.05
Resolves disputes	.26	.44	−.02	.21	.36	.08
Does housework	.02	−.06	.65	.16	.06	.22
Does the shopping	−.12	.53	.42	−.06	.58	.10
Takes children to school	−.05	.16	.67	−.22	.09	.77
Plays with children	.40	.06	.44	.14	.03	.67
Helps children with homework	.21	.12	.55	−.01	.13	.70
Teaches manners to children	.44	.39	.07	.37	.16	.30
Contributes financially	.11	.73	−.16	−.03	.71	−.08
Manages finances	−.08	.77	.07	−.02	.74	−.03
Gives pocket money to children	.02	.64	.16	.06	.59	.11
Supports career of children	.23	.56	.01	.20	.48	.12

The three factors explained 49.21 percent and 41.10 percent of the variance in the analysis of the roles of father and mother, respectively. Highest loading of each item is italicized.

variance (first five eigenvalues: 5.94, 1.79, 1.31, 1.16, and 1.01). Each of the three factors showed the patterning of high and low loadings as found in the analysis of the father's roles, with one remarkable exception (see Table 7.2). Whereas the item dealing with housework had a loading of .65 on the third factor in the analysis of the roles of the father, the loading was only .22 in the analysis of the roles of the mother. The mean of the mothers across all 5,482 participants was 5.47 ($S = .99$) on a seven-point scale compared to a mean of 2.61 ($S = 1.49$) for the fathers. It is very clear that mothers do most of the housework in all the countries studied. The scores of the mothers were very high in all countries and showed very little variation. Owing to the very small variation in the scores, the item showed small correlations with all other items, leading to low loadings on all factors. The two items with the double loadings in the analysis of the roles of the father went to the first factor in the analysis of the mother.

The cross-cultural stability was not optimal. The factorial agreement indices for the three factors were .95, .88, and .71. Greece, France, Cyprus, and Indonesia showed low values on the third factor. An inspection of the factor loadings in these countries did not suggest any specific patterning. The agreement indices of the factors of the father were slightly higher than those of the mother, presumably because of the slightly stronger factor loadings in the factor analysis of the father. The roles of the father seem to be more clearly defined than the roles of the mother.

A final analysis addressed the similarity of the three factors found for the father and the mother. The three factors showed agreement indices of .98, .97, and .87, respectively. So, it seems that the first two factors showed a high level of correspondence, while the somewhat lower value of the third factor can be explained by the differential loadings of the item about housework in the two analyses. In summary, the same sets of three factors can be used to describe the role of the father and the mother in all 27 countries, although the comparisons of scores on the childcare factor should be carried out with caution, as some countries showed slightly different factors.

Grandparents and uncles/aunts

As can be seen in Table 7.3, factor analyses of the roles of the grandfather showed the usual two-factorial structure (explaining 49.09 percent of the variance; first four eigenvalues: 9.34, 1.96, 1.06, and 0.95). The items about taking care of the grandchildren and playing with grandchildren showed loadings of about the same size on both factors.

Table 7.3 *Factor loadings of the roles of the grandfather, grandmother, and uncles/aunts (Georgas et al.) (pooled solution)*

Role	Grandfather		Grandmother		Uncles/aunts	
	Expressive	Instrumental	Expressive	Instrumental	Expressive	Instrumental
Emotional support to X[a]	.71	.00	.72	-.01	.72	.00
Emotional support to parents	.76	-.08	.73	-.07	.76	-.10
Keeps the family united	.80	-.02	.78	-.02	.79	-.02
Keeps a pleasant environment	.83	-.03	.81	-.03	.83	-.05
Conveys traditions to X	.76	-.04	.74	-.02	.71	.00
Conveys religion to X	.65	-.03	.67	-.07	.60	.05
Preserves family relations	.76	.00	.75	-.01	.75	.02
Supports X	.66	.13	.65	.13	.68	.12
Takes care of X	.29	.44	.34	.40	.35	.41
Protects the family	.53	.30	.52	.29	.48	.33
Resolves disputes	.24	.48	.23	.48	.16	.54
Does housework	-.04	.57	.10	.54	-.00	.64
Does the shopping	-.05	.69	-.05	.67	-.04	.70
Takes X to school	-.07	.71	-.09	.69	-.11	.72
Plays with X	.41	.38	.38	.38	.33	.42
Helps X with homework	.00	.67	-.03	.66	.03	.68
Teaches manners to X	.58	.23	.60	.19	.46	.32
Contributes financially	-.02	.75	-.05	.74	-.06	.78
Manages finances	-.13	.79	-.14	.77	-.15	.81
Gives pocket money to X	.20	.56	.20	.55	.12	.62
Supports career of X	.23	.53	.24	.50	.22	.52
Babysits X	.24	.49	.30	.43	.21	.51
Helps parents with their work	.03	.61	.00	.64	.06	.60

Note:
The two factors explained 49.09 percent, 47.23 percent, and 49.16 percent of the variance in the analysis of the grandfather, grandmother, and uncles/aunts, respectively. Highest loading of each item is italicized.

[a] X involves grandchildren in the analysis of grandparents and nephews/nieces in the analysis of uncles/aunts.

The analysis of the grandmother also yielded a two-factorial structure, explaining 47.23 percent of the variance (Table 7.3). The same two items showed double loadings. A computation of the equivalence of the two factors found for both grandparents showed the similarity of both factors (agreement index = 1.00 for both factors).

The analysis of the roles of uncles and aunts also showed the two-dimensional structure (explaining 49.16 percent of the variance; see Table 7.3). All items showed the highest loading on the expected factor, although the differences were not large for some items. Interestingly, the same two items of the previous analysis (taking care of and playing with nephews and nieces) showed double loadings. For each of the three positions the structural equivalence was good (with median agreement indices well above .95).

Siblings

Factor analyses of the roles of the siblings (son of 10, daughter of 10, son of 20, and daughter of 20 years of age) also showed the two-factorial structure (Table 7.4). The percentages of variance explained were 42.72 percent, 42.59 percent, 42.86 percent, and 42.65 percent, respectively. Again, the items showed the loadings in line with expectations. Furthermore, with a few exceptions (e.g., the role of the 10-year-old son in the Ukraine) all factor agreement indices were well above .90. The median agreement coefficient across all the analyses of the siblings was .97. A final analysis addressed the equivalence of the factors as found for the four siblings of Table 7.4. Very high agreement indices were found (.99 and higher), which strongly suggests that the factors found were identical across the siblings.

Emotional distance

The scale measuring bonds or Emotional Distance (Georgas, Mylonas, Bafiti et al., 2001) with kin and non-kin showed a very good agreement in all countries, except for Germany (.40). The items constituted a single factor (see Table 7.5). In the hypothesis tests two scores derived from the scales are used, namely emotional distance to nuclear family members and extended family members. It may be noted that in keeping with the literature the concept is referred to as Emotional Distance, while the scale is scored in the opposite direction (of emotional closeness). On both scales high scores indicate strong emotional ties.

Table 7.4 *Factor loadings of roles of the siblings (Georgas et al.) (pooled solution)*

Role	Son 10 yrs		Daughter 10 yrs		Son 20 yrs		Daughter 20 yrs	
	Expressive	Instrumental	Expressive	Instrumental	Expressive	Instrumental	Expressive	Instrumental
Emotional support to grandparents	.66	-.13	.66	-.11	.65	-.12	.59	-.07
Emotional support to siblings	.72	-.07	.72	-.07	.68	-.01	.68	-.04
Keeps the family united	.77	-.08	.77	-.09	.81	-.08	.80	-.09
Keeps a pleasant environment	.77	-.06	.77	-.06	.77	-.01	.78	-.04
Conveys traditions to siblings	.59	.19	.59	.18	.59	.14	.60	.14
Conveys religion to siblings	.53	.24	.53	.22	.53	.15	.55	.12
Preserves family relations	.65	.11	.64	.12	.65	.08	.68	.06
Does housework	.14	.57	.19	.56	.10	.45	.19	.47
Does the shopping	.01	.65	.00	.65	.00	.66	-.03	.67
Takes siblings to school	.01	.60	.01	.61	.00	.65	.02	.63
Plays with siblings	.34	.08	.35	.07	.31	.31	.33	.29
Contributes financially	-.11	.65	-.11	.63	-.09	.68	-.10	.69
Babysits siblings	.07	.62	.07	.63	.11	.58	.15	.53
Helps parents with their work	-.02	.69	-.01	.68	-.06	.70	-.07	.71

The two factors explained 42.72 percent, 42.59 percent, 42.86 percent, and 42.65 percent of the variance in the analysis of the roles of the roles of son of 10, daughter of 10, son of 20, and daughter of 20 years of age, respectively. Highest loading of each item is italicized.

Table 7.5 *Factor loadings of emotional distance (Georgas et al.)*
(pooled solution)

Emotional distance from	Loading
Mother	.38
Siblings	.44
Father	.41
Grandparents	.55
Cousins	.54
Uncles/aunts	.61

The first factor explained 25.35 percent of the variance. Loadings of positions not used in the computation of the emotional distance to nuclear and extended family (i.e., neighbors, friends, newspaper journalists, colleagues, acquaintances, priest, primary-school teachers, prime minister, shopkeepers, writers, spouse/date, fellow students, members of parliament, high-school teachers, newscasters) are not represented here.

Self-construal

In initial analyses, 20 items of the Self-construal Scale (Singelis, 1994; Singelis and Brown, 1995; Singelis and Sharkey, 1995) were analyzed, yielding the expected patterning of high and low loadings on both factors. However, the two-factorial solutions of about half of the countries did not reveal the same two factors. More specifically, agreement indices of less than .90 were obtained in more than half of the countries for the independence factor; the interdependence factor revealed low values in only two countries. The problems of the independence factor were not clearly patterned. Therefore, it was decided to adopt the strategy of splitting the scales as in the analysis of the personality and values scales. Initial analyses showed that items "I should take into consideration my parents' advice when making education/career plans" and "Even when I strongly disagree with group members, I avoid an argument" of the interdependence scale had to be eliminated as they challenged the equivalence in several countries. The final, nine-item scales showed unifactorial solutions with loadings between .35 and .65 (see Table 7.6). The independence scale showed a median agreement index of .96, but too low agreement values were found in four countries (France: .69; Indonesia: .81; Japan: .82; United Kingdom: .89). In each case different items (with either low or negative loadings) were responsible for the low values. The agreement was excellent for the interdependence scale, with a median of .98 and all values well above .90.

Table 7.6 *Factor loadings of independence and interdependence (Singelis et al.) (pooled solution)*

Scale/item	
Independence	Loading
Enjoy being unique	.43
Act as independent person	.44
Direct and forthright	.49
Comfortable when praised	.43
Speaking up not a problem	.53
Act the same way	.62
Do the best for me	.41
Take care of myself	.44
Act the same way	.51
Interdependence	
Respect modest people	.36
Sacrifice self-interest	.58
Cooperate	.52
Relationships are important	.50
Happiness depends on others	.53
Stay in the group	.57
Respect group decisions	.65
Maintain harmony	.65
Go along with others	.44

The two factors explained 23.09 percent and 29.24 percent of the variance in the analysis of the independence and interdependence scale, respectively.

Personality

In initial analyses all personality variables from the Williams, Satter-white, and Saiz (1998) Personality Traits Scale were analyzed jointly. In line with the underlying theoretical model, which is the currently popular five-factor model of personality (e.g., Allik and McCrae, 2004), five factors were extracted. Subsequent analyses showed that this five-factorial structure was not at all stable across cultures. This finding is not consistent with the literature. The evidence for the structural equivalence of the model is impressive, sometimes with the exception of Openness (e.g., De Raad, 1994). One of the possible reasons for the poor support of the structural equivalence could be that we used an instrument to measure the five factors of personality for which the structural equivalence has never been tested. Another problem could be the considerable reduction of items needed in the current study; there were 30 items in our instrument while the original instrument has 240 items, so our factor solution cannot be expected to be as stable as a solution based on the full instrument. Therefore, we adopted another strategy and analyzed the measure as consisting of five independent scales. For each of the five scales the same factor equivalence procedure was followed. The pooled solution, which represents the factor loadings in the "average country" (Table 7.7), showed the expected unifactorial bipolar arrangement of items. The absolute values of the loadings ranged between .40 and .70, with one exception. The negative pole of Openness was not well defined. The item about rigidity showed a loading of −.03 and the items about inhibition and conservatism −.26.

The factorial agreement of the Agreement, Conscientiousness, Extraversion, and Neuroticism scales were very good; the median agreement index is well over .95. Yet, that does not mean that the agreement is perfect. For example, even for Conscientiousness, the scale with the highest median agreement, there was a single country (South Korea) that did not reach the lower threshold of .90. An inspection of the factor loadings showed that the value of .89 was due to the weak loading (−.01) of "organized." It was not clear to what extent this problem is due to sample particulars, translation problems, or a relationship between the item and the construct that differs from other countries.

The most problematic scale was Openness, with a median value of .89. Particularly for Algeria (.24), Saudi Arabia (.31), and Nigeria (.32) the scale did not show the unifactorial, bipolar structure as expected and found in the global solution. The countries with these low values did not show similar deviances of the global pattern among themselves. Therefore, it was assumed that particulars of the sample or administration caused the problems. As noted before, this is not the first study to observe problems with the equivalence of the Openness Scale. A comparison of the median agreement indices per country showed that some countries such as Pakistan and Nigeria had average values well below .90. A further inspection of the factor loadings did not suggest a patterning behind the deviant loadings.

It is clear that any comparison involving data in which one or more countries did not show the desired structural equivalence has to be interpreted with caution. The question had to be addressed of how to proceed with using the scales in the countries with low values. From a statistical perspective different approaches can be adopted. The first is to eliminate the problematic items so as to end up with a set of equivalent items. This approach was not adopted, as it would reduce our already short scales even further; moreover, in most countries all items performed well. The second would be to eliminate the whole country. For

Table 7.7 *Factor loadings of personality (Williams et al., 1998)* *(pooled solution)*

Scale/item	Loading
Agreeableness (32.76 percent)[a]	
Understanding	.61
Sympathetic	.55
Considerate	.56
Quarrelsome	−.52
Deceitful	−.57
Rude	−.62
Conscientiousness (40.07 percent)	
Organized	.69
Reliable	.49
Responsible	.66
Careless	−.60
Lazy	−.63
Disorderly	−.70
Emotional stability (31.76 percent)	
Stable	.54
Optimistic	.50
Calm	.47
Moody	−.53
Irritable	−.67
Anxious	−.64
Extraversion (39.61 percent)	
Outgoing	.62
Sociable	.69
Active	.57
Withdrawn	−.60
Shy	−.65
Quiet	−.64
Openness (25.28 percent)	
Imaginative	.65
Adventurous	.72
Spontaneous	.67
Rigid	−.03
Inhibited	−.26
Conservative	−.26

Note:

The scales were analyzed in separate factor analyses.

[a] Numbers after scale names refer to the proportion of variance accounted for by the factor.

obvious reasons, it is not attractive to remove every country that shows a value lower than the threshold level in any of the equivalence analyses. The third approach adopted here (as well as in the subsequent analyses) was to inspect any patterning in the deviances and to compare the equivalence problems across scales so as to identify problematic samples.

Family values

The Family Values Scale (Georgas, 1989, 1991, 1993, 1999) was intended to measure two factors, Hierarchical roles of father and mother and Relationships within family and with kin. Initial analyses showed that four items ("Parents shouldn't get involved in the private lives of their married children," "Parents should help their children financially," "The children should work in order to help the family," "The parents shouldn't argue in front of the children") did not show loadings in various cultural groups and were eliminated. As can be seen in Table 7.8, the remaining items in the pooled solution revealed the expected patterning across the two orthogonal factors. All countries showed agreement indices well above the threshold level of .90 (with overall

Table 7.8 *Varimax-rotated factor loadings of family values (Georgas et al.)* *(pooled solution)*

Item	Hierarchy	Relationships
Father head of family	.69	.23
Good relationships with relatives	.16	.56
Mother's place is at home	.69	.02
Mother go-between	.59	.14
Parents teach behavior	.09	.60
Father should handle money	.75	.06
Children take care of old parents	.11	.58
Children should help	−.09	.60
Problems are solved within the family	.08	.60
Children should obey parents	.32	.62
Honor family's reputation	.28	.63
Children should respect grandparents	.08	.69
Mother should accept father's decisions	.70	.13
Father is breadwinner	.72	.12

The two factors explained 44.36 percent of the variance. Highest loading of each item is italicized.

medians of .96 for Hierarchy and .98 for Relationships) except for the loadings on the hierarchy factor in Pakistan (.83) and the loadings on the kin relationships factor in Ghana (.89). The low values were due to some low loadings in these countries as compared to the pooled solution.

Values

The 24 items from Schwartz (1992, 1994a) measuring six values (Embeddedness, Hierarchy, Harmony, Intellectual autonomy, Affective autonomy, and Mastery[1]) were first analyzed in a single analysis. The expected two-factorial structure was not stable across countries. As in the previous analysis, the relatively small number of items (Embeddedness was measured with six items, the others by three items each) could also challenge the equivalence. The same procedure of splitting up the instrument into separate unifactorial scales was also followed here. The procedure was effective in that with the exception of Mastery in Algeria (with an agreement coefficient of .68), all scales in all countries showed values above .90; across all comparisons the median agreement was 1.00, which points to excellent structural equivalence. The pooled solutions are given in Table 7.9; all items showed positive and in most cases high loadings.

INTERNAL CONSISTENCY

In the next step of the analyses the Cronbach alpha internal consistencies were computed for the scales. Each factor found in the structural equivalence analyses was taken as a scale. In most analyses this meant that all items were assumed to constitute a single scale. Reliability analyses at both individual and country level are reported. The former is based on the individual responses ($N = 5,482$) to scale items. The latter deals with the reliability at country level. Each country makes up one observation ($N = 27$). The latter analysis is carried out because many analyses (and most hypotheses) deal with differences at country level, and the reliability of the constructs at country level cannot be assumed but has to be demonstrated.

For the Self-Construal, Personality, and Values scales the individual-level reliabilities were fairly similar, with an average of .62 (range of α:.45–.75). The values at country level were slightly higher ($M = .69$,

---

[1] As noted in Chapter 6, *Egalitarian Commitment* was omitted in a number of countries, and rather than not employing the questionnaire, we proceeded with six scales instead of seven.

Table 7.9 *Factor loadings of values (Schwartz) (pooled solution)*

Value and item	Loading
Embeddedness (35.59 percent)[a]	
Family security	.54
Respect for tradition	.64
Honoring elders	.70
Social order	.63
National security	.66
Reciprocation of favors	.34
Hierarchy (59.55 percent)	
Authority	.81
Wealth	.69
Social power	.81
Harmony (60.66 percent)	
World of beauty	.71
Unity with nature	.83
Protecting environment	.79
Intellectual autonomy (51.31 percent)	
Broadminded	.61
Creativity	.78
Curious	.75
Affective autonomy (56.05 percent)	
Pleasure	.78
Exciting life	.68
Enjoying life	.78
Mastery (50.34 percent)	
Independent	.80
Daring	.67
Choosing own goals	.65

Note:
[a] Numbers behind value names refer to the percentage of variance explained by the factor.

range of α: .27–.90). The low value of .27 is due to a small, negative correlation between "daring" and "choosing own goals" (the other correlations were positive). Internal consistencies at country level also tended to be higher for the other scales (presumably owing to aggregation effects in these data). Family Networks, Emotional Distance, and Family Values showed higher values, both at individual and country level (the latter had an average of .81 and the former of .79). It can be concluded that although the internal consistencies of particularly the scales related to values, self and personality were only moderate, the values are acceptable given the relatively small number of items of most of the scales.

The expressive role had high reliabilities both at individual level (overall mean $\alpha = .84$, $S = .04$) and country level (overall $M = .91$, $S = .04$). The Instrumental roles (for father and mother this was split into finances and childcare) showed lower values. The overall mean was $\alpha = .68$ ($S = .08$) at individual level and .62 ($S = .22$) at country level. Higher reliabilities of the expressive roles (presumably because of their slightly larger number of items) were found in every country. The lowest country average was found for Algeria (.69) and the highest for Hong Kong (.83). The distribution of internal consistencies did not show clear outliers. Furthermore, an inspection of the patterning of these values did not suggest any country-level characteristic (such as temperature, affluence, or religion) with which these values would be related.

It can be concluded that the averages of the internal consistencies of the various scales ranged from acceptable to good, that the differences across countries were not large, and that the expressive roles tended to have higher internal consistencies than the instrumental roles.

GENDER DIFFERENCES

The next analysis addresses the differences in responses given by female and male participants (no data on gender were available for Indonesia). Because the sample size in this study is large, relatively small differences in average scores between females and males can result in statistical significance but, in fact, these differences may be very small from a psychological perspective. Thus, interest was more in the size and "psychological significance" rather than the statistical significance of the differences, that is, effect sizes. Two kinds of effect sizes are reported in this section. The first is used in reporting results of an analysis of variance with gender and country as independent variables and psychological measures as dependent variables. The effect size we report is the proportion of explained variance (η^2) resulting from the independent variables. This number refers to the proportion of variance resulting from the total score variation (i.e., across individuals and countries) that is due to gender differences. The total score variation consists of both (random) unsystematic sources of variance resulting from unreliability of the measures as well as systematic differences across individuals, gender, and countries. Cohen (1988) proposed values of η^2 of .01, .06, and .14 to distinguish small, medium, and large effects. An advantage of this measure of effect size is that it can be used for independent variables with any number of levels; it can be used to compute effect sizes for both countries and genders. A disadvantage of this measure is that is not directional. An effect size of .14 is large; yet, it does not indicate which level (country or gender) showed larger or smaller values relative to the others. Therefore, we also employed another effect measure which is directional (although it can be used only for independent variables with two levels, such as gender). Cohen's d is defined as the difference of the averages of the male and female students, divided by their pooled standard deviation. The numbers can be interpreted as z scores: values above zero refer to higher average scores of males; values below zero refer to higher average scores of females. Cohen's d is said to be small, medium, or large if its absolute values are larger than .20, .50, or .80, respectively.

The multivariate effect size of gender for the Self-Construal Scales (Singelis et al. 1995) was zero and not significant. The interaction was significant ($p < .01$), though very small ($\eta^2 = .01$). More specifically, the value of Cohen's d of the Independence Scale was $\eta^2 = .03$ and for the Interdependence Scale $\eta^2 = .01$.

The multivariate effect size of the scores on personality (Williams, Satterwhite, and Saiz, 1998) was statistically significant ($p < .01$) but small; the proportion of variance accounted by gender, η^2, was .03, while the interaction of gender and country also showed a small effect size of .01 (interactions effects of all analyses reported here are discussed at the end of this section). More specifically, female participants scored higher on Agreeableness when averaged across countries ($d = -.23$), Conscientiousness ($d = -.20$), Extraversion ($d = -.15$), and Openness ($d = -.09$), while males scored higher on Emotional Stability ($d = .15$).

For the Family Values Scale (Georgas, 1989; Georgas et al. 2004c), the multivariate main effect of gender and interaction of gender and country were highly significant ($p < .01$); their effect sizes were ($\eta^2 = .04$ and .01, respectively). An inspection of the univariate results showed that the significance was entirely due to the Hierarchy Scale. Males showed much higher scores on the scale than females ($d = .42$; $p < .01$), while the differences on the Kin Relationship Scale were nonsignificant and very small ($d = -.02$). Most differences we find are in line with the gender literature (Brannon, 2002; Maccoby and Jacklin, 1975; Williams and Best, 1982, 1990).

The multivariate effect sizes of gender and the country by gender interaction on Schwartz's values questionnaires were significant ($p < .01$) and small ($\eta^2 = .02$ and .01, respectively). Females showed higher scores on Embeddedness ($d = -.14$) and Harmony ($d = -.13$), while males scored higher on Hierarchy ($d = .19$). The differences on the other scales were so small that even with the current sample sizes the gender differences were not significant (Intellectual Autonomy: $d = .01$; Affective Autonomy: $d = .03$; Mastery: $d = .03$; all $ps > .05$).

The three family network variables (geographical proximity, frequency of visits, frequency of telephone calls) and Emotional Distance from nuclear and extended family (Georgas et al., 2004a) showed a similar patterning of small, but consistent gender differences. The family network variables were statistically significant ($p < .01$), although the multivariate effect size was small ($\eta^2 = .01$), as was the effect size of the interaction ($\eta^2 = .01$). The d values of the gender differences were $-.01$ (geographical proximity), $-.10$ (females visit relatives more), and $-.18$ (females telephone relatives more). The multivariate effect sizes of Emotional Distance (to the nuclear and extended family) were .003 for the main effect of gender and .01 for interaction of gender and country. The average emotional distance (Cohen's d) was $-.11$ for the nuclear and $-.18$ for the extended family. The consistency of d values of all variables tested is remarkable and suggests that daughters have a somewhat closer emotional relationship with the members of the nuclear family and close kin. The effect is probably not due to acquiescence as similar effects were not found for the other psychological variables.

The last set of variables involved the Family roles (Georgas et al., 2004b). The meaning of gender differences is different from the previous analyses. In the previous analyses the cross-cultural stability of gender differences in psychological functioning was examined; in the analysis of the family roles the participants did not report about their personal preferences or practices but about patterns in their own family. Systematic differences of male and female participants are more problematic than in the previous analyses as they point to systematic differences in males and females as observers of family patterns. Large interactions of gender and country would exacerbate this problem, as they would mean that these systematic observer effects vary across countries.

All family roles were examined in a single multivariate analysis of variance. The multivariate effect sizes of both the main effect of gender and the interaction of country and gender were significant ($p < .01$); the first explained 7 percent and the second 1 percent of the variance. The former effect, a medium size, is due to the global gender difference across all positions and roles; Cohen's d of the difference of the global means of male and female students was $-.12$. The negative sign is in line with the findings on the network variables and emotional distance, despite the difference in psychological meaning of both kinds of variables. That is, females tend to be more in agreement with each of the three roles.

In most of the previous analyses the interaction component was significant but small. In analyses we conducted (but not reported here), the nature of the deviations was explored by using factor analysis of their correlations and cluster analysis of their distances. No particular patterning was found in either analysis. Therefore, it seems likely that at least some of the effects may be due to sampling particulars, small sample sizes of either gender in some of the countries, and other presumably less relevant sources of variation.

The analyses to be reported further in this Chapter, exploration of country differences and tests of hypotheses, could have been carried out on the data after correction for differences in gender composition of the samples (by applying weights to individual-level data so as to make the gender ration identical across countries). This was not done for three reasons. First, it would have meant that Indonesian data could no longer be used as no gender data were available for Indonesia. Second, the proportion of females in the sample, which ranged from .22 in Ghana to .89 in France ($M = .62$, $SD = .16$), was not systematically related to the scores on the family roles. The latter finding suggests that a correction for differential gender composition does not lead to a systematic change in the patterning of findings. Third, the overall correction would affect the mean score of a country to only a limited extent, as most of the gender differences were relatively small.

In conclusion, although gender differences were found with some variables, the effect sizes indicate they do not appear to be very large across countries. The largest differences appear to be in the direction of females having somewhat higher average scores. This was found in a number of family roles, particularly the expressive roles of mother, grandmother, daughters, but even with father, grandfather, and sons. Females visit and telephone relatives more frequently. Females are somewhat more Agreeable, Conscientious, and Extroverted on the personality scales, and they have higher scores on Embeddedness values. Males have somewhat higher scores on Emotional Stability, Schwartz's Hierarchy values, and Hierarchical family values (Georgas et al., 2004b). However, it is important to emphasize again that the effect size of these differences, the percentage of variance explained, was relatively small and does not allow us to conclude that there are large gender differences in most of the findings.

EDUCATIONAL LEVEL OF PARENTS

A potentially important source of individual and country differences in family-related measurement instruments is the educational level of the parents. It could well be that parental educational level is associated with particular parenting styles and family practices. The relationship of family-related scales and parental education was investigated at individual and country level separately. Parental educational level was measured as the number of years of schooling averaged for both parents and coded into four categories. No attempt was made to further examine the nature of the differences of schooling in the various countries so as to provide a more fine-grain scoring system.

No data were available for Indonesia and South Korea, which reduced the sample size to 4,981 participants in 25 countries. Some data on educational level were missing in some countries.

The variation in parental education was large. The global average was about 10 years of schooling. An analysis of variance was computed in order to estimate the effect size of the country differences. The country differences were highly significant ($F(24, 4980) = 73.16$, $p < .01$) and explained not less than 26 percent of the variation in parental education, which points to large cross-cultural differences. A closer inspection of the country means (not further reported here) did not suggest that students living in more affluent countries tended to have better educated parents. The correlation was .27, which is not significant in a small sample of 25 observations.

The correlations between parental education and the family variables (Family Networks, Family Roles, and Emotional Distance) at *individual* level were very low. Most of the means of the correlations were close to zero while the standard deviations were sizeable. This pattern suggests that within counties the correlations were not strong. Although not further documented here, the same pattern was found when the educational level of father and mother were correlated separately with the family variables. Furthermore, a cluster analysis of the correlations of the parental educational level and family variables per country (25 countries × 25 family variables) did not suggest any patterning of the correlations. Therefore, it seems fair to conclude that there are no salient correlations between parental educational level and family variables that generalize across countries.

At *country* level the Family Network and Emotional Distance scales did not show any significant correlations. For the family roles some significant correlations were found; more specifically, the financial and care roles of the mother ($r = .57$ and $.40$) as well as the instrumental–material/economic role of the grandfather and grandmother ($r = .40$ and $.54$) were all significantly related to parental education ($p < .05$). A similar pattern of positive (though nonsignificant) correlations was found for the other positions. If we focus on the patterning rather than on the significance of the correlations (and disregard the significance levels), the correlations point to the presence of very weak negative correlations between parental education and expressive roles and a somewhat stronger (though still modest) positive correlation between parental education and instrumental–material/economic roles.

In summary, we did not find correlations between parental education and family-related variables at individual level in the 25 countries. Some correlations were significant in some countries; however, their significance was sample- or country-specific and did not generalize across the 25 countries of our study. At the country level we found a pattern of weak negative correlations between parental education and expressive roles and a pattern of slightly stronger positive correlations between parental education and instrumental–material/economic role roles. Particularly at the individual level we can safely ignore the influence of parental education on the family variables studied here. This observation implies that parental education does not need to be involved as a covariate in the analyses reported in the remainder of the Chapter.

SIZE OF CROSS-CULTURAL DIFFERENCES

The current section describes the size of cross-cultural differences in all psychological variables (i.e., family networks, family roles, emotional distance, personality, self-construal, family values, and values) at country-level and also at the individual level. The current section describes different kinds of analyses. First, some analyses consider the data at individual level ($N = 5,482$) and treat individuals as replications within countries. Second, some analyses consider the data at country level ($N = 27$); each country is represented by its mean, which is derived from aggregating individual scores. Third, some analyses deal with sets of countries clustered on the basis of Affluence, Relatedness or Religion. Table 7.10 gives the clustering of the countries in terms of affluence and relatedness.

The last religion cluster comprises of a mixture of Buddhism, Hinduism, and Traditional Beliefs. As the first four clusters are more homogeneous and are based on a substantial variation in the percentages, it was decided to omit the last cluster from the hypothesis tests.

Psychological and family variables

Table 7.11 gives an overview of the averages and standard deviations of the psychological scales at country level ($N = 27$; a more detailed table can be found in the next Chapter). It is remarkable that for all psychological variables the mean scores are much above the scale mid-points of 4 (score range: 1 to 7), possibly because most items dealt with positive, desirable attitudes. The standard deviation of the family value

Table 7.10 *Country clusters in terms of affluence, relatedness, and religion*

	Low	Medium	High
Affluence	Algeria, Ghana, India, Indonesia, Nigeria, Pakistan	Brazil, Bulgaria, Chile, Cyprus, Georgia, Greece, Iran, Mexico, Saudi Arabia, Turkey, Ukraine	Canada, France, Germany, Hong Kong, Japan, South Korea, Spain, The Netherlands, UK, USA
Relatedness	Algeria, Ghana, India, Indonesia, Nigeria, Pakistan	Brazil, Bulgaria, Chile, Cyprus, Georgia, Greece, Hong Kong, Iran, Japan, Mexico, Saudi Arabia, South Korea, Spain, Turkey, Ukraine	Canada, France, Germany, The Netherlands, UK, USA
Religion			
Roman Catholic	Brazil, Canada, Chile, France, Mexico, Spain,		
Protestant	The Netherlands		
Christian	Germany, UK, USA		
Orthodox	Bulgaria, Cyprus,		
Islamic	Georgia, Greece,		
Buddhist/	Ukraine		
Hindu/	Algeria, Indonesia, Iran, Nigeria, Pakistan,		
Traditional	Saudi Arabia, Turkey		
	Ghana, Hong Kong,		
	India, Japan, South Korea		

Hierarchy is larger than the others. The means and standard deviations of emotional distance are striking; the global mean of the scale measuring distance to the nuclear family is 6.16, which is very high, while its standard deviation is only 0.18. The emotional distance is smaller ($M = 4.68$) and its standard deviation is much larger ($SD = .43$). Clearly, a close emotional tie with the nuclear family and a weaker relationship with the extended family is universal in our data.

Means and standard deviations of Family Networks and Family Roles are given in Table 7.12. It is interesting to compare the means of the male and female positions. Consistently higher scores were reported for female positions; for instance the mean of mother across the three scales (i.e., expressive role, finances, and childcare) is 4.62, while this value for the father is 4.12. Similarly, the mean score is 3.50 for grandmother and 3.25 for grandfather, 3.58 for the 20-year-old daughter and 3.40 for the 20-year-old son, and 2.72 for the 10-year-old daughter and 2.64 for the 10-year-old son. The importance of the various family positions

Table 7.11 *Means, standard deviations across countries, and proportion of variance (η^2) accounted for in psychological variables by country and clusters of countries based on affluence, religion, and relatedness*

Scale	M	SD	Country	Affluence cluster	Religious cluster	Relatedness cluster
				Proportion of variance accounted for		
Emotional Distance						
Nuclear	6.16	.18	.04	.01	.01	.01
Extended	4.68	.43	*.09*	.02	.04	.00
Self-Construal						
Independent	4.78	.34	**.17**	.02	.01	.01
Interdependent	4.85	.49	**.29**	.04	.02	.05
Personality						
Agreeableness	5.60	.32	**.14**	.04	.05	.02
Conscientiousness	5.16	.42	**.17**	.05	*.06*	.03
Emotional stability	4.56	.28	*.09*	.01	.02	.02
Extraversion	4.72	.28	*.07*	.00	.03	.01
Openness	4.56	.31	*.13*	.01	.05	.01
Family values						
Hierarchy	4.46	1.06	**.54**	**.33**	**.32**	**.37**
Kin	5.99	.45	**.29**	**.18**	*.12*	**.15**
Values						
Embeddedness	5.71	.49	**.29**	**.20**	**.20**	**.14**
Hierarchy	4.51	.53	**.16**	.05	*.06*	*.06*
Harmony	5.45	.37	*.11*	*.09*	*.06*	*.07*
Intel. autonomy	5.60	.31	*.09*	.01	.01	.00
Affect. autonomy	5.75	.36	*.13*	.01	.05	.02
Mastery	5.74	.25	*.07*	.02	.02	.00

All scales have a minimum score of 1 and a maximum score of 7. Nonsignificant and small effect sizes ($\eta^2 < .06$) are printed in regular font, medium effect sizes ($.06 < \eta^2 < .14$) in italics, and large effect sizes ($\eta^2 > .14$) in bold.

for the Family Roles showed an interesting pattern. As could be expected, parents showed the highest scores ($M = 4.37$), indicating that they play the most central role in vital family functions, both expressive and instrumental. They are followed by the 20-year-old children ($M = 3.49$), who are followed by the grandparents ($M = 3.37$). Uncles and aunts showed a mean of 2.89, while the lowest scores were obtained for 10-year-old children ($M = 2.68$). Finally, means of expressive roles were larger than means of instrumental–material/economic roles, with the

Table 7.12 *Means and standard deviations across countries, and proportion of variance (η^2) in family variables accounted for by country and clusters of countries based on affluence, religion, and relatedness*

			Proportion of variance accounted for				
Scale	M	SD	Country	Affluence clusters	Religious clusters	Relatedness clusters
Family networks						
Geographic proximity	3.42	.51	**.17**	.02	.08	.07
Visits	4.22	.37	.11	.06	.05	.07
Telephone calls	3.22	.58	**.17**	.07	.05	.06
Family roles						
Father expressive	4.40	.42	**.19**	**.14**	.13	.10
Father finances	4.70	.41	**.19**	.11	.10	.06
Father care	3.25	.30	.08	.01	.02	.02
Mother expressive	4.89	.32	**.20**	.13	.11	.07
Mother finances	4.61	.33	.13	.00	.02	.00
Mother care	4.37	.40	**.15**	.01	.09	.02
Grandfather expressive	3.91	.45	**.17**	.11	.07	.06
Grandfather instrumental	2.58	.33	.12	.03	.01	.03

Grandmother expressive	4.15	.40	**.17**	.08	.06	.04
Grandmother instrumental	2.85	.29	*.09*	.00	.03	.01
Uncles/aunts expressive	3.37	.43	**.16**	.04	.04	.02
Uncles/aunts instrumental	2.41	.31	*.12*	.04	.01	.05
Son (20) expressive	3.72	.31	*.11*	.06	.04	.02
Son (20) instrumental	3.08	.25	*.09*	.07	.03	.06
Daughter (20) expressive	3.89	.35	**.15**	.07	.06	.03
Daughter (20) instrumental	3.26	.26	*.09*	.05	.03	.03
Son (10) expressive	3.33	.30	*.12*	.03	.01	.01
Son (10) instrumental	1.95	.23	*.08*	.02	.02	.03
Daughter (10) expressive	3.41	.31	*.13*	.03	.02	.01
Daughter (10) instrumental	2.03	.24	*.08*	.02	.02	.02

All scales have a minimum score of 1 and a maximum score of 6 (except for geographic proximity which has a maximum score of 7). Nonsignificant and small effect sizes ($\eta^2 < .06$) are printed in regular font, medium effect sizes ($.06 < \eta^2 < .14$) in italics, and large effect sizes ($\eta^2 > .14$) in bold.

exception of the financial role of the father, which was globally the most important role of the father.

Proportion of variance (η^2) accounted for in psychological and family variables

The nature and size of the cluster differences were further explored in series of analyses of variance with either country or cluster membership as the independent variable and the scale scores as dependent variables. These analyses are at the individual level. Four kinds of analyses are reported. The first is based on an analysis of variance with country as the independent variable (27 levels) and a psychological measure as the dependent variable. The second analysis is at the individual level ($N = 5,482$) and is based on a clustering of the countries in three Affluence clusters (see Table 7.10). It may be noted that the three levels of Affluence are used as a nominal classification in the analysis. The third analysis addresses Religion and examines the effectiveness of a split in religious clusters (five levels; see Table 7.10) to address country differences in psychological variables. The final analysis addresses the country clustering in terms of Relatedness (three levels; see Table 7.10). All main effects of country were found to be significant ($p < .01$), which is not surprising for our large sample size. Therefore, we were more interested in the size of the cross-cultural differences, as measured by the proportion of variance accounted for by cluster membership (η^2) and in the nature of the cluster differences, which were explored in post hoc analyses. The latter analyses are given for referential purposes and are not discussed here in detail (the next section examines to what extent their pattern follows expectations).

The first set of analyses of variance can be seen as defining an upper limit of the effect sizes that can be found in the clustering of the countries. By definition the effect size of a clustering cannot be larger than the effect size found in the first analysis. However, the question to be addressed is to what extent the two ways of clustering countries (which use very few levels compared to the 27 levels of the first analysis) yield effect sizes comparable to the country variation. If a particular clustering captures much country variation, an effect size will be found for the clustering that is similar in size to the effect size of the first analysis. On the other hand, a country clustering that yields very small effect sizes does not provide an explanation of the country differences observed.

The effect sizes of the psychological variables can be found in Table 7.11, and the effect sizes of the family variables can be found in Table 7.12. The effect sizes of the country differences of the first analysis pointed to large differences. All effect sizes were medium or large, with the exception of Emotional Distance to the nuclear family for which a value of $\eta^2 = .04$ was found. The average effect size was $\eta^2 = .18$ for the psychological variables and $\eta^2 = .16$ for the family variables. These values are very large if one takes into account that the scores are derived from scores of individuals and that even for fairly reliable instruments a sizeable proportion of the variance is random error, which reduces the effect size of countries. Particularly high effect sizes were found for the values Embeddedness (Schwartz, 1992) and Hierarchy (Georgas, 1989; Georgas et al., 2004c). Both point to large cross-cultural differences in more traditional and more modern countries. We return to this issue in the next section on hypothesis tests. Furthermore, the expressive roles of family members showed somewhat larger cross-cultural differences than did the instrumental–material/economic roles (with average effect sizes of $\eta^2 = .26$ and $\eta^2 = .11$, respectively).

The cluster means of family network variables and family roles are presented in Table 7.13. This table also indicates which mean scores differed at least .50 SD (a medium or large effect size) from each other. An inspection of the Family Network variables shows that the countries in the medium level of both Affluence and Relatedness tended to show the highest scores on geographic proximity, frequency of visits, and telephone calls. As for Religion, the Christian Orthodox showed the highest means. Curvilinear effects (in which the medium level of Affluence or Relatedness showed much higher or lower means than the other levels) were not found for any family role. Rather, these showed either linear effects or no effects at all. The most common pattern was a decrease of scores across the levels of Affluence (with in some cases medium or large effect sizes in the comparison of the countries in the low and high affluence clusters). The opposite pattern was found for Relatedness; scores on the family roles tended to increase with Relatedness. The comparisons of the Religious clusters showed medium or large effect sizes only in some comparisons of Protestant and Islamic countries. The expressive roles of both the father and the mother were more salient in Islamic countries. The other family positions showed the same pattern of higher scores in Islamic countries than in Protestant countries, although the effect sizes tended to be small. The financial role of the father was also more salient in Islamic countries than in Protestant countries; the same was found for the instrumental role of the 20-year-old son. The parental instrumental roles (finances and childcare) showed an interesting pattern. The financial role of the father decreased with Affluence and increased with Relatedness, while the financial role

Table 7.13 *Mean scores on family network variables and family roles per country clustering (affluence, religion, and relatedness)*

	Affluence			Religion					Relatedness		
	Low	Medium	High	Cath.	Prot.	Orth.	Muslim	Buddh.	Low	Medium	High
Family networks											
Geography	3.60	3.66	3.25	3.28	$2.68_{O,M}$	3.73_P	3.56_P	3.84	$2.80_{M,H}$	3.71_L	3.60_L
Visits	3.98	4.50	3.95	4.24_P	$3.66_{C,O}$	4.60_P	4.17	3.98	3.84_M	4.48_L	3.98
Telephone	2.72_M	3.61_L	3.29	3.18_O	3.37	$3.88_{C,M}$	3.09_O	3.05	3.23	3.53_H	2.72_M
Father											
Expressive	$4.98_{M,H}$	4.48_L	4.01_L	4.08_M	4.08_M	4.53	$4.93_{C,P}$	4.17	4.09_H	4.31_H	$4.98_{L,M}$
Finances	5.16_H	4.85_H	$4.32_{L,M}$	4.51_M	4.52_M	4.94	$5.12_{C,P}$	4.34	4.49_H	4.63_H	$5.16_{L,M}$
Childcare	3.44	3.22	3.20	3.42	3.39	3.32	3.27	3.00	3.47	3.13	3.44
Mother											
Expressive	5.25_H	5.00_H	$4.54_{L,M}$	4.75_M	4.76_M	5.01	$5.22_{C,P}$	4.54	4.73_H	4.80_H	$5.25_{L,M}$
Finances	4.61	4.61	4.58	4.70	4.69	4.81	4.50	4.43	4.64	4.58	4.61
Childcare	4.32	4.48	4.29	4.56	4.63	4.78_M	4.19_O	3.97	4.62	4.31	4.32
Grandfather											
Expressive	4.41_H	4.00_H	$3.43_{L,M}$	3.68_M	3.66_M	4.04	$4.31_{C,P}$	3.52	3.63_H	3.76_H	$4.41_{L,M}$
Instrumental	2.87	2.56	2.41	2.40	2.68	2.77	2.62	2.55	2.55	2.47	2.87
Grandmother											
Expressive	4.53_H	4.24	3.71_L	4.03	4.06	4.20	4.47	3.68	4.01	3.98	4.53

Instrumental	2.88	2.86	2.74	2.76	3.07	3.13	2.74	2.64	2.95	2.76	2.88
Uncle/aunt											
Expressive	3.61	3.47	3.08	3.48	3.28	3.29	3.60	2.99	3.32	3.27	3.61
Instrumental	2.78_H	2.35	2.29_L	2.44	2.46	2.30	2.58	2.34	2.45	2.28_H	2.78_M
Son 20											
Expressive	3.95_H	3.83	3.44_L	3.69	3.54	3.79	3.94	3.43	3.57	3.67	3.95
Instrumental	3.47_H	3.08	2.86_L	3.02	2.85_M	3.09	3.31_P	3.01	2.91_H	3.00_H	$3.47_{L,M}$
Daughter 20											
Expressive	4.15_H	3.99	3.58_L	3.85	3.77	3.91	4.16	3.53	3.79	3.80	4.15
Instrumental	3.51_H	3.32	3.01_L	3.21	3.00	3.42	3.39	3.10	3.08_H	3.21	3.51_L
Son 10											
Expressive	3.19	3.48	3.10	3.40	3.12	3.38	3.27	3.12	3.16	3.35	3.19
Instrumental	2.15	1.89	1.88	1.86	1.79	1.87	2.02	2.09	1.79	1.91	2.15
Daughter 10											
Expressive	3.25	3.57	3.18	3.50	3.23	3.44	3.36	3.16	3.27	3.42	3.25
Instrumental	2.21	1.98	1.94	1.93	1.85	1.97	2.10	2.15	1.86	2.00	2.21

Cath. = Roman Catholic cluster. Prot. = Protestant cluster. Orth. = Christian Orthodox cluster. Buddh. = Buddhist/Hindu/traditional beliefs cluster. Subscripts following denote indicate medium and large effect sizes. For Affluence and Relatedness the subscripts L, M, and H indicate that the cell mean differs at least .50 SD (a medium effect size) from the score in the low, medium, and high level, respectively. For example, the letter M in the first cell of telephone calls (2.72_M) indicates that this mean of 2.72 differs at least .50 SD from the mean of 3.61 of the medium-affluence cluster. The subscripts C, P, O, M in the means of the religions indicate that the means differ from the Catholic, Protestant, Orthodox, and Muslim mean, respectively. The last cluster (Buddhist/Hindu/Traditional Beliefs) is not considered because of its heterogeneity.

155

of the mother was unrelated to both Affluence and Relatedness. In Roman Catholic and Protestant countries the financial role of the father was less important than in Islamic countries. Childcare shows even fewer cluster differences. Apart from the scores of the mothers, which were higher in the Orthodox than in the Islamic countries, no cluster comparison yielded a large effect size, strongly suggesting the childcare is a domain with small cluster differences.

The psychological variables showed a pronounced pattern of cross-cluster similarities and differences (see Table 7.14). The Emotional Distance, Self-construal, and Personality Scales showed very few medium and large effect sizes. The same was true for Intellectual Autonomy, Affective Autonomy, and Mastery. However, the other values, Embeddedness, Hierarchy, and Harmony, showed much more cluster variation. These three values decreased with Affluence and increased with Relatedness. The religious clustering also showed various substantial effect sizes for the same values. The Roman Catholic and Protestant clusters often showed much lower means than did the Orthodox clusters. Family Values largely replicated this pattern of cluster differences. These values increased with Relatedness and decreased with Affluence; the Islamic and (to a somewhat lesser extent) Orthodox Cluster showed high scores while the Roman Catholic and Protestant clusters showed lower scores.

The analyses of the three different country clustering methods yielded largely similar results. The patterning of the relatively large and small effect sizes across the scales was similar across the four analyses; for example, Georgas' Hierarchy and Schwartz's Embeddedness showed large values in each analysis, while emotional distance to the nuclear family yielded relatively small effects in all analyses. Moreover, the effect sizes of the psychological variables of the three types of clustering are largely identical ($\eta^2 = .07$ for Religion and $\eta^2 = .06$ for the other clusters). This value means that the three affluence and the five religious clusters can capture on average 35 percent ($= 100 \times (.06 + .07 + .06)/(3 \times .18)$) of the country variation. Affluence and Relatedness are more effective than Religion despite their slightly lower effect sizes, because the latter uses five categories while the former two need only three categories to arrive at the same effect size. The three kinds of clustering can explain on average 36 percent ($= 100 \times (.05 + .05 + .04)/(3 \times .13)$) of the country variation in the family variables. Affluence and Relatedness are also slightly more powerful here for the same reason as in the first analysis. Moreover, Affluence, Religion, and Relatedness explain 49 percent, 39 percent, and 26 percent in the expressive roles, respectively. These numbers are lower for the instrumental–material/

Table 7.14 *Mean scores on emotional distance, self-construal, personality, family values, and values per country clustering (affluence, religion, and relatedness)*[a]

Domain/scale	Affluence			Religion					Relatedness		
	Low	Medium	High	Cath.	Prot.	Orth.	Muslim	Buddh.	Low	Medium	High
Emotional distance											
Nuclear	6.24	6.22	6.00	6.17	5.90	6.28	6.19	6.05	6.02	6.14	6.23
Extended	4.68	4.85	4.45	4.82	4.35_O	5.10_P	4.59	4.39	4.57	4.69	4.68
Self-construal											
Independent	4.91	4.86	4.68	4.93	4.79	4.82	4.81	4.67	4.77	4.77	4.91
Interdependent	5.17_H	4.83	4.72_L	4.84	4.57_O	4.98_P	4.95	4.87	4.60_H	4.84	5.17_L
Personality											
Agreeableness	5.72	5.62	5.35	5.60	5.53	5.57	5.73	5.22	5.59	5.46	5.72
Conscientiousness	5.38_H	5.23	4.83_L	5.18	5.15	5.19	5.35	4.66	5.19	4.99	5.38
Emotional stability	4.57	4.59	4.42	4.60	4.61	4.60	4.56	4.29	4.64	4.47	4.57
Extraversion	4.67	4.76	4.63	4.86	4.95	4.65	4.72	4.38	4.89	4.64	4.67
Openness	4.50	4.60	4.47	4.75	4.75	4.45	4.54	4.24	4.73	4.48	4.50
Family values											
Hierarchy	$5.86_{M,H}$	$4.52_{L,H}$	$3.75_{L,M}$	$3.62_{O,M}$	$3.47_{O,M}$	$4.43_{C,P,M}$	$5.61_{C,P,O}$	4.74	$3.27_{M,H}$	$4.45_{L,H}$	$5.86_{L,M}$
Relationships with kin	$6.51_{M,H}$	6.01_L	5.63_L	5.84_M	5.70_M	5.93_M	$6.41_{C,P,O}$	5.76	$5.70_{M,H}$	5.87_H	6.51_L
Values											
Embeddedness	6.17_H	5.89_H	$5.28_{L,M}$	$5.36_{O,M}$	$5.30_{O,M}$	$5.94_{C,P}$	$6.20_{C,P}$	5.51	$5.26_{M,H}$	$5.71_{L,H}$	$6.17_{L,M}$
Hierarchy	5.06_H	4.54	4.33_L	4.23_M	4.31_M	4.37_M	$5.00_{C,P,O}$	4.73	4.19_H	4.53	5.06_L
Harmony	5.78_H	5.63_H	$5.07_{L,M}$	5.34	$4.97_{O,M}$	5.57_P	5.77_P	5.30	4.96_L	5.49_L	$5.78_{L,M}$
Intellectual autonomy	5.54	5.68	5.50	5.73	5.51,	5.68	5.54	5.45	5.54	5.62	5.54
Affective autonomy	5.62	5.80	5.74	5.83	5.92	6.04	5.64	5.42	6.02	5.69	5.62
Mastery	5.81	5.86	5.60	5.76	5.64	5.91	5.81	5.59	5.64	5.77	5.81

Note:
[a] See footnote to Table 7.13 for an explanation.

157

economic role (Affluence: 30 percent; Religion: 31 percent; Relatedness: 27 percent).

It can be concluded that large cross-cultural differences were found in nearly all scales examined, especially in Schwartz's Embeddedness and Georgas' Hierarchy values. Moreover, the clustering of countries in terms of Affluence, Religion, and Relatedness was effective in that about 35 percent of the country variation could be accounted for by differences in affluence, religion, or relatedness. More specifically, the effectiveness of Affluence in explaining country differences in expressive roles was remarkable.

HYPOTHESIS TESTS

This section focuses on relationships between country-level indicators (such as the ecological and sociopolitical variables) and psychological variables, such as the family-related variables. It consists of two parts. The first discusses the correlations between country indicators and the psychological variables. The hypotheses that were formulated in Chapter 5 for some of these correlations are tested here. The second part examines the country-level indicators in more detail; it integrates these variables, and examines the relationship of the integrated variables with the psychological variables.

In order to be consistent with the previous analyses, the presentation of the correlations deals more with effect sizes than with significance of correlations (Cohen's proposed cutoff values of .10, .30, and .50 for small, medium, and large effect sizes in (absolute values of) correlations). For our current sample sizes ($N = 27$) correlations are significant at 5 percent level if their absolute values are larger than .38 and at 1 percent level if these are larger than .48.

Ecocultural Framework, ecological and sociopolitical variables, psychological variables and family variables

According to the Ecocultural Framework, the three ecological indicators (i.e., Affluence, Temperature, and Percentage of Population Working in Agriculture) are expected to show a similar pattern of correlations. Affluence is expected to have a positive correlation with Education and an inverse relationship with Agriculture. We hypothesized that the Percentage of the Population Working in Agriculture and Temperature would be positively related to family network variables (i.e., Geographic Proximity and Frequency of Visits), while Affluence would show the opposite pattern. As can be seen in Table 7.15, the correlations of the

Table 7.15 Correlations across all family positions with affluence, religion, family networks, and psychological variables (N = 27 countries)

		Family networks			Emotional distance (Georgas et al.)		Self-construal (Singelis et al.)		Personality traits (Williams et al.)					Family values (Georgas et al.)		Values (Schwartz)					
		Geogr	Visits	Telep	Nucl	Ext.	Indep	Inter	Agree	Consc	Emot	Extra	Open	Hiera	Kin	Embed	Hier	Harm	Intel	Affect	Mast
Affluence		-48	-27	26	-39	-29	-23	-28	-43	-43	-28	01	-02	-68	-64	-70	-49	-82	-11	25	-32
% working in agriculture		31	-10	-44	33	26	26	24	44	54	35	06	06	69	64	63	73	70	09	-09	35
Highest temperature		18	-09	-05	-08	-34	-16	-08	-05	02	-15	-07	-18	39	29	32	40	21	-07	-14	09
Education		-24	-15	35	-29	-05	-29	-18	-42	-48	-30	-07	-05	-59	-60	-64	-55	-79	-22	33	-32
Religion	Catholic	-23	03	-04	02	18	08	01	06	02	00	38	40	-49	-21	-53	-44	-16	32	10	-02
	Protestant	-65	-60	-13	-34	-23	13	-21	01	05	24	29	27	-41	-25	-42	-07	-61	-15	25	-20
	Orthodox	23	45	54	25	51	07	15	02	09	11	-09	-21	-02	-01	24	-13	18	12	34	33
	Muslim	24	20	-05	21	-16	-07	03	28	23	03	03	-03	62	56	69	37	49	-21	-32	06
Family networks	Geograph	–	53	25	17	34	02	24	-08	-06	-15	-11	-15	46	30	41	36	31	-25	-25	12
	Visits	53	–	38	64	38	12	20	01	12	09	15	06	-01	11	29	34	34	12	34	22
	Telephone	25	38	–	-27	26	-16	-04	-13	-17	-28	08	-17	-28	-18	01	03	-14	-07	-02	15
Emotional distance	Nuclear	17	64	-27	–	34	31	26	26	42	48	26	33	10	32	35	00	45	32	-02	29
	Extended	34	38	26	34	–	53	52	55	53	44	26	24	03	27	20	19	11	00	-03	26
Self-construal	Independ.	02	12	-16	31	53	–	64	40	52	12	31	31	10	27	24	12	12	-18	-06	15
	Interdep.	24	20	-04	26	52	64	–	34	12	12	-12	06	22	36	24	34	11	00	34	-17
Personality traits	Agreeable	-08	01	-13	26	55	40	34	–	86	70	44	41	15	64	45	14	34	-01	02	05
	Consc.	-06	12	-17	42	53	52	12	86	–	78	63	40	19	64	56	34	46	13	18	32
	Emot. stab.	-15	09	-28	48	44	12	12	70	78	–	54	56	03	41	56	30	19	16	22	31
	Extraversion	-11	15	08	26	26	31	-12	44	63	54	–	71	-18	34	33	12	10	23	36	38
	Openness	-15	06	-17	33	24	31	06	41	40	56	71	–	-30	00	14	07	-03	31	38	32
Family values	Hierarchy	46	-01	-28	10	03	10	22	15	19	03	-18	-30	–	75	78	62	56	-39	-42	07
	Kin	30	11	-18	32	27	27	36	64	64	41	34	00	75	–	86	48	57	-21	-27	18

Table 7.15 (cont.)

		Family networks			Emotional distance (Georgas et al.)		Self-construal (Singelis et al.)		Personality traits (Williams et al.)				Family values (Georgas et al.)				Values (Schwartz)				
		Geogr	Visits	Telep	Nucl	Ext.	Indep	Inter	Agree	Consc	Emot	Extra	Open	Hiera	Kin	Embed	Hier	Harm	Intel	Affect	Mast
Values	Embedded	*41*	29	01	*35*	27	20	24	*45*	**56**	*33*	14	-14	**78**	**86**	–	**57**	**69**	-14	-20	*33*
	Hierarchy	*36*	-16	-24	00	03	19	-06	14	*34*	*30*	12	07	**62**	*48*	**57**	–	*50*	00	01	*49*
	Harmony	*34*	*31*	-14	*45*	19	11	12	*34*	*46*	19	10	-03	**56**	**57**	**69**	*50*	–	*38*	-26	*47*
	Intel. aut.	-25	12	-07	*32*	-03	00	-18	-01	13	16	23	*31*	*-39*	-21	-14	00	*38*	–	*33*	**62**
	Affect. aut.	-25	-03	28	-02	27	-06	-26	02	18	22	*36*	*38*	*-42*	-27	-20	01	-26	*33*	–	**55**
	Mastery	12	22	15	29	26	15	-17	05	*32*	*31*	*38*	*32*	07	18	*33*	*49*	*47*	**62**	**55**	–

Correlations are significant at 5 percent level if their absolute value is at least .38 and at 1 percent level if their absolute value is at least .49 ($N = 27$). Decimal points omitted. Zero and small effect sizes (absolute value of correlation, $r_s < .30$) are printed in regular font, medium effect sizes ($.30 < r < .50$) in italics, and large effect sizes ($r > .50$) in bold.

160

Percentage of the Population in Agriculture and Temperature with Proximity of Residence were in the expected direction, but the correlations were not strong ($r = .31$ and $.18$). The correlation with Affluence was stronger ($r = -.48$). Frequency of Visits showed small negative correlations for all three indicators. Frequency of Phone Calls showed a correlation of $-.44$ with the Percentage of the Population Working in Agriculture and of $-.05$ with Temperature. Affluence showed a correlation of $.26$ with Frequency of Phone Calls. The analyses provided incomplete support for the hypotheses. Although the sign of most correlations was in the expected direction, the strength of the association tended to be weak, in particular for Temperature.

Ecological variables and psychological variables

A second set of predictions involved the association of the ecological variables and psychological variables. It was expected that the Percentage of the Population in Agriculture and Temperature would be associated with close Emotional Distance and an Interdependent Self-construal, high Hierarchy and Kin Family values; an opposite pattern was expected for Affluence. As in the previous analysis, the correlations of Temperature tended to be weak and to have the expected sign. The correlations of the Percentage in the Agriculture and Affluence were stronger and in the expected direction. The correlations (absolute values) with Emotional Distance were around $.30$ and with both Self-construals around $.25$. Strong effect sizes were found for both family values ($r = .66$) and three personal values (Embeddedness, Hierarchy, and Harmony; $r = .68$). It can be concluded that our predictions were confirmed for all three indicators in most cases, although the relationships of the psychological variables tended to be weaker for Temperature than for the other two indicators.

Fairly strong correlations of $.45$ were found with Agreeableness and Conscientiousness. Emotional Stability showed a medium effect size of $r = .33$, while Extraversion and Openness were unrelated to the ecological variables. Mastery showed a medium effect size ($r = .34$); both intellectual and affective autonomy did not show any relationship with the ecological variables.

Sociopolitical variables and psychological variables

Two kinds of sociopolitical variables were studied, namely Education and Religion. As predicted, the patterning of Education was strikingly similar to the pattern for Affluence; the correlation of the rows for

Affluence and Education in Tables 7.15 and 7.16 was .95. The direction of these relationships was always correctly predicted. Correlations with an absolute value of at least .30 were found for Making Phone Calls ($r = .35$), Agreeableness ($r = -.42$), Conscientiousness ($r = -.48$), Emotional Stability ($r = -.30$), Hierarchy in the Family ($r = -.59$), Relationships with Kin ($r = -.60$). Furthermore, strong correlations were also found for Embeddedness ($r = -.64$), Hierarchy as a personal value ($r = -.55$), and Harmony ($r = -.79$).

The correlations of Religion (based on percentage of adherents in each country) showed an interesting pattern. Catholicism showed positive medium effect sizes for Extraversion ($r = .38$) and Openness ($r = .40$), and Intellectual Autonomy ($r = .32$), and negative medium and large effects for Embeddedness ($r = -.53$), and Hierarchy as a family value ($r = -.49$) and as a personal value ($r = -.44$). Family network variables were not associated with Catholicism ($r < .25$). The percentage of Protestants in a country showed a large, negative effect size for Proximity of Residence ($r = -.65$), Frequency of Visits ($r = -.60$), and Harmony ($r = -.61$). Negative effects of medium size were found for Emotional Distance to Nuclear Family ($r = -.34$), Hierarchy in the Family ($r = -.41$), and Embeddedness ($r = -.42$). Although the variables with sizeable effect sizes were quite different for Catholicism and Protestantism, the overall patterning was fairly similar, as expected (the two rows of correlations showed a correlation of .56). The two religions had a negative relationship with interpersonal features; the relationships with intrapersonal features tended to be positive, but were often very weak.

The percentage of Orthodox adherents showed an entirely different pattern of correlations. Positive correlations above .50, pointing to large effects, were found for Making Phone Calls ($r = .54$) and Emotional Closeness to Extended Family ($r = .51$), while a medium effect was found for Visits to the Family ($r = .45$). Affective Autonomy ($r = .34$), and Mastery ($r = .33$) also showed medium-size effects. As expected, the correlations for the percentage of Muslim adherents were the opposite of those found for Catholicism and Protestantism; the correlations of the rows of Tables 7.15 and 7.16 for Islam, on the one hand, and Catholicism and Protestantism, on the other hand, were $-.74$ and $-.76$, respectively. The strongest relationship between the percentage of Muslims and the psychological variables was positive and involved both Family Values (Hierarchy: $r = .62$, Kinship Relationships: .56). Medium-size correlations were found for two individual values, being Hierarchy ($r = .37$) and Harmony ($r = .49$). Affective Autonomy showed a negative correlation of $-.32$.

Table 7.16 Correlations of the family roles for each family position with affluence, religion, family networks, and psychological variables (N = 27 countries)

	Father			Mother			Grandfather		Grandmother		Aunt/Uncle		Male 20 yrs		Female 20 yrs		Male 10 yrs		Female 10 yrs	
	Exp.	Fin.	Care	Exp.	Fin.	Care	Exp.	Instr.	Exp.	Instr.	Exp.	Instr.	Exp.	Instr.	Exp.	Instr.	Exp.	Instr.	Exp.	Instr.
Affluence	**-65**	**-58**	11	**-61**	11	16	**-61**	-19	-48	05	-37	-28	**-55**	**-66**	**-51**	**-69**	-33	-38	-29	-41
% working in agriculture	**71**	**67**	14	**71**	03	01	**64**	42	**55**	19	39	**66**	46	**82**	44	**73**	05	**59**	04	**59**
Highest temperature	50	31	-05	37	-25	-44	35	-04	33	**-40**	30	19	29	30	31	-03	15	28	16	23
Education	**-55**	**-45**	03	**-54**	15	22	**-52**	-04	-44	21	-43	-29	**-52**	**-56**	**-50**	**-49**	-39	-44	-37	-46
Religion Catholic	**-56**	-34	22	-32	24	32	-33	-28	-17	-03	04	01	-13	-13	-17	-10	12	-17	12	-19
Protestant	-31	-21	32	-19	17	25	-34	-13	-23	06	-07	12	-28	-36	-19	-35	-38	-23	-33	-25
Orthodox	13	24	15	16	34	49	15	34	06	**53**	-14	-20	07	01	00	27	10	-15	05	-10
Muslim	**73**	**53**	-25	**58**	-47	**-51**	**57**	-01	**53**	-33	35	06	**56**	39	**61**	21	23	05	26	06
Family networks Geograph	37	41	-20	24	-32	-17	34	37	21	-03	12	13	23	38	17	24	12	01	08	00
Visits	17	39	03	17	-15	18	23	08	21	04	16	-18	26	13	24	20	32	-34	29	-31
Telephone	-09	03	01	-10	05	18	-15	00	-17	06	-24	-45	-15	-39	-14	-32	-07	**-65**	-07	**-63**
Emotional distance Nuclear	35	**51**	26	47	07	29	**48**	27	**53**	29	40	26	47	**52**	45	**58**	**40**	11	37	14
Extended	15	43	34	31	17	**54**	27	28	23	36	25	33	28	30	24	48	20	-12	16	-09
Self-construal Independ	14	31	47	25	21	33	11	-01	11	-04	33	42	25	21	24	25	12	06	09	03
Interdep	21	23	24	21	07	05	17	07	12	-08	12	15	17	25	14	16	-04	00	-10	-04
Personality traits Agreeable	37	**54**	22	**56**	-11	20	**40**	02	40	05	30	27	44	41	49	49	22	01	23	06
Conscient.	47	**67**	40	**68**	-05	42	**53**	18	**54**	22	**52**	**50**	**57**	**52**	**62**	**66**	28	06	31	12
Emot. stab.	24	46	36	45	15	41	33	05	33	21	43	39	44	30	44	46	29	05	30	11
Extraversion	11	34	44	38	10	**51**	25	10	38	24	49	33	41	20	44	35	18	-39	22	-33
Openness	-09	17	23	18	12	34	07	-01	22	14	39	36	17	08	18	21	06	-26	09	-22
Family values Hierarchy	**79**	49	-17	**60**	-27	-38	**70**	33	**58**	-04	44	37	**65**	**62**	**62**	47	34	**51**	31	**50**
Kin	**80**	**65**	22	**79**	-16	-05	**78**	28	**72**	01	**63**	43	**85**	**69**	**84**	**62**	44	21	43	23

Table 7.16 (cont.)

Values	Father Exp.	Father Fin.	Father Care	Mother Exp.	Mother Fin.	Mother Care	Grandfather Exp.	Grandfather Instr.	Grandmother Exp.	Grandmother Instr.	Aunt/Uncle Exp.	Aunt/Uncle Instr.	Male 20 yrs Exp.	Male 20 yrs Instr.	Female 20 yrs Exp.	Female 20 yrs Instr.	Male 10 yrs Exp.	Male 10 yrs Instr.	Female 10 yrs Exp.	Female 10 yrs Instr.
Embedded	**88**	**72**	05	**82**	-21	-12	**79**	*30*	**68**	03	**54**	*30*	**79**	**59**	**79**	**60**	*44*	22	*43*	26
Hierarchy	**56**	*47*	01	**50**	-03	-11	*44*	*30*	*35*	06	*42*	**60**	*36*	*47*	*33*	*42*	04	*46*	04	*47*
Harmony	**55**	**54**	-10	**58**	-02	-05	**52**	21	*46*	11	28	20	*48*	**65**	*45*	**68**	*32*	*44*	*30*	*48*
Intel. aut.	-25	-14	19	-05	**58**	36	-19	-12	-12	21	-07	01	-13	05	-20	27	00	16	-01	19
Affect. aut.	-11	02	*42*	04	*44*	**60**	00	17	04	*45*	17	27	-08	-18	-09	09	-14	-27	-12	-22
Mastery	26	*32*	*33*	*36*	*48*	*43*	29	25	29	*35*	*40*	*39*	*34*	28	25	*46*	19	10	17	14

Correlations are significant at 5 percent level if their absolute value is at least .38 and at 1 percent level if their absolute value is at least .49 ($N = 27$).
Decimal points omitted. Zero and small effect sizes (absolute value of correlation, $rs < .30$) are printed in regular font, medium effect sizes ($.30 < r < .50$) in italics, and large effect sizes ($r > .50$) in bold. Exp. = expressive role. Fin. = financial role. Care = childcare role. Instr. = instrumental role.

Table 7.17 *Spearman's rank order of the correlations of the four main religions, across all scales*

Religion	Catholic	Protestant	Orthodox
Catholic	–		
Protestant	.53**	–	
Orthodox	.06	−.08	–
Islamic	−.72**	−.62**	−.35*

Note:
$^{*}p < .05.$ $^{**}p < .01.$

In order to identify the overall patterning of these correlations across the four types of religions, Spearman's rank order correlations were computed across the various scales of the of Tables 7.15 and 7.16; results are reported in Table 7.17. This analysis was aimed at comparing correlations of the four religions with personality, values and family values, self-construals, and family networks and family roles. We found the expected patterning. The correlations between Catholicism and Protestantism were positive and significant ($\rho = .53$, $p < .01$). Islam showed significant, negative correlations with the three Christian churches (Roman Catholic: $\rho = -.72$; Protestant: $\rho = -.62$; Orthodox: $\rho = -.35$; all $ps < .05$). The correlations between the Christian Orthodox percentages on the one hand and Catholic and Protestant Christianity on the other hand were very small. It appears, in summary, that we found some evidence for the two expected clusters of correlations. The first cluster is based on a juxtaposition of Catholicism and Protestantism on the one hand and Islam on the other. Catholic and Protestant countries showed negative associations with expressive and instrumental roles, while Islamic countries showed the opposite pattern (with a strong positive correlation of .56 for expressive roles and a median of only .05 for the instrumental role). Orthodox countries constitute the second cluster. The instrumental role showed a median correlation of .24 in the Orthodox countries; the other correlations of Orthodox countries were close to zero. As for the other scales, the major source of differences of the first cluster is correlations with hierarchy-related variables (which are positive for Catholicism and Protestantism and negative for Islam). The Christian Orthodox Church has its own independent pattern of correlations with the psychological variables (which did not confirm our hypothesis).

Table 7.15 contains several correlations with large effect sizes, for which no hypothesis was formulated. A first example involves the strong positive intercorrelations of .60 of the personality scales (at country level). A much lower value of .21 was found at individual level (the latter figure is based on scores that were standardized per country in order to eliminate confounding country differences in scale scores). The positive correlations of the scales were also found by Williams et al. (1998), possibly owing to the role of response sets such as social desirability (Poortinga and van de Vijver, 2000). The two family values (Hierarchy and Kinship Relations) showed large effect sizes ($r = .75$). The patterning of Schwartz's six values pointed to the existence of two larger value clusters (with high within-cluster and low between-cluster correlations). The first one is formed by the more interpersonal values of Embeddedness, Hierarchy, and Harmony, and the second by the more intrapersonal values of Intellectual Autonomy, Affective Autonomy, and Mastery. Relatively strong, positive correlations were also found between Emotional Distance and all personality scales and between Georgas et al.'s Family Values and Schwartz's Embeddedness, Hierarchy, and Harmony.

Ecological and sociopolitical variables and family roles

As the hypotheses about the relationships of roles only involved a distinction between expressive and instrumental roles, another table was composed, containing the median correlations across the nine family positions (father, mother, etc.) (see Table 7.18). The Percentage of the Population Working in Agriculture and Temperature were assumed to be positively associated with both family roles, while Affluence was assumed to have a negative relationship. The median correlations of the Percentage of the Population Working in Agriculture were .46 and .59 with the expressive and instrumental roles, respectively. The correlations were (again) lower for Temperature, namely .31 and −.03 (the latter relationship is clearly at odds with the hypothesis). The median correlations of Affluence were −.51 and −.28, as expected. Highly similar values of −.50 and −.29 were found for Education. These correlations confirmed our expectation.

In summary, the ecological variables and sociopolitical variable of Education showed a pattern of negative relationships with the expressive role and weaker associations with the instrumental role. For Religion, the expected opposite pattern of correlations of Muslim and Orthodox countries on the one hand and Catholic and Protestant

Table 7.18 *Median correlations between country-level indicators and expressive and instrumental roles (N = 27 countries)*

Country-level indicator		Expressive	Instrumental
Affluence		−.51	−.28
Percentage of population working in agriculture		.46	.59
Highest temperature		.31	−.03
Education		−.50	−.29
Religion	Catholic	−.17	−.10
	Protestant	−.28	−.13
	Orthodox	.07	.24
	Muslim	.56	.05
	Buddhism/Hinduism/Other	−.09	.01
Family networks	Geographical	.21	.01
	Visits	.23	.04
	Telephone	−.14	.00
Emotional distance	Nuclear	.45	.27
	Extended	.24	.33
Self-construal	Independence	.14	.21
	Interdependence	.14	.07
Personality traits	Agreeable	.40	.20
	Conscientious	.53	.40
	Emotional stability	.33	.30
	Extraversion	.38	.24
	Openness	.17	.14
Family values	Hierarchy	.60	.37
	Kin	.78	.23
Values	Embedded	.79	.26
	Hierarchy	.36	.42
	Harmony	.46	.21
	Intellectual autonomy	−.12	.19
	Affective autonomy	−.08	.17
	Mastery	.29	.33

countries on the other hand replicated our findings in the analysis of the other psychological variables.

Psychological variables and family variables

A final analysis concerned the relationships between the psychological variables (at country level) and the family variables. As can be seen in Table 7.16, personality factors were unrelated to the family network variables. Embeddedness, Hierarchy, and Harmony were positively related to proximity of residence, while the two autonomy values showed (weaker) negative correlations. Frequency of visits and telephone calls were less systematically related to values. Self-construal scores were not strongly related to the family network variables related either. Emotional Distance showed positive relationships with proximity of residence and frequency of visits (closer emotional ties are associated with more proximity and more frequent visits). Frequency of phone calls did not show strong relationships with Emotional Distance. The two family values, Hierarchy and Kin Relationships, showed positive relationships with proximity of residence, while the relationships with frequency of visits and phone calls were weak.

The relationships between psychological variables and family roles tended to be stronger. Most of the correlations were positive, although slightly stronger for the expressive role (median $r = .36$) than for the instrumental role ($r = .24$). All personality factors had a median correlation of well above .30 with both Family Roles, except for Openness, which was unrelated to roles. Embeddedness was the value with the strongest median correlation (of $r = .79$) with the expressive role, its relationship with the instrumental role was much weaker (median $r = .26$). Positive correlations were also found for Hierarchy, Harmony, and Mastery. Zero correlations were found for both autonomy values. The median of both self-construal scores were just above zero, which suggests that Family Roles are unrelated to independent and interdependent self-construals at country level. Emotional Distance to both the nuclear and extended family were positively related to Family Roles (median $r = .30$ across roles and positions, indicating that countries with stronger family emotional ties report on average higher scores on both Family Roles. Finally, both Family Values showed strong, positive relationships with both roles (median $r = .45$ across all roles and positions); countries with stronger family values showed higher scores on both expressive and instrumental roles across all positions.

It can be concluded that psychological country characteristics were more strongly related to Family Roles than to Family Network Variables and that the relationships were somewhat stronger for the expressive role than for the instrumental role. Proximity of Residence is the only Family Network variable that shows relationships with "relational and hierarchical" psychological characteristics, such as Embeddedness and Harmony. For the Family Roles a related and more pronounced pattern was found; strong relationships with these psychological characteristics were found, while country features that deal with independence (such as Intellectual and Affective Autonomy) were unrelated to Family Roles.

Family Change Model

On the basis of Kağıtçıbaşı's Family Change Model (see Chapter 3) two kinds of hypotheses were formulated (see Chapter 5). The first deals with living conditions including urban–rural, SES, and level of affluence, reflecting socioeconomic development. The second deals with culture, reflecting culture of relatedness–separateness.

Living conditions and family patterns

To deal with the first kind of prediction of the Family Change Model, changes in family patterns with increased Affluence are examined. It was predicted that both expressive roles and instrumental roles would decrease in importance with growing affluence. The current study is not longitudinal, which precludes a direct test of the second hypothesis. However, by comparing the relationship of both roles with Affluence, an indirect test can be carried out of the adequacy of the model. Therefore, the hypothesis is tested that both the emotional role and the material role decrease across the Affluence range. This hypothesis is tested at country level ($N = 27$).

A set of regression analyses (at country level) was carried out with Affluence as the independent variable and the Family Roles as dependent variables. The regression coefficients of Affluence are hypothesized to be below zero for both the expressive role and the instrumental role. The regression coefficients are given in Table 7.19. Most regression

Table 7.19 *Raw regression coefficients predicting the emotional (Expressive) and economic (Instrumental) roles of the family members at country level on the basis of affluence*

Position	Expressive	Instrumental
Father	$-.27^{**}$	$-.24^{**}$ (Finances) and .03 (Care)
Mother	$-.19^{**}$	.04 (Finances) and .06 (Care)
Grandfather	$-.28^{**}$	$-.06$
Grandmother	$-.20^{**}$	.02
Uncle/aunt	$-.16$	$-.09$
20-year-old male	$-.17^{**}$	$-.16^{**}$
20-year-old female	$-.18^{**}$	$-.18^{**}$
10-year-old male	$-.10$	$-.09^{*}$
10-year-old female	$-.09$	$-.10^{*}$

Note:
$^{*}p < .05.$ $^{**}p < .01.$

coefficients are below zero, as expected. The global median is $-.13$. The median regression coefficient is $-.18$ for the expressive role and $-.09$ for the instrumental role. These differences are small and confirm the earlier observation that cluster differences are smaller for the instrumental role than for the expressive role. Even without a statistical test of the significance of these dependent regression coefficients, it is clear that the pattern of findings is in line with the prediction according to which both the material/instrumental role and the emotional/expressive role should decrease across the Affluence range.

The Family Change Model recognizes the parallel associations of Affluence and Education and the inverse association of Percentage of Population Working in Agriculture (indicating rural living conditions) with family patterns (see Chapters 3 and 5). Regarding these associations, similar predictions are made with the Ecocultural Framework. Therefore, the relevant results reported previously for Ecocultural Framework also hold for the Family Change Model. To avoid repetition, the predictions of the Model presented in Chapter 5 will be mentioned here in general terms.

Increased Affluence and Education and decreased Percentage of Population in Agriculture were predicted to be associated with greater distance of residence and reduced frequency of family contacts; decreased emotional roles and emotional closeness; decreased material/instrumental family roles; less material/instrumental role of the child; decreased prevalence of interdependent self; less hierarchy and decreased kin relationships; and less personal embeddedness. These associations are borne out by the above findings and those presented previously with regard to the Ecocultural Framework. They refer to systematic relationships between living conditions and family/self patterns that are in line with a contextual sociocultural approach to the (changing) family.

In conclusion, various hypotheses derived from the Family Model were supported. First, the emotional/expressiveness role of the family was important in all relatedness clusters. Even in the independence cluster, which showed the lowest expressiveness scores, the global means were still relatively high and they are higher than the means of the instrumental role for each position. Secondly, both the expressive and the instrumental role decreased in importance with increased Affluence (although the decrease in the former was more pronounced than in the latter). Thirdly, the instrumental role of children decreased more (than others') with increased affluence. If we do not take the financial role of the father and the mother into account, the current results suggest that the instrumental role of children is more influenced (decreased) by Affluence than is the instrumental role of any other family member. This is in line with the predictions of the Family Change Model regarding decreased material/economic value of the child with economic development.

Culture of relatedness–separateness clusters

To deal with the second kind of prediction deriving from the Family Change Model, country clusters were formed predicting a specific patterning of high and low scores on emotional/expressive and material/ instrumental roles/Interdependencies across the three clusters of Relatedness (see Chapter 6). The Family Model of Interdependence was proposed to be prevalent in agrarian, collectivistic contexts (culture of relatedness; see Table 7.10 for a listing of the countries in the first relatedness cluster). Countries in this cluster should have high values in both roles. The Model of Emotional Interdependence was proposed to be prevalent in urban and relatively more affluent contexts but with a culture of relatedness (the second cluster). It should have high values in expressive roles but lower values in Instrumental Roles. The Family Model of Independence is proposed to be prevalent in industrial individualistic contexts (culture of separateness; third cluster of Table 7.10). Countries in this cluster are expected to show low values of both the emotional and material roles/interdependencies. This hypothesis is tested at individual level ($N = 5,482$).

In order to test the hypothesis, analyses of variance were carried out, with cluster membership (three levels) as the independent variable and the Family Roles as dependent variables. The results are given in Table 7.12. The Family Network scales showed medium-size cross-cluster differences (with effect sizes between .062 and .074). Proximity of residence of parents and children was smallest in the (high-relatedness) interdependence cluster and lowest in the (low-relatedness) independence cluster. Participants in countries of the middle cluster reported the most visits ($M = 4.48$) and participants in the independence cluster the smallest number ($M = 3.84$). Frequency of telephone calls was also highest in the middle cluster ($M = 3.53$ vs. 3.23 for the independence cluster and 2.72 for the interdependence cluster). Emotional Distance showed remarkably small differences across the three clusters. Emotional Closeness (low Distance) to the Nuclear Family varied slightly across the clusters, but the scores were high for all clusters (the lowest average, found in the independence cluster, was 6.02 on a seven-point scale). The effect size was .005, which indicates that across the three clusters of relatedness the emotional closeness to the nuclear family was invariably high. Emotional Closeness to the Extended Family was greater, but again, the range of the scores was small (4.57 to 4.69) and the effect size was only .001. These findings support the hypothesis that Emotional Distance is only marginally related to (affected by) Relatedness.

The Family Change Model predicts a specific patterning of high and low scores on both roles across the three clusters. Emotional/expressive roles should be higher in the interdependence cluster than in the independence cluster; also, scores on emotional/expressive roles should be higher than scores on material/instrumental roles in all three clusters. As can be seen in Table 7.13, the averages of the emotional/expressive role increased with Relatedness for most positions. The effect sizes tended to decrease from the top to the bottom of the table (from the parents to the 10-year-old children). Although sizeable, even the most substantial decrease in scores was less than one unit on the six-point response scale. Thus, the emotional/expressive role remains important in the family. The average score of the emotional/expressive role was larger than the average score of the material/instrumental role for all family positions (except for the financial role of the father, which was the highest score of the father in each cluster). This finding provides strong evidence for the vital importance of the emotional/expressive role of the family.

As predicted by the Family Change Model, scores on instrumental roles tended to decrease with Relatedness, even though the effect sizes were small for most positions. This was not always the case. For example, very small cluster differences, which did not show a decrease, were found for the childcare role of the father and the financial and childcare role of the mother. Indeed, the main prediction of the Family Change Model is with regard to the decreased material value (instrumental role) of the (grown-up) child.

AN INTEGRATION OF COUNTRY CHARACTERISTICS

The hypotheses specified relationships between country characteristics (e.g., relatedness and religion) and psychological variables (e.g., family roles). We assumed in our hypotheses that the ecological variables, Affluence and two religions (Catholicism and Protestantism) would show identical patterns of correlations with the psychological variables. These hypotheses may incorrectly convey the impression that all context variables in the ecocultural variables are interchangeable. The four sets of variables are based on a conceptual classification. However, conceptual distinctness does not necessarily imply statistical independence. An important issue not yet considered involves the unique contribution of a defined country characteristic to the observed effects. For example, a

Table 7.20 *Factor loadings of country-level affluence indicators*

Variable	Loading
Affluence[a]	.95
Education[b]	.88
Relatedness[c]	−.93
Percentage of population working in agriculture	−.87

Notes:
Country scores can be found in Table 6.4.
[a] Indicators: Gross National Product per capita in US$, energy use per capita (in kg of oil equivalent), electricity consumption per capita in kilowatt hours, unemployment rate, percentage of population employed in industry, percentage of population employed in services, imports (in US$), exports (in US$).
[b] Indicators: total adult illiteracy, pupil/teacher ratio education at first level, enrollment ratios at first, second, and third level of education (see Chapter 6).
[c] Three levels (higher scores refer to higher levels of relatedness).

hypothesis test dealing with religious differences should ideally control for all country differences other than religion (often indicated in the literature as "all other things being equal"). This argument, which is the cornerstone of experimental designs, does not necessarily hold when comparing naturally occurring entities, such as countries. This section first examines relationships between the sets of country characteristics we have used (ecocultural variables, sociopolitical variables, religion, and relatedness).

It turned out that some country characteristics showed strong inter-correlations. A factor analysis of the economic indicator Affluence (Gross National Product, energy use, electricity consumption, unemployment rate, percentage of population employed in industry, percentage of population employed in services, and imports), the Education indicator (adult illiteracy rate, pupil/teacher ratio education at first level, enrollment ratios at first, second, and third level of education), percentage of the population working in agriculture, and relatedness constituted a very strong factor, which explained 82.3 percent of the variance; loadings are presented in Table 7.20. As could be expected, Relatedness and Percentage of the Population Working in Agriculture (which in developing and developed economies is also a measure of industrialization) showed negative loadings, while Affluence and Education showed positive loadings. Both Temperature and Religion constituted separate clusters. The correlations of the clusters can be found in Table 7.21. The Protestant countries in the study were the more affluent countries ($r = .53$, $p < .01$) and the Muslim countries were the less affluent

Table 7.21 *Correlations between the combined affluence indicator, average maximum temperature in the hottest month, and the four main religions of the current study (N = 27)*

Variable	Affl.	Temp.	Cath.	Prot.	Orth.
Affluence (combined)					
Temperature	−.31				
Percentage of Roman Catholics	.30	−.24			
Percentage of Protestants	.53**	−.17	.11		
Percentage of Christian Orthodox	.01	−.32	−.30	−.29	
Percentage of Muslims	−.52**	.49**	−.44**	−.31	−.21

Note:
**$p < .01$.

countries ($r = -.52$, $p < .01$). The correlations of Temperature and Affluence had opposite signs. Islamic countries tended to be warmer ($r = .49$, $p < .01$). Finally, in their correlations with Affluence and Temperature, Islamic countries and Christian countries showed correlations with opposite signs (although not all correlations were significant). The latter confirms our findings of multidimensional scaling.

In summary, for the current set of countries the conceptual classification of the contextual variables into ecological variables (Percentage of population engaged in agriculture, Highest monthly temperature, Affluence) and sociopolitical variables (Education and Religion) was found not to be two separate classes of variables, since several of their constituent elements showed strong relationships. Empirically, these contextual variables can be rearranged into three groups of variables: (1) Affluence, as measured by indicators of the level of economic development of a country (including Education); (2) Ecology, as measured by temperature; (3) Religion, as measured by the percentage of adherents to the four denominations of the current sample: Roman Catholic, Protestant, Christian Orthodox, and Muslim. This classification of variables is more or less in line with Georgas, van de Vijver, and Berry's (2004) classification, with one adjustment. Whereas Georgas et al. (2004c) found that the economic factor was also related to temperature (i.e., average daily maximum temperature in the hottest month), the current set (which is based on a much smaller set of countries) found a weaker correlation.

These three new indicators were used in regression analyses in order to detect their association with the psychological and family variables. The analyses were carried out at country level, because the hypotheses involve mechanisms at this level. However, an analysis at country level has a sample size of "only" 27 cases. The number of predictors (afflu-ence, temperature, and religion) would be large relative to the number of observations, which would make it difficult to find any significant coeffi-cients. Therefore, it was decided to split up the analyses and to examine the association of each religion in separate regression analysis. For example, the association with Agreeableness was studied in four regres-sion analyses. In the first affluence, temperature and the percentage of Roman Catholics were used as the predictors, in the second the latter was replaced by the percentage of Protestants, in the third by the percentage of Christian Orthodox, and in the fourth by the percentage of Muslims. So, for each dependent variable of interest four regression analyses were carried out, each time with a different religion as inde-pendent variable. In addition to significance, consistency of associations between predictors and dependent variables was examined.

The results of the regression analyses of the psychological variables are presented in Table 7.22. The prediction of personality traits at country level was not very successful. Agreeableness and Conscientiousness were negatively predicted by Affluence, while the contribution of Affluence to the explanation of the other traits was limited. The regression coeffi-cients of Temperature were small, nonsignificant, and negative in most cases (median $\beta = -.11$). Mostly positive, though nonsignificant associ-ations were found for religion (.11). Only one of the 20 squared multiple correlations was significant. It is fair to conclude that relationships between the country characteristics studied here and personality ranged from absent to weak. These results largely confirm findings that positive personality aspects such as agreeableness and conscientiousness are negatively related to Affluence (Allik and McCrae, 2004; van de Vijver, 2006; van Hemert, van de Vijver, Poortinga and Georgas, 2002).

Schwartz's values questionnaire yielded high squared multiple correl-ations for Embeddedness, Hierarchy, and Harmony (median $R^2 = .58$, .43, and .66, respectively, all $ps < .01$). The largest contribution came from Affluence, which showed a negative association in all analyses. Roman Catholicism was negative related to Embeddedness ($\beta = -.34$), while Christian Orthodoxy and Islam were positively related ($\beta = .28$ and .45, all $ps < .01$). The analysis of the individualistically oriented values (Intellectual Autonomy, Affective Autonomy, and Mas-tery) showed nonsignificant multiple correlations. It can be concluded that the collectivistic values are strongly and negatively influenced by Affluence, while the individualist values are not influenced by Affluence; the same pattern was reported by Georgas et al. (2004). Temperature and Religion did not show strong associations with values. The lack of an association between religion and personal values may seem unexpected.

Table 7.22 *Regression analysis with affluence (combined score), temperature, and religion as independent variables and psychological variables as the dependent variable*

Dependent Variable	Religious Denomination	Affluence (combined)	Temperature	Religion	Adj. R^2
Emotional distance					
Nuclear family	Roman Catholic	−.54[*]	−.23	.01	.17
	Protestant	−.56[*]	−.23	.03	.17
	Christian Orthodox	−.48[*]	−.15	.22	.21[*]
	Muslim	−.51[*]	−.25	.06	.17
Extended family	Roman Catholic	−.38	−.41	.18	.14
	Protestant	−.35	−.44[*]	.04	.11
	Christian Orthodox	−.22	−.29	.44[*]	.31[**]
	Muslim	−.40	−.37	−.19	.13
Self-construal					
Independent	Roman Catholic	−.38	−.25	.12	.04
	Protestant	−.64[*]	−.29	.46	.17
	Christian Orthodox	−.34	−.25	.05	.02
	Muslim	−.43	−.20	−.20	.05
Interdependent	Roman Catholic	−.40	−.18	.09	.03
	Protestant	−.38	−.19	−.00	.02
	Christian Orthodox	−.35	−.16	.11	.03
	Muslim	−.42	−.16	−.11	.03
Personality					
Agreeableness	Roman Catholic	−.49[*]	−.17	.14	.10
	Protestant	−.67[*]	−.21	.34	.16
	Christian Orthodox	−.44[*]	−.18	.04	.08
	Muslim	−.36	−.27	.23	.12
Conscientiousness	Roman Catholic	−.50[*]	−.11	.11	.11
	Protestant	−.78[**]	−.15	.48[*]	.25[*]
	Christian Orthodox	−.44[*]	−.08	.15	.12
	Muslim	−.44	−.16	.08	.10
Emotional stability	Roman Catholic	−.32	−.25	−.01	.00
	Protestant	−.64[*]	−.27	.49[*]	.17
	Christian Orthodox	−.29	−.20	.15	.02
	Muslim	−.34	.06	.01	.00
Extraversion	Roman Catholic	−.07	.01	.40	.03
	Protestant	−.19	−.07	.36	−.03
	Christian Orthodox	.02	−.09	−.11	−.11
	Muslim	.10	−.10	.01	−.11
Openness	Roman Catholic	−.11	−.11	.40	.06
	Protestant	−.24	−.19	.39	.01
	Christian Orthodox	−.07	−.28	−.30	−.00
	Muslim	.04	−.21	.10	−.09
Family values					
Hierarchy	Roman Catholic	−.64[**]	.12	−.26	.63[**]
	Protestant	−.73[**]	.16	.02	.56[**]

Table 7.22 (*cont.*)

Dependent Variable	Religious Denomination	Affluence (combined)	Temperature	Religion	Adj. R^2
	Christian Orthodox	$-.71^{**}$	.17	.01	$.56^{**}$
	Muslim	$-.60^{**}$	.07	.27	$.61^{**}$
Values Embeddedness	Roman Catholic	$-.60^{**}$	.05	$-.34^{*}$	$.59^{**}$
	Protestant	$-.76^{**}$	.10	.10	$.49^{**}$
	Christian Orthodox	$-.63^{**}$	.20	$.28^{*}$	$.56^{**}$
	Muslim	$-.51^{**}$	$-.06$	$.45^{**}$	$.62^{**}$
Hierarchy	Roman Catholic	$-.50^{**}$	.18	$-.26$	$.46^{**}$
	Protestant	$-.78^{**}$	.21	.32	$.46^{**}$
	Christian Orthodox	$-.58^{**}$	.22	$-.01$	$.39^{**}$
	Muslim	$-.60^{**}$	.25	$-.06$	$.39^{**}$
Harmony	Roman Catholic	$-.87^{**}$	$-.04$	.10	$.66^{**}$
	Protestant	$-.91^{**}$	$-.06$	.10	$.66^{**}$
	Christian Orthodox	$-.81^{**}$	.00	.17	$.68^{**}$
	Muslim	$-.80^{**}$	$-.09$	.12	$.66^{**}$
Intellect. autonomy	Roman Catholic	$-.24$	$-.05$	.38	.03
	Protestant	$-.17$	$-.12$	.06	$-.10$
	Christian Orthodox	$-.11$	$-.08$	.12	$-.09$
	Muslim	$-.29$	.02	$-.37$	$-.01$
Affect. autonomy	Roman Catholic	.33	$-.04$	$-.02$	$-.00$
	Protestant	.29	$-.04$	.05	.00
	Christian Orthodox	$.41^{*}$	.09	.38	.14
	Muslim	.24	.04	$-.21$	.03
Mastery	Roman Catholic	$-.35$	.00	.09	$-.01$
	Protestant	$-.46$	$-.02$	.22	.02
	Christian Orthodox	$-.24$	.10	.33	.09
	Muslim	$-.39$	.05	$-.17$	.00
Relationships with kin	Roman Catholic	$-.68^{**}$	.08	.01	$.43^{**}$
	Protestant	$-.84^{**}$	.06	.25	$.47^{**}$
	Christian Orthodox	$-.67^{**}$	.08	.02	$.43^{**}$
	Muslim	$-.56^{**}$	$-.03$	.29	$.48^{**}$

Note:
Values in cells denote standardized regression coefficients.
$^{*}p < .05.$ $^{**}p < .01.$

However, there are at least two explanations for this finding. Firstly, some important religious values such as submission to a Supreme Being may be either universal or not covered well by the questionnaire. Secondly, the relationship between religion and values may be strongly influenced by Affluence. For example, Harmony showed a correlation of $r = .49$ with the percentage of Muslims and of $r = -.54$ with the percentage of Protestants (both ps $< .01$). However, the very strong correlation between Affluence and Harmony of $r = -.83$ ($p < .01$) rendered correlations of the religions nonsignificant.

The regression analyses of the two self-construal measures showed similar results. No squared multiple correlation reached significance, although it is remarkable that the regression coefficients of Affluence and Temperature were negative in each analysis. This similarity may seem unexpected, as independence and interdependence are often supposed to be negatively correlated. However, the scores at country level showed a very strong positive correlation between both of $r = .64$ ($p < .01$), which can explain the similarity in sign of the regression coefficients.

Both family values, Hierarchy and Relationships with Kin, were strongly influenced by the country characteristics (median $R^2 = .59$ and .45, respectively, both $ps < .01$). These effects were due to the negative association with Affluence (median $\beta = -.41$ and $-.39$). Religion and Affluence had small regression coefficients, which were positive in almost all cases.

Compared to family values, Emotional Distance showed weaker associations with country characteristics. Affluence and Temperature invariably showed negative regression coefficients (median $\beta = -.44$ and $-.27$), which reached significance in some cases. The proportions of variance accounted for by the predictors were modest (median $R^2 = .17$).

It seems fair to conclude that the psychological variables that were examined showed substantial variations in their associations with country characteristics. The most strongly affected were Personal and Family Values (notably Embeddedness, Hierarchy, Harmony, Family Hierarchy, and Relationships with Kin). It is noteworthy that all these aspects are strongly relational. Affluence had a negative influence on all these values. The impact of Temperature was very limited (with only one significant coefficient in 68 analyses). The influence of religion (which had six significant coefficients) was slightly higher. Clearly, Affluence was the most salient predictor and it was more effective in explaining interpersonal aspects than intrapersonal aspects. These findings support a model in which increasing Affluence is assumed to affect social aspects much more than individual aspects of psychological functioning. The findings regarding Self-construals were not in line with this conclusion, possibly owing to the measurement problems with these scales found in the equivalence analyses (see the first section of this Chapter).

Family Network Variables (proximity of residence of parents and children, frequency of visits, and frequency of telephone calls) showed some relationships with the predictors (see Table 7.23). Not surprisingly, Affluence was positively related to Telephone Calls). Temperature

Table 7.23 *Regression analysis with affluence (combined score), temperature, and religion as independent variables and family networks and family roles as the dependent variable*

Dependent variable	Religious denomination	Affluence (combined)	Temperature	Religion	Adj. R^2
Family networks					
Geographic	Roman Catholic	−.40	.04	−.06	.09
proximity	Protestant	−.02	.09	−.60**	.33**
	Christian Orthodox	−.38	.12	.19	.12
	Muslim	−.42	.06	−.01	.08
Visits	Roman Catholic	−.13	−.10	−.08	−.12
	Protestant	.39	−.06	−.80**	.31**
	Christian Orthodox	−.04	.02	.39	.04
	Muslim	−.04	−.19	.22	−.08
Telephone	Roman Catholic	.42	.05	−.11	.04
calls	Protestant	.67*	.09	−.42	.14
	Christian Orthodox	.52**	.24	.55**	.33**
	Muslim	.49*	−.02	.23	.06
Father					
Expressive	Roman Catholic	−.50**	.26	−.34*	.62**
	Protestant	−.68**	.31*	.13	.52**
	Christian Orthodox	−.54**	.39*	.22	.56**
	Muslim	−.42**	.16	.43**	.64**
Finances	Roman Catholic	−.48*	.11	−.17	.29*
	Protestant	−.67**	.13	.22	.29*
	Christian Orthodox	−.45*	.25	.33	.37**
	Muslim	−.41*	.03	.30	.32**
Childcare	Roman Catholic	−.01	.00	.20	−.09
	Protestant	−.21	−.05	.41	−.01
	Christian Orthodox	.10	.04	.21	−.08
	Muslim	−.09	.10	−.34	−.04
Mother					
Expressive	Roman Catholic	−.54**	.17	−.12	.38**
	Protestant	−.75**	.18	.28	.42**
	Christian Orthodox	−.52**	.27	.24	.42**
	Muslim	−.45*	.08	.31	.43**
Finances	Roman Catholic	−.04	−.21	.18	−.03
	Protestant	−.05	−.25	.10	−.05
	Christian Orthodox	.10	−.12	.36	.07
	Muslim	−.22	−.04	−.57*	.16
Childcare	Roman Catholic	.04	−.38	.20	.14
	Protestant	−.05	−.42*	.22	.13
	Christian Orthodox	.20	−.25	.47*	.32**
	Muslim	−.08	−.26	−.43	.22*

Table 7.23 (*cont.*)

Dependent variable	Religious denomination	Affluence (combined)	Temperature	Religion	Adj. R^2
Grandfather					
Expressive	Roman Catholic	$-.53^{**}$	.15	.12	$.35^{**}$
	Protestant	$-.68^{**}$	.17	.18	$.36^{**}$
	Christian Orthodox	$-.53^{**}$	.23	.17	$.36^{**}$
	Muslim	$-.44^{*}$	.06	.32	$.40^{**}$
Instrumental	Roman Catholic	$-.20$	$-.16$	$-.25$	.00
	Protestant	$-.38$	$-.13$	.17	$-.04$
	Christian Orthodox	$-.20$	$-.03$	.27	.02
	Muslim	$-.32$	$-.07$	$-.14$	$-.04$
Grandmother					
Expressive	Roman Catholic	$-.44^{*}$	.20	.02	.18
	Protestant	$-.62^{*}$	.18	.29	$.24^{*}$
	Christian Orthodox	$-.41^{*}$	.22	.07	.18
	Muslim	$-.29$	.07	.35	$.26^{*}$
Instrumental	Roman Catholic	$-.01$	$-.44^{*}$	$-.14$	.07
	Protestant	$-.20$	$-.43^{*}$	.23	.09
	Christian Orthodox	.06	$-.26$	$.46^{*}$	$.26^{*}$
	Muslim	$-.15$	$-.33$	$-.25$	.10
Uncles/aunts					
Expressive	Roman Catholic	$-.39$	.23	.22	.12
	Protestant	$-.56^{*}$	.18	.37	.17
	Christian Orthodox	$-.35$	.16	$-.11$	.09
	Muslim	$-.27$	.15	.14	.09
Instrumental	Roman Catholic	$-.43^{*}$	.10	.14	.09
	Protestant	$-.74^{**}$	.05	$.54^{*}$	$.27^{*}$
	Christian Orthodox	$-.42^{*}$	.03	$-.14$	.08
	Muslim	$-.51^{*}$	.18	$-.28$	.12
Son 20 years					
Expressive	Roman Catholic	$-.52^{*}$	.15	.06	$.22^{*}$
	Protestant	$-.67^{**}$	.12	.27	$.27^{*}$
	Christian Orthodox	$-.48^{*}$	.16	.08	$.22^{*}$
	Muslim	$-.34$	.00	.38	$.32^{**}$
Instrumental	Roman Catholic	$-.73^{**}$	.10	.11	$.49^{**}$
	Protestant	$-.88^{**}$	.07	.28	$.53^{**}$
	Christian Orthodox	$-.69^{**}$	.10	.06	$.48^{**}$
	Muslim	$-.71^{**}$	.09	$-.03$	$.48^{**}$
Daughter 20 years					
Expressive	Roman Catholic	$-.45^{*}$	.17	.02	.18
	Protestant	$-.66^{**}$	.15	.34	$.26^{*}$
	Christian Orthodox	$-.44^{*}$	.18	.02	.18
	Muslim	$-.24$	$-.01$	$.49^{*}$	$.34^{**}$
Instrumental	Roman Catholic	$-.76^{**}$	$-.25$	.06	$.43^{**}$
	Protestant	$-.85^{**}$	$-.26$	.17	$.45^{**}$
	Christian Orthodox	$-.68^{**}$	$-.17$	.26	$.50^{**}$
	Muslim	$-.77^{**}$	$-.23$	$-.08$	$.44^{**}$

Table 7.23 (*cont.*)

Dependent variable	Religious denomination	Affluence (combined)	Temperature	Religion	Adj. R^2
Son 10 years					
Expressive	Roman Catholic	−.30	.12	.25	.01
	Protestant	−.23	.08	−.01	−.05
	Christian Orthodox	−.22	.10	.07	−.05
	Muslim	−.19	.03	.12	−.04
Instrumental	Roman Catholic	−.50*	.12	−.03	.23*
	Protestant	−.67**	.11	.24	.27*
	Christian Orthodox	−.52**	.11	−.04	.23*
	Muslim	−.70**	.29	−.46*	.37**
Daughter 10 years					
Expressive	Roman Catholic	−.26	.14	.24	−.01
	Protestant	−.22	.10	.05	−.06
	Christian Orthodox	−.18	.11	.03	−.06
	Muslim	−.12	.04	.18	−.04
Instrumental	Roman Catholic	−.52*	.05	−.06	.23*
	Protestant	−.68**	.05	.22	.26*
	Christian Orthodox	−.54**	.06	.00	.22*
	Muslim	−.71**	.21	−.42	.34**

Note:
Values in cells denote standardized regression coefficients.
*$p < .05$. **$p < .01$.

was unrelated to the Family Network Variables. It is interesting to note that Protestant and Orthodox countries showed different relationships. The percentage of Protestants showed negative and in some cases very strong associations with each of the three dependent variables (the value of β was −.80 for frequency of visits and −.60 for geographic proximity, both ps < .01), while the opposite was found for the percentage of Christian Orthodox. The two other religions did not show a strong patterning. The effects of the percentage of Christian Orthodox adherents and Affluence are both positive and go in the same (positive) direction, which is remarkable as in most analyses Affluence and Religion showed regression coefficients with opposite signs.

The expressive roles of the father and the mother were both negatively associated with Affluence (median β = −.52 and −.53, coefficients of all tests were significant). The patterning of the other variables was also similar for both parents, although more pronounced and more often significant for the father than for the mother. Temperature showed low, positive regression coefficients in all analyses, which were significant (only) for percentages of Protestant ($\beta = 31$, $p < .05$) and Orthodox adherents ($\beta = 39$, $p < .05$). Furthermore, the data suggested that the four Religions did not affect the expressive role in the same way. Negative regression coefficients were found for Catholicism, although only the value of the father was significant ($\beta = -.34$, $p < .05$), while the other religions showed positive regression coefficients. Yet, it should be acknowledged that the relationships were weak and only one of these was significant: the positive regression coefficient of Islam in the prediction of the father's expressive role ($\beta = .43$, $p < .01$).

The instrumental role of the parents, split up into finances and childcare, yielded squared multiple correlations that were lower than found in the analyses of the expressive role. Apart from this agreement, the findings were quite different for both parents. The financial role of the father diminishes with Affluence (median $\beta = -.47$; all four coefficients were significant, $p < .05$), but this was not the case for the mother (median $\beta = -.05$, the coefficient was not significant in any analysis). The childcare role of the father was unrelated to any country characteristic. For the mother negative coefficients were found for Temperature (median $\beta = -.32$, while Religion yielded heterogeneous results (significant only for Christian Orthodox, $\beta = .47$, $p < .05$). It is interesting to note that Affluence was unrelated to the childcare role; we found no evidence for the view that with modernization (i.e., increase of Affluence) the father assumes a more active role in childcare. A final observation concerns the comparison of the size of the squared multiple correlations for both parents. The median value of the father was .31, while the value of the mother was .19. This finding suggests that the roles of the father are more affected by changes in Affluence than are the roles of the mother; however, it should be realized that this interpretation is tentative (for the current limited sample size tests of differences of dependent multiple correlations require much larger differences in observed values in order to be significant).

Hierarchical power   A prediction based on the family literature in Chapter 1 was that Hierarchical power of the mother has increased in higher affluent countries, as compared to father. The two family roles are: "*Father–mother* is the protector of the family," and "When there are arguments or disputes, *father–mother* makes the decision regarding the manner of solution."

The simple correlation between level of affluence and paternal power was very high and indicated a negative relationship between power and affluence, ($r = -.70$, $p < .01$, as also with maternal power ($r = -.60$, $p < .01$). However, at the individual level, means of the three affluence clusters of countries indicated an interaction between level of maternal and paternal power. Paternal power in low-affluence countries was higher than maternal power, while no differences in means of father and mother were found in medium-level affluent countries, but maternal power was higher than paternal power in high-affluence countries.

A second hypothesis was that fathers in all societies do less housework (cleaning, cooking, washing) than mothers. The simple correlation between level of affluence and housework was very high for fathers ($r = .60$, $p < .01$), but no significant correlation was found for mothers ($r = -.08$, ns). However, at the individual level, means of the three affluence clusters of countries indicated an interaction between housework and mother and father. The means of housework for fathers increased according to level of affluence of the countries, but there were no differences for mothers across the three affluence levels.

Further evidence for the interpretation that Affluence influences the role of the mother more than the role of the father was found in the analysis of the grandparents. Higher values were found for the grandfather (median $R^2 = .22$) than for the grandmother (median $R^2 = .22$). The Expressive Roles of both grandparents were negatively related to Affluence (median $\beta = .53$ for grandfather and .43 for grandmother). The regression coefficients of Temperature and Religion were positive in almost all analyses, though no coefficient reached significance. The absence of any influence of Affluence on Instrumental, found for the parents, was replicated for the grandparents. It can be concluded that the expressive role of both grandparents becomes less salient with increases in Affluence, in particular for the grandfather, and that cross-cultural differences in their instrumental role (which were large according to Table 7.23) are affected by other country characteristics than those studied here.

For the uncles and aunts only one of the eight squared multiple correlations was significant. Affluence invariably yielded negative regression coefficients, which were significant for the instrumental role (median $\beta = -.47$), the regression coefficients of Temperature all have a positive sign, but did not reach significance. The coefficients of the religions were both positive and negative; one of these was significant: the percentage of Protestants was positively associated with the instrumental role of the uncles and aunts ($\beta = .54$, $p < .05$).

The final analyses involved the children. In all 32 analyses (4 children $\times$ 2 roles $\times$ 4 religions) Affluence had a negative sign. This consistency points to a decrease in both expressive and instrumental roles with an increasing Affluence, although the effect seems slightly more pronounced for the 20-year-old children (median $\beta = -.61$) than for

Table 7.24 *Regression analysis with affluence (combined score), temperature, and religion as independent variables and aggregated family roles as the dependent variable*

Dependent variable	Religious denomination	Affluence (combined)	Temperature	Religion	Adj. R^2
Expressive	Roman Catholic	−.50*	.21	.01	.27*
	Protestant	−.66**	.19	.25	.32**
	Christian Orthodox	−.48*	.24	.10	.28*
	Muslim	−.36	.08	.35	.35**
Instrumental	Roman Catholic	−.49*	−.16	.04	.10
	Protestant	−.74**	−.18	.41	.22*
	Christian Orthodox	−.39*	−.04	.36	.32*
	Muslim	−.63**	−.03	−.37	.20*

Note:
Values in cells denote standardized regression coefficients.
*$p < .05$. **$p < .01$.

10-year-old children (median $\beta = -.41$). Furthermore, Temperature showed a positive sign in most analyses, but never reached significance, while the regression coefficients of Religion tended to be small and have different signs across roles and positions, except for Islam, which showed small negative coefficients for the instrumental role and small positive coefficients for the expressive role. Finally, the values of the squared multiple correlations were higher for the instrumental role than for the expressive role (with median values of .10 and .40, respectively). This is a reversal of the pattern found for all adult rules.

Across positions means of emotional roles tended to differ across countries in the same way, which suggests the existence of positive correlations across the positions. If the expressive roles of the eight positions are considered as items of a scale, an internal consistency of .96 is found. Similarly, if the instrumental roles are taken to constitute a single scale, an internal consistency of .83 is found. Both values point to consistent country differences in both roles. Regression analyses were then carried out with the same predictors as before (Affluence, Temperature, and the four Religions) and the scale scores on the expressive role and instrumental role as dependent variables (see Table 7.24). The same pattern of findings emerged as reported before: Affluence yielded negative and significant predictors in all analyses, while the influence of Temperature and Religion was much weaker. Furthermore, the expressive role revealed slightly larger squared multiple correlations than did the instrumental role.

It is remarkable that in most analyses Affluence had a negative sign (the mean beta across all analyses was $-.38$), indicating that higher levels of Affluence are associated with lower levels of most psychological scales and family roles. Aggregated across the regression analyses, Temperature had a negligible impact (average beta of $-.01$). The pattern of Religion showed more variation. The percentage of Christian Orthodox and Protestants had an average beta of $.15$, which indicates that these religions were associated with psychological variables and that Affluence and these religions seem to have an opposite influence. The average beta was $.02$ for Islam and $.04$ for Roman Catholicism.

It can be concluded that the regression analyses of the family roles were fairly consistent in that Affluence was the main predictor and that the influence of Temperature and Religion were much weaker. Affluence and Religion often showed opposite relationships with the psychological variables and family roles. The influence of the various religions was not the same; the percentage of Christian Orthodox and Protestant adherents often showed stronger relationships than did the percentages of Muslim and Roman Catholic adherents. Furthermore, the country variables we studied were slightly more effective in predicting the Expressive Role than the Instrumental Role for adults (parents, grandparents, and uncles/aunts), while the opposite was found for children (20-year-old son and daughter, 10-year-old son and daughter).

8   Synthesis: how similar and how different are families across cultures?

James Georgas, John W. Berry, and Çiğdem Kağıtçıbaşı

The study of the diversity of types of families and family change through-out the world during the past 200 years has largely been the province of family sociology and cultural anthropology, but more recently psych-ology and psychiatry have taken an active interest. The co-authors in this study are all psychologists and their primary interest is in the cross-cultural analysis of psychological phenomena. The design of the study was based on four hierarchical levels: ecological and sociopolitical char-acteristics of societies, family roles, family networks, and psychological variables. Thus, the project emphasized the study of the psycho-logical variables of emotional closeness, self-construal, personality, family values, and general values and their relationships within eco-logical and sociopolitical features of societies, family roles, and family networks. The data from the countries of this project form a rich and complex mosaic of interrelationships across and within these four hierarchical levels.

The project has both a cross-cultural or comparative dimension and an indigenous dimension. The cross-cultural dimension is based on quanti-tative analyses of data from 27 countries, while the indigenous dimension reflects a qualitative analysis of cultural features of the 30 countries in the study, as well as descriptions of the relationships between the ecological and sociopolitical, family, and psychological variables by authors from these countries.

This chapter discusses three related themes that underlie the findings presented in Chapter 7. The first theme deals with how families differ in cultures across the world. Are there differences in family networks, family roles, and psychological variables among countries with different ecological, sociopolitical, and relatedness systems? The second theme

This chapter describes all main results of the study in a non-technical way. It can be read independently of the previous chapter. The reader who is interested in a description of details and technical aspects of the analysis is referred to Chapter 7.

concerns how families are alike across cultures. That is, to what degree are these features of family similar in countries throughout the world? A third theme involves family changes in societies throughout the world as a result of social changes, such as economic level, education, political systems, the global influence of television, and of communication through telephones, email, and the internet. These are usually referred to as *modernization, globalization* or *economic development*. For some family sociologists, cultural anthropologists, and psychologists, these changes are considered to lead to an inevitable convergence of the types of family structure, function, and of psychological relationships in the Majority World toward those characteristics found in North America and Northern Europe. This study looks at alternative explanations.

The complexity of the study based on so many variables and countries created a mountain of data on which the co-authors sat. A strictly empirical methodology leading down from the peak might have resulted in staggering along paths through the trees only to discover that we were walking in circles, or in following a stream which led to a cliff, requiring us to turn back again. In order to provide some bearings, we employed two compasses to help lead us down the mountain. Berry's Ecocultural Framework (Chapter 2) and Kağıtçıbaşı's Model of Family Change (Chapter 3) were employed as heuristic devices. Their significance for this project lies, particularly in the case of the Ecocultural Framework, in acting as a kind of map which differentiates cultures in terms of their ecological and sociopolitical contexts. A basic assumption is that ecological and cultural features provide large-scale contexts that shape the family and individual behavior. That is, family and individuals are adaptive to specific features of the ecocultural context and to changes in them. Family change can thus be seen as adaptation to the ecocultural context. The Model of Family Change also provides a map that alerts us to where to look for family and individual phenomena and links among them. These two frameworks were central in formulating hypotheses as to how ecological, sociopolitical, and culture of relatedness characteristics of societies might be related to family networks, family roles, and psychological variables in different cultures.

An epistemological orientation in this study is based on an old adage of Kluckhohn and Murray (1950, p. 15), with apologies for the gender-biased language:

> Every man is in certain respects
> like all other men,
> like some other men,
> like no other man

Kluckhohn and Murray were referring to three hierarchical levels of personality: universal traits, taxonomies of traits, and individual traits. The upper two levels also refer to nomothetic methods while the lowest refers to idiographic methods. The adage also applies to the current project. As our focus is on cultures as well as on individuals, Kluckhohn and Murray's adage might be paraphrased as, "Cultures are like all other cultures, like some other cultures, like no other culture." As outlined in Chapter 2, we have adopted a universalist perspective, which holds that all cultures share universal features, and all individuals share common psychological processes. Within this worldwide commonality, in which all cultures share some features, there are groups of cultures that share customs and psychological features, but are different from other groups of cultures. And single cultures have specific and possibly unique features and meanings, such as, language, myths, meanings, and symbols.

The comparative quantitative analyses in this study represent the nomothetical approach, while the family portraits represent the indigenous (idiographic) approach at the country level. However, it is important to emphasize that the study is weighted more toward the comparative than the indigenous approach. The implications are that we seek to find similarities and differences in families among the countries.

A second orientation has to do with the search for universals across countries as well as differences between countries. In most psychological research, we search for statistically significant differences between groups. This is also the case here. But in this study, we also pay special attention to comparisons in which there are no statistically significant differences. In this case, findings of no differences between countries are very important in that these variables may represent universals across cultures.

A third orientation, related to the above, has to do with patterns of similar findings across numerous countries. One advantage of studies with large numbers of countries is the emergence of patterns of differences or similarities in data. In studies with only a few countries, statistical differences may lead to certain, possibly invalid, conclusions regarding differences or similarities between countries in psychological variables. But with large numbers of countries, the patterning of the results enables more valid conclusions.

A fourth orientation concerns the independence of cultures in studies with large numbers of countries. Each country is not an independent unit in terms of cultural characteristics. That is, the 27 *countries* in our sample do not necessarily denote 27 independent *cultures*. This lack of independence among cultures is usually referred to as Galton's problem (Naroll, Michik and Naroll, 1974). Thus, our orientation was to attempt to group countries into cultural zones with common cultural character-istics, based on ecological and sociopolitical measures. In this way, the findings can be generalized to clusters of countries that share certain cultural level features, rather than just ordering the 27 countries on the basis of values on the variables. This procedure was followed using clusters of countries based on the variables of Affluence, Religion, and Relatedness, as will be described in detail below.

The chapter is divided into six sections. The first section describes the variables employed in the Ecocultural Framework and the Model of Family Change. The second section summarizes the cross-cultural simi-larities and differences of family roles, their relationships with ecological, sociopolitical and relatedness variables, and the family roles for each family position. Section three summarizes the relationships between the psychological scales and the cross-cultural patterning of similarities and differences in family roles. Section four presents a synthesis of the findings and addresses the question of which aspects of family are universal and which are culture-specific, together with the evaluation of the hypotheses based on the Ecocultural Framework and the Family Change Model. Section five discusses the limitations of the study. Section six presents the conclusions of the study.

THE VARIABLES OF THE ECOCULTURAL FRAMEWORK AND THE MODEL OF FAMILY CHANGE

The variables employed in the theoretical models of the Ecocultural Framework and Model of Family Change are summarized below.

Ecocultural Framework

Two sets of endogenous variables were identified in the Ecocultural Framework outlined in Chapter 2. Ecological variables are those that define natural habitats and establish contexts within which human popu-lations adapt; they are then linked to the emergence of cultural arrange-ments (including family structures) and the development of individual behaviors. Sociopolitical variables are those that impinge upon estab-lished cultural groups and on individuals within them, leading to a process of acculturation and cultural and psychological change. In earlier usage (e.g., Berry, 1976) these two sets of exogenous variables were combined to form a single index that was used to predict cultural and psychological outcomes.

Ecological variables

Agriculture   Agricultural societies, as discussed in Chapters 1, 2, and 3, have been widely described in the sociological and anthropological literature for almost two centuries as closely related to family systems, family roles, values and attitudes. Agricultural subsistence is an integral part of the Ecocultural Framework. The main country level measure used in this study was the percentage of the population engaged in agriculture. The Ecocultural Framework was originally aimed at understanding the transition from nomadic hunting and gathering societies to sedentary agricultural societies (Berry, 1976); the percentage of persons working in agriculture, which is of course higher in agricultural societies, was a good indicator of this process. The current study mainly involved students from agricultural, industrial, and post-industrial societies. The percentage of the population working in agriculture *increases* when a group changes from hunting and gathering to agriculture. However, the percentage of persons working in agriculture *decreases* with a change from agricultural to industrial societies; this process continues with the transition from an industrial to a post-industrial society. It was argued in Chapter 2 that the percentage of persons working in agriculture should be associated with various family features, such as closer geographic proximity of family members, more frequent visits, higher scores on expressive and instrumental childcare, closer emotional bonds, a more interdependent self-construal, more agreeableness and conscientiousness, high scores on family hierarchy and kin family values, and higher scores on hierarchy (as a personal value) and embeddedness.

Temperature   Whiting (1981) reported how infant care is patterned by cold and warm temperatures in different regions. For example, mothers and infants slept in the same bed in cultures with hot and mild winter temperatures and did not use cradles, but mothers and infants slept apart and used cradles in societies with cool and cold temperatures. Drawing on the Ecocultural Framework, the current study tests the hypothesis that lower temperatures have psychological consequences that happen to coincide with those expected for a lower percentage of persons working in agriculture.

Affluence   Industrialization and urbanization have, together with agriculture, been key issues in changes from the extended family to the nuclear family system, as well as changes in family roles and values, according to the sociological and anthropological literature. The current study used a variable called *Affluence*, which combines various economic measures at the country level (Georgas, van de Vijver, and Berry, 2004c). Georgas et al. used archival data to measure Affluence: Gross National Product per capita, energy use per capita, electricity consumption per capita, unemployment rate, percentage of population employed in industry and services, imports, and exports. We expected that the relationships articulated for percentage engaged in agriculture (see above) would be found for Affluence, but in an inverse direction. Moreover, this ecological variable has links to sociopolitical variables, since many of the changes in Affluence, and its current levels, have come about through contact with other cultures. Hence, we expected that there would be relationships between Affluence and other variables in the study that will be described for sociopolitical variables (see below).

The countries were cluster analyzed based on affluence level, resulting in three country clusters: (1) High Level Affluence: United States, Canada, Germany, Japan, France, the Netherlands, United Kingdom, Hong Kong, South Korea, and Spain; (2) Middle Level Affluence: Greece, Saudi Arabia, Ukraine, Mexico, Bulgaria, Chile, Cyprus, Brazil, Turkey, Iran, and Georgia; (3) Low Level Affluence: Indonesia, Pakistan, India, Algeria, Ghana, and Nigeria listed in order of declining index of affluence (see also Table 7.11).

Sociopolitical variables

As we noted in Chapter 2, sociopolitical variables in the Ecocultural Framework are those that have impinged on a society from outside their traditional culture. The resulting process of acculturation brings about changes in their established cultural practices and individual behaviors. Over time, these changes modify the original ways that societies and families operate in adaptation to their ecological contexts. In this study we lack longitudinal observations, and hence are not able to observe change directly. However, we have used two variables to represent these external influences: Religion and Education. These influences have had an impact for highly variable periods of time. Religious conversion has taken place for over 2,000 years, and continues at the present time. Education, in the sense of formal Western-type schooling, is more recent in many societies in our sample.

Religion   Two ways of measuring religion-related concepts have been proposed in the literature (e.g., Inglehart, 1997). The first refers to degree of religiosity of individuals (e.g., as measured by church attendance among Christians or living in compliance with religious regulations such as Ramadan among Muslims). Another way to measure religion, employed in the current study, is to categorize the dominant religious dogma of countries in terms of the percentage of the population belonging to religious denominations. We chose this latter approach for two reasons. First, the dominant religion of a country influences societal institutions and, directly or indirectly, the values and behavior of the individual, regardless of the degree of religiosity or the religious beliefs of the individual. That is, citizens of a multicultural country may be adherents of different religions, and may not be influenced by the dominant religion of the country, but their life and social values are influenced by the institutions of the country, such as laws, system of education, and customs that were established earlier when there was one dominant religion. Second, unlike religiosity, the percentage of adherents of a country gives us access to religion as a social institution and theories about its role.

In his classic book, *The Protestant ethic and the spirit of capitalism* ([1904]1958), Weber argued that Calvinistic Protestantism set the stage for capitalism by introducing laws and social institutions permitting economic and banking activities, introducing interest on loans, all leading to capitalistic enterprise. Perhaps the most profound concept of Protestantism was that salvation could be attained by the individual and not necessarily through the church, as espoused by Catholicism. This concept of the individual relationship between God and man influenced the development of individualism and individualist values in the life course. Calvinistic Protestant dogma shaped cultural institutions in Europe and North America, such as the democratic systems of government, laws permitting and regulating private enterprise, laws protecting the rights of individuals. The constitutions of Protestant countries codified these religious values as laws and social institutions which continued to be in effect for centuries. This is the case, for example, in the United Kingdom, the United States, and Switzerland at the present time, even though these countries have undergone great economic, educational, and other social transformations during the past centuries. Huntington's (1996) thesis that the basic institutions of eight major cultures, with religion as a basic constituent, have persisted for centuries is an extension of this Weberian thesis.

In a large-scale study of nations, Inglehart and Baker (2000) found that religious values in Protestant, Orthodox, Islamic, and Confucian cultures continued to explain a significant percentage of the variance, even after controlling for the effects of economic development. Georgas et al. (2004c) found that Religion and Affluence at the country level were related to values in separate and contrasting ways. Some religions are related to more emphasis on interpersonal aspects, such as power, loyalty, and hierarchy, together with low Affluence. Other religions, (particularly Protestantism) and higher scores on Affluence, were associated with more emphasis on intrapersonal aspects, such as individualism, utilitarian commitment, and well-being.

Education   Education was measured by the archival variables: total adult illiteracy, pupil/teacher ratio education at first level, enrollment ratios at first, second, and third levels of education. These country-level indices are on the whole measures of *access to education*. This measure of education differs from the variable Parental education, which was assessed at the individual level of the respondents.

Family Change Model

The general contextual orientation of the Family Change Model situates the family in the sociocultural environment, in particular addressing culture and living conditions (urban–rural SES and level of affluence) (Kağıtçıbaşı, 1996a, p. 77; see also Chapter 3). A specific expectation regarding Affluence deriving from Kağıtçıbaşı's Family Change Model was that both emotional/expressive and material/instrumental roles would decrease with Affluence.

Relatedness

To examine patterns of variables as predicted by Kağıtçıbaşı's Family Change Model, countries were divided into three clusters; as just noted, this was first done on the basis of Affluence. A second clustering was based on a general indication of the "culture of separateness–culture of relatedness" (individualism/collectivism) distinction (Kağıtçıbaşı, 1990; see also Chapter 3 and Chapter 7). The two ways of clustering the countries showed a patterning of: low affluence/high relatedness; medium affluence/medium relatedness; and high affluence/low relatedness (except for Hong Kong, Japan, South Korea, and Spain, which were categorized as medium relatedness; see Table 7.11). The corresponding three family models (Kağıtçıbaşı, 1990, 1996a, Chapter 3) are the family model of interdependence, the family model of emotional interdependence, and the family model of independence. The expectations deriving from the Family Change Model were for relatively weaker family bonds (interdependencies) and weaker emotional/expressive roles in the high affluence/low relatedness cluster (family model of independence), and relatively stronger family bonds and emotional/expressive roles in the low affluence/high relatedness cluster. The third pattern, medium affluence/medium relatedness, were expected to be in between. An additional expectation of the Model was that there would be generally high levels of emotional bonds in all the families, despite the above distinctions.

Integration of the country characteristics of the Ecocultural Framework and Family Change Model

The ecological, sociopolitical, and relatedness variables showed salient associations in our sample of 27 countries. This does not invalidate their independent theoretical background, but attests to the strong inter-relationships of institutions at country level, such as affluence and education. We identified three sets of characteristics. The first was temperature, while the second involved the dominant religious dogma of the country. The third combined the economic indices of the Affluence factor, the percentage of population engaged in agriculture, the education indices, and the relatedness variable. This combined measure is called the *Socioeconomic Index*, and will be referred to frequently in the remainder of this chapter.

FAMILY ROLES[1]

This section summarizes the universal patterning of the family roles, followed by a description of the domains of large and small cross-cultural differences in these roles and other family scales (networks and values). The final part contains a more in-depth exploration of the cross-cultural similarities and differences of the roles for each family position.

The universality of the structure of family roles

The core of the questionnaire, and indeed of the project, focused on family positions, roles, and functions. The family positions were: father, mother, grandfather, grandmother, aunts/uncles, 20-year-old male, 20-year-old female, 10-year-old boy, and 10-year-old girl. In total, 22 roles were examined for each of these positions (see Table 6.4 for a detailed

---

[1] The study also involved the examination of gender differences. This chapter does not discuss these differences and the reader is referred to Chapter 7, p. 142 for a full presentation of the size and patterning of these differences and their implications.

description).[2] Three main roles were found for father and mother: *expressive/emotional* (e.g., providing emotional support to children, grandparents, and wife/husband; keeping the family united; keeping a pleasant environment); *financial* (e.g., contributing financially to the family; managing finances; giving pocket money to children; supporting career of children); and *childcare* (e.g., taking children to school; playing with children; helping children with homework). Two main roles were found for the other seven family positions: *expressive* (e.g., providing emotional support; keeping the family united; conveying traditions) and *instrumental* (e.g., contributing financially; babysitting; helping parents with their work). Note that the financial and childcare roles of mother and father are instrumental roles. The analyses demonstrated a remarkable cross-cultural stability in the patterning of the 22 roles.

It was notable that the factor analyses of the family roles resulted in two factors resembling Parsons' (1943, 1949) *expressive* and *instrumental* roles. They also resemble Durkheim's (1888, 1892, 1921) description of the last two stages of family change, in which the paternal family is reduced to the conjugal or nuclear family and in which the relationships between parents and children change from material or economic basis to "personal motives." The two factors are also similar to Kağıtçıbaşı's (1990, 1996a) emotional interdependencies and material/economic interdependencies roles. She focuses more on changing intergenerational relationships in the family with changing lifestyles, based on the findings of the Value of Children Study (see Chapter 3).

We found firm evidence that expressive/emotional and instrumental/material roles are distinct from one another and are common across the countries in this study. These are potential universals in families in all cultures.

---

[2] The following 22 roles were examined: providing emotional support to children; keeping the family united; trying to keep a pleasant environment in the family; conveying traditions, manners, and customs (e.g., reads, tells stories) to children; conveying the religious tradition to children; contributing to the preservation of family relations (e.g., family gatherings during the holidays, anniversaries); supporting (the grandparents or grandchildren or nephews/nieces) when in need (illness, financial problems, etc.); taking daily care (cooking, shopping); protecting the family; making the decision regarding the manner of solution when there are arguments or disputes; doing housework (cleans, cooks, washes); doing the shopping, pays bills, etc.; taking the children to school; playing with the children; helping children with homework; teaching good behavior to children; contributing financially to the family; managing the family finances; giving pocket money to children; supporting (at the beginning of their career) the children; babysitting when the parents are not home; helping the parents with their work (fields, shop or family occupation). Not all roles apply to all positions; the reader is referred to Table 6.4 for a detailed overview.

Cultural differences and similarities in family variables

With a sample of 5,428 participants, it is not surprising that all country differences in scores at the individual level turned out to be statistically significant. Hence, the analyses were more directed toward identifying the patterning of the country differences. Areas of salient similarities and dissimilarities were found. Strong emotional ties with the nuclear family were universal in our data (the mean score was fairly close to the scale maximum for parents and children), while the ties with the extended family were much more variable. Another universal feature involved the higher score of the female positions (of mother, grandmother, and 20-year-old daughter), which means that women assume a more active role in family roles in every country studied. Interestingly, the rank order of the other positions of family roles is also universal. Grandparents follow the parents in their importance in family roles; the 20-year-old children play a less salient role, while the 10-year-old children play the least important family role.

Of all the family variables studied (roles, family networks, and values), the smallest cross-cultural differences were found for Emotional Bonds with the nuclear family and the largest cross-cultural differences were found for the Family Hierarchy Values Scale. Furthermore, the expressive role showed much more cross-cultural variation than the instrumental (financial) role.

A first attempt at understanding the patterning of cross-cultural differences was made by defining country clusters on the basis of three criteria: Affluence (3 levels: low, medium, and high); Relatedness (3 levels: low, medium, and high) and Religion (5 levels: Catholic, Protestant, (Christian) Orthodox, Muslim, and a combination of Hindu, Buddhist, and Traditional Beliefs). The clustering was most effective for Affluence; about half of the country variation in the expressive role and Hierarchy (the scales with the largest cross-cultural differences) could be accounted for by Affluence; about 40 percent could be explained by Relatedness and about 25 percent by Religion. Cross-cultural differences in the instrumental role were explained by about 30 percent by each of the clusters.[3] The score differentiation was largely between more affluent societies on the one hand and more agricultural and less affluent countries on the other hand.

Two important conclusions can be drawn. The first involves the presence of systematic country-level differences in family-related

---

[3] These percentages are not additive. See Chapter 7.

variables. Although the samples in each country showed much intra-cultural score variation, we also found large cross-cultural differences. The second refers to the patterning of the cross-cultural differences. Each of the clustering criteria (i.e., Affluence, Relatedness, and Religion) captured part of the cross-cultural variation. These results yield a promising start for testing the hypotheses based on the two theories that guided this project. However, as noted in the previous section, the clustering criteria are not independent and the issue of their partial overlap is taken into account in the hypothesis tests.

Cross-cultural differences and similarities in family variables per role[4]

Parents   The roles of the father are given for each affluence level in Figure 8.1 and for each religious cluster in Figure 8.2; Figures 8.3 and 8.4 present the same for the Mother.[5] The first striking observation is the higher scores and smaller variation of scores of the mothers, which means that mothers everywhere are more actively involved in the family than fathers. Also, fathers in most countries score highest on the financial role while mothers score highest on the expressive/emotional roles. Another important finding involves the strong relationship between socioeconomic level and scores on expressive/emotional roles. Countries with low socioeconomic level (i.e., countries with high percentages of the population engaged in agriculture, low levels of industrialization, services and access to education) tend to have higher scores on expressive/emotional roles. In countries with higher monthly temperatures, higher expressive roles were found for both parents (as well as both grandparents and 20-year-old females). These findings support the predictions of the Ecocultural Framework and Model of Family Change.

Comparisons of means of the four religious clusters indicated that Muslim mothers and fathers showed the highest scores on the expressive role, followed by Orthodox, while Protestants and Catholics showed the lowest scores. The difference between Muslim and Orthodox countries and Protestant countries supports predictions based on the Ecocultural

---

[4] The results of the analyses of the previous Chapter are combined here, which implies that no sharp distinction is maintained between the results of each specific analysis. The reader is referred to the previous Chapter for an understanding of which analyses were employed to draw the conclusions.

[5] It is important to differentiate between the relatively few gender differences of the respondents and the many gender differences in the family roles. The responses of the male and female students differed very little on the variables. However, a number of differences were found between the Expressive and Instrumental family roles of mother and father and other family positions as well as on other variables.

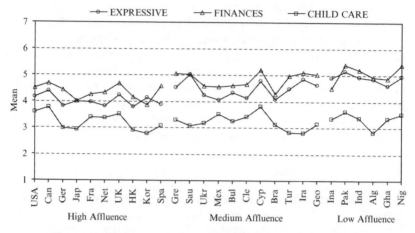

Figure 8.1. Mean scores on family roles of the father according to level of affluence.

Note to figure. Countries are ordered along the horizontal axis according to their decreasing score on Affluence (USA has the highest score on affluence and Nigeria the lowest). The separations reflect high, medium and low affluent societies. The vertical axis displays the seven-point Likert response scale.

Explanation of country symbols: Alg = Algeria; Bra = Brazil; Bul = Bulgaria; Can = Canada; Cle = Chile; Cyp = Cyprus; Fra = France; Geo = Georgia; Ger = Germany; Gha = Ghana; Gre = Greece; HK = Hong Kong; Ind = India; Ina = Indonesia; Ira = Iran; Jap = Japan; Kor = South Korea; Mex = Mexico; Net = The Netherlands; Nig = Nigeria; Pak = Pakistan; Sau = Saudi Arabia; Spa = Spain; Tur = Turkey; UK = United Kingdom; Ukr = Ukraine; USA = United States.

Framework; however the prediction that Catholic countries would show identical relationships to Orthodox and Muslim countries was not sustained.

The instrumental/material role of the parents was split into finances and childcare (see Figures 8.1 and 8.2). The financial role of the Father (manages finances, contributes financially, gives pocket money to children, supports career of children, does the shopping) was positively related to level of agriculture of countries and negatively related to level of education, affluence, and the socioeconomic index (in line with the prediction of the Ecocultural Framework). No correlation was found for

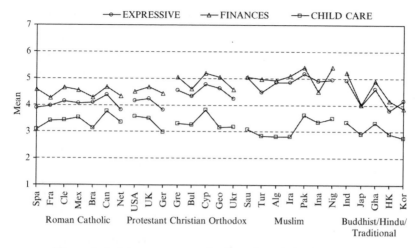

Figure 8.2. Mean scores on family roles of the father according to dominant religious denomination of countries.

Note to figure. Countries are ordered according to their main religion. For example, Roman Catholicism is the religious denomination with the largest number of adherents in Spain. Within each religious cluster, countries are ordered according to their decreasing percentage of adherents. For example, Spain is the country with relatively speaking the largest percentage of Roman Catholics, while the Netherlands is the country in which Roman Catholicism is the largest religion, but has the lowest percentage of Roman Catholics within the Catholic country cluster.

the mother's financial role (contrary to the prediction of the Ecocultural Framework). This finding might be related to the literature that describes the changing roles of women in high affluent societies such as the United States, Canada and northern Europe. In these societies the financial role of the mother has not diminished; rather, it is common to see that the mother works and manages financial aspects of the family. This possibility is supported by the observation that in 1990, 61 percent of nuclear families in affluent countries had both parents in the workforce (Bernardes, 1997; Gottfried, Gottfried, Bathurst, and Killian, 1999).

The relationship between father's financial role and high temperature was positive. However, the relationship between the childcare role of mother and highest temperature was negative; that is, in warmer

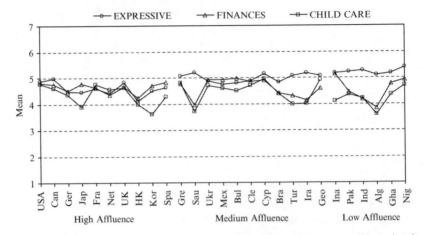

Figure 8.3. Mean scores on family roles of the mother according to level of affluence.

Note to figure. See Figure 8.1 for an explanation of the country names and their rank order in the clusters.

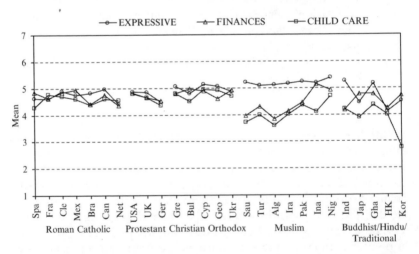

Figure 8.4. Mean scores on family roles of the mother according to dominant religious denomination of countries.

Note to figure. See Figures 8.1 and 8.2 for an explanation of the country names and their rank order in the clusters.

climates, mothers are *less* involved in child care than in colder climates, but they are *more* Expressive. This, at first glance, paradoxical finding might be explained by the presence of other family caretakers in warmer climates. These countries are primarily agricultural societies with extended families; that is, grandmothers, aunts, and older daughters commonly help care for the younger children. This finding is consistent with Whiting's (1981) findings that infant care is patterned by cold and warm temperatures in different regions.

The socioeconomic level of countries was not correlated with the childcare role (plays with children, helps children with homework, takes children to school, does housework) of father or mother. The hypothesis of the Ecocultural Framework regarding childcare was not supported. This also suggests a universal finding, namely that the affluence level of a country is not related to how much mothers or fathers perform childcare roles; they do it similarly everywhere.

Interestingly, this global pattern is not shown by all items constituting the childcare factor. Let us take a closer look at the cross-cultural patterning of the item dealing with housework. Inkeles (1998), one of the proponents of modernization theory, has questioned the degree to which increased economic development of countries leads to convergence in all realms of societal institutions. He writes that there are cultural forces that resist convergence, and family is one of these societal institutions. He explains that some widespread changes in family relationships did not occur in certain societies undergoing modernization, even when the objective conditions for such changes were met, and attributes this resistance to higher-order cultural values. One example he gives is husbands not helping wives in household chores, even in advanced industrial societies and after wives have entered employment. This hypothesis was tested by selecting the family role, "does the housework (cleans, cooks, washes)." The correlations between agriculture, education, affluence, and housework differed for mothers and fathers. Countries with higher level of affluence and education reported more housework by fathers than agricultural countries. However, there was no correlation between socioeconomic levels of countries and housework for mothers. That is, across different socioeconomic levels of countries women do approximately the same level of housework, but men from higher socioeconomic countries do more housework than men from lower socioeconomic countries. However, men from higher socioeconomic countries still do less housework than women. The same relationship was observed for 20-year-old males; they, too, tend to be more actively involved in housework in countries with higher levels of socio-economic development. Interestingly, the workload of the 20-year-old daughters follows the opposite trend; they tend to work less in the house in countries with higher levels of socioeconomic development. These latter relationships should not convey the impression that the workload is equally shared by the two genders.

The means of the three country clusters on socioeconomic level indicate that mothers perform a higher level of childcare roles than fathers in all countries. This is another potential universal suggesting that even in affluent societies, fathers do not assume an increasingly active role in childcare. These findings are further supported by the family portraits (see also Chapter 4), where it can also be observed that mothers in all countries continue to do most of the childcare and work in the home. Bonke (2004a, 2004b) reports that Danish men continue to do less housework than women in a country in which laws provide for gender equality in the workplace and also grant fathers the opportunity to take parental leave to care for the children. Also many of the men who took parental leave and were interviewed early in their marriages had returned to more traditional family roles by the time they were interviewed years later. Bonke is uncertain whether the small number of men involved in household roles and the "short duration of modernity" are a result of resistance to changes among men and/or women (i.e., individual reasons) or because the time is not yet ripe for such change (i.e., structural reasons). Our data do not permit us to clarify whether further increases in affluence will lead to a further increase in the housework workload of adult males.

Comparisons of means of the four religious clusters for the financial role indicated that the highest average scores were obtained by Muslim fathers, followed closely by Orthodox fathers, and the lowest were for Protestant and Catholic fathers. However, no differences were found between the religions for the mothers' financial role, or for fathers' childcare role. Also, the comparison of the different religions regarding the childcare role of mothers indicated that Orthodox mothers had the highest means, but Muslim mothers the *lowest* means. The pattern of relatively high scores of Muslim mothers on the Expressive role and low scores on the Financial roles, together with lowest childcare role of Muslim fathers, points to a pattern of stronger role differentiation among Muslim parents than with other religions.

Other family positions   A salient and universal finding was that scores on the Expressive role were higher than on the Instrumental role (see also Table 7.16). The Instrumental roles of the other family members, notably of the 10-year-old children, tend to be limited in our samples. Finances and childcare are almost universally more parental roles; the only exception to this pattern is the childcare role by the father, which is not strong in any sample studied.

It was previously noted that the expressive role became less salient with increased country level of affluence for both parents. This pattern was replicated for all other family positions, which makes the decreased expressive role of family members together with increased affluence one of the most salient findings of the current study. This is in line with the predictions of the Family Change Model and the Ecocultural Framework. Affluence has less impact on the instrumental role. However, these findings should not be interpreted as indicating that the expressive role of the family is no longer important in affluent societies. Quite to the contrary, the expressive role remains very important, even in high-affluent countries.

The instrumental role yielded a more differentiated pattern for the various positions. It may be noted that only the following instrumental roles of the 20- and 10-year-old sons and daughters were included in the questionnaire: playing with children, babysitting, taking the children to school, housework, shopping, helping the parents with their work, and contributing financially to the family. No significant differences were found across cultures in the instrumental role for the grandparents and uncles/aunts, which replicated our findings for the parents. However, the results were more clear-cut for the children. Their instrumental role diminished with increase in affluence (and decrease in agriculture). In more traditional, agricultural communities, the children continue to take on many household tasks, help in the childcare of younger siblings, and help the parents in the fields or the stores. Thus, the Ecocultural Framework hypotheses for instrumental roles of children, in contrast with mother and father and grandmother, were supported. In this context the similar prediction of the Family Change Model regarding the decreasing economic/utilitarian value of children for parents with increased affluence is also borne out. This is a key factor underlying a change from the Family Model of (total) Interdependence, where the economic/utilitarian value of the child is important, to the Family Model of Emotional Interdependence, where the child's economic/utilitarian value for the family becomes negligible. This is also in line with the recent findings of the Value of Children Study (Ataca, Kağıtçıbaşı, and Diri, 2005; Kağıtçıbaşı and Ataca, 2005) which showed a remarkable decrease in parents' perceptions of children's material/economic contribution to the family over a thirty-year period in Turkey (see Chapter 3).

The significant relationships between temperament and some roles tended to become nonsignificant in the regression analyses, indicating that the influence of temperature was indirect and mainly influenced by the socioeconomic index. Regression analyses in which the independent influence of the socioeconomic index, religion, and temperature were studied, showed zero or weak effects of the latter two variables; the most potent predictor was the socioeconomic index (and hence, also the percentage of the population working in agriculture, as well as relatedness).

THE PSYCHOLOGICAL SCALES AND FAMILY ROLES

This section first summarizes the cross-cultural differences and similarities in scores on the family network scales and the psychological scales then provides a description of the relationships of the family network and psychological scales with the family roles.

Cross-cultural differences in family network and psychological scales[6]

Family networks

As discussed in the first three Chapters, agricultural societies with high percentages of the population engaged in economic subsistence on small farms are characterized by extended families whose members usually live in close geographic proximity to each other. These individuals live either in the same household or in nearby towns, and they frequently visit kin while cooperating on farming activities and everyday family activities and chores. The hypothesis of the Ecocultural Framework that countries with low socioeconomic levels (i.e., a high percentage of the population engaged in agriculture, low scores on educational indices, and a low level of affluence) would live in closer geographical proximity with kin was confirmed (see Figure 8.5). However, the prediction that individuals in agricultural societies would visit kin more frequently than in affluent countries was not borne out.

This seemingly complex pattern was further examined by looking at the intercorrelations between the three indicators of family networks (proximity of residence, frequency of visits, and telephone calls) at country level; these were found to be positively related. So, there are more interactions with parents and kin (assuming that proximity of

---

[6] More details can be found in Tables 7.12, 7.14, 7.16, and 7.17.

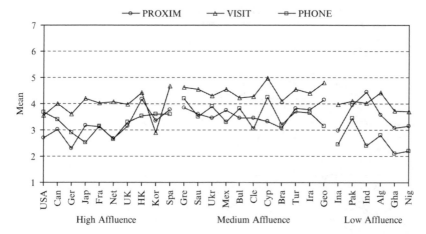

Figure 8.5. Mean scores on family network variables according to level of affluence.

Note to figure. See Figure 8.1 for an explanation of the country names and their rank order in the clusters.

residence is also an indirect measure of frequency of contact) in some countries than in others. A closer inspection of the data revealed that two variables showed opposite correlations with socioeconomic level; propinquity of residence is negatively related to socioeconomic level (adult children in more affluent countries tend to live further away from family and kin), while frequency of telephone contact and visits is positively related to socioeconomic level. However, inspection of Figure 8.5 (see also Table 7.16) indicates that the highest frequency of tele-phone calls and frequency of visits were in countries in the *medium*, and not high, affluence cluster. So, in higher socioeconomic level countries, children live further away from parents and kin. But in countries with medium socioeconomic level, children maintain more frequent contact (more visits and telephone calls) with parents and kin. Visits with family and kin in high socioeconomic countries is indeed at the *same* level as low socioeconomic countries, while telephone calls with kin are second to medium affluence countries but higher than low affluence countries. This may be an indication that in countries with increasing socioeco-nomic level, perhaps in urban areas, contacts with family and kin are even at a higher level than low affluence countries.

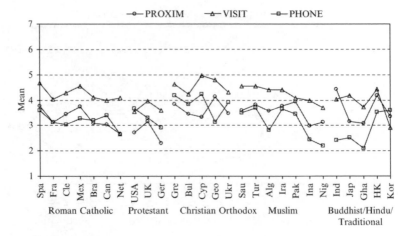

Figure 8.6. Mean scores on family network variables according to dominant religious denomination of countries.

Note to figure. See Figures 8.1 and 8.2 for an explanation of the country names and their rank order in the clusters.

Religion plays an interesting role in this frequency of contacts. Countries with more Protestants (which are also countries with a relatively high socioeconomic level) tend to show fewer contacts, while countries with more Christian Orthodox show the opposite pattern and have more contacts. The Orthodox countries showed the highest scores on telephone calls and visits. The data strongly suggest that family network variables are influenced by religious values (see Figure 8.6).

Our data do not suggest a strong relationship between Affluence and frequency of family contacts. Contacts with the extended family may differ slightly between the more affluent cultures of northern Europe and North America and the less affluent cultures; however, these differences are relative and point to the presence of active family network relationships between members of the nuclear family and kin also in Western societies. The literature on family networks in North America and northern Europe (Marks and McLanahan, 1993; Milardo, 1997; Olson et al., 1989; Segalen, 1986) supports these speculations. Uzoka (1979), in a review of studies in the United States and other countries, concluding that the nuclear family is embedded in a network of extended kin who provided social support, stated it most succinctly as, the "myth of the nuclear family . . . as structurally nuclear but functionally atomistic"

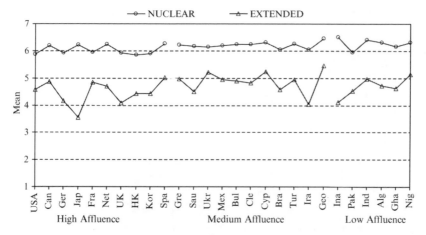

Figure 8.7. Mean scores on emotional bonds with nuclear and extended family according to level of affluence.

Note to figure. See Figure 8.1 for an explanation of the country names and their rank order in the clusters.

(p. 1096). Our findings indeed show close family relations across the countries.

Finally, the third variable tested, Temperature, was unrelated to the family network variables.

Emotional bonds

The means of the emotional bonds with the nuclear and extended family showed a clear pattern; the means across the Affluence levels are given in Figure 8.7. As could be expected, it was universally found that the bonds with the nuclear family were much stronger than with the extended family. Moreover, the bonds with the nuclear family showed means close to or above six (on a seven-point scale) in all countries. So, in all countries the emotional bonds with the nuclear family were very strong. We did not find support for an erosion of emotional ties to the nuclear family in Western societies.

The relationships of Emotional bonds with socioeconomic level, Religion, and Temperature tended to be absent or weak. It appears that the predictions of the Ecocultural Framework and the Model of Family Change were not strongly supported; both models correctly predicted the direction of the relationships, but only weak relationships were found.

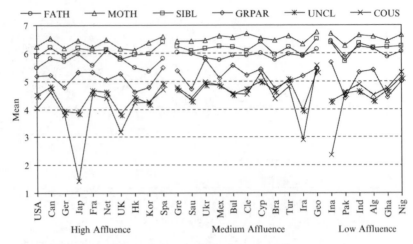

Figure 8.8. Mean scores on emotional bonds with specific family members according to level of affluence.

Note to figure. See Figure 8.1 for an explanation of the country names and their rank order in the clusters.

Figure 8.8 shows the degree of emotional closeness of mother, father, and siblings of the nuclear family and grandparents, uncles/aunts and cousins, in terms of means of each country for each of the Affluence clusters. The similar pattern, of closest emotional bonds with mother, second with siblings, and only third with father in all countries is remarkable. It might have been expected that the young adult respondents in this study might feel emotionally closer to the father than to their siblings. Similar results to those of the present study were found in a study with 16 countries (Georgas et al., 2001). This is a robust universal. It is important to emphasize again that these findings are the perceptions of young adults. The perceptions of the degree of emotional closeness with father, mother, and siblings might be different if parents or grandparents were asked to rate them. This is an interesting question for future research.

Self-construal

Analyses of the Self-construal Independence and Interdependence scales showed that these scales were problematic. When all respondents were analyzed together as a single sample, the two expected factors (one for each subscale) were found. However, when we repeated the analyses for each country separately, we could not find the expected two factors (subscales) in many countries. The underlying structure is apparently not very stable across countries, which reduced its suitability for cross-cultural comparisons. We split the instrument into two scales (based on the expected two factors) and treated the subscales as separate scales. The cross-cultural stability of these scales was fair for the Independence Scale and high for the Interdependence Scale, but we still found unexpected correlations with other measures. Contrary to the usual pattern, there was a high positive correlation between the two scales.

It was expected that low Affluence countries would have higher levels of Interdependent Self-construal, but it was unexpected that higher levels of *Independent* Self-construal would also be found in these low Affluence countries. This finding may be an artifact of the positive correlation between the two Self-construal scales. The relationships of both scales with socioeconomic level and Temperature were weakly negative. Comparisons of means of the four religious clusters indicated that Orthodox countries had the highest level of Interdependent Self-construal and that this was significantly different from Protestant countries. However, interpretation of this finding must be made with caution, again, because of the problematic nature of the scale.

We would speculate that it may be that "autonomy" items in the *Independent* Self-Construal subscale are endorsed by our young and educated samples of university students who also value "relatedness" items in the Interdependent subscale. This may parallel other findings in our study, such as the rejection by our respondents of family hierarchy, but endorsement of close family–kin relationships, as will be discussed later in this Chapter.

However, in order to avoid confusion in the remainder of the Chapter between Singelis' Self-construal concepts of Independent and Interdependent Self and Kağıtçıbaşı's concepts, analyses and interpretation of the findings will employ her terms, such as the "Autonomous-related self," based on findings related to family roles and values, rather than the Self-construal results. In any case, Kağıtçıbaşı (2005) rejects the use of the term "Independent Self-construal" because it connotes both "autonomous" and "separate," while "Interdependent" connotes both "related" and lacking "autonomy."

Personality traits

The multiple regression analysis indicated that higher socioeconomic level was slightly related to lower scores on all personality variables, although significance was reached only for those that may be termed the "positive personality variables" of Agreeableness and Conscientiousness. This finding is consistent with expectations based on the Ecocultural Framework. Our scales yielded high positive intercorrelations at country level, which were also observed by Williams, Satterwhite, and Saiz (1998). These findings cast doubt on the discriminant validity of the scales and could point to the influence of response styles, such as social desirability. The observation that the strongest relationships were found for positive personality scales is in line with the finding by van Hemert et al. (2002) that social desirability is negatively related to Affluence. In the largest study published to date, which involved 51 countries, McCrae et al. (2005) found positive correlations between Affluence on the one hand and Extraversion, Agreeableness, and Openness on the other hand. The present study did not find a significant relationship for either Conscientiousness or Openness. Although the correlations between personality variables and country-level characteristics are not consistent across studies and instruments (cf. Allik and McCrae, 2004; van de Vijver, 2006; van Hemert et al., 2002), the current results confirm findings in the literature that the relationships are not very strong. Religious denomination was not related to the five personality traits, nor was Temperature.

Family values

The multiple regression analysis found that the socioeconomic level of countries was highly related to both family values (i.e., hierarchical roles of mother and father, and family and kin relationships). Neither Temperature nor Religion added much to the prediction. It is interesting to note that the percentage of Protestants and Roman Catholics showed negative correlations with both family values, while the percentage of Muslims showed positive correlations; however, after controlling for the association between Religion and Affluence in the regression analysis, the relationships were no longer significant.

The relationships of Affluence in the regression analyses were in the direction as predicted by the Ecocultural Framework and the Model of Family Change. Low Affluence countries have higher means on both of these family values, hierarchical roles and relations with family/kin, than high Affluence countries. Neither Religion nor Temperature added any predictive power. The amount of variance explained by Affluence ranged from 45 percent to 65 percent, indicating that the relationships are very strong and that family values are heavily influenced by socioeconomic level; higher country socioeconomic level is associated with less hierarchy

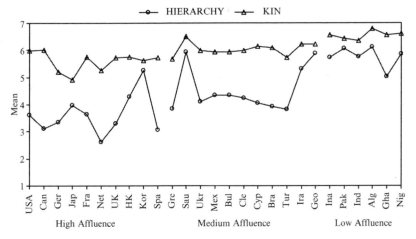

Figure 8.9. Mean scores on family values according to level of affluence.

Note to figure. See Figure 8.1 for an explanation of the country names and their rank order in the clusters.

and looser relationships in the family, as predicted by the Ecocultural Framework and Family Change Model.

The means of the countries on both family values per affluence level are given in Figure 8.9. The very high scores on the relationships with family and kin are the most striking findings in the figure. Our earlier observation about emotional bonds was replicated here; higher socioeconomic level seems to induce somewhat looser family relationships and ties but they are still very strong in all countries, even in the most affluent countries. These findings bear out the hypotheses deriving from the Ecocultural Framework and the Family Change Model.

Although hierarchical roles values in the family are strongly influenced by socioeconomic level, Religion also plays a role. The Islamic and Christian Orthodox countries showed the highest scores on hierarchical role values.

The differences in hierarchical family values suggest changes in the social power of the parents. Figure 8.10 presents the power of the father and the mother per level of affluence based on two family roles: "father/mother is the protector of the family" and "When there are disputes, father/mother makes the decision regarding the manner of solution." Two important conclusions can be drawn from the figure. The first involves the reduction in social power of both parents with higher levels

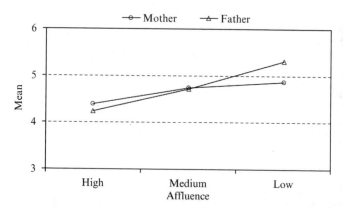

Figure 8.10. Mean scores on social power of parents according to level of affluence.

Note to figure. See Figure 8.1 for an explanation of the country names and their rank order in the clusters.

of Affluence. It is reasonable to assume that with an increasing level of Affluence, power is more shared between parents and children. The second involves the difference in social power between mother and father. Whereas in low affluence countries, father has *more* power than the mother, in high affluence countries father has less or equal power than the mother. So, the social power of the mother is less with high Affluence countries, but the power decrease of the father is stronger.

Another interesting finding is that the means of relationships with family and kin are higher than hierarchical roles in all countries. This finding, paradoxically, might imply that relationships with kin are more important than hierarchical relationships within their nuclear family. Let us look at this matter more carefully. This pattern of relationships is similar to studies in Greece (Georgas, 1999; Georgas et al., 2004a) in which young people rejected, as did students in this study, those values of the traditional extended family that are associated with the hierarchical roles of father and mother; that is, father's autocratic role and economic and social power, the strict obedience of children, and of the dutiful and acquiescent mother. On the other hand young people in the study in Greece agreed with some values of the traditional extended family, such as the importance of maintaining relations with relatives, respect for grandparents, offering help to parents, obligations toward the family. The rejection of the power of the father and strict hierarchical relations in the family, and also in society, might well provide an explanation for the higher means of family and relationships with kin than hierarchy in the 27 countries of this study. Thus, it does not appear to be that relationships with kin are more important than those with members of the nuclear family. An alternative hypothesis is that young people are rejecting the autocratic power of the father and the hierarchical role relationships in the family, as well as the unequal power relationships between males and females.

The prevalence of the emotionally interdependent family (Kağıtçıbaşı, 1990, 1996a; and Chapter 3) with the family culture of relatedness, but not the traditional totally interdependent family, is implicated by this finding. As predicted by the Family Change Model, this is particularly the case given the characteristics of individuals in our sample, who are young and educated. Even though we are not dealing with values in the model, but rather with family/kin relationships, the emotionally interdependent family culture appears to be the norm here. In this family context, autonomy emerges together with relatedness, resulting in the autonomous-related self. This situation explains why hierarchy (which suppresses autonomy) is rejected, but close emotional family bonds are accepted by the young people in our study.

Values

The results of the multivariate analyses of Schwartz's values were very similar to those of family values. Countries with high socioeconomic level tended to have lower levels of the collectivist values of Embeddedness, Hierarchy, and Harmony, as compared to countries with low socioeconomic levels (see Figure 8.11). The simple correlations between percentage of population engaged in agriculture and these three collectivist values were also in the same direction as predicted by the Ecocultural Framework. Religion was also related to these values. Muslim countries had the highest means, followed by Orthodox countries. Muslim countries had the highest means on Hierarchy and these means differed from the other three religions. The pattern with Harmony was similar to Embeddedness. In a regression analysis, socioeconomic level showed, again, a stronger association with these values than did Religion or Temperature. The same pattern, that is, collectivistic values being higher in low Affluence countries, was reported by Georgas et al. (2004c) employing the country-level data from Schwartz (1994). It is remarkable that country-level characteristics were unrelated to the individualist values of Intellectual Autonomy, Affective Autonomy, and Mastery. It is a recurrent theme in our findings that interpersonal aspects

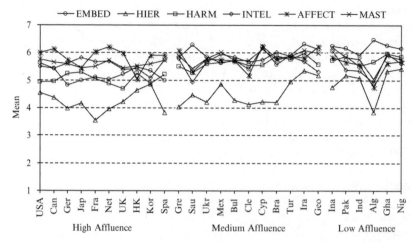

Figure 8.11. Mean scores on Schwartz's values according to level of affluence.

Note to figure. See Figure 8.1 for an explanation of the country names and their rank order in the clusters.

(e.g., collectivistic family and personal values) behave more in line with expectations than intrapersonal aspects (such as most personality scales).

Relationships with family roles

This section explores the relationships between the family roles and both the family network scales and the psychological scales.

Family roles and family networks

The relationships between family roles and family networks were relatively weak. The correlations of the expressive/emotional role with propinquity of residence and frequency of visits were positive, while the correlation with frequency of phone calls was negative. Most correlations between the instrumental roles and family networks were nonsignificant, except for the negative correlations with frequency of phone calls for the children (the strongly negative correlations for the younger children remained highly significant even after partialling out socioeconomic level). The predictions of the Ecocultural Framework were only partially supported here: the sign of the correlations was usually in line with expectations, but the correlations were weak and hardly ever reached statistical significance.

Family roles and emotional bonds

The findings regarding the relationships between emotional bonds and the expressive role were remarkable. Across all family positions, higher values of the Expressive role were associated with stronger emotional bonds with members of the nuclear family (the median correlation across the various positions was .45). The correlations for members of the extended family were weaker, though in the same direction (median correlation of .24).

The instrumental role was also positively related to emotional bonds. The distinction between nuclear family and kin was not found here; the median correlation (across all family positions) was .27 for the nuclear family and .33 for kin. However, these correlations vary according to gender and the family position. The correlations between the emotional bonds with the nuclear family and father's financial role and the instrumental roles of the 20-year-old males and females were in the .50s, while those of mother and grandmother were very low. Also, the correlations between the emotional bonds with extended family members of father and the 20-year-old females were in the .40s. It can be concluded that countries with stronger emotional bonds in the family tend to rate the expressive and instrumental roles higher across most family positions.

It is interesting to look into more detail at the relationships between emotional bonds and Affluence. Bonds with nuclear family members become somewhat weaker with higher Affluence; the same trend, though much weaker, was found for kin. The opposite trend (stronger ties with increasing affluence) was found for relationships with friends and spouses/dates (note that both categories refer to students' closest friends). So, the slightly decreasing emotional bonds within the nuclear family (and to a lesser extent, the extended family) may well be replaced or compensated by stronger ties with non-kin in more affluent countries.

It is not clear why emotional bonds with kin are less affected by Affluence than bonds with the nuclear family. One possible explanation may be related to the impact of the decreasing power differential within society and also within families in more affluent countries. Hofstede's ([1980]2001) work indicates that there is a salient negative relationship between power distance and affluence; more affluent countries tend to be more power-sharing. Analogously, with increasing affluence, family members tend to increase power-sharing and the traditional parental power in families is slightly affected. The extended family will be affected less than the nuclear family by this process, as there was less power-sharing with the extended family anyway.

Another potential explanation is that maintaining close contacts and communication with members of the extended family – grandparents and fathers-in-law, aunts and uncles, collateral kin on both sides – is necessary in order to maintain equilibrium between kin groups in agricultural societies and that the necessity to maintain an equilibrium between kin necessitates not showing preferences toward emotional closeness with specific kin. Close ties and cooperation are necessary in agricultural communities or in corporate activities of extended families. Much of the emotional closeness is ritualized in various family celebrations – weddings, baptisms, funerals. But there are differences between rituals and values of how one *should* display emotional closeness with members of the extended family on the one hand, and the *actual* degree of emotional closeness with them on the other. Although there might appear to be true emotional closeness and interaction with a favorite nephew or aunt, one must always be careful not to "rock the boat" by openly showing favoritism toward them, lest it result in resentment or even open conflicts between the different kin. Although common sense might suggest that the relationships between kin are close, harmonious, and happy in countries with functionally extended family systems, there are often resentments and jealousies below the surface within the extended family, for example, because of perceived economic favoritism of the grandparents to certain sons and daughters, or because one member of the family has been successful, or because the brother is the economic patriarch of the family and is perceived as showing favoritism to a sister, etc. (see Chapter 1 on history of family systems). Hence, showing emotional favoritism openly in the extended family may have *perilous* consequences for the desired harmonious relationships with kin. One learns to try to treat members of the extended family equally in social situations, so as not to lead to conflicts with kin.

Family roles and self-construal

The relationships between the independent and interdependent self-construals on the one hand and the family roles on the other hand were not very strong. For both self-construals, most correlations were positive, though not significant. This pattern of findings is difficult to explain. Different correlations might have been expected for independent and interdependent self-construals. The failure to find a meaningful patterning is probably a consequence of the poor psychometric properties of the instrument; more specifically, as mentioned earlier, we found that the scales were not equivalent across cultures and that, contrary to expectation, the correlation between the independent and interdependent self (at country level) was positive and strong. Derlega et al. (2002) also found poor psychometric properties of the instrument among students outside the United States.

Family roles and personality traits

When aggregated across both expressive/emotional and instrumental family roles and positions, each personality trait (Agreeableness, Conscientiousness, Emotional Stability, Extraversion, and Openness) showed a positive correlation. The relationships tended to be stronger for the expressive role. The median correlations were about .39 for the first four factors, while Openness showed a slightly lower correlation of .17. The median correlation for the instrumental role was slightly lower (.27), and again the correlation for Openness was somewhat lower (.14). The lack of differentiation in the correlations of the personality traits may be a consequence of their strong positive intercorrelations at the country level (see p. 137). It can be concluded that we found significant correlations between personality factors and both expressive/emotional and instrumental roles for various family positions. The relationships were always positive. The psychological implications of this finding are uncertain, as social desirability might have influenced the size and patterning of the cross-cultural differences. This impression is reinforced by McCrae et al.'s (2005) study in which five independent personality factors were found both at individual and country level.

Family roles and family values

The relationship of expressive/emotional family roles to hierarchical family values and to relationships with family and kin were the highest among all the psychological variables. The median correlation was .60 for hierarchy and .78 for relationships with family/kin. Countries with higher scores on the expressive roles tended to have higher scores on family hierarchy. This stronger family orientation is also found for the instrumental roles, although the median correlations are much smaller (.37 for hierarchy and .23 for relationships with family and kin).

Low affluence countries tend to have higher levels of expressive family roles and higher levels of hierarchical family and relationships with family and kin values as compared to high affluence countries. These are, of course, societies with functionally extended family systems. Combined with previous findings, the picture that emerges is one of families with slightly stronger ties and more intense contacts (both emotional and economic) and a more traditional family orientation in less affluent countries.

Family roles and Schwartz's values

The patterns of relationships between expressive/emotional and (though somewhat weaker) instrumental roles and Schwartz's Embeddedness, Hierarchy, and Harmony values were also almost identical with those of family values, which might be expected as a result of the high correlations between the Georgas and Schwartz values. Low affluence countries, with high percentages of the population engaged in farming, tend to have higher levels of expressive family roles and to have high levels of Embeddedness (family security, respect for tradition, honoring elders, social order, national security, reciprocation of favors), Hierarchy (authority, wealth, social power), and Harmony (world of beauty, unity with nature, protecting environment), as compared to high affluence countries. This pattern is in keeping with expectations derived from the Ecocultural Framework.

Schwartz's values were also highly correlated with both family values (i.e., hierarchical roles and relationships with family and kin). Indeed, it is interesting to note the pattern of means of the six Schwartz values. The country means of Schwartz's Hierarchy values are the lowest of the six scales, while the means of Embeddedness are the highest. This finding appears to be similar to the pattern of the lower means of the hierarchical roles and higher means of relationships with family and kin values, respectively. Embeddedness and emotional bonds are more relevant than hierarchy, both as personal values and as family values among educated young adults, as they tend to be both autonomous and related with family/kin. As we have noted previously, these are important characteristics of the emotionally interdependent family.

SYNTHESIS

What is different across countries?

In the introduction to this Chapter, we presented Kluckhohn and Murray's conceptualization of three levels of the study of relationships between culture and personality: universal traits, taxonomies of traits, and individual traits. We paraphrased this adage so as to be applicable to cultures. The second level, "Cultures are like some other cultures," implies a taxonomy or clustering of cultures according to ecological and sociocultural variables, and discovering differences in features of family roles and psychological variables. That is, groups of cultures share certain features of family roles and psychological variables, but also differ from other groups of cultures on these variables. This section discusses the cross-cultural differences in family roles and psychological variables.

Our theoretical frame of reference, based on the Ecocultural Framework and the Model of Family Change, predicted a specific pattern of cross-cultural differences. In line with these hypotheses, we found that (1) level of affluence based on economic indicators and energy level of a country, (2) percentage of the population engaged in agriculture, (3) level of access to education, and (4) level of relatedness, are powerful predictors of family variables and, indeed, of several psychological variables (see Georgas et al., 2004a). The same was also found for socioeconomic level, an index based on the combination of the first four indices. Furthermore, religious denominations (Protestantism, Catholicism, Islam, and Orthodox Christianity) are also related to a number of family and psychological variables, although to a lesser degree, and their impact is often confounded with Affluence. The level of highest temperature of a country appears to have very limited relationships to family variables, especially after controlling for Affluence.

Countries with high levels of socioeconomic development have lower means on family values (hierarchical roles and relationships with family and kin), and three of Schwartz's values (Embeddedness, Hierarchy, and Harmony), and both expressive/emotional and instrumental/material family roles.

Probably the most important psychological variable differentiating societies in this study is values associated with hierarchical roles of father and mother. These values of extended family types, characteristic of agricultural societies, which grant the father economic and social power within the family, which socialize children to be obedient, and which prescribe the role of the dutiful and acquiescent mother, are the most closely tied to the socioeconomic level of the countries. This robust pattern of relationships supports predictions stemming from the Ecocultural Framework. The Family Change Model also predicts that with changing lifestyles (urbanization and education) the shift from the totally Interdependent Family Model to the Emotionally Interdependent Family Model entails the development of the Autonomous–Related Self. This is because obedience-oriented parenting decreases and autonomy in childrearing increases (Kağıtçıbaşı, 1996a, 2005). Autonomy implies rejection of hierarchy, the common pattern we find in our educated university student samples. Since this is a cross-sectional study, and not a longitudinal one, the degree to which the differences in these hierarchical values across countries are related to social *change,* or to cultural *features* of the societies, is open to debate.

Another major difference between countries was the relationship between the expressive/emotional and the instrumental/material family roles. Much greater differences were found for the expressive/emotional than the instrumental roles. In addition, countries with highest monthly temperatures were related to higher emotional/expressive roles of parents, grandparents, and 20-year-old females, to the father's increased financial role, and also to the mother's increased childcare role.

Another important difference between countries was the relationship between socioeconomic level and the financial role of fathers and mothers. Fathers in low and medium affluence countries are more involved in financial roles than in high affluent countries. Fathers deal more with financial matters than mothers in low and medium affluence countries, but this difference was not found in high affluence countries. This finding is consistent with the literature, as discussed above, in regard to women in high affluence societies such as the United States, Canada, and northern Europe, in which the mother works and contributes financially to the expenses of the family.

An interesting constellation of relationships at the country-level was found between socioeconomic level, expressive/emotional family roles, hierarchical family role values, relationships with family and kin values, Schwartz's Embeddedness, Hierarchy, and Harmony values and the personality traits Agreeableness, Conscientiousness, and Harmony. These variables are all highly intercorrelated. High scores on the variables in this constellation are characteristic of agricultural societies with extended family systems in which interpersonal, collectivistic orientations and activities are highly valued, such as the family roles of keeping the family united, maintaining a pleasant family environment, conveying religion and traditions to children, preserving family relations, supporting grandparents, and protecting the family. This pattern also included the family values regarding the importance of maintaining relations with relatives, of respect for grandparents, of offering help to parents, of obligations toward the family; values related to Embeddedness, Hierarchy, and Harmony; and hierarchy and relationships with kin. The patterning of these relationships is broadly consistent with predictions based on the Ecocultural Framework.

These findings of relationships among socioeconomic level and variations in values and family roles in different societies is consistent with the family change literature for the past two centuries, as discussed in Chapters 1 and 3. Comte perceived the reduction of patriarchal authority in the stem family as result of the introduction of egalitarian relationships in France after the Revolution, thus setting the stage for the analysis by family sociology of the relationship between family change and social change. The subsequent theories of Le Play, Marx, Morgan, Spencer, Durkheim, and Parsons analyzed changes in such relationships as a result of industrialization, urbanization, and political changes, with the primary focus on the transformation of the extended type of family to the nuclear family.

Cultural anthropology was less concerned in the past with family change and social change, but focused more on the detailed description of the different types of family structure, family roles, and values in societies throughout the world, and how they related to ecological characteristics. Two of these anthropological studies served as a basis for the Ecocultural Framework. In the first, the relationship between differentiated social roles and social stratification in agricultural extended families was described by Nimkoff and Middleton (1960). In the second, the relationship between the socialization of children in agricultural societies for responsibility and obedience, and for achievement, self-reliance, and independence in hunting and gathering societies was described by Barry, Child, and Bacon (1959). The relationships in this study between family expressive and financial roles and the family and general values in societies with different socioeconomic levels, whether as a result of social and family change or as a characteristic of cultural features of these societies, support the finding of these early studies and the predictions based on the Ecocultural Framework.

It seems fair to conclude that countries with high socioeconomic levels have lower levels of expressive/emotional and financial family roles, hierarchical family values and relationships with family and kin values, Embeddedness and Hierarchy values, and Personality traits of Agreeableness and Conscientiousness, and live further away from kin; the opposite is found with countries with low socioeconomic levels and high levels of Relatedness together with high percentages of the population engaged in agriculture. These findings support a model, broadly related to the sociopolitical variables in the Ecocultural Framework, in which the increasing socioeconomic level of countries is assumed to affect social and family aspects much more than individual aspects of psychological functioning.

Religion, in addition to the socioeconomic level of countries, is a source of variation across cultures. The dominant religious dogma of countries was related to certain family and psychological variables, although to a lesser degree than socioeconomic variables. Christian Orthodox and Islamic countries tended to have the strongest family orientation. Some of these countries are in the lowest Affluence cluster, and some are in the cluster of countries with an intermediate level of Affluence. Muslim fathers and mothers had the highest scores on expressive/emotional roles, followed by the Orthodox, Protestant, and Catholic countries. Muslim fathers also had the highest financial roles, followed again by the same order of religions. Christian Orthodox mothers had the highest scores on the childcare role, but Muslim mothers had the lowest means. And Orthodox countries had the highest means on visits with and telephone calls to family and kin.

What is invariant across countries?

We return here to Kluckhohn and Murray's assertion that "Cultures are like all other cultures." That is, cultures most likely share universal traits, in this case, features of family roles and psychological variables.

The absence of differences in mean scores or relationships between variables across countries (universals) can be a significant *psychological* finding. However, making a judgment as to whether or not the absence of differences represents a psychological universal is often problematic. In this type of study, with many countries and many variables, the decision as to whether or not a finding is universal is facilitated by searching for patterns. The patterns may be that countries across the range of socioeconomic levels do not differ on psychological variables. Or, stated in another way, the same pattern of relationships is found across countries with different socioeconomic levels.

The most robust potential universals were found with emotional bonds. The mean scores of emotional bonds with the nuclear family did not differ across countries. Another important universal was the patterning of closeness of emotional bonds with members of the family across countries. The closest emotional bonds were with mother, followed by siblings, and third with father. Emotional bonds were stronger with the nuclear family than with the extended family in all countries. In addition, the relationship of emotional bonds with members of the nuclear family was only weakly related to the socioeconomic level of countries, and surprisingly, socioeconomic level was not related to emotional closeness with kin.

Potential universals were also found with family roles, in addition to the differences in family roles across countries described in the previous section. Expressive roles were invariably higher than instrumental roles for all family positions. Mothers scored on average higher on the expressive roles and the childcare roles while fathers scored higher on the financial role. In addition, the financial role of mothers was not related to the socioeconomic level of countries, nor was the childcare role of fathers. Mothers across all countries performed more housework (cleaning, cooking, washing) than fathers. Older children played a more important role in maintaining family functions; they had higher scores on both expressive and instrumental roles.

These findings suggest a cross-culturally robust set of universal basic structures and functions in the family. It is indeed tempting to conclude from this study that many basic family functions show remarkably small cross-cultural differences; however, this would be an oversimplification. The differences we found, (notably the differences in hierarchy and power differential in family) were meaningfully related to country characteristics, notably to socioeconomic level, and possibly to other cultural characteristics which we have not studied in this project.

An integration of the ethnographic descriptions of family and culture with the quantitative findings

The discussion up to now has been based primarily on the quantitative findings. The 30 country portraits present qualitative descriptions of each country, family, and family change from an indigenous perspective. The main themes across the family portraits described in Chapter 4 provide an additional perspective in the sense that the authors address the structure and function of the traditional family and specific changes in family structures and functions in recent history. This allows the possibility of interpreting some relationships found in the cross-sectional student data as reflecting *changes*, rather than qualifying them as only "differences" because the design of the project is not diachronic. Parsons' (1949, 1965) distinction between instrumental parental roles related to survival and expressive roles related to the maintenance of morale and cooperation, mentioned above, are also relevant to the country portraits. The former roles are more assigned to the father, in that it is his task to provide the link with society and the material goods by being the breadwinner and head of the family. The latter roles are more assigned to the mother, in that she was responsible for the emotional equilibrium within the family. However, the country portraits report changes in the traditional distribution of roles between father and mother. With the increasing economic independence of women working outside the house, the position, social power, and authority of the man and father as provider has come increasingly under pressure.

There appears to be a cluster of related changes that show coherence and that can all be linked to the shift in economic subsistence from agricultural to industrialization and urbanization that is largely due to sociopolitical factors. This shift has opened up new opportunities, particularly for separate and more distant nuclear family households at the cost of the traditional residence near the extended family, higher education, and employment for women outside the home. It is not clear to us whether the diminishing sacrosanct status of marriage should be seen as part of this cluster or as an independent phenomenon with different cultural roots (notably the widespread availability of birth control techniques, increasing one-parent families, the acceptance in some societies of homosexual relationships and legality of marriage, increasing divorce rates, etc.).

Where are less extensive changes to be noted in the country portraits? Here we can make two observations. First, the role of the mother as primary caretaker in the family appears to have been subject to change to a far lesser extent than that of the father as authority figure and breadwinner. Second, the breaking up of common residence for the extended family appears to have a limited effect on affective ties and practices of mutual support between parents and children (both at a young age when parents care for children, and at an old age when these roles are reversed).

In an influential definition of the family that we mentioned in Chapter 1, Murdock (1949, p. 2) distinguished structurally three types of family organization: the nuclear family, i.e., a married man and woman with their offspring, and two composite forms, the polygamous family based on marriage relationships, and the extended family based on blood relationships. In all instances the nuclear family serves as the basic structure to which Murdock attributed four functions:

In the nuclear family or its constituent relationships we thus see assembled four functions fundamental to human social life – the sexual, the economic, the reproductive and the educational. Without provision for the first and third, society would become extinct; for the second, life itself would cease; for the fourth, culture would come to an end . . . No society, in short, has succeeded in finding an adequate substitute for the nuclear family, to which it might transfer these functions. (1949, p. 10–11)

The claim of universality of the nuclear family has been criticized by many (e.g., Reiss, 1965). However, as Ingoldsby (1995) argued, the exceptions do not deny the general rule and for practical purposes Murdock's definition is useful and informative. In the broad perspective provided by the country portraits Murdock's four functions can be clearly identified and they can be used to help to organize the findings from the portraits.

With increasing socioeconomic development, the sexual function appears to become less exclusively tied to marriage and reproduction.

The advancement of contraceptive technology since the middle of the twentieth century has led to a separation of sexual expression from reproduction. Probably through this development the importance of sexuality in establishing and affirming affective bonds in couples, whether formally married or not, has become more evident.

In respect to the reproductive function, the most striking changes are in the number of children. As noted by many authors of the country portraits, this number has been strongly decreasing, sometimes already to a level well below that needed for population replacement. This happens particularly in high affluence societies, where parents should be able more easily to afford a larger family. Moreover, children born to unmarried women and increasing divorce rates mean that a substantial number of children, particularly in Western societies, do not grow up, at least for part of their childhood, in a nuclear family.

The country portraits show that the importance of the economic function of the family has been declining; most visibly in Western societies where extensive alternative societal support systems provide the economic security that one could in the past (and in many societies still can) find only with one's own family. The consequences of lessening economic constraints are most evident in the less central role of the father, as previously discussed. The portraits describe another factor that reinforces this trend, namely the increasing participation of women in the labor market. In agricultural societies, married women were also often economically productive, but they did not receive wages that would have made them economically more independent from their husbands.

In contrast to the economic function of the father, the educational function of the family, which is mainly the mother's role, has remained much the same as it was in the past. The socialization and caretaking function that is instrumental in the upbringing of new generations emerges from the 30 country portraits as the function of the family that has been most resistant to change, and the mother has remained the central figure in this process.

Evaluation of the theoretical frameworks

Particular findings confirmed or did not confirm the theoretical orientations of the Ecocultural Framework and the Family Change Model that guided this project. We will not repeat these findings here, but will attempt to provide an appraisal of the extent to which the main findings of the study provide support for the theoretical background in more general terms.

Ecocultural Framework

As outlined in Chapter 2, the ecological approach to the study of cultural variation was developed by the anthropologists Forde and Kroeber. It was subsequently elaborated to include psychological variables by Whiting (1974), Berry (1976) and others. In these studies, there was an explicit limitation to where close connections between habitat, culture, and behavior would be likely to be found. In subsistence-level societies, where direct ecological engagement is a daily reality, people (both collectively in societies and as individuals) had to confront physical constraints and to make use of opportunities as they interacted with their environment. They had few resources that could provide any alternative other than to adapt to these ecological realities. This project is the first to extend the use of the Ecocultural Framework beyond subsistence-level societies.

A number of predictions about relationships between ecocultural and family and psychological variables were proposed in Chapter 5, based on earlier findings with subsistence-level populations. However, in this project, we have sampled not only individuals who live within predominantly agricultural societies, but also those in industrial and post-industrial economic systems; these latter two are obviously not at the subsistence-level. With so many resources available to them, close connections between habitat, culture, and behavior are less likely to be found in such societies. Nevertheless, we made predictions about societies based on the percentage who are engaged in agriculture (even though many have begun to experience urbanization and industrialization), and to contrast their practices and behaviors with samples in more industrial or post-industrial societies. The three clusters based on the Affluence index (which is the inverse of the agriculture index) contain countries that have made the transition from agricultural to industrial societies at different times. The high Affluence cluster contains the Western nations of North America and northern Europe, societies that were the first to industrialize and urbanize over 200 years ago. This cluster also contains the East Asian countries, Japan, South Korea, and Hong Kong, which have more recently industrialized. The low Affluence cluster (that is, with a high percentage engaged in agriculture) is characterized by agricultural subsistence and a low level of industrialization. The middle level cluster contains countries which have begun to industrialize and urbanize during the past few decades and which are in an active stage of economic and cultural change that is associated with industrialization and urbanization.

On the basis of these ecological and sociopolitical influences, and the various ways of responding to them, we predicted and found a number of links across societies between ecological, sociopolitical, cultural, social, and behavioral phenomena. In line with the Ecocultural Framework, we found that affluence and the percentage engaged in agriculture are related to a number of family variables. A more general index of socioeconomic status (combining some ecological and sociopolitical variables) was more frequently and more consistently related to cultural, family, and psychological variables.

To highlight a few of these relationships with some of the family variables, we found that the percentage of the population engaged in agriculture was predictive of proximity of residence; the relationship with Affluence was even stronger. Frequency of phone calls was negatively related with both the percentage in Agriculture and with Affluence. Countries with low socioeconomic development (i.e., countries with high percentages of the population engaged in agriculture, low levels of industrialization, services and access to education) had higher scores on expressive/emotional roles, and in countries with higher monthly temperatures higher expressive roles were found for both parents. Contrary to prediction, however, was the finding of a near universal for childcare roles: there is no variation in the higher caregiving provided by mothers across cultures, nor in the lesser care-giving provided by fathers. In keeping with expectations, the expressive role became less salient with increased country level Affluence for both parents and for all other family positions; this decrease in expressive role of family members with increased Affluence provides support for the Ecocultural Framework. However, with respect to the instrumental role, there was little variation across cultures for mother, father, and grandmother, suggesting another universal. Despite this lack of variation for parents, the instrumental role activities of children diminished with increase in Affluence (and decreased in relation to percentage in Agriculture). That is, in more traditional, agricultural communities, the children continue to take on many household tasks, caring for younger siblings, and helping the parents in family economic activities.

With respect to some of the psychological variables, we found that, as expected, higher socioeconomic level was related to lower placement on the two personality variables of Agreeableness and Conscientiousness. With respect to values, we found that the socioeconomic level of countries was related to the two family values of hierarchical roles of mother and father, and family and kin relationships. Low affluence countries had higher means on both of these family values than high affluence countries. That is, there are some personality differences, and less hierarchy and looser relationships in the family as societies move away from agriculture toward industrialization and greater economic wealth. Religion is also an important predictor: Islamic and Christian Orthodox countries showed the highest scores on hierarchical role values.

While many of these expectations were borne out, there was also a failure to confirm some hypotheses derived from the Ecocultural Framework. There were a number of reasons for this. First, predictions about differences relating to ecocultural variables may be undermined by the existence of *universals* in cultural and behavioral phenomena. In many cases, we observed such invariance, and have suggested that they were examples of universal family structures and functions. Second, there are some methodological issues; some relationships were weaker than expected and did not reach significance, possibly because we had a sample size of only 27 countries. Moreover, the student samples, although convenient, might not have been the best to test the hypotheses. It could well be that a replication with other samples (such as hunting and gathering and agricultural peoples as well as university students), and in more countries, would provide additional evidence for the validity of the theoretical framework. And third, the correlational patterns for roles were different; we found stronger correlations for the expressive role than for the instrumental role. Our theoretical framework does not specify why we should expect this difference.

Family Change Model

The predictions of the Family Change Model (Kağıtçıbaşı, 1990, 1996a; and Chapter 3) regarding the relations between contextual variables and family variables were parallel to those of the Ecocultural Framework. This is because the family change model also fits with the Ecocultural Framework and situates the family and self within the ecocultural context. In particular, as predicted by the Family Change Model, the most significant indicator of living conditions, Affluence, was found to have a marked, negative effect on emotional/expressive and material/instrumental) family roles. In contrast, percentage of population in agriculture, the main indicator of rural living conditions, was positively related to both emotional and material family roles. More specifically, with increasing affluence, people's proximity to, and bonds with family and kin, decreases; emotional family roles weaken; instrumental family roles also weaken, especially that of the child, with decreasing material/utilitarian value of the child for the family; there is less hierarchy and less intense kin relationships; and finally, there is less personal embeddedness. On the other hand, emotional closeness to the nuclear family is only weakly related to the level of affluence. The corresponding relations with percentage in agriculture are in the opposite (and predicted) direction. Educational access at the country level, as an important indicator of socioeconomic status and thus a component of living conditions, has the same predicted effects as affluence. The combined economic and educational variables converge to the expanded notion of socioeconomic index, as used in this project.

Thus to a large extent the predictions of the Family Change Model are borne out by our results. Delving further into the predictions and implications of the model, we find that, to start with, the two distinct family dimensions, the emotional/expressive and the material/instrumental, emerged from the factor analyses of the family roles. This basic finding supports the Family Change Model, which construes these dimensions as two types of family interdependencies. The fact that both types of interdependencies (roles) decrease with affluence is in line with the predictions of the model; however, there are also differences among the three clusters based on a combination of affluence and culture of relatedness. While the high affluence/low relatedness cluster has the lowest levels of both emotional and instrumental/material roles, the latter role is highest in the low affluence/high relatedness cluster, again providing support to the Family Change Model. Though lowest in the high affluence/low relatedness cluster, emotional family roles are high in all clusters. This is in line with the recent Value of Children Study findings, already referred to (Ataca and Kağıtçıbaşı, 2005; Kağıtçıbaşı and Ataca, 2005), which showed that the economic value of children decreased with socioeconomic development over a 30-year period but that the psychological value of the child remained high across different socioeconomic groups in Turkey.

Another important finding of the present study, the sharp decreases in family hierarchy values with higher socioeconomic levels while relationships with family/kin remain high, point to the apparent prevalence of the Family Model of Emotional Interdependence, as predicted by the model. This pattern involves autonomy of the individuals together with relatedness, thus the "autonomous-related self" (Kağıtçıbaşı, 1996b, 2005) is particularly salient for our young and educated sample.

STUDY LIMITATIONS

The current study has various limitations. We list the most important. One limitation is due to the sampling of participants, that is, university students. Groups of university students (mainly psychology students) are not representative of their age cohorts, let alone of the larger population. Our findings might have been different if representative samples had been included. For example, the values regarding family roles may represent the perceptions of this younger generation and may not be the same as those of older respondents. On the other hand, university students are likely to represent the cutting edge of changes in the family. Imminent family changes will probably be expressed earlier by university students, as they represent the younger generation of the society, the most highly educated of their cohort group, and the most likely to adopt changes.

A second limitation is that the data reflect attitudes or perceptions of the respondents, and may not represent actual behaviors. It would be a major challenge for our findings if the relationship between attitudes and behaviors were to be very different across the countries of investigation. We do not have any evidence for systematic cross-cultural differences in this relationship. The attitudes as expressed by the student samples may also be susceptible to distortion by response styles, such as social desirability and acquiescence. This limitation is not unique to the current study but is characteristic of studies based on self-reports. It is known that response styles show systematic differences across cultures. More affluent countries tend to show less social desirability and acquiescence (van Hemert, van de Vijver, Poortinga, and Georgas, 2002; van Herk, Poortinga, and Verhallen, 2004). On the other hand, these studies also showed that more educated persons tended to show less influence of response styles. So, it is probably fair to conclude that our student samples were not very susceptible to response styles. However, we do not have quantitative evidence to establish the size of the effects.

Finally, we recognize that because short forms of some psychological variables have been employed with the Self-construal scales (Singelis, 1994; Singelis et al., 1995), Personality Traits (Williams et al., 1998) and Values (Schwartz, 1994b), the concepts these instruments are assumed to measure may not be entirely represented. It is not likely in our view that the cross-cultural differences would have been very dissimilar to what we found, if the full instruments had been administered. However, longer instruments would have provided a more detailed view and would have allowed more precise conclusions about the relationships between these constructs and family-related variables.

CONCLUSIONS

The goals of the family project were to investigate how families in countries in different geographical areas around the world are similar and how they are different in their family networks, family roles, and psychological variables. Differences in families across cultures may be related to the extent to which families are changing throughout the world as a result of changes in social, technological, media, information technology, increase in education, reduction of agriculture as the primary form of economic subsistence, and other cultural changes. Differences may also reflect family patterns embedded in the context of cultures throughout the world, as a result of the specific historical development, social structure, language, customs, symbols, and the plethora of cultural features characteristic of societies.

On the other hand, as societies share certain cultural features, families throughout the world might share some common features. Countries that are contiguous to each other share a variety of cultural features. Murdock (1969) clustered countries into geographical zones. Indeed, people intuitively cluster countries into geographical zones and assume similar cultural characteristics, such as "European families," "African families" or "Asian families." The countries in our study were separated into three clusters, based on socioeconomic level, and into five religious denominations. Analyzing the results in terms of cultural zones, that is, similar cultural features of different countries, is more powerful than treating each country as an independent unit. It enables the identification of similar patterns of findings in countries with similar cultural features.

Thus, the features of the cultural clusters, affluence and religion, cut across geographical zones. For example, the high affluence cluster contains countries in North America and Europe, but also East Asia. However, culture is an extremely complex concept which includes all features of patterned human activity. The ecological and sociopolitical measures of culture we employed in our study are only a few of the myriad number of potential measures of culture. On the other hand, these measures were chosen because of their inclusion in the two theories, and because of their demonstrated relationships to family features in many studies; more so with socioeconomic measures than with religion and temperature.

Another goal was to attempt to infer the direction of future changes. Can the changes in family be explained by modernization theory and globalization theory, in which economic and other structural changes in societies throughout the world are assumed to lead inevitably to the same morphological changes as in the families of Western societies?

What are the main findings?

What is different and what is similar or universal in families across cultures? The main conclusion is a combination of cross-cultural differences and similarities in family characteristics across cultures.

What is different in families across countries?

The Ecological, Sociopolitical, and Relatedness indices   The Socio-economic index was the most powerful source of variation of the family and psychological variables. It was composed of Affluence, Percentage of the population engaged in Agriculture, Education, and Relatedness. The Relatedness index was based on the Affluence level of the country, so that its relationship with the variables is very highly correlated with the Socioeconomic index (see Table 7.11). Religious denominations of countries was also a significant source of variation, although less so than the Socioeconomic Index. Highest Monthly Temperature was minimally related to only a few variables.

Let us begin with those family and psychological variables in which differences were related to the Socioeconomic index of the countries.

The highest relationship with socioeconomic level of countries in the project was with hierarchical values of mother and father. That is, low socioeconomic, primarily agricultural countries have higher hierarchical family values as compared to high socioeconomic countries. Similar relationships in the same direction, but somewhat lower, were found with relationships with family and kin values, Schwartz's values Embeddedness, Hierarchy, and Harmony, the expressive/emotional roles, and some instrumental/expressive roles. However, fathers are more involved in financial roles in low and medium socioeconomic countries than in high affluence countries. Also, fathers have higher financial roles in low and medium affluence countries than mothers, while no differences between mothers and fathers were found in high affluence countries. The relationships with personality traits Agreeable-ness and Conscientiousness were also in the same direction, more so in low affluence countries, but very low. Finally, in regard to family net-works, kin and family live further apart in high affluence countries, but in medium affluence countries family and kin visit and telephone more frequently than in both high and low affluence countries.

In addition, the variables socioeconomic level, expressive/emotional family roles, hierarchical family role values, relationships with family and kin values, Schwartz's Embeddedness, Hierarchy, and Harmony values and the personality traits Agreeableness, Conscientiousness, and Har-mony were all highly intercorrelated.

The religious denominations across countries   The dominant reli-gious denominations of countries – Catholic, Protestant, Christian Orthodox and Islam – were related to a lesser degree than was the Socioeconomic Index to some variables. Comparisons of means of the four religious clusters indicated that Muslim fathers and mothers had the highest scores on expressive/emotional roles, followed by the Orthodox, Protestant, and Catholic countries. Muslim fathers had the highest means on financial roles, with the same order of religions. Christian Orthodox mothers had the highest means on childcare roles, and Muslim mothers the lowest. Orthodox countries had the highest means on visits with and telephone calls to family and kin.

Temperature   Fathers in countries with high monthly temperatures had higher scores on the financial role than in countries with low monthly temperatures. Mothers in warmer climates were less involved in the childcare role than in colder climates. Mothers in warmer climates have higher expressive roles. These relationships were relatively weak.

What is similar or universal in families across countries?

Which family and psychological variables do not differ across countries? Can we describe them as universal phenomena common to human beings, regardless of the very powerful variable of socioeconomic differences between countries?

Emotional bonds were the most robust universal. Emotional bonds were stronger with the nuclear family than with the extended family in all countries. Although the relationship of emotional bonds with members of the nuclear family was related to the socioeconomic level of countries, this correlation was weak. Surprisingly, however, socioeconomic level was not related to emotional closeness with kin. A universal was the patterning of closeness of emotional bonds with members of the family across countries, in which the closest emotional bonds were with mother, next with siblings, and last with father.

Although expressive and instrumental roles were related to the socioeconomic level of countries, potential universals were also found. Expressive roles were higher than instrumental roles for all family positions across countries, whatever the socioeconomic level of the country. Mothers scored higher than fathers on expressive roles and childcare roles across countries, again whatever the socioeconomic level, and fathers similarly scored higher than mothers on the finance role, except in high affluence countries. In addition, the financial role of mothers was not related to the socioeconomic level of countries, nor was the childcare role of fathers. Mothers across all countries performed more housework (cleaning, cooking, washing) than fathers. Older children played a more important role than younger children in maintaining family functions; they had higher scores on both expressive and instrumental roles.

Family change or just differences between cultures?

A third theme of this Chapter was the issue of family changes in societies throughout the world. The first issue is whether the design of the project, which is not diachronic, can allow us to claim that we have actually measured changes in families across culture. We have been very careful on this issue, since the differences between countries that we found may reflect differences in families across cultures and not necessarily family change. On the other hand, the family portraits of each country provide support for changes in family roles and values in many countries in this study. A second issue is whether family changes will lead to convergence of family features according to modernization and globalization theories.

Let us begin with the assumption that some of the findings may be indicative of family change across cultures. According to the Ecocultural Framework, both human behavior and the family would adapt to changes in the ecocultural context. The Family Change Model would also view changes in the family and human behavior as a result of economic development. If so, what might be the dynamics of changes in family networks, family roles, and psychological variables with socioeconomic changes from societies with an economy of agricultural subsistence to more complex industrial or post-industrial societies?

Based on the results of the family networks, it would appear that people move away from the family home, presumably to get a better education and also to find work in urban areas. But it would appear that contact with the family and kin are maintained to a large degree, even in high affluence countries.

The family roles expressive/emotional roles and the instrumental/expressive roles appear to be common across all countries. However, high and low affluence cultures differ in terms of these roles. Whether these differences are related to the traditional family roles of cultures throughout the world, or to the degree to which they change with increasing affluence is more difficult to answer. It would appear that in higher affluence countries, fathers and mothers share the financial roles more than in low and medium socioeconomic countries, in which fathers are more concerned with financial matters than mothers. It also appears that in high affluence societies, mothers have, perhaps, the same or more power in the family than fathers, while the opposite is observed in medium and low affluence societies. On the other hand, there are certain universals across cultures, whatever the socioeconomic level of the countries. Mothers have higher expressive roles and childcare roles than fathers across countries. Also, the childcare role of fathers is at the same level across countries, mothers do more housework than fathers, and fathers do about the same level of housework across countries. And older children have higher scores on both expressive and instrumental roles than younger children.

What about the psychological variables? Perhaps the strongest evidence from this study that supports the hypothesis of family change is the hierarchical role family values of mother and father. They are strongly related to socioeconomic level, but a perusal of the countries at the medium socioeconomic level, (such as Greece, Bulgaria, and others) that were recently agricultural cultures, indicates the strong rejection of these hierarchical roles values related primarily to the autocratic power of the father in agricultural extended families. Schwartz's Embeddedness, Hierarchy, and Harmony values show the same profile. That is, the dynamics appear to be that with increasing societal affluence, better educational facilities and opportunity for work are created for both males and females. Increased knowledge and the opportunity to earn money apart from the family lead young people to reject the authoritarian role of the father. On the other hand, the rather weak relationship of level of country Affluence with personality traits Agreeableness and Conscientiousness may or may not be a good index of family change. Finally, emotional bonds with members of the nuclear family and the extended family are universal across countries with different levels of affluence. This is an indication that although affluence may bring changes in roles, to a certain degree, and definitely to values, emotional closeness with the family does not change. Shifts toward higher autonomy and lower hierarchy in families with socioeconomic development appear to be compatible with continuing close family relations.

Let us look in more detail at the elements in the above scenario. What are the psychological consequences of the decrease of the traditional extended family systems and the increase of nuclear family systems? Do they mean the withering away of kin relations and the autonomy of the nuclear family as Parsons theorized? The issue is related to the definition of the nuclear family, as discussed in Chapter 1. That is, the nuclear family is not necessarily the same as the household, which is the notion employed in demographic studies. Many demographic studies do not refer to kin relationships or to family networks. In addition, demographic data often confound the nuclear and extended family members. These are some reasons why the methodology of the present study did not include structural definitions of the family, that is, whether the respondents declared they lived within a nuclear or an extended family, based on demographic data on types of families from each country. We employed Murdock's concept of the nuclear family as one nucleus within the constellation of nuclear families that make up an extended family. That is, a nuclear family is one of a number of nuclei of a constellation of two parallel nuclei of the grandparents on each side of the family, together with the nuclei of granduncles and aunts, uncles and aunts, sisters and brothers, cousins, etc.

One of the findings in this study, in the quantitative data set as well as the qualitative country portraits and supported by the literature, is that family networks do not differ much between high affluence and low affluence countries, except for living further apart. Studies of living arrangements during different historical periods indicate that families often lived and slept together in one room. Separating houses into rooms, and children sleeping separately from parents, are relatively recent in many cultures, as is each sibling having its own room. In many societies throughout the world, with increased affluence, newly married couples purchase or rent a separate house. This is often accomplished through aid from their parents, who build, buy, or rent a separate house for them. From a psychological viewpoint, individuality is a basic psychological phenomenon that does not exist only in Western societies. The degree to which these agricultural societies control the social expression of individuality, whether through values, laws, or traditions, has been documented by cultural anthropology and sociology. However, certain psychological needs of the individual may be universal and transcend the institutions, values, and traditions of societies. One of these is the need for psychological privacy, even in extended family systems. From a psychological point of view, we would speculate that a separate household might represent the need for privacy of the young couple and some degree of psychological separation from the parents, particularly of the wife of the husband from the mother-in-law and the father in-law.

The issue for us was less a matter of where the various family members live or of the family structure, but rather the degree of psychological closeness, interaction, communication, and support. Does living apart from one's parents imply that the psychological bonds with family members are withering? The findings indicated that emotional closeness with members of the nuclear family was only marginally related to socioeconomic level, and the average emotional closeness across the three country clusters based on affluence did not differ much across countries. Although emotional closeness was distinctly lower for extended family members, these score levels did not differ much in countries with different socioeconomic levels throughout the world, for reasons discussed above. On the other hand, the picture in the literature that in societies with clans and closely bound extended family systems, all the members of extended families and kin live harmoniously and are cooperative and happy does not appear to be entirely accurate. Cooperation in extended family systems, particularly in the area of economic subsistence, land rights and use, inheritance and other matters, requires a delicate equilibrium between families so as to avoid disputes that can lead to open conflicts and be detrimental to the entire clan or community.

The relationships between family members and kin are regulated through societal values, particularly in agricultural communities, which dictate how one *should* behave toward family and kin. The findings suggest that these family values are related to the socioeconomic level of the country and that they are still in effect in primarily agricultural countries, but less so in more affluent countries. However, the means of a number of high affluence societies on the family and kin values, specifically Canada, the United States, the United Kingdom, France and Germany, are in fact lower than the average of the middle affluence societies. An explanation might be that these are multicultural societies with large numbers of immigrant families. That is, the country scores on these family values are based on individuals from different ethnic backgrounds within these countries and there is considerable intracultural variability.

It appears that values related to hierarchical relationships within the family, and hierarchical values in general, are the most important indicators of family change. The young respondents in our study increasingly reject the authoritarian model of the father who makes all the decisions in the family and the role of the submissive and conforming mother and children, a tendency also reported in the family portraits. It is significant that this pattern was prevalent in the countries in the middle range of affluence level, suggesting changes in functional aspects of the family. On the other hand, family values related to maintaining relationships with family members and kin have changed much less than hierarchical roles within the nuclear family. As discussed above, the emerging autonomy in changing families in more developed, urban-educated sectors of the less affluent countries is an explanatory factor here. Kağıtçıbaşı's Family Change Model (1996a, 2005, Chapter 3) indeed proposes that autonomy emerges (thus less acceptance of hierarchy) while relatedness continues to be important in the Family Model of Emotional Interdependence.

We would further speculate that this may be related to the demographic findings discussed in Chapter 1: that although young couples increasingly establish separate households from the parents, these households tend to be geographically close to the parental household. In these households, grandparents often offer financial aid, help in household tasks, and care for the children while the mother works.

One possibility is that the different level of expressive/emotional roles as a function of socioeconomic levels across countries is less an indication of family change and more an indication of traditional cultural differences between agricultural societies with more extended families and affluent societies with more nuclear family systems. For example, although emotional closeness with members of the nuclear family differs very little across countries, higher level of expressive/emotional roles is related to closer emotional bonds with members of the nuclear family across countries. There were similar findings with instrumental roles, except for childcare, in which mothers in all societies are more involved than fathers, as well as in family tasks such as cleaning, washing, and cooking. That is, the design of our study makes it difficult to differentiate the degree to which some of these differences in family roles between countries reflect family change or deeply rooted cultural values.

The role of the father as authority figure and breadwinner has changed more than that of the mother as primary caretaker. In addition, residence far from kin does not lead to psychological isolation from kin, or to significant lessening of communication by telephone.

Another indicator of family change is the increased power of the mother in the family. The many changes in traditional family roles reported in the country portraits together with the findings in the study based on the student samples, suggest that the mother's engagement in the workforce, her higher level of education and her economic contribution to the nuclear family have resulted in a lessening of authority of the father. The mother has become at least as or more powerful than the father in affluent societies. Much of the family power may have shifted down in affluent countries and is now shared among parents and children, who enjoy more autonomy than in traditional family contexts.

One conclusion stemming from this study is that while families are changing in different cultures throughout the world, based on the findings with the psychological variables, close emotional relationships remain with members of the nuclear family and communication with kin is still frequent, even in affluent Western societies. Individual autonomy is attained but not at the cost of relatedness with close others, as indeed proposed by the Family Change Model. We cannot generalize to the different types of one-parent families, simply because this was not one of the goals of the project.

The final question was whether the types of families in low socioeconomic developing societies will converge with the types of nuclear and one-parent families in high affluence Western societies as predicted by modernization theory and globalization theory.

Modernization and globalization theories have come under increasing criticism from social and behavioral science, including economists. Harrison (2000) states that the assumption of economists that the economic policies and mathematical economic models developed in Western countries will have the same result in all cultures, has had limited success in underdeveloped countries. Inkeles (1998), a leading proponent of modernization theory, argued that some family patterns are constant across countries and over time, which suggests that some human needs are resistant to any change of social organization. Huntington (1996) has argued that cultural values, including religion, have replaced ideological distinctions after the end of the cold war. Inglehart and Baker (2000) also agreed with Huntington's theory that although modernization theory could explain some aspects of cultural change, religion also explained the influence of long-established cultural zones. Georgas et al. (2004c) found that religion and affluence were related to psychological variables in separate and in sometimes contrasting ways. Some cultural anthropologists (Yanagisako, 1979) argue that modernization theory provides an "excessively broad hypothesis" for the explanation of the decline of kinship structures.

That changes in the economy of countries, from subsistence level to industrial, service, and post-industrial economies, result in social changes and in changes in the family is not a matter of contention. The issue is whether these changes, driven by an economic engine, result in convergence of the same types of family structure and function as found in Western societies. Intercultural contacts or socioeconomic development do not necessarily or inevitably lead to the homogenization of world cultures or of individual behavior. This because the process of acculturation, which follows from such sociopolitical influences, takes many forms, including a rejection of change, and the creation of new cultural ways of living (Sam and Berry, 2006). For example, in the past, acculturation of immigrants to a multicultural society was assumed to take the form of assimilation of the individuals to the culture of the host society. However, acculturation can take various forms (Berry, 2003) rather than just assimilation, including rejection of the new influence or integration of the various cultural elements. The adaptation of family structure and function to changes in different societies can also take these other forms, and not just become more like the dominant model assumed by modernization theory. Also, the universals found in this study, such as emotional bonds with the family and kin, the patterning of emotional bonds with members of the nuclear family, the different gender differences in childcare and housework, are certainly not a result of globalization, but reflect basic similarities in human behavior across cultures.

The findings in this study challenge, to a large degree, assumptions of modernization and globalization theories. We have found that hierarchy is rejected by young people and that hierarchy is negatively associated with socioeconomic development (therefore significant family change), but there is nevertheless valuing of close family ties. Therefore, we believe that the hypothesis that families in all societies will eventually converge to the separate-independent nucleated family of Parsons' and others' models of Western societies is not correct.

In closing, we would speculate that while families will change in all societies, many findings in our study, particularly the psychological universals, support the position that although changes will occur with increasing socioeconomic development of countries, many cultural patterns in family life will continue to exist.

Part II

9   The Algerian family: change and solidarity

Mustafa M. Achoui

A HISTORICAL OUTLINE OF ALGERIA

The history of Algeria goes back to pre-classical times. The *Amazighan* (Berbers) are the earliest inhabitants identified historically in Algeria. Today, the majority of Algerians are Arabic-speaking with about one-fifth of Algeria's population still speaking the different dialects of *Tamazight* (Berber) especially in Kabiliya, Aures (*Shawiya*), Ghardaya (*Mouzabi*) and Ahhagar (*Touareg*). The majority of Algerians, however, are "Arabized Berbers" and the distinction between Arabs and Berbers in Algeria is linguistic rather than ethnic (Richard, 1980).

Since the introduction of Islam to Algeria in the seventh century, several dynasties have been established. *Almohads*, for example, governed and unified Algeria with the whole of North Africa and Spain during the twelfth and the thirteenth centuries. After the decline of the Almohad dynasty, three states emerged in North Africa, one in today's Algeria, which existed until the early sixteenth century. The Ottoman administration of Algeria stretched from 1518 until the colonization of Algeria by the French army in 1830. The great revolution for independence lasted seven years, from 1954 to 1962.

The population of Algeria is 33 million inhabitants. The birth rate has increased from 1.46 percent in 1999 to 1.69 percent in 2005. Algiers is the capital of the country, with four million inhabitants (Office Nationale des Statistiques, 2005).

THE ECOLOGICAL FEATURES

Algeria is the largest country in Africa after Sudan, with a surface of 2381,741 km^2 and a long Mediterranean coast of 1,200 km. Almost nine-tenths of its total area is desert. The highest mountain in the extreme south is the *Ahaggar* (Hoggar) with a peak of about 3000 m. Two mountain chains dominate the northern part of the country, crossing from east to west. Vast plains between the two chains permit the

243

cultivation of different crops. The climate of northern Algeria is of the Mediterranean type.

ORGANIZATION AND INSTITUTIONS OF SOCIETY

Economic organization

After independence, the flight of the French settlers left a large vacuum in all domains. Consequently, the country faced a serious state of disorder and uncertainty (Achoui, 1983). After decades of implementing a socialist regime, Algeria remains heavily dependent on hydrocarbons (oil and gas), accounting for about 95 percent of its export earnings. The country ranks fifth in natural gas and fourteenth in oil reserves in the world.

The GDP in the country is distributed as follows: 10 percent agriculture, 69 percent industry, 21 percent services. The government is still the largest employer (29 percent of the labor force) followed by agriculture 25 percent, construction and public works 15 percent, industry 11 percent and other 20 percent (Office Nationale des Statistiques, 2004). Traditionally, the small agricultural properties require cooperation between the extended family members in order to survive and to keep the family property undivided as long as possible. Facing an economic crisis in addition to political turmoil, Algeria is burdened with a heavy foreign debt. The poverty rate in the country was estimated in 1999 to be 23 percent of the population. The most difficult problems that the country is currently facing are unemployment (27.3 percent in 2001), low economic growth, foreign debts, insecurity, housing crisis, and late marriage. These problems have had an impact on the family and social bonds in Algeria. The actual economic crisis in the country is worsened by internal migration to the urban areas. The percentage of labor force is estimated to be 58.9 percent in urban areas and 48.1 percent in rural areas (Office Nationale des Statistiques, 2004).

Political institutions and legal system

Historically, the social life of Algerians in small communities in the mountains and in the desert was regulated on the basis of consensus. Usually, consensus was reached after informal consultation and discussion. The consultation was shared and practiced by all mature males of the community. However, the wisdom of aged people was given more weight. This practice is mainly the result of three factors: ecological, cultural, and religious. In the early 1970s, the government introduced a socialist approach to development on the basis of a planned economy. The riots of October 1988, however, put an end to the socialist regime in Algeria. The successive regimes tried to move toward liberalism in economics, but with less success because of the social and political instability in the country. The current political system in the country is republican and parliamentarian.

The education system

One of the priorities of the governments after independence was building schools even in remote areas. Schools are open to both genders, who share the same classes at all educational levels. Hundreds of vocational schools are also open to both sexes in different regions of the country. The actual total literate population was estimated in 1995 to be 61.6 percent (73.9 percent of males and 49 percent of females). Interestingly, the proportion of female students in high schools is, for the first time in the Algerian history, higher than that of males, reaching 52.5 percent in 1997. The total schooling rate in Algeria was 83 percent in 1998. However, the general rate of schooling is still higher among males than females: 85.3 percent of males and 80.7 percent of females in 2001 (Office Nationale des Statistiques, 2004).

Religion

Algerians are *Sunni* Muslims. Islam is considered in the constitution as "the state religion." However, a secular elite does exist and is very influential in the state apparatus. Islam was considered to be an important factor in national unity throughout the history of Algeria. The religiosity of Algerians can be seen in Friday's prayer, in which the mosques are full of believers from different strata, ages, and genders especially in large cities. Another indicator is the month of *Ramadhan*, the Muslims' fasting month. The number of people who attend prayers in the mosque during this month increases sharply, which indicates that the majority of Algerians fast during this sacred month.

BONDS WITH GROUPS IN THE IMMEDIATE COMMUNITY

French colonization since 1830 had disturbed the social and economic systems in Algeria. Thousands of peasants had been deprived of their fertile lands and were driven to remote areas. In these geographically remote areas, the Algerians ran their civil and social affairs relatively independently from the French central government in Algiers. Consequently, civil affairs such as marriage, divorce, and even disputes were carried on usually on the basis of Islamic jurisprudence, customs, and traditions. Traditionally, the Algerians, who were mainly farmers, herders and pastoral nomads, lived in small communities which consisted of families related through blood and marriage. Each community was governed by an informal council, which included all its adult males and was headed by a wise and aged man. Several families formed the larger lineage or clan. Clans usually form a tribe (*Kabilah* in Arabic) or (*Adthroum* in *Tamazight*). Loyalty is mainly to the family rather than to the clan and the tribe. Regionalism is a concept that is widely used in Algeria to refer to social bonds that govern interests among people on the basis of their belonging to the same geographical region.

THE FAMILY

Marriage

In regard to endogamy, marriage was restricted in the traditional family to potential spouses from the extended family and same religion, Islam *Sunni,* which can be translated as Orthodox. In today's family, especially in large cities, marriage is less restricted. In regard to exogamy, Islam does not forbid marriage between first cousins. Marriage to first cousins used to be the norm rather than the exception in the traditional family. This trend is decreasing, especially in large cities, in which other criteria such as education, beauty, and family status are the main criteria for selecting a spouse. Polygamy is very rare in Algeria although the "Family Code" allows it under very restricted conditions (Family law). In the revised family code, the husband must first obtain his wife's consent before marrying a second wife.

Divorce is permitted in Islam as the last resort when a conflict between the couple is unresolved. The parents and relatives usually intervene to reach a compromise for solving the problems between the couple. However, the divorce rate is increasing in Algeria while the marriage rate is decreasing. The rate of divorce was about 2 percent in 1992. The main stated reasons for divorce are sexual problems (maladjustment), parents' interference, and interpersonal problems among the couples (Main reasons for divorce, 2000).

In the traditional family, decisions to marry were made by both families. Although fathers were believed to play the major role in the decision, mothers played a greater role, more hidden but more influential, in this decision. Marriage used to be an arranged affair, especially among relatives. Marriage is becoming more and more a personal choice with only the blessing of the parents. Educated males and females tend to marry on the basis of either their own choice or their parents' choice with their consent. The average age at first marriage is 31.3 among males and 27.6 among females. The marriage rate decreased from 6.0 percent in 1990 to 5.4 percent in 1998. This rate, however, increased slightly again in the year 2000 to reach 5.8 percent (Office Nationale des Statistiques, 2004).

Obtaining a spouse in the traditional family in Algeria was usually arranged on the basis of formal and informal contracts, as is the case in all Muslim societies. The bride is given a dowry according to Islamic law. The dowry (bride price) is the responsibility of the groom or his family. Traditionally, however, the bride is supposed to bring with her a small dowry, e.g., housewares.

Family structure

The traditional Algerian extended family structure is patrilineal in terms of lineal descent, in which kin of both sexes were related through the men only. The Algerian family can also be described as patriarchal in that the father or the grandfather had the legal power and the social norms, which supported his authority.

The extended family includes three generations or more, grandparents, sons/fathers, daughters/mothers, children, and grandchildren, in which grandfather was the head of the family in terms of authority structure, and with collatoral kin (cousins, uncles and aunts, nieces, and nephews), and with affinal relationships (parents-in-law, children-in-law, and siblings-in-law). Beyond these lineages were the patrilineal clans called *Adhrum* by the Berbers and *Firq* by the Arabs, in which kinship was assumed and the links between individuals and families were close. The largest units consisted of tribes that were aggregations of clans claiming common or related ancestors (Metz, 1993).

Boutafnoushat (1984) asserted that the Algerian family characteristics might be summarized as follows:

- The Algerian family is an extended family which contains several small families under what is called "the large house" (*Al-Dar Al-Kabirah*) in rural areas and "large tent" (*Al-Khiama Al-Kabirah)* among the Bedouins tribes. Usually, about 20–60 persons live collectively in one large family. Each extended family may include between three and four generations.
- The Algerian family is patriarchal and extended. In Berber areas and other regions of the country the extended family includes three to four generations but sooner or later it divides to several families, which go

through the same cycle again. Nevertheless, the extended family type, as Boutafnoushat asserts, is founded on two bases: (1) blood relationships (*Asabiyah*), which implies economic, social, and ethical integration among the members of the extended family, clans, and tribes; and (2) relationship with land, which implies developing strong relationships with and love of the land of the ancestors.

Residence after marriage was *patrilocal*, in that the married sons resided in or near the father's residence, or that of kinsmen. The married daughter resided with or in a separate home near the father-in-law and mother-in-law, and under their authority. In general, married sons and daughters live with or very near to their parents. However, because of a housing crisis in large cities, most of the newly married sons live with their parents even if they are permitted to live separately. The newly married couples are supposed to show respect and obedience to their parents and grandparents. In return, they get their blessings and help. Usually, the grandparents, especially grandmothers, care for their grandsons and granddaughters. The sons and daughters carry on their fathers' or family's names besides their first names. Women keep their family names even when they get married. This is in fact true in all Muslim countries. Thus, the Algerian family is still dominantly an extended family, although a new trend toward becoming a nuclear family is developing slowly among young educated people, especially in urban areas. The average size of the Algerian family in 1998 was about 6.68 persons.

Family roles and functions

The roles and functions of the traditional Algerian family were grounded on religious (Islamic) and traditional values, which appear to be common to agricultural societies. Obedience to parents, respect for old people, mutual cooperation and helping are the bases of these values. Married women play a hidden but a significant role in almost all aspects of life. They are supposed to be obedient to parents and husbands, to care for the upbringing of the children, participate in agricultural activities, to be good housewives, and preserve their chastity before and after marriage. Fathers represent the family and work as breadwinners either on their land or for somebody else. Grandfathers have the authority over all family issues, especially regarding financial matters and ownership of land and other properties during their lives. Their property is not usually divided among children until they die. While males are expected to help their fathers in daily or seasonal agricultural activities, females are expected to help their mothers in housekeeping and to serve their fathers and brothers. The children are usually disciplined by fathers and mothers. However, mothers and grandmothers tend to play the role of mediators and/or protectors of children. The grandparents take care of and protect their grandsons and granddaughters, provide advice to their children and relatives, and mediate in conflicts. Uncles, particularly father's brother(s) play a significant role when fathers are absent or dead. In the case of divorce, children of both sexes remain under the mother's custody until she decides to remarry. According to the Algerian Family Code, boys stay under their mother's custody until age 10. This age can be extended to 16. For girls, however, the age of custody is extended to 18 or until they get married. The right of custody is given, according to the law, first to the mother, then to the maternal grandmother, next to the aunt (the sister of the mother), and then to the father (Family Law).

CHANGES IN THE FAMILY

Today, about 60 percent of the total population lives in urban areas, which further complicates the housing crisis in the already crowded cities. Furthermore, the high cost of living, unemployment, insecurity, and political instability have weakened the social bonds to a large extent. However, overcrowding and housing shortages often forced people of a given kinship to scatter throughout a city, which decreased the solidarity of migrant groups (Metz, 1993). The other aspect of change is women's work in different institutions and activities. Even though the rate of women's participation in the labor force was about 25 percent in 2000, this rate will inevitably increase in the future because of the high percentage of females at different levels of education. The attitude toward women working outside their family's property is changing dramatically. Therefore, more women are joining the labor market every year.

Demographics

Compared to the high birth rate in the 1970s, birth rate has decreased to about 1.7 percent. Unemployment has also decreased from 30 percent to 15 percent. This percentage is very high, especially since 60 percent of Algerians are city dwellers. Furthermore, about 27 percent of the active total population is less than 30 years old (Office Nationale des Statistiques, 2004).

Family values

Boutafnoushat (1984) asserts that the concept of *Aylah* means a small family, which includes the couple and their children, while *Osrah* means the extended family, which includes three to four generations. This implies that the concept of family in English and some other languages does not have the same meaning as in Arabic language. The concept of *Osrah*, as Boutafnoushat (1984) maintains, carries on the sacred values of the tribe. Traditionally, the members of the family are supposed to support and help each other whenever there is a need, even in large cities. Usually, priority in helping is given to the sons and daughters over the parents, sisters, brothers, grandfathers, grandmothers, aunts, uncles, cousins, and other relatives. This help is extended to members of other families who belong to the same clan or tribe. The other difference between concepts in different languages, which might carry a hidden value, is the difference between the concepts that are used in *Arabic* to refer to "uncle," who is the father's brother (*a'amm* in Arabic), and "uncle" who is the mother's brother (*khal* in Arabic). The same difference exists between the father's sister (*a'amma*) and mother's sister (*khala*). These differences in semantics and values do not exist in English and Latin languages.

The family members are expected to support and help each other and defend the family honor and dignity. Traditionally, males carry on the responsibility of representing and defending the family values and social status. However, females are responsible for their chastity and their family's honor.

Religious holidays and social events such as *Eid Al-Fitr, Eid Al-Adha*, marriages, circumcisions, seventh days or *Akika* (new borns' birthday celebrations) are happy occasions in which Algerians express their adherence to values of mutual support, help, sympathy, and respect to parents and relatives in general. Furthermore, sad occasions such as sicknesses, accidents, and deaths are occasions for showing sympathy toward relatives. People feel more obliged to demonstrate their support under these circumstances. This sympathy is extended to neighbors and friends in the cities, and to clan and tribe members in rural areas.

10   Botswana

Adebowale Akande, Bolanle Adetoun,
and Johnsto Osagie

A HISTORICAL OUTLINE OF BOTSWANA

Botswana was formerly called Bechuanaland protectorate: At independence, it had hardly anything in terms of either infrastructural development or human resources development; in fact, it was classified as one of the 25 poorest countries in the world. It received self-governance from Britain in 1965 and on September 30, 1966, Botswana became independent. Botswana is the oldest democracy on the continent of Africa. The Basarwa are the earliest inhabitants of Botswana. Much of their earlier history and culture is recorded in rock paintings, folk tales, and songs. Their proper name is *San* meaning "person," but they are commonly known by the derogatory name "Bushmen." The San were later followed by the Tswana. Botswana has 1,643,000 inhabitants. The ethnic groups include Tswana (Setswana, 79 percent, Kalanga (11 percent, Basarwa (3 percent), and others including Kgalagadi and white (7 percent). The term for the nationals, *Batswana*, refers to the country's people rather than the ethnic group or origin. *Setswana* is the national language. Gaborone is its capital.

THE ECOLOGICAL FEATURES

Botswana has a semi-arid, warm climate, generally conducive to good health. Botswana, a landlocked country in southern Africa, is large (582,000 km^2) relative to its population of fewer than 2 million. Eighty-seven percent of the population lives in the eastern part of the nation, where the average annual rainfall is about 550 mm, sufficient for both arable and livestock agriculture (Setiloane, 1975). It is a predominantly flat to gently rolling tableland with the Kalahari Desert to the southwest and the delta swamps and river plains to the north. The lowest point is the junction of the Limpopo and Shashe Rivers, 513 m, and the highest point is the Tsodilo Hills, 1,489 m.

ORGANIZATION AND INSTITUTIONS OF SOCIETY

Economic organization

Botswana has maintained one of the world's highest growth rates since independence in 1966. Through fiscal discipline and sound economic fundamentals, Botswana has transformed itself from one of the poorest nations in the world to a middle-income country with a per capita GDP of US $6,600 in 2000. Manganese and some gold and asbestos were the only known minerals in Botswana at the time of independence. Huge copper and nickel, coal and antimony deposits have since been found, as well as soda ash and salt. The country's three diamond mines and stones collectively make up one of the largest diamond reserves in the world. Diamond mining has fueled much of Botswana's economic expansion and currently accounts for more than one-third of GDP (US$ 5.1 billion) and for three-fourths of export earnings (Bank of Botswana, 2001). Beef is Botswana's second largest export; it is of a very high quality and is an ingredient of most local recipes or menus. Seventeen percent of the land has been set aside for the maintenance and development of natural parks and wildlife sanctuaries and a further 20 percent of available land surrounding these areas has been allocated for wildlife management. After diamond mining and cattle ranching, the country relies heavily on tourism as an integral part of its economy, and is deeply committed to the conservation of its wildlife and heritage. The other important type of land use is grazing, especially of cattle, with some goats and sheep. Livestock is normally kept apart from the lands at grazing stations known as cattle posts, over 150 km from the town in some instances. The herdsmen, either the adolescent sons of the owner or his servants, normally maintain a hut or two at the cattle post. The head of the household comes to check on the cattle from time to time; a considerable portion of his time being spent traveling between the town and his cattle post and the lands (Setiloane, 1975). Unemployment and HIV/AIDS have been problems in Botswana, and the devastation of AIDS threatens to destroy the country's future (Akande, 2000). A disturbing scenario is becoming commonplace. Older males are intentionally seeking out younger girls owing to their mistaken belief that teenage females have a low incidence of HIV or other sexually transmitted diseases and that younger girls are "a bargain" when compared to older women. Conversely, young females often feel that they hold control over, and are manipulating, older men for material goods, cash, or career mobility. Many HIV-infected men feel that they can rid themselves of the HIV virus by engaging in unprotected sexual acts with virgins or female babies or taking showers immediately after intercourse.

Political institutions and legal systems

In the past, Botswana had small communities which largely managed their own affairs; sections organized their more important rituals together. It is only the great traditional festival called "succession ceremony" that is celebrated by all of Botswana at one time. It is the elders who are responsible for such collective decisions to be made, and the junior generation who must see that their decisions are carried out if anyone does not voluntarily abide by them. Essentially, the responsibility of the elders is to monitor the welfare of the people by their mediation through the performance of rituals for the health of the cattle. The elders also have responsibility in everyday matters – deciding whether a newcomer may settle in the community or settling disputes that arise within it (Silitshena, 1982). After independence in 1966, Botswana became a multiparty parliamentary republic operating under a constitution and a bicameral legislature. The upper house consists of a 15-seat advisory House of Chiefs representing different ethnic groups. The National Assembly has 40 elected members and four appointed members. There have been seven peaceful elections since independence. Administratively, Botswana is divided into six modern towns (Francistown, Gaborone, Lobatse, Jwaneng, Orapa, and Selebi-Pikwe) as a way of developing industry and diamond-related businesses in the nation's 10 districts (Central, Chobe, Ghanzi, Kgalagadi, Kgatleng, Kweneng, Ngamiland, North-East, South-East, Southern). The central government upholds the rule of law and monitors all aspects of life.

The educational system

Education is, in theory, universal and free up to junior secondary level. Qualitative changes in primary and secondary education in recent years have concentrated on teacher training and certification, on equipment and importation of expatriate teachers for the advancement of science and maths education. The curriculum has moved away from its original South African model and modified so as to be similar to the Nigerian model. The Botswana education system follows a 7+3+2 structure. There are seven years of primary education, at the end of which pupils write the Primary School Leaving Examinations (PSLE). Some of these learners proceed to Form One, which is the first year of the three years of the junior secondary school course. At the end of the Junior Certificate (JC) program learners write examinations which qualify them for entry into senior secondary education. The senior secondary school curriculum is covered in two years. Those who do not meet the JC examinations requirements have to leave the education system and perhaps enroll in vocational and technical institutions such as the brigades training centers. One of the giant strides taken by the government to promote vocational education in Botswana is the establishment of the Brigade movement. Brigades are community-focused, post-secondary further education institutions "aiming at vocational training oriented to the needs of communities" (Leburu-Sianga and Molobe, 2000). The main higher education institutions are the University of Botswana, Botswana Polytechnic, Molepolole College of Education, and Tonota College of Education. Just as in other African countries, in order to develop a curriculum that addresses issues of access, quality, relevance, mass education, and preparation for the world of work, the Department of Teacher Training and Development (TTandD) has phased out the two-year Primary Teaching Certificate and introduced a three-year diploma course. Colleges of education now offer only diploma courses. Among Botswana's contributions to global culture are words derived from Setswana in foreign dictionaries – *Kalahari*, *Tsetse*, and *Tilapia*.

Religion

The religion of the Batswana is basically one of ancestral veneration. It is now estimated that about 68 percent of Batswana hold indigenous beliefs (ancestral veneration) while around 32 percent of the population are Christians (Letamo and Majelantle, 2001). An all powerful god is believed to exist – called *Modimo* – who is the creator and holder of destiny. The Batswana believe in life after death in a world located underground. The ancestors reward those who respect and venerate them and punish those who do not (Government of Botswana and United Nations Development Report, 1997). The two most popular churches are now the Zion Christian Church among the working class and the Roman Catholic Church among the middle-class professionals. Male circumcision is not accepted as traditional practice in Botswana (Akande, 2000).

BONDS WITH GROUPS IN THE IMMEDIATE COMMUNITY

The Botswana communities apply the rule of allegiance and hostility to control their families and clans. The total goal of the society is to uphold the respect for life, property, one's honor, and rule of law. Men's social orientation is toward larger, impersonal status groups, whereas women's social orientation is toward close dyadic relationships. It appears women are more emotionally knowledgeable, sensitive, and skilled than men, especially in the way they establish bonds with groups in their community. Women provide the predominance of care for Botswana infants and children. The mother seems to assume almost total responsibility for their physical well-being, making sure they are well fed, fully clothed, and protected from hazards. And if a mother is temporarily absent, other women, e.g., grandmothers, sisters, aunts, are available to take care of young children. Emotions are not used to differentiate oneself from others – indeed the norm in traditional Botswana society is to fit in with others, avoid conflict, and express solidarity or commitment to the family or the clan or a group. When pleasing events happen, there is an inclination to not overly celebrate the good fortune but rather to acknowledge that things can take a bad turn next time. Similarly, when bad fortune befalls, the despair is frequently counterbalanced by the self-instruction that things can turn out well the next time around. The Botswana people conceived a tribe as consisting of the descendants of a single ancestor, the clans and lineages, and of land rights. There was often fighting within tribes as well as between tribes, and fighting for alliances with other families and clans. A group of villages within an area might fight one another, but they were expected to form an alliance against external enemies, so that people who were your opponents one day might be your allies the next. It is considered wrong to join with outsiders against neighboring communities or clans or to refuse support to the neighboring communities or clans if aid is requested (Akande, 2002). When neighboring villages were raided the enemy herds were seized and captives were adopted into the families of the captors and their hostage daughters were married within the family. But nowadays, the rules of alliance and aggression are not usually followed.

THE FAMILY

Marriage

In regard to endogamy, in the traditional family of the past, marriage was not restricted to potential spouses of the same tribe or clan. In regard to exogamy, rules still exist that prohibit establishing marriage relationships with one's nuclear family, and members of extended family, including cousins up to second degree.

Social sanctions against divorce were strong in the traditional family. If a marriage broke up it was usually because the woman left or the man left. Grounds for divorce included adultery, external pressure, childlessness, and autocratic behavior of the partner.

In the traditional family, the decision to marry was made by both families, with fathers or the male member of the family (in the death or absence of the father) taking charge.

Obtaining a spouse. In some clans, girls were often betrothed at birth to youths between 13 and 21 years of age, who then had to wait until the prospective bride grew up. All through this long period the future son-in-law was expected to do odd jobs for the girl's father. The marriage was finally ratified by a payment of *bogadi* or *lobola* (bride price) to both the bride's clan section and to her father. In present-day Botswana, there is no clear-cut dowry or *bogadi*, depending on both families and their understanding of their culture. In Botswana today, educated grooms and brides seek to choose their spouses from different ethnic groups and clans other than their own. The husband is the breadwinner of the family and pays the bills even if the wife is employed, unless there are some concessions on the part of the wife. However, one can say that the Botswana family is gradually becoming nuclear, but as a way of continuation of interaction, close relatives still live near to each other. In some cases married sons and daughters prefer to live either with their parents or grandparent(s) or next to them in a separate house or bungalow or apartment.

Family structure

The traditional Botswana extended family structure could be said to be tribal and patrilineal in terms of lineal descent, in which kin of both sexes were related through the men only. It could also be referred to as patriarchal in that the grandfather or the father had the legal power and social norms which supported his authority.

The extended family included three generations, grandparents, sons/fathers, daughters/mothers, and children, in which grandfather was the head of the family in terms of authority structure, and included collateral kin (cousins, uncles and aunts, nieces and nephews), as well as affinal relationships (parents-in-law, children-in-law, and siblings-in-law), or best man/maid of honor at the marriage of offspring, or bonds with others through mutual obligations.

Residence after marriage was patrilocal, in that the married sons resided in or near the father's residence. The married daughter was traditionally supposed to live in or near the house of the father-in-law. The mother-in-law had authority over the daughter-in-law. Most cases of divorce are said to be attributed to the constant conflict or rivalry between the daughter-in-law and the mother-in-law in Botswana. However, young couples now try to avoid this problem, by choosing to be independent from the in-laws or parents even if as a sort of social obligation they need to live near them.

Family roles and functions

In the traditional family of the past, the father in Botswana was the breadwinner and the mother was the housewife. The grandparents were highly respected and played a significant role in deciding about many family matters. Women were not expected to work outside the house, but were supposed to care for the children (Akande, 2002). The traditional *tswana* and *kalanga* social order is fundamentally based on polygyny and even to some extent today, most men aim for and attain control over several wives. Large households with many wives and children established the social foundation for a man to assume the status of a "big compound head" and the economic basis for controlling a substantial productive operation (Bainame, Letamo, and Majelantle, 2002; Letamo and Majelantle, 2001). In present-day Botswana, women are as educated as men and, with rapid economic changes, about 43 percent of women work outside the home. This might be due to westernization, or financial reasons or as a way of attaining self-fulfillment.

CHANGES IN THE FAMILY

Demographics

In today's Botswana more girls than boys attend primary schools, but more boys attend secondary schools and tertiary institutions. Botswana has one of the highest rates in Africa of one-parent female-headed families. Formal marriage by *bogadi* or bride price and female monogamy have declined, and women are now becoming de facto heads of household. Botswana is also experiencing a falling birth rate (Akande, 2002). Females used to marry at a very tender age, between 11 and 15, but now young people, particularly educated women, tend to delay getting married because of the expenses associated with marital life.

Family values

There are dramatic changes in traditional family values. People do not uphold exaggerated patriarchal norms as before. Brides do not want to marry into families with an excessive patriarchal structure. The imperative passed to daughters from mothers whose view of feminine obligation has been to preserve both family relationships and the family as a whole, no matter what the personal cost, is a thing of the past. In present-day Botswana, women do not stay in a bad relationship. Botswana couples who want "it to work" work together and build a sense of solidarity and support by learning to live together creatively. Women are no longer something that is allocated distributively to households in the form of female children, and then later, still distributively, to other households in the form of wives. While some women still uphold the traditional values of conciliation, responsibilities for children, and maintaining ties with the extended family, they do not believe they have to act in a passive manner, projecting shyness, reserve, and a display of failing, fear, and incompetence in their everyday life.

CONCLUSIONS

As a closing point, in today's Botswana, we have a somewhat mixed system of family. It is not a totally nuclear or a totally extended family. Despite the influence of colonization, apartheid, westernization, and high tech, some families in Botswana still believe in their culture and worldview, although with some differences (Akande, 2002). People now hold an awareness of the other. The pursuit of self-esteem has become a central preoccupation in Botswana society. This is where the people feel they can experience a much deeper satisfaction and joy that comes with learning and creating, giving, and connecting with others.

11 The Brazilian *jeitinho:* Brazil's sub-cultures, its diversity of social contexts, and its family structures

Cláudio V. Torres and Maria Auxiliadora Dessen

A HISTORICAL OUTLINE OF BRAZIL

Brazil was "discovered" by Europeans in 1500, and after a long period of Portuguese colonization, was declared independent in 1822, becoming the Empire of Brazil. The country was successfully ruled by two emperors until the declaration of the Republic, in 1889. The proclamation of the Republic, in 1889, signals the end of slavery in Brazil and the beginning of the urbanization, and consequently industrialization processes. The Republican military project also included the organization of the modern family, called *new family* in agreement with a bourgeois organization pattern. In this organization, the "modern woman" should be educated to perform her duties as a mother and also educated to provide financial support to the household. The Republican project was basically focused on the modernization of the white family of European origin, that is, the traditional family. This picture became worse when the military left the process, and the oligarchies assumed control of the country.

Since its independence from the Portuguese crown in 1822, Brazil has been in a continuous process of industrialization. In fact, this started in 1806 with the relocation of the Portuguese Court to Brazil after having escaped from Napoleon's invasion in Europe. Brazil has had five Constitutions, the first in 1934, and others in 1946, 1967, 1969, and 1988. The latter Constitution was developed by the dictatorship government, which ruled the country for 20 years after the military coup in 1964.

Brazil's present-day population is approximately 180,000,000 inhabitants, most of them (over 40 percent, as indicated by the Brazilian census of 2002) from a *mulato* or *mestiço* ethnicity, Portuguese terms that refer to interracial mixtures or black and white and/or native origin. Brasília is its capital, with approximately 2,500,000 inhabitants, and is located in the central region of the country and right at the center of its geographical distribution. Brazil is an important member and one of the creators of the Mercosur – the free trade agreement of South America.

ECOLOGICAL FEATURES

Brazil is the largest country in South America, with a territory of more than 8,000,000 km^2. The range of vegetation and geographical features in the country is extremely vast, varying from deserts, to sub-tropical weather, to rainforests, including the Amazon Forest, which covers a quarter of the national territory. Average temperature varies between 15 and 35 °C, depending on the region of the country. The majority of the population lives on the coast of the Atlantic Ocean.

Owing to its wide territorial extension and its colonization process in the sixteenth century, Brazil is very heterogeneous in cultural terms, with different groups being formed by the European immigration and the African slavery commerce. For Ribeiro (1997), the country has a cultural division that originates from its social-economic history. Brazil has an extensive variety of weather and soil, which would be determinants of the division into distinct Brazilian sub-cultures (Torres and Dessen, 2004).

ORGANIZATION AND INSTITUTIONS OF SOCIETY

Political institutions and legal system

Today, Brazil is governed by the Constitution of 1988, written two years after the end of the dictatorship as a mark of the re-establishment of democracy in the country. Recently, the labor party was elected to the federal government, and an ex-union leader was inaugurated president. Yet, most of the Brazilian federal government is still highly centralized.

As one would expect, the social movement of Brazil and of Latin America in general, did not follow the rest of the world. Social-cultural networks and solidarity campaigns have always been present in the history of Brazil. For Carvalho (2000), these networks represent a necessary condition for the survival of, for example, low-income families. For instance, the large families characteristically found in the northeast and other rural regions of the country, function as a way of maximizing income and social support, and affecting relationships, in order to obtain better jobs, housing, and health conditions.

The educational system

Elementary and high-school education in Brazil is still limited to very few. There is still a high percentage of illiteracy – 32 percent in official numbers (http://www.mec.gov.br). Yet, it should be noted that once an individual simply learns how to sign his or her name, but nothing else, this individual is officially not considered to be illiterate anymore. Until the end of the military dictatorship in 1986, the State was considered to be solely responsible for the educational system. The Constitution of 1988 represented an evolution in this concept, giving the State the duty of providing the family with educational and social resources. However, lower class families of African origin have not benefited from a specific policy directed toward the family and education since the nineteenth century. Parallel to the public educational system, private elementary and secondary schools provide a fair level of education for those who can afford reasonably high tuition fees. Paradoxically, the public and tuition-free universities of the country, recognized by their high level of education and research in South America, receive mostly students who graduate from this private educational system. Recently, two of the most important public universities of the country, University of Brasília and the State University of Rio de Janeiro, have implemented a quota system for students of African-Brazilian origin, and another well-known institution, the State University of São Paulo, has started discussions to do the same. All these initiatives have been highly criticized by the media and by the Brazilian bourgeoisie in general.

Religion

Religion is a very important topic in the Brazilian culture. Considered to be the largest Catholic country in the world, the truth is that Brazil is an eclectic country, where the Christian religion mixes with the African-based religions in an almost perfect union. This religious syncretism can be seen in most Brazilian cities, with people attending a Catholic service and an African cult sometimes in the same night. Brazilian history is marked by a strong influence of the Catholic Church, which has been present since the beginning of the Portuguese colonization. After the separation between Church and State at the end of the nineteenth century, the Catholic Church in Brazil started developing strategies that resulted in a Catholic educational policy of broad impact. In relation to the family, it "received a Catholic religious treatment with strong European connotations, based on an idea of a standardfamily, patriarchal, with a clear presence of morality and sexual control, typical from this ideology" (Neder, 1998, p. 34).

BONDS WITH GROUPS IN THE IMMEDIATE COMMUNITY

Schwartz (1994b) observed that Brazilians scored low in intellectual and emotional autonomy, which is related to Hofstede's (1980) dimension of individualism (Smith and Bond, 1999) and high on conservatism and hierarchy (correlating with Hofstede's notion of power distance). Pearson and Stephan (1998) found Brazilians to be significantly more collectivist than other countries. We can observe that in Brazil there is little room for participation in problem-solving and that participation in decision-making is not encouraged to a large extent (Nogueira, 2001; Torres, 1999). As observed elsewhere (Droogers, 1988), social and political structures in Brazil are still evolving, especially after the 20-year military dictatorship regime. It is expected (Santos, 1998) that the globalization process and the developing privatization of Brazilian institutions might require a new class of educational, organizational, and social leaders; leaders skilled in managing change, especially to reduce social problems, such as those found in the increasing Brazilian division between the richest and the poorest social classes. However, any managerial practice, leadership, or educational model cannot be directly applied to the Brazilian context without accounting for the proper cultural differences.

There is also some suggestion in the literature (Nogueira, 2001) that verticalism would be a preferred cultural manifestation in this country. Thus, we could understand the Brazilian national culture as one of vertical-collectivism. Inequality is not only accepted, but also expected in this cultural pattern (Singelis, Triandis, Bhawuk, and Gelfand, 1995). Yet, although the concept of culture assumes that members of the same culture are subjected to similar social influences, we can find larger differences among the sub-cultures within a country than between cultures across countries. Following this rationale, Torres and Dessen (2004) suggested a variation in the Brazilian's preferred cultural pattern, which would get increasingly more individualist and less vertical as one moves away from the northern to the southern regions of the country.

Also, we should note that the Brazilian's worldview is the one of the *jeitinho*, discussed by Amado and Vinagre-Brasil (1991). *Jeitinho* (or literally, "little way") is a Portuguese term that is difficult to translate, but which means that a problem should be accepted as given, and that "there might be no ways to reach the goal, but in a certain way we will achieve it anyway" (Droogers, 1988, p. 699). Smith, Peterson,

Ayestaran, Jesuino, and Ferdman (in press) observed a great similarity between the Brazilian *jeitinho* and the notion of improvisation found in other Hispanic cultures. Taken together, these results suggest that in the Brazilian context there is little room for participation, and that social hierarchy is accepted.

THE FAMILY

Cândido (1972) has defined Brazil as a large family, with few formal rules and a consensus toward the authority of the father. The Brazilian contemporary family has a hierarchical structure, one where the husband/ father has authority and exerts his power over the wife and children (Romanelli, 2000), providing closer proximity between the mother and children. This structure is reflected in a division of labor that clearly dichotomizes the "masculine" and "feminine" tasks. The Brazilian family has been influenced by demographic, economic, and social changes, which have resulted in changes in the structural relations of the family and in the redefinition of the traditional model of the nuclear family.

In Brazil, the family can be understood as a social group within a social-cultural context. Partly as a result of the globalization process in the country during the past 20 years, the family gained the role of promoting relationships that prevent the social isolation resulting from growing poverty or urbanization in the country (Biasoli-Alves, 1997; Dessen and Braz, 2000; Romanelli, 1997), demonstrating its importance in the protection, support, creation, and maintenance of social relationships. Also, changes in the basic economic conditions caused by globalization and modernization, such as the internal migration, and new patterns of consumption, have influenced the perception of the family. In relation to the new patterns of consumption, for instance, the Brazilians' frustrated consumer expectations led to an increase in illicit earning, delinquency, drug dealing, and other forms of social exclusion. These factors have an impact on parent–child relationships, children's relationships, and the transmission of social values, particularly in poor families (Dessen and Biasoli-Alves, 2001). A fundamental tension relates to these shifts in social relations in the face of little change in the patriarchal authority, where men still attempt to exert power on their wives and children.

Marriage

Nowadays, there are not strong social restrictions in the choice of partners, although there used to be some pressure in the past to prohibit unions of Europeans with Japanese immigrants, independent of their gender. When the couple makes the decision to get married, the families have a direct influence in terms of avoiding unions between individuals of different social classes. Divorce was institutionalized in Brazil only in 1977, owing to the negative influence of the Catholic Church. In 85 percent of divorce cases (Neder, 1998), the mother is responsible for the care of the children, and the property acquired after the marriage is distributed equally between the partners. A decrease in formal (religious and/or legal) marriages has been observed in the last decades, along with an increase in consensual unions.

Family structure

There is not a single model of family organizating in Brazil. The nuclear bourgeois family, originating from the European patriarchal family model, does not represent the "only historical possibility of family organization to guide the ordinary life in the path of progress and modernity" (Neder, 1998, p. 28). African slavery is a cornerstone of the Brazilian society and the organization of the Brazilian family. Yet, there was not such a thing as an African family structure, but several types of family organizations. This implies the presence of different structures, such as matriarchal and patriarchal, on top of differences in religion, language, and tradition. The violence that characterized the slavery in Brazil was responsible for the separation of couples, and parents and their offspring, creating sometimes irreversible losses. Although the end of slavery in Brazil happened more than a hundred years ago, the lower-class families of African origin show, until today, a pattern of loss of family bonds. This pattern can be seen, for example, in the migrations from rural to metropolitan areas or in other forced family separation.

CHANGES IN THE FAMILY

Demographics

In regard to demographic statistics, the traditional idea of the Brazilian family, one of a couple with sons and daughters, which in 1981 represented 65 percent of homes in Brazil, represented only 61 percent in 1990. Between 1981 and 1990, the average number of persons per family dropped from 4.5 to 4.1, both in urban and rural areas, although it is still usual to find large families in rural areas (Ribeiro, Sabóia, Branco, and Bregman, 1998). The average number of children ranges from 2.5 to 1.9 children per couple, depending on the region of the country (northeast and southeast, respectively). Official data estimate that one-third of Brazilian children live with a single parent. It should also be noted that the proportion of Brazilian families living in precarious conditions is high. More than one-third (http://www.ibge.gov.br) live below the line of poverty. In the rural areas, families are even poorer, with 65.8 percent of them living below the line of poverty. In urban areas, 27.9 percent of the families in 1990 lived below the poverty line, but there are reasons to believe that this number has increased since then (Ribeiro et al., 1998).

Family relations

In the early decades of the twentieth century, the family was larger, with more children, and with daily contact between generations, who sometimes lived under the same roof. At that time, the traditional values endorsed by adults during socialization process were directed primarily at girls. The responsibility for all domestic tasks was handed down from one female kin member to another (Biasoli-Alves, 1997). Marriage was arranged for daughters and women did not need to study or plan for an independent life. In the middle of the century, from 1930 to 1970, a change was coupled with a reduction of in-group activities and an increase in solitary activity within the home. Television came to dominate the spacing and timing of family interactions, even though in most households strong inter-generational links persisted. Family values shifted to allow secondary school girls to enter professional life, as long as such involvement did not interfere with their family responsibilities. Women in Brazil prioritized their domestic responsibilities, while the provider role remained firmly associated with the husband. At the end of the twentieth century, more middle-class women entered higher education and professional life, which facilitated their social contacts and raised questions about the persistence of the gender bias at home. Even today, in dual-earner couples, the woman continues to run the house and care for the children and her husband. In relation to boy/girlfriends and sexuality, parents attempt to enforce clear and conservative rules about their daughters', but not their sons' behavior (Romanelli, 1998). Biasoli-Alves (1997) suggests that Brazilian society ended the twentieth century adapting to profound changes in beliefs about relationships within the home, focused upon notions of the "ideal child", the nature of maturity (e.g., autonomy) and new beliefs in acceptable childcare strategies (e.g., close supervision in a highly stimulating environment), along with different understandings of the public roles of women and men.

FINAL COMMENTS

It is important to emphasize that daily life in very poor families differs from that in working-class families, as the former usually experience family relationships which reflect strong pressing economic needs (Ribeiro et al., 1998). Children are required to participate in activities to maintain the family, including domestic tasks and paid labor. Considering that there are few studies in Brazil examining family interactions and the socialization process in poor families when it comes to, for instance, child employment, school, and the home environment, we should be careful about making simplistic links between poverty and problems of family relationships in developing countries like Brazil.

The agreements and disagreements amongst scholars in relation to a generic family model for Brazil reflect the interest of researchers, especially historians, for investigations that show "how difficult it is to conceive a unique image that can be applied to all different social segments in various moments of our history" (Samara, 1992, p. 61). In this Chapter we did not have the intention of characterizing the multiplicity of the Brazilian families or their lifestyles, which would be, we believe, an impossible task because of the enormous diversity of social and family contexts in Brazil. Rather, we can affirm that the transformations that have happened in Brazilian families have resulted not only in changes in their structural relations, but also in the redefinition of the traditional model of a nuclear family. As these transformations are still happening, we still cannot define with clarity a new model of functioning for Brazilian families in face of the changes in the broad society.

12   Britain

Robin Goodwin, Sophia Christakopoulou,
and Vicky Panagiotidou

A HISTORICAL OUTLINE OF BRITAIN

Great Britain (England, Scotland, and Wales) forms part of the United Kingdom, which also includes Northern Ireland. The name "Britain" is probably derived from Celtic origin, reflecting Celtic rule in pre-Roman times. Britain was ruled by Rome from AD 43 to AD 409 and was last successfully invaded by the Normans in 1066. The second half of the twentieth century witnessed the dismantling of the British Empire and the rebuilding of the United Kingdom into a modern European nation. The United Kingdom was a founding member of the United Nations and of the Commonwealth, is one of the five permanent members of the Security Council, and has been a member of the European Union since 1973.

Britain's current population is approximately 60 million, of whom one in six are over 65 years old. One in fifteen of Britain's inhabitants are from non-white ethnic groups. Nearly half of them were born in Britain from parents who had emigrated from the former British colonies in Africa, Asia, and the Caribbean since the 1950s.

ECOLOGICAL FEATURES

Britain is an island situated in northwestern Europe, surrounded by the Atlantic Ocean, English Channel and the North, Celtic, and Irish Seas. The landscape is varied, from the mountains of Wales, Scotland, and Northern England, through the flat expanses of the Midlands and Eastern England to the rolling hills of the South. The climate is generally cool to mild with frequent cloud and rain. The temperature rarely extends beyond the range of -10 to $+30\,^\circ$C.

ORGANIZATION AND INSTITUTIONS OF SOCIETY

Economic organization

Over the last century Britain has enjoyed a strong manufacturing base, which grew out of the Industrial Revolution of the nineteeth century. Recent decades have seen a rapid decline in manufacturing industry, which now employs 19 percent of the workforce, and a growth in the services sector, which employs 80 percent of the workforce (Office of National Statistics, 2002). Less than 1 percent of the population works in agriculture. Unemployment rates are currently low (around 5 percent of the workforce) with rates particularly low in the wealthier areas, largely situated in the southeast of the country.

Political institutions and legal system

Britain is a constitutional monarchy. Through the centuries, political power passed gradually from the Crown to the people's elected representatives. The king (or queen) is the head of state, but political power rests mainly with the two Houses of Parliament – the House of Lords and the House of Commons – the latter being the more powerful and important body. Britain's constitution is unwritten, partly statutes, partly common law and practice. Recently Britain has implemented a degree of devolution. In 1999 the Scottish parliament and the Welsh and Northern Ireland assemblies were set up with varying degrees of power.

The education system

Approximately 99 percent of the total population aged 15 and over has completed five or more years of schooling, the large majority in secondary school. Around one in three of young people in England and Wales, and 40 percent in Scotland, go to University (Office of National Statistics, 2002). The conversion of many polytechnics to universities in the early 1990s means that there are now 87 universities in the United Kingdom. There are five million students in further and higher education (58 percent female, 42 percent male) 2.2 million of whom are in higher education (55 percent female, 45 percent male) (Office of National Statistics, 2002).

Religion

Britain is a predominantly Christian country. Although there are only approximately 7.9 million "active" faith members in Britain, 40 million Britons claim to be Christians. Other significant religions are Islam (approximately 1.5 million adherents), Hinduism (0.5 million), Sikhism (0.5 million) and Judaism (300,000) (Office of National Statistics, 2002).[1]

BONDS WITH GROUPS IN THE IMMEDIATE COMMUNITY

One of the significant characteristics of local communities in Britain is the informal networks of kin and friends that offer support and assistance to individuals and families. Recently there has been an extensive debate about the loss of community in local neighborhoods in Britain and the dispersal of social support networks. However, recent studies (Christakopoulou and Dawson, 2000) have demonstrated that there are still strong bonds among established residents in various local communities and informal networks of family and friends that interact frequently and provide support and help on a reciprocal basis. Women are very important in forming relationships across the neighborhoods, with children playing a central role in the formation of these social networks.

THE FAMILY

Marriage

One of the major changes in family patterns in recent decades, and a contributory factor toward the trend for later first marriage, has been the growth in cohabitation before marriage. Over the last two decades, cohabitation rates have risen markedly, with 1 in 6 adult non-married people now cohabiting. Consequently, more than 52 percent of births in the United Kingdom are outside of marriage, and cohabitation does not necessarily end when children arrive. Forty percent of current co-habitees in the British Social Attitudes Survey (2001) had children

---

[1] Sectors of Britain's ethnic minorities have grown substantially over the past decade, with birth rates particularly high amongst Britain's Muslim population. Figures for ethnic minority membership, and the religions observed by these minorities, are therefore likely to be underestimates: actual numbers should be clarified when the results from the 2001 National Census are released.

(Park, Curtice, Thomson, Jarvis, and Bromley, 2001). For those who do cohabit there is little formal governmental recognition. English law does not give cohabitees the same rights and responsibilities towards one another as it gives spouses, which has implications for property disputes and the like (Standley, 1993). For the great majority of Britain's population, the choice of a spouse has no restrictions, although norms prevent marriage to members of the nuclear family and first cousins. The decision to marry is made by the individuals involved, with or without the consent of the parent.

Obtaining a spouse amongst the white community is usually left to the individuals, although more indirect social pressure from family as well as friends over partner choice is, of course, still important. There are no official dowries amongst this community. Amongst Britain's ethnic minorities, and in particular amongst British Asians, marriages are frequently arranged by parents and go-betweens mainly on caste, religious, and social class lines (Ghuman, 1994), although there is usually some choice as to whether or not to accept the partner (Goodwin, Adatia, Sinhal, Cramer and Ellis, 1997). Arranged marriage is particularly prevalent amongst Britain's Muslim populations (primarily from Pakistan and Bangladesh) (Beishon, Modood and Virdee, 1998).

Britain has moved away from traditional fault grounds for divorce to ones designed to allow for divorce with less acrimony. With the implementation in 1971 of the Divorce Reform Act 1969, which introduced the irretrievable breakdown of marriage as the sole ground for divorce, the number of divorces increased dramatically. The rise continued in the 1980s and 1990s. Divorce rates fell slightly recently to an annual rate of 12.7/1,000 married people. Social sanctions against divorce are generally not strong in Britain. Although a few decades earlier there was a strong social stigma attached, even for the apparently innocent party, as divorce became more common, its social and moral significance diminished considerably. However, there is a great deal of hostility to divorce amongst Britain's Pakistani and Bangladeshi communities (Beishon et al., 1998).

Family structure

The typical British family is nuclear in structure (Goode, 1963; Millar and Warman, 1996), a structure that preceded industrialization (Finch, 1997; Kağıtçıbaşı, 1996a). Seventy percent of families consist of dependent children living with both their birth parents (Lewis, 2000). However, since the 1960s there has been a decline in the proportion of traditional households consisting of a couple family with dependent children. In 1961, 38 percent of the households in Great Britain were of this type but by 1998–9 this had decreased to 23 percent. The proportion of extended family households has also declined from 3 percent to 1 percent. Moreover, the proportion of unmarried and divorced one-parent family households with dependent children has more than trebled to 7 percent in 1998–9. In addition, 30 percent of couples do not have children, and one-person households amount to 29 percent (Office of National Statistics, 2000).

As in many societies across the world, affinal relationships can be "challenging," with the mother-in-law seen as a constant source of chiding, although, of course, families vary greatly on this. Lineal and collateral relationships also vary greatly and are highly individualistic: in Finch's words, "people are treated as unique persons rather than occupants of positions in a kinship universe" (Finch, 1997, p. 131). This is reflected in the distribution of property after death, with this distribution largely dictated by the choice of each testor (Finch, 1997).

Postmarital location is typically *neolocal* – apart from the relatives of both spouses. However, Britain's ethnic minority groups exhibit very different patterns of family structure. Those of Caribbean origin are more likely to cohabit and have a number of dependent children. South Asians are more likely to be married (Ballard and Kalra, 1994; Modood, Berthoud, Lakey, Nazroo, Smith, Virdee, and Beishon, 1997) and may live in "semi-extended" arrangements, with separate nuclear households existing in close proximity (Owen, 1996). South Asians are also more likely to have created their own kin network in Britain, with family members brought in from overseas.

Family roles and functions

Although the overwhelming majority of people in Britain do not live in three-generational households, most are involved quite actively in three-generational family relationships. The bond between parent and child remains strong when the child leaves home and has its own family. The support the parental generation gives continues, although the type and the extent of this support are affected by the parents' economic situation and the geographic closeness to their child's family (Allan, 1985). Contact with relatives is likely to depend on whether or not partners have children, with those with dependent children more likely to see their relatives more frequently than those without such children (McGlone, Park, and Smith, 1998). The web of assistance between the family members is not sustained by a rigid set of rules of obligations, but rather by a series of guidelines within which negotiations are conducted. These guidelines concern reciprocity, the balance of independence and dependency and the importance of protecting the moral identity of giver and receiver (Finch and Mason, 1993).

In terms of gender roles, Millar and Warman (1996) describe a "gender fault' " where beneath an egalitarian surface there are still clear gender divisions. Women still do three-quarters of the housework, spending an average of 18.5 hours a week on household tasks (compared to 6 hours for men). The majority of Britons express support for a "traditional" division of labor in the family, although this conventional viewpoint is less popular amongst those aged under 30 (Dench, 1996). Ferri and Smith (1996) found that the more mothers were involved in work outside the home, the more fathers shared equally in childcare and housework. Father's hours of employment also affected their own contribution to childcare – those who worked long hours did less at home, regardless of their wife's employment situation. However, considerable gender segregation in roles remained, and even in families where both parents worked full-time, mothers took the main responsibility for domestic life. Thus, for example, the woman who worked full-time in a dual-earning family took the prime role in looking after the children in 28 percent of cases and shared this responsibility with her partner in a further 69 percent of examples. Only in 1 percent of cases did fathers taken the prime role in childcare in the dual-earning family.

Both fathers and mothers tend to assume that women are more sensitive to children's needs than men. Mothers frequently say they prefer to look after the children and run the home, reflecting the persistence of traditional family views in Britain (Lewis, 2000). Fathers view providing income for the family as their central role and are most likely to work as a means of providing for the family. The woman's activities were seen as complementary to this (Warin, Solomon, Lewis, and Langford, 1999).

The wife makes the decisions in areas of domestic life that the couple claims as not very important such as food purchases, house decoration, children's clothing. Husbands have far more say in big decisions that involve more expense or disruption such as moving house and overall financial control. Wives are being consulted over any major decisions, but in the end it is the husband who decides (Edgell, 1980).

CHANGES IN THE FAMILY

Demographics

There has been a steady decline in the number of marriages per 1,000 persons in Britain, although there was a slight increase in marriage rates during 2000 (Office of National Statistics, 2000). Fewer couples now marry in church and the number of marriages where both partners were marrying for the first time in 2000 accounted for just 58 percent of marriages. There is also a tendency in recent years for people to marry for the first time somewhat later in life. The average age of first marriage for men was 30.5 in 2000, and 28.2 for women (Office of National Statistics, 2002).

The average family size is decreasing and is projected to fall below two children per woman for women born around 1960, and over 20 percent of women born after 1965 will remain childless (Office of National Statistics, 2002). Women are now having children much later in life, with a 41 percent increase in the number of women aged over 40 now giving birth (now 9.3/1,000 women) (Office of National Statistics, 2001). There is also a high rate of teenage pregnancies. In 1995, the United Kingdom had the highest rate of live births to teenage women, over twice the European Union average (Office of National Statistics, 2000).

Family values

The majority of the adult population can be classified as being very "family-centered." This outlook is similar amongst both non-manual and manual working groups, although it is strongest amongst older people (McGlone et al., 1998). A "belief" in conventional marriage remains strong (Dench, 1996; Lewis, 2000). However, contacts with relatives are declining, with weekly contact with the child's grandmother falling by 9 percent to 50 percent between 1986 and 1995. This has occurred because of increasing geographic distance between relatives, and a decline in phone contacts, and has occurred most markedly amongst non-manual workers with dependent children (McGlone et al., 1998). Family members are still connected by a network of mutual aid that takes many different forms, ranging from childcare and caring for the elderly to intergenerational financial and moral support. However, which family members offer help under what circumstances is highly variable. Kinship relations remain very important, but there is a lack of agreement about what obligations should exist in families (Finch and Mason, 1993). Ethnic minority families are likely to perceive that they are different from white families in showing greater commitment to parenting and providing greater disciplining of children (Beishon et al., 1998), although it is unclear to what extent this is only a perceived distinction.

Gender roles

The division of labor within the home has changed from the traditional pattern, according to which the husband is the breadwinner and the wife looks after the home/children, to a neo-traditional pattern, in which both partners are in paid employment and while the wife does most of the domestic labour in the home, she expects and usually gets some help from her husband (Mansfield and Collard, 1988). Fathers are now playing an increasingly prominent role in childcare. Although mothers are still more heavily involved in looking after the children, fathers now spend an increasing amount of time with their offspring (Lewis, 2000).

CONCLUSIONS

Britain began the twentieth century as a leading example of the Western European system of kinship based on the nuclear family. After World War II, divorce, separation, cohabitation, and single parenthood began to rise. The end of the century found Britain a leader of extramarital and teenage births, divorce, and rising cohabitation (Office of National Statistics, 2000). As a result, family in Britain is characterized by its diversity in structure and functions. Contributing factors to this diversity are the significant ethnic minority population with their own family traditions, and the changes that have occurred in family during recent decades.

Although family life revolves mainly around a nuclear unit, and a married or cohabiting couple with dependent children is still the most common family household in Britain, there is an increase in other family types, with the one-parent family household being the predominant alternative.

Despite these changes, the "image" of the two-partner family, with at least one child and probably still enjoying their first marriage, continues to be pervasive across most communities in Britain, with traditional marriage forms strongest amongst Britain's Asian communities and religious groups in the majority community. Gender roles have certainly changed over the past few decades but probably not as much as sometimes reported in the British media. Thus, although there has been some change in line with the ecological demands raised by changing work structures, with more men helping to look after their offspring, women at work maintain their "dual roles," retaining prime responsibility for "traditional" household chores. Finally, although most adults live apart from their parents and extended family, emotional bonds remain relatively strong. Thus proclamations of "The Death of the Family" (Cooper, 1971), in Britain at least, are premature.

13 Bulgaria: socialism and open-market economy

Elena Krasteva and Velislava Marinova-Schmidt

A HISTORICAL OUTLINE OF BULGARIA

Bulgaria was established as an independent nation-state in 1878, having rebelled against the Ottoman Empire, under whose domain it had been for 500 years.

After World War II the monarchy was replaced by a republic, which was ruled by the Bulgarian Communist Party. During its rule (1945–1989) the Bulgarian society adopted an urban and industrial character. The main changes during this period were: collectivization of the agricultural household; nationalization of industry and the land; reduction of private property; and changes in the ratio between industrial and agrarian development favoring industry and exclusive emphasis on the development of the productive sectors. In 1989 the social system changed. The Communist Party gave up its monopoly of power and the new established government was a coalition of several parties. After that, Bulgaria turned toward the realization of social and political reforms as well as the transformation into a market economy.

The present-day population of Bulgaria is approximately 8,300,000 inhabitants. Sofia is the capital, with 1,100,000 inhabitants. Bulgaria has 238 towns and 4,445 villages. Bulgaria became a member of the European Free Trade Association in 1999 and is currently a pre-integration member of the European Union; it is also a member of NATO and the United Nations.

ECOLOGICAL FEATURES

Bulgaria is situated in southeastern Europe, in the center of the Balkan peninsula. Its total area is 111,000 km^2, 30 percent of which is mountainous, and the remainder consists of plains, valleys, and hills. The mountains of Rhodopes, Rila, and Pirin are the spine of the country. The area is rich with rivers and natural sources of mineral water. The climate is temperate continental with four clearly defined seasons. In the region of the Black Sea the climate is coastal Mediterranean.

ORGANIZATIONS AND INSTITUTIONS OF SOCIETY

Economic organization

The ecological features shaped specific types of subsistence that remained unchanged for centuries. The mild climate, as well as the fertile soil, resulted in favorable conditions for the development of agriculture and animal husbandry. Agriculture is the traditional occupation of Bulgarians. The broad valleys permit the cultivation of crops. Large and small cattle are reared in the mountains. The cities are commercial and cultural centers. During recent decades services related to tourism have increased. Since 1989 the economic situation in the country has been characterized by a restructuring of the economy. The main occupations of Bulgarian people nowadays are commerce and agriculture.

Political institutions and legal system

In the period between the fourteenth and eighteenth centuries the Ottoman rulers destroyed the Bulgarian state institutions and the Orthodox religious structure. Bulgarian people lost their political, legal, and religious rights. All power in the Ottoman feudal system was concentrated in the figure of the sultan. Traditional Bulgarian culture survived only in smaller villages, which were often ignored by the centralized Ottoman authorities. Church life there experienced relatively little influence from the Greek Orthodox Church as well, because of the geographically isolated locations of the villages. Therefore, during the Ottoman domination, the villages became isolated repositories of Bulgarian culture, religion, social institutions, and language (Curtis, 1992). The political system in modern Bulgaria is a parliamentary republic. Since 1990, the president has been the head of the state and the prime minister is the chief executive and the head of the government (Council of Ministers). The members of government are elected by the National Assembly. The unicameral legislature (National Assembly) consists of 240 delegates, who are directly elected by the Bulgarian people for a 4-year mandate.

The educational system

During the centuries of Ottoman rule the socialization of children was accomplished exclusively by the family and the community. The father taught his craft to the son and the mother taught the daughter household matters. In the beginning of the twentieth century, state educational institutions assumed the socialization of children. The educational system of modern Bulgaria is accessible to all. In recent years there has been a tendency toward the creation of more private schools and private universities. Bulgarian parents value education highly and help their children financially during their studies (Spasovska, 1985a).

Religion

The Orthodox Church has played a significant role in the preservation of the Bulgarian language, national identity, and values. At the present time 85.7 percent of the population is Christian Orthodox.

BONDS WITH GROUPS IN THE IMMEDIATE COMMUNITY

In the agrarian communities of Bulgaria there were very close relations among the members who were organized into large extended family groups (zadruga), which safeguarded order and security in the community. Each member was protected by the community. The problems of the community were solved among the members, who demonstrated collective consciousness and mutual assistance in cases of external danger (Hadjiiski, 1995). At the present time the ecology of the big cities results in more anonymity and a loosening of the close relationships among the inhabitants of the same neighborhood.

THE FAMILY

Marriage

With regard to endogamy, in the traditional family of the past, marriage was restricted to the choice of spouse from the same religion, mostly Bulgarian Orthodox, while in the modern family the marital choice has no restrictions. In regard to exogamy, norms prohibit marriage within the nuclear family, between first cousins and with the family of the godfather.

Social sanctions against divorce were strong in the traditional family although the Orthodox Church permitted divorce for three reasons. At the present time, the legislature still maintains laws with moral and financial sanctions against the divorced. The sanctions were established by law in 1985 and after the law was passed, the number of divorces in Bulgaria diminished. The percentage of marriages that terminated in divorce was 10 percent in 1965, 15 percent in 1975, 21 percent in 1985, and 19 percent in 1990. This is a relatively low percentage in comparison with the rest of the East European countries, lower in comparison with Western European countries, and somewhat higher than in South European countries, e.g., Albania, Greece, Italy, and Serbia.

In the traditional family decisions to marry were made with the agreement of the fathers of both families. There were strict norms about the age, the kind of premarital contacts and the behavior of men and women. Strong community sanctions prohibited an individual from marrying until his/her elder brothers and sisters had married. Today an individual decides whom to marry without the consent of the parents.

Obtaining a spouse in the traditional family was not related to legal transfer of property from the father of the bride to the family of the groom. There was an unofficial dowry, that is, the father of the bride would offer money or property to the young couple in order to aid them in setting up a household. There was a silent agreement that the family of the groom should provide a home for the couple to live in and the family of the bride should help with the furniture. This practice is still in operation today, though mainly in the villages (Hadjiiski, 1995).

Family structure

The traditional agrarian extended family (*zadruga*), from the end of the nineteenth century was patrilineal; it included from two to four families, in which kin of both sexes were related through the men only. The basic nucleus was the pair of parents joined by the families of one or more married sons (lineal family) (Telbizov, 1946).

The Bulgarian extended family included three or more generations. Unmarried sons or daughters were included as members (Makaveeva, 1991). The father was the patriarch of the family, who made decisions for all the members who were under his protection. In the extended family there were close relations among parents-in-law, children-in-law, and siblings-in-law (affinal relationships), among grandparents and grandchildren (lineal relationships), and among uncles, nieces, and nephews (collateral relationships).

Residence after marriage was patrilocal, because the sons who married remained in the house of their father with their family, and the daughters who married resided in the house of their father-in law.

Family roles and functions

The main characteristic of the agrarian extended family was the guiding role of the parental couple. The norms prescribed the father as the major authority in all spheres of family life. Mother came second in the family hierarchy, with the role of wife and housekeeper. The descriptions of the traditional roles of the family members which follow are based on Makaveeva (1991).

Father

Paterfamilias and head of the family . . . Behaves with authority and dignity . . . Should possess the social performance and the ability to provide a good economic situation for the family . . . Handles the finances . . . Coordinates the work of the family members . . . Distributes duties among the family members . . . Takes part in the family labor until old age . . . Decides the fate of all who are under his protection . . . Represents the family in the community . . . Owner of the mobile and immobile property of the family . . . The power of the father ends with his death.

Mother

Second in the family hierarchy . . . Subordinate, modest, obedient . . . Always willing to attend to her husband and his parents . . . Regulates the housework . . . Looks after the children and takes care of the needs of the family members for clothes and food . . . Controls daughters and daughters-in-law . . . Sometimes takes part in the hard agricultural work along with men . . . Being a woman, the mother does not inherit paternal property.

Parents

Both are responsible for transmitting social and practical experience to children.

Women

Should not have children if they are not married . . . Do not have right to paternal property . . . Should have a big dowry . . . Should be good mothers, wives, and housekeepers.

Children

Owe respect and obedience to their parents and to adults in general . . . Should help with the housework . . .The elder son usually takes the leadership after the death of the father and inherits the greater part of the paternal property . . . The roles of the other sons and daughters differ according to their age . . . The roles of the daughters-in-law differ according to the position of their husbands in the family . . . The wife of the elder son usually takes the position and the responsibilities of the mother upon her death.

CHANGES IN THE FAMILY

Demographics

The number of marriages per 1,000 persons in Bulgaria has been declining since 1960, reaching 4.7 in 1993 (Sugareva, 1996). Only 5 percent of women are not married at the age of 30 to 34 and this percentage has not changed in the last three decades. Women in Bulgaria marry at a younger age in comparison to women in the rest of the European countries. The average age of marriage for women in Bulgaria is 21.

The decline of the birth rate began later than in the rest of Europe and Eastern Europe. Since 1990 Bulgaria has a negative birth rate because of the many young people who have left the country. The number of births per 1,000 women of childbearing age in Bulgaria was 59.9 in 1980 and 44.3 in 1991 (Kojuharov, 1992).

Family values

Findings from contemporary studies (Iachkova, 1997) show that the family occupies the first place in the values of Bulgarians. Family, health, and good children are the three main values of Bulgarians without differences according to gender, age, social position or economic level.

Changes in the structure of the family imply changes in family values. The body of research on this topic testifies that many traditional values are still preserved among Bulgarians – namely those which are associated with mutual help in the extended family, good relations among the family members, responsibilities of children toward relatives, and re-sponsibility of parents toward children. Young people in Bulgaria do not reject these values. The only factor that is rejected by Bulgarians is associated with the hierarchical roles of the father and mother, that is, the absolute power of the father over the finances and all the significant matters in the family and the subordinate position of the mother and her role of housewife and good mother.

CONCLUSIONS

Family structure and function in most European countries today are in a transitional state. These changes, which began in northern Europe and include a number of Western European countries and the United States, are not occurring at the same rate in Bulgaria.

Today's Bulgarian family is experiencing a double transition. On the one hand there is a transition from traditional to new family forms and behavior, as observed in all developed societies. In Bulgaria this transition began later and is occurring at a more rapid rate. On the other hand, there is a transition from totalitarian to democratic social structures, which is taking place in the entire Bulgarian society and has its impact on the family as well. Analysis of this double transition is possible with the understanding of three factors: (1) the general tendencies of the development of the family in Europe, (2) the specific features of south eastern Europe, and (3) the nature of the transformations that have taken place in Bulgarian society since 1990 and their impact on the family (Sugareva, 1996).

In the conditions of transition to a modern economy there are two contradictory directions: on the one hand toward conservation of the traditional values, and on the other hand toward change and adaptation to the new conditions. The Bulgarian family is changing in order to adapt to the new social realities. What is the essence of the changes in the family in Bulgaria?

The traditional family in Bulgaria two centuries ago corresponded to the type found in agrarian societies and to the traditional type of demographic reproduction with high birth rate and high degree of mortality. Its main characteristics were domination of the father, many children, and several generations residing under the same roof. The traditional family pattern was widespread in the whole country until the beginning of the twentieth century and, in the villages, until the 1960s.

Profound changes appeared in the structure of the Bulgarian family after the World War II, when the socialist system was established. It acquired the features of a monogamous family in which new needs and activities developed. The global changes in the economic and cultural life of the nation in the period of socialism played a decisive role in creating a new type of family relations. The old traditional roles of the family members diminished and the actual equality between man and woman was strengthened.

The dominating communist ideology set the model of the working woman. The economic activity of women was higher than 90 percent for ages the 20 to 44, which is higher than the percentage in the West European countries and in most East European countries (Klinger, 1990).

This high economic activity was the main factor that changed the position of the woman in the family. The woman continued to take care of the housework and the children, and in addition worked to maintain the family. In many families the woman became the social and financial head of the family. This shift in the distribution of family power is the main characteristic of the modern family in Bulgaria today. The relations between the parents changed from typically traditional with the dominance of man to democratic, where husband and wife are linked with feelings of love and tenderness in a relationship of equality.

The above does not mean that the extended family has lost its presence in modern Bulgaria and has separated into small nuclear families, characteristic of an industrialized society. Very important family values associated with maintaining contact with relatives, children respecting adults, children's obligations toward parents, and parents' responsibilities toward, children are still valid today and are accepted also by the young people in Bulgaria. In fact, the members of the nuclear families maintain close contact with relatives, telephone and visit them regularly, offer them emotional and economic help. The families have the nuclear structure where two generations live under the same roof, but function as an extended family.

In the cities, where the model of the nuclear family is strong, a new type of inter-generational relationship can be observed. The different generations show a marked preference and a tendency to live "close at a distance" (Spasovska, 1985b), that is, in separate apartments but close to each other. This type of model of contact preserves the strong emotional bonds and the psychological proximity between the generations in conditions of stated independence and non-interference in the conjugal relationship. The preference for living under the same roof is characteristic of the elderly and in the agrarian regions, while the preference for living "close at a distance" is characteristic of residents of the cities and of those with higher educational levels (Spasovska, 1985b). The preference for a family of three generations, which exists in the villages as well as in the cities, shows that the traditional patterns are still strong. The maintenance of this type of family is based on particularities in the lifestyle in the region and benefits the mutual assistance between the generations.

The conclusion is that the modern family in Bulgaria has preserved several characteristics of the extended family, primarily in its function, in spite of all the changes in the social and economic situation of the country during recent decades. The traditional agrarian extended family has not simply separated into small nuclear families in the urban environment; it has just changed its configuration, keeping the maintenance of contact with the larger kin.

14 Canada

Kyunghwa Kwak and John W. Berry

A HISTORICAL OUTLINE OF CANADA

In its short history Canada has become a diverse and pluralistic modern society, both in terms of its geography and the contacts among its cultural groups. When the first European explorers – mainly from France and Britain – arrived on the east coast of Canada in the 1500s they found a land populated by less than half a million Aboriginal peoples. The Inuit lived along the coastal edges and islands of the Arctic; First Nations, or Aboriginal, peoples inhabited the rest of the land. As the population of French and British colonialists grew, settlers expanded westward for trade and land by colonial policy and war. Following the American Revolution of 1776, colonists loyal to Britain came up from America and settled in Canada. The eighteenth and nineteenth centuries saw a steady flow of British immigrants on the one hand, and Chinese, Italian, and Irish workers on the other.

In the early twentieth century, many settlers originating from Eastern European countries came to the Canadian prairies to farm. After the 1930s, with the growth of cities, the tide of immigration flowed to urban centres, where the majority of Canadians resided and worked. Between 1946 and 1954, 96 percent of the immigrants admitted to Canada came from Europe. In the 1950s the federal government's immigration policy had been to fill the country's needs in the natural resource and industrial sectors; the policy later shifted toward acceptance of professionally educated workers. In the 1960s, Canada halted its previous preferential treatment of British, French, and American citizens (with, for example, The Chinese Immigration Act of 1923; Canada's Immigration Act, 1952) and finally implemented immigration policies which did not officially discriminate on the basis of race, color, or religion. Some legal landmarks have also contributed to the shape of Canadian society, particularly the statutes of official bilingualism (1969; 1987), multiculturalism (1971; 1987), and The Canadian Charter of Rights and Freedoms (1982).

Since the 1980s, the majority of immigrants have come from Asia, Africa, and the Caribbean, a far cry from the earlier predominance of immigrants of European origin; most choose to live in large cosmopolitan cities such as Toronto, Montreal, and Vancouver. As a result of this shift, visible minorities have risen to 11.2 percent of the population in 1996; Canada has since become an even more diverse multicultural nation. Despite this influx of immigrants, and despite lingering questions surrounding Québec's place in Canada, Canadian national identity has remained strong.

ECOLOGICAL FEATURES

Canada is the second largest country in the world after Russia, with a total area of 9,970,610 km^2 and spanning a distance of 5,514 km from east to west and 4,634 km from north to south. Canada's immense size has created some problems for its scarce population of just over 30 million (31,413,990 in 2001). For reasons of agriculture, climate, economics, and geography, over 90 percent of the Canadian population lives within 200 km of the Canada–United States border. Over three-quarters of all Canadians live in urban areas (77 percent in 1996); in fact, about one-half of all Canadians currently live in Canada's 10 largest cities. Roman Catholicism remains the single largest denomination (48 percent), professed mainly by those of French, Irish, and Italian origin, followed by various strains of Protestantism (37 percent) and Asian religions (4 percent).

Canada is a Federal State consisting of 10 provinces and three Territories. Originally a federation of only four Eastern provinces, the country grew to incorporate the Western Provinces (British Columbia, Alberta, Saskatchewan, and Manitoba) and the Northern Territories from 1867, the date of Canada's confederation, until 1949, when Newfoundland and Labrador entered the confederation. The ethnic mix varies by region and province. For example, in Newfoundland 95 percent of the population are of British origin, while in Québec the British comprised only 8 percent. In two provinces, Manitoba and Saskatchewan, the majority of the population is neither British nor French. Ontario and British Columbia are the two provinces where most ethnic groups have chosen to reside. The Province of Québec is predominately of French origin, and the Territory of Nunavut of Inuit origin; their social institutions and policies – language, education, civil law – reflect these origins accordingly.

Until 1971, the number of persons per family in Canada remained fairly constant. Since then, although the number of families has increased, the numbers of persons and children per family have been in a steady decline, 1.7 children living in a household in 1971 as compared to only 1.3 in 1991. On the other hand, since the 1980s, immigration continues to expand Canada's population and rich ethnocultural diversity. As the number of Asians and Aboriginals has increased, the proportion of British origin has decreased, making up only 37 percent of the population in 2001. Education and health care are now being transformed to reflect the needs of cultural groups and regional variations and to promote diversity and multiculturalism.

STRUCTURE AND FUNCTION OF THE FAMILY IN CANADA

In a culturally diverse society such as Canada, it is inaccurate to talk about the family structure without considering various differences including culture of origin, immigration history, and socioeconomic background. As the composition of Canada's population has changed, the typical family pattern has also changed from that of a nuclear family to various other forms of family. Close physical and emotional ties with extended family members are more apparent for some ethnocultural groups than others; recent immigrants from southern Europe and Asia as well as First Nation Indians are some examples. Among Canadians the incidence of intergroup marriage also varies greatly according to the couple's ethnic origins.

Although a great deal of variation exists among families across all ethnocultural groups residing in Canada, economic, legal, and social changes help explain significant trends in Canadian family life.

Economic changes

Canadian household income has shifted from single to dual (e.g., 34 percent in 1967 vs. 62 percent in 1986). In the labor force, the participation rate by Canadian men between the ages of 25 and 55 has been more or less constant, hovering around 93 percent from 1971 to 1991, but that of Canadian women has increased dramatically, from 44 percent to 77 percent during the same period. Working outside the home and contributing to the family income has consequently changed power relations within the marriage and the family. This, in turn, has also contributed to a rising divorce rate. As a result of marriage break-ups, many single-parent families live in poverty, especially those headed by the mother. The cost of living for families has also increased, in part because of prolonged residence of children at home and a longer life span for the older generations (female 81 and male 75 years old in

1996). Owing to the significant increase in cost of living but only a very limited increase in family income over two decades, the children of the 1990s are considered to be the first generation of Canadians who face the prospect of being less wealthy than their parents, even though Canadians continued to enjoy a high standard of living (GNP CDN $26,420 in 1996) compared to the rest of the world.

Legal changes

In working conditions and family relations there have been important improvements in children's rights and the status of women. The Family Law Reform Commission initiated major changes in family law from the late 1970s throughout the 1980s. Significant changes included equal responsibility shared by both spouses for the support and care of the children, both within marriage and after separation. The custody of children is usually awarded to mothers upon divorce, and child support can be enforced by the court when the noncustodial parent defaults on payments. The Canadian Charter of Rights and Freedoms (1982) has been used to challenge a number of issues relating to family law, too. For example, like mothers, both biological and adoptive fathers have a right to parental leave. Also, family members have the right to decide not to continue medical treatment if there is no hope of recovery for the patient.

Social changes

Although women increasingly work outside the home, comprising 58 percent of the workforce in 1996, the majority of Canadian women are employed in fields traditionally assigned to women, and household and domestic tasks continue to be unequally shared by the husband and wife. Women in Canada with paid work outside the home still spend an average of four hours a day on childcare and household chores. Overall, women do much more of the household work than men, twice or three times more when they hold a full-time job, and five times more when they hold a part-time job. Although women's income contributes to the family's total earnings, lower wages for women than men for the equivalent job ensure that domestic labor and power are still not shared equally at home. With more emphasis on individualism and independence, people feel less bound to be content with an unhappy marriage or to be swayed by social pressure. Serial monogamy is becoming more prevalent, and more couples are choosing to live together in common-law unions. More couples are delaying childbearing or planning to remain childfree. Thus Canadian families have undergone many variations in lifestyle and family structure, as compared to families of earlier times. One persistent issue, however, remains women's devotion to family and home and its rightful appreciation.

ETHNOCULTURAL GROUPS AND THEIR FAMILIES IN CANADA

Turning to the specific families from the four important ethnocultural categories, the following reviews them in terms of their history and current standings in Canada.

French-Canadian families

Preceding the British settlers, the French *habitant* families were fairly self-sufficient and raised a large number of children per family for centuries. The family was patriarchal and roles of family members were clearly defined. Even though the mother was the center of the home, the father ruled, and the wife and children were expected to obey. After 1950, with increased urbanization and industrialization, social mobility among French-Canadians and geographical dislocation of family members contributed to diminished contact among kin members. Marriage with a non-French Canadian, non-Catholic, or non-French speaking spouse were also significant factors for lessened contact among the extended family. Since the late 1960s, both the birth rate and the marriage rate in Québec have declined. In fact, these were lower than the national averages. In 1988, the former was 13.1 per 1,000 compared to 14.6, and in 1985, the latter was 6.4 per 1,000 compared to 7.8 in the rest of Canada. While Québec's divorce rate has been close to the national figure since 1977, its marriage rate has been lower than the national average. These changes had been the result of a decline in the Roman Catholic Church's influence, delayed marriages and the practice of birth control, as well as eased social pressures and fewer legal impediments for common-law relationships and divorce.

British-Canadian families

British settlers engaged in many occupations and lived in wider regions across the country and they were also not a homogeneous group in religion, politics, or social status. The emigration of many United Empire Loyalists from south of the border after the American War of Independence (1775–80) made the British population larger than the

French, and further contributed to the establishment of the English legal system in Upper Canada. In recent times, among British-Canadians, exogamy has been increasing and couples, up to 30 percent of young couples, more often choose to live in common-law relationships. Divorce is also on the rise. Over 50 percent of new marriages end in divorce, although most choose to remarry, a situation which often leads to blended families with children from the previous marriages. Similar socioeconomic status tends to prevail in the choice of marriage partner. In general, a nuclear family is the standard, and independence among family members is expected. Family relationships across generations vary greatly depending on proximity and opportunity for travel. Traditionally, fathers exerted stronger authority outside the home, mothers, inside. The British family is, however, in transition from a rather sedentary, extended, permanent, patriarchal-dominated institution to one more variable in structure and role allocation in order to accommodate demands of greater mobility, higher fragmentation, and more egalitarian relationships.

Aboriginal families

By 1996, the Aboriginal community accounted for 3 percent of Canada's population, including 554,000 Indians, 21,000 Métis, and 41,000 Inuit. Métis, descendants of intermarriage between Native-Indians and Europeans, have been officially recognized as Aboriginal people since 1982, but their Aboriginal rights and collective group boundaries are currently being challenged in the Canadian Supreme Court, and hence are not included here.

Inuit families

Among the eight main tribal groups of the Inuit, there is considerable variation in lifestyle, which bears upon social grouping and family relationships. Traditionally, because of the harsh environment, families were not large. Most marriages were monogamous and patriarchal as the bride came to live in the groom's community, whose familiar hunting territory was nearby. Kinship ties extended significantly beyond the nuclear family in order to maximize the use of resources and extend cooperation, as in hunting for food. After World War II, the Inuit moved into settlements to be centralized in order to gain stability for the family and a better life for future generations. The extended family has retained its significant role in these settlements, but throughout these transitions the role of Inuit women, especially, has changed. Many acquire income through employment outside the home or the sale of homemade handi-craft work. More recently, social, economic, and political forces appear to be a greater threat to the stability of the Inuit family than the physical environment. The younger generations in particular suffer from psycho-logical and behavioral maladaption brought on by poverty, physical isolation, and bicultural conflicts. Currently, however, the cultural heri-tage of strong family bonding, coupled with community leadership, could do much to assure collective stability ahead.

Native-Indian families

Native-Indian families were traditionally self-sufficient and matri-archal, as the strongest family bonds were between mothers and their children. Sex roles were clearly defined, and hierarchical authority was given to older men, but children were treated with respect. The bride selected her male partner for monogamous marriage. Newborns were nursed by breast-feeding for two to three years, and girls were preferred to boys. In the Native-Indian families, no physical punish-ment was employed in the disciplining of children. Young men were initiated into adulthood by spending weeks alone in the forest.

The Native-Indian family has several distinctive features compared to the average Canadian family. In 1985 single-parent families compose 20 percent, but the family size is larger, with 4.5 individuals. Although their marriage rate is lower, the birth rate per Native woman is 3.15, com-pared to 1.7 for the rest of the Canadian population. Life expectancy still remains about 10 years shorter for both males and females when com-pared to the Canadian national average. Living on reserves, many Native Indians are unskilled and endure prolonged periods of unemployment. Their standard of living, sense of identity, and cohesion of tribe and family have steadily declined; transmission of their culture to the next generation remains in jeopardy. Yet, increasingly, Native peoples are gaining new political power, which in turn may have a positive impact on social structure and family life.

Other ethnic families

Ethnic immigrant families may experience hardship when the younger generation relinquishes ethnic collective traditions and welcomes more individual norms. The choice of spouse is customarily of great import-ance to ethnic families; however, the practice of endogamous marriage varies widely across ethnic groups.

Portuguese-Canadian families

Portuguese-Canadian families tend to be traditional, patriarchal, and Roman Catholic. They maintain an extensive communication network among kin members in Canada. A man's closest relationship is usually with his brother or father rather than with his wife. With a higher education level, however, younger generations are becoming more egalitarian in their family relations, and many young families desire more freedom from the expectations of their relatives.

Italian-Canadian families

Italian-Canadians have close and extended families. Upon arrival in Canada, it is common for Italians to live with relatives until they can establish their own home. Relatives often live near one another, and frequently meet for family events. Within the home, children are expected to show gratitude for the sacrifices made by their parents, and, as adults, to support their ageing parents. Women, especially daughters, are fairly restricted in their social activities, whereas sons or men are more free in their social exchanges. Among Italian-Canadians ethnic endogamy has been declining but religious endogamy between Roman Catholics persists.

Chinese-Canadian families

In the 1960s after the Canadian laws allowed more non-white immigrants, Chinese immigrants started to arrive, principally from Hong Kong. Since then Chinese-Canadian families have become upwardly mobile and have moved into suburban areas. Currently Chinese-Canadian families are slightly smaller than the average Canadian family, but many more families live in extended-family households. Families make financial sacrifices so that children can obtain a good education. Grandparents play an important role in keeping the Chinese tradition alive in the family. As the result of a few key political events in China, notably the Tiananmen Square Massacre (1989) and the return of Hong Kong to China (1997), the number of Chinese immigrants to Canada has dramatically increased and their ethnic network has been correspondingly strengthened.

CONCLUSIONS

Making allowances for some regional and cultural variations in Canada, we can observe that nuclear, monogamous and egalitarian families predominate over extended, hierarchical arrangements. On the other hand, current changes in family structure show a decline in family size, number of children, and the extended family network, whereas the rates for common-law unions, inter-ethnic marriage, divorce, and single-parent families are climbing. In spite of increased income per family, today's younger generations and new families may not enjoy the same standard as previous generations, because of higher expectations about their standard of living. More specific laws exist to protect different members of family and family relations. Finally, Canadian society more readily accepts various types of family; however, within the family, erosion of the division of labor by gender has been very slow.

15 Chile: new bottle, old wine

Francisco Donoso-Maluf

A HISTORICAL OUTLINE OF CHILE

Chile became an independent republic in 1810–1818 by rebelling against almost 300 years of Spanish colonization. By the 1830s, Chile was able to build one of the most orderly and stable political systems in Latin America (Collier, 1985; Heise, 1979). Contrary to its democratic tradition, from 1973 to 1990 Chile lived under a military regime led by General Augusto Pinochet, with systematic gross human rights violations. The recent political transition toward democracy has been intertwined with a free market economic model.

The current population of Chile is 15 million inhabitants, one-third of whom live in its capital, Santiago. At present, just 4.6 percent of the population considers itself as belonging to some of the surviving indigenous ethnic groups, most of whom (87.3 percent) claim to be Mapuches (Instituto Nacional de Estadísticas, 2003).

ECOLOGICAL FEATURES

Located between the Cordillera de Los Andes and the Pacific Ocean, Chile is a narrow country, 4,270 km long and with an average width of 177 km, in southwestern South America. Chile is mountainous, with less than 20 percent of its surface flat. With the exception of some military posts, the vast Chilean Antarctic territories remain uninhabited. Chile has a very variable climate, with the northern desert of Atacama, rich in

The empirical work for the Chilean Chapter of the research "Family Structure and Function Across Cultures: Psychological Variations" was possible thanks to the financial support of both The Research Committee of the University of Athens and the Dirección de Investigación de la Universidad de La Serena (DIULS).

I want to express my gratitude to Professor José Luis Saiz for his thoughtful guidance at a preliminary data analysis stage, as well as to our students team of the Department of Psychology of the Universidad de La Serena for their very valuable collaboration in data collection and coding processes.

mining ore, a central template region where 65 percent of the population is concentrated and whose land is fertile for agriculture, and a southern area with a cold and rainy maritime climate, suitable primarily for cattle and sheep raising.

ORGANIZATION AND INSTITUTIONS OF SOCIETY

Economic organization

Until the 1930s, most of the Chilean population was dispersed in rural areas, which were mainly economically organized under the estate system (*hacienda*) until the 1960s, when the Agrarian Reform was implemented. The impoverishment of rural areas and the fall of saltpeter exports by the early twentieth century resulted in progressive urbanization. After a model centered on national industrialization as a way to replace imports (1929–1973), Chile implemented a free market model together with the restructuring of the State. Since the early 1990s, Chile has shown unprecedented economic growth rates (GDP averaged 8 percent during 1991–1997) and rising levels of exportations in areas such as fruit, forestry, fishing, and mining, while copper remains the main Chilean export. However, such progress has tended to coexist with three chronic problems: (1) a very sensitive national economy in respect to world economy changes; (2) a poverty index that during the 1990s averaged as much as one-fourth of the population; and (3) a strong income concentration, currently of 61 percent, in the richest quintile of the population, while just 3.3 percent in the poorest (Comisión Económica para América Latina y el Caribe, 2002; Programa de las Naciones Unidas para el Desarrollo, 2002a).

Since the middle of the 1970s economic activity has been characterized by services (49 percent of male labor force and 82 percent of female), industry (31 percent of male and 14 percent of female) and agriculture (19 percent of male and 5 percent of female). Women's participation rate in the labor market has increased from 23 percent in 1985 to 37.6 percent in 2000 (Programa de las Naciones Unidas para el Desarrollo, 2002a).

Political institutions and legal system

Four main diachronic political-institutional steps can be pointed out in Chile. The first was a strong and early option for a presidential system over a parliamentary one, through the 1833 Constitution. Second, a non-conflictive split between the State and the Catholic Church took place, through the 1925 Constitution. A third step, also related to the 1925 Constitution, was the so-called "social question," which allowed the rise of the Chilean middle classes and the conquest of considerable social rights by/for/to the lower classes. The fourth step is related to a modernization process initiated under Pinochet's authoritarian regime, which involved a new institutional foundation in different spheres (social, political, economic) through the 1980 Constitution.

The educational system

Free and compulsory public education was initially seen as a unilateral imposition from the State, especially among rural families, where child labor was more valued than education (Gonzalbo, 1999; Serrano, 1999). Today, 94.6 percent of Chilean population (94.8 percent male and 94.4 percent female) is literate (Instituto Nacional de Estadísticas, 1999). Despite this, considerable differences in the quality of education between the current various types of primary and secondary schools (fully public, subsidized, and private) persist. In a similar way, the historically elitist nature of Chilean university education remains, and has been exacerbated since the 1980 reforms, when public universities began to charge tuition fees. At the present time, 4.1 percent of Chileans aged 5 years and older have completed education at pre-primary level, 41 percent at primary, 36 percent at secondary, and 16 percent at tertiary, while 2.7 percent have had no schooling. There are no significant gender differences at any educational level (Instituto Nacional de Estadísticas, 2003).

Religion

Today, 70 percent of the Chilean population is Catholic, while 15.1 percent is Evangelical and 8.3 percent is either atheist or agnostic (Instituto Nacional de Estadísticas, 2003). Except for the 1960s–1980s, the Catholic hierarchy has maintained a historical conservative orientation, which currently involves considerable influence over diverse State policies (i.e., sexual education for youth programs and contraception methods) and over important parliamentary sectors in order to prevent a divorce law in Chile.

BONDS WITH GROUPS IN THE IMMEDIATE COMMUNITY

Regarding the Chilean traditional family, mainly in its rural context, it is necessary to point out that the estate or *hacienda* was not only a production unit, but also a social-cultural one. According to Donoso (1989) and Orrego-Luco (1983), the estate could be represented as a family itself where the landowner (*hacendado, patrón*) and his family had the parental role while "their" servants (*inquilinos*) and their families performed the role of obedient children. The landowner simultaneously represented both protection and exploitation: somebody whose discourse emphasized the sacred value of marriage among his servants and, at the same time, imposed an "open sexuality" (Valdés, 1995) over their wives, daughters, aunts, and/or sisters. As a result, a large number of "illegitimate children" or *huachos* have been documented as a significant component of the traditional Chilean family (Montecino, 1993; Salazar, 1990; Valdés, 1995).

THE FAMILY

Marriage

According to legal and religious norms, marriage as much in the traditional as in the current family, has been exogamous, although marriage of first cousins has been permitted.

Until 2004, Chile was one of the last countries in the world that had not legalized divorce. The old legal framework – unaltered since 1884 – allowed only a "divorce without bond dissolution," which impeded remarriage. The usual solution for this obstacle was the annulment of civil marriages through a fraudulent legal procedure. As this way was not always affordable, most couples used to opt for a de facto separation, which not only impeded a new marriage but also involved a serious legal vacuum. After divorce without bond dissolution, the mother maintained custody of the children, the father was in charge of food provision, and liquidation of patrimony was legally shared. In the cases of annulments and de facto separations, many of the relationships between men and women used to be of an informal (and, consequently, unstable) nature.

The new Civil Marriage Law (2004) allows couples to be divorced after being separated for at least a year, if both spouses agree. If only one party agrees, the waiting period is three years. A judge can approve a divorce without a waiting period if one of the spouses proves violations of marital duties by a partner, such as violence, homosexuality, prostitution, drug addiction, or a criminal conviction. Couples seeking a divorce must also go through a mediation process. After divorce, the partner who could not develop a laboring or professional career as a result of his/her dedication to housework or childcare receives an economic compensation from the ex-spouse. Decisions about custody of children and food provision are made at the Family Tribunals.

During the past decade, some legal changes have allowed the overcoming of previous ways of filial segregation (i.e., food pension, inheritance, etc.) by eliminating the juridical distinction between "legitimate" and "illegitimate" children.

From 1992 to 2002, married Chileans decreased from 51.8 percent to 46.2 percent, separations increased from 3.4 percent to 4.7 percent, and annulments from 0.3 percent to 0.4 percent, respectively (Instituto Nacional de Estadísticas, 2003).

In traditional upper-class families, where marriage was mainly a strategy to obtain economic and social advantages (Bravo, 1990), decisions to marry were generally made by the fathers, partially influenced by close relatives. In the *hacienda*, decisions to marry among servants were usually made by the landowner or his wife, in order to avoid their "immoral" cohabitation. Outside the estate, in the small plot families, decisions to marry were freer, coexisting with considerable and unstable cohabitation (Salinas, 1994; Valdés, 1995). Although in today's Chile decisions to marry are made by the bride and the groom, some racial, religious, and social-economic aspects that may influence individual choices still persist. Currently, the main reasons for marriage are love (60 percent), pregnancy (36 percent), and the desire to leave the parental home (26 percent) (Comisión Nacional de la Familia, 1993).

Despite the patriarchal and contractual nature of marriage in the traditional family, obtaining a spouse did not always involve the unilateral father's dowry to the groom. In fact, usually the families of both the bride and the groom contributed – money, land, a house in upper-class marriages and animals, clothes, or some money in lower-class marriages (Cavieres, 1990). Today, such contributions tend to be more restricted, especially in middle- and lower-class marriages (some money, furniture or appliances).

FAMILY STRUCTURE

The traditional Chilean extended family structure could be described as patrilineal according to its lineal descent, and patriarchal in respect to the paternal and/or grandpaternal centralization of power, authority and patrimony, which was formally (legal) and informally (social norms/ customs) supported.

The extended family could include up to three generations, with collateral kin (cousins, uncles and aunts, nieces and nephews) and affinal relationships (parents-in-law, children-in-law and siblings-in-law), in addition to *compadrazgo* (bonds with relatives or friends through baptism of the children).

Residence after marriage was usually patrilocal. However, mainly as a result of the lack of both land or house space, residence was also near the wife's relatives.

Beyond this, another kind of traditional family structure – mainly in rural areas – was characterized by the absence of father, unmarried mothers and their illegitimate children or *huachos*. In fact, the *huacharaje* (Salazar, 1990) was also found outside the estate, where the *peones* or *gañanes* (wandering agrarian workers) practiced an open sexuality within wide geographical areas. Generally, these unmarried women and their children remained within their poor rural extended families (Montecino, 1993; Valdés, 1995).

Family roles and functions

In roles of the traditional family members, the father, who worked in order to provide food and other goods to his family ("breadwinner"), was the main decision-maker, and in charge of imposing discipline and respect over the children; the mother was in charge of housework and childcare; while the children were to respect and obey their parents and relatives. Children usually worked to help the fathers, particularly in agricultural areas (Cavieres, 1990, 1997). When siblings were numerous, older children (mostly older daughters) used to help mother in raising the children. Father usually worked with grandfather, when he was the owner of a piece of land. Mother shared housework with her mother-in-law. Grandparents and uncles/aunts had some degree of authority over the grandchildren/nephews/nieces, even when the children's parents were present.

CHANGES IN THE FAMILY

Demographic changes

The rate of marriages per 1,000 persons has decreased from 7.0 in 1968 to 6.6 in 1992. Cohabitation (free union) has increased from 5.7 percent in 1992 to 8.9 percent in 2002 (Instituto Nacional de Estadísticas, 2003). The rate of births per 1,000 persons has decreased from 37.5 in 1960 to 18.7 in 1997 (Instituto Nacional de Estadísticas, 1999). However, the number of births out of wedlock has increased – mainly among younger and poorer women – from 17.5 percent in 1965 to 34.3 percent in 1990 and 47.7 percent in 1999 (Servicio Nacional de la Mujer, 2001).

New family structures

Today's Chilean family has an average size of 4.7 members in the lowest quintile income families and 3.1 members in the highest quintile; and of 3.6 members in urban families and 3.5 in rural (Comisión Económica para América Latina y el Caribe, 2002; Instituto Nacional de Estadísticas, 2003). Currently, poverty affects 16.6 percent of families while indigent families reach 4.6 percent (Feres, 2001).

The transition from the extended family to the nuclear family began in the 1970s. In 1970, the nuclear families were just 30.3 percent, while the extended reached 64 percent. In 2002, the nuclear families were 57 percent while the extended were 21.9 percent (Instituto Nacional de Estadísticas, 2003). Despite such a structural transition, extended family life retains an important place in Chilean society. Although couples are expected to set up their own households, they remain in close contact with the members of their larger families. Children generally get to know their cousins well, usually on weekends – in order to *tomar once* (to have an afternoon snack) – and on holidays, when time is spent in the company of relatives. It is also common to find children living for extended periods of time for educational or other reasons in households headed by relatives, sometimes even cousins of their parents. These extended family ties also provide a network of support in times of nuclear family crises. It is also usual for close friendships among adults to lead to links that are family-like. For example, children often refer to their parents' friends as "uncle" or "aunt" (Hudson, 1994).

One-parent families have increased, reaching 16 percent in 1992 (8.8 percent nuclear, 7.2 percent extended). Owing to the need for economic support as well as help in family roles fulfillment, a considerable amount of lower-and middle-class one-parent families include other relatives in the same household, thus becoming extended families. By the early 1990s, 43 percent of the one-parent families were extended (Muñoz and Reyes, 1997).

Increasing female heads of households

Female heads of families have increased, reaching 28 percent in 1998 and 31.5 percent in 2002 (Arriagada, 2002; Instituto Nacional de Estadísticas, 2003). Furthermore, 83.9 percent of one-parent families were headed by women in 1992, and 87.9 percent in 1998 (Muñoz and

Reyes, 1997; Comisión Económica para América Latina y el Caribe, 2002). Because women's incomes are lower than men's, these families are strongly associated with poverty and children's incomes may become significant (Reca, Pérez, and Espíndola, 1996).

Family values

Marital relationships

A good marital relationship is most valued by men while maternity and relationships with children are mostly valued by women. Men and women continue to value the traditional parental roles of the husband as provider and the wife at home with children (Comisión Nacional de la Familia, 1993). With the increase of women's participation in the labor market, the persistence of these traditional values in men produces conflicts in marital relationships. Arriagada (2002) has underlined the tense coexistence between the new family values (higher autonomy, motherhood as an option, female economic independence) and the old ones (subjective dependence, pregnancy in adolescents, persistence of sexual division of housework).

Parental relationships

Children report that parents pay special attention to their school performance, particularly of sons. Children point out that their relationship with their mother is better than with their father (Comisión Nacional de la Familia, 1993). According to Programa de las Naciones Unidas para el Desarrollo (2002b), Chilean youth has become highly critical in respect to both the father's authority and what they consider parents' authoritarianism, distrust, carelessness, and lack of affective expression.

Family and the public sphere

Chilean family concerns have become part of the public political agenda, particularly since the early 1990s. This can be seen in two main areas: (1) the numerous state, government and NGO programs focused on family issues (family welfare, intra-familial violence, gender equality in family roles, etc.); and (2) the progressive role of the Chilean family as a source of empowerment for its members (family associations asking for housing, health services, better education for children, etc.) (Comisión Económica para América Latina y el Caribe, 2001).

CONCLUSIONS

Contrary to the linear conceptions of social processes – as proposed by the modernization paradigm – Latin American societies seem to show that traditional structures and functions may be transplanted or reproduced in modern/urban contexts (Brunner, 1990). At the same time, such a peculiar landscape is useful as a reminder that fractures between social structures and functions are possible (Berger and Luckmann, 1999). Thus, the unavoidable question here is: What has changed and what has remained in the Chilean family?

Some diverse social and demographic changes have been apparent during the last 30–40 years. On the one hand, there have been decreasing rates of marriage and birth, etc.; on the other hand, there has been an increase in the number of births out of wedlock along with the considerable abandonment of pregnant women by their partners: in 1996, 22 percent of pregnant women and 46 percent of pregnant girls younger than 19 years old reported not having a partner (Comisión Económica para América Latina y el Caribe, 2000). Whether or not this represents a persistence of the old problem of *huacharaje* in Chile, could certainly be part of a long discussion; however, as Arriagada (2002) has pointed out, this phenomenon seems to be more an expression of traditional patterns than of modern ones.

Second, as reported in some other national contexts, the transition of the Chilean family from the extended to the nuclear system has not resulted in isolation of the latter (Bott, 1971; Segalen, 1996). Kinship networks in Chile remain active and psychological support is bilaterally kept between nuclear and extended family members, involving what Kağıtçıbaşı (2002) has called an "emotional/psychological interdependence." In methodological terms, this seems to demonstrate – as Georgas, Mylonas, Bafiti, et al. (2001) have underlined – that we can get a much more comprehensive view of family by considering the functional relationships between members of the nuclear family and their kin than by focusing only on its structural dimensions centered on household.

Third, despite the decrease of the father's authority, the assumption of motherhood as an option and the increasing rates of women's participation in economic activity, some traditional family values that reinforce gender inequality still persist, even in women. Of course, this is highly related to gender socialization, which reinforces women's "subjective dependence" (Arriagada, 2002).

Fourth, despite efforts of current democratic governments to conciliate economic growth with social equality, most social and educational achievements of Chilean children remain conditioned by social class and urban/rural location of their families. Rural families present higher levels of poverty, which usually results in the interruption of schooling, particularly of girls. This strengthens the "poverty circle" within what some authors have called "modernization with exclusion" (Arriagada, 2002).

To sum up, in analyzing the Chilean family and its ecocultural context, we can see a paradox. On the one hand, while the Chilean social context has exhorted some systemic-functional changes in population (higher schooling, competitiveness, individual criteria for decision-making), many of the principal traditional social structures and moral premises have remained, to a great extent, unaltered (a retrograde legal framework in respect to some issues, conservative religious influence over politics and public affairs, social inequality, social exclusion). On the other hand, while the Chilean family has faced structural changes (i.e., from extended to nuclear, one-parent, etc.), many of its main extended traditional functions remain (usual contact among relatives, kinship networks for psychological support, etc.). Whatever its nature, this separation between change in family structure and persistence in family functions in Chile seems to indicate that relatedness between family members is much more than a mere complement of autonomy.

16   Cyprus

Neophytos Charalambous

A HISTORICAL OUTLINE OF CYPRUS

Cyprus is the third largest island in the Mediterranean. Its unique proximity to Europe, Asia, and Africa and its strategic position has resulted in its occupation by various conquerors over the centuries. Since the Myceneans settled on the island over 3,000 years ago, establishing the Hellenic civilization, Phoenicians, Romans, Crusaders, Franks, Venetians, Turks, and British have left their mark on the island. The Republic of Cyprus was established as an independent state in 1960 after a rebellion against the British Empire, which was in control at that time. In 1974 Turkish troops occupied the northern part of the island. The de facto division of the island still exists, although Greek Cyprus has recently joined the European Union and a solution for unification with the Turkish Cypriot northern section is presently being sought. The total population of Cyprus is 760,000 inhabitants, 670,000 in Greek Cyprus in the south and 100,000 in Turkish Cyprus in the north.[1] Nicosia is the capital, with 250,000 inhabitants.

ECOLOGICAL FEATURES

Cyprus is 225 km long and its maximum breadth is 96.5 km. Its area is 9,251 km². It has a central plain with two mountain ranges in the north and south and a few scattered narrow coast plains. The climate is temperate, Mediterranean, with hot, dry summers and cool winters.

---

[1] Since the division of Cyprus, there is little shared demographic or other information between the two communities. This portrait of the Cypriot family will necessarily refer only to the Greek Cypriot community. In order to avert unnecessary redundancies, the term "Cypriot" in the text will be used to refer to "Greek Cypriots."

ORGANIZATION AND INSTITUTIONS OF SOCIETY

Economic organization

Before 1974, the Cypriot economy was largely agriculture-based. The main products were citrus fruits, olives, grapes, potatoes, carrots, and other vegetables. It had a small manufacturing sector, which produced consumer goods such as clothing, shoes, cement, and wines primarily for the domestic market and some for export. Since 1974 in Greek Cyprus, agriculture, which accounted for 37 percent of GDP before 1974, was 4.2 per cent in 1997 while manufacturing accounted for 11.9 percent. Tourism generated annual earnings equivalent to 19.3 percent. The per capita GDP approaches US$ 16,000. The present labor force in Greek Cyprus is 73 percent in services, 22 percent in industry, and only 5 percent in agriculture.

Political institutions and legal system

The Republic of Cyprus operates under the terms of the 1960 constitution as amended in 1964. It consists of three independent branches: executive, legislative, and judicial. At the district level, a district officer coordinates village and government activities. At the village level, there have been councils since Ottoman times, each composed of a village head and elders. Under the Ottoman empire, the village head and elders were elected by the villagers. In the British period and after independence, the village heads were appointed by the government and then chose the elders. Legislation in 1979 provided that village and town government officials were elected every five years.

Education

The development of education in Cyprus has been rapid. During the nineteenth century the percentage of educated people was small. It increased steadily during the first half of the twentieth century and very rapidly after independence. The percentage of literacy was about 64 percent in 1946, rose to 81 percent in 1960 and is 99 percent today. Education has always been regarded important in Cyprus and educated people were highly esteemed. Six years of elementary education and six years of secondary school are provided and attendance is mandatory between the ages of 5 and 15. The University of Cyprus was established in 1988 and private colleges have also been established. Numerous

Greek Cypriots attend foreign universities, mainly in Greece, The United Kingdom, and the United States. The percentage of students studying at university level in 1999/2000 was 69 percent, 41 percent abroad and 28 percent in Cyprus.

Religion

About 80 percent of the population of Cyprus is Greek Orthodox and 18 percent Muslim. Religious observance varies. In traditional rural villages, people attend services frequently, women more than men, and elderly family members are usually responsible for fulfilling religious duties on behalf of the whole family.

BONDS WITH GROUPS IN THE IMMEDIATE COMMUNITY

The power of the ingroup, composed not only of the members of the extended family but of the in-laws and distant relatives, has been lessened, since the individual today joins a variety of other in-groups. Attendance at weddings, christenings, and funerals is a very good indicator of the bonds with the community. Weddings in the past were a major social event lasting three days, and provided the opportunity for kin, friends, and acquaintances to meet, enjoy themselves, and show their respect and solidarity. The number of participants was the best indicator of one's social network. Traditional wedding ceremonies and feasts continue in the villages and even in some urban neighborhoods. They are attended by thousands of guests from the nearby villages and sometimes from all over the island. Another aspect of the wedding is that the presents contribute to the economic support of the newly-weds. The traditional coffee shop, the *kafeneion*, which has been the place of entertainment and socialization with one's fellow villagers, is still preserved in the villages and even in some neighborhoods in the towns. Various kinds of associations (athletic, cultural, religious, social, occupational) are substitutes of the bonds of migrants and refugees with their villages (Attalides, 1981).

THE FAMILY

Marriage

For the Cypriot, family is traditionally the most important in the hierarchy of values, and marriage has been a means of social integration and the ultimate purpose of a person's life, especially for women. The creation of a family is regarded the main reason for marriage. In the past, marriages were arranged by the parents or through the mediation of a matchmaker, since romantic love was not highly regarded in the Cypriot society. Until the first half of the twentieth century the parents of the couple used to agree orally on the dowry they would give to their children, with the groom's parents providing the house and the bride's parents providing the furniture. After the 1950s a dowry contract was signed by both parties at the engagement in the presence of the priest. Since then, the obligation to provide the house was transferred to the parents of the bride. However, the dowry contract was abolished by the church in 1980 and the arranged marriage has been replaced by the love match. Recent research indicated that 50 percent of Cypriots are against the dowry, while 48 percent believe that both families of the couple must contribute (Popular Bank of Cyprus, 2002).

Concerning endogamy, in the traditional family, marriage was confined to spouses from the same religion and the same village or the nearby villages. In today's family choice of spouse does not have any ethnic or religious restrictions and is a matter of personal choice of the man and the woman. In regard to exogamy, marriage was not allowed with members of the nuclear family and first cousins. These norms are in effect in the present-day family.

Although divorce was very rare in the past, the Orthodox Church permitted three divorces per person. Since 1990 Cypriots have the choice of civil marriage. However, the vast majority continues to prefer the ecclesiastical marriage. Before the New Family Law was enacted divorce matters were handled exclusively by the ecclesiastical courts. Since 1990 divorces have been handled by the Family Courts in which the church has its representative. The new family laws contain provisions regarding the equality of rights after divorce, the allocation of property and child custody.

Family structure

The traditional extended family included grandparents, parents, and children with collateral and affinal relationships. In addition, the inclusion of best men at the marriage or others involved in the baptism of the children, and who are often not members of the extended family, contributes to close bonds and the mutual respect of their families.

A separate home for the nuclear family has always been recognized as a prerequisite for the couple's economic independence and well-being. One of the main concerns of the parents is to secure a house for their children. Residence of the couple has usually been determined by the location of their parents' residence. In the past the new couple used to settle in the house of either the husband's or the wife's parents. Another pattern is for the young couple to settle in their own house near the wife's parents, who have to build the house. Sometimes the wife's parents may live in the same house or in a nearby auxiliary house. The trend, however, is towards the neolocal pattern of residence.

Demographics

Marriages have increased from 7.7 in 1980 to 13.8 in 2000 (Statistical Service of the Republic of Cyprus, 2003) contrary to the declining trend in the European Union, and this appears to be the highest marriage rate in Europe. Age of marriage age has also risen, from 26.3 in 1976 to 28.8 in 2000 for men, and from 23.7 in 1976 to 26.0 in 2000 for women. The birth rate per thousand has been declining from 20.4 in 1980 to 12.6 in 2000. The total fertility rate for 2000 was 1.84 children per woman. Until 1974 divorce was quite rare in Cyprus and great stigma was attached to the woman who had divorced. During the last three decades the divorce rate has risen steadily from 0.27 in 1974 to 1.77 in 2000. There are several reasons for this: the liberation of women, their better education and economic independence, the alternatives available to the divorcees, and the lessened disapproval of divorce by the community.

Family roles and functions

In the traditional Cypriot family the roles of the spouses were clearly separated. The husband/father had undisputed authority over his wife and children. He was the head of the family and the "pillar of the home." He worked in order to earn a living for the family and managed all the economic family matters. He was the leader and protector of the family. He was also the decision-maker and represented the family in its social relations.

The wife/mother had a primarily a caretaking role. She cooked, cleaned, and looked after the children. Her purpose in life was to be a good mother, an obedient wife, and a good housekeeper. The Greek Orthodox Church reinforced this role. During the wedding ceremony the priest advises that "the woman should obey and fear her husband."

In the contemporary Cypriot family roles are changing. Women's higher education, sexual liberation, economic independence, and self-sufficiency have contributed to a steady change in the traditional values and attitudes toward the functioning of the Cypriot family and the allocation of roles of the spouses. In Mylona's study (1986) the majority of women said the decisions concerning the purchase of household items, personal items, and their employment are taken jointly by both spouses. It appears that the contemporary family pattern has replaced the patriarchal one and it is based on mutuality, cooperation and equality.

Cypriot parents do all in their power to equip their children with what is necessary for a better life. Traditionally, their dual purpose in life was to endow their daughters with a good dowry and their sons with a good education. In today's family, education of the daughters is also a main concern. Parents in Cyprus are characterized as overprotective. They help their children with their homework, they support them financially, they look after their grandchildren, they "live for their children." Research findings of Mylona (1986) indicated that for the woman of Cyprus the greatest desires are a good start in life and a good education for their children.

Children are expected to study hard, they should obey and respect their elders, should tell their parents what they do, honor the name of the family, and take care of their elderly parents.

The ingroup is something more than the extended family and includes best men, godparents, in-laws, friends and sometimes the whole village. The appropriate behaviors toward members of the ingroup are cooperation, protection, solidarity, and mutual support, especially during times of need. The ingroup functioned as a system of collective responsibility and solidarity against outside threats from outgroups. Relationships with outgroups were often characterized by distrust and contention. In the past, outgroups might be other families within the community or another nearby community. Nowadays, the power of the ingroup has been decreased, since the individual joins a variety of other ingroups.

CONCLUSIONS

The researcher of the Cypriot society should take into account some particular factors that affect family structure and function. It is worth noting that Cyprus is one of the youngest states, since it achieved independence only in 1960. It is also a small area with a small population, and these factors affect family relations, e.g., geographic proximity, residence, and frequency of contacts. Close national bonds with Greece and the remnants of the British colonial administration are two additional factors that affect the lifestyle and the culture of the Cypriots. It must also be noted that the present study refers only to the Greek population of Cyprus since the de facto division of the island is still in effect.

The transition from the extended family pattern to that of the nuclear family has not been linear. The extended family was replaced by the nuclear family only in its structure. The Cypriot family preserved the characteristics of the extended family and traditional kinship patterns continue. In a study which investigated the relationship of family bonds to family structure and function across five cultures, Greek Cypriot students along with Greek students demonstrated that they preserved the closest emotional bonds, geographic proximity, and more frequent contacts with members of the extended family, indicating functional differences between the individualist (Britain, Germany, the Netherlands) and collectivist (Cyprus, Greece) cultures (Georgas, Christakopoulou, Poortinga, Goodwin, Angleitner & Charalambous, 1997). These findings suggest that the theories of depersonalization of the nuclear family are not confirmed and seem to be a myth.

Change and development in the society of Cyprus came at a very rapid rate. Economic and political factors caused a swift change in the Cypriot society in general and to the Cypriot family in particular. The first noteworthy change is that the patriarchal role of the father decreased while the role of the mother is increasing. Today's Cypriot woman has acquired a much higher status in the society and the family as a result of her higher education and her economic independence. Although traditional values, attitudes, and stereotypes still affect the society and the family, Cypriot women are striving toward equality and mutuality. Today's women are searching for a new identity and are trying to compromise between their new extended roles both outside and inside the home. They are burdened with many responsibilities and find it difficult to cope with today's multiple roles. However, younger couples manage a more democratic allocation of domestic tasks. There is no doubt that male authority has weakened and the position of Cypriot women is on the way to equality. On behalf of the state, new legislation has been passed and international conventions have been ratified on the elimination of discrimination against women. Despite this, it is well known that the process of change is not a matter of legal arrangements but that it starts from the minds and hearts of the people.

Another change concerns the relationships between parents and children. Although today parental control has decreased there is still very close interdependence, especially on the part of the parents. It is said that parents are more dependent emotionally on their children than the children are on their parents. Their three major concerns are to educate their children, help them find a good job, and secure a successful marriage.

Summing up, we could draw the following final conclusions concerning the Greek Cypriot family:

The first conclusion is that despite social, political, and economic changes the family remains the strongest institution in Greek Cypriot society and the major purpose of a person's life.

Second, the process of change from the extended to the nuclear family pattern is confined only to its structure, since there is evidence that the Cypriot family preserves all the functional characteristics of the extended family.

Third, the Cypriot family is at a developmental stage between conservatism and modernization. In Schwartz's cross-cultural research on value priorities (1994b), Cypriot teachers appeared most conservative among 36 cultures and they give emphasis on the maintenance of the status quo, propriety, preserving the traditional order, including the social order, obedience, respect for tradition, family security, and self-discipline.

Fourth, the Cypriot, like the Greek family, is at a transitional stage from collectivism to individualism. From this contextual perspective the Cypriot family pattern corresponds to the synthetic model of human relatedness or pattern Y (Kağıtçıbaşı, 1990, 1996a), according to which there is independence on the material dimension and interdependence on the emotional dimension. It is the model that characterizes industrialized collectivist societies (Georgas et al., 1997).

17 Portrait of family in France

Gérard Pithon and Olivier Prévôt

A HISTORICAL OUTLINE OF FRANCE

The French Republic is a Western European country bordered by the countries of Belgium, Germany, Switzerland, Italy, and Spain, and by mountains (Alps and Pyrenees) and oceans (Atlantic and Mediterranean). Its population is around 60 million, with its capital, Paris, having around 2 million inhabitants and with around 11 million living in the capital region (*Encyclopédie Hachette Multimedia 99*, 1999). Around 1850, three-quarters of the population was rural; by 1934 it was 50 percent and is now mostly urban or suburban (*Encyclopédie Microsoft Encarta en ligne*, 2005).

France covers 550,000 km^2, and is divided into 22 regions and 96 departments. There are also 120 overseas possessions, some of which are an integral part of France (departments), while others are territories. Families in the overseas departments and territories are more vulnerable and fragile than in Metropolitan France. The present description of the French family is limited to metropolitan France (i.e., in Europe). Nevertheless in metropolitan France there are large variations in family structure and culture by region, urbanization, and religion.

The present borders of France were largely fixed by the fourteenth century. Prior to that, many groups came together to form the French people, including Gallo-Romans, and "barbarian" invasions from the east and north. Starting with Clovis (481–511, King of the Franks), Roman Catholicism and the French language served as unifying forces. It was mainly the French Revolution (in 1789), with the abolition of the monarchy and the emergence of the secular French Republic, that promoted the development of modern French society (LeGoff, 1985). Its ideals of liberty, equality, and fraternity served as the platform for liberal reforms in France and elsewhere in Europe during the eighteenth century.

ECOLOGICAL FEATURES

France spans northern and southern of regions of Europe and has maritime, alpine, and continental climates. The contrasts of lowlands with high plateaus, mountain peaks with valleys, and cold, wet regions with sunny, warm ones, makes it the most varied in Europe. Despite these large variations, about three-quarters of the land is suitable for various kinds of agriculture.

ORGANIZATION AND INSTITUTIONS OF SOCIETY

Economic base

France has the world's fourth largest economy, behind the United States of America, Japan and Germany, varying from second in agricultural exports and services, to fifth in industrial production. Unemployment in 1995 was over 10 percent (3 million unemployed; 26 million employed). This was due mainly to a rapid growth in population compared to growth in jobs, combined with losses in the industrial and agricultural sectors. However, these losses were partially compensated for by an explosion of employment in the service sector. From 1806 to 1996, the active working population dropped from 65.1 percent to 4.9 percent in the agricultural sector (Institut National de la Statistique et des Etudes Economiques, 1999). It increased from 20.4 percent to 26 percent in the industrial and building sector. It had increased regularly up to 37.4 percent to 1974 then it dropped suddenly. In contrast, it exploded from 14.5 percent to 69.1 percent in the service sector (commerce, finance, health, tourism, and education). Unemployment continues to affect particularly women, those under 25 years or over 50 years of age, and immigrants.

Education

The University of Paris was founded in the twelfth century. However, the basic principles of the educational system stem from the French Revolution: education is public, centralized, hierarchical, and state run; primary education is secular, free, and obligatory; although some private education exists controlled and partly subsidized by the state. According to Fourastié (1983), 8 percent of the working population has three years of university level after the baccalauréat (the secondary school final exam which allows the entry to a university), 27 percent has a first degree, 43 percent works with a professional qualification, and 22 percent of the population comprises non-qualified workers.

Religion

Religious wars between Protestants and Catholics ravaged France in the sixteenth century, ending in 1598 with the Edict of Nantes, giving religious freedom to Protestants. Both religions influenced marriage practices, including the marriage of children in order to protect family interests. However, Protestants accepted the dissolution of marriage (divorce) more easily than Catholics. When the Edict of Nantes was revoked in 1685, large-scale emigration of Protestants to Switzerland, Germany, The United States, and Canada took place, affecting the balance between the two religions. The secularization of French society following the Revolution was accompanied by a decline in religious practice. In 1905, the political management of church and state were separated. At the present time about 75 percent of the population respect the rules and celebrations of the Catholic Church. Because of immigration from North Africa, Islam has become the second most common religion, followed by Protestantism and Judaism. In 2003, for the first time, the French government has helped the Islamic communities to have one national organization that federates the main Islamic French communities. Although all these religions co-exist peacefully nowadays, there are some tensions, mainly because of political conflicts in various parts of the world.

FAMILY

Although beset by the same problems that affect other families in Europe, the family in France continues to fulfill the same essential functions: begetting, educating, and socializing children, developing their skills and economic responsibilities and transmitting the cultural heritage of their society.

Households

France has more than 21.4 million households, defined as those who live under the same roof. Among these households there are 7.7 million couples with children (36 percent); 6.1 million couples without children, not born yet or who have left home (29 percent); 1.2 million single-parent families, unmarried, divorced, widowed or living alone with one or more children (6 percent); 0.6 million multiple households which have many generations under the same roof or the same generation who live together (3 percent); and finally 5.8 million people living alone (26 percent): unmarried, widowed or divorced, of which 3.7 million are women (64 percent) and 2.1 million are men (36 percent) (Institut National de la Statistique et des Etudes Economiques, 1999).

Le Play (1806–1882), who is the founder of empirical sociological research on the family, contrasts the stem family with the nuclear family. Stem families combine three generations: parents who own the house, their oldest son and his wife and their children, and the unmarried brothers and sisters of the oldest son. Traditionally, the oldest son inherited all the property without having to divide it. In contrast, the nuclear family, which was a product of the industrial revolution, was made up of parents and their children. It is supposed to be more unstable (Le Play, 1871).

Segalen (1996), and Attias-Donfut, Lapierre, and Segalen (2002) explained what has disappeared within the French family and what still exists nowadays. It was the bourgeois model of the family that disappeared in the nineteenth century represented by a "stable" marriage (under the authority of the father; the mother kept the household and took care of the children). Today, a more "geometrically variable family model" exists: the classic conjugal family, the single-parent family, the blended family, and the homosexual family. But, the strength of parental relations is still very strong, especially nowadays with a longer life expectancy; therefore two, three or four generations can have strong ties.

Evolution of rights within the family

There has been a rapid evolution of the rights within the family. In 1810 the adultery of a man was punished with a simple warning, while an adulteress was punished with a penalty of prison. From 1938 the obligation of obedience of the woman to her husband was abolished, but the husband still decided the place of residence and whether his wife could or could not work. It was only in 1996 that wives were granted the right to practice a profession without the authorization of their husbands. The Neuwirth Law authorizes contraception, but does not yet publicize it except in the medical reviews. "The parental authority" takes the place of paternal authority in 1970. The married couple together assure the moral and material direction of the family. Nevertheless, the mother exercises the authority over a natural child, even if both parents acknowledge it. The notion of head of the family is thus done away with. In 1975 the voluntary interruption of pregnancy was temporarily authorized;

divorce by mutual consent was allowed; the place of residence was decided mutually, and the married couple could opt for two different residences. In 1979 the law on the voluntary interruption of pregnancy was permanently adopted; in 1993 shared parental authority was generalized with regard to all the children (legitimate or natural), whatever the situation of their parents (marriage, separation, divorce). At the time of the Conference of the Family in June 2001, the socialist government instituted parental leave, allowing fathers 14 days' leave, while keeping full salary. Since 2001 legislation has given children the possibility of carrying the name of one of the two parents or the two hyphenated; but they currently take the name of the father in most cases.

Equality between women and men has improved even if women's rights have been scoffed at for too long. The patriarchal family has disappeared; the patrilineal family is no longer an obligation.

Decrease in marriages

Houchard (2000, p. 18) summarizes the marriage situation: "less often, later, less long." Thus, from 1920 to 1995 the number of marriages decreased from 623,000 to 254,000 (Mermet, 1999). Nevertheless, according to Houchard (2000), since 1996 the number of marriages has increased in France (reaching 304,300 in 2000), which remains an exception in Europe. Galland (1991) attempted to explain the decrease in the number of marriages as a consequence of raising the school-leaving age resulting in a later entry into active life, especially for girls, who gain from the possibility from pursuing longer studies. It is also due to the recent economic crisis and the unemployment of youth, which delays their family life.

From 1972 to 1992 the median age of marriage increased for men from 24.5 years to 29 years while for women it increased from 22.5 years to 27 years. Couples are marrying later and later, and men are 4.5 years on average older than their wife (Institut National de la Statistique et des Etudes Economiques, 1999).

Cohabitation

This ideology stems from mass movements and protests (students and workers) in 1968, which praised the liberation of morals, free union, and equality between men and women. From 1970 cohabitation became an alternative to marriage or regarded as a form of trial marriage.

Daguet (1996) stressed that cohabitation became the main way of entering the life of a couple in the 1980s, which then formed the basis of becoming a lasting life of the couple of today: "In 1975 the non-married couples were not yet 3 percent . . . it changed to 12.4 percent in 1990. In 1965 only 10 percent of new couples began their life together without marrying, thirty years later, the proportion has risen to 90 percent" (Daguet, 1996).

Births and deaths

The overall numbers of births decreased steadily from 1950 to 1994. The raw birth rate changed from 20.5 per 1,000 inhabitants in 1950, to 12.5 per 1,000 in 1994. By contrast, the rate of births outside marriage increased for the same years from 7 percent to 36 percent (Institut National de la Statistique et des Etudes Economiques, 1999). With regard to the average number of children of fertile women, France is just above the middle of the European countries.

Divorce

According to Daguet (1996), from 1962 to 1990 the number of divorces increased 3.5 times, compared to an increase of married couples of 1.7 times. The Catholic religion opposes divorce, but this injunction seems to have little effect these days.

NEW FORMS OF FAMILIES

The new forms of families in France are one of the major recent phenomena. Single-parent families and blended families increased regularly (Cadolle, 2000). "One quarter of the marriages celebrated each year involves a couple in which at least one of the partners has already been married" (Mermet, 1999).

The engagement period, where the future wedded partners are morally committed to marry one day, has no legal value. Marriage between related persons is prohibited. An exception can be made for marriages between uncle and niece or between aunt and nephew. Marriage is possible when there is no blood bond between the marriage candidates: adopted brothers and sisters, or father-in-law and daughter-in-law or mother-in-law and son-in-law when the person who has created the alliance is dead.

But to live together without marriage is a right. The civil code recognizes the stable unions between two people of different sex or the same sex, even without a legal contract. Since 1999 a legal contract (*Pacte Civil de Solidarité*) allows two persons of the same sex or of different sexes to live together. However two persons of the same sex cannot be married, adopt or have children with medical assistance. It is a source of conflicts between the political parties. A mayor from the Ecological Party has been condemned by a court for having authorized a marriage between two homosexuals; the marriage was not legalized and the mayor was dismissed for six months. There is a hierarchy of different legal protections: the weakest partner is more protected in a formal marriage, and less so in cohabitation. These protections affect the obligations between partners, patrimonial rights, the right of succession, and of income.

FUNCTIONS AND ROLES OF FAMILY

The management of domestic activities and the sharing of family tasks are a part of the social competence that is evolving rapidly today. Kauffman (1993) mentions questions which confront all couples today: "Who does what?" "How should domestic activities be shared?" Formerly, the woman had to assume nearly all responsibility for household activities and stayed at home. The new idea of sharing between men and women in all areas of society suggests that household tasks must be shared equally, all the more as a growing number of women have a job.

When the two partners of a couple work (and if the father is under 45 years old) it is mainly the woman who experiences constraints linked to the number of children. The sharing of domestic activities remains traditional: men spend a little more time doing odd jobs and shopping while women spend much more time taking care of children, ironing, doing the laundry, housework, cooking, and washing the dishes.

The authority of the father is put more and more into question. The Roman model of "paterfamilias" has progressively disappeared, giving way to a familial community or "the equal democratic model." These evolutions accompany a change of values and practices in the family and society, mainly the work activity of women and their changing economic and identity autonomy.

Thus, the family structure has changed in its management and in its internal distribution of power. It seem more fragile, but better adapted to contemporary democratic requirements. These changes seem to accompany an increase in single-parent and blended families. The bonds of affinity, the sharing of interests, and the responsibilities of raising children born from different former unions, organize themselves in these blended families without considering the blood ties between the children. Nevertheless, the raising of adolescents accompanied by the professional development of youth has become one of the growing preoccupations of French society, as well as the increase of juvenile delinquency and youth unemployment. Many authors (e.g., Franza, 1999) do not hesitate to associate these worrying facts, which are more frequent in the vulnerable sectors of society, with the instability of the family bond. More and more parents call special phone numbers, dedicated to helping families, in order to explain that they cannot deal anymore with their adolescent. Prevention and repression are two classical ways of intervention that the various governments use to some extent. Parental education, with the idea of primary prevention, is one type of action that must be developed (Pithon, Ho Can Sung, and Brochain, 2003; Pithon, Terrisse, Gordon, Prévôt, and Vallerand, 2004). Another type of measure is to separate the recidivist delinquent from his surroundings and to put him in Special Educational Centers (Franza, 1999).

The major changes in function and structure of the family are rapid and incontestable. The French family is monogamous, mainly nuclear in an urban setting, sometimes more spread out in a rural setting. This emergence of nuclear families, especially in urban settings in industrial societies, to the detriment of traditional spread out families in a rural setting (Parsons, 1949) does not explain, however, the new transgenerational solidarities that seem to be gathering strength (Attias-Donfut and Segalen, 1998; Georgas et al., 2001; Attias-Donfut, Lapierre, and Segalen, 2002). A study by Roussel and Bourguignon (1976) shows that 75 percent of married children live less than 20 km from their parents. A study by Cribier (1981) reveals that in Paris, retired people intensify their relationships with their married children. Thus their social networks are maintained in part thanks to these relations. The children can even help them financially in order to maintain the apartment or secondary home. As Bawin-Legros (1988, p. 33) recalls, all the surveys carried out regularly in France by CREDOC and in Belgium by the INUSOP, indicate that "the family value appears at the head of essential values, even among the youngest members of our societies."

18   Georgia

Nana Sumbadze

A HISTORICAL OUTLINE OF GEORGIA

After more than a century of Russian occupation and 70 years of being a part of the Soviet Union, Georgia declared its independence in 1991. The population of Georgia is about 4,600,000, 57.8 percent of which is urban. The majority are ethnic Georgians (70.1 percent), while the large minorities are Armenians (8.1 percent), Russians (6.3 percent), and Azeris (5.7 percent) (State Department of Statistics for Georgia, 2000). Georgia adopted Christianity in the fourth century. The majority of the population belongs to the Eastern Orthodox Church. There are also significant numbers of Armenian Gregorians, Catholics, and Muslims. The state languages in Georgia are Georgian and Abkhazian (in the territory of the Autonomous Republic of Abkhazia). Georgian has its original alphabet, dating back to the fifth century AD or even earlier. Georgia is a presidential republic. The parliament has 235 seats, elected through a mixed-proportional and majority-voting system. Georgia strives for integration with Europe. In 1999 the country became a member of the Council of Europe.

ECOLOGICAL FEATURES

Georgia is situated to the south of the Caucasian mountains, bordering Russia in the north, Turkey and Armenia in the south, Azerbaijan in the east. Its Western part is washed by the Black sea, while the north is dominated by the high mountains of the Great Caucasus range, with some of the highest peaks above 5,000 m. The climate ranges from subtropical Mediterranean to continental. The location and difference in altitude contribute to the diversity of relief, climate, and soils, which in their part determine the diversity of agriculture, way of living, and traditions.

ORGANIZATION AND INSTITUTIONS OF SOCIETY

Economic organization

Georgia is traditionally an agrarian country, even if the majority of the population is now urban. Rich soil, abundance of sunny days, and different climatic conditions permit the cultivation of a wide variety of agricultural produce. Georgia is famous for its wine. Sub-alpine meadows allow for herding of cattle and sheep. Industry is predominantly concentrated in the large cities, and since the collapse of the Soviet Union, is at standstill. The future of the country is now more dependent on its location as a crossroads between Asia and Europe, and on the restoration of the ancient Silk Road for transporting goods, and as a route for the gas and oil pipelines from Caspian Basin to Europe through Turkey, rather than on the development of industry.

Political institutions and legal system

Three periods in Georgian society in the past century, separated by two major events, are important to an understanding of Georgia's political institutions. The first event was the Socialist Revolution of 1917 and the second was the declaration of independence in 1991. Before the 1917 October revolution, Georgia was characterized by a low level of industrialization, high dependence on agriculture, and the concentration of the population in rural areas. During the Soviet period, many traditional values were questioned or even rejected officially. Gender equality was proclaimed, industrialization was intensified. The increase of education and industrialization resulted in the urbanization of the population. Disruption of the Soviet Union induced changes in the political and economic systems. The transition to a market economy was very painful for the population. Mass unemployment, high level of corruption, and inefficient handling of finances by the state, has resulted in more than half of the population being below the poverty line (UNICEF, 2000).

The educational system

Traditionally, education is highly valued by Georgian society. Almost the entire population of the country is literate. Education is free and consists of 11 years, of which 9 years are compulsory. Twenty percent of the economically active population has a university degree (Government of Georgia and United Nations Development Report, 1996). The first university in Georgia, Tbilisi State University, opened in 1918. Recently, in addition to state education, numerous private schools and universities have opened throughout Georgia. This accounts for the growth in the number of people with university education, increasing from 137 per 1,000 of population to 201 during the last 10 years.

BONDS WITH GROUPS IN THE IMMEDIATE COMMUNITY

Close kinship ties and high levels of mutual support characterize the social fabric of Georgian communities. Obligations toward family members, kin, and friends are considered a priority and are placed before obligations to the state and society at large. Although Georgia is undergoing a process of rapid change, the society still rests on the conception of the traditional family characterized by respect for elders, frequent and intensive communication, and high levels of mutual assistance.

FAMILY

Marriage

Before the Soviet period, traditionally, most marriages were arranged. In the isolated mountainous area of Western Georgia-Svaneti, the arranged marriage soon after the child's birth, known as "cradle engagement" was a tradition for a long period. Marriage within the same religion and ethnic group was almost a norm, although inter-ethnic marriages with Ossetians and Armenians were accepted. Marriage between people related to each other through blood kinship was prohibited up to sixth generation. Social norms regarding marriage became more relaxed during the Soviet period, despite the fact that communist ideology never achieved full support in Georgia. Young people freely chose their partners and love was proclaimed to be the basis of a happy family life. However, the norms differed according to gender. It was more acceptable for a man than a woman to marry outside one's ethnic group.

During the past 10 years, westernization and individualization, especially in urban areas, have resulted in more freedom in the choice of a spouse. Marriages of women and men to Americans and westerners in general, are highly approved. Women marrying foreigners outnumber men marrying foreign women. Marriages between Christians and Moslems have been and are still quite rare.

In the not so distant past, premarital sex for women was strictly prohibited. However, some parts of Georgia had quite unusual traditions in this regard. In a mountainous region of Pshavi the tradition of premarital sex after reaching maturation was a commonly approved practice. The more "friends" the girl had, the better was her reputation and chances of good marriage. However, the meeting place of young people, their behavior, vows exchanged – all were predetermined by customs and norms, and strict sanctions were imposed for their violation. Such sanctions first of all concerned premarital pregnancy, which was considered to be extremely shameful. If the couple were kin, or lived in the same village, they were severely punished. Instances of punishment by death in the case of incest were known, although ostracism and expulsion from the village were more common.

There were never any strict regulations related to dowry in Georgian society. It was and still is usual for the bride's family to provide the newly-weds with bedding, kitchen utensils, and bedroom furniture. It was also widespread in older times to give the bride a copy of the book of "The Knight in the Panther's skin," a poem by the medieval Georgian poet Rustaveli. The bridegroom's family as a rule gave jewelry to the bride.

The wedding feast was usually quite large and was organized and financed by the family of the bridegroom. The bride's family usually had a smaller party before the wedding ceremony. The bridegroom with his best men and close circle of friends and kin, called *makari* came to the bride's home to accompany her to the party. The same tradition is still kept today with the only difference that wedding parties are smaller, especially in cities.

Owing to difficult economic conditions, the number of registered marriages declined dramatically from 37,000 in 1990 to 14,000 in 1999. The number of divorces also declined from 9,000 in 1990 to 1,600 in 1999, but the decrease is significantly greater for divorces than for marriages.

The legal procedures for divorce have not changed much and are quite simple. A court ruling is needed for divorce, for the custody of the children and property issues. As a general practice, the child's custodian is the mother, but the father retains the right to spend a specific amount of time with the child, and is required to pay for the maintenance of minor children. The court can also oblige the father to provide his ex-wife and children with a dwelling. Children as a rule carry the father's family name. In marriages between different ethnic groups, the children are commonly considered to have the father's ethnicity.

Family structure and roles

Political and economic changes have had an impact on the family structure, patterns of family life and family roles; however, the Georgian family still retains many of its traditional features and remains a central institution for the socialization of children, as well as for the satisfaction of its members. Children are traditionally treated in a relaxed and affectionate manner. Children's health, proper development, and good education are considered as the most important goals of the family, to which much is sacrificed (Hentschel, Sumbadze, and Schoon, 2001). In the pre-Soviet period, the family was patriarchal. It usually consisted of three generations, and the eldest male was considered to be the head of the family and with unquestioned authority. His wife had power over her daughter-in-law, who was supposed to do the chores outlined by her mother-in-law. Children had almost no say in family decisions and were supposed to obey elders. At the beginning of the twentieth century when agriculture was the main source of the family's income, and where agricultural land was not scarce, the number of children was correlated with economic conditions; families with many children had more "hands" and greater possibilities to be better off. Thus, families were quite large in rural areas and having six or more children was common.

The Soviet period brought many changes in the family. Industrialization resulted in migration of the population to towns and cities and increased opportunities for education. Communist ideology had a significant impact on families, although it never gained full support in the country and much of it was more declarative than actually practiced. Free choice was declared the sole basis for marriage. Increase of educational level, ease of divorce, free abortion, the necessity for women to join the workforce, and increased migration all contributed to the decrease of family size. In towns, the meager salaries did not permit couples to have many children. Dual-earning families became a norm.

Today as in the past, the newly-weds usually live in the husband's house, which means living with his parents and unmarried siblings. There is a growing tendency of newly-weds renting an apartment, particularly among affluent urbanites, but economic conditions do not allow most to do this. Even more, parents and married children who had previously lived apart, now often live together in order to reduce household expenses. With the current underdeveloped social security system and the lack of institutionalized means of assistance (pensions are extremely low and high unemployment does not permit young families to pay for kindergarten) living together is attractive for all three generations.

Usually a nuclear family consists of four members, but the pattern is slightly different in urban and rural areas. Twenty-three percent of urban families consist of four and 17 percent consist of three members, while about 20 percent of rural families are composed of six or more, and 18.4 percent have four members (State Department of Statistics, 2001).

In the past, families celebrated the New Year together at the paternal home. This norm is continued today. After the celebration, the younger members of the family usually go out. Despite the changes described above, families still retain traditional family roles; father is usually the breadwinner and mother is the housekeeper. Women are the primarily caretakers, responsible for the children's upbringing, providing love and support. Therefore neither women's importance nor their role in the family changed much in contrast with men, who become more alienated from family members with age. The emotional and social ties of the woman within the family remain constant and are a source of satisfaction (Sumbadze, 1999). Although the traditional family was patriarchal, women have never been devoid of power in families, but this power has never been, and still is not acceptable to be manifested openly. An old Georgian word for women, *dedakaci* can be translated as "mother-man," and the word "spouse" means, "one who is in the same yoke," connoting gender equality. Discussing the family at the beginning of twentieth century, a famous Georgian poet, Vaza-Pshavela, wrote "In a family, woman is the master. She has great power over the young and the old. The upbringing of children, which is of utmost importance, is in her hands, she decides the fate of her children. The future of a child depends on her nurturance of its young and sensitive soul and mind. That is why it is necessary that mother be educated, to show kindness, to know how to bring up children, as in this way she can either ruin or revive the nation" (Oboladze, 1990, pp. 31–32). The woman's role in family life has increased in today's Georgia. In an economy with high unemployment, women proved to be more ready to adapt to new realities than men, and in many cases became the main breadwinners in families. Computer and foreign language skills, which are more readily found among the young have become decisive in getting employment. Therefore, in many families, parents who are still in their productive years must rely on the income of their children. Through financial independence, and sometimes by making people with traditional higher authority dependent on them, women and children have gained more power in the family. At the present time, many husbands who were authoritarian in the past, do all the housework in the family, while not so long ago they imperiously demanded it from their wives.

Georgia is characterized by low geographic mobility. In the past, unmarried children living outside the capital usually left the parental house only when attending university. Many graduates would not return to the village but stayed in the urban area. Thus, a common pattern is for parents in rural areas to provide their offspring with agricultural produce, and, in return, to receive financial help from their children. In the past, urban dwellers usually stayed at home at least until marriage. This pattern has changed. There were universities in only three or four cities 10–15 years ago, but at the present time they are in almost every town. As a result more young people stay in the parental home. But owing to a new phenomenon – emigration of the young for economic reasons – the structure and the role division in families is changing. The money sent home by immigrants comprises about 5 percent of the average household's income. If the initial wave of emigration was composed mainly of young men who left for Russia, at the present time, women are increasingly migrating to many countries.

Social support

Survival of many families in the last decade was possible only as a result of the support system deeply seated in traditions of Georgian society. Kinship and other social ties and obligations toward others are highly valued. Social support, in addition to that of family members and kin, is usually also provided by the best man of a married couple, godparents, friends, neighbors, and colleagues. There are commonly shared norms concerning provision of the support in the community. Even in cases of extreme difficulties, when surveys asked respondents to name the biggest inconvenience of the present austerity, the answer was frequently the impossibility of providing social support and of attending social events that entailed expenditure. Families usually obtain financial assistance in cases of death of a family member and at weddings. In rural areas, the family is usually assisted in building a house and in doing domestic and agricultural work requiring many hands – this is called *nadi*. The host would commonly provide the workers with food and drinks.

Interaction among family members is high even when they do not comprise a household. Coming to the funeral of a family member is a norm fulfilled by a majority of persons, even by those who live in a different country and the travel is expensive. The number of kin in a family is increased by the baptism of a child. The invitation to be a godparent is an honor and refusal is a grave insult. The godparent is considered to be an important person for the child, who is expected to play a significant role in the course of the child's development, to attend his or her birthdays and all big parties of the family, and to provide help to the child in case of need.

CONCLUSIONS

It can be concluded that many changes occurred during the past century in the structure and function of the Georgian family. These changes were determined by large-scale social and economic developments which characterized the twentieth century. These changes were forced on the population, but the Georgian culture served as a stabilizing and balancing factor that allowed many traditions and practices of Georgian families to be retained during this difficult Soviet period.

The past ten years have been marked by economic difficulties and impoverishment, which have negatively affected the size of families and their functioning. But they also had a positive effect, having activated women and young people, making them sometimes the main earners of the family and in this way undermining the absolute nature of father's authority, thus empowering women and children in their family life.

Strong family ties and a well-functioning support system still characterize Georgian society; during recent hardships it even acquired a survival value. But the primacy of kinship values and the tight system of assistance together with its beneficial effects also have a negative side. They sometimes serve as a breeding ground for illegal and criminal networks. The concentration of economic and political power among a small number of family clans is a serious problem that Georgia faces today.

19 Germany: continuity and change

Heidi Keller

A HISTORICAL OUTLINE OF GERMANY

The history of the German nation begins with the constitution of the empire (Reichsverfassung) that the German constitutional national assembly approved March 28, 1849. The honor of the head of the German empire was awarded to a reigning German sovereign who held the title "Emperor of the Germans" (*Kaiser der Deutschen*) bequeathed to his descendants. The German Reich comprises three phases: the phase of the emperors from 1871 to 1918 with the Prussian Wilhelm II being the last emperor, the republic of Weimar (Weimarer Republik) from 1919 to 1934 with the presidents Ebert and von Hindenburg, and the Third Reich from 1934 to 1945 with Adolf Hitler being the president and the chancellor of the Reich in one person. It is noteworthy that the constitution of the Reich had a law that regulated that no German state within the Reich is allowed to apply a different legislation to other Germans which discriminates these as foreigners.[1]

Nevertheless, Germany's recent history is overshadowed by the Nazi regime that not only tried to eliminate the Jewish population of Germany but also conquered larger parts of Europe in order to expand the "German Reich." As a consequence of World War II, the Allies (France, Great Britain, USA, USSR) divided Germany and its capital, Berlin, into four zones in May 1945. In October 1949 the German Democratic Republic was founded with a strong obligation to the socialist ideology of the former Soviet Union. In May 1955, the Federal Republic of Germany became a sovereign state and a member of NATO. At the same time, the Warsaw pact was formed with the GDR as a member. Although the two German states held official diplomatic relations, the borders were closed with an "iron curtain" that divided Eastern and Western Europe. In November 1989 the Berlin wall was opened.

---

[1] "Kein deutscher Staat darf zwischen seinen Angehörigen und anderen Deutschen einen Unterschied in bürgerlichen, peinlichen und Prozessrechten machen, welcher die letzteren als Ausländer zurücksetzt."

Reunification, which had not been anticipated by the majority of the population in the East and the West, was proclaimed on October 3, 1990 accompanied by an overarching emotional enthusiasm in both parts of Germany.[2] Since then Germany has been a federal republic with 16 states and approximately 80 million inhabitants. Berlin again became the capital of the united Germany in 1999, replacing Bonn, which had been the capital of West Germany from 1949 on.

ECOLOGICAL FEATURES

Germany is located in central and northern Europe and covers a geographical variety of alpine regions, mountains and highlands, plains and seashores. Its climate is mostly temperate with somewhat cold winters and mild summers It rains through the year in all parts of Germany. Since the 1970s, the unlimited striving for economic growth and prosperity has been criticized from a growing ideological movement that understands human beings as parts of global ecosystems. The Green party, which emerged from initiatives at that time, emphasizes environmental concerns as part of the government policy, especially in environmental education, consumer protection and consumer information (for which a ministry has been introduced), and environmental and nature protection.

ORGANIZATION AND INSTITUTIONS OF SOCIETY

Economic organization

After the industrial revolution of the nineteenth century, Germany changed from an agrarian society into an industrialized, knowledge and service society. Today about 31 percent of the population is employed in industry, 68 percent in the service area, and about 1 percent in the agrarian area. There are major differences between individual German states regarding the economic organization. Essentially the states with a higher level of industrialization, mainly in Western Germany, are economically more prosperous. Urbanization covers 87 percent of the population. Germany is the most industrialized country in Europe, and is found behind the USA and Japan on rank three in a global comparison.

---

[2] This enthusiasm, however, was soon replaced by soberness when the dramatic changes that reunification implied, especially for the eastern part of the population, penetrated daily life. "Moaning Easterners" and "all-knowing Westerners" became metaphors for the deep gaps between the two societies (McKenzie, 1995).

The technological and scientific know how as well as the elaborate infrastructure formed the basis of economic success. Yet, since the 1990s, the German economy has experienced a strong recession, resulting in excessive national debts and substantial consequences for economy and welfare.

Political institutions and legal system

Germany is a federal[3] and constitutional democracy. The federal state is responsible for the common interest of all people with unitary regulation, whereas the 16 individual states regulate everything else (e.g., education). The presidents of the state governments (*Ministerpräsidenten*) form the constitutional organ of the *Bundesrat*, which guarantees the participation of the states in federal (legislative) and European matters. The parliament, the *Bundestag*, is composed according to the outcome of the election of representatives of the legal political parties. The major aspects of public and private life are codified in the law corpus. The German state promotes the protection of citizens, the promotion of equal rights and the support of minorities.

The educational system

Children begin school at six. Ten years of schooling are mandatory. The school system comprises four years of primary school and differentiates thereafter into *Hauptschule* (five years) with a consecutive work-oriented education (apprenticeship), graduation after 10 years of schooling (*mit-Reife*), or in the *Gymnasium* with the "maturation test" (*Abitur*) after 12 to 13 years of schooling, depending on the state. Moreover, an integration of these types of schooling exists (integration school, *Gesamtschule*). Germany has 84 universities and 243 other institutions of higher education. The percentage of the native German population that does not complete primary education (*Hauptschule*) is 8.6 percent (53.5 percent are women). Ten years of schooling (*mittlere Reife*) is completed by 41.7 percent of native Germans (56.6 percent women), and *Gymnasium* (including the advanced technical college certificate) is completed by 25.5 percent of native Germans (44.7 percent women; Statistisches Bundesamt, 2002).

---

[3] Federal is derived from the latin *foedus* which means union (*Bund, Bündnis*).

Religion

The percentages of religious denominations in Germany are: 42.9 percent Roman Catholics, 41.6 percent reformed and traditional Lutherans (Protestants), 2.7 percent Muslims, and 12.8 percent other religions. Active participation in church and church-based community life is dramatically decreasing over the generations.

BONDS WITH GROUPS IN THE IMMEDIATE COMMUNITY

Community life in rural areas is transparent because of co-residency of families over generations with implied social control. Communal organizations (*Vereine*), often gender-segregated, preserve local customs, which may go back to pre-Christian times, and socialize the youth into community life (Hüwelmeier, 1997). Community life in urban areas is rarely bound by traditions but relies on individual activities with similar minds. During recent decades, some residential areas, suburbs or even single streets have organized parties in order to facilitate bonding and a sense of local identity. Citizens of foreign origin have a lively community life in their own community centers.

THE FAMILY

Marriage

Marriage in Germany is largely the result of self-selection with no specific regulations concerning endogamy. There is, however an implicit expectation of the family to marry a "fitting" partner with respect to social class, education, religion, interests, and the like. Accordingly the reported frequencies of bi-cultural marriages are very low; however, the consent of both German and immigrant parents for inter-ethnic marriages of their children is increasing (with the exception of immigrants from the Far East, (Keller, Zach, and Abels, 2005). The German law prevents marriage between blood relatives.

Divorce

Although the newly married have the goal of staying together until death parts them, as they promise themselves and their communities in the religious ceremony, divorce rates have increased continuously since 1992. Seventy percent of the divorces in East Germany and 50 percent in the West affect minors (Vaskovics, Garhammer, Schneider, and Job, 1994). Although most of the parents share joint custody, the majority of children live with their mothers. A considerable number of divorced parents remarry divorced partners with children. Family structures become bi-nuclear with a substantial increase in complexity and dynamics of family relationships.

Obtaining a spouse

The traditional German family started with economic input from both parents' sides. Whereas the husband's parents invested in education so that he could support his own family,[4] the wife's parents provided her with the *Aussteuer*, which basically comprised the table and bed linen. Girls worked for years on their *Aussteuer* by sewing and stitching patterns (often a monogram) into it. Although these traditions have widely disappeared, parents still tend to help their children start their independent households with economic support.

Family structure

The stereotypic German family is a nuclear family: a married couple with their one to two children. Germans typically start a family at the end of their twenties with the husband being two to three years older than the wife. Pregnancy or the prospect of having children in the near future is an incentive for getting married. The typical German family has 1.3 children (Zach, 2003).

Every tenth family living with children in Germany is a family of foreign origin. Non-marital living arrangements and single parents are less numerous in families of foreign origin as compared to ethnic German families. Fewer families of foreign origin are childless, and the number with more children is greater than ethnic German families, although the birth rates decrease while they are living in Germany, with the exception of Turkish families.

Family roles and functions

The roles of the family members in the traditional German family are rooted in the norms and values that characterized the Prussian state

---

[4] In situations of economic hardship, education of boys is considered as more important than the education of girls.

during the nineteenth century. Values that characterized the army, such as discipline, obedience, and authority penetrated the public life and exerted a major influence on the educational values and practices (Ahnert, Meischner, and Schmidt, 1995). The second major impact on the value systems of the German family arose from Protestantism. Protestantism, especially in its pietistic branches, stressed individual responsibility, freedom and inwardness (Ahnert, Krätzig, Meischner, and Schmidt, 1994), and thus laid ground for individualism as a major cultural value. Protestant individuality and achievement ethics combined with Prussian authority and obedience form the characteristics of "Germanness" (Keller, Zach and Abels, 2005).

Father

The father provided the economic security for the family and represented the moral authority. He decided the major matters for the family. He was emotionally distant from the children and served mainly as a punishing institution.

Mother

The mother was the keeper of the house and raised the children. Although she supported the father's authority, she could also intervene in conflicts between father and children. The life of the mother was ruled by three Ks, *Küche* (kitchen), *Kirche* (church), and *Kinder* (children).

Children

Children were expected to be obedient and industrious. They were supposed to be seen but not heard when they were young. They were expected to remain close to their parents and support them in old age.

Grandparents

If the grandparents were alive and lived close by, their functional roles for the family were comparable to the parents' roles, with a distant grandfather and a nurturant, indulgent grandmother.

Godmothers and godfathers

Godparents were the secure base for the children if their parents could not raise them. Usually they were siblings or cousins of the parents and came from both parents' sides. They were registered during the baptism ceremony and stayed close to the children throughout childhood and adolescence.

CHANGES IN THE FAMILY

Demographics

Marriages are postponed until both husband and wife have completed their education and started a career and often follow, not precede pregnancies. There is a substantial number of one-parent families, i.e., 35 percent in 1997. Since 1991 the number of single households has increased by 12.1 percent and the estimate for the year 2015 is a further increase to 36.4 percent (Statistisches Bundesamt, 1999). There are also patchwork families who are mainly composed of divorced parents. Additionally, there are gay families who have attained a legal status recently, and finally there are individuals who deliberately decide not to have children and families (Keller, Zach, and Abels, 2005).

Family values

The traditional family values beyond the regulations of the family relationships extended to the continuation of the lineage, which was guaranteed by male offspring who carried on the father's name, and the continuation of the family profession or trade. This continuation established old age security for the parents (*Altenteil* = part of the elderly). Sociopolitical changes and feminism have rendered traditional family values largely obsolete. However, traditional values have not completely disappeared; the acceptance of family values has instead become individualized and a matter of choice. Family values have become modernized in the sense that equal rights for males and females and the increasing participation of females in the labor force have created different expectations for the family as an institution. Family values have also become polyethnic by integrating families from different ethnic and cultural backgrounds with different value systems into the society. The impact of family values on family life and their intergenerational transmission, moreover, largely depend on the quality of relationships among members of families. The early experience of close parent–child relationships affects closeness throughout the lifespan with acceptance of intergenerational obligations. Emotional insecurity and rejection create interpersonal distance and separation early during the lifespan with often irreparable emotional damage at both ends.

OUTLOOK

It is difficult to portray families in societies that have a fast pace of life, a high potential for change from generation to generation and an increasing complexity of daily life. Moreover, in the era of globalization, developments in individual societies interact in a multiplicity of obvious and non-obvious ways. Accordingly, the public awareness as expressed in the coverage of media adapts the interpretation of the traditional institutions of societies to the modern zeitgeist. Demographic and sociographic surveys as well as – politically highly controversial – census data update the current status of families in Germany on a regular basis. The reports inform us that the traditional family is disappearing, that single households are vastly increasing, that the elderly population increases disproportionally, that the elderly are isolated from their children and lonely, and that the new fathers take equal responsibilities in caring for their children on a day-to-day basis. On the other hand, psychological and sociological studies inform us that the majority of youngsters want to have children, marry, and found a family. The goal of life is seen in meaningful relationships with a partner and raising children; most adolescents also want to maintain good relationships with their parents (Keller, Zach, and Abels, 2005). How do these controversial pieces of information fit together? One aspect that contributes to these discrepancies is that the accessible information about families relies mostly on cross-sectional studies. Family, however, is not a static concept but changes in predictable and unpredictable ways. In order to get the full picture of families in Germany and elsewhere, we have to adopt a longitudinal perspective. The statistical data about single households, for example, need to be related to different phases of family development. In an individualistic society like Germany, children leave the parental household usually when they have finished school. They live in single households or share apartments with peers from then on until they find a partner with whom they want to live. Often young couples live together for some time before they marry. Once they start a family in their late twenties and early thirties, the majority return to traditional family roles with the mother going on maternity leave and the father being the main breadwinner. Single mothers are usually not single by choice, but as a result of broken relationships. Marriages break up on a large scale after a few years, which may lead to temporary single households again, before mothers and fathers may remarry. Owing to a longer life expectancy, women often survive their husbands (80.6 vs. 74.4 years, Federal Statistical Office for 1997–1999) and form again single households. Thus, life trajectories can consist of many different phases, which can only be foreseen and planned to some degree at the beginning of the family life.

Nevertheless, the institution of family seems to be a stable unit that has survived diverse sociopolitical ideologies. Student revolts, feminism, and the provocation of social hierarchies during the 1960s and 70s proclaimed the abandonment of traditional patterns of family life and living in communes instead, where every person had equal rights, including the children. Interestingly, the children who had been brought up under the ideology of complete liberty returned themselves to rather traditional lifestyles including the formation of traditional families. Obviously, beyond their sociological characteristics and their psychological functions families have biological roots that qualify the family environment as the best place for cultural learning.

20   Ghana

Benjamin Amponsah, Charity Akotia,
and Akinsola Olowu

A HISTORICAL OUTLINE OF GHANA

Ghana derived its name from the ancient Ghana Empire in the Western Sudan, which fell in the eleventh century. Formally known as Gold Coast, Ghana was the first black colony in sub-Saharan Africa to gain independence from the British on March 6, 1957 and became a republic in 1960. The ruins of about 30 castles dotted around the coast of Ghana are evidence of four centuries of the presence of Europeans who traded in ivory, gold, and slaves. The population of Ghana is 18,800,000. Accra is its capital with a population of 1,605,400 inhabitants. The major ethnic groups are the Akan (49 percent), Mole-Dagomba (16.5 percent), Ewe (12.7 percent), and Ga-Adangbe (8 percent) (Ghana Statistical Service, 2000).

ECOLOGICAL FEATURES

Ghana is located in West Africa on the Gulf of Guinea. It is bordered on the west by Côte d'Ivoire, on the north by Burkina Faso and by Togo on the east. Ghana has an area of 238,533 km^2. Ghana is primarily a lowland country. The northern part of the country is grassland showing a dry transitional expanse between the Sahara desert to the north and the southern tropical region. The weather varies by region, but in general it has a tropical climate with annual average temperature between 26 °C and 29 °C. Annual rainfall varies from more than 2,100 mm in the southwest to 1,000 mm in the north. During the dry season (August to February), the Sahel brings dry winds, called *harmattan* throughout the country.

ORGANIZATION AND INSTITUTIONS OF SOCIETY

Economic organization

Ghana is rich in natural resources such as gold, diamond, bauxite, manganese, timber, and cocoa, most of which are export commodities.

336

Agriculture is the mainstay of Ghana's economy. After decolonization in 1957, Ghana enjoyed economic and political advantages unparalleled elsewhere in tropical Africa. The foundation of prosperity then was solidly based on the production and export of cocoa, of which Ghana was the world's leading producer. Ghana had a well-developed transportation and road network, relatively high per capita income, low national debt, and sizable foreign currency reserves. During the last thirty years, the growth and prosperity enjoyed by Ghanaians started experiencing substantial economic declines in all spheres of national life. However, from the early 1980s and continuing into the 1990s, serious economic restructuring and reforms embodied in the Economic Recovery Program were vigorously pursued to rebuild the shattered economy and to restore the luster of Ghana's name.

Political institutions and legal system

Historically, most traditional political systems in Ghana were centralized, with kings and chiefs exercising administrative, legislative, and judicial controls in their political units (e.g., the Akans, Ga-Adangbe, Ewe, the Gonja, Dagomba, Mamprusi, Wala, etc.). In the traditional system, politics and law were fused and embodied in kings and chiefs whose legitimacy were derived from their ancestors. During colonization, the British policy of indirect rule utilized these kings and chiefs in government and administration, thus traditional authorities retained their jurisdiction over the internal affairs of their communities. Independence ushered in an era of constitutionalism. The democratic experiment was overthrown in 1966, which was followed by alternating military and civilian governments until January 1993 when the military government gave way to the Fourth Republic after presidential and parliamentary elections in late 1992. The Fourth Republican constitution divides power among a president, parliament, cabinet, council of state, and an independent judiciary. Governments are elected by universal suffrage. Ghana's struggle towards democratization has gained a stronger ground with the success of its 1996 multiparty elections. Today, Ghana is a welcome African example of legitimate democracy and successful economic reform. Administratively, there are 10 regions divided into 110 districts, each with its own District Assembly. Under the districts are various types of councils, including town or area councils, zonal councils, and unit committees at the lowest level.

The legal system is based on Ghanaian common law, customary law (traditional), and the 1992 constitution. The Ghana Law Reform Commission established in 1968 has been reviewing statutory and customary laws. Among the successes of the Commission's work are the Mainten-ance of Children Decree 1977 and the Intestate Succession Law 1985. The Maintenance of Children Decree establishes Family Tribunals to hear complaints about maintenance of children during the subsistence of marriage and after divorce. The Intestate Succession Law provides protection for spouses and children in communities where they are not entitled to shares of their deceased estates.

The educational system

The formal Western-style classroom education was introduced into Ghana (then Gold Coast) by missionaries as early as 1765. Many of these educational institutions, established by Presbyterian and Method-ist missionaries, were located in the southern part of the country in what became the British Gold Coast Colony. In an effort to achieve the goal of conversion of the natives, the churches made baptism a condition for school enrolment. In 1952 the government drew up the Accelerated Development Plan for Education. The program, which became a reality in 1961, was designed to provide education for every child aged six and above. The central government took responsibility for the entire educa-tional system and funded schools through the Ministry of Education. Compared to its neighbors in the West African sub-region, Ghana's educational system was relatively advanced at the time of its independ-ence in 1957. Presently, the educational system comprises primary schools, junior secondary schools, senior secondary schools, polytechnic (technical and vocational) institutions, teacher-training colleges, and university-level institutions. Universal education remains an unrealized goal. However, most children have access to primary and junior second-ary schools. The literacy rate is about 64.5 percent (70 percent and 51 percent for males and females respectively).

Religion

Statistics vary with regards to the religious dispersion in Ghana. One reason for this variation is that many Ghanaians regarded as Christian or Muslim also embody several aspects of traditional indigenous beliefs into their religion. However, it is estimated that 69 percent of the population is Christian (including Orthodox, Pentecostal and charis-matic) 15.6 percent Muslim, 8.5 percent traditionalist, and 6.9 percent others (Ghana Statistical Service, 2000). Although the presence of for-eign religions is strong in Ghana, traditional religious practices have largely retained their influence because of their intimate relation to family loyalties and customs. In traditional society the belief system is expressed in a supreme being (*Nyame* in Akan and *Mawu* in Ewe). In almost all the varieties of traditional religion in Ghana, veneration of ancestors and the spirits is recognized as part of the order in their universe. Visits to the shrines are popular among the uneducated and those in rural communities. However, some educated Ghanaians including Christian "converts" sometimes show divided loyalties and do pay homage or consult the traditional oracles in times of trouble.

BONDS WITH GROUPS IN THE IMMEDIATE COMMUNITY

The extended family system is the hub around which traditional social organization revolved. For example, among the matrilineal Akans, which is the best known indigenous system in Ghana, maintenance of the family bond is of paramount importance. In order to ensure the bond of unity in the immediate community, respect for life, family dignity and protection of property, there was always insistence on conformity to traditional norms. Violations were severely sanctioned. Almost invariably, the individual's loyalty to his or her lineage overrides all other loyalties. If a person marries a group member from outside, he/she does not become an automatic member of that group, although he/she is expected to protect and respect the interest of the spouse's lineage. The headman and his elders are responsible for the allocation of land and had to manage conflicts within and without the unit; they presided over ceremonies for infants, supervised marriages, and arranged funerals. In general the headman and the elders are custodians of the political and spiritual authority of the group, and ensured the security of the community. These obligations that bind the group together also grant its members the right of inheritance. The extended family, therefore, functions as a mutual aid society in which each member has both the obligation to help others and the right to receive assistance from it in case of need.

THE FAMILY

Marriage

Traditional law in many communities in Ghana prevents certain categories of kin from marrying owing to the closeness of their relationship. The most widespread example of this marriage prohibition in Ghana is that of lineage or clan exogamy, which forbids a man to take a wife from his own group, lineage, subclan, or clan (Nukunya, 1992). With regard to endogamy, there are prescriptions or preferences for marital unions among certain kinfolk in traditional Ghana. However, there are still enforceable rules preventing marriage and sexual relations in the nuclear family. For example, among the Akan and the Ewe, marriage between first cousins is permitted and even encouraged. However, the rules of exogamy ensure that the partners must be cousins belonging to different lineages. There are serious social sanctions against breaches in marital relationships. However, divorce may still occur especially after family tribunals have failed to resolve breaches of marital bond. Some of the reasons that may lead to divorce include witchery, adultery, barrenness, impotence, battering, and family pressures.

Obtaining a spouse

Marriage is between two families and it binds not only the couple and their close relations but also more distant kinsfolk, neighbors, friends, and even villages. There is an elaborate procedure in selecting a potential spouse. The relatives of the "to be" spouses make sure that their affines are not noted for witchery or wizardry and do also not suffer from any debilitating diseases such as leprosy, epilepsy, insanity, and the like. The individuals must also be respectful and hardworking. These elements must be satisfied before consent is given. For marriage to be legal in the traditional system, three general processes needed to be observed which included marriage payment, the formal handing over of the bride by her parents to the bridegroom and his parents, and the marriage ceremony itself (Nukunya, 1992). The marriage payment varies from place to place and according to circumstances. This may involve two bottles of gin *tiri nsa* and an agreed sum of money. The situation in northern Ghana is slightly different since drinks are not emphasized. Presently, the Ghanaian traditional system of marriage is shifting toward nuclear as a result of urbanization, modernization, and the empowerment of women. However, the impact of the extended family on couples is still much felt in both the traditional and the urban settings.

Family structure

As in most societies in Africa, the Ghanaian social organization survives on a strong extended family system. The extended family can extend to three or four generations in a direct line which may consist of parents, siblings, uncles, cousins, aunts, grandparents, and great grand-relations. For the Ghanaian then, the extended family is a source of pride, strength, and assurance. In times of difficulty, they all share the cost of relief and also share the times of joy together. Even when there is spatial separation of blood relations, family ties remain intact and emotionally in terms of financial assistance and loyalty.

The extended family structure in Ghana may be a matrilineal, patrilineal, or double unilineal descent system. Among the matrilineal Akans, members of the extended family (*abusua*) include the man's mother, his maternal uncles and aunts, his sisters and their children, and his brothers. A man's children and those of his brothers belong to the families of their respective mothers. Consequently, in inheritance, a man's nephew (sister's son) will have priority over his own son. In 1984, legislation was introduced to change this traditional pattern of inheritance.

Among the matrilineal Akans, residence after marriage was matrilocal. The wife and her children traditionally reside at their maternal house, where she prepares meals to be carried to her husband at his maternal house, especially in the evenings. For the patrilineal and double-descent peoples of northern Ghana, residence was invariably patrilocal or virilocal. That is, the couple may live in the compound of the man's father or in his own house if he has one. Also, among the patrilineal Ewe in southeastern Ghana, all of the sons and grandsons of one male ancestor together with their wives, children, and unmarried sisters may be found in one stead.

Irrespective of the family composition (matrilineal, patrilineal or double unilineal descent system), power relations are patriarchal, in that each family unit is usually headed by an elder male, who may have inherited that status from his ancestry. Elderly female members of matrilineal descent groups may be consulted in the decision-making process on issues affecting the family, but almost invariably, the men wield more influence. In all the traditional systems, polygyny as a conjugal arrangement is on the decline for economic and religious reasons, but where it is practiced, sleeping rosters with the husband were, are still are, planned for the wives.

Family roles and functions

Traditionally, the husband or the father is the breadwinner and the mother generally is a housewife bringing forth children and taking care of them. However, as an economic unit, all members of the family are expected to contribute to the maintenance and survival of the family. Division of labor was in respect of age and sex. The entire extended family was responsible for the socialization of children; but it was generally the man's responsibility to exact punishment to the children. A wife is expected to be treated tenderly with love and understanding. The husband must also give periodic gifts to the wife; take responsibility for her problems including her debts. The wife in return must also show respect and obedience. She is not expected to call the husband by his personal name but a name that will address him as her master (Nukunya, 1969). These relationships are undergoing rapid change, as more women are now educated and attaining economic independence.

CHANGES IN THE FAMILY

Demographics

The very difficult economic conditions from the 1970s and the effects of modernization have brought more pressure to bear on the Ghanaian traditional family. For example, the fertility rate, which was 6.4 children per woman in 1988 had dropped to 4.6 children per woman in 1998 (Ghana Statistical Service, 1998). The median age of first marriage for women is approximately 18.9 years, while the median age at first birth is 20 years. Although there is a drive toward monogamous marriage, instances of polygynous unions are still high. It is estimated that approximately 28 percent of currently married women are in polygynous marriages (Ghana Statistical Service, 1994).

Family values

The Ghanaian family system is in transition. The emphasis on the nuclear family and the strengthening of marital ties has relegated to the background those of kinship, especially in the urban settings. With the promulgation of the Intestate Succession Law of 1984, which regularized the procedures for inheritance in Ghana, it is now the responsibility of parents to bring up their children and provide the necessary security for their upkeep and well-being. Women are encouraged to be assertive and active in their roles and it is no longer fashionable for a man to marry an uneducated or an unemployed woman. Early betrothal and marriage of young girls under 18 years is now frowned upon. Prolific childbearing is no longer a cherished value. Society is coming to terms with the fact that women are equal partners in marriage and must be accorded the respect and dignity they deserve. Although there is a gradual weakening of influence of the patriarchal extended family in the urban family, the influence of the extended family is still strong, especially in the rural areas. Children also have an important role to play in the family arrangement. They are seen as a social investment and have the obligation to take care of their parents in their old age. Children are expected to help their parents in household chores, show respect, and uphold family values.

CONCLUSIONS

One important issue that comes out clearly in the Ghanaian social system is its dual but interrelated nature. Although the greater majority of the citizens still live almost entirely in rural areas, and observe and venerate ancestral customs and practices, the effects of modernization associated with urban life have affected the social behavior, beliefs, and values of all Ghanaians. There is constant interaction between the people irrespective of their residential status. Ideas, goods, and services flow constantly between urban and rural areas, which invariably blurs the distinction between so-called traditional and modern life. In contemporary Ghana, modernization is grafted onto traditional roots, and although traditional social relationships are undergoing major transformation to fit the needs of modern life, they continue to endure primarily through the kinship system. The transition into the modern world has been slow for women. This is based on the view that despite the efforts of government and non-governmental organizations in the promotion of girl-child education, activities aimed at promoting the well-being and development of women, the high rate of female fertility and the high drop-out rate of women in the educational ladder in Ghana are indications that women's primary role continues to be largely child-bearing.

It is interesting to note that in the more affluent urban centers family life approximates to Western lifestyles in varying degrees. In such areas, both parents in the family negotiate family decisions. With children spending increasing amounts of time away from home with peers and relevant others, more of their values reflect that of their peers, teachers, and adults who do not share the values of their lineage. We can conclude that despite the influence of modernization and urbanization, the extended family continues to be the cornerstone of social welfare arrangements in Ghana.

21   Greece

*Kostas Mylonas, Aikaterini Gari, Artemis Giotsa,
Vassilis Pavlopoulos, and Penny Panagiotopoulou*

A HISTORICAL OUTLINE OF GREECE

Greece was established as an independent nation state in 1822, having
rebelled against the Ottoman Empire. Its present-day population is
approximately 10,500,000 inhabitants. Athens is the capital, with
4,500,000 inhabitants. Greece became a member of the European
Union in 1981.

ECOLOGICAL FEATURES

Greece is in southeastern Europe, situated at the base of the Balkan
peninsula, with mountains as its spine and hundreds of islands in the
Aegean, Ionian, and Cretan seas, few fertile plains, and, even today,
small isolated communities in the mountains and on the many islands,
and relatively large cities on the plains and by the sea. Its climate is
Mediterranean with hot and dry summers and mild winters.

ORGANIZATION AND INSTITUTIONS OF SOCIETY

Economic organization

The ecological features of Greece shaped specific types of subsistence
patterns which remained unchanged for hundreds of years. The plains,
essentially broad valleys between mountains, permitted some cultivation
of crops. Cities, often located near the sea on the serrated coastline,
became trading and mercantile centers. In the mountains, the herding of
goats and sheep, and vine and olive oil cultivation were widely found.
Fishing was the standard mode of subsistence in communities by the sea,
together with merchant shipping. During the past 20 years, the traditional forms of subsistence patterns have given way to decreased agriculture (20 percent), increased industrialization (20 percent) and
services (60 percent) primarily related to tourism.

Political institutions and legal system

Historically, the many small communities throughout Greece were partly self-governed, most likely because the geographical conditions made effective political control of these isolated communities by a central government almost impossible, either by the Ottoman Empire or by the governments of Greece after its establishment in the early 1820s. This relative autonomy and self-government in the communities, in which essentially each set their own traditions, customs and right to judge their own members according to local customs and norms, was a critical factor that affected the Greeks' social perception of law, fairness, government, and suspicion of central government – attitudes that have been sustained until the present time (Friedl, 1962). However, in modern Greece, central government controls all aspects of life. Since the 1980s, institutional changes regarding women's rights have been codified by new laws.

The educational system

After the establishment of the Greek state and the formation of the first Greek constitution of 1823, education was limited to the very few. The University of Athens was established in 1837, with male students only until 1890, and one of the highest values of the traditional agricultural family was to send at least one of the sons to the university, even if this required selling of land to finance his education (Gari and Kalantzi-Azizi, 1998; Tsoukalas, 1982). At the present time, the Greek education is an integral part of the EU educational system. Approximately 90 percent of the population is considered literate and the percentage of males and females enrolled in tertiary education is 47.4 percent and 46.3 percent, respectively.

Religion

The population is 98 percent Christian Orthodox. Although the proportion of people attending church regularly in the urban areas is about 10 percent, recent polls indicate that the great majority of the population believe in the Orthodox religion.

BONDS WITH GROUPS IN THE IMMEDIATE COMMUNITY

The small isolated autonomous communities were characterized by suspicion of outsiders and tight social control of their families or clans.

Violations of local social standards or religious customs provoked the reaction and sanctions of the entire community. The members of the community judged and punished those who violated their customs, whatever the law of the central government, either Ottoman or Greek. The collective responsibility of the community members, the respect for life, the respect of family honor and property, and the institutions collectively supported by the community, were carefully protected. On the other hand, the inter-family relationships within the community were often characterized by hostility and contention.

THE FAMILY

Marriage

In regard to exogamy, in the traditional family of the past, marriage was restricted to potential spouses from the same village and of the same religion. In today's family, choice of a spouse has few restrictions. In regard to endogamy, the Orthodox religion prohibited marriage of the nuclear family and first cousins, but marriage of second cousins was permitted, although in isolated villages these restrictions on marriage between first cousins were sometimes overlooked.

Obtaining a spouse

Traditionally, decisions to marry were made by the two families, with the father – or the eldest brother in case of the father having passed away – making the decision. Today, the decision whom to marry is made by the individual with or without the consent of the parents. In the traditional family, marriage was usually arranged on the basis of contracts, in which the father's dowry of a house to the groom represented legal transfer of property (Cassia and Bada, 1992; Friedl, 1967; Psychogios, 1987). However, regional variations in property transmission were observed. Pastoralists with extended families and neolocal island farmers gave a trousseau to daughters at marriage; continental farmers presented land and trousseaux to daughters. Women from the islands had a comparatively freer status, e.g, on the island of Naxos daughters were endowed from the patrimony and sons from the matrimony. In the present day, there is no official dowry, but social norms are directed toward the father buying property ready for when the daughter marries, or buying a car for the married couple after marriage.

Social sanctions against divorce were strong in the traditional family, although the Orthodox Church permitted three divorces for both men and women. The patriarchal rights of the head of the family were codified in terms of the father; in case of divorce the father retained the property, became custodian of the child, maintained control of family finances, etc. The Greek constitution of 1975 and later laws contained provisions regarding gender equality, including the married woman's right to maintain her family name and equal rights after divorce regarding control of property and child custody. According to Eurostat (1995) the lowest increase in divorce rates in the European Union are in Greece and Ireland. Greece had a rate of 0.4 in 1965 as compared to a 0.6 average of the 15 EU countries, and a 0.7 rate in 1993 as compared to a 1.7 average of the EU countries.

Family structure

The traditional Greek extended family structure could be described as patrilineal in terms of lineal descent, in which kin of both sexes were related. It can also be described as patriarchal in that the father or the grandfather had the legal power and the social norms which supported his authority.

The extended family included three generations: grandparents, sons/fathers, daughters/mothers, and children, with the grandfather being the head of the family in terms of authority structure. The family was related to collateral kin (cousins, uncles and aunts, nieces and nephews), and maintained affinal relationships (parents-in-law, children-in-law, and siblings-in-law), as well as *koumbari* (bonds with a family through baptism of the children, or "best man/maid of honor" at the marriage of offspring), or bonds with others through mutual obligations.

Residence after marriage was patrilocal, in that the married sons resided in or near the father's residence or that of kinsmen. The married daughter resided with or in a separate home near the father-in-law. In Athens, residence was almost always in the home of the father-in-law and the mother-in-law had complete authority over the daughter-in-law.

Family roles and functions

The traditional roles of the family members have been described based on perceptions and attitudes towards Greek family values, roles, and duties (Vassiliou, 1966) and on traditional Greek family values (Georgas, 1991). Roles in the traditional Greek family can be described as follows: *father* takes the lead role in the family and handles all financial matters; *mother* accepts her husband's decisions, is always there – in the home – living for her children, as her first goal should be to be a good mother;

parents are protective and supportive; *children* are obedient, respectful, and caring for their parents when they become old; finally, *women* should not have children outside marriage and should return to their family homes if separated.

Triandis and Vassiliou (1972) described the Greek ingroup as composed of more than the extended family, including e.g., best man at the wedding, the godfather, in-laws, friends, with the criterion that they showed concern and support during times of need. The appropriate behaviors toward members of the ingroup were cooperation, protection, and help, while appropriate behaviors toward members of the outgroup were competition and hostility. Also, a key central value of the ingroup, which encompasses many other values, was *philotimo* (Vassiliou and Vassiliou, 1973). *Philotimo* can be loosely translated as "honor," but it has a special meaning for the Greek ingroup, i.e., "to give to others," "to be correct in fulfilling your obligations," "to sacrifice yourself for others," "to respect others."

CHANGES IN THE FAMILY

Demographics

The number of marriages per 1,000 persons in Greece has been declining in Greece from 9.4 in 1965 to 5.4 in 1994 (Eurostat, 1996). The same trend was found in the 15 EU nations, but the number of marriages in Greece was following a steeper declination than the average of the EU nations, i.e., 7.8 in 1965 to 5.2 in 1994.

Greece has the lowest rate of one-parent families in the EU. The number of births per 1,000 women of childbearing age in Greece has been declining from a rate of 2.39 in 1970 to 1.35 in 1994, but this still remains somewhat higher than the EU average. In general, in Greece there is a close association between marital status and fertility rates, with 98 percent of births within marriage, the highest percentage among the 15 state-members of the EU (Kotzamanis and Maratou-Alibrante, 1994).

Family values

The Greek constitution of 1975 preserved the traditional norms of family life (article 1388), until 1983, when the new Greek Family Law (23/2) introduced alterations in respect to the duties and rights of Greek family members. In studies of traditional family values, three factors emerged (Georgas, 1986, 1989, 1993; Papademou, 1999). The strongest factor was *hierarchical roles of father and mother*, with values related to the traditional roles of the patriarchal extended family, in which father was the head of the family, who acted in an authoritarian manner (punishes children when disobedient), controlled the finances (handles the money in the house . . . is the breadwinner), while mother was submissive, conciliatory, a housewife, caring for the children (accepts the decisions of the father . . . yields and is compromising . . . is always there for everyday matters . . . her place is in the home). A second factor was *responsibilities of parents toward the children*, e.g., parents shouldn't argue in front of the children; should teach their children to behave properly; the problems of the family should be solved within the family. The third factor was *responsibilities of children toward the family and the relatives*: children should take care of their parents when they become old; obey their parents; help with the chores of the house; respect their grandparents; maintain good relationships with one's relatives. In contrast with the rejection of hierarchical roles of father and mother (Safilios-Rothschild, 1971), young people did not reject values associated with responsibilities of the parents toward the children and responsibilities of the children toward the family and the relatives. These latter values were not only related to responsibilities of children to the family but also to the importance of maintaining ties with members of the extended family, that is, traditional values of the Greek extended family system.

Thus, the findings indicated that children, adolescents, and young people in Greece do not reject all the values of the traditional extended family, but only those associated with the traditional hierarchical roles of father and mother, son and daughter. The results also suggested that father's power within the family has lessened and mother's has increased, although the two-spouse family roles seem to remain traditional (Lambiri-Dimaki, 1972; Maratou-Alibrante, 1995). On the other hand, young people in Greece agreed with values of the traditional extended family in regard to the importance of maintaining relations with relatives, of respect for grandparents, of offering help to parents, of obligations towards the family, etc.

The analysis of the transition of the Greek traditional extended family system to the nuclear family system was based on methods of social support theory (Bengtson and Schrader, 1982; Roberts, Richards, and Bengtson, 1991). The findings indicated that the types of residence patterns and interactions with kin in Athens are very similar to that of the traditional towns. Grandparents, aunts, uncles, and cousins reside very near the nuclear family, even in Athens, either in the same apartment building, in the neighborhood, or in the community. They visit each other frequently and telephone each other frequently. In addition, it appeared that they also telephone each other frequently even when the kin live outside Athens (Georgas, 2000; Maratou-Alibrante, 1999).

CONCLUSIONS

Is today's Greek family extended or nuclear? Many family values of the extended family, as discussed above, particularly those related to relationships with kin, are still accepted, even by young people. Thus, one can conclude, at least on the basis of the evidence presented, that aspects of the extended family are still active in Greece and in Athens. It appears that the form of the rural extended family in Greece has been transplanted to Athens. Thus, one can characterize the Athenian family type as an urban extended family.

These conclusions also provide a partial answer to why the percentage of nuclear families in Greece was at the average of EU nations and slightly higher than Germany (Eurostat, 1995). We first have to add that the same panel also found that the number of three-generation households in Greece, over 20 percent, was the highest in the EU. However, just comparing demographic statistics is not enough. One has to look at the interactions between the members of the constellation of nuclear families which constitute the extended family, and not just at demographic statistics regarding the nuclear family itself, in order to understand the degree of maintenance of ties between the nuclear family and other kin.

In addition, historical and ethnographic information (Mousourou, 1985) is also vital in interpreting these results. Common residence of two or three generations is one way of differentiating between the nuclear and the extended family. Nuclear family households have been found (Georgas, Mylonas, Bafiti, et al., 2001) to be more prevalent in affluent countries. For example, an adult son or daughter can afford, because of the high level of GNP in Western Europe, to rent or buy an apartment and live separately from his/her parents. This is more difficult in a less affluent society such as Greece. However, as discussed above, one of the values in modern Greek society, stemming from older traditions of property transmission (Cassia and Bada, 1992), is that the father/potential-grandfather plans for a separate residence for the daughter, even before adolescence, for when she marries. Economics of Greece are an imperative at this point. A typical process of many fathers/potential-grandfathers with a piece of property or an old house in Athens or another city would be to make an arrangement with a building contractor. The arrangement was that the father would provide the property and the contractor would finance the construction of the apartment building, with the provision that the father would retain two or three apartments, e.g., one for him and his wife, and two for the daughters, and the contractor would sell the other apartments. This explains why such a large proportion of Athenian families live in the same apartment building. Although some family values have changed, they are primarily those related to some traditional roles of father and mother. The father has lost some of the autocratic power over the mother and the children, and as "nature abhors a vacuum" this power has been absorbed by the mother, and to a large degree, by the children. However, this does not mean that the extended family system is decomposed into isolated nuclear units. In fact, family values associated with maintaining close contact with relatives, children respecting grandparents, children's obligations toward parents, are still accepted by young people in Athens and in Greece. Nuclear family members in Greece maintain close contacts with relatives; they visit them regularly, or if living at some distance, telephone them frequently (Georgas, Christakopoulou, Poortinga, Goodwin, Angleitner, and Charalambous, 1997). Indeed, in comparing the frequency of these contacts with other cultures, Greece has one of the highest rates of visits and telephone contacts with relatives. According to the definition of the nuclear family – two generations in a household – each of these families is structurally nuclear, but functionally, their ties are that of an extended family or joint family; that is, the Greek family appears to be phenomenologically nuclear but functionally extended.

When these changes in the Greek family were compared with other countries, demographic statistics indicated that rate of divorce, the number of one-parent families, the number of children born to unmarried women in Greece remain the lowest in the EU. The social support data described above were used (Georgas et al., 2001) in a cross-cultural study with 16 countries: Canada, USA, Mexico, UK, the Netherlands, Germany, Czech Republic, Ukraine, Bulgaria, Yugoslavia, Greece, Cyprus, Turkey, Hong Kong, China, and India. In terms of means of geographic proximity, Greece was fourth after Cyprus, India, and China. Cyprus and Greece had the highest means of meetings with siblings, aunts/uncles, and cousins. Greece also had the second highest means, after Greek-speaking Cyprus, of telephone contacts with grandparents, aunts/uncles, and cousins. These are indications that residence patterns, interaction, and communication with kin are relatively close in comparison with other countries that also have an extended family system.

The conclusions about changes in the family in Greece appear to be that although affluence has been increasing in recent years, the traditional extended family has not decomposed into isolated nuclear families, but has changed its configuration. Its morphological equivalent is the extended family system in the urban setting with a continuation of contacts with its network of kin.

22 Hong Kong, SAR China: transitions and return to the motherland

Peter W. H. Lee, Sunita Mahtani Stewart, and Kitty K. C. Chan

A HISTORICAL OUTLINE OF HONG KONG

Hong Kong is situated at the southeastern tip of the Chinese mainland. Hong Kong Island, Kowloon, the outlying islands, and the New Territories are collectively included as "Hong Kong," spanning an area of 1,100 km². Hong Kong became a British colony in 1841 after the Opium War. It began with a population of 3,650 scattered over 20 villages, and 2,000 fishermen living aboard their boats. Hong Kong received an unparalleled influx of immigrants from Guangdong and Shanghai in 1948–1949 after the defeat of the Chinese Nationalist Government. By mid-1950, the population had swelled to 2.2 million, and it currently stands at 6.8 million (Information Services Department of Hong Kong SAR, People's Republic of China, 2002b). In 1997, Hong Kong was reunited with Mainland China as a Special Administrative Region (SAR) under the one-country–two-systems principle. Hong Kong was promised a continuation of its pre-existing capitalistic and political system for fifty years.

ECOLOGICAL FEATURES

Mountains dominate Hong Kong's natural terrain. The main island of Hong Kong and nearby Kowloon peninsula are populated with high-rise residential and office buildings. Rural and farming land in the New Territories are increasingly rebuilt into residential complexes, giving rise to new towns. Hong Kong is linked with good roads, extensive railway and underground networks, and efficient public transport services. Communication and travel within Hong Kong can be made with ease. Hong Kong is one of the most densely populated places in the world with a land population density estimated to be 6,480 per square kilometre in 1999 (Information Services Department, 2002b).

ORGANIZATION AND INSTITUTIONS OF SOCIETY

Economic organization

Hong Kong is a centre of commerce and trade. It had a labor force of 3.4 million in 1998 (Information Services Department, 2002b). The working population consists of 32 percent managers, administrators, professionals, and associate professionals. The proportions of clerical (18 percent), service and shop sales workers (14 percent) have remained relatively stable. The proportion of plant and machine operators and assemblers, has dropped significantly with the relocation of most manufacturing industries to southern China because of the cheaper labor cost. Likewise, agricultural and fishing industries have shrunk to a negligible 0.4 percent of the total industry sectors. To date, manufacturing, construction, financing, insurance, real estate, and business services make up 30 percent of the total industry. The remaining bulk of industries and services comprise electricity, gas and water (0.4 percent), wholesale, retail and import/export trades, restaurants and hotels (32 percent), transport, storage, and communications (11.1 percent), community, social, and personal services (26 percent).

Political institutions and legal system

Hong Kong became a Special Administrative Region of the People's Republic of China (HKSAR) on July 1, 1997. The constitutional structure of the HKSAR is set out in the Basic Law, which lays down its administrative policies for 50 years after 1997. The long years of British rule leading to a capitalist lifestyle and popular education resulted in a complex mix of traditional and western philosophies. There are evident changes towards equalitarianism, increased individualistic consciousness, greater wish for autonomy, freedom, anti-authoritarianism, anti-traditionalism, and a more intense striving for achievement (Yang, 1996).

Economic growth, easy access to information, the rise of a well-educated middle class, a vocal media and more women joining the workforce served to catalyze shifts from traditional to "modern" values. The Western emphasis on individual autonomy frequently conflicts with culturally defined ideals of reverence to authority and subservience of personal needs. While child discipline places great importance on respecting authority, "listening and not answering back," superficial conformity of the children often exists alongside superficial reticence with unexpressed rebellious dissent. This is particularly so as children generally become better educated than their parents, and smaller families lead to increasing parental indulgence and tolerance.

The educational system

A mix of Eastern and Western teaching has long influenced education in Hong Kong. The educational policies have always aimed at preserving the basic elements of traditional Chinese values while incorporating advances made in the west at the same time. Schools are highly subsidized, with an average of one-quarter of the Government's total annual budget for education. The percentage of population aged 15 and above by educational attainment by sex is: 20 percent of males and females with primary education; 22.5 percent males and 15.6 percent females with junior secondary education; 25.9 percent males and 26.7 percent females with senior secondary education, 12.7 percent males and 13.6 percent females with post-secondary but non-degree courses, and 13.9 percent males and 11.5 percent females with degree/university education.

Religion

There are 600 Buddhist and Taoist temples and 800 Christian churches and chapels representing a mix of traditional and Western influences in religion. About 4 percent of the population was estimated to be Roman Catholic, 4.5 percent other Christian denominations, 1 percent Muslim. While no official estimates are available, popular adherence to some form of Buddhism and Taoism is highly prevalent to the extent that the Buddha's birthday has been designated as a public holiday since 1999 (Information Services Department, 2002a).

BONDS WITH GROUPS IN THE IMMEDIATE COMMUNITY

The immediate family and extended family group are the primary groups of bonding. Extended family groups have shrunk over the past decade with a definite trend towards smaller family size. Outside the immediate family, there are few other groups of close bonding.

THE FAMILY

Marriage

In regard to endogamy, there is no restriction on choice of spouse, even across races. It is common to see Chinese ladies courting and marrying

Caucasians. There is a parallel trend for arranged marriages of Hong Kong males from lower socioeconomic strata with Mainland Chinese girls, usually from rural areas. In regard to exogamy, norms prohibited marriage within the nuclear family and first cousins.

Social sanctions against divorce continue to soften over the years. The divorce rates have witnessed a steady increase, from 1.2 percent of all marriages in 1991, rising to 1.9 percent in 1996 and 2.7 percent in 2001. In case of divorce, there are no set rules for retention of property, or child custody, which is usually worked out through negotiation. When negotiations break down, the couple may seek adjudication in a court of law. In Hong Kong, decisions to marry are usually made by the couples, virtually independent of parental approval. Final "approvals" are sought from parents when everything has been practically decided. The fathers of both families serve the function of ceremonial endorsers. There is no official dowry. However, by custom, the female brings along gold pieces and ornaments as gifts from her own parents. The two families also agree on the size of the wedding banquet and the quantity of ceremonial cakes the male family would supply to the females' families and friends.

Family structure

The Hong Kong family structure could be described as patrilineal in terms of lineal descent, in which children carry on the family line of the male only. It is also patriarchal in that the father assumes normative authority. However, mothers take on an active and decision-making role on domestic issues.

The extended family includes three generations: grandparents, sons/fathers, daughters/mothers, and children. The father is the head of the family in terms of authority structure, with collateral kin (cousins, uncles and aunts, nieces and nephews), and affinal relationships (parents-in-law, children-in-law, and siblings-in-law). In some families, the family kinship extends to godparents of the children, who are usually good friends of either parent.

Residence after marriage is not fixed. In Hong Kong some couples choose to live with the husband's family, primarily for cost savings. It is unusual for the husband to agree to reside with the wife's family of origin. However, couples prefer to live on their own away from either family of origin. Hong Kong is itself a very small place, and commuting is cheap and efficient. The general preference is not to reside in the parental household after marriage. The main consideration is financial viability. Working couples with children may choose to live near their parents for easier access and support.

Family roles and functions

The traditional roles of the family members have been much diluted with western influences and increasing financial independence. Some examples of the roles-values of the Hong Kong Chinese family are as follows.

Father

Usually head of the family . . . contributes the major bulk of family income . . . punishes the children (more severely) . . . gives a dowry to the daughter . . . the breadwinner . . . supports children practically through life – "children are children for life and will always be children" . . . expected to take care of elderly parents.

Mother

Intermediary between father and children . . . place is in the home, but increasingly takes on employment and even develops a career . . . despite this, the mother is still expected to take on the predominant share of household chores . . . more devoted to her children than the father . . . usually accepts the decisions of the husband but could also be assertive and insisting on her own way, especially in domestic affairs . . . expected to be there for everyday matters . . . women's first goal in life is a good mother and wife, as well as being dutiful to parents.

Parents

Teach children to behave properly . . . help children strive for academic excellence with promises of a good secure job and livelihood . . . keep children from going astray and associating with bad peers . . . help children financially . . . help children decide on their career choice . . . strive to leave some savings and estates to children if possible.

Women

Shouldn't have children if they are not married . . . be a capable wife and devoted to supporting the husband . . . support and take care of aging parents, sometimes to the extent of not getting married.

Children

Shouldn't talk back to parents . . . should be humble and obedient . . . should study hard and get good results . . . should always behave in a socially expected and law abiding manner and not shame the family's name . . . obligated to care for parents when they become old . . . obey their parents during all stages of their development.

Moore (1974) noted amongst Chinese a strong emphasis on filial piety, harmony between man and nature, man as a social being, and a preference for tolerance. Hsu (1971) noted in the Chinese an overriding importance placed on familial and social rather than individual homeostasis. The Chinese place a strong preference on rules, social order, harmony, and public duty. The family is the pivotal and fundamental unit of social organization, as a basic resource of support and as the roots and determinants of an individual's orientations and life goals. Yang (1995) reported Yeh's (1990) notion of familism in the Chinese as a multifaceted system of cognitions, affects, intentions, and behaviors. Great importance is placed on harmony and solidarity, lineage prolongation and expansion, family prosperity, and family sentiments. The Chinese pattern of socialization has been regarded by some scholars as a form of collectivism (Triandis, 1987), which calls for subordination of personal goals, interests, and welfare for the sake of the family.

CHANGES IN THE FAMILY

Demographics

The proportion of never married persons among males of age 15 and over decreased from 36.5 percent in 1991 to 33.9 percent in 2001. In females, the proportion was 29 percent in 1991 and rising slightly to 30.1 percent in 2001. Over the last decade, the number of domestic households increased by 30 percent from 1.58 million to 2.05 million. The average household size decreased from 3.4 to 3.1 (Information Services Department, 2002b). The dependency ratio within the households (i.e., number of persons under aged 15 per 1,000 persons aged between 15–64) decreased from 420 in 1991 to 383 in 2001 reflecting the downsizing of the typical family and a reduction in birth rates.

Family values

Responsibility toward the family, interdependency of the family members, and respect for parents (Feldman and Rosenthal, 1991) remain as key values. Nuclear and small-size families are becoming the norm over traditional extended families. As early as 1949, Levy noted that "the traditional family is being wiped out without being replaced" in Hong Kong. With smaller family size, children in the family are afforded more attention, nurturance, and indeed indulgence. At the same time, the burden of responsibility and family obligations becomes heavier as fewer family members are available to share out. As children still feel obliged to offer financial and emotional support to their parents for life, the stress to achieve success may have become more intense. With the erosion of the extended family, important relations are increasingly built with a wider group of individuals outside the family (Lau, 1981; Wu and Tseng, 1985). Respect for the elders seems to have weakened considerably (Goodwin and Tang, 1996) as productivity and achievement are increasingly valued.

The emphasis on socially desirable and culturally approved behaviors, and social harmony (King and Bond, 1985; Wu and Tseng, 1985) has undergone drastic changes in definition and form as the Hong Kong society evolved from its traditional Chinese roots to increasing western influence, and came from poverty to affluence and back to stringency in the years after 1997. Currently, the family in Hong Kong is still in a state of flux having just recovered from the strong emigration drive prior to the political hand-over in 1997. It is a time when families who had gone abroad are coming back to the homeland. Traditional Chinese values relating to family obligations, subjugation of individual needs to the greater social order, filial piety, are weakened as the individual in the family is confronted with the challenges from within Hong Kong after the political transfer of 1997 as well as of globalization in the twenty-first century.

Of particular impact after the political transfer are the economic downturn, the growing distrust of the government, increasing demands for democracy, and the growing gap between the rich and the poor. An interesting trend is also evidenced as Hong Kong people develop more trust, comfort, and a better sense of integration with Mainland China given the evident and continuous support from the Motherland, especially during the period of economic stringency and the SARS outbreak in 2003.

The family structure in Hong Kong clearly changed in response to the impending political changes. Families were disrupted as children were sent abroad to study, or whole families emigrated leaving the elderly behind, or spouses and children were sent abroad to "sit the immigration prison sentence" (the residency requirement) while husbands remained in Hong Kong to continue to generate income for the family's livelihood. Since 1994 and continuing beyond 1997, there is a clear trend towards late marriages and increasing numbers of single males and females during the prime marriageable ages (Information Services Department, 2002b).

In the post-1997 era, Hong Kong evidenced much difficulty and distrust in the process of adjusting to a new government viewed with at least some degree of skepticism. The unprecedented downturn in the world's economy was untimely and unfortunate for the new SAR government as it was still courting trust from the people of Hong Kong. The economic bubble in Hong Kong burst overnight. With much anxiety and resentment, the Hong Kong Chinese seemed to have lost their previous zeal and sense of direction. Not without reason, some public commentators labeled the society as "a society filled with angst and grudge." The HKSAR government served conveniently as the scapegoat to be blamed for the common people's own reckless investments and disastrous speculations. Many families are faced with the previously unheard of phenomenon of "negative asset," where the housing loan previously contracted into largely exceeds the market value of the asset. A wider rift between the well-to-do and the underprivileged has become evident. The disadvantaged projected their frustrations with anger and resentment as they struggled at the fringe to make ends meet. Alongside economic adversities, demands for democracy and the so-called rights of the people became more prominent. The demand for betterment of individualistic well-being and needs in a society of flux became more reminiscent of those of the west.

Unfortunately in the current society of flux, the emphasis over the previous decade on small families with indulgence and over-protection of one to two children may precede a generation of youngsters who might be less stress tolerant and resilient compared to the previous generation. It would indeed be an interesting study to trace in progression and reciprocal influence the effects on Hong Kong families and their children of the impact of the Chinese historical heritage, through economic affluence as a British colony, reunion with China, economic downturn alongside the world's recession, to the current new era of changing economic activities and further opening up of economic, cultural, and social boundaries to the west as well as Mainland China.

CONCLUSIONS

The Chinese in Hong Kong share cultural roots by virtue of their common heritage. Regardless of their place of abode, Chinese are influenced by a long-standing value system which to date remains influential. Tseng, Lin, and Yeh (1995) referred to "Chinese" as people who belong to the ethnicity of China – an ethnic group with roots in the Hua-Xia region of central-northern China. Having a Chinese surname signifies one's family of origin and also legitimizes one as being "Chinese." The

Chinese identify and take pride in their traditional roots arising out of three thousand years of cultural heritage. The Chinese as a group share various behavior patterns and thinking styles (ethnic character) as well as beliefs and values (culture), which reinforces the former. Despite the pervasive influence of a common historical heritage, students of ecocultural influences of a particular ethnic group need to be mindful of the idiosyncratic influences in a particular locale on the psyche of the people studied. In understanding the ecocultural influences on the people of Hong Kong, heterogeneity influences versus homogeneity factors (Tseng et al., 1995) should both be heeded.

Today's Hong Kong family is clearly edging toward being smaller in size and nuclear in core. The traditional Chinese family values and heritage have remained, although they are also likely to have been diluted with drastic social changes including emigration, repatriation, fewer children (with resultant indulgence and greater tolerance for misbehaviors), changing economy, and increasing economic stringency. The strong preference on rules, social order, harmony, and public duty remains evident. The grip of the parents on children, however, seems to have loosened as children are wooed by western individualistic and materialistic influences as well as the trends and fads of neighboring Asian countries (Japan in particular). Likewise, the influence of Mainland China on Hong Kong is going to be increasingly seen as China opens itself more and more to the world, and Hong Kong people become less wary of the Chinese communist influence. There is a growing sense of Chinese nationalistic feelings in the people of Hong Kong. It is anticipated that as Mainland China and Hong Kong draw nearer to each other, the two regions will become less dissimilar in family and cultural orientation.

23   India

Janak Pandey

A HISTORICAL OUTLINE OF INDIA

India, home of more than a billion people, is one of the oldest civilizations in the world and therefore it has a rich history of traditions, religions, sociopolitical struggles, and reforms. The present form of the republic of India came into being in 1947 after around 200 years of British rule and after a prolonged predominantly non-violent freedom struggle. The independence resulted in a bloody partition (as India and Pakistan), the memories of which still linger. India continues to be a member of the Commonwealth of Nations, and it claims to follow the policy of non-alignment, which is lately becoming less relevant in the increasingly globalizing world.

ECOLOGICAL FEATURES

India is the fifth largest country in the world and occupies a strategic and dominant position in South Asia. The climate is predominantly tropical, except in the north, but owing to its large size and varied topography (high mountains, large plateaus, and long river basins) the country has varied climatic conditions at different places. Agriculture is the primary means of subsistence mainly because of the fertile soil and plenty of rainfall. India can be divided into two very distinct groups of rural and urban, with a larger section of the society living in villages and subsisting on agriculture. Since independence, there has been a concerted effort towards industrialization, which has also led to a growth in migration to the cities. As a result, though agriculture still remains the main source of livelihood, there has been diversification into a number of other professions. In addition, economic categories and social stratification in the form of castes exists among the majority Hindus (80 percent) and also in some minorities such as Shia Muslims. Although economic class and social castes are highly correlated, they are not the same.

The present analysis is focused on one of the largest states of India, Uttar Pradesh, located in the north central part of the country.

ORGANIZATION AND INSTITUTIONS OF SOCIETY

Political institutions and legal system

India has a both unitary and federal political structure, necessary to keep together a diverse country of many languages, religions, and cultures. The country is governed by a strong central (federal) government. Each of the 28 states has a provincial government. India is a secular democratic republic with quite distinct social justice leanings in its constitution. Although the country has a majority of Hindus, secular ideals and guarantees of equal rights and equal opportunities to each community are constitutionally and socially valued. The Indian constitution provides for a separation of powers and autonomy to the executive, the legislature, and the judiciary. There exists the practice of universal adult franchise irrespective of class, gender, and education. The Indian political system consists of multiple political parties at national and regional levels. Another characteristic of the Indian political governance is decentralization. In the vast rural areas power is vested in the villages through the *Panchayati Raj* (village government) system. The political unity of diverse cultures and regions becomes difficult at times because of secessionist movements in some parts of the country. After independence in 1947, a number of legal reforms generally have been in favor of social justice and human rights.

The Educational system

The British introduced their educational system during the colonial period. However, major educational expansion covering the masses started only after independence in 1947. In the last two decades, with concentrated efforts, illiteracy has been reduced greatly. The revised Programme of Action of 1992 of the National Policy for Education 1986 envisaged compulsory education of satisfactory quality to all children up to 14 years of age before the turn of the twenty-first century. To operationalize the revised policy, a number of schemes such as operation Black Board, Non Formal Education, District Primary Education Programme, National Literacy Mission, and many more have been launched in the last two decades.

Provisional figures of the recent census of 2001 and comparison with 1991 reveal that all states without exception have shown increases in literacy level with the overall literacy rates increasing 13.2 percentage points (from 52.2 percent in 1991 to 65.4 percent in 2001), the female literacy rates increasing 14.9 percentage points (from 39.3 percent to 54.2 percent) as against 11.7 percent (from 64.1 percent to 75.8 percent) for males. Traditionally, India has been very rich in indigenous educational systems, which predominantly remained limited to certain upper castes, such as Brahmins. A large percentage of the Indian population did not have access to formal education. Nevertheless, they have an extensive store of folk knowledge covering almost all areas from astronomy to astrology. The number of persons who opt for higher education in India well exceeds that of most of the Western countries. With the literacy campaign launched by the government, and a reservation policy that was adopted to improve the lot of the backward and deprived classes, formal education has received a boost and more and more states are achieving or nearing the target of total literacy.

Religion

India is the place of birth of two of the world religions – Hinduism and Buddhism. The largest number of people are followers of Hinduism (80 percent) with Islam being the next most practiced religion (18 percent). The other religions are: Christianity, Buddhism, Jainism, and Sikhism. Religion is a defining feature of Indian culture and it is a guiding force for the people. The followers of diverse religions co-exist peacefully and are generally tolerant of religious differences. But at times, the religious differences are sources of major inter-group tensions and conflicts.

BONDS WITH GROUPS IN THE IMMEDIATE COMMUNITY

Although Indian society is highly stratified in terms of caste and class, it is characterized by close ties within the community. These bonds are sought to be enforced and strengthened in all types of social interactions, ranging from making friends, granting favors, to marriage. Each community has its distinct sets of norms of social and moral behaviour and each person identifies with these. Any infringement by a member is frowned upon and often severely sanctioned.

The communities are quite closely knit. Caste-based affiliations become the basis for formation of communities and play a major role in any social interactions. Sharing of worries, living space, and food, is a practiced norm. It is considered a neighborly right to get involved with each other's problems – even personal ones. Most of the time there is sufficient and open communication between different groups and communities, except during communal and caste tensions when they break down.

Traditionally, every caste has its proper place and duties, particularly in villages. Conformity to caste-based occupations provides interdependence and mutual support in a village community. However, owing to upward occupational mobility of lower castes and welfare measures of democratic civil society, traditional role-relationships of caste have undergone change. Villages used to be almost self-sufficient economically. In the barter economy of villages, the peasant supplied food and craftsmen (e.g., smiths, carpenters, potters, weavers) met other needs of the community.

THE FAMILY

India is culturally so varied that every possible form of family and marriage patterns may be found. However, the two predominant religions – Hindu and Muslim – have a number of castes and sub-castes, economic hierarchies, and regional variations. The most prominent cultural patterns of the two communities are discussed. *Varna Ashram* guides the family life of Hindus.

Marriage

Traditionally, the Hindus give a lot of importance to the caste in matters of marriage. With some exceptions in urban areas, one can marry only within one's caste. Inter-caste marriages create furore in the community and are often not acceptable to the family. Even in the Muslim community, preference is for marrying within the caste in cases where such stratification exists. Hindus and Muslims differ on the dimension of exogamy. Hindus, except some tribal communities and some in the south, often consider the *Gotra* outside which one should marry. Marriage between siblings and cousins is prohibited among the Hindus, whereas amongst the Muslims it is quite common to find marriage between cousins, and often preferred. Marriage is regarded as necessary in the life of a Hindu because it provides him an entry into the *Grihasthashram* (the stage of a householder) and the opportunity to beget a son without whom he cannot be released from the cycle of life, birth, and rebirth. Ideally the marriage must take place within one's caste (*varna*) and economic level, but in practice it often occurs even within one's sub-caste or *jati*. A Muslim marriage, unlike the Hindu, is not a religious sacrament but a secular bond wherein prohibitions are comparatively fewer. Muslim men are allowed up to a maximum of four wives at a time, but Muslim women do not enjoy the same right. Divorce also is almost exclusively the husband's privilege and it is not binding upon him to give a cause. Divorce is not commonly practiced among the Hindus, though legally there is a provision for it. Divorce is not easily accepted amongst the larger population in either of the religions. However, when it occurs, the children stay with either the mother or the grandparents.

The choice of spouse is generally a prerogative of the parents, usually the father, more so in the case of girls. Until recently, the potential bride or groom had no say in the matter – the marriage being arranged by the parents or some older relatives if the parents were not present. Nowadays the earlier absolute discretion of the parents is being substituted by patterns where the children have power to veto the parents' choice, and often make their own choice, which may be quite opposed to the wish of the parents (Sinha, 1988). Also, intercaste marriages are becoming more frequent, caste and status being relegated to the background and material considerations and family accomplishment are becoming the new criteria (Sinha, 1991). The new trend emphasizes the selection of the life partner based on love, with or without the consent of the family elders (Khatri, 1970). Especially in urban India things have changed considerably in the past few years, and now a lot of young people opt for spouses of their own choice even against the wishes of the parents, though getting parental approval is generally considered desirable, if not essential.

Dowry is one major characteristic of the Hindu marriage. The parents give presents to their daughters and legally it is her property but usually the husband and the in-laws control it. The size of the dowry the parents can afford is a major consideration during the contractual discussion between the potential in-laws. Except for some communities in the south, the girl is supposed to leave her parental house and live with the husband and his family.

Family structure

The Hindu society exhibits a more or less uniform familial pattern. To a Hindu, the family is a sacred institution deriving sanction from religion and social traditions that are being fortified by myths and legends. Wadia (1966) asserts that the family structure and the commitment toward family responsibility have not waned, even in the face of multidimensional changes in the country. The family as an institution has survived what Sinha (1988) calls "cacophonic changes" in the social set-up, even if there have been some transformations in its nature. The Hindu family can be described as patrilineal and joint wherein the father's authority reigns supreme and residence is patrilocal. Property passes from the father to the sons and descent is recognized along the male line. The family pattern amongst the Muslims is also more or less uniform and is the manifestation of the interaction between Islamic laws and Hindu influence.

Still, the joint character of the Indian family shows signs of disintegration, filial solidarity being more in evidence than fraternal cohesion (Gore, 1968). However, an important characteristic of the family in India is that even though structural changes are pushing it toward nucleation, attitudinally the members are still connected to each other, and major decisions, especially those involving finances are being taken jointly (Sinha, 1988, 1991).

Over time, even Muslims, particularly the Shia community, have developed a highly stratified caste system. The Muslim family, like the Hindu, is patrilineal, stem, and patrilocal. The eldest male runs the family and the women, who generally observe *Purdah* (non-transparent veil), do the domestic work. Property is not held jointly by the sons, as among the Hindus, and is inherited according to a very elaborate code which takes even fractions into account. The total result of the inheritance laws gives them a strong patrilineal character. Adoption does not provide inheritance rights. The Muslim family is extended like that of the Hindus but may not consist of all the relatively distant kin, who find their place in a Hindu joint family.

Residence after marriage for the newly-weds is with the groom's parents in most cases. However, with all the other changes that are occurring, often there is a need to leave home and go to some other city in search of work. In such cases the newly-weds live separately from the husband's parents. In the typical Indian family, be it a Hindu or a Muslim one, relationships with relatives, even those who are very distantly related, are maintained and renewed specially on occasions such as marriage or death when all members of the extended family gather together. Thus, affinal and collateral relationships are very strong.

Control and institutionalization of divorce

Generally when changes occur in the family, the control resides with the elder family members and social organizations very seldom are involved in them. In the case of divorce, the law provides that the sons up to age five and the daughters up to age seven will be under the mother's custody, unless it is demonstrated that this would be detrimental to the child's development. A lot of Indian families being joint ones, it often happens that once the parents are divorced, the children are left in the care of grandparents, though the parents may still take major decisions about them together or singly. The role of social institutions in these family matters is quite negligible so far, but seems to be gradually becoming important, particularly if the father is supposed to pay for the maintenance of the wife and children even after divorce.

Family roles and functions

Mother

The mother in the Indian family is given respect and almost a goddess like status, at least theoretically. She is responsible for the upbringing of the children and also takes care of their need for love, care, and protection. The Indian male is said to have a very dependent relationship with his mother and finds it very difficult to wean himself out of her influence. The priority for the mother in the Indian family is the well-being of her husband and children and to this end she is expected to make all efforts and sacrifices. Her life is defined and programmed in terms of her family, the unity and progress of which is considered her responsibility. She is the homemaker.

Father

The father is generally perceived as the "breadwinner" as in most other patriarchal societies. He is responsible for giving a respectable standard of living to the family and he also has the role of disciplining the children. Though the mother is the one who is responsible for the emotional needs of the children, it is the father who takes decisions regarding important matters about the children, especially when finances are involved, since he controls the finances.

Grandparents

Grandparents have traditionally had a very important role to play in the family as the custodians of culture and conventions, but this role is gradually being eroded as more and more people are moving out of their family homes in search of jobs, and are opting for a nuclear family set-up. Grandparents take care of the grandchildren in the absence of their parents and they are the ones who may be credited for instilling the traditional values in the new generation because they are the storehouse of folklores and myths. Even when uneducated, grandparents play an important role in familiarizing their grandchildren orally with the religious texts and epics.

Aunts and uncles, cousins and other members of the extended family

These relations supplement the roles of the father, mother, and grandparents. It is common that an aunt is instrumental in bringing up a child when the mother is busy with household chores or with another young child. Apart from the daily intermingling and sharing of responsibilities, these relatives show solidarity in times of need, troubles, and important occasions like marriage, death, unemployment etc., when they rally together as a family.

In many extended families, one's cousins provide friendships and they are the ones with whom one can share secrets and apprehensions when young, and often also when one is grown up.

Children

Children in the family are expected to respect their elders and care for the younger ones. They should excel in studies and give a helping hand at home when necessary. They should obey their parents and look after them when the parents grow old. After adolescence, the children may enjoy a friend-like status with the parents, at least in urban centres.

Degree of power

The eldest male in the family is conventionally vested with almost all the powers related to finances and decision-making. The women generally have no choice but to abide by the rules, many of which regulate their behaviours and activities. With the changing family patterns, some degree of autonomy has come into women's hands also, but still very little. Older women such as the mother and the grandmother do command respect but they still do not participate in taking major decisions. Because of social expectations that they should provide love and affection, women, especially the younger ones, are not able to assert themselves. In matters of career, it is invariably the woman's career that takes second place in the event of a conflict of interests. The women are encouraged to be submissive and dependent and any striving towards independence is generally frowned upon.

24   Indonesia: traditional family in a changing society

Bernadette N. Setiadi

A HISTORICAL OUTLINE OF INDONESIA

Until the seventeenth century Indonesia consisted of many kingdoms. Mostly Hindu and Buddhist kingdoms were in power between the seventh and fourteenth centuries, while the Islamic kingdoms started in the fifteenth century. The year 1602 was the beginning of the Dutch colonial dominance, which lasted for about three and a half centuries. During the Japanese occupation, Indonesia declared its independence as a nation state on August 17, 1945, but the struggle against the Dutch continued until 1949. With a population of approximately 205,000,000, Indonesia is the fourth largest country in the world. Jakarta is its capital, with over 8,000,000 inhabitants.

ECOLOGICAL FEATURES

Indonesia is a vast archipelago of about 5,100 km spread east to west across the equator between Asia and Australia and between the Indian Ocean and the Pacific Ocean, covering an area of 1,919,700 km^2. The country has 6,000 inhabited islands among more than 13,000 islands. About 60 percent of the population lives on the island of Java, which makes up about 7 percent of the country's total land area. Most of the big islands have volcanoes, many still active. The lands are generally fertile, even though in the last 10 years unwise use of the forest and land has significantly damaged the environment. It has two seasons, one dry from June to September and one rainy from December to March. The average daily temperature fluctuates between 27 °C and 37 °C.

ORGANIZATION AND INSTITUTIONS OF SOCIETY

Economic organization

The majority of Indonesians live in the rural areas as farmers. The many kinds of crops include rice, rubber, tobacco, coconut, fruits, and various kinds of spices. In the coastal areas fishing is the standard mode of subsistence. Indonesia is also rich in natural resources such as petroleum, tin, natural gas, nickel, and timber. In line with economic growth, many cities have become trading centers and have factories. As a consequence, there has been a steady increase of urbanization in the last 20 years. In 2001, those engaged in agriculture constituted 44 percent of the total population, manufacturing 18 percent, and services 38 percent. Many young people left their traditional jobs as farmers to work in factories or trades in the big cities. As a country with great scenic beauty and rich cultural diversity, Indonesia has great potential in the area of tourism. Unfortunately, all these potentials have not been fully realized.

Political institutions and legal system

Indonesia is a republic with central and provincial governments. The Dutch occupation for three and a half centuries significantly influenced the present legal and judicial system, mostly in business and criminal cases. In civil law such as marriage and inheritance, the country also acknowledges Islamic law and *Adat* (indigenous) law. In a country consisting of thousands of islands, many remote island communities are not yet touched by the legal system and follow their own traditions in settling disputes or other community issues.

The educational system

Under Dutch colonization, education opportunity for Indonesians was limited to the children of those who worked for the Dutch and the aristocrats. Since independence, all Indonesians have equal opportunity for education. Compulsory basic education is six years. In addition to the state school system, the Islamic school system, where the percentage of the religious courses is higher, also exists. The literacy rate is approximately 91 percent for men and 80 percent for women (Indonesia Human Development Report, 2001). There are about 93 percent males and females enrolled in primary school (Haub and Rogers, 2002), but 55 percent males and only 48 percent females are enrolled in secondary schools (Sass and Ashford, 2002).

Religion

There are five formal religions in Indonesia: Islam, Protestant, Roman Catholic, Buddhist, and Hindu. In the islands, some communities are still animists. More than 85 percent of the population is Muslim, making Indonesia the world's largest Muslim country.

BONDS WITH GROUPS IN THE IMMEDIATE COMMUNITY

There are more than 300 ethnic groups in Indonesia, each with its own customs and traditions. Many of the communities, especially those in the provinces, live in accordance with their customs. Those who have moved to the big cities still maintain contacts with people from their place of origin. They usually have meetings or ceremonies where they can meet people from the same ethnic group. Through these meetings they maintain strong bonds with others who come from the same extended family, village, or ethnic group.

THE FAMILY

In a country with over 300 ethnic groups, the social structure and functions of the family vary widely. Since more than half of the population lives on the island of Java, for the purpose of this portrait the description of the family is based on what is generally observed in Java.

Marriage

In the past, marriage in a traditional family was restricted to potential spouses from the same or neighboring village, with the same social status and from the same religion. Regarding exogamy, marriage was not allowed within the nuclear family, between first cousins and second cousins. These restrictions are still observed at the present time even though marriage between second cousins is sometimes tolerated. The improvement of the transportation system has enabled people to travel, and as a consequence the number of marriages with potential spouses from distant regions has increased. Higher level of education also increases the tendency among young people to find their own future spouses. But one fact remains unchanged. Whoever the potential spouse is, she/he needs the parents' approval to marry. In more traditional families, older members of the extended family, grandparents or older uncles/aunts from the father's or the mother's side, are often consulted by the parents. During the approval process, similarity in social status and religion are still among the important criteria. The young man's family will go to the young woman's family to officially ask for her hand in marriage. They usually bring an official bride price, consisting of dress and jewelry, the value of which depends on the social status of the two families. In more traditional families, all the costs for the marriage ceremony, including reception for hundreds of guests, is the responsibility of the bride's family. In families where this tradition is not strictly observed, the groom's family helps with the cost.

Young couples that marry without the approval of their elders are given sanctions, which vary according to the reason for disapproval. A son or daughter who marries someone from a different religion can be disowned by the parents, while less serious differences can result in disharmonious relationship with the in-laws. In many cases the birth of the first grandchild provides the reason to lift the sanction.

Divorce is generally disapproved but not harshly sanctioned. In most occasions the husband initiates the divorce. It is more difficult for the wife to initiate the divorce unless her family supports her. Those who are divorced young usually remarry. Among the middle-class, the husband and wife equally divide the earnings they have accumulated during their married life. Among the less educated, the husband often leaves the wife and children without sufficient support. The divorcee usually returns to live with her parents. Polygamy is acceptable among the Muslims. Obtaining a divorce is more complicated among the non-Muslims because they must undergo a long process until the civil court judge makes the decision. Among the Muslims who follow Islamic law, the divorce process is shorter. Child custody depends on the age of the child. If the child is under age, the mother usually maintains custody of the child. Older children can choose their custodian.

Family structure

The majority of Indonesians, especially those who live in Java, can be considered as bilateral in terms of lineal descent, in which kin of both sexes were related through the men and the women. In this system, men and women have the same rights in the family, regarding family inheritance. In practice, however, quite often the sons receive a larger share than the daughters.

Even though the nuclear family is the basic family unit, one finds many three-generation families in Indonesia. There are two main types: (1) the married son/daughter brings his/her family to live with the parents; (2) the elderly grandparents live with their son/daughter's family. In both types the male – the grandfather in the first type and the father in the second type – is the formal leader of the family, especially in dealing with the community and external affairs. Regarding the domestic affairs, it is the grandmother or the mother who has a more significant role.

Residence after marriage

There are, in general, no specific rules about where the newly married couple will live after marriage (bilocal). It depends on the economic condition of the parents and the couple. In the villages, very few young couples can afford their own house. They usually move into one of the parents' houses, whoever has more rooms. If both parents can afford it, the couple move more often to the woman's parental home (matrilocal) or they live alternately in both parents' houses. In the cities, young couples with independent incomes prefer to live in their own house at the onset of marriage, but even in these cases, young couples prefer to live near their parents' house. In these arrangements, the grandchildren are often entrusted to the care of the grandparents when their parents are working.

In the rural areas, those who are married are considered fully-fledged community members with all their responsibilities including participation in the community affairs. In the cities, married children who live with their parents are often exempted from obligations to the community.

Family roles and functions

As indicated above, many young couples stay at their parents' home until they can afford to have their own house. In the Javanese family, women are usually better in maintaining relationships with their blood relatives (Geertz, 1961). That is why parents who are old or do not have sufficient financial support prefer to live in their daughter's house if they can make a choice. Thus, even though nuclear family is the preferred form, there are still many three-generation families.

The father is the head of the family and is expected to be the main breadwinner. His role as the head of the family is reflected in the interaction with the community as protector of the entire family, and in making important decisions such as marriage of the children, buying property, and in punishing grave misbehavior of the children.

Mother plays a very significant role in maintaining harmony within the family. She keeps the family united during hard times and provides emotional support to all family members. The mother is expected to spend more time with the children and therefore to be responsible for their care and discipline. According to Magnis-Suseno (1984), mother's role in the family is more significant than the father's. Mother is the center of the family. She manages the money and is influential in important decisions such as the choice of schools, jobs, and spouses for the children. In difficult times the mother usually keeps the family intact.

Both father and mother are expected to be responsible for their children's welfare, formal education, as well as religious and moral education. Children are expected to respect and obey their elders. When their parents are old they have the duty to care for them. In most families, especially in the rural areas, daughters are supposed to help their parents doing household chores, while the sons help in the field. Older daughters often take over some of the mother's responsibilities in the house such as cooking, washing, and taking care of younger siblings. Adult children are expected to marry. There is strong pressure for those who have reached marriage age, especially the daughters, to marry. Married couples are expected to have children. Not being able to have a child is an acceptable reason for divorce by either husband or wife, or for the husband to take a second wife (Kasto, 1982).

Grandparents are respected for their age and wisdom. They are expected to give advice in matters related to tradition and religious education as well as family matters. Grandmother often helps in supervising house chores and the children, especially when both parents are working. In many cases, there are strong bonds between the grandparents and their grandchildren because grandparents have more time for them, and play with them but do not consider disciplining the grandchildren as their duty.

One can only expect and demand the full support of members of the nuclear family. Married children have the duty to respect and take care of their parents even if they do not live in the same house, neighborhood or city. This can be observed in the custom where thousands of families who live in big cities go to their hometowns or villages every year to pay respect to their parents during the *Idul Fitri* celebration. In addition to their obligations toward the members of the nuclear family, there are also other obligations toward members of extended family such as grandparents, grandchildren, uncles, aunts, and cousins. One is expected to support relatives from the extended family in times of need such as death and sickness in the family as well as offering help in important celebrations such as weddings. How much one feels obliged to help will depend very much on the proximity of their houses and the frequency of contacts (Geertz, 1961). The same kind of support is also expected from neighbors in the rural areas and in the lower income communities in the cities.

CHANGES IN THE FAMILY

Three factors play dominant roles in family change: better educational opportunities, economic development, and progress in information technology. When Indonesia gained its independence, the majority of the population was illiterate and only a small number of the elites had university education. Fifty years later, approximately 85 percent of the population is literate and each of the 26 provinces has at least one state university and several private universities. One direct consequence is the increase of the marriage age. While about 2,180,000 marriages took place among those below 19 years old in 1980, they significantly decreased to about 1,360,000 in 1995. With better education, the divorce rate of this group had also decreased from around 9 percent to 5 percent during the same period (Badan Pusat Statistik, 1996).

Improvement of economic conditions, infrastructure, and communication has enabled people to travel farther and means that they are no longer limited to marriage with people from nearby areas. Mixed marriages between people from different ethnic backgrounds place more stress on the young couple because they have to deal with in-laws who have different customs and expectations from their own. As a consequence there is a greater need among young couples to live separately from their parents. Nevertheless, most still maintain close relationships with their parents by visiting them regularly, asking them to baby-sit or to take care of the children when they work.

Improved education has also resulted in the increase in women entering the labor market. However, the roles expected from the mothers have not changed much. Working mothers are still expected to be responsible for house chores. They get little help from their husbands, who consider their main duty in the family as limited to being the breadwinner and the protector of the family. Husbands with a higher level of education have started assisting their wives in taking care of the children, but quite often it is limited to playing with the children after work or during holidays (Nurhaena, 1995). This unbalanced development and change in the role of mothers and fathers puts greater stress on working mothers because they are still expected to be the main emotional provider for all the family members, do all the house chores, and take care of the children within the limited time they have outside their working hours. One solution taken by many is to have a maid or a helper who does the house chores, so that mothers, and sometimes fathers, can spend their limited time playing with the children, helping them with their homework, and supervising them in developing various life skills.

CONCLUSIONS

What can we say about families in Indonesia today? Progress in education, economic, and information technology has not yet had a big impact on family life in Indonesia. Even though there has been a steady increase of urbanization, getting married and forming a family is still the expectation of young people and their parents. It is true that young people marry at a later age and prefer to have their own home from the beginning of their married life, but the pattern of relationships with their parents has not changed significantly. Whenever possible, many prefer to have their house near their parents so they can keep close contact with them. Even when they live in different cities, they try to visit their parents regularly.

Most young people accept the idea that they should take care of their parents and take them into their homes when the parents are too old to live on their own. Old people's homes are for those who do not have children to care for them; it is still considered improper by the society if children put their parents in these homes.

The impact is probably seen in the changes of the pattern of relationships with the extended family members. Better infrastructures have enabled people to work further away from their region of origin. Higher education has also resulted in more wives entering the labor market. Within the limited time available, the young families have to concentrate on their own family, which results in diminishing contact with extended family members. Grandparents are probably the exception because when both parents are working, many young couples entrust the care of their children to them.

In spite of the many changes and progress in various areas of life, the nuclear family is the least affected. All the functions and the roles within the nuclear family remain intact.

25   The Iranian family in a context of cultural diversity

Shahrenaz Mortazavi

A HISTORICAL OUTLINE OF IRAN

Iran, the "bridge of turquoise," forms a vital bridge situated between two bodies of water, the Caspian Sea and the Persian Gulf (Beny, Nasr and Bakhtiar, 1975, p. 3). Iran has an ancient civilization and it has been inhabited from earliest times. Nearly 3,000 years ago, because of the bitter cold and the infertility of the soil, the Aryans living in the northern lands migrated to the southern plains of the Iranian plateau and gave their name to it. "Iran" is the shortened form of "Aryan." The Arians founded the Pars dynasty, which gave its name to Persia, the other name of our country. King Darius (550–486 BC) enumerates 23 ethnic groups as the people of the Achaemenian empire. Iran's greatest period of glory and grandeur as well as hardship and agony were during this period (Sarvestani, 1998).

Iran has many unique features as well as wide variability in its ecology, inhabitants, arts, and customs. Diversity in climate has made the country rich in produce in some regions and poor in others. Diversity and contrasts are equally evident in culture, arts, and in local dialects and languages. Farsi or Persian is the official language for literary expression and scholarly exchange. It is written with Arabic letters. Azari Turkish, Arabic, Dari (the language spoken by Zoroastrians), and a number of local dialects are also spoken in different parts of the country. Musical notes and instruments have been known for thousands of years in Iran. Persepolis, the site of a monumental palace near Shiraz is an excellent example of ancient Iranian architecture. Beautiful Iranian mosques (for example in Isphahan) reveal among others, Iranians' love of arts and their respect for religion.

Cross-cultural research shows that our national culture is moderately high in collectivism (Hofstede, 1980; Mortazavi and Karimi, 1992). The population is composed of different subcultures and tribal groups such as Kurds, Lors, Balutch, Arabs, etc.

The remains of the biblical Queen Ester and her foster father Mordecai are believed to lie in a tomb in Hamadan. Ester married an Iranian king and pleaded for the protection of her fellow Jews in exile. Tolerance and protection were granted and have largely continued. The ancient foundation of Ester's tomb hints at prehistoric dates. A Jewish colony has settled around Ester's tomb since at least AD 225 (Waite and Heydari, 1995).

Turkmans coming originally from the steppes in the north settled in the northeastern parts of Iran. They are mostly horsemen. Lors, Quashqais, and Bakhtiaries are other nomadic groups settled in the west and near the south of our country. Kurds and Turks are settled mostly in the northwest.

Ethnic diversity is reflected in dress, in folklore, in religions, in languages, and in dialects. Because of the high diversity in geographical features of the country on the one hand (high mountains, deserts and seas, rivers etc.) and of the moderate role of the media in some farther parts of the country on the other, impressive variability in subcultures and contrasting social values is pervasive.

ECOLOGY

Iran is a high plateau; its highest snow-covered peak is at 5,671 m, 850 m higher than Mont Blanc. Two deserts cover about one-third of the country. At the Caspian Sea, the sea level is minus 20 m. In this part of the country, the sky is often covered by thick clouds as distinct from the rest of the country, which is generally sunny.

ORGANIZATION AND INSTITUTIONS OF SOCIETY

Economy

The Islamic Republic of Iran belongs to the Third World countries. In 1988 GNP was about US$2,000. Since then, not much progress has been reported with respect to GNP. Iran's economy is mostly dependent on its oil reserves. The export of Iranian handmade carpets, dried fruits, and some spices, such as saffron, plays a modest role in the country's economy.

Governmental statistics reveal that from 1956 to 1996, the number of families has tripled from 4 to 12 million. In 1996, about 32 percent of Iranian families consisted of three persons, 47.0 percent of four to six persons and 21 percent of more than seven (Amani, 2001). Iran's population was about 60 million in 1996. The Iranian population is very young with a mean age of 24. Life expectancy is 71 years and there is high population growth, which is decreasing (3.9 percent in 1986 and

1.5 percent in 1996).The rapid population growth has had a negative impact, among others, on the educational system. World Bank statistics show that in 1996 the urban population was about 62 percent of the total population. All these statistics suggest the necessity of creating enough jobs for the youth to overcome different economic and social problems, such as unemployment, addictions, etc.

The Third World has its sociopsychological problems, such as problems concerning need satisfaction. For example, some psychological and physiological needs, for security (financial, job, etc.), are not fulfilled very well or are only occasionally met (Mortazavi, 2000). Relatively high unemployment has its consequences, such as the migration of unskilled workers to big cities like Tehran, Tabriz, or Shiraz, where there are better possibilities for survival. An investigation in 80 rural guidance and secondary schools for girls situated in 15 Iranian provinces (the country comprises of 26 provinces and the Province of Tehran was not included in this sample), revealed that 45 percent of the rural pupils' fathers were working in a city or were working winters in a city and summers in their own villages (Mortazavi, 1996).

Education

Statistics of the Ministry for Higher Education for 2004 show that 60 percent of Iranian students are female and only 40 percent are male. Referring to Governmental statistics for 2002, the percentages of male and female pupils in all three levels (primary, secondary, and tertiary levels) are nearly equal. The percentage of schools in rural distincts is 30.1 percent and it is 69.9 percent in urban environments.

Religion

Iranians are mostly Islamic Shiites. Armenians, Assuris, Jews, and Sunnis are some of Iran's religious minorities. Governmental statistics for 1996 indicated about eighty thousand Christians (1.3 percent of the population) and thirty thousand Zoroastrians (0.5 percent of the population) and twelve thousand Jews in Iran. Armenians and Assurians are settled mainly in the northwest.

THE FAMILY

Interactions in the Iranian family

In most Iranian families, interactions are regulated by Islamic *Shia's* laws and rights as well as by traditional ways of life and customs. Some

Islamic rules and rights, deduced from the Islamic holy book, the Koran, are stable over time and cannot be changed by democratic methods, for example by asking people about their preferences. But some other regulations can be interpreted differently in different times. For example, laws regarding children's custody after divorce or the husband's death are changing now and a mother can obtain her child's custody under certain circumstances. The new laws and rights for women (Shojaii, 2004), allow the mother custody of her children (boys and girls) from birth to the age of seven.

Child custody, financial provision for the wife, and some other aspects of the social life, e.g., divorce, are controlled by Islamic laws (indirect control). From this point of view a marriage is considered as an agreement. The marriage contract includes some clauses that allow different circumstances or predicaments for divorce, a wife's financial provisions, proprietary rights of the wife, etc. Without such agreements, the husband can divorce his wife and under some circumstances he has the right to have more than one wife (polygamy). The statistical center of Iran reports a mean divorce rate of 8 percent of marriages for the country in 1996.

In our religion exogamy is allowed with first cousins. Women have control over their property and they have right of ownership. Inheritance law allows a daughter half as much as a son.

In bigger cities, newly married couples prefer to be independent and live apart from their parents and relatives. Young couples prefer mostly to have their own home, but emotionally they stay close to their parents. Iranian collectivistic oriented parents prefer to keep their children near them. In rural societies, young couples reside mostly with or near the husband's parents (patrilocal). Relationships with relatives are not limited (collateral), although Islamic laws related to gender separation are considered in some social interactions, especially in more traditional families.

In Iranian families, the breadwinner is mostly a man (the father, the husband or the older son), but families with women as the head of household are not few. For example, in 1996, they comprised 8.4 percent of Iranian families (Amani, 2001, p. 48). The relative high percentage of families with women as the head of household is related to historical factors, as well as to the fact that Iranian women have control over their property. Widows (with or without children or unmarried single women, etc.) can survive, because of their relative economic independence with some regional exceptions. Mostly, women preserve their family name after marriage.

In a research on "school spaces," a representative sample of guidance and secondary schools indicated that 81 percent of pupils' families were nuclear in the province of Tehran. Nuclear is defined here as a family comprising father, mother and their children, living in a single residential unit such as a room, an apartment or a house (Mortazavi, 1996). Pupils from nuclear families showed more signs of psychological distress than those living in extended families ($t = 2.16$, $p < .03$). In 14 other provinces of our sample (10,824 pupils) more than 88 percent of pupils lived in extended families. These observations indicate deep changes in family structures, which have begun in the province of Tehran, where the media is having an important role in people's social values and life.

CHANGES IN THE FAMILY

Because of the emotional and economic interrelatedness of family members in collectivistic cultures, especially in rural areas, young couples live near or next to their parents. Collectivistic parents also try to house their children near themselves and they help each other in various ways. In cities, it is not possible to find easy solutions for such cultural values and motivations. Population growth is an important influential factor with respect to the change in family structure and social life. The process is accompanied by a crisis in traditional collectivistic values and lifestyle. For example, in the Province of Tehran there is not enough space for housing the exploding young population. Consequently, priority is given to building 70 m^2 apartments for Tehran and its environment. Such restricted spaces cannot be adapted easily to extended family life. In such new residential areas, complementary institutions, which facilitate the functioning of individualistic nuclear families such as kindergarten and homes for the aged parents, are rare.

The crisis becomes more relevant because younger generations and those living in big cities, who are influenced by Western individualistic values through the media, are influenced at the same time by the collectivistic values of their parental families. They feel responsible for their older parents. Socially and morally, putting grandparents into homes for the aged is still considered an improper decision.

Conflicting values and conditions can be observed in many more situations. For example, in a cross-cultural research (Watkins, Mortazavi and Trofimova, 2000) with samples from America, Russia, Hong Kong, and Iran, it was shown that samples of Iranian students, especially girls, were simultaneously giving more importance to independent and interdependent aspects of their self-concept than all other samples, although Iran belongs to collectivistic cultures. This observation contradicts earlier findings, since giving importance only to interdependent aspects of the self is reported to be a main aspect of collectivism. These findings were reaffirmed in another study on collectivism, self-concept, and parental roles in Iranian and American families as related to age and gender (Mortazavi, unpublished manuscript). This comparative research showed that the Iranian younger generation (students) compared to the Iranian older generation (staff members of an Iranian university) and to American respondents (students and university staff-members) were simultaneously giving significantly more importance to independent and interdependent aspects of their self-concept measured by Adult Sources of Self-Esteem Inventory (ASSEI) (Elovson and Fleming, 1988).

In many cases, the coexistence of individualistic and collectivistic values leads to conflicting situations and to stressful interactions in our social life. For example, the older generation, who have mostly lived in an extended family know that grandparents' presence is a shelter for children in every respect. The younger generation stresses the fact that extended family life can be a source of difficulties for young parents. Both perspectives are reliable and lead to unsolved conflicts and to unpredictable situations.

An interaction between ecological variables such as population growth, cultural values, and family structure is observed in the following example. In an interview with a sample of women living in very poor, hot, and southern provinces with very high birth rate and unemployment, it was investigated how women justified their high birth rate. Most of the interviewed women answered that in that part of the country, each man's self-esteem and hope of prosperity was dependent on the number of his sons. This perspective is a valid one, with respect to the harsh ecological conditions of this part of the country and to people's tribal life style.

A comparison of such examples with the lifestyle of the young generation in Tehran and other bigger cities reveals a high diversity in social life and the impact of ecological variables on the structure of Iranian families.

Family roles and functions

The father and the mother and specially their respective parents have traditionally differentiated roles in Iranian families. A pilot study with 80 Iranian students revealed high variability in family members' roles.

In Farsi there are different concepts and names for the sisters of each parent (i.e., *Khaleh* is the mother's and *Ammeh* the father's sister) and for their brothers (*Daii* is the term used for the mother's brother and *Amoo* for the father's brother). Therefore, two indices for family members' roles could be computed. One index was computed for the roles of "father and of his relatives" (the father and his father, his mother, his sisters and brothers) and another for the social roles of "mother and of her relatives" (the mother, her father, her mother, and her sisters and brothers). In a study by Mortazavi (unpublished manuscript), the following roles were differentiated:

- Roles expected from "the mother and of her relatives": housekeeping and taking care of children – teaching children good manners – keeping harmony – maintaining relationships – providing emotional support.
- Roles expected from "the father and of his relatives": paying costs as well as financial support of the family members.
- Roles expected from all members of the extended family: keeping family united, face saving and economical management as well as shopping.

In another study with Iranian and American students (representing younger generations) and with samples of staff-members of an Iranian and of an American university (representing elder generations), social roles for mother, father and grandparents were described by referring to the researcher's experiences in Iranian (collectivistic) families. As expected, these roles correlated with collectivism (measured by an index computed from Schwartz's value scale (1992, 1994a) and with an Iranian scale for collectivism (Mortazavi and Karimi, 1992)), but not with an index computed for individualism. Significant differences were observed with respect to the mother's role between Iranian samples representing both generations. It was shown that the social role of the mother is undergoing significant changes from the younger generation's perspective.

In summary, in Iranian families, the father is traditionally responsible for the family's finances. The father and his father have highest legal power in the family. The father's high status in the family's hierarchy is reflected on the one hand in his right to make decisions about all family members and on the other in respectful interactions of family members and relatives with him by different symbolic ways of verbal and proximal behaviors, i.e., the amount of his personal space, his territorial behaviors, his larger inter-individual distances with other family members, etc. (Kazemi-Mortazavi, 1978).

The mother is traditionally responsible for housekeeping and taking care of children. In most Iranian families, from early childhood, girls are growing up with various responsibilities, such as helping the mother in the household and taking care of younger siblings, being helpful to the guests and to grandparents. It seems that such responsibilities lead to their high competences in social life. Consequently, in some subcultures, especially those living in the northern parts of the county, the mother has much influence on the father's decisions and she decides specially about the family's inner social life. With some exceptions, the Iranian mother mostly has control over her family members' social-emotional life without showing (in contrast to the father) overt signs of power.

In recent decades, especially in urban environments, Iranian mothers have to work outside their household to upgrade the family's finances or to help the family to survive. This fact is leading to deep changes in the traditional social role of the Iranian "mother."

26   Japan: tradition and change in the Japanese family

Yukiko Muramoto

A HISTORICAL OUTLINE OF JAPAN IN THE MODERN ERA

The modern era of Japan began in the late 1860s, when the Meiji Restoration stopped the system of feudalism. The first European-style constitution provided a parliament, while keeping the sovereignty of the emperor: head of the army and navy, and with executive and legislative powers. Worship of the emperor was emphasized and taught at schools. After World War II a profound change took place in Japanese society. The new constitution gave power to the people and made Japan a peaceful democratic nation. In direct contrast to the Meiji constitution, the emperor now has no power related to government, but is still considered the symbol of Japan and of the unity of the Japanese people.

ECOLOGICAL FEATURES

Japan is a long archipelago consisting of about 7,000 islands, located off the coast of northeast Asia between the Sea of Japan and the North Pacific Ocean. It is around 3,000 km in length from northeast to southwest, with an area of around 380,000 km^2. Hokkaido, the island farthest to the north, is as cold as Canada, while island chains farther south have similar climates to the Caribbean islands. Three-quarters of the land is made up of mountain chains. The present population of the nation is approximately 127 million inhabitants. Tokyo is its capital, with 12 million inhabitants. The urban areas are densely populated; more than 40 percent of the population live around the three largest metropolitan areas of Tokyo, Osaka, and Nagoya.

ORGANIZATION AND INSTITUTIONS OF SOCIETY

Economic organization

Postwar Japan is a highly industrialized country. The percentage of the working population in primary industries (e.g., agriculture, forestry, and fisheries) was only 5.3 percent in 1998, compared with 31.5 percent in secondary industries (e.g., manufacturing, mining, and building) and 63.2 percent in the tertiary industries (e.g., commerce and service).

Large corporations in Japan have applied a special system of employment with two basic elements: lifetime employment and seniority. Many employees are recruited directly upon graduation and are guaranteed lifelong employment with the firm. Salary and promotion in the company increases proportionally with the number of years with the company. In the 1990s, however, this traditional system began eroding. The Japanese economy is no longer expanding as during the 1970s and 80s. The companies can no longer afford to promote a system where seniority is more important than job performance. Also, recruitment of new employees is undergoing change. New employees are being recruited when needed, and people are changing jobs more frequently.

Political institutions and legal system

The Japanese system of government is similar to the British parliamentary system. The Diet, composed of two Houses, is the highest organ of state power and the sole law-making organ of state. Executive power is vested in the Cabinet, which consists of the prime minister and around 20 ministers of state and is collectively responsible to the Diet. Judicial power is vested in the Supreme Court and inferior courts. At the local level, there are 47 prefectures and more than 3,000 subordinate municipalities, which are each ruled by their own governors and assemblies. The local governors are directly elected by the residents.

Educational system

The current system consists of six years of elementary school, each three years of junior and senior high school and four years of university or two years of junior college. Compulsory education includes elementary school and junior high school. According to the 2000 statistics by Ministry of Education, Science and Culture, 97.0 percent of students who graduated from junior high school also went to high school and 45.1 percent of those who graduated from high school went on to university or junior college. Most high schools and universities require applicants to take an entrance exam. Many students attend cram schools after regular school, in order to enter the best institutions.

Religion

The two most important religions in Japan are Shinto and Buddhism. Shinto is the indigenous faith of Japanese people since ancient times, while Buddhism was introduced to Japan in the sixth century. The two religions have co-existed for a long time and even complemented each other to a certain degree. Many Japanese today tend to claim that they do not believe in any religion. However, they follow some religious customs in ceremonial occasions such as weddings and funerals.

SOCIAL RELATIONS AND GROUP BONDS

Group-oriented society

It is often argued that the fundamental social unit in Japan is not the individual in the Western sense but the group (e.g., Menon, Morris, Chiu, and Hong, 2000; Triandis, 1994). In her distinguished work of Japanese society, Chie Nakane, a Japanese anthropologist, pointed out that Japanese tend to stress the situational position in a particular "frame," rather than personal attributes (Nakane, 1970). According to her analysis, the group in Japan is not perceived as an organization in which individuals with common attributes are bound by contractual relationships and still thinking of themselves as separate entities. Rather, the Japanese group is "my" or "our" group that is perceived as an integrated agent in itself.

The emphasis of group consciousness leads Japanese to differentiate their behavior by whether the situation is *uchi* or *soto* (Lebra, 1976). *Uchi* literally means "inside," whereas *soto* means "outside." Japanese use the term *uchi* colloquially to refer to their house, family, the company where they work, and other ingroups.

Three domains of relationships

The *uchi–soto* dichotomy is an important criterion for defining social relations in Japan, but not a sufficient one. Lebra (1976), as well as Doi (1973) and Inoue (1977), defined three domains of interpersonal situations among Japanese.

First is the "intimate" relationship, characterized by communication of unity and spontaneous expression. In this relationship, people understand each other without saying anything, because they have a feeling of oneness. Social nudity of actors is also allowed. The intimate interaction is facilitated by settings that are tension-reducing. The ideal setting in that respect is one's home. In other words, the intimate relationship is typically built up among family members.

Second is the "ritual" relationship, characterized by dignity and humility. In this relationship, people need to protect others' face as well as one's own. For saving face of both others and themselves, people often resort to indirect and ambiguous communication based on *omoiyari* (empathy) to others.

Third is the "anomic" relationship, characterized by a totally novel or anonymous situation. In this relationship, others are defined as outsiders. People tend to behave in a shameless and heartless manner, because their actions cannot be guided and controlled by a set of norms.

THE FAMILY

Marriage

Marriage has been traditionally considered to be an arrangement between two families rather than a joining of two individuals. Before the war, marriage was described as "going to be a bride" in the sense that it was a physical movement whereby the wife enters and becomes a member of the husband's household. Even today, wedding receptions are often hosted formally by the two fathers of the groom and bride.

Nevertheless, the Western concept of marriage, in which two individuals meet and fall in love without the formal intercession of a go-between, is being gradually adopted in Japan. Arranged marriage is decreasing year by year, although it is still a form of spouse selection. Only 10 percent of all marriages in 1995–1999 were arranged (National Institute of Population and Social Security Research). Marriage based on love, rather than arranged marriages, prevails more in urban areas than rural areas, and more among younger couples than older couples.

The divorce rate (the number of divorces per 1,000 persons) was 2.0 in 1999. Although the rate is gradually increasing these days, divorce is still less frequent compared to Western countries. The proportion of households headed by single mothers is only about 1 percent of all the Japanese households.

Family structure

Before World War II, three or four generations often lived together in Japanese families. In traditional Japanese families, father filled the role of patriarch with absolute authority over others. The first-born son, a future household head, held a superior status to that of his younger siblings. A bride traditionally held the lowest status in the family. The welfare of the *ie* (family) took precedence over any one member.

In contemporary families, however, non-traditional family structure is increasing, with the average number of family members decreasing dramatically. The average family had 4.1 members in 1960, but 2.7 in 2000, according to the national census. The percentage of nuclear families was 58.4 percent in 2000. Married sons do not necessarily reside in or near the father's residence. Married daughters are sometimes connected to their parents more closely than married sons. The absence of grandparents in the family is considered as one factor that creates a discontinuity between generations and lessening of traditional sense in Japan.

Gender roles in the family

The traditional gender role norm, "A husband works outside and a wife should concentrate on the home," becomes weaker but still remains in Japan. The 2000 national survey held by the Institute of Population Problems revealed that Japanese wives' approval and disapproval of this norm were almost fifty–fifty, although it varied depending on their age and occupation. According to the survey, in more than 80 percent of families in all age groups, more than 80 percent of housework is done by a wife. Grandmothers and daughters tend to help mothers doing household chores more than grandfathers and sons do. This indicates that the gender role in family is taken over across generations.

Mother–child bonds

When a child is born into a family, a Japanese mother minimizes the physical and psychological distance between herself and the child by staying close to the child and by gratifying the child as much as possible (Azuma, 1986). This type of socialization creates the bond of *amae* (dependence) (Doi, 1973). A child's strong dependency needs, both emotional and existential, are satisfied by the mother's indulgent devotion to the child. As children grow up, they are expected to transfer themselves from the secure world with their mothers to outer societies. A mother's job is to prepare her child for adult life and to become a mediator between the home environment and the external environment (Kim, 1994). In this sense, a Japanese mother psychologically represents the family, although the formal head of the family is the father. She holds a stable and powerful position inside home, and plays an important role in keeping the home environment pleasant for all other family members.

CHANGES IN THE FAMILY

Facing the aging society

Japan is aging rapidly with a low birth rate, longer lifespan, and increase in age at which men and women marry. Out of a current population of 126.9 million, 17.3 percent are over their 65 years of age, and the figure may reach 28 percent in 2025, according to statistics by the Japanese government. The percentage of households with people over 65 was 32.2 percent in 2000. The trend toward a nuclear family causes a new problem of elderly-only households. The percentage of elderly-only households is 20.2 percent and is still increasing.

Later marriage and fewer children

The birth rate in Japan has been steadily decreasing. The number of births in 2001 was 1.175 million as compared to the previous record low of 1.177 million in 1999. Japan has witnessed a declining number of births since the children of postwar boomers were born in the 1970s. Meanwhile, more Japanese young people prefer to remain single longer, which also contributes to the aging population and drop in birth rate. According to the national census in 2000, 69.3 percent of Japanese 25- to 29-year-old men were single as compared to 54.0 percent of women in the same age group. Japan's fertility rate, which stood at 1.36 in 2000, is far below the 2.1 needed to keep the population steady without immigration.

Working wives and mothers

Japanese women have made some gains since implementation of the Equal Employment Opportunity Law in 1985. However, working wives and mothers still lag far behind men in terms of their living environment. According to the 1996 national survey held by the Ministry of Labor, the average time spent doing housework in a day was 4 hours and 56 minutes for full-time housewives, and 3 hours and 18 minutes for working wives. In contrast, the average time husbands spend in housework was less than 10 minutes, regardless of whether or not their wife works.

In 1992, the Child Care Leave Law went into effect, allowing employees, both men and women, to take a leave of absence until their children reach the age of one. Workers with preschool children may also get reduced hours in place of a leave. This law applies only to full-time regular employees, and does not guarantee payment of salary while on leave. In 1995, the law was revised to include family care provisions (e.g., parent care). The national survey revealed that 56.4 percent of women who gave birth in 1998 took a leave of absence, whereas only 0.42 percent of their husbands took it.

In sum, the working environment for Japanese wives and mothers has improved, albeit only slightly. This slowness might be a cause of the later marriage and fewer children, as was mentioned above.

PSYCHOLOGICAL MEANING OF FAMILY

Expectation of being understood

As Lebra (1976) indicated, the ideal family relationship in Japan is characterized by "a feeling of oneness" among members. Family members are expected to understand each other without saying anything. To examine this notion empirically, Muramoto (2003) asked Japanese college students to indicate to what extent they thought each family member understands them, by illustrating the level of their understanding on a scale from 0 to 100 percent (0 not at all understanding them, and 100 completely understanding them). The respondents were also asked to indicate to what extent they understand themselves, by illustrating in the same way as above. As a result, they expected their parents and siblings to understand them to a very large extent. The respondents estimated, on average, that mother understands 72 percent of them, father understands 65 percent of them, and siblings understand 63 percent of them, while they understand 77 percent of their own. Especially, some respondents answered that their mother understands them more than they themselves do. In contrast, they did not expect their extended family members to understand them very much. They estimated, on average, that grandparents understand less than 50 percent of them, and uncle or aunt understands only 38 percent of them.

An indirect self-enhancement through the family's eyes

Japanese are likely to maintain and enhance their self-esteem indirectly by getting support from their family members, rather than a direct self-enhancement (e.g., Muramoto, 2003). In a series of studies on achievement attribution, Muramoto asked Japanese college students and adults to recall their positive and negative life events and to attribute these events to various internal and external factors. They were also asked to estimate how other people around them would attribute their success and failure. Results showed that, in attributing one's success and failure, the respondents tended to emphasize external factors (e.g., luck, chance) for success more than for failure, indicating "self-effacing" attribution. In estimating attributions made by others, however, the respondents tended to expect that their parents and siblings would emphasize internal factors (e.g., ability, effort) for success more than for failure. These results suggest that Japanese do not try to enhance or protect their self-esteem explicitly, but that they do so implicitly by using an indirect way. They may maintain their own positive self-regard by mutual and reciprocal support with their family members.

CONCLUSIONS

"What is your home for you?" In the 2000 national opinion survey in Japan, the typical answers to this question were "the place to have a happy time with family" (62.5 percent), "the place to take a rest and relax" (59.4 percent), "the place to strengthen the family bond" (43.6 percent), and "the place where both parents and children keep growing" (34.0 percent) (multiple answers were available). In the 1995 social survey in Tokyo area, Japanese clearly distinguished family from other social groups in terms of the following aspects: (a) financial support, (b) psychological support, (c) sharing emotions, (d) *amae* (dependence), (e) firm bonds, and (f) permanence of the relationship (Muramoto and Yamaguchi, 2003). It was also found that Japanese are likely to maintain and enhance their self-esteem indirectly by getting support from their family members, rather than by direct self-enhancement (Muramoto, 2003). These results indicate that the absolute importance of the family still remains among Japanese, although the Japanese family is strongly influenced by the ongoing transformation of the socioeconomic context. The various social changes in Japan have carried new roles and functions to the contemporary family, and will keep carrying further potential to the future family.

27 Mexico

Rolando Diaz-Loving

A HISTORICAL OUTLINE OF MEXICO

Mexico's most recent pre-Colombian emergence is highlighted by the foundation of Tenochtitlan by the Aztec culture in the year AD 800. These warrior latecomers took over much of the territory previously inhabited by very advanced cultural groups such as the Mayans and the Olmecas. The current Mexican territory was a mosaic inhabited by numerous and diverse indigenous peoples who interbred biologically and culturally with the Spanish conquerors from 1519 to 1810. After 300 years, the independence movement against the Spanish monarchy began in 1810. Mexico became independent in 1821. During the nineteenth century, a reform movement separated the church from the state, having a profound impact of on the political, social, and economic configuration of the country. A century after the independence movement, the Mexican revolution gave birth to a new civilian legacy, and to political stability and a single party rule for the rest of the twentieth century. With the new millennium, Mexico has jumped into a new experience; an opposition party has won the presidential election and is now ruling the country.

According to the 2000 results of the XII Population and Housing Census, Mexico's present-day population of approximately 97,483,412 inhabitants makes Mexico the eleventh most populated country in the world. Average annual population growth rate for the period 1990–1995 was 2.1 percent and dropped to 1.58 percent a year for the period between 1995 and 2000. Mexico City (Federal District) is its capital, with 13,096,686 inhabitants, although the metropolitan area for the city holds more than 22 million people (Instituto Nacional de Estadistica, Geografia e Informática, 2001). Mexico is a member of the North American Free Trade Agreement.

ECOLOGICAL FEATURES

Mexico is in North America in the Western hemisphere, west of the Greenwich meridian; it shares a 3,152 km border with the southern extreme of the United States, and is north of the Central American countries of Guatemala and Belize. To the west is the North Pacific Ocean and to the east the Caribbean Sea and the Gulf of Mexico. The country covers an area of 1,964,375 km^2, of which 1,959,248 km^2 are on the mainland and 5,127 km^2 are islands; it is the fourteenth largest country in the world. The country's territory is very irregular and is characterized by mountains, plains, valleys, and plateaus. Mexico has an amazing variety of landscapes: swamps, deserts, tropical jungles, and alpine vegetation, many fertile plains, and small, isolated communities in the mountains, relatively large cities of over a million inhabitants on the plains and by the sea. Its climate varies from humid and warm (southeast and near the sea), to "moderately cool" in the mountains (in the middle of the country), to moderate and temperate in the southwest and hot and desert in the north. Owing to its geographical location, shape, climate, water, and geology, Mexico has a wide variety of ecological characteristics that are unique worldwide; they include a wealth of different soils, and a diversity of flora and plant communities that feature practically all those known throughout the world. Some parts of the country contain almost no vegetation and some areas are covered in snow all year. Conversely, there are lush rain forests where the vegetation reaches a height of 40 m in areas with over 4,000 mm of annual rainfall. Between these two extremes, there is a large variety of shrub communities, forming extensive, varied bush land, grassland, conifer and elm oak forests in almost all mountain systems, palm groves and jungles with varying degrees of foliage life, highly developed mangroves in the southern parts of both coasts, and pioneer plant communities in coastal dune areas. Large non-renewable resources such as petroleum and silver reserves deserve special mention. At the start of 2000, oil reserves stood at 58.204 billion barrels, and Mexico is the world's foremost silver producer; output reached 2,482,809 kg in 2000.

ORGANIZATION AND INSTITUTIONS OF SOCIETY

Economic organization

Mexico's Gross Domestic Product for the year 2001 was 618,031.4 million dollars, and its distribution was as follows: agriculture with a participation rate of 4.3 percent; industrial sector at 26.4 percent, of which manufacturing industry constitute 72.4 percent; and the service sector 69.3 percent, the latter includes communal, social and personal services at 35.6 percent. According to results of the National Employment Survey 2000,

39,633,842 people are economically active, this figure represents 55.7 percent of the population aged 12 years and over.

Political institutions and legal system

In accordance with its Constitution, Mexico is a representative, democratic and federal republic governed by three branches of power: the executive, the legislative, and the judiciary. The country is made up of 32 political-administrative entities (31 free, sovereign states, and the Federal District, the seat of the Executive, which is also where the nation's capital is located). Each president governs for one six-year period, with no re-election. Each state has a governor and municipal presidents head smaller demarcations.

The educational system

For 2000, the population aged 15 years and over registered an illiteracy rate of 9.5 percent. In the same year, 92.3 percent of the population aged 6 to 14 years attended school. In addition, for the school year 1999/ 2000, preschool enrolment was 3.4 million; elementary school, 14.8 million; secondary school 5.3 million; high school 3.0 million; and 1.6 million in higher education. The two largest higher education institutions are federal. In addition, each state has at least one public university and several private institutions. It should be noted that only seven out of every 100 Mexicans has access to the middle and higher education systems.

Religion

At the present time, 87.99 percent of the population is Catholic, 5.19 percent is Protestant and the rest belongs to other religions. In general, females and older people take religion more seriously than men and the younger population and attend church on a regular basis. Observance and violations of religious customs are still central to the entire community.

BONDS WITH GROUPS IN THE IMMEDIATE COMMUNITY

Large urban centers, medium size cities, and many small rural communities hold the Mexican population. As one moves from the countryside to the urban centers, the gregarious and open arms tradition of the Mexicans tends to diminish. However, even in Mexico City, people are still generally friendly and willing to assist strangers. Tight social and family premises continue to socialize children into amiable, courteous, respectful, and self-modifying behavior patterns, which create for harmonious relations between individuals. The rules of interpersonal behavior are extended at the group and institutional level. Intra group and intra family relations are expected to be cordial, and people will actually prefer to incorporate someone or a group into an extended family format, rather than confront them or have any type of hostility or contention.

THE FAMILY

Historic development of the Mexican family

The Mexican family has been molded by the events that have shaped the history of the country. Its roots are in the customs and traditions of our indigenous ancestors. These very varied groups strictly followed rules and rites in regard to marriage. Indigenous Mexicans gave equal power and status to males and females, although they established clear differential behavioral patterns and specific training that allowed them to function separately and adequately in the family.

With the arrival of the Spanish in Mexico, social structures, among them the family, were uprooted and profoundly modified. Monogamy and extended families became prevalent and special emphasis was placed on loyalty and cohesion. The centuries that followed the Spanish conquest saw marriage fall into the arms of the Catholic Church, whose principal objective was "decency." Under these conditions, family honor was a must and sex was basically the territory of marriage, with virginity until marriage becoming paramount. The church also sanctioned marriage and indicated the appropriate behaviors and roles to be played by the family members. Given the long tradition of favoring male offspring in the Catholic rural perspective, parents gave dowries for their female children to get married and start a family. In this patriarchal arrangement, the family lived close to the father's family and the father was to be the provider and director; the mother was expected to give tenderness, caring, education, and protection to the children; the sons and daughters were supposed to return love and show respect and obey their parents. Marriage was arranged by the social groups and families even before their birth of the spouses to be, and separation was not acceptable. As a matter of fact it was almost impossible, given the moral codes, the prohibition voiced by the church, and the functional reliance of the family on the fathers. With the influence of the church and the traditional family, endogamy was prevalent, with marriage occurring frequently between men and women of the same religious and socioeconomic background.

Stemming from its Hispanic heritage, marriage was conceived throughout the nineteenth century and a good part of the twentieth, as a stable union destined for procreation. In this format, the place of the female is the home and her role is motherhood, which, by the way, gives her ample veneration, admiration, and respect. On the other hand, males must love and respect their spouses, but are allowed to have fleeting romances. In addition, the father is responsible for the children only if he knows they are his or if he loves his wife. The combination of roles and expectations for males and females within the family creates an interesting outcome, Mexican women are supposed to be adaptable, obedient, and in need of protection and security; however, the woman is the one who really holds the power in house, which increases as the relationship extends. In fact several historians have descried the family as a place of an absent father, a mother that governs, many children, and little sex.

CHANGES IN THE FAMILY

The transition of the Mexican family into the new millennium has witnessed many changes, but has also dragged with it many monolithical structures from the past. On the one hand, more and more people are marrying according to on their own free will and are doing so in uncharted relationships. Not only are they selecting their spouses; they are increasingly doing so even without the consent of their parents. On the other hand, as recently as 1990, 82 percent of marriages were performed in churches, 93.3 percent of Mexicans live in an extended or nuclear family, males on average marry at 26 and females at 23, the groom's parents go and ask for the girl's hand and females invariably take on the husband's family name.

Social sanctions against divorce are as strong as ever. Nevertheless, in legal terms, people can divorce as many times as they wish, provided they wait for a year before getting married again. The marital contract can be made with joint or with separated ownership of goods, and children can decide with which parent they wish to live after the age of seven. According to the Mexican Institute of Geography and Information, one out of every two urban marriages will end up in divorce, with a smaller percentage for rural areas. Additionally, females file over 60 percent of divorces and the average age for divorce is 32 years for females and 34 for males. Families provided for by fathers were down to 79.9 percent in the year 2000 and males who dedicate themselves exclusively to household chores have increased to 0.7 percent. Obviously, these numbers reflect a small and slow change, but still a change from the old traditions.

Family structure

Something to keep in mind in the description of the Mexican family is that the geographic diversity of Mexico is paralleled by the social diversity of the country. In this regard, we should stress that there is a variety of Mexican families. In fact Leñero (1982) was able to identify 20 categories and 53 family types, depending on the social context (degree of urban or rural development and social class), the structure (nuclear or extended; exogenous or endogamous), the power dynamics (patriarchal, matriarchal, or single-parent), and the stage of the relationship (courtship, newly-weds, etc.), which have a definite effect of the family interaction and composition. Although nuclear families are becoming more common, extended families continue to exist, especially in lower socioeconomic levels and in rural areas. From census data for the year 2000, 74.2 percent of Mexican families live in nuclear dwellings. The nuclear families further subdivide into 11,313,242 nuclear families with children 1,432,165 nuclear families without children, and 1,759,722 single-parent families. However, even in these cases of housing independence, there continue to be strong economic ties to the families of origin, which transcend to the grandchildren. In fact, these clans of affiliative and functional support have re-emerged with the current economic difficulties, and in spite of increasing migration, nuclear families in urban areas try to live close to their parents.

Family values

The study of the norms that regulate the thoughts, feelings, and behaviors within the Mexican culture, as well as the formation of national character, have been deeply researched and described by Díaz-Guerrero (1994). Based on his analysis, it is clear that interpersonal behavior is directed and determined, in part, by the extent to which each subject addresses and believes the cultural dictates. In order to assess the adherence to the Mexican socio-cultural norms, he extracted the historic-socio-cultural premises from sayings, proverbs, and other forms of popular communication. Content analysis makes it evident that these proverbs show the central position that family plays within this culture. Two basic propositions describe the Mexican family: (a) the power and supremacy of the father, and (b) the love and absolute and necessary sacrifice of the mother. Constructed around these two cardinal premises, over 80 percent of the population indicate these premises are correct and guide their life. Analyses of the responses to the statements yield a central traditionalism factor called Affiliative Obedience vs. Active Self-Affirmation, stressing that, "children and people in general should always obey their parents," and that "everyone should love their mother and respect their father," which means children should never disobey parents and should show respect in exchange for security and love from them. From this point of view, it is evident that Mexico is built on a strict hierarchical structure, where the respect for somebody reflects the power that is offered to persons with higher social hierarchic level.

The changes related to gender in contemporary Mexican families and the sense of traditionalism are both evident in the Machismo vs. Virginity–Abnegation factor, which refers to the degree of agreement with statements such as "men are more intelligent than women," "docile women are better," "the father should always be the head of the home," and "women should remain virgin until marriage." Interestingly, abnegation reflects that both men and women believe that it is important to first satisfy the needs of others and then of themselves; that is to say that self-modification is preferred over self-affirmation as a copying style in relationships. Finally, the importance of Family Status Quo and Cultural Rigidity in relation to the roles played by men and women in the family, appears in proverbs like "women always have to be faithful to their husbands," "most girls would prefer to be like their mothers," "women should always be protected," "married women should be faithful to the relationship," "young women should not be out alone at night," and "when parents are strict, children grow up correctly."

Integrating the different factors that form the socio-cultural premises of the Mexican family depicts the rules and norms that specify the relationship patterns, but also the expectancy and stereotypes formed by people outside the group. Another important point is that premises and stereotypes are tendencies in particular groups – they give a general idea of the character of a group, but there are also individual differences and variability. Not all Mexicans defend and live by the socio-cultural premises – some are rebels to the culture; for example, Mexican students become counter-culture when they call for liberty and equality in a culture made of interdependence and respect.

CONCLUSIONS

If we were to depict the Mexican family, its past and its future, a good way to synthesize would be to focus on the family roles, values, and functions. Generalizing, the father has been the perennial official head of the family, who is supposed to command respect and punish the children. By 1992, males were the main provider in 53.3 percent of families, both parents shared being the main provider in 16.9 percent of the cases, and females appeared as the main provider in 8 percent of the families.

Without hesitation, we can affirm that the mother is still the most sacred and important element of the family. The mother is the affectionate intermediary between the father and the children whose unquestioned place is the home. However, nowadays, women are more than compromising good mothers, women are developing personally outside the home sphere and do not only live to take care of a husband and children. More and more, women choose to stay in school, select a career, work outside the home, decide to get married and when to have children.

The coalition formed by the parents, in good Catholic tradition, continues its legacy of teaching their children to behave properly, provides economic and emotional support, insures social and intellectual growth and believes that they shouldn't argue in front of the children. In spite of these premises, the truth includes a growing number of separations. In turn, children shouldn't talk back to their parents, they must be obedient and never doubt the words of their parents. In addition, they should care for their parents in their old age and help with the household chores. In short, they should always respect their parents and older persons in the family.

As can be seen by the description offered herein, the Mexican family is varied, but has some distinctive characteristics that emanate from its common history. In the same tenor, there is no doubt that families are being impacted by advances in technology, education, and services, but the majority of families remain committed to the legacy left behind by the ancestral indigenous peoples and the Catholic Spanish conquerors.

28 Mongolia: traditions and family portrait

Tuya Buyantsogt

A HISTORICAL OUTLINE OF MONGOLIA

Mongolia is a country with a history that dates back to the times of the Khunnu Empire. Mongolia today still evokes images of Genghis Khan's warriors and the steppe-dwelling nomads who created the world's largest continuous land empire in the thirteenth century. The country is now experiencing the most recent of the many waves of change that have enriched the national culture of Mongols.

Mongolia, which in 1921 became the first socialist country in Asia, saw its state grow very rapidly – extending its influence ever deeper into people's daily lives. In Mongolia, the state owned every cow, sheep, yak, and goat. It owned the enterprises within which people worked. And it repressed any political opposition or alternative ways of thinking – a process that included closing down hundreds of Buddhist monasteries.

Since socialism in the world collapsed Mongolia has chosen its own way of development, and it has been undergoing profound political and socioeconomic changes since 1990. The essence of this process consists of: political democratization; advancement of human rights and fundamental freedoms; transition to a market economy, and vindication of the equality of different forms of property; implementation of an open foreign policy and international activities; recognition of the important role of a rational environmental policy in ensuring sustained development; and revival of the best national traditions in every sphere of life. These unprecedented developments have found their embodiment and legal guarantee in the new constitution ratified by the parliament in 1992, as well as the national legislature amended and renewed in recent years. The foundations of a truly democratic and humane civil society are now being laid.

As in other countries undergoing simultaneous political, economic, and social restructuring, Mongolia is now experiencing a difficult and crucial period. The most sudden and destructive economic crisis occurred because of the discontinuance of the financial and economic assistance from the former Soviet Union, which used to supply the largest proportion of resources needed for the country's investment, as well as foodstuffs and other essential consumer goods. Dramatic changes of the recent past affected the vulnerable groups of the population, especially women and children. Many qualified jobs have been eliminated in society. The government has, however, made commendable efforts to build a new system of social protection. In 1994, it established mechanisms for social and health insurance, which now covers around 90 percent of the population. Efforts to reduce pressure on the budget have involved some degree of privatization of services – permitting the expansion of private education, for example, and some private healthcare. However, there is a danger of heightened inequity. Moving toward a market economy has widened the gap between rich and poor. The second danger is that weakening of the public provision of basic services will stifle future human development. Mongolia's successful entry into a global economy will require a healthy and educated workforce that can cope with the ever-changing demands of the marketplace. Social service expenditure has to be seen less as a cost and more as an investment in the capacities of the Mongolian people.

Mongolia's average population density is only 1.3 persons per km^2, and much of the country is indeed sparsely populated. Most of Mongolia's 2.4 million people live in cities and towns. These urban clusters are often separated by vast distances. Poor roads greatly increase that separation. The present shortage of fuel and spare parts for vehicles also tends to magnify distances. Domestic air service, once quite adequate, has been severely curtailed for similar reasons. Communications infrastructure is also quite limited, further contributing to the isolation of communities and families. In rural areas, nomadic and semi-nomadic ways of life are still common. Delivery of services to communities and families is particularly problematic.

ECOLOGICAL FEATURES

Mongolia is a land-locked country situated in Central Asia and is bordered by the Russian Federation on the north and the People's Republic of China on the east, south, and west. The total area is 1,566,500 km^2. It extends for 2,405 km from its Western border point to the eastern one and 1,263 km from the north to the south. The total length of the border line is more than 7,600 km. Mongolia is on the whole a mountainous country, with an average altitude of 1,580 m above the sea level. All these physical and geographical factors contribute to the unique severity of Mongolia's climate: hyper-continental climate, with annual extremes of temperatures (+/− 25°C), long winters, intense solar radiation, sustained winds, and low precipitation. Given these environmental constraints, potential for agriculture is limited (of the 126 million hectares of arable land, only 1.3 million are actually cultivated). The livestock population − over 25 million head, or more than 10 times the human population − has to survive hard winters on sparse pastureland of 122 million hectares. Livestock accounts for 70 percent of all agricultural production, which amounts to 40.4 percent of GNP, and involves 34 percent of the economically-active population. Global warming has heightened Mongolia's exposure to a number of regular natural disasters.

Drought. A large part of Mongolia consists of arid and semi-arid areas, and around one-quarter is affected by drought every two or three years.

Floods. Overgrazing, deforestation, and soil erosion are thought to be increasing the frequency and duration of floods.

Fires. As the climate has become drier, there have been an increasing number of fires. In 1998 alone, there were 132 outbreaks of fire causing damage to the environment and infrastructure.

Dust and snow storms. Climatic change is also thought to be associated with severe snow and dust storms of recent years. In 1996–1997 storms and snowfalls that covered 20 percent of the territory resulted in the deaths of over 600,000 animals.

Unfavorable climate and geographic conditions, and particularly Mongolia's remote hinterland location, make the costs of manufacturing, construction, transportation, social services, and provision of essential commodities, such as clothing, roughly three to five times higher than corresponding expenditures in those developing countries with more benign climates and favorable geographic settings.

ORGANIZATION AND INSTITUTIONS OF SOCIETY

Political institutions and legal system

The organization of the political system of Mongolia had been unique since the third century BC, including the period of Genghis Khan in the eighth century when the new regime of United Mongolia was at its peak of development. Until 1990, Mongolia was a country with a socialist orientation under the single-party system, based on the ideology of "workers' leadership." Social, economic, and political reform processes of the 1990s developed simultaneously and all in a peaceful manner. The government of Mongolia is the highest executive body in the state. The government implements the state laws passed by the parliament of

Mongolia in accordance with its duties and commitments to direct economic, social, and cultural development. The Parliament is composed of 76 full-time members. The new democratic constitution established the legal and political framework for a pluralistic society that respects human rights and freedoms. Civil liberties and other rights are legally guaranteed. The equality of men and women in political, economic, social, and cultural affairs is reaffirmed. The right to own private property is fully recognized and strongly encouraged. These and other provisions establish legal basis for further economic and social transformations.

Economy

As Mongolia has a severe climate, dispersed population, and a wide expanse of unproductive land, the economy relies heavily upon agriculture, in particular animal husbandry and mining. Since 1990, Mongolia's economy has suffered substantially owing to the withdrawal of Soviet aid for development. However liberalization seems to have had its positive effect on the economy, leading to a boost of small-scale agricultural entities. Both agricultural and industrial growth have been positive since 1994. By 1996, the average monthly earnings of an urban family of four were $40 and of rural families $30. An estimated 36 percent of the population lives in poverty. In 1998, the GDP per capita was estimated at $452. The share of 1998 by sector at constant price indicates that the products of the agriculture sector made up 32.8 percent of the total GDP, followed by the industrial sector with 24.1 percent and the trade sector with 18.9 percent. The percentage of people employed in agriculture and animal husbandry was 48.5 percent, in industry 11.9 percent and in other sectors 39.6 percent.

In 1990, the Mongolian government chose to carry out its economic reforms at a rapid pace. Like most of the transition countries of Eastern and Central Europe, it opted for "shock therapy." The Government quickly liberalized prices and privatized herds of livestock. And especially after 1996, it opened up the economy to the outside world.

The educational system

One of the main achievements of Mongolia in the twentieth century has been the establishment of a public education system with universal access. Since the democratic reforms, there have been substantial changes in the structure, methodology, and orientation of the educational system. Primary and secondary education have remained free of charge, whereas higher and vocational education have not. Although there is still free access to primary and secondary education, in the academic years of 1990–1997 school enrolment rate dropped sharply. In 1990, the school enrolment rate for 8- to 15-year-old children was 98.6 percent compared with 82.3 percent in 1997. However, in 1998–1999 the enrolment rate increased and reached 90.6 percent in 1999. School enrolment rates differ by gender and location. In Mongolia education level in rural and urban areas differs considerably. Moreover, in rural areas there were about twice as many males and females (5.7 percent) with no primary schooling as in urban areas. In 1998, the urban average for higher education was 19.6 percent and the illiteracy rate was 1.3 percent compared with rural averages of 4.4 percent and 2.2 percent and respectively. In every education level girls' enrolment rate is higher than that of boys. According to the Living Standards Measurement Study of the World Bank (2000), the school enrolment rate for female children in secondary schools, including technical vocational schools was 48.3 percent, in specialized and non-degree schools was 9.4 percent, and in higher educational institutions 7.6 percent. Thus, school drop-out rate depends largely on probability of joining the next level of schooling. As mentioned in "The human development report 2000," 70 percent of university students are females. In the future this will contribute to unequal gender distribution of the educated population. The share of males in primary education aged 10 and over was 23.8 percent against 23.1 percent of females, the share of males in secondary and non-degree tertiary education was 56.9 percent against 57.7 percent, and the share of males in degree and higher education was 7.6 percent against 7.7 percent according to the data of the year 2000. Further development of the education sector in Mongolia will depend on the country's economy. Overall, interactions between economic development and development of the education sector are important. In particular, the development of the human resource potential of the Mongolian people through the contributions of its education and human resource sector is an essential element of future prosperity.

Religion

Mongolia, as an ancient nation, has its own history of spiritual life. The religion is Buddhism, which is separate from the state. Religious freedom is practiced in the country and it is guaranteed by the constitution of Mongolia. At present, there are more than 120 Buddhist temples with thousands of monks, "lamas." Other religions are also allowed.

Since 1990, a Buddhist reawakening has been gently sweeping Mongolia. One aspect of this is the effort to reopen the monasteries and temples in the capital city of Ulaanbaatar and rural areas. Buddhist traditions were nearly wiped out during seven decades of socialism. A major step in the revitalization of Buddhism was the visits of the Dalai Lama, the high priest of Lamaism, which is the form of Buddhism practiced in Mongolia and Tibet. The Dalai Lama began public teachings in Mongolia to prepare Mongolians to receive a form of spiritual initiation known as the *Kalachakra*. Unlike the other tantric practices that are related to the individual, the *Kalachakra* is typically given to large gatherings. Finding a knowledgeable teacher is not easy for many Mongolians. Of the 2,000 monks in Mongolia today, about half are over 75. Few monasteries are left in the country, and there are few monks who are qualified to teach other monks. Some programs to support Buddhist learning in Mongolia have begun. The Tibet Foundation, an organization based in London, has been supporting projects in Mongolia since 1990. A program called "Buddhism in Mongolia" has sponsored Mongolian monks and nuns to study in Dharamsala, India, the Dalai Lama's home-in-exile from Tibet. Teachers from India have traveled to Mongolia to assist Mongolian monks.

The Mongolian government is also trying to take some responsibility in the Buddhist revival. While it does not openly fund Buddhist causes, it does help finance textbooks and articles that include information about Buddhism. And although the government will not pay for the construction of monasteries, it funds some programs to rebuild monasteries that were destroyed in the 1930s.

FAMILY

According to the information on community health and nursing of the World Health Organization, family is a relationship in the community of two and more persons. In Mongolia monogamy exists. In the ancient times in the higher classes, polygamy existed secretly because the noble people were not allowed to marry within the same class, but the tradition decreed them to marry with the common people so as to demonstrate they were all part of one community and also to mix their blood with that common people.

The husband is the head of the family. Traditionally, divorce could be initiated by either husband or wife. When there was a serious conflict between them and it was impossible to continue their marriage, the wife was returned to her own family. But nowadays the situation has changed and divorce is controlled by laws. The possibility of divorce neutralizes the superior right of a husband and helps to establish normal communication within the family.

The wife is responsible for the housework and the care of the children. Mongolian women have equal rights with men. Mongolian women are able to herd animals, to ride horses, and also to participate jointly with men in ceremonies, holidays, and preaching in rural areas. In cities there are many women successfully running big companies and some women have been elected in governing boards of the state.

In order to consider the relationships within the family, it is necessary to mention some specific aspects of the society. One of the characteristics of Mongolian society is its relatively small population. The rural areas are based primarily on traditional animal husbandry, but in the urban areas they are based on industry as in European countries. Some researchers express this as "one state–two cultures." Some might disagree with this statement, but for others it seems true. This kind of difference influences family relationships.

Traditional customs are followed by many families. The model of the classic family is that of the herdsman, although the inhabitants of big cities have an increasing influence on the whole life of Mongolia. Although in the last few years migration from the rural to the urban areas has increased and people's occupations have changed as well as their place of residence, the traditional aspects of society have not basically changed very much.

Family structure

Until the thirteenth century, Mongolians lived in large extended families of three or four generations: great-grandparents, grandparents, fathers, mothers, sons, and daughters. From that time the large extended families broke down and today families live separately in their own dwellings within their own nuclear family. On the other hand, Mongolians in rural areas still lead a nomadic way of life looking for a new pasture for their animals. Thus smaller nuclear families have increased. But a tradition of respect for the elders of the extended family still dominates.

Many people still live in a traditional unique national dwelling *(ger)*, which can be easily set up and dismantled, shipped, and put up again, fully preserving its original shape. When the son marries, the *ger* is put up and the son's family lives separately from the extended family. In the extended family the hearth and the image of Buddha are objects of worship, and they are still kept. Following our traditional custom of marriage, a new *ger* is built for a son and livestock and property is given.

Later, parents of the son live near his family and their daughter follows her husband and lives near her father-in-law's family.

According to the 2000 Population and Housing Census, the family structure of Mongolians has changed substantially. Because of the transition to democracy, changed economic conditions and preferred lifestyles of Mongolians, the family structure today is: 35,400 households (6.5 percent of the population) are single; 340,000 households (63.0 percent) are nuclear; 15 3,000 households (27.8 percent) are extended and 14,700 families (2.7 percent) are mixed from the total of 541,000 households throughout Mongolia.

CHANGES IN THE FAMILY

Today in Mongolia the traditional values of the father as the head of the family have changed. In a recent survey of the Ministry of Social Welfare and Labor, 13 percent answered that the head of the family is the mother. The 2000 Population and Housing Census indicated that 83.7 percent of families are headed by fathers and 16.3 percent by mothers.

The proportion of legal to unmarried couples above 15 years old is 87 percent to 13 percent respectively, or one unmarried couple to eight marriages. The percentages of married couples according to age are 1.27 percent for 15–19-year-olds, 25 percent for 20–24-year-olds, 24 percent for ages 25–29, and 15 percent for ages 30–34.

In modern Mongolia the role of working mothers and women is increasing. The mother not only works, but also cares for the family and does most of the housework, while the father only gives his salary. Mothers have more roles than fathers but on the other hand mothers strongly influence all aspects of the family.

In Mongolia a law was passed recently, regulating family life. The changes in the law, reflecting changes in family life in recent years, are related to joint ownership of the property, legal confirmation of marriage, divorce, and adoption of children.

29 The Netherlands: tolerance and traditionalism

Peter Cuyvers

A HISTORICAL OUTLINE OF THE NETHERLANDS

The Netherlands originated from a union of regions (Republic of Seven Provinces) led by the provinces of South-Holland and North-Holland, and with members of the House of Orange as military leaders. Under the Oranges the country gained independence in an Eighty Years War against Spain that ended in 1648. After the French revolution the Netherlands became a kingdom. Its present population is just over 16 million inhabitants, of whom approximately one-quarter is concentrated in the densely populated area around Amsterdam and Rotterdam. The Netherlands was one of the founding members of the European Union.

ECOLOGICAL FEATURES

The Netherlands is a small and densely populated area in northwest Europe, of which the history and ecological system is dominated by the sea and the large rivers. Large parts of the country, called polders, are below sea-level and have to be protected by dikes. The same goes for the substantial landwinnings from an inland sea made in the twentieth century. The cooperation needed to protect the land has become a token for the political model of constant communication in search of joint solutions, called the "poldermodel." It may well be that this cooperation model has still deeper roots in the coexistence of approximately equal Protestant and Catholic religious groups and the strong merchant orientation of the provinces of Holland in the period that they dominated the world seas (first half of the seventeenth century).

This contribution is mostly based on P. Cuyvers, A. Kuijsten, and H. J. Schulze, (in press). Family change and family policies: The Netherlands. In P. Flora, S. Kamerman, and A. Kahn (eds.), *Family change and family policies in the west*. Vol II: *Family change and family policies in consociational democracies. Belgium, Switzerland and the Netherlands*. Oxford: Clarendon Press.

ORGANIZATION AND INSTITUTIONS OF SOCIETY

Economic organization

The merchant origin of the wealth of the Netherlands is still visible in its present economy, which is dominated by financial service institutions (banks and insurance companies) and Rotterdam as largest port in the world. Mercantile power also resulted in colonies of which Indonesia, especially, was considered the "pearl in the crown." Agricultural and industrial development lingered until the end of the nineteenth century but boomed in the twentieth century. Nowadays the majority of the population is employed in the services sector.

Political institutions and legal system

The political system in the Netherlands was created in a constant struggle between the civil rule in the original regions and the House of Orange, originally employed by the provinces as military officials (City-Holders). The House of Orange was usually supported by the common citizens and was eventually able to acquire royal power, but was forced to accept a parliamentary democracy in the nineteenth century. After this the Netherlands very quickly evolved into a centralized state, though regions and municipalities remained as layers of executive power. Another quite specific characteristic of the executive system is the very large extent to which public tasks such as education, healthcare, and broadcasting are assigned to institutions with an independent status by law even if they are fully funded by government. This system originates from a struggle for hegemony between the main religious groups: this struggle was "pacified" in the nineteenth century by giving Protestants and Catholics the right to govern their own schools (see below). In the twentieth century this practice of creating separate "pillars" of institutions was found in many walks of life (youth clubs, sports, etc.). It also proved a useful instrument in accommodating the emerging socialist movement, enabling it to create, for instance, its own socialist radio and (later) television network.

The educational system

The link between education and the struggle for hegemony of religious groups led to an extended network of primary schools in the nineteenth century. In the twentieth century secondary education was made available for all by government funding. At present 20 percent of the young men and the same percentage of young women is enrolled in tertiary education. All students over 18 years of age receive a stipend dependent on their parents' income.

Religion

The number of citizens considering themselves members of a religious organization sharply decreased after World War II to approximately one out of five. On the other hand still over 80 percent of the population professes belief in the existence of a "higher presence." As a result of immigration after World War II, the number of Muslims increased to approximately one million, making Islam the third religion of the country. Contrary to the remaining small "strongholds" of traditional Christians (mainly Protestants in rural areas), Muslims cluster in the centers of big cities. In the beginning of the century this has provoked increasing concern in the public debate, owing to the foundation of a number of Islamic schools and the building of large religious houses.

BONDS WITH GROUPS IN THE IMMEDIATE COMMUNITY

Until recently the Netherlands has been a rather open society, accommodating in the past huge groups of (religious) refugees from other European countries. For centuries public life in cities and villages was controlled by civil authorities, organizing both security and support systems for the poor, the latter in cooperation with church authorities. This enabled nuclearization of the family in an early stage of its history.

THE FAMILY

Marriage

Since by the seventeenth century the nuclear family was the dominant household,[1] marriages within the kinship network at an early stage were seen as rather improper (though occasionally allowed for cousins). As for exogamy, the selection of partners in the Netherlands for a long time was characterized by cultural (group) restrictions. Marriages between partners of different religions were almost inconceivable until the second half

---

[1] In the city of Leiden for instance a record shows in 1648 an average household size of just over four, but also in smaller towns in past centuries families averaged just over two children and really large families were the exception (van den Brink, 1996).

of the twentieth century, when religion lost its social power. The same went for marriages between people of different social classes, such as working class with middle class (or blue and white collar).

Within these social and religious groups, obtaining a spouse was largely considered to be a matter of personal choice of the partners themselves, as long as they made a choice within the prescribed religious and social boundaries. Permission from the father to marry was needed till the age of 27 until the beginning of the twentieth century, but was lowered to 18 for men and 16 for women. Dowry usually took the shape of the customary paying of the wedding by the parents of the bride and the giving of presents such as the linen and crockery by the rest of the family. In general the social approval for marriage further was linked to the potential of the male partner to sustain a family.

Divorce was prohibited by law until the second half of the twentieth century (divorce law of 1971), except in the case of adultery. After a growing practice of admittance of adultery (the so-called "big lie"), divorce with mutual consent became legal. Thereafter, divorce rates have boomed up to one out of three marriages, gradually stabilizing to the present rate of one out of four marriages overall. In 2002 the Netherlands Family Council and the Central Statistics Office published a national family report using new life course analysis and distinguishing between stages in the life cycle, showing different dissolution figures for cohabiting couples (50 percent), married couples (25 percent) and married couples with children (15 percent). See "Demography" for a further description (Nederlandse Gezinsraad/Netherlands Family Council, 2001).

Family structure

By the seventeenth century the nuclear family dominated the social structure. Within the family the man officially was the "head" of the union; married women and children were devoid of legal rights. Legally equal rights for men and women were established late in the twentieth century: until 1957 a wife was not able to make any legally-binding decisions without her husband's consent and until 1986 the husband still held the decisive vote in matters such as the education of children.

Extended families were relatively rare, though until far into the twentieth century it was quite usual that children "married into the parental home" because there was a housing shortage. However, in such a situation the young couple was still considered to be independent, parental authority over children stopped at the moment of their marriage. On the other hand, because of the same housing shortage and the continued habits of the "rural period" old parents in need of care used to live with one of their children. This practice quickly decreased after 1950 when old age homes became common. At present just over 300,000 aged live in these homes; the vast majority of people over 65 (or even 75) still live independently, because of increased health and are supported by an extended professional home care system (Hortulanus, 1983).

Family roles and functions

The roles in the family in the Netherlands were dominated for centuries by the values of the higher middle-class or "bourgeois" citizens. Other models, such as the aristocratic way of leaving childcare to servants or boarding schools, or the necessity in the working class of mothers participating in gainful employment, met with strong disapproval. This resulted in a very strong ideology of motherhood, especially when the increasing wealth enabled the working class to adopt the petit bourgeois family model in the second half of the twentieth century. The ideal of the breadwinner-family was strongly supported by the political and religious elite after World War II, resulting for instance in an official agreement between labour unions and employers to pay male workers enough to sustain a family and to limit the wage of women (Labour Foundation, 1947, quoted in Bussemaker, 1997).[2]

In the traditional model fathers were (sole) earners, carrying the responsibility for the welfare of the rest of their family and having the "final authority" over children. "Wait till your father comes home. . ." was a common threat to disobedient children). Mothers were (and still are) in control of the housekeeping, shopping, cooking: they are seen as master of their *own* domain in which fathers have nothing to seek. It should be noted that children in the middle-class model are expected to be obedient and respectful, but also are entitled to love and good care; parents have a responsibility for their upbringing and education. Finally there is a very strong conviction that the nuclear family is entitled to privacy: it is considered very inappropriate to pay unannounced visits, not only for friends but also for family members and even for one's own parents (Kooy, 1992).

---

[2] The Labour Foundation – now replaced by the Social-Economic Council – was the official body through which employer organizations, labour unions, and the national government negotiated central agreements on the development of wages and the social system.

CHANGES IN THE FAMILY

Demography

The changes in the family structure in the Netherlands are best described from the perspective of the "modern life course." The most prominent feature of the modern life course is the dissolution of the classical "iron triangle" between marriage, leaving the parental home, and family formation. Nowadays over 90 percent of youngsters cohabitate before marriage. Since partnership dissolution for cohabitating couples is over 50 percent, there is in fact an extended period of partner selection in which individuals live as singles for shorter or longer periods. Almost all cohabitating couples who stay together for a longer period eventually decide to marry, one out of three after the birth of their first child. The overall divorce rate for married couples is 25 percent, the divorce rate for couples with children is just under 15 percent. Family formation is postponed: the average age to become a parent is almost 30 for females and 33 for males. The birth rate is approximately 1.65. It should be noted that the decrease in birth rate is caused to a large extent by the increase in childless women, at present almost 20 percent. The average number of children for mothers is just over 2.

Family values

In several studies of the Netherlands Family Council (Cuyvers and Latten, 1999; Nederlandse Gezinsraad, 2001; van der Avort, Cuyvers, and and de Hoog, 1996) two distinctive characteristics of family ideology in the Netherlands have been distinguished: *tolerance* and *traditionalism*. Together they build a paradox: on the one hand the Netherlands is one of the most liberal countries in the world with respect to acceptance of (post)modern lifestyles and diversity of living arrangements. On the other hand, the Netherlands has a surprisingly low rate of female employment and a very strong ideology of motherhood compared to other modernized Western countries.

As far as tolerance is concerned, personal freedom of choice in relations is widely respected. Children are supposed to choose their own friends, adolescents their own partners for the "dating and mating" experience. Sexual freedom is respected and parents who do not allow their children to sleep with their partners in the parental home are considered a bit old-fashioned. As stated before, cohabitation before marriage is the choice of a large majority (90 percent). Presently cohabitation is becoming quite popular with older partners (who establish a second relationship after divorce). Though homosexuality still meets some resistance in the lower classes and traditional religious groups, it is officially accepted: same sex couples have the same right as male/female couples to marry or register their partnership. (For example, several members of parliament – including some from the Christian-Democrat party – have had official homosexual partnerships.) Within families, ways of relating and communicating are also regarded as a matter of choice. Fathers, mothers, and children are considered to be autonomous individuals, each of them having a right to think and act independently. A prominent social scientist (de Swaan, 1988) has called the family in the Netherlands a *negotiation household*. Authority in a family – if present at all – should not depend on a specific position but on the result of the ability to find a majority for one's viewpoint. After leaving the parental home relations with other family members are seen as non-obligatory, with the exception of one's own parents. But even this social obligation will fall short if there is a personal conflict. In sum, the personal element in family relations is seen as far more important than the aspect of social obligation.

As for traditionalism, the family landscape in the Netherlands is dominated by nuclear families with a breadwinner and a mother with no paid job at all or a rather small one. Though employment rates for the younger generations of mothers are rising, still almost half of them have no job/income at all and in families with two earners the female share averages only one-quarter of the family income. Just over 5 percent of the families with children are "real" dual earner families with the mother working approximately the same number of hours as the father. Within these quite traditional families conflict between the generations seems to be rather absent. The rather high level of income means that most children have their own room at an early age with a lot of personal possessions such as CD-players, game computers, and television sets. They can afford fashionable clothing, first from the parental income, later paid for by the small jobs almost every child over 16 has. Attitude surveys (Sociaal en Cultureel Planbureau, Nederland 1995) show that the younger generations seem to be a bit more conservative than their parents, but only slightly so. Leaving the parental home takes place at an average age of 22 for girls and 23 for boys. The years after the age of 18 that children spend in the parental home in almost complete financial and sexual freedom are usually called the "Hotel Mamma" period.

Though there is a growing debate on the educational capacities of parents – as a result of rising youth crime records – it is generally recognized that over 85 percent or even up to 95 percent (Nederlandse

Gezinsraad, 2001) of families function quite smoothly, having found a balance between freedom and authority.

CONCLUSIONS

The family in the Netherlands has been the nuclear family for centuries. That is, the guiding image has been the (petty) bourgeois ideal of the closely knit unit of parents and their children, building the well-known "haven" of Christopher Lasch (1979). From the very start of the Republic of Seven Provinces, both aristocratic and agricultural family patterns have met severe criticism, mainly based on their neglect of the interests of the child. Children should not be left to professional carers nor be confronted with the necessities of working life at an early age. Of course, this family model has been unattainable for the majority of the population for quite a long time. In fact, it lasted until the boom after World War II, when the ideal of the breadwinner family with its own family home became reality for most.

As a consequence of this ideal the modernization of the nuclear family into an equality-based model in the Netherlands at least had a false start. In a recent survey three-quarters of the men *and* women in the Netherlands responded with a firm "no" to the statement that a woman *should* contribute to the family income. (In all other EU countries over 60 percent of the men and women thought a woman should.) This may seem strange in a culture also emphasizing equality between partners within families. The explanation probably is to be found in the strong adherence to the ideology of free choice: for many respondents their reply is based on a desire to return to the old days of separate roles, for many others their reply is based on the conviction that any obligation for a certain role should be disapproved of.

Though the ideology of freedom and equality is firmly rooted in the Netherlands, there also is a strong counter-tendency, probably concurrent with a deeply rooted cleavage between the upper social strata and the lower and middle social groups. For example, lower and middle groups have been and still are strong supporters of the monarchy, whereas the cultural avant-garde has republican tendencies. Modern family patterns were strongly advocated by this same avant-garde – dominating, for instance, the media – in the past decades. The "elite" is concentrated in the so-called "Randstad," the area between Amsterdam and Rotterdam. Since in the past decades there has been a lot of migration of the highly educated to these areas, there seems to be sort of a split between this city-dwelling cultural elite and the middle classes who are still living in rural areas or moved out of the city to suburban areas. One of the more material characteristics of this split is that the distance between the generations literally became larger as a result of the migration in highly educated groups. For lower- and middle-class families it still is quite common to live within a couple of minutes from the parental home. The general pattern therefore seems to be that most families in the Netherlands accept diversity of lifestyles and living arrangements as a (good) result of more personal freedom, but do not really wish to change traditional patterns for themselves.

30 Nigeria

Yuwanna Jenny Mivanyi

A HISTORICAL OUTLINE OF NIGERIA

Nigeria came into existence as a nation in 1914 (Buah, 1960), a result of the amalgamation of the northern and southern regions and boundary adjustment with Cameroon by the British government led by Lord Lugard and supported by the efforts of missionaries, after a struggle of 40 years. Nigeria became independent in 1960. Currently, Nigeria's population is 122,443,748, and its capital, Abuja, has a population of 511,471. In 1963, Nigeria joined other African nations to form the Organization of African Unity (which was recently renamed the African Union in 2002). Nigeria is also a member of the Economic Community of West African States (ECOWAS). There are over 300 ethnic groups in Nigeria, of which the Hausa, Igbo, and the Yoruba groups dominate in the north, east, and west, respectively. However, no one language is used nationally, despite the attempt to employ a lingua franca over two decades ago.

ECOLOGICAL FEATURES

Nigeria is situated in West Africa, bounded by the Niger Republic, the Atlantic Ocean, the Republic of Cameroon, and Benin. Nigeria has a varied ecology, with a stretch of highlands in the northeast, rainforest in the southeast, and desert in the northwest. There are 36 states; the largest and oldest city is Ibadan in Oyo State, with its weather-beaten roofs, and with a population of 1,228,663 and 287,077 households in 1991. A household in Nigeria connotes a compound where several persons live together under the same roof or in the same building, sharing the same source of food, and think of themselves as a unit. In the 1991 census there were 17,909,705 families constituting 96.6 percent of all households.

The climate is differentiated by dry and wet seasons, longer rainy seasons in the south and longer dry seasons in the north. The temperature varies from 14°C in winter to 35°C in March and April, and between

25°C and 30°C in July and August in most parts of Nigeria, except Lagos which is relatively humid in virtually all seasons. The climatic conditions are due to Nigeria's situation between latitudes 03 and 15 degrees north of the equator and longitudes 04 and 14 degrees east of the prime meridian.

ORGANIZATIONS AND INSTITUTIONS OF SOCIETY

Economic organization

Although the ecological and climatic variations influenced different types of subsistence patterns in traditional Nigerian society, the economy was mainly based on agriculture. Along the two major rivers – Benue and Niger – the tributaries at the coast and the Atlantic Coast itself, fishing is also a means of subsistence. In addition, root crops like cassava, cocoa yam, and yams were cultivated.

In northern Nigeria assorted grain production predominated through shifting cultivation. Grains include maize, guinea corn, wheat, millet, sorghum, rice, and soya beans. Vegetables such as lettuce, onions, okra, tomatoes, and spices such as pepper and garlic, were grown in both dry and rainy seasons. In addition, skeletal production of yams, sweet potatoes, and cassava was carried out on the sporadic lowlands of the savannah. Animal husbandry was, and is still, common in the savannah vegetation in northern Nigeria. Mechanized agriculture was introduced in the late 1970s but did not replace manual labor, especially in the rural settings. The large-scale manual agriculture is basically responsible for the migration of youth of age 17–30 years from rural to urban settings. Census figures show that the percentage of the population engaged in agricultural/animal husbandry, fishing, and hunting in Nigeria in early 1990 was 35.6 percent, with 3.3 percent in services, and 1.5 percent in administrative and managerial.

Political institution and legal systems

In traditional Nigeria, the political, social, and legal systems worked under the extended family structure. Clusters of family compounds formed villages. These family compounds were surrounded by farmlands for farming and rearing animals. Through this spacious farmland allocation, neighbors were so far apart that they had no basis to quarrel over animal intrusion into each other's land. For every family compound or cluster there was a head. In the north and west there were specific laws regarding land ownership, which the British colonialists used to govern the people after capturing their land. Specially in the northern region, among the Hausas, there existed the ward head *(mai Anguwa)*, village head *(Dagachi)*, district head *(Hakimi)*, and emir *(Sarki)*. In 1804 when Usman Danfodio conquered the area, the Heads adopted the Islamic system. The "indirect rule" worked well in the north because of the structures already in existence. British colonialists attached only resident representatives to the then existing Heads to oversee affairs. In the west there were the *Obas*. In the eastern region the indirect rule was enforced but it failed because there were no specific laws regarding property ownership, as in the north or west (Buah, 1960). The Hausa States, Fulani States, Jukun Kingdom, Nupe Kingdom, Oyo Empire, Borno Empire, and Benin Empire were composed of their descendants who still rule today in Nigeria. However, because of the consolidation of Christian and Islamic legal systems for over a century, in addition to the formal legal system, the traditional political and legal systems weakened, to some extent, but their effectiveness is maintained in their communities.

The educational system

Nigerians did not embrace Western education until the 1930s. In the past, most Nigerian communities sent the children of slaves or "nonentities" to school. Even today there is an imbalance in the acceptance and development of Western education in Nigeria by regional location and by sex. The southern regions accepted Western education earlier than the northern region of Nigeria, almost 60 percent to 40 percent respectively. The adult literacy level by 1998 was 57 percent, of which 39 percent was female and 62 percent male. The average primary school enrolment was 81 percent, 75 percent girls and 86 percent boys (UNICEF/National Planning Commission, 1998). The gradual awareness of the benefit of Western education is obvious even in the remotest Nigerian hamlets. It has reached the extent that communities now vote people into political office based on the spirit of "give and take." Political aspirants may be pressured to promise building a school or state how many needy children would be sponsored for education in the community. As a result of the demand for university education there are over 30 universities and 150 polytechnics and colleges of education in Nigeria.

Religion

There are two major religions in Nigeria: Christianity (50 percent) and Islam (45 percent), while 5 percent are either traditional indigenous religions or free thinkers. Both Christianity and Islam came to Nigeria long before 1914 when Nigeria became a nation. While Christianity is embraced more in the south, because the Christian missionaries first settled there, Islam is embraced more in the north, especially the Hausa States, because the Islamic Jihad of Othman Danfodio came to Nigeria through the northern states in 1804. In most families in Nigeria Christians and Muslims co-exist, except the Hausa Fulani and some Igbo communities, where it is possible to find families that are 100 percent Muslims and 100 percent Christians, respectively.

BONDS WITH THE IMMEDIATE COMMUNITY

Historically, strong ties existed among the family clusters and communities, because they were economically and socially interdependent through trade by barter and inter-family and community marriages. For example, the nomadic Fulanis in the north reared cattle. Milk was given in exchange for maize, guinea corn, or groundnut. Village markets were also means of interaction in building friendships. People respected each other's customs. There were friendly jokes between communities; communities could refer to each other as "slave" and "master" (as among the Kilbas, Higgi, Buras, Margi, the Hausas, and the Nupes; the Fulanis and the Tiv) in northern Nigeria. Such communities believed they were kith and kin; their ancestors had common roots of existence.

As the Nigerian society became polyethnic in residential patterns as a result of urbanization and schooling, fear and ethnic strife also increased. Christian converts had to renounce their customary beliefs and move out of traditional cohorts. Assertion of superiority in beliefs by one group over the other resulted in continuous strife between and/or among religious adherents and communities. In Kaduna State the dichotomy between Christian and Islamic legal practices recently caused strife between Christians and Muslims resulting in clashes that led to thousands of deaths in 2000. The religious clashes also triggered sporadic ethnic group grievances nationally, while the Hausas are predominantly Muslims, "the other groups" are predominantly Christians. Some "uncultured" persons are even using religion as a means to be elected into government offices, thereby weakening the family and community ties needed for the survival of Nigeria as a nation.

THE FAMILY

Marriage

Traditionally, marriage took place among families of the same community and also among second cousins. Marriage among first cousins takes place only among the Fulanis and the Hausas. Emphasis on one's religious beliefs is paramount rather than ethnicity in choosing life partners. Many Nigerians believe that inter-ethnic marriage is the likely factor that will persevere in maintaining friendship ties naturally and nationally.

In the traditional Nigerian society most ethnic groups practiced polygamy. Among the Kilbas, Margi, and Buras in Adamawa State, usually the first wife advised her husband to bring her a companion (another wife). Children of different wives of the same husband interacted as brothers and sisters without differentiation. Each of the wives was a mother to every child. Children slept together according to age and sex. With the inception of Christianity polygamy was and is discouraged among its converts. Islam does not prohibit polygamy as long as the husband treats the wives equally. Whether equality is practiced or not is better synthesized by the participants.

A point of note is that affluence is the predisposing factor to polygamy among Christian deviants and Muslims in Nigeria. Polygamy is not generally practiced in the same manner and serenity nowadays as it was in the days of old. Among the traditional communities, divorce was generally seen as an irresponsible act that brings a stigma to the families of the couple. There was only one instance where divorce could take place without social sanctions against the act, when a girl married a man against her parents' wish. Among the Kilbas, if a girl eloped with a man of her choice, she could later leave the man to go and marry the man of the parents' choice. She then stayed with this (latter) husband for a year or two years to pacify her parents, after which she could go back to the first husband. This practice is extinct now. Divorce and separation are currently increasing. Islam permits divorce up to three times for women. After three divorces the woman must re-marry before reconciling to the husband who divorced her if she still loved him and/or if he also still loved her. The Western legal system allows divorce, but there are conditions on children's maintenance, if any children existed between the couple. In 90 percent of Nigerian communities, after divorce, the father was given custody of the children. Today, the matrimonial decree of 1970 regulates which parent maintains custody of the child, although the court's decision is still not accepted by many couples. With the enactment of the Convention for Eliminating all forms of Discrimination Against Women (CEDAW) in 1975 by the UN, Nigerian women have equal rights with the men after divorce, regarding child custody and maintenance.

At the present time decisions to marry are still determined by parents, even if friendship or courtship was initiated by the couple. The man pays a bride price, which varies from community to community and family to family. In some communities in northern and southern Nigeria bride price may vary according to the bride's level of education. The university graduate has a higher bride price than the bride who has secondary or primary school education. Obtaining a spouse is chiefly initiated by the male but finalized by both families. Christian adherents are subjected to biblical expectations as processed by each local Assembly. It all depends on how committed to the Christian doctrines the local Assembly of the girl was, since the bride price is determined from her vantage point. The dowry for Muslims is called *sadaki* which cannot be less than N2,500 as determined by the religion.

Family structure

The Nigerian family structure is patrilineal in kinship, traced through the father and grandfather. The extended family is composed of the grandparents, the sons/fathers, daughters/mothers and, cousins, aunts/uncles, nieces/nephews and in-law relationships (affinal). The oldest male on the father's side is usually the head of the family. This extended family chain exists currently, despite the nuclear family practices. Mivanyi (1988) says the family structure is better called the combined nuclear–extended family system.

Residence

Historically the couple's residence after marriage was patrilocal. Changes have occurred because of acculturation brought about by Westernization and urbanization. However, Mivanyi shows that the young couple is still strongly under the influence of the husband's father and mother. The couple in urban areas does not stay near the grandparents. A few grandparents come to visit their grandchildren, but the urban families visit their kin in the villages regularly.

Family roles and functions

In the traditional Nigerian family the father was the head of the family. He owned the farmland and the house, and was the authority on family decisions, including marriage. The mother was submissive and obedient to the father. She supplemented the father's authority over children and family matters. She was the head in the absence of the father. In the polygamous family the senior mother assisted the father. Parents taught their children to be obedient. The father "provided" and the mother "maintained." Women who were not married were not expected to have children, except adopted children. Illegitimate children were not accepted in the families.

Demographics

Information on the Nigerian family can be traced to the Christian missionary education in the nineteenth century. However, much interest has been invested in the family study in the early 1990s with government initiated programs like the Better Life for Rural Women (BLFRW), Family Support Programme (FSP), supported by International agencies like USAID, UNDP, UNIFEM, and UNICEF. In the traditional communities of the past, every person of marriageable age had to marry. Young widows compulsorily married into their late husband's family, i.e., the brother of their late husband. Widowers were freer to marry within their immediate or neighboring community. In present-day Nigeria marriage is important but not compulsory. Single parenthood is on the increase (Adeniyi & Mivanyi, 1999). By 1998 the mean age of marriage was 16.9 years, but in some states, mainly southern, the average age may be 30.5 years. These are significant changes. The fertility rates are 6.5 percent and 5.5 percent for northerners and southerners respectively, while the national rate is 6.0 percent. The cost of marriage in some communities discourages some young men from marriage. Such men would prefer to own a car and a house, and have a "comfortable" job before marriage.

Family values

Acculturation has brought about changes in family values, which now include decisions on *"what type* of family to form," *"where,"* and *"who* does *what."* Economics dictate the structure and the function of the modern family. In the extended family, the means of survival was basically farming. The family compound was inherited. Membership was ascriptive; husband/wife plus paternal grandparents (sometimes with maternal grandmother), paternal uncles/aunts, cousins, nephews/nieces, and others formed a pattern of settlement. Some family settlements could be larger than others, depending on the number of integrated households occupying the family land. The oldest male took charge of this extended family. Husbands owned farmlands. Wives and children worked for the husband/father. At a specified age (which varied from one community to the other), the male child was given a portion of land. The female child was being prepared for marriage. Role selection or role stratification was virtually non-existent since important roles were ascribed by age and sex. Obedience and discipline were inculcated into role performances.

CHANGES IN THE FAMILY

A few couples choose to stay with grandparents/parents only to care for them, or for the parents themselves to care for their grandchildren, as the need arises. A situation that is arising in the Nigerian family is that wives/mothers and children are staying in separate locations from the husbands/fathers because of constant transfers of the husband/father (Omolara, 1995). The membership of a family could still be as large as 30 persons and as small as 6 (Mivanyi, 2002). Family functions in Nigeria are really becoming more structural (theoretical) than practical, unintentionally, depending on who among the members of the family is "more privileged" to carry out what function, economically and socially. Kitchen chores are no longer reserved for the girl child or the mother. In some families the father's power is minimally felt, while the mother's increases. Increase in formal education gives freedom to the child too early. Individualism, in all facets of family life, is strengthening among family members.

CONCLUSIONS

The extended family structure still exists in Nigeria, although not to the same extent as in the past. Migration of people through urbanization, formal education, and inter-ethnic marriages are dislodging the "tightness" of the extended structures of the family, both physically and psychologically. Hence family structures and functions are becoming liberal. The family as an institution in Nigeria will continue to remain, although the structure and function are changing. The leadership of the family, for example, may eventually depend on either the father or the mother, or on equal partnership. Control is likely to be ascribed to the person providing for the needs of the family members. It is likely also that the more responsible the public institutions, including religious institutions, become, the greater will be the attachment of individuals to them, thereby reducing family bonds and authority.

31 Pakistan: culture, community, and familial obligations in a Muslim society

Riffat Moazam Zaman, Sunita Mahtani Stewart, and Taymiya Riffat Zaman

A HISTORICAL OUTLINE OF PAKISTAN

Although Pakistan is a recent political creation, the roots of its culture and society can be traced back to the Indus Valley civilization (*c.* 2500–1600 BC). For the last 1,000 years, the regions that constitute Pakistan today have been predominantly Muslim. The rule of the Muslim Mughal Empire in India formally came to an end in 1857, when the British (who had originally entered India as traders in the early seventeenth century) placed India directly under the crown and made Queen Victoria the Empress of India. For the following hundred years India was a British colony, and in 1947 when the British left India, Pakistan became an independent nation and a national homeland for Muslims. After Partition, East Pakistan, which had many linguistic and cultural differences from West Pakistan, seceded to become Bangladesh in 1971. Pakistan's present-day population is approximately 140 million, making it the seventh most populous country in the world. Islamabad is its capital, with a population of 805,000.

ECOLOGICAL FEATURES

Pakistan is bordered by India in the east, China in the north, and Iran and Afghanistan in the west. The landscape of the country is diverse; it has a coastline on the Arabian sea, long stretches of desert, fertile plains, and some of the highest mountain peaks in the world. Pakistan is divided into four provinces: Sindh, Punjab, Baluchistan, and The North-West Frontier Province (NWFP). More than half of the people of Pakistan live in the plains of the Punjab, which are irrigated by the five tributaries of the River Indus and make up a quarter of Pakistan's total land area. About a quarter of its population lives in Sindh, which takes up 17.7 percent of the land area and is more urbanized than the Punjab. The

427

remaining population is scattered throughout the deserts of Baluchistan and the mountains of the Frontier Province. Neither of these provinces is as urbanized or agrarian as Sindh and Punjab and they are populated mostly by tribes.

The climate, like the landscape, consists of extremes. The monsoon season brings rain, but there is little rain for the rest of the year. The climate of the deserts is hot and dry all year round, while temperatures in the northern areas can drop to below freezing in the winter months, which last for more than half the year. The Punjab plains experience hot, long summers and short, cold winters, while the coastal areas of Sindh usually experience warm weather all year round.

ORGANIZATION AND INSTITUTIONS OF SOCIETY

Economy

The economy of Pakistan is mostly agrarian, especially because most of the population is sustained by the crops grown in the Punjab. These crops form the backbone of Pakistan's exports. Pakistan's major crops are cotton, wheat, rice, and sugarcane. The growing trend of industrialization and urbanization has meant that Pakistan has developed industrial counterparts to its agrarian base, namely strong textile and sugar industries and steel, cement, fertilizer, electric goods, and shipbuilding industries. Employment by sectors of economic activity are: agriculture (48 percent), industry (18 percent), and services (34 percent). Urbanization has also meant that many people have moved from rural areas into larger cities in search of work. Pakistan's largest cities are Islamabad, Karachi (a megacity with a population of 13 million), Lahore, Peshawar, Quetta, Rawalpindi, Hyderabad, Multan, Sialkot, and Faisalabad.

Political and social trends

The figure of Mohammed Ali Jinnah, the founder of Pakistan, is the only national symbol in Pakistan that united all social classes. Even today, he is seen both as a religious reformer and as a secular visionary. After his death in 1948, the conflicts between the classes became more apparent, as national identity was left to Pakistan's successive governments, none of which was able to command the same unity as Jinnah. As a result, Pakistan is still struggling between two identities; the westernized elites believe that there is progress in secularism and look toward Western models of nation-building, while the vernacular classes see the Western model of development as threatening to a religious identity and hope to increase the role of Islam in guiding all aspects of life and creating national institutions of law and order.

The Muslim League, which was the only political party in Pakistan after independence, was unable to secure a lasting government, and this set a precedent in later years for military rule. In many ways, Pakistan's leaders have struggled to secure a base for power; Ayub Khan's government in the 1960s was military, progressive, and secular, Bhutto's government in the 1970s was socialist, and Zia-ul-Haq's military government in the 1980s was focused on restoring Islam to the realm of social and political life. Pakistan's governments are an external manifestation of conflicts that take place at a familial and societal level where the elite westernized classes own most of the country's wealth and often hold posts in the government, while the class of Muslim scholars, the *ulema*, have little say in government, but hold enormous influence within the masses. The conflict between secular, Western values, and more conservative, Muslim values is arguably the most intense among the emerging middle classes, where children of Urdu-speaking parents have access to English education and media, and face conflicts with their parents whose values differ from those they are taught at school.

Education

Three kinds of educational systems exist in Pakistan. Private schools, in which the medium of instruction is English, are found in most large cities, whereas public schools, in which Urdu is the medium of instruction, are found in both rural and urban areas, more in the latter than the former. Schools run by mosques are known as *madrassas,* where children are instructed in religious texts, namely the Koran, and taught Arabic and Persian. Of these schools, *madrassas* are a legacy of Muslim rule, while private English schools are a legacy of British rule. The overall literacy rate of Pakistanis is 42.7 percent, with this figure being 55.3 percent in males and 29 percent in females (Government of Pakistan, 2002). There is a large variation in literacy levels between genders, provinces, and rural and urban populations. The province of Baluchistan has the lowest overall literacy rate (24.5 percent) while the provinces of Punjab and Sindh have the highest in the country, 43.8 percent and 43.6 percent respectively. The larger cosmopolitan cities, Karachi, Lahore, and Islamabad, have overall literacy rates of 65.9 percent, 69.1 percent, and 77.2 percent, respectively. Females as percentage of total school enrollment are: primary 43 percent, secondary 41 percent, and tertiary 40 percent.

Religion

Even though the presence of autonomous tribal areas has meant that the population of Pakistan is linguistically and ethnically diverse, 95 percent of Pakistanis are Muslims. The remaining population is composed of Christians, Parsis, and Hindus. Since Pakistan was made for Muslims, religion has been an important uniting factor.

CULTURE AND THE MUSLIM COMMUNITY

While many cultural factors have contributed to the family system that exists in Pakistan, religion remains a dominant influence. As a result of the central role of Islam many similarities can be traced between family structures in Pakistan and those that exist in other Muslim countries where a majority of the citizens are practicing Muslims. On the other hand, Pakistani culture has incorporated within it many customs of the predominantly Hindu culture of South Asia that had existed for many years prior to Muslim dominance in the region. For instance, while there is no social stigma attached to widows and divorced women in Arab Muslim countries, in Pakistan such stigmatization is common, as it is in India. The "dowry" system (money, property, and other gifts given to the woman by her family) that is practiced by Pakistanis is a derivative of Hindu customs, even though the expense of weddings in Islam is to be borne entirely by the groom's family, and is the norm in many Muslim countries. It is interesting to note that these two family customs, which are a residue of years of intermingling between Muslims and Hindus, both work to the disadvantage of women.

Within the national consciousness Islam generally takes precedence over other cultural factors. It is able to cut across social and economic classes, even though emphasis given to it and its role may vary in the life of Pakistani families. Family and community figure prominently in both the religious principles and the history of Islam. The Koran, which Muslims believe to be the revealed word of God, not only provides spiritual guidance, but is also considered to be a source of guidance for legislative and judicial procedures. Historically, Muslims believe that they are part of a larger *Ummah,* which can be translated roughly as a nation or community. What binds and characterizes this community is a belief in one God, Allah, the Prophet Mohammad as His messenger and the *Sharia* (Islamic Law) as the guide to all aspects of a Muslim's life.

THE FAMILY

Pakistani culture, like many others, is not monistic. Cultural variations are related to ethnicity (Balochi, Sindhi, Punjabi, Pakhtun, etc.), socio-economic factors, literacy, and whether a family is rural or urban. Within the urban setting, cultural norms within a town may differ from those in a megacity like Karachi. Nevertheless, a hierarchical structure is generally maintained, as is a segregation of work and duties between genders.

Family structure

The most prevalent family structure living under one roof is an extended one, both vertically and horizontally, and may include three generations, grandparents, sons with their wives and children, and unmarried siblings. Therefore, one household may include several cousins being raised together. Cousins are generally referred to as brothers or sisters, sometimes adding the prefix "through-my-maternal-aunt" or "through-my-paternal-uncle." There is no word equivalent of "cousin" in the Urdu language. Similarly, generic words such as "aunt," "uncle" or even "grandparents," have no equivalent in Urdu. The terms used are specific to each relationship, i.e., a *khala* is always the mother's sister and a *phuphee* the father's.

Nuclear families are less prevalent, and generally found in urban settings. In most cases though, parents reside with married sons, usually the oldest one. In the last two decades as increasing numbers of young adults have migrated to the West, there are now instances of elderly parents living by themselves. Pakistani society is partrilineal and patri-local. According to Islamic law all sons inherit equal portions of the property and each daughter half of this amount. A married woman can hold property in her name on which the husband does not have any claim. Property and other assets can be gifted in one's lifetime to any family number.

According to the Islamic law, a divorced woman has custody of her children until the age of seven years, after which custody is generally determined on the welfare of the child/children. In all cases the father remains the legal guardian and is financially bound to provide for the children; however, in reality this does not always happen.

Marriage

In Islam, Muslims must marry Muslims, men are permitted to marry women who are *Ehle Kitab*, i.e., women from among the People of the

Book (Christians and Jews). Women can marry non-Muslims only after the prospective spouse converts to Islam. By and large people prefer to marry within their own ethnic groups. Marriages between first cousins and relatives are not uncommon, since they are sanctioned in Islam. While divorce is allowed in Islam it is socially not accepted, and therefore the rate of divorce is low in Pakistan. Remarriage for a divorced woman is difficult, especially if she has children. In cases where a woman remarries, her parents may take on the responsibility of raising her children from her first marriage. Islam allows a man to have up to four wives, with a stipulation that he treats them with fairness and equality. The Muslim Family Laws Ordinance of Pakistan promulgated in 1961 made it mandatory for a man seeking a second wife to get permission from an Arbitration Council. The request for permission is to be submitted together with a statement of "the reasons for proposed marriage and whether the consent of the existing wife or wives has been obtained" (Ahmed, 1982). A marriage without permission of the Arbitration Council may attract penal action, but it does not invalidate the other marriage. Unfortunately, owing to low female literacy rates and an androcentric, patriarchal structure of Pakistani society, this Ordinance may not have served as a major deterrent to men who wish to take a second wife. Nevertheless, polygamy is not very common in Pakistan and this may be due to economic constraints.

Obtaining a spouse for the adult child is the responsibility of the parents, with help from the extended family. Since marriage is a union of two families rather than two individuals, parents look for compatibility between the two families. Typically, the boy's parents take a *rishta* (marriage proposal) to the girl's parents. In modern, urban families where there are more opportunities for young men and women to socialize with each other, marriages often take place by choice. In such cases too, consent and approval of the parents is required. The two main marriage ceremonies are the *Ruksati*, a reception given by the bride's family, followed by a *Valima* (a dinner for family and friends), given by the groom's family. After marriage, the wife resides with the husband's family, which includes his parents and his siblings. In more "modern" families, couples may reside independently, though close bonds with their families of origin continue. This pattern of material independence with emotional interdependence has been seen to evolve in collectivistic cultures where urbanization and industrialization are on the increase (Kağıtçıbaşı, 1996b).

Family roles and functions

The family structure is strictly hierarchical, where power structures are clearly defined along sex and age; wisdom is attributed to age and therefore grandparents and other "elders" in the extended family command respect and loyalty. Open expression of negative feelings toward parents and elders is neither allowed nor accepted (Zaman, 1992). Gender roles are clearly differentiated with the separation of domains "inside" and "outside" the home.

Pakistan, like other collective cultures, places greater value on obedience, fulfilling of duties and obligations than "rights" of the individual family member. Parenting promotes respect for elders, interpersonal harmony and stresses mutual interdependence rather than individual autonomy (Stewart, Bond, Ho, Zaman, Dar, and Anwar, 2000). Parental warmth, which is a universal parenting dimension, is coupled with parental control, which is more for female than male children. Maintaining family *izzat* (honor) and social approval are important aspects of childrearing (Stewart, Bond, Zaman, McBride-Chang, Rao and Fielding, 1999). Typically, the father is the head of the family and the chief breadwinner, until the adult sons can contribute to the family's finances. The woman's responsibility as a mother is to manage the home and children, and take care of her parents-in-law. In general, maintaining family harmony is the wife's responsibility. Mothers in Muslim families have a central role, in that Traditions of the Prophet are said to ascribe heaven to be under a mother's feet. In other words, devotion to the mother is the path that leads to Paradise. Respect, reverence, and looking after the mother is a fundamental duty of children. Mothers wield considerable power and influence through their adult children, especially the sons. In many traditional families, the matriarch can be a force to be reckoned with. This is often a source of conflict between the mother-in-law, daughter-in-law, and son/husband triad.

In joint families, it is the obligation of sons to pool their incomes to maintain their families, and take care of their unmarried sisters. In traditional homes, an older brother may postpone his marriage until his sisters have been married first. Daughters are perceived as *amanat*, which is a "keepsake," i.e., something you are taking care of until it is returned to the one to whom it rightly belongs. The true home of a daughter is considered to be with her husband and in-laws. Following marriage, the emotional bond of daughters with their family of origin, especially the mother, remains strong. In a qualitative study (Stewart, Zaman, and Dar, under review) of middle-class mothers, respondents emphasized the importance of preparing their adolescent daughters to adjust to their marital lives. As one respondent stated "we prefer sons but love our daughters more."

It is interesting to note that in a recent study (Stewart, Zaman, Chang, Dar, and Bond, under review) while "autonomy" as a perceived need was endorsed by adolescents (boys as well as girls) and their mothers, its relative importance to relatedness as a need was rated as less important. Thus, in the Pakistan culture both men and women are equally enmeshed within strong family bonds where interrelatedness, responsibilities, and needs of others take precedence over autonomy and independence.

32   The Saudi society: tradition and change

Mustafa M. Achoui

A HISTORICAL OUTLINE OF SAUDI ARABIA

The Arabian Peninsula is the homeland of Arabs. Arabs are descendants of the Semitic tribes, which still maintain tribal affiliations today. Arabia was the cradle of Islam. Islam started with the revelation of the Holy Koran in Meccah in AD 610. In 622, the prophet Mohammad migrated to Al-Madinah and established the first Islamic state.

The contemporary history of the actual Saudi Arabia kingdom is traced back to 1744. In that year Al-Shaikh Mohammad Ibn Abdul Wahhab met prince Mohammad Bin Sa'ud in Al-Daraiya. The two agreed to call for Al-Tawheid (oneness of Allah/God) in establishing religion as a way of life. 1902 marked the history of the new Arabia. In 1904 King Abdul Aziz Ibn Sa'ud had recovered all the territory in Al-Najd, the central part of the country. In 1927 the British, who had established Arabia as a protectorate in 1915, acknowledged the independence of the two kingdoms of Al-Hijaz in the Western region under Al-Sharif Al-Hussein, and Al-Najd in the central region under Abdul Aziz Ibn Sa'ud. In 1932, these two kingdoms were unified and named the Kingdom of Saudi Arabia under the leadership of King Abdul Aziz. The population of Saudi Arabia is about 21,009,900 (including about seven million foreigners). Seventy-seven percent of the population is urban and 23 percent is rural. Riyadh is the capital, with 4,300,000 inhabitants.

ECOLOGICAL FEATURES

Saudi Arabia consists mainly of deserts in the north and south and its surface is 2,149,690 km^2. The highest mountains are along the length of the country's narrow Red Sea coastal plain. Temperatures are cooler

This research is sponsored by King Fahd University of Petroleum and Minerals, Saudi Arabia. The author wishes to acknowledge the help of Dr. Bazid Khalid in collecting data.

during winter (between 14°C and 23°C), and extremely hot during summer (between 30°C and 50°C).

ORGANIZATION AND INSTITUTIONS OF SOCIETY

Economic organization

The ecological features of Saudi Arabia shaped specific traditional types of subsistence patterns until oil production began in 1938. Saudi Arabia has the largest crude oil reserves, approximately 25 percent, in the world. Since 1970, planning for development was introduced as a modern way of organizing economic activities and changing the society. The traditional forms of subsistence patterns, such as growing palms and vegetables and keeping camels and sheep have given way to increased oil-related businesses and industrialization. Despite industrial development, oil and petroleum products still account for more than 90 percent of the income. Because of this economic development, most people in the country have become urban dwellers. About 79.2 percent of the labor force is in the government sector. The private sector employment constitutes only 16 percent of the total workforce. The labor force employment stands at 16 percent in agriculture, 20 percent in industry, and 74 percent in services.

Political institutions and legal system

Historically, the Bedouin tribes throughout the Arabia had a measure of self-governance. The head (*al-shaykh*) of the tribe had absolute authority over the tribe (*al-kabilah*). Generally, the *shaykh*, who is usually a wise and old man, governs people who form clans and tribes on the basis of consensus (*ijma'a*) in an informal council. The political system in the country is a monarchy and its legal system is based on *Shari'a* or "Islamic legislation."

The educational system

According to Al-Saif (1997), the percentage of illiteracy among the population (above 15) was 48.9 percent in 1982, higher among females (69.2 percent) than among males (28.9 percent). However, the level of literacy is improving. According to 1999 statistics, about 4,5000,000 students were enrolled in educational institutions from kindergarten to higher education. The percentage of females attending elementary schools and universities is almost equal to that of males. Interestingly, the number of females (124,785 students) in higher education is higher than the number of males (114,795 students).

Religion

Saudi Arabia has a very prestigious religious status in the Muslim world because it houses the Muslims' two holy shrines: *Al-Masjid Al-Haram* (The holy mosque) in Meccah and the *Al-Masjid Al-Nabawi* (Prophet Moham-med's mosque) in Al-Madinah. More than two million Muslims perform pilgrimages (*Haj*) to Meccah every year. Saudis are all Muslims. Islam plays a significant role in all Saudis' aspects of life. The mosque as a religious and a social system plays a significant role in satisfying the people's spiritual and psychosocial needs, such as affiliation and socialization among people who live in the same neighborhood (Al-Khalifa, 1990).

BONDS WITH GROUPS IN THE IMMEDIATE COMMUNITY

The traditional social bonds in the Saudi society are based on blood relationship in the same tribe (*Al-Kabilah*). Traditionally, individuals' loyalty is mainly to the tribe and its leader. The tribe is the basis of the society. Social distinction is not made on the basis of wealth but on the basis of honor, generosity, and trustworthiness (Al-Khariji, 1983). How-ever, social distinction is made also on the basis of which tribe one belongs to.

Structurally, tribal groups are defined by common patrilineal descent that unites individuals in increasingly larger segments. Although tribes may differ in their status, all lineage of a given tribe is considered equal. Cole (1973) noted that four to six patrilineally related lineages are grouped together in a clan. The community bonds with groups in the immediate community of the traditional isolated communities and tribes were characterized by the power of ingroup, composed not only of the members of the extended family, but of distant relatives and in-laws. Consequently, the ingroup within the Saudi tribes is essentially collect-ivistic in nature. However, this characteristic is moving more toward individualism in the large cities. The power of the traditional ingroup has lessened, and the individual is able to join a variety of ingroups, a characteristic of complex societies, such as associations, and clubs (Al-Saif, 1997).

Today, the traditional social bonds and social relationships are changing in the Saudi large cities because of urbanization and rapid economic development. They are, in fact, becoming weaker in kind and number (Al-Masa'ad, 1995). In remote areas, social bonds are stronger than in cities. Islamic jurisprudence and traditions are the basis of regulating social bonds such as marriage, divorce, and inheritance.

THE FAMILY

Marriage

In regard to endogamy in the traditional family, marriage was restricted to potential spouses from the same tribe. However, some of these restrictions vary in different regions of the country. In the central part of the country, for example, these restrictions are more observed while they are less observed in the Western region such as in Meccah and Jeddah. In regard to exogamy, the dominant marriage pattern is among first cousins, primarily to the sons and daughters of the uncle/father's brothers. Marriage with the sons and daughters of mother's sisters and brothers used to be less frequent than with father's relatives. Now, the trend is in the opposite direction. The main reason is the increasing influence of the mothers on the selection of their son's wives (Al-Saif, 1997). However, young and educated people tend to select their wives from different tribes, groups, and clans. The groom or his family should present a dowry (bride price), which usually consisted of jewelery or any valuable thing, to the bride. This is an obligatory duty of the groom or his family toward the bride, according to Islamic teachings. No marriage would be considered legal without this dowry, regardless of its value. The husband, according to Islamic teachings, is in charge of his family's and must be the one who shoulders the family's financial burdens even if his wife is working or rich, unless she makes concessions.

The divorce rate in Saudi Arabia is increasing. The total number of registered divorce cases in the kingdom was 17,528 in 1998. This number represents 23 percent of the total marriages in the country in the same year. This percentage was 22 percent in 1989. The national rate of divorce was about 1.35 percent in 1999. The main causes of divorce according to Al-Saif (1997) are women working, polygamy, family pressures, family interference, and sexual maladjustment.

Polygamy is another phenomenon that is dramatically changing and decreasing because of urbanization, education, development, and cost of living. Generally, educated and employed women gain more independence and consequently reject polygamy. Some parents and young females put monogamy as a condition before marriage. Putting such conditions is acceptable by the Islamic teachings. Ghraib (1991) found that 86.8 percent of husbands in the Gulf (Qatar, Kuwait, United Arab Emirates, Oman, Bahrain, and Saudi Arabia) have only one wife, 9.6 percent have two wives, 1.1 percent have three wives and only 0.3 percent have four wives; 74.7 percent had married their relatives; and 25.5 percent live with their extended families. Al-Saif (1997) found that in

Saudi Arabia, only 4.8 percent of parents approve of their daughters marrying a husband who has another wife. This rate is much lower than the previous rate of 14.5 percent.

In the traditional family, decisions to marry were made mainly by both families. Although, fathers are believed to play a major role in decision-making regarding this issue, mothers in reality play a greater role, more hidden but more influential, in this decision. Married women in Saudi Arabia as is the case in all Muslim countries preserve the names of fathers' families and tribes as a part of their identity, according to Islamic teachings.

Family structure

The traditional Saudi extended family structure could be described as tribal and *patrilineal* in terms of lineal descent, in which kin of both sexes were related through the men only. It could also be described as patri-archal in that the father or the grandfather had the legal power and social norms that supported his authority. The characteristic type of family in Saudi large cities is moving towards nuclear, although relatives tend to live near each other even in large cities that are expanding horizontally more than vertically. Therefore, interaction among relatives can be achieved more easily. The extended family included usually three generations: grandparents, sons/fathers, daughters/mothers, and children, in which grandfather was the head of the family in terms of authority structure, and with collateral kin (cousins, uncles and aunts, nieces and nephews), and with *affinal* relationships (parents-in-law, children-in-law, and siblings-in-law).

Residence after marriage was *patrilocal*, in that the married sons res-ided in or near the father's residence. The married daughter is tradition-ally supposed to live in or near the house of the father-in-law. The mother-in-law has authority over the daughter-in-law. Even in large cities one might notice that married children are supposed to live near to their parents if not in the same house. The trend among educated married spouses is to be independent from the parents even if they are supposed to live near them as a social obligation.

Family roles and functions

Traditionally, the father in the Saudi family is the breadwinner and the mother is the housekeeper. The grandparents are highly respected and play a great role in deciding about many family issues. Women are not expected in traditional families to work outside the house, family prop-erty and ingroup boundaries. Consequently, the rate of Saudi women in the labor force is still minimal (about 6 percent). However, rapid economic change has influenced the family functions in Saudi Arabia. Since 1970, almost all young females have attended school. Consequently, marriage is delayed and the percentage of non-married girls is increasing. Al-Khariji (1983) argued that the higher the female education, the lower her chance of marriage unless she married before finishing her studies. On the other hand, Al-Saif (1997) stressed that a new trend is developing. Saudi families, in general, do support women working outside the family, on condition of respect for Islamic traditions and not mixing with men. He reported that 52 percent of Saudi women are inclined to work outside the family for financial reasons, and 50 percent are motivated to work in order to achieve self-actualization and gain a social role and status. He maintained that the spouses do support their wives working, despite the associated shortcomings of being outside the home. Al-Saif (1997) also mentioned that the social and economic changes in Saudi Arabia since 1970 created changes in some roles and social status of many individuals and functions in the society. He maintained, however, that the relationship between the roles and the status is not always positive. For example, the role of women in society is changing positively but their status is still traditional. Parents and grandparents play a significant role in resolving any family conflicts. Female children are expected to help their mothers while male children are expected to help their fathers. Female children should also help and serve their fathers and brothers at home. However, maids in Saudi rich and middle-class families are taking over most of the mother's functions such as caring for children, cooking, and cleaning.

CHANGES IN THE FAMILY

Demographics

The government "Chart" states in article 9 that: "The family is the nucleus of the Saudi society." Some sociologists such as Al-Saif (1997) think that this new organization of society is positive because it stresses the importance of the family rather than the tribe or the individual. The marriage age is, for example, an indicator of the impact of urbanization on the Saudi family. Females used to marry at a very early age: between 13–16 years old. This tradition is changing. The age of marriage among females is now between 20 and 25 years of age. Males used to marry between 15 and 18. At present, the majority of young males prefer to delay their marriage. About 60 percent of Saudi youths prefer not to get married early because of the expenses of marriage (Al-Saif, 1997). Late marriage of both males and females might be attributed to several factors, such as increasing years of schooling for both sexes, high expenses of marriage, especially the cost of the dowry (bride price), desire to live independently, and the desire to select their spouse freely (Al-Badran and Al-Rwished, 1989). The birth rate in Saudi Arabia, however, is one of the highest rates in the world (3.5 percent).

Family values

Al-Saif (1997) stated that about 80 percent of the households in Riyadh were originally Bedouins. The majority of the inhabitants live in neighborhoods with people with whom they share mainly the same values, traditions, and blood relationship. However, the social relationships in the Saudi large cities are changing. The social bonds are becoming weaker in kind and number (Al-Masa'ad, 1995). This leaves room for the emergence of more pragmatic relationships.

Unfortunately, there are no available studies about changes in different values. However, sociological studies regarding marriage, values, social bonds, and social change show in general, as indicated above, that family values are changing especially in large cities such as Riyadh, Jeddah, and Dammam because of urbanization, industrialization, and education. Nevertheless, the practices of veiling and gender separation, and the values related to these practices, have not changed. There is little expressed desire for such change because these practices were grounded in fundamental tribal-familial values, sanctioned and institutionalized by the *Ulama* (religious scholars) and the central government.

CONCLUSIONS

Since 1972, the family in Saudi Arabia has been undergoing changes in structure, functions, roles, and status. This change might be attributed to such factors as urbanization, industrialization, education, telecommunication, and the mass media. The family is becoming nuclear in large cities, although most relatives leave near each other in the same neighborhood. This phenomenon explains partially the tremendous horizontal expansion of large cities in Saudi Arabia. The social bonds among relatives and people who belong to the same tribe are still strong. Contact with family members during religious holidays and special events such as marriage is clearly observed. Modern communication technology makes it easier to get in touch with relatives, regardless of their location. Social change because of industrialization, urbanization, and education is clearly observed, especially in large cities. In addition, the attitudes and values that are related to female education and women working outside home or family property are becoming more positive and supportive.

33   The South African family

Adebowale Akande, Bolanle Adetoun,
and Maggie Tserere

A HISTORICAL OUTLINE OF SOUTH AFRICA

After the British seized the Cape of Good Hope area in 1806, many of
the Dutch settlers (the Boers) trekked north to found their own republics. The discovery of gold (1866) and diamonds (1867) spurred wealth
and immigration and intensified the subjugation of the original indigenous Africans. The Boers resisted British encroachment, but were
defeated in the Boer War of 1899–1902. The resulting union of South
Africa operated under a policy of apartheid – a notoriously difficult
phenomenon to characterize. This is evident by the hugely divergent
adumbrations apartheid has received in literature on South African
politics and history. South Africa's present population is approximately
43,647,658 inhabitants, its area of land is 1,217,912 km^2. Pretoria is its
capital, with 1,080,187 inhabitants. In addition to the capital, important
cities are Cape Town (2,350,157), Johannesburg (5,700,000), and
Durban (1,378,792). South Africa is a founding member of the African
Union.

The apartheid project

No blueprint or apartheid grand plan existed by 1948 when the Her-
stigte Nationale Party (HNP) was victorious at the polls (Norval, 2001).
Formed in 1914, the party banned liberation movements including the
Pan-Africanist Congress (PAC) and African National Congress (ANC)
and jailed thousands of activists and political leaders, among them
Nelson Mandela during it rule. It used a "womb to tomb" surveillance
plan for the subjugated African populations, as well as the overtly racist
construction of the black Africa or North Africa (Mandela, 1994; Mbeki,
2002; Norval, 2001; Seepe, 2004).

The apartheid government eventually negotiated itself out of power
and in 1994 the new government led by Mandela and his ANC
party extended democracy to the rest of the population and encouraged

442

reconciliation. Thabo Mbeki became president in 1999 after Mandela retired. The New National Party (NNP) that rebranded from the National Party disbanded to join ANC (those they had oppressed) in August 2004.

ORGANIZATION AND INSTITUTIONS OF SOCIETY

Economic organization

South Africa is an anomaly, having a very visible first world infrastructure that coexists with abject poverty comparable to the worst parts of Africa. It has abundant natural resources. It produced almost half of the world's gold and is one of the ten producers of diamonds, as well as copper and several valuable minerals in the world. Its only resource deficiency is oil. The country has one of the strongest economies in the continent, backed by a comprehensive transportation system, media/ high-tech capability, electric power grid, and a major manufacturing sector. The major manufactures include processed food, beverages (like wine), clothing, textiles, chemicals, iron and steel, machinery, and automobiles. The chief seaports are Durban, Cape Town, Port Elizabeth, East London, Saldanha Bay, and Mossel Bay. Despite inadequate irrigation and just about 10 per cent amount of arable land, the country still grows a large amount of wheat, corn, sorghum, peanut, potatoes, cotton, citrus fruits, sugarcane, and tobacco. Also, large numbers of dairy and beef cattle, goats, hogs, and sheep are raised. The country has a large fishing industry and a tremendous amount of fishmeal is produced.

By 2004, services contributed almost 62 per cent of GNP while industry contributed 35 per cent and agriculture only about 3 per cent. While Africans, coloreds and Asians make up 68 per cent of the workforce, the economy is mainly controlled by Afrikaans-speaking and English-speaking Europeans.

Political institutions and cultural system

South Africa is a multiparty parliamentary republic (Seepe, 2004). It is a fragmented, heterogeneous, and complex society (Murray, 1994). It is a diverse community with 11 official languages. Despite the influence of Christianity and Islam, the majority of the African population still upholds traditional values, language, religion, and customs. These values derive from a distinctive African cosmology characterized by acceptance of a masculine supreme entity as a creator, and acceptance of the belief in ancestral spirits and supernatural powers. With respect to language the Africans can be divided into four main groups, namely the Nguni, the Sotho, the Tsonga Shangaan, and the Venda. The Nguni language group comprises four subgroups of the Zulu-speaking peoples, the Swazi, the Ndebele, and the Xhosa-speaking peoples. The traditional political system is characterized by kings, paramount chiefs, and ward herdmen. They have a deep-rooted fear of incest and therefore prefer exogamic marriages. Initiation ceremonies are performed when children reach the age of puberty, which is considered to be the onset of adulthood. During the ceremony, knowledge and values concerning manhood, procreation, morals, sexual skills, birth control, and pregnancy are passed on to either the boy or girl concerned. Great emphasis is placed on marriage, the solemnization of which can last for days. African art and cultural singing have made a unique contribution to South African cultural life. To the Africans murals and beadwork are not merely decorative. Before the existence of written language, they were the primary form of communication, (Asante, 1993). Different colors carry different meanings, which carry messages pertaining to the social status of a person, so that one can see if a woman is married and how many children she has.

African culture demands people to try to fit in with their social groups. The African self is defined as a relational entity that is made meaningful in reference to the pertinent social relationships to which the self is a part (Akande, 2004). Indeed African individuals see themselves as "fractions" who do not become whole until they have fitted in and occupied their proper place within social groups. For Africans, the feeling of well-being means a sense of acceptance by others. The Africans' concept and use of time is different from the Western people. Traditional Africans live according to the natural rhythm of the seasons rather than insistence on rigidly maintaining schedules to the click of a digital clock (Akande, 2000).

The educational system

A social class stratification strategy was zealously pursued by the National Party Government. Even men of God both in Afrikaans churches and universities (with the exception of intellectuals like Dr. Beyers Naude) were rallied to use their knowledge and pulpits to give credence to this project. Simply put, the strategy was geared at positioning Europeans at the peak of the pecking order, coloureds and Indians (Asians) followed, and at the bottom of the heap, the Africans (called Kaffirs). Laws and policies were used to uphold this hierarchy stringently.

The era of the 1980s represents a turning point, not only in the political history of South Africa but also to the future prospects of the majority of children and youth. Quite a number of unprecedented, "miraculous" developments happened between 1990 and 1996. For example, 1996 marked the passing of the constitution of the Republic of South Africa, which guarantees specific rights to every child, equal access to education and a fair, appropriate treatment for children/ youths accused of having committed a crime (Sachs, 1992).

Higher education is not free in South Africa. The number of universities and polytechnics (or technikons) has been scaled down from 36 to 21. There is still a lot of discrimination regarding staff appointment in the system.

Higher Education in South Africa is seen as a "white masculism" paradigm which is inhospitable to Africans because it consists of concepts, of modes of learning or pedagogy, of epistemology which are peculiar to either Greek or Jewish origin or time or ideology and are not part of the African canon of experience (cf. Makgoba, 1997; Makgoba and Seepe, 2004; Mthembu, 2004). In fact the transformation in higher education has just begun.

Some leaders in this transformation include Professor Sipho Seepe (Acting Vice Chancellor of Vista University); Professor Thandwa Mthembu (Deputy Vice Chancellor at WITS); Professor Tyrone Pretorius (Deputy Vice Chancellor at UWC); Professor Malegapuru Makgoba (Vice Chancellor of UKZN); Professor Kwesi Prah (Director of CASAS); Professor Ad Akande (Director of IRC) and Professor Dolina Dowling (Pro-Vice Chancellor of Bond SA). Some celebrity academics include Professor Bankole Omotoso "Yebo Gogo" and Professor Sipho Seepe. Omotoso is famous for his ingenuity in commercial advertisement-making while Seepe is known for his critical writings/speeches as a public educator.

Religion

South African religion has been a unique blend of Christianity and traditional African beliefs. The Khoisan peoples believed in a supreme being who presides over daily life and controls elements of the environment. In addition, they believed that the sun and the moon were gods and their legends and myths refer to god who can transform himself into animals or human forms.

The Zulus and Xhosas ("red blanket people") believed in a Supreme Being, or high god (*Qamata* or *Tixo*), supported by a group of ancestral spirits – a different pantheon on spiritual beings in the community. The thinking is that the rituals performed by human beings could not influence the actions of the supreme deity, but were just to honour or placate lesser spiritual beings, and sometimes to ask for their intervention. The supreme deity was believed to be a remote transcendent being who possessed the power to create the Earth, but operated beyond human comprehension or manipulations, whereas the ancestors were once human. Some importance is attached to the position of the diviner or *sangoma* in the society. The Europeans practice mainly Christianity and Asians practice Buddhism, Islam, and Hinduism.

BONDS WITH GROUPS IN THE IMMEDIATE COMMUNITY

The family has been regarded as a social and economic unit usually headed by a married man. The women's role within the unit has been associated with service and dependency. Female dependence is emblematic of the established gender and authority relations of the society. For South African women, this dependency on males was not only regarded as the norm but also as a badge of respectability in their community. This is underscored by the hostile attitude toward those women who were not contained within a male-headed family unit, and who had been unable to fulfill the female destiny of marriage and motherhood. Those women who did not live under the protection of a man were regarded as social anomalies or dreadful old maids who constituted a sexual threat to the married and a ready prey to the twin dangers of sexual impropriety and abject poverty. As adults, in sibling households, sisters often took over housekeeping roles supported by the brothers in a financial and emotional bond not dissimilar to the conjugal. Men own the land, which they inherit from their fathers, and could be allocated houseyard land upon marriage. Conversely, women rarely own any principal means of production and they do not have any say in kin-group decisions. The patriarchal extended family is the central social unit, in which the senior man has sole authority over every individual, including the younger men.

Among the other groups (Europeans) in South Africa, there is a protection by the community of the respect for life, respect for one's belongings and a person's honor. Violations of ethical standards or religious rites can provoke the reaction of the community.

THE FAMILY

Marriage

The dominant structure of the society – the family – is somehow breaking down in South Africa. However, the most complex, confusing, sometimes bittersweet and sometimes joyous of human relationships could still be said to be the marriage relationships (Hendrick and Hendrick, 2001). Historically, and even today, before a male was recognized as an adult with the right to marry, he first had to go through the initiation process and be circumcised. Until such time he was perceived as a boy and irresponsibility on his part was expected and condoned. However, females are not circumcised (except South Sotho women). Because of xenophobia, some societies are still against marrying persons from other ethnic groups or countries in Africa. However, this is gradually changing. In regard to endogamy, in the past, specific rules channeled people into marriages within particular groups. Individuals are encouraged and at times forced to marry within ethnic and religious groups, similar class and socioeconomic backgrounds. The custom demands that girls remain virgins until they married, if a girl was not a virgin her father would receive less lobola for her (although this is not true today). In regard to exogamy and incest taboos, there are still rules that prohibit marriage and sexual relationship with one's most closely related biological kin, and between parents and children and brothers and sisters.

Divorce is frowned upon by most people. The maternal father will always aspire to keep the marriage intact in order to avoid being asked to return the lobola. The culture accepts the dominance of males, with occasional beatings usually perceived as an acceptable form (once, not grossly in excess) of spousal control. Most wives believe that their spouses are likely to take other women as wives or companions. Historically, the decision to marry or obtaining a spouse was a family affair, which was finally ratified by a payment of lobola. Prearranged marital agreements are usually entered into by guardians or parents even before the birth of their children. Regarding marital consent, the bride and groom have less legal standing over their marriage than do their parents. This is as a result of the fact that a bride does not simply marry the groom – in African custom she weds the groom and his family. Procreation is one of the most highly valued milestones in African communities. The birth of a child is a great blessing and it is an indication that a person will be better taken care of in declining years – "children are the living messages we send to a time we will not see." Hence, in the olden days, if a woman was unable to conceive, it was customary for a younger sister "to stand in" for her and bear a child for the spouse.

Family structure

The traditional African extended family structure could be said to be tribal and patrilineal in terms of lineal descent, in which kin of both sexes were related through the men only.

The extended family included three generations, grandparents, sons/fathers, daughters/mothers, and children, in which grandfather was the head of the family in terms of authority structure, and with collateral kin (cousins, uncles and aunts, nieces and nephews), and, as well as with affinal relationships (parents-in-law, children-in-law, and siblings-in-law), or best man/maid of honor at the marriage of offspring, or bonds with others through mutual obligations (see the Chapter on Botswana).

Residence after marriage was patrilocal, in that the married sons resided in or near the father's residence. The married daughter is traditionally supposed to live in or around the house of the father-in-law. The mother-in-law has authority over the daughter-in-law. Most cases of divorce are said to be attributed to the constant conflict or rivalry between the daughter-in-law and mother-in-law in South Africa. However, young couples now try to avoid this problem, by choosing to be independent from the in-laws or parents even if as a sort of social obligation they need to live nearby them. This is also the case among whites and other groups in South Africa.

Family roles and functions

In the traditional family, the father in South Africa is the breadwinner or wage earner and the mother is the anchor and nurturer of the family (Nhlapo, 1992). The grandparents are highly respected and play a great role in deciding about many family matters.

CHANGES IN THE FAMILY

Demographics

Profound changes have reshaped South African family life in recent years. In over a decade of democracy, divorce rates have doubled. The number of divorces today is twice as high as in 1995 and three times higher than in 1980. The rapid upsurge in the divorce rate has resulted in a dramatic increase in the number of single-parent households or what used to be known as broken homes. The number of households consisting of a single woman and her children has tripled since 1983. A sharp increase in female-headed homes has been accompanied by a startling increase in the number of couples cohabiting outside marriage. The majority of contemporary women now believe that both partners should have jobs, do household chores, play family roles, and take care of children. What can one say accounts for these upheavals in family life? One of the most far-reaching forces for change has been a sexual revolution far more radical than the mid-twentieth century "revolution in morals and manners." Contemporary South Africans are much more likely than their predecessors to postpone marriage, to live alone, and to engage in sexual intercourse outside marriage.

Family values

The changes that have taken place in family life and values have been disruptive and uneasy and have reshaped the family into a major political battleground. For instance, courtship became more romantic and stylized, women increasingly became the "moral guardians" of the culture, with men needing to have their unbridled passions controlled by women's modesty. Courtship has moved to the practice of dating. Men and women could go out together for an evening by foot or by motorcar, and once again the rules and the power shifted (Akande, 2002; Hendrick and Hendrick, 2001). Just as in America, feminism has played a big role in transforming South African family values. Some feminist activists and literature denounced the current tempo of marriage as "slavery" and "legalized rape." And they critiqued the idea that childcare, nurturing, and housework were the apex of a woman's accomplishments or her sole means of fulfillment. This movement awakened the South African women to what they viewed as the evil of oppression called "sexism."

CONCLUSIONS

The emerging South African family can be described as "the saturated family," whose members feel their lives are scattered in amorphous business. The technologies of psychosocial saturation (e.g., car, ill-gotten wealth, TV, cell phones) have created family turmoil and a sense of discontinuity and fragmentation (cf. Gergen, 1991). The home is no longer a refuge of harmony, understanding, peace, and quiet but the site of dispute and violence between individuals of different ages and gender.

Overall, there is need to call for more complexity in our conceptualization of the family. Without a doubt, the family will remain one of the hottest social and political issues in the years to come.

34 South Korea

Uichol Kim and Young-Shin Park

A HISTORICAL OUTLINE OF SOUTH KOREA

Korean history can be divided into five separate periods: Old Chosun, the Three Kingdoms Period, Koryo Dynasty, Yi Dynasty, and the modern era. These periods span a total of 4,335 years. According to legend, the nation of Chosun (meaning "The Land of the Morning Calm") was founded by a mythical figure known as Tangun. Tangun is said to have unified 3,000 tribes into a single nation and ruled for about 1,200 years before he retreated to a mountain. Chosun subsequently split into various tribes, and they were later united to form the Three Kingdoms consisting of Koguryo, Paekjai, and Shilla.

Shilla was able to unify the peninsula in AD 676 and Buddhism was adopted as the official religion. Confucianism was adopted in the sixth century, influencing the governmental and educational system. In 918, Wanggun founded the Koryo Dynasty, which lasted until 1392, when General Yi Song-gye founded his own dynasty. He established Confucianism as the guideline, not only for government, but also for the private life of the people. In the nineteenth century, Korea retreated into a stringent isolationism and became known as the "Hermit Kingdom." As a staunch Confucian state, Korea resisted all attempts to modernize, until forcefully colonized by Japan in 1910.

With the liberation of Korea from Japan in 1945, Korea was arbitrarily divided along ideological lines by the Soviet Union and the USA. The Korean War erupted in 1950, in which more than three million people lost their lives and the border on the thirty-eighth parallel was eventually reestablished. The division of the two Koreas is still a political reality with the Republic of Korea to the south and the Democratic People's Republic to the north. Currently, there are 48 million people living in South Korea and 22 million people living in North Korea.

ECOLOGICAL FEATURES

The Korean peninsula is approximately 1,000 km in north–south length, and 216 km wide at its narrowest point, with a total area of 220,958 km^2 (approximately the size of the British Isles). In terms of terrain, hills and mountains characterize Korea, accounting for nearly 80 percent of the territory. Korea's climate is temperate, tending toward the continental type with four distinct seasons and typical temperate zone flora and fauna.

ORGANIZATIONS AND INSTITUTIONS OF SOCIETY

Economic organization

In the traditional agrarian society, people settled along the river basins, in between mountain ranges and along the seashores. The population of today's South Korea has become urban, with 90 percent of the population living in urban areas. North Korea remains closed and isolated with all facets of the society being controlled by the communist government. South Korea has adopted capitalism, commercialism and industrialization. It has grown rapidly, with heavy industries (e.g., ship-building, steel industry and automobile industry) and has become one of the major international exporters of electronic goods (e.g., TVs, cellular phones and semiconductors).

Political institutions and legal system

Confucianism provided the main philosophical basis for governing Korean people for centuries. With Western encroachment, communist ideology was adopted by North Korea. From 1945, communist leader Kim Il-sung controlled all facets of North Korean society and his son, Kim Jong-il, succeeded him as the absolute ruler. In South Korea, authoritarian presidents, with the support of the United States, maintained dictatorial control of the country from 1945 to 1987. In 1987, nationwide demonstrations against dictatorship forced the transition to a democratically elected president and National Assembly. The political and legal system consists of three branches: executive branch, legislative branch and the judiciary. The legal system represents a blend of Confucian, German and American influences.

Educational system

In the fourth century, Confucianism was adopted and the National Confucian Academy was established in 373. The National Examination system was established in 788, which selected individuals on the basis of merit for government positions. Western education was introduced through contact with the Western missionaries. With the colonization of Korea, Japan forcibly implemented the German *Volk* school system. From 1945, South Korea adopted the educational system of the United States. The current educational system is a blend of the Confucian, German, and American systems. In international studies of educational achievement, Korean students are ranked at the top in performance in reading, mathematics, and science (Baldi, Perie, Skidmore, Greenberg and Hahn, 2001; Organization for Economic Co-operation and Development, 2004).

Religion

The native religion of Korea is Shamanism (nature-worship). It blended unobtrusively with Buddhism and Confucianism, which entered Korea two thousand years ago. Christianity was introduced more than two hundred years ago. Currently, around 27 percent report being a Christian, 25 percent Buddhist, and 40 percent profess no religion.

BONDS WITH GROUPS IN THE IMMEDIATE COMMUNITY

As a traditional agrarian society, the extended family served as the network and three generations were considered the basic unit of a family. The National census was developed more than a thousand years ago. It kept records of all family members and subsequent generations. Confucianism provided the philosophical basis of viewing society as the extension of the family; it provided an ethical code of behavior for individuals and family members and this code was implemented through a network of regional governments, which was tightly controlled by the central government.

THE FAMILY

Marriage

In regard to endogamy, traditional marriages were restricted to within the same hereditary class. The vast majority belonged to the peasant class and around 10 percent were the landed aristocrats. In regard to exogamy, Confucian law strictly forbade marrying a person from the same region with the same surname. This law was enforced until recent years.

Social sanctions against divorce were severe. Since the family served as a basic unit, divorce was considered as the last resort (e.g., a woman failing to give birth to a son). Divorce for a woman was considered disastrous, since she would be denied access to her children, inheritance, and would become a social outcast. With modernization and affluence, divorce laws have been changed recently with the women having equal rights to men.

In the traditional family, a decision to marry was made by parents of both families, with the father having the final word. If grandparents were alive, they played an important role in the decision-making process. Currently, parents play an advisory role, but their blessing and support are considered to be essential. If the parents oppose the marriage, many young people spend months trying to convince and coax their parents to approve the marriage.

A professional go-between or a well-known acquaintance provided a bridging role in introducing a spouse in the traditional family. The parents of the groom provided a home for the couple to live in and the parents of the bride provided the furniture, clothing, and household goods. This system still exists in modern Korea with the parents of the groom being expected to purchase the house and the parents of the bride being expected to furnish the home with all the necessary appliances, furniture and household goods.

Family structure

The traditional family structure was *patrilineal* and *patriarchical*. The lineage was defined through the father, who held the authority, power and resources. Once a daughter was married, she was no longer considered a part of her childhood family. Inheritance was passed down to the sons, with the oldest son inheriting the largest sum.

Three generations constituted the basic family unit, with grandparents and parents living with their children. Unmarried paternal uncles and aunts would typically live together in the same house. Collateral kin on the father's side would typically live in the same neighborhood. Affinal kin (i.e., in-laws) would typically live in another village, some distance away from their daughter.

The place of residence after marriage was patrilocal after three years of marriage. The husband would spend his first three years after marriage with his wife's family and then live out the rest of his life with his parents.

Although the patrilineal system is still being maintained in modern Korea, the authority of the patriarch has been eroded. Currently, newly-weds live by themselves and both parents are considered to be equally important.

Family roles and function

In Korea, family serves as the basic unit and the conceptions of past and future are not abstract ideas, but they are relationally defined. Parents represent the past and the children represent the future. Since the children represent the future of the family, tremendous emotional, financial and social investments are made for them and in them. Parental devotion and indulgence are two important features of the traditional socialization practice that still remain in modern Korea. Parents view unselfish devotion and sacrifice to their children as their basic role and duty. Korean parents see their children as extensions of themselves. Children's accomplishments become their own and they vicariously fulfill their own dreams and goals (Park and Kim, 2004).

A mother represents the inner world of the child and the father represents the outside world. The role that a father and mother play is both different and complementary. It is summarized in a popular Korean phrase "strict father, generous mother." In a mother–child relationship, a mother shows her devotion to her child through sacrifice and indulgence (i.e., it flows downward, from a mother to a child). In a father–child relationship, children are required to display their devotion to their father through obedience, respect and compliance (i.e., it flows upward, from a child to a father).

Father

The father represents the family and makes decisions for the family. As the head of the family, the father represents a link between the family and the outside the world. Through the father, children are linked across time (i.e., through his lineage) and across space (i.e., through his position in a community). One of the prime responsibilities of the father is to have a son who can continue the family line. The other main responsibility is to educate his son. As the head of the household, he holds the authority to represent the family, to speak and act on behalf of the family, but not against the family. For example, property was the communal possession of a family, and not the father. Although the father had the right to dispose of the property, the other family members also had rights to the property. An arbitrary decision by the father against the family was considered uncustomary and an illegitimate act (Kim, 1995). A father had the authority, duty and responsibility of handling family property on behalf of the family and not for himself.

Mother

A mother is responsible for raising the children, ensuring that the children respect and obey their father, taking care of elderly parents and relatives and managing household affairs. She socializes her sons and daughters differently. The son is taught to lead and become a breadwinner and the daughter is taught to support her future husband and family. The mother is responsible for managing the household affairs, including household finance, maintaining social relationships and ensuring that the children are properly socialized. She is also responsible for ensuring that the daughter-in-law is respectful to her son and actively participates in the socialization of the grandchildren.

Grandparents

The age of 60 represents a full cycle in one's life. It represents a second birth. At this age, the father typically passes his property and power to his eldest son and the son becomes responsible for managing the family affairs. He takes on the role of the grandfather. Similarly, the mother passes her role and responsibility to the eldest daughter-in-law and takes on the role of the grandmother. They no longer hold major responsibilities and they are to be taken care of and indulged like children.

Women

In traditional Korea, individuals are defined by their roles as a mother, father, brother or sister and not by categories such as gender. Women as mothers or sisters had traditionally supportive and subservient roles. With modernization, women now have equal rights. Women have equal rights in the case of divorce and also in the case of inheritance.

Children

Children are not viewed as a separate entity but the most important part of the self and family. When children are born, they are perceived as helpless beings that need to be indulged and cared for. When a child is born, a mother remains close to the child to make the child feel secure, to make the boundary between herself and the child minimal, and to meet all of the needs of the child. Children's strong dependency needs, both emotional and physical, are satisfied by their mother's indulgent devotion, even if it means a tremendous sacrifice on her own part. As children mature, they sense that it is through the mother that they obtain gratification, security and love. As such, children become motivated to maintain a close relationship. The mother uses her strong emotional bond with the child to encourage the child to transfer and extend himself or herself to the father, siblings, relatives, friends and teachers when children enter school.

CHANGES IN THE FAMILY

With modernization, urbanization and industrialization, the traditional extended families have virtually disappeared. In 1975, the average size of household was more than five, but this has been reduced to three in 2002 (Korea National Statistics Office, 2003). Currently, fewer than one in ten families have three generations living under one roof.

Many young people have moved to cities, and rural villages are now sparsely populated. Fertility rate has also seen a dramatic decrease: 6.0 in 1960, 4.7 in 1970, 2.7 in 1980, 1.6 in 1990, and as low as 1.2 in 2004. Coupled with urbanization, the rate of marriage has decreased from 10 per 1,000 persons in 1980 to 7 in 2000. The divorce rate has increased from 0.6 per 1,000 in 1980 to 2.5 in 2000.

Family values

The traditional family structure, type, size and residency have changed significantly in the past 40 years. These societal changes brought forth some changes in family values and some values remain constant. The traditional focus of the past, emphasizing the role of ancestors and grandparents, has changed to focus on the children. The traditional focus on sex-role differentiation has changed to sex-role equality in which women have equal access to learning, power and resources. The traditional focus on having many children and boy preference has changed to having just one child and not having any gender preference. Although family structure, type and size have changed, the importance of family has not declined. In an intergenerational study of adolescents, adults and elderly, harmony in the family was rated as the most important value for all three samples and this result has been consistently replicated over many generations (Kim, Park, Kim, Lee, and Yu, 2000).

CONCLUSIONS

In the traditional agricultural communities, the family served as the unit of survival. People had many children so that the family line would continue, to ensure adults were provided for when they became old and weak, and to ensure siblings were able to take care of each other when the parents passed away. In traditional Korea, Confucianism helped to maintain the conservative, patriarchical and agrarian society (Kim, 1995). Power was concentrated in the hands of few and men had access to power and resources. The rights of women were virtually non-existent and their identity was defined by their role as a daughter, wife and mother.

Modernization, industrialization and urbanization helped to transform Korean society and family. From 1965, the Korean economy grew at a rapid pace, along with educational, social and democratic reforms. Although many people assume that Korea has simply adopted Western lifestyles, this is not the case. The past-oriented Confucian philosophy was replaced by the future-oriented version (Kim, 2001). Koreans no longer invest much of their time and energy on their ancestor or parents, but on their children, who represent their future.

In modern society, family members, relatives and the number of children no longer determine whether one succeeds in life. It is much more important to have educational, financial and professional knowledge to have a high quality of life. Modern life provides people with more resources, time and freedom of choice. Koreans live longer, are healthier and wealthier, and with more modern conveniences than ever before. The family values have changed from past-orientation (i.e., ancestors and grandparents) to future-orientation (i.e., the success of children). Although family structure, size and residency have changed, the importance of family and maintaining harmony within the family have not changed for many generations. It is the most important life-goal for Koreans of all ages.

35   Spain: tradition and modernity in family structure and values

Hector Grad

A HISTORICAL OUTLINE OF SPAIN

The foundation of the Spanish state is frequently placed at the unification of the kingdoms of Castile and Aragon at the end of the fifteenth century. Absolutism, the strength of the Catholic Church and Inquisition, and the decadence of the colonial empire led to the virtual disconnection of Spain from the European scene. The liberal revolution (1812) implied a renewed link of Spanish society to the rest of Europe and the diffusion of Enlightenment ideas. The defeat of the Republican regime in the Civil War (1936–1939) closed a period of social and cultural progress. The subsequent dictatorship by General Franco imposed social and political conservatism, besides economic and cultural isolation. After Franco's death (1975), the restoration of democracy led to the 1978 constitution and to joining the European Union in 1986. The present population of Spain is 41 million inhabitants living in an area of 506,000 km^2. The capital, Madrid, is the largest city, with 3 million inhabitants.

ECOLOGICAL FEATURES

Most of Spanish territory is in the Iberian Peninsula in southwestern Europe. Spain has offshore territories in the Mediterranean Sea, in the Atlantic Ocean opposite the Sahara coast, and in Africa (north of Morocco). The center of the peninsula is a large plateau surrounded by mountains north and south. Its climate is continental with cold and rainy winters and hot and dry summers in the plain; it is mild and rainy in all seasons on the northern and western coast; and it is Mediterranean with hot and dry summers and mild winters on the eastern coast. A large part of the central plain and the southeastern coast is semi-desert.

ORGANIZATION AND INSTITUTIONS OF SOCIETY

Economic organization

The ecological features and the traditional structure of land ownership shaped the agricultural production of Spain. Small holdings were typical of the northern and northwestern regions, while large state units were characteristic of the western and southern regions. Thus, there are crops in the north and center (including large vineyards), and herding of cows, goats, and sheep, and cultivation of olive oil in the east and south, and fishing in the northwest and the south. Modern, work-intensive, fruit production has expanded in the southeast since the 1980s.

Industrialization began in the late nineteenth century, focused in Madrid in the central plain, Catalonia in the northeast, and the Basque Country in the north – leading to a first wave of internal migration from poorer agricultural regions to the industrial cities. A second migration wave, including emigration to America and northern European countries, followed the economic and political hardships after the Civil War. A third internal migration followed the industrial growth and social modernization between 1960 and 1980, increasing the urban population from 57 percent to 73 percent. Support from the EU and, national and regional support to agriculture and alternative services recently balanced this emigration from rural areas. Consequently, the 2001 urban population rate was 76 percent, close to the EU average.

Small and medium enterprises are the most frequent organization of production and services. Industry, agriculture and fishing, and market-targeted services represent 27 percent, 4 percent, and 50 percent of GNP respectively. Textile, metal, and chemical factories, agriculture and fishing, and tourism are the main economic activities.

In spite of economic growth above the EU average, the Spanish labor market combines high unemployment and precarious jobs. The unemployment rate remains the highest in the EU at 11 percent for the total population, but 16 percent for females, in 2002. It is worth noting that the figures are much higher for youth: 31 percent for ages 16–19, 21 percent for ages 20–24, and 15 percent for ages 25–29, while female rates are 40 percent, 26 percent, and 19 percent respectively (Instituto Nacional de Estadística, Reino de España, 2003). These figures are combined with the highest rates of temporary jobs in the EU, since only 26 percent of men, and 21 percent of women in the 16–29 age range enjoy a fixed contract (Cruz and Santiago, 1998).

Political institutions and legal system

Historically, various social, economic, and political processes have contributed to the strengthening of regional identities, alongside the development of the Spanish state and identity. Demands for cultural and political autonomy received significant support in Catalonia, the Basque Country, and Galicia, since the late nineteenth century. The 1978 constitution intended to achieve a balance between accepting these demands and the existing centralist state, establishing a parliamentary monarchy and a quasi-federal structure based on 17 autonomous regions. In this organization, the administration of most of the educational, welfare, and development services was decentralized and cultural, i.e., local languages and political rights were recognized in these regions.

The constitution established no official religion, but there are preferential institutional arrangements with the Roman Catholic Church, which still retains considerable social and political influence in some regions and social groups.

Democracy and the integration into the EU facilitated the change of laws regarding legal aspects of the family (divorce, family status for cohabiting couples, equal status for descendants outside marriage) as well as the status of women in family and society (e.g., equal opportunities in education and job access, contraception and abortion rights).

The educational system

The General Educational laws of 1857, 1970, and 1990 established free and compulsory education in Spain at the primary, intermediate (to age 14), and first stage of secondary (to age 16) level. According to educational statistics (Ministerio de Educación, Cultura y Deportes, 2000), primary schooling was complete for both genders, secondary schooling rate rose to 94 percent of the relevant 1999/2000 cohorts (96 percent for females), and illiteracy fell to 2.6 percent in 2001. The private sector, in many cases religious institutions, provides a significant portion of primary and secondary education.

While higher education was previously attended by a minority, the recognition of the right to higher education and the expansion of secondary education made feasible the extension of higher education. Therefore, the population of university students increased from 657,447 in 1979/80 to 1,581,415 in 1999/2000, representing 27 percent of the relevant cohorts (29 percent among women).

Religion

In recent national surveys (Centro de Investigaciones Sociológicas, 2002a, 2002b), 82 percent of the adult population was Roman Catholic and 16 percent was secular or agnostic. Nevertheless, attendance at services is low among believers: 49 percent reported never attending, 20 percent reported attending at least once a week. Furthermore, 18 percent and 38 percent reported being "not at all" and "not much" religious, and the corresponding figures for ages 18–24 were 30 percent and 45 percent. As a result of immigration, Islam has become the second religion in population size (with 200,000 believers).

BONDS WITH GROUPS IN THE IMMEDIATE COMMUNITY

Beyond differences between rural and urban areas, Spanish traditional culture shared a collectivist orientation with other Mediterranean cultures (Triandis, 1995; Triandis, Bontempo, Villareal, Asai, and Lucca, 1988). This orientation emphasized the centrality of interpersonal hierarchical relations within kinship and other close ingroups. The self was defined in terms of interdependence with significant others, and individual goals were subordinated to those of ingroups. This interdependence affected behaviors both within and beyond the family context. Thus, values that serve to strengthen social bonds and preserve interpersonal and social harmony – like loyalty, humility, conformity to social norms and traditions – are specially reinforced.

In line with this view, psychological well-being was found to depend on social relations, and specifically on friendship bonds (Requena, 1994). People preferred to maintain numerous, albeit superficial, friends rather than few and close relationships (whose emotional engagement and responsibilities were perceived as stressful). The Basque *cuadrilla*, a long-lasting social and cultural peer reference group, is a good example of these relationships.

Furthermore, this interdependent orientation is reflected in the concept of honor – seeking and maintaining a respected reputation. Honor is mainly centered on family reputation, but also comprises gender-specific codes of individual behavior for its achievement and maintenance, stressing chastity, sense of shame in social relations with men and decorum for females, and responsibility for the protection of family honor, virility, and toughness for males. As in other Mediterranean cultures, honor was found as a core value in traditional, especially southern, Spanish culture (Gilmore, 1987; Peristiany, 1965). Recently, familiar and social interdependence, social power, and honor were found to be more important as individual values in Spain than in northern Europe (Rodriguez Mosquera, Manstead, and Fischer, 2002).

Modernization, urbanization, and affluence have reinforced individualist orientations and more instrumental and egalitarian interpersonal relations with a greater diversity of ingroups in Spain. Thus, a more independent self-concept, besides the search for individual distinctiveness, has developed in younger generations. However, these processes have been relatively rapid, and are still recent. In consequence, collectivist and individualist orientations may coexist with varying intensity, often in a contradictory way, in the person. On the one hand, this may lead to the differential application of certain collectivist norms to ingroup members and of certain individualist norms to other social groups. On the other hand, individuals in modern Spanish society may receive support from a network of social bonds, beyond the nuclear family, that would help them cope with many stressful personal and social situations. This social support, for instance, may explain the smooth social coping with high unemployment during the last twenty years.

THE FAMILY

Marriage

In regard to endogamy, established social relations and social control in the rural traditional family promoted marriage within the same village, and this tradition is still prevalent in rural society. In the urban family, choice of a spouse is an individual decision constrained by the social context of personal relationships. In regard to exogamy, the law prohibits marriage up to third-degree relatives.

In traditional Spanish society, formal and informal regulations strongly backed by the church affected family and wider social relations banning divorce. Law regulated divorce in 1981, providing equal rights in divorce demands and the subsequent distribution of property and child custody. Consequently, recent statistics (Eurostat, 2002b) placed the Spanish divorce rate (1.0 percent) the fourth lowest in the EU, but the highest among the Mediterranean and Catholic countries.

The traditional family had a large influence on the marriage decisions of offspring. In the context of the preferential system of inheritance (see below), non-preferred daughters were provided with dowries and non-preferred sons with financial aid to emigrate. Modernization and individualism shifted both the selection of the partner and the decision to marry to the couple, while dowry became limited mainly to traditionally oriented ethnic or social class groups.

Family structure

Contreras (1991) noted regional differences in the traditional family structure in Spain. Extended families with bilateral inheritance (where a favored descendant inherited from both parents, and the non-favored descendants were compensated by dowry or by aid to migration) was characteristic of the rural north. In general, this kinship structure was patrilineal in terms of lineal descent, kin of both sexes were related through the men only, and the residence after marriage was patrilocal. Where male absence was frequent (western and northern coast, as well as the Pyrenees region), the traditional kinship shifted to matrilineal, with matriuxorilocal residence after marriage, i.e., the new family unit resided in or near the residence of wife's mother or her relatives.

In the eastern, southern, and central rural regions, the large nuclear family with unspecific lineal descent, neolocal or ambilocal residence after marriage and bilateral equalitarian (divided) inheritance was the most frequent traditional kinship structure. Neolocal residence was sometimes delayed, each partner staying at his or her parents' home. The bilateral inheritance in all these kinship structures was reflected in offspring keeping both paternal and maternal family names.

Modernization and migration have eroded these traditional structures, bolstering a nuclear family system that was already typical of cities and central and southern regions. Data from 1970, 1981, and 1991 showed that the proportion of all types of extended family declined from 20.7 percent to 15.2 percent and 10.6 percent of households (Alberdi, 1995). Furthermore, extended families were concentrated in the rural areas of the northern regions (where they were traditionally common). In other regions, they were restricted to urban middle- and upper-class households (Flaquer and Soler, 1990).

Family roles and functions

Values related to hierarchical relations of power and gender were typical of the traditional family in Spain. Power relations within this family were clearly patriarchal, to the extent that legal rights and social norms supported the husband's authority on family life and decisions, e.g., control of the wife's income during the Franco dictatorship (Alberdi, 1995, 1999).

CHANGES IN THE FAMILY

Demographics

The main change in the Spanish family has been the increase of cohabitation and single-person households, and recently also single-parent families (Alberdi, 1999). Average household size decreased from 3.9 in 1970 to 2.8 in 2001 (Instituto Nacional de Estadística, 2003). This trend is an outcome of the increasing number of single households, the fall in the birth rate, and the delay of youth emancipation in that period.

According to Instituto Nacional de Estadística (2003), the percentage of single households increased from 9.9 percent in 1981 to 20.7 percent in 2001, mainly as a reflection of elderly people living alone (8.0 percent of households), but also because of single young households and single-parent families (5.7 percent in 1980, 8.2 percent in 1991, and 12.0 percent in 2001). According to Instituto Nacional de Estadística (2002) and Eurostat (2002b), the rate of marriage decreased from 7.7 in 1975 to 5.1 per 1,000 inhabitants in 2001, close to the EU average. In line with this trend, the proportion of newborns to unmarried women, in relation to total number of newborns, increased significantly from 3.9 percent in 1980 to 19.5 percent in 2001, although it is still the third lowest in the EU.

The decreasing household size was partially due to the fall in the birth rate in Spain. Fertility decreased from 2.8 children per woman in 1975 to 1.2 in 2001, the second lowest and the lowest rates respectively in the EU in those years (Eurostat, 2002a; Instituto Nacional de Estadística, 2002).[1]

However, the reduction in household size was moderated by a delay in young people leaving home and an increase in age of marriage. According to Instituto Nacional de Estadística (2003), the proportion of single persons rose between 1981 and 2001 from 40 percent to 85 percent for age 25, and from 20 percent to 56 percent for age 29. Moreover, the proportion of youth living in the family home rose from 59 percent to 70 percent at age 24–25, and from 25 percent to 50 percent at age 26–29 (Instituto de la Juventud, 2000). Thus, 73 percent of age 25, 50 percent of age 28, and still 35 percent of age 30 were single and living in the family home in 2001 (Instituto Nacional de Estadística, 2003). Several studies (Iglesias de Ussel, 1995; Instituto de la Juventud,

---

[1] Recent increments in the fertility rate are mainly due to the contribution of the young immigrant population, which has risen from 350,000 in 1991 to 1,570,000 in 2001 (Instituto Nacional de Estadística, 2003).

2000; Valero, 1995) have attributed this trend to social conditions (economic difficulties resulting from unemployment and precarious jobs, expensive flat rents, and scarce welfare support to young people and their families); as well as to educational reasons (the prolongation of study period resulting from the extension of higher education); and to cultural factors (importance of family bonds in Catholic and Mediterranean cultures, tolerance of parents allowing young people to enjoy their own way of life and feelings of comfort at their parents' home).[2]

Family values

Modernization did not affect to a great extent family value orientations in Spanish society. Large segments of young people endorse the centrality of the family framework,[3] traditional family values, and maintaining good relationships with parents (Centro de Investigaciones Sociológicas, 1999). The meaning of family, however, shifted from the institutional realm to the field of personal relationships among family members (Iglesias de Ussel, 1990), and hierarchical relations were clearly weakened (Alberdi, 1999).

Nevertheless, traditional gender roles and division of work are still in force despite gender-equality legislation, education, and institutional advertising. According to Instituto de la Juventud (2000), 36 percent of young women perceived gender-related discrimination, while the most frequently cited experience in this regard was their parents' bias within the family. Also, up to 44 percent of young men reported they never participate in housework, e.g., cleaning up, babysitting their children or younger brothers and sisters, cleaning their room.

Family relationships are central and demand time, as well as economic and emotional resources in Spain (Alberdi, 1999). The dominance of the nuclear structure with neolocal residence after marriage results in infrequent co-residence of generations. Therefore, family-value orientation leads people to invest considerable time in family communication and visits.

[2] These attitudes were reflected in survey findings of the 15–29-year-old population: for 98 percent the family was "very or quite important," 97 percent were "fairly satisfied" with their family (Centro de Investigaciones Sociológicas, 1999), and for 50 percent staying at the family home was "more comfortable" (Elzo and Orizo, 1999).

[3] In spite of increasing cohabitation and single-person households among young Spanish people, survey data has shown that marriage commitment continued to be important for them. For 46 percent of men and women between 15 and 29, marriage is in general "quite important," and only 17 percent consider it "not at all important" (Centro de Investigaciones Sociológicas, 1999). Therefore, both forms of alternative relationship seem to be first steps toward the "formalization" of couples, rather than definitive forms of union.

Family networks involve mutual support. Sons and particularly daughters are expected to help and care for parents, and eventually to take them into their home in case of need. On the other hand, parents help young families with practical (e.g., caring for children) and financial support.[4] Iglesias de Ussel (1995) noted that families often make use of their social networks and relationships to help their children find jobs, a pattern shared by many southern European countries in contrast to northern European countries (Mendras, 1997).

CONCLUSIONS

Ethnographic studies have indicated that the nuclear structure with neo-local or ambilocal residence after marriage, and bilateral equalitarian inheritance, was already common in the traditional family in Spain. The modernization and democratization of society promoted non-traditional structures (cohabitation, single-person household and parenting), facilitated the rise in the rate of newborns of unmarried women and of divorce, and stressed interactional orientations and non-hierarchical family values.

In spite of the rise of individualist orientations, Mediterranean and Roman Catholic collectivist values still affect family decisions and behaviors of young people in Spain. Large segments of young people seem to endorse the centrality of family structure, its social supportive bonds, and the traditional family values (referring to gender roles and marriage). These value trends are reinforced by the social reality of youth in Spanish society, where high unemployment and the weakness of welfare state support make it difficult to gain independence in leaving the parental home or in getting married. Following economic uncertainty, marriage rates and, specially, birth rates have declined during the last 20 years.

In this complex situation, the increase of single elderly people and the dependence on immigrants to ensure population replacement and welfare are both symptoms and challenges to present familial and social structures in Spain. In the context of the expected social and economic convergence in the EU, these processes raise the question of whether the actual integration of traditional and modern family patterns will be maintained or whether new family values will be reinforced following further improvements in wealth, employment, and welfare provisions in Spain.

---

[4] Moreover, the under-development of family welfare policy in southern European countries seems to assume that families would provide this support for young people. In turn, this policy implicitly reinforces the ideological assumption that family is the main provider in society (Flaquer, 2000; Papadopoulos, 1998).

36   Turkey

Bilge Ataca

A HISTORICAL OUTLINE OF TURKEY

The Republic of Turkey was established in 1923 after the overthrow of the Ottoman sultan, the Islamic caliphate, as a secular nation state with a parliamentary government. Its present day population is approximately 67 million. Istanbul is the largest city with about 10 million inhabitants, and Ankara, the capital, is the second largest city with about 4 million inhabitants. The history of Turkey consists of, first, the history of Anatolia before the coming of the Turks and of the civilizations – Hittite, Thracian, Hellenistic, and Byzantine. Second, it includes the history of the Turkish peoples, including the Seljuks, who brought Islam and the Turkish language to Anatolia. Third, it is the history of the Ottoman Empire. Finally, Turkey's history is that of the Republic established in 1923.

ECOLOGICAL FEATURES

Turkey is situated on the northeastern Mediterranean basin with 800,000 km² of land, 97 percent of which lies in the Anatolian Peninsula, Asia, and 3 percent in Thrace, Europe. The coastal regions are characterized by a Mediterranean climate with hot and humid summers, and mild and rainy winters, while the inland is cold and snowy in the winter and hot and dry in the summer.

ORGANIZATION AND INSTITUTIONS OF SOCIETY

Economic organization

The Turkish society is in a rapid transformation from a traditional, rural, agricultural, patriarchal society to a modern, urban, industrial, and egalitarian one. Beginning with the republican era, state policies supporting industrialization, as well as migration from rural areas to the cities, have resulted in 60 percent of the population working in the industry and services sectors, while the remaining 40 percent work in the agriculture sector at present. The leading industry and services sectors are automotive and textile, and tourism, respectively. The main agricultural products are grain in the inland region and cotton and fruits in the coastal districts. From the founding of the Republic in 1923 to 1950, the proportion of the population living in urban areas grew from 13 percent to 19 percent; however, by 2000, nearly 70 percent of the population had become urban (State Institute of Statistics, Republic of Turkey, 1991, 2001).

Political institutions and legal system

Republican Turkey, a single-party regime until 1946, is now a multi-party system with democratic elections conducted every five years. The institutional structure is based on the separation of powers principle, by which legislative, executive, and judiciary functions are given to different hands. However, the military has been a significant political institution, making three coups in 1960, 1971, and 1980. The current constitution, accepted in 1982, mandates secular, egalitarian democracy. Women were given rights of election in 1934.

The educational system

When the Republic was established in 1923, the literacy rate was 11 percent and the Arabic alphabet was being used. After the Republic was founded, the educational system that had long been diversely executed under the private spheres of foundations was unified. In 1928, the Latin alphabet was adopted. At present, all educational activities in Turkey are under the supervision of the government and the literacy rate is 87 percent. Eight years of elementary education are compulsory, and further education is encouraged by the state. Istanbul University was established as the first university in 1846. Today, there are 60 universities in Turkey.

Ethnic and religious composition

The Turkish society is mostly composed of ethnic Turks. Several ethno-cultural groups such as Kurds, Armenians, Greeks, Circassians, Gypsies, Laz, Syriacs, and Sephardic Jews are also represented; however, with the exception of Kurds, who make up approximately 20 percent of the population, these groups are small. Approximately 98 percent of the population is Muslim, with the remaining being Jews and Christian groups (Greeks, Armenians, Syriacs). Two major divisions of Islam,

Sunni and Alewite, are represented, with the Sunni being more numerous. The official language is Turkish; however, various languages such as Kurdish, Armenian, and Greek are spoken within the communities.

THE FAMILY

Turkey is at the crossroads between the East and the West, and its social and cultural mosaic reflects this characteristic. Present-day Turkey is characterized by a heterogeneous population, a variety of cultural influences, geographic and ecological variation, and rapid, ongoing social and economic transformations, so much so that it is almost impossible to portray a Turkish family prototype. However, despite the huge demographic shift over the last 50 years, the Turkish population is largely rural, either by current residence or by origin. Although 70 percent of the population now lives in cities, a very large proportion of the urban residents were born in villages or are the children of village-born parents. While this is a very dynamic group, it remains close to its rural, traditional values, and practices (Kağıtçıbaşı and Sunar, 1992; Sunar, 2002). Also, in spite of the major transformations, cultural values, norms, and attitudes have not changed equally rapidly; in the context of interpersonal, family, and gender relations, the culture can still be characterized as traditional, authoritarian, and patriarchal (Sunar and Fisek, in press). Hence, for the sake of comprehensiveness, the following discussion will focus on the salient features of the traditional, rural Turkish family, and where relevant, the newly emerging trends of modern, urban families will be related to this general pattern.

Marriage and divorce

The present Civil Code, an adaptation from the Swiss legal system, was introduced in 1926 by the new Turkish Republic. It abolished Islamic family law, religious jurisdiction, and polygamy. The legal age of marriage was increased to 18 years, and the marriage partners' consent became a requirement. The husband's one-sided disownment of the wife was made illegal. Today, only civil marriage ceremonies and legal forms of divorce are officially acknowledged. Arranged marriages are common in rural areas, whereas in cities it is generally the couple themselves who make the decision to marry.

Family structure

The majority of Turkish households (including rural) are nuclear in structure (Berik, 1995; Delaney, 1991; Starr, 1989; Timur, 1972). The extended family household remains a cultural ideal in many regions (Bastug, 2002), and many households pass through a "transitional extended family" phase following the marriage of a son (Timur, 1972). However, most of all, the Turkish family can be characterized as "functionally extended" with much social support and interaction among close relatives, who also live close to each other (Kağıtçıbaşı, 1982a; Kandiyoti, 1974). Close family members feel responsible for each other and also for distant kin. Ties between parents and children, between siblings, and between the children of siblings are extremely close. Children of both sexes remain with their parents until they get married; close ties with parents involving frequent interaction continue after marriage as well (Bastug, 2002; Hortacsu, 1989). Hence, individuals grow up in a "culture of relatedness" (Kağıtçıbaşı, 1985, 1996b) where they frequently interact with a wide network of relatives, including grandparents, aunts, uncles, and cousins (Bastug, 2002). This pattern persists against increased urbanization and industrialization (Duben, 1982). Even in middle-class urban settings, it is likely that family households will include at least one grandparent or another elderly relative. A study of such three-generation households showed that the elderly relatives preferred to reside with their adult children and it was not out of financial need or need for physical care (Sunar, 1988).

A basic structural feature of the Turkish family is generational and gender hierarchy (patriarchy). The traditional Turkish family is male-dominated; father is the absolute authority in the family. Adults dominate children, who do not have many rights until they are grown up and married (Olson, 1982). In an observational study of family interaction, Fisek (1995) found that generational hierarchy, expressed in terms of parental control and nurturance, was high regardless of the educational or clinical status of the family, maternal employment, and family size. Male dominance is the norm in the Turkish family; women are regarded as lower in value, prestige, and power than men (Fisek, 1982, 1993; Kağıtçıbaşı, 1982a; Kandiyoti, 1988; Sunar, 2002). This hierarchy is reflected mainly in role differentiation, including a strict division of labor based on what is domestic labor and what is not (Fisek, 1993). The status of a task depends mainly on whether it is men's or women's work (Fisek, 1993; Kağıtçıbaşı and Sunar, 1992). Overall, a combined gender/ generational hierarchy is in effect such that the father is stronger than the mother, who is in turn stronger than the children in the Turkish family (Fisek, 1995).

Gender hierarchy is based on the dominant value of the traditional social system, the concept of honor (*namus*), which refers to the sexual behavior (chastity) of the women. Honor is maintained by men in the family by controlling the sexual behavior of their female relatives (wives, daughters, sisters, etc.) (Kağıtçıbaşı and Sunar, 1992; Meeker, 1976). Illegitimate sexual contact with a man leads to loss of the protector's honor. The maintenance of family honor dictates considerable restriction of female behavior; hence, it reinforces male dominance and female subordination. It is more of a social affair, reflecting the other-directed character of social relations, the significance of others' evaluations, and the importance given to shame. In this sense, the honor tradition also contributes to the closely knit relationships of the traditional family. One is dependent on the behavior of the family members in order to be an honorable member of the community. The communal nature of honor thereby strengthens the close ties of the individual with family, kin, and the community (Meeker, 1976; Ozgur and Sunar, 1982; Sunar and Fisek, in press). However, honor as a value lost its power among the urban, educated middle class. Male–female relations are less closely controlled and more autonomy is given to young people in the management of their lives. Western-style dating is common; cohabitation without marriage is occasionally seen (Sunar and Fisek, in press).

Family roles and functions

Olson (1982) characterized the Turkish marital relationship as comprising a "duofocal family structure" in which husbands and wives maintain their separate social networks with their close-knit same-sex friends and/or relatives. This pattern of distinct sex roles with a separation of spheres of activity and a lack of sharing between spouses is observed also in towns and among rural migrants in cities (Kağıtçıbaşı, 1982a; Kandiyoti, 1977, 1982). However, it is moderated in dual-income and highly educated urban families (Fisek and Sunar, 2003).

In the traditional families, spousal relationships are centered around economic maintenance and childrearing, rather than emotional companionship (Olson, 1982). The husband is responsible for making the major decisions about the household; communication is not a high priority (Kağıtçıbaşı, 1982a; Kandiyoti, 1977; Olson, 1982). However, increased education and urban residence are leading to changes in the marital relationship in the direction of more egalitarian attitudes and intimacy expectations between spouses (Ataca and Sunar, 1999; Fisek, 1993, 1995; Imamoglu, 1994; Kağıtçıbaşı, 1986). The wife is more involved and the husband is less dominating in the family decision-making (Ataca and Sunar, 1999; Imamoglu, 1991).

Based on the male authority and the interdependence among family members, two sets of traditional childrearing practices related to sex-differentiation and to interdependence can be identified. The wide difference in the status and power of males and females results in different attitudes and childrearing practices. For example, in rural areas there is a strong preference for having sons rather than daughters. This preference is associated mostly with the economic value of the son in contributing to the family's welfare through financial and practical help and care in old age, but also with the desire to carry on the male line and the status that accrues to the mother of a son (Kağıtçıbaşı, 1982b, 1996a). Girls and boys are socialized differently in order to prepare them for their adult roles. There is a widespread tendency to educate sons more than daughters. Official statistics show higher literacy rates and higher levels of educational attainment for males than females at all ages. Turkish parents allow more independence and aggressiveness in their sons and expect more dependence and obedience in their daughters. Compared to boys, girls are much more closely supervised and limited in their permissible activities, particularly in later childhood and adolescence (Ataca, 1992; Başaran, 1974).

Consistent with this sex-differentiated socialization, there is a clear preference for same-sex interactions. Turkish youth prefer same-sex friends, next to their mothers, for communication (Hortacsu, 1989). In a study that examined the importance of relationships for need satisfaction, parents, same-sex siblings, and same-sex friends emerged as the individuals with whom university students and middle-aged adults had the most meaningful relationships (Hortacsu, Gencoz, and Oral, 1995). Looking also at the functionality of relationships, they found that same-sex siblings were rated as important as mothers for satisfaction of disclosure during childhood, adolescence, and youth, and that during youth, same-sex friends and same-sex siblings were rated equally important for understanding, instrumental help, trust, and self-development (Hortacsu, Gencoz, and Oral, 1995).

Urban parents show less boy preference and stress the psychological value of children such as the loving relationship between the parent and the child (Ataca and Sunar, 1999); this trend has also increased over three generations (Sunar, 2002). An interesting finding is that urban middle-class mothers perceived daughters, more than sons, as a prospective help in old age (Ataca and Sunar, 1999). This shift has been accompanied by other changes, such as more equal treatment of sons and daughters, and greater autonomy in the family (see Ataca and Sunar, 1999; Kağıtçıbaşı, 1982b; Sunar, 2002). Urban parents encourage children of both sexes similarly to pursue professional educations (Acar, 1991; Erkut, 1982). Hence, the way in which children are perceived and valued by parents appears to be a function of social circumstances and social change (Kağıtçıbaşı, 1985).

Family relationships, characterized by a high degree of material and emotional interdependence, reflect on childrearing practices (Sunar, 2002). Children are reared in an atmosphere of mutual emotional attachment and loyalty among family members with considerable control. Control in childrearing is the norm in Turkey and does not connote lack of love, as might be the case in Western cultures, rather, it is an aspect of the overall surveillance and control of all members of the family (Kağıtçıbaşı, 1982a; Kağıtçıbaşı and Sunar, 1992). In order to maintain the harmonious operation of a closely interdependent family, obedience, dependence, loyalty, conformity, and quietness are encouraged, and autonomy, initiative, activity, and curiosity are discouraged in both sons and daughters (Fisek, 1993; Kağıtçıbaşı, 1982b; Kağıtçıbaşı, Sunar, and Bekman, 1988, 2001; Sunar, 2002).

Mothers express their affection openly, both verbally and through physical means like hugging and kissing the child, and they also encourage the child to reciprocate (Kağıtçıbaşı, Sunar and Bekman, 1988). Although expression of anger toward both parents is not encouraged, it is strictly not tolerated for fathers. Many fathers are affectionate and playful with their small children; however, as children grow up, authority and respect start dominating the relationship, and by the time a child reaches adolescence, there is considerable distance from the father in terms of communication. Recent research showed that urban youth felt emotionally closer to their mothers than to their fathers (Hortacsu, Gencoz, and Oral, 1995; Sunar, 2002); they also communicated more with their mothers than with their fathers (Hortacsu, 1989). Fisek's (1995) study with urban families showed that closeness to mother and to father were defined differently. Information about self and decisions were shared more in father–child pairs, whereas emotional sharing and touching were more evident in mother–child pairs.

Gender-specific parent–child relationships also show variations. While the father and daughter relationship may be characterized by affection and tolerance (Kandiyoti, 1977; Sunar, 2002), the father and son relationship is more formal and authoritarian (Kiray, 1976). The mother and daughter are close (Fallers and Fallers, 1976; Hortacsu, 1989; Kiray, 1976; Olson, 1982); however, the closeness of the mother–son relationship is noteworthy (Kağıtçıbaşı, 1981; Kandiyoti, 1977; Kiray, 1976). One reason for this closeness is the fact that a son confers status upon his mother in the traditional Turkish family. Another reason is the emotional distance between the woman and her husband, coupled with her isolation in the domestic arena, which in turn, lead her to seek closeness with her children, mainly with her more valuable son (Fisek, 1982, 1993).

The findings of a study of childrearing practices in three generations of urban middle-class Turkish families showed both continuities and changes over generations (Sunar, 2002). All three generations reported parental behaviors that emphasized the importance of the family over the individual. Much emotional closeness in the family was also indicated, especially between mothers and children, and to a lesser extent between fathers and daughters. There is also consistency in sex-differentiated childrearing. Sons were given more autonomy whereas daughters were more closely supervised and controlled. It was also reported that urban middle-class parents in all three generations attributed a higher value to daughters compared to rural and rural-origin groups. There were also some changes observed over three generations. There was a trend toward increased encouragement of emotional expression, but suppression of negative emotions within the family. There was also a trend toward increased equalitarian treatment of sons and daughters despite the continued relative restriction of daughters. Parents' authoritarian control decreased by increased use of rewards and reasoning as methods of discipline and encouragement of independence over generations.

CONCLUSION

The Turkish culture is a blend of the Eastern and the Western cultural features. At present, it is characterized by much heterogeneity and social change, which led to the emergence of not one, but many Turkish family prototypes. Although it is safe to assume a rural, traditional, patriarchal pattern that would be applicable to a large portion of the population, modern/Western features are very much in existence, especially in the urban centers of western Turkey. An emerging coexistence of the traditional and modern/Western characteristics is clearly seen in the Turkish middle-class urban family, which portrays a synthesis of the more positive aspects of both collectivistic and individualistic cultures (e.g., close relationships with more individual autonomy) while avoiding their negative aspects (e.g., authoritarian discipline and interpersonal alienation) (Sunar, 2002; Sunar and Fisek, in press). In a culture making the transition from an agricultural to an urban, industrial economy, Kağıt-çıbaşı (1996a) portrays this family as emotionally (but not economically) interdependent, and predicts "a *combination*, or *coexistence*, of individual and group (family) loyalties" (p. 89). This new synthesis of the traditional and the new patterns that meet the challenges of a changing world are likely to continue in the foreseeable future.

37 Ukraine

Irina Zhuravliova

A HISTORICAL OUTLINE OF UKRAINE

Ukrainians have lived in the territory of present-day Ukraine for millennia. The roots of the Ukrainian nation are found in the Trypillian culture, which evolved in the Middle Dnipro region in the third millennium BC, the heritage of the Scythian tribes, and the Chernykiv culture. More than 1100 years ago Kievan Rus' – Ukraine – a powerful European medieval monarchy, was established (Sybstelniy, 1991).

During 1917–1921, eastern Ukraine became the theater of war of six different armies and the events of those years had a revolutionary significance for the social, economic, and national evolution of Ukraine. The Russian Bolsheviks were forced to take into account national sentiment when they established Soviet rule in Ukraine (Zinkewych and Hula, 1993). For decades the Ukrainian Republic was a constituent member of the USSR and despite its dependence on Union decisions and structures, the international status of Ukraine as a state in its own right increased over the years.

On July 16, 1990 the Supreme Rada of Ukraine adopted an important historic document – the "Act" – proclaiming Ukrainian state sovereignty, independence, and indivisibility of power within the boundaries of Ukrainian territory, and independence, and equality in conducting foreign relations. On August 24, 1991 the Supreme Rada, in effecting this declaration and proceeding from the right to self-determination, proclaimed the independence of Ukraine.

ECOLOGICAL FEATURES

The main characteristic of Ukraine's geography is its plains, which compose 70 percent of the country's land area. The remaining 25 percent of the land consists of hills and tablelands, and only 5 percent are the Carpathian and Crimean Mountains. Ukraine is rich in minerals, has coalfields, iron, manganese, nickel, and uranium ores (Lappo, 1984).

The climate of Ukraine is temperate and continental with variations such as temperate Mediterranean at the south and coastal type at the Black Sea. Because of its position, situated in the center of great trade routes, Ukraine was influenced by several civilizations and has often been a target for foreign invaders.

The total land surface of Ukraine is 603,700 km^2 and its population is 10 million people, of whom 80 percent are Ukrainians; the remaining 20 percent are Russians, Byelorussians, Moldavians, Polish, Hungarians, Greeks, etc.

The ecological circumstances of Ukraine were ideal for the development of river, sea, and road connections. The development of transportation gave people the opportunity of maintaining their financial, political, productive, and cultural relationships with each other, and to move to new lands.

Today, means of transport (railway, roads, planes, rivers, sea system) and means of information (television, radio, newspapers, and magazines) are numerous and well developed.

THE ORGANIZATION AND INSTITUTIONS OF SOCIETY

Economic organization

The ecology of Ukraine provides an ideal environment for various human subsistence activities, such as the cultivation of the land, animal husbandry on the level plains, arboriculture on the table lands, fishing and merchant shipping in the coastal areas and rivers.

The vast plains with very fertile black soil led to the forming of the first large agricultural communities in Europe (Sybstelniy, 1991, p. 17–28). Some historians believe that the quality of the land was of great importance in shaping how the land was cultivated and different types of subsistence patterns. The cultivation of the land in Ukraine was based only on the extended family and not collectively with the cooperation of other families from the community as in Russia (Pavliouk, Goryn and Kyrchiv, 1997; Sybstelniy, 1991).

By the end of the nineteenth century and the beginning of the twentieth, trade and industrialization in Ukraine gradually increased (Shablia, 1995). After the integration of Ukraine into the Soviet Union new laws relating to the economy were promulgated, such as the ban on the acquisition of property and property ownership by families and the institution of individuals working as laborers in collective farms. The consequence of the sudden changes in the organization of the society caused the economic crisis of 1930, during which almost 8 million people died from hunger in the countryside of Ukraine (Zinkewych and Hula, 1993).

Industrialization increased rapidly after World War II. The entire period of the socialist regime was characterized by internal immigration. New industries were developed and continue to function to the present day, e.g., mines, ore extraction, energy production, chemical machine construction, textile factories, and food production. The agricultural economy, as in the past, holds an important position in the economic system of the country (Shablia, 1995).

Political institutions and legal system

During the medieval period, community councils ruled the agricultural communities. These councils were largely independent. With the development of the financial trade relationships and the transition to the state private property and of family-owned property in the fifteenth century, the power of the community council decreased. The council also became submissive to the central administration.

From 1922 to 1991, Ukraine was one of the Soviet Union's republics, and submitted to the total control of the central government. This period was characterized by the strong influence of socialist ideology on every institution of society, and also on people's psychology.

Today, Ukraine is a presidential parliamentary democracy. The president, the parliament representatives, and the members of the peripheral administration are elected. Private ownership, the control of the economic crisis, and the reassurance of better living circumstances for the citizens help to explain the present political condition of Ukraine.

The educational system

The principles of the Ukrainian education are based on Slavic tradition. The family and the community were the most important sources of socialization. Parents were responsible for the upbringing, morality, and proper social behavior of their children. From the time of Kievskagia Rous in the twentieth century, the main purposes of children's socialization were that the child would become the perfect worker and patriot (Kon, 1988).

During the Soviet regime, a major part of children's socialization was undertaken by the national education institutions: the kindergarten, the nursery school, and the primary school, because both parents had to work. The present educational system consists of primary school (3 grades), intermediate school (4 grades), high school (5 grades), higher education (3 years), tertiary school (4.5 or 5 years). The first three stages are compulsory. Teaching is in the Ukrainian language, contrary to the period of the Soviet regime when teaching was in Russian for a large number of schools.

The reformation of modern Ukraine though, and also the Ukrainians' needs, demands a further improvement of all means of information. Education and the media have been the main means of the Ukrainian language reaching the new generation.

Religion

The history of Ukrainians' religious life can be divided into four periods; the pre-Christian, the Christian, the period of governmental atheism, and the present period, characterized by the return of people to their religious traditions. According to Pavliouk, the Christianization of Ukrainians' ancestors was a great and positive influence, while at the end of the twentieth century, the opposite phenomenon was observed. The latter change was the result of the long-lasting religious prohibition (Pavliouk, Goryn, and Kyrchiv, 1997). From recent demographical researches, we can conclude that the majority of Ukrainians are Christians and Mennonites.

BONDS WITH GROUPS IN SMALL COMMUNITIES

As far as bonds of groups within the small communities are concerned, there is some information found in folklore research. According to these studies, the relationships within villages were intimate and strong. Some of the community's functions were the order and security of all its members and the protection of the villagers' property. Conflicts between the members of a community were solved inside the community. In case of external danger the members of the community showed ingroup identity and solidarity for the confrontation of those dangers.

Nowadays internal migration, from the small communities to urban areas, has resulted in the loss of the small community's bonds. Inhabitants of big cities communicate and maintain firm relationships more often with friends from their working environment or studies and not much with the representatives of the community (Kravets, 1966).

THE FAMILY

The study of the evolution and the special characteristics of the Ukrainian family has interested many researchers and sociologists in many periods, but information on this subject is limited (Kravets, 1966). It is believed that researchers took into consideration only some aspects of family evolution and relationships.

A review of the Ukrainian bibliography relative to the family reveals some difficulties in interpretation as a result of opposing views concerning the traditional form of the Ukrainian family. Some researchers exclude the collective element from the development of the Ukrainian family, believing that the family structure has always been nuclear. Others, such as Kravets (1966), argue that during the historical evolution the extended family existed before the nuclear family and that the appearance of the nuclear form was the consequence of socioeconomic changes.

The present report on the characteristics of the Ukrainian family is based on recent historical and folklore studies.

TRADITIONAL FORMS OF THE UKRAINIAN FAMILY

The basic forms of the family are the nuclear or simple family and the complex or extended family. A distinctiveness of the Ukrainian family is considered the tendency to form nuclear, simple families, quite early in the historical evolution of the family. By the end of the nineteenth century and the beginning of the twentieth, the number of nuclear families increased to 84 percent, with only 16 percent consisting of variations of the complex family (Pavliouk, Goryn and Kyrchiv, 1997). Sometimes, because of economic and social events, an inverse process was observed, in that people were trying to unite their families. This was happening because each house had to be represented by one person on occasions such as bond slavery or big disasters.

The Ukrainian bibliography, depending on the place of residence, defines two family types – the agricultural and the urban – each with their variations. The agricultural families are distinguished as families of farmers, families of workers who occasionally work in nearby villages or towns, and families of intellectuals, who are very few. Urban families are separated into workers, employers, and intellectuals.

Agricultural families

The organization of the complex agricultural family is patriarchal, which means that the established traditional practice is maintained in which the father is the leader of the family. In the agricultural extended family, the strong social power of the father and the traditional hierarchy of the family roles are obvious. Father is responsible for the financial and professional coordination of the family, for the distribution of the responsibilities among the members of the family, for the management of the family budget, and the control of the expenditure. The father's will is the "law" for all family members.

Work was an obligation for men and women (Borisenko, 1998). Women did all the housework and working in the fields. Women were also responsible for the upbringing of the children and taking care of their husbands. Men were occupied with agriculture, repairing agricultural tools, and the storage of fuels and construction materials. Men would never do women's work. All family members would attend community gatherings, in order to help a family or to celebrate a traditional or family occasion (Kravets, 1966).

Working-class families

At first, the working-class family had much in common with the agricultural, and there are still families consisting of members of three generations. Most of these still occupy themselves with agriculture, maintaining some family traditions. However, one can observe some changes in the relationships within the family and the allocation of family duties and roles, which denote the establishment of a more equal status between spouses, parents, and children.

The number of children in the agricultural family is reducing at a rapid pace since there is no longer the need for "many hands" for the cultivation of land, along with the fact that the workers' life conditions were very difficult at the beginning of the century (Boiko, 1980). As in the agricultural families, education through work is dominant in the socialization of children. The majority of working-class families (like the families of clerks and intellectuals) are located in urban centers, where their degree of dependence on the state and other social, political, and economic institutions is increasing. Compliance with traditional values, customs, and family or community institutions is decreasing, because some of these values do not fit well in today's society.

THE MODERN UKRAINIAN FAMILY

Family structure

Industrialization and the domination of the Soviet Union, which exercised a powerful ideological influence at the beginning of the twentieth century, caused changes in the political, economic, and social sector, and they, in their turn, affected the structure and functions of the Ukrainian family decisively. As in other industrialized countries (Goode, 1963), there is also a prevalent tendency in Ukraine to a transition from the extended type of family to the nuclear family. The Ukrainian bibliography claims that most of the families are nuclear in type, especially those in urban centers, and the extended type is limited to some provincial areas of Ukraine.

Zatsepin's (1991) book on the new family emphasizes the existence of an aspect of perpetuity in the extended family, in which members of more than two generation groups live together in some phases of family life, about 70 percent of newly wedded couples up to the age of 20 are members of extended families, and when it comes to older couples aged 30 and above, 20–25 percent live together with one of the parents of either of the spouses.

Young people in Ukraine marry quite early, and through lack of financial resources, often live with the parents of one of the spouses or receive financial aid from their parents or even their grandparents (Kochetov, 1987; Zatsepin, 1991). Another clue that relates to the financial cooperation between the members of the family becomes evident from the fact that most of the families, not only in provincial areas but also in urban centers, own stretches of land around the city which are cultivated by the parents, usually with the help of the married children.

Financial support and cooperation between the members of the Ukrainian family are preserved to an extent because they provide functional elements, and they probably are the result of the combination of two parameters – political and economic: political, because they can be considered as a continuation of the remnants of socialist ideology, which forced people to collective labor, formation of cooperatives and mutual assistance; and economic as a result of adjustment to recent economic reforms.

Marriage and divorce

In the early 1990s the ratio of marriages per 1,000 people of the whole population was 9.3–9.5 percent, but this was reduced to 7.6 percent in 1992. In recent years, this has fluctuated: 8.2 percent in 1993, 7.7 percent in 1994, and 8.4 percent in 1995 (Zadoenko, 1999).

According to the Civil Code of Ukraine regarding Marriage and Family, marriage is based solely on the mutual agreement of the couple. The age limit for women is 17 years of age and for men 18. Until the 1990s most women married between the ages of 20 and 24, but a gradual decrease in age was anticipated (Kochetov, 1987). The highest frequency of marriages for men is in the age group 20 to 24. But the frequency of marriages has been decreasing in all age groups for both men and women.

The ratio of divorces has increased, from a total of 156,700 in 1974, to 183,400 in 1985, 222,600 in 1992, and a decrease to 188,200 in 1997.

Family roles

In regard to family roles, although both spouses contribute financially to their household and the repute of the man as the head of the family is not that powerful, the woman is more occupied with housework than the man (Drouzhynin, 1996). However, in the last 15–20 years in the new families, men have tended to become more involved in housework and the upbringing of children (Kabloukov, 1989). Also, the parents of the couple provide important help when it comes to the care of children and housework (Alexandrova, 1990), which is a fact that increases the frequency of gatherings and invigorates the emotional bonds between the members of the wider family.

CONCLUSIONS

The broader economic, political, and social changes in Ukraine have affected the connection of psychological variables with Ukrainian family schemes, with the types of relationships, and the quality of these relationships. In Ukraine the nuclear family is in force because of its structure, while the functional elements prove the existence of intimate emotional bonds, economic cooperation up to a degree, and support from the members of the wider family, especially people from the third generation.

These arguments are enhanced by results regarding an important psychological element of the modern Ukrainian family: values. Members of the sample in this study reject values that have to do with traditional hierarchical roles of men and women, and widely accept values regarding mutual assistance and solidarity between the members of the wider family and positive family relationships. The acceptance of some family values by the Ukrainians proves the preservation and functionality of these family values. These results also bear out the perpetual relative stability they ascribe to values.

38 Family in the United States: social context, structure, and roles

Basilia Softas-Nall and Denis G. Sukhodolsky

A HISTORICAL OUTLINE OF THE UNITED STATES

Compared to most nations of the world, the United States is a relatively young nation. The British colonies in America declared independence from Great Britain in 1776. The United States of America was established as an independent nation following the Treaty of Paris in 1783. The rest of the 50 states joined the first 13 in the nineteenth and twentieth centuries. When the United States declared independence from Great Britain, that declaration of independence stated that all men have the right to "life, liberty, and the pursuit of happiness." Consequently, these values have become central in the philosophy of American individualism. Currently, the country's population is a little over 278 million people, of which 69.1 percent are Caucasian, 12.5 percent are Hispanic, 12.3 percent are black, 3.6 percent are Asian, 0.9 percent are Native American, and 7.9 percent reported other racial backgrounds (US Census Bureau, 2000). Thirty-three million adults in America live in households where at least one other adult family member has a different religious identity. American families often have ties to the cultures from which they originated. The degree to which each family identifies with the culture of origin varies, but the diversity in American families is partially due to the diversity in the cultural backgrounds of the population.

ECOLOGICAL FEATURES

The United States is located in North America and stretches from the Atlantic Ocean to the Pacific Ocean. It is bordered by Canada on the north and Mexico on the south. The country also has several overseas territories, including the states of Alaska and Hawaii. The terrain is varied with a vast central plain, mountains in the west, hills and low mountains in the east, rugged mountains and broad river valleys in Alaska, and volcanic topography in Hawaii. The climate is mostly temperate, but tropical in Hawaii and Florida, arctic in Alaska, semiarid in the plains, and arid in the southwest.

THE ORGANIZATION AND INSTITUTIONS OF SOCIETY

Economic organization

The US economy is market-based, with private individuals and business firms making most of the decisions with limited regulation by the government. The advances in technology have created a gradual development of a two-tiered labor market where the top 20 percent own more than 80 percent of the nation's wealth, and this gap has continued to grow (Galbraith, 1996). In 2000, 30 percent were in professional occupations, 29 percent in technical, sales, and administrative support positions, 13.5 percent in service industries, 24.6 percent in mining, manufacturing, and transportation, and only 2.5 percent in farming and fishing.

Political institutions and legal system

The United States has a federal republic type of government with a strong democratic tradition. The legal system in the United States is based on English common law. The three branches of the federal government, executive, legislative, and judicial, have checks and balances of power over each other, including judicial review of legislative acts. Each of the 50 states has a strong state government, responsible for executive, legislative, and judicial systems within each state. Certain powers are reserved for the federal government, including printing of money, entering into treaties with other countries, and military operations.

The educational system

Each state has an autonomous educational system with compulsory education of children to a certain age, usually 16. After high school, most students attend some form of higher education. Historically, higher education began as the responsibility of churches. With land grants, each state began to open its own colleges and universities. In the early 1800s, industrial schools began, which were based on teaching basic science and industrial and agricultural applications. Currently, each state usually runs several colleges and universities, each with its own geographical region or general subject of responsibility. Approximately 97 percent of the population is considered literate. In 2000, 84 percent of Americans aged 25 and older had completed at least high school and 26 percent had a Bachelor's degree or higher. Today, more than 150 languages are spoken in American schools. About 3.5 million students will come from homes where English is not the first language.

Religion

Regarding the main religions, 56 percent of the population is Protestant, 28 percent is Roman Catholic, 2 percent is Jewish, 4 percent belongs to other religions, and 10 percent reported no religious affiliation.

FAMILY STRUCTURE AND ROLES

The traditional model of marriage was based on the development of a family and the acquisition of property (Sperry and Carlson, 1991). Roles within the marriage were closely associated with sex-role stereotypes, and if a person did not want to fulfill those roles, he or she would not marry. The modern model of marriage became common following World War II. The keys in the modern modes are love and choice. People come together because they love each other and want to be together. The roles that each person plays in the relationship are negotiated and can be variable and vague (Sperry and Carlson, 1991). In the last 25 years, family forms have dramatically changed and single-parent families and families with working mothers are more common, while the number of married-couple households has declined (Steil, 2001).

Marriage

In regard to endogamy, today's American family has no universal restrictions. Within a family, there may be rules about who is appropriate to marry and who is not, but these are variable across the country. From 1980 to 1999, the number of interracial marriages almost doubled. More than 50 percent of Americans are marrying out of their ethnic group (US Census Bureau, 2000). In regard to exogamy, marriage between members of the nuclear family and first cousins is prohibited in most of the country. The rates of divorce and remarriage are high in the United States. Since 1970, approximately one out of every two marriages ended in divorce, although this trend has started to decline in recent years (Steil, 2001). Cohabitation and divorce research has suggested that traditional marriage norms against separation and divorce are weaker in urban than in rural environments (Bulcroft and Bulcroft, 1993). There is little, if any, social stigma against divorce. The decision to marry is made by the man and woman entering the union. The consent of the parents or other groups in the society is not necessary. Most states still require that marriages only be between a man and a woman, but one state, Vermont, allows homosexual marriages. There is no official dowry. In many marriages, it is customary for the bride's family to pay the cost of the wedding, but this is not mandatory. Once children marry, they are expected to manage financially on their own with little or no support from their families of origin. In the 2000 census, the number of Americans living alone was 26 percent of all households and surpassed for the first time the households of married couples with children (Schmitt, 2001). Adult status is extended to individuals based upon age, and it does not matter if someone is married or not. Some cultural groups within the United States are more likely to marry than others. For example, Caucasian and Hispanic women are much more likely to be married (60 percent) than are black women (39 percent) (US Census Bureau, 2000).

Family structure

Generally, the family structure in the United States is considered to be nuclear. However, the percentage of married-couple households with children under 18 has declined to 23.5 percent (US Census Bureau, 2000). Single-parent families are the fastest growing type of family, and from 1990 to 2000 the number of single-parent families grew almost five times faster than the number of married couples with children (Schmitt, 2001). Of the single-parent families, 90 percent of black families, and 85 percent of black and Caucasian families are headed by women (US Census Bureau, 2000). These families often have financial difficulties. In 1997, almost half of single-parent families had incomes below the poverty line (US Census Bureau, 2000). There is heterogeneity in intergenerational relationships within this country. This heterogeneity can be traced to historical trends such as mobility, divorce rates, single-parent families, grandparents and other family members raising children, increased visibility of gay and lesbian couples and families, and a shift away from the family as the primary source of social support (Carter and McGoldrick, 1999; Silverstein and Bengtson, 1997). Many people have very close relationships with extended family, but many also create important relationships with people not related to them at all. Families establish and maintain relationships which help the members of the family whether or not the relationships are with relatives or non-relatives. The nature of the family now is based on voluntary commitments by its members and does not have the permanence of families found in the middle of the twentieth century (Cheal, 1993). This voluntary commitment by parents has left many children without parents to raise them. A grandparent often takes in these children. Today, more than 3.7 million children live in households headed by grandparents. These children live with their grandparents for a variety of reasons, including substance abuse by a parent, child abuse, teen pregnancy, parents' inability to care for the child, death of a parent, AIDS, and unemployment (Williamson, Softas-Nall, and Miller, 2003).

Post-marital residence

The post-marital residence is related to the convenience of the couple. Sometimes the couple moves into a place together, sometimes one moves into the current home of the other, and sometimes they live with family members until they can afford to live on their own, but the booming economy has allowed more younger people to leave home and live on their own (Schmitt, 2001). The location of the post-marital relationship is generally related to the location of the couple's job(s). Many adult children must move away from their parents to maximize their economic and occupational options (Silverstein and Bengtson, 1997). Corporate employees and their families are transferred (Kiechel, 1987) and more move with the hope of finding new and better jobs. Families who live far from other family members use modern communication devices to keep in touch, even over long distances (Silverstein and Bengtson, 1997). Relationships with relatives vary for different families. Although some families continue to live near other family members, many families are scattered across the country. Adult children are not isolated from their parents, but interact and assist even over large geographic distances. Commonly, the national or ethnic origin of the family can play a role in the type of relationships people have with their family members (Burton, 1996).

Control and institutionalization of divorce

In the United States, the family usually is given the first chance to determine how changes in the family will occur after the divorce. If the husband and wife cannot make decisions together, the courts will step in and make final decisions regarding child custody, property, and financial provisions. The majority of the states allow for no-fault divorces. These divorces do not require either party to claim that there is abuse or infidelity in the marriage; a person must just ask for a divorce and one will be granted. In most divorces, property acquired by the couple during the marriage is split equally, no matter who acquired which property and no matter what role each had in the cause of the divorce. Traditionally, some alimony was paid to the wife when the husband was the only breadwinner, but this is becoming less common as more wives have careers of their own. Custody of children is often shared between the parents (joint custody), and this is now the assumption as long as both are interested in having contact with their children and are reasonably capable of doing so. Physical custody of the children still often rests with the mother, and child support is often paid by the father unless he has the children for half the time or more (Zill and Rogers, 1988).

Family roles and functions

Traditionally, the husband/father would be responsible for being the breadwinner, financial planner, and household mechanic. The wife/mother would be the homemaker and childcare provider (Sperry and Carlson, 1991). However, these traditional roles are changing. Following World War II, a marriage pattern based on the egalitarian idea of companionship and traditional divisions of household labor started to emerge (Weiss, 2000). As could be expected, younger age groups have less traditional attitudes than older age groups, but there has been a decrease in all age groups in the proportion that hold traditional attitudes. Attitudes regarding gender roles have become more egalitarian. When people from younger generations marry now, both husbands and wives are less likely to assume that the husband will be responsible for financially providing for the family (Wilke, 1993). The current generation of married adults has further changed the family roles. Men are regretting their disengagement from the family and women seek assistance in the raising of the children, so new roles are being negotiated in marriages (Weiss, 2000).

Husband and father roles

The role of the husband/father in the family is changing. Men are not usually required to be the sole breadwinner anymore. In 1960, 42 percent of families were solely supported by a man, and in 1988 only 15 percent of families were solely supported by a man (Wilke, 1993). In two-parent nuclear families, married men's participation in household work and childcare has been increasing (Steil, 2001). However, fathers are still less likely to be involved in parenting than mothers. In families where the parents are divorced and not living together, almost four times as many children are detached from their fathers as are detached from their mothers (Furstenberg and Nord, 1985). Some theorize that the weaknesses in the relationships between fathers and children is partially caused by early family socialization which puts mothers in the nurturing role, and by the courts who hand down custody decisions that favor mothers over fathers (Hagestad, 1986; Rossi, 1993).

Wife and mother roles

Sixty-seven percent of mothers with children under school age and 77 percent of mothers with school-age children work (US Census Bureau, 2000). Between 1982 and 1992, employed mothers doubled their use of daycare for preschool age children. The people reaching adulthood now are the children of the women who entered the workforce in the 1960s and 1970s, and these adults have a much more liberal view about women's roles (Brewster and Padavic, 2000). According to Wilke (1993), women are essential to the financial support in 38 percent of families. However, even when the wives are working, they continue to do twice as much housework as their husbands, and 80 percent of the cooking, cleaning, and laundry. Mothers also spend more time alone with their children and are primarily responsible for planning, organizing, supervising, and scheduling the activities for the children (Barnett and Shen, 1997; Chadwick and Heaton, 1999).

Children

As the economies transformed from agrarian to industrial, families had fewer children, but the likelihood that each child would live to adulthood dramatically increased (Kain, 1990). As children's mortality rates and the number of children born to each family decreased, American parents began taking special interest in the raising of children. As family structures have changed, fewer children have a parent at home dedicated to their care. In addition, the distance between many children and their extended families allows for less support for them from the community beyond their parents (Farrell, 1999). More children become enrolled in preschool programs, and children start school earlier and stay in school longer than they did in the past (Zill and Rogers, 1988). Public education for all children is provided through the twelfth year of education (not including preschool and kindergarten). If children attend college, many are at least partially supported by their parents during this process. Adult legal status is usually reached at age 18, but many children are supported by their parents after that age. It is not uncommon for children to work part-time, often starting between the ages of 14 and

17. However, children are not usually required to work to add to the family income, but work for their own spending money and non-essential expenses. In general, children in the United States today have the role of going to school while being supported by their parents during their development, while career choices, place of adult residence, and marriage usually happen sometime after legal adult status is achieved.

CONCLUSIONS

The family in the United States has changed dramatically during the history of the country, but the most significant changes have been in the years since World War II. At that time, the ideas about gender roles within the family began to change significantly. Since that time, many people have chosen or been required to move away from their families of origin. This geographic distance from extended family has also changed the look of the "typical" American family. A final change in the American family has been the changing attitudes toward divorce, single parents, and same sex couples. The look of American families is becoming increasingly diversified, so that each family is able to define for itself how the family will work.

Appendix

QUESTIONNAIRE

The following questionnaire is a part of a research project that concerns family. This includes roles, behaviors, activities, and relationships between the members of the family.

There are no right or wrong answers. We also remind you that the questionnaire is anonymous and all information provided by you will be confidential. Please do not leave any questions unanswered.

Thank you for your cooperation.

Gender: Male □   Female □

Age (in years):_____

Are you presently residing in your place of
    permanent residence?   □ Yes   □ No

Family status:

_____ Single and I live by myself
_____ Single and I live with my parent(s)
_____ Married without children
_____ Married with children
_____ Divorced
_____ Widowed
_____ Other (please clarify)

Number of years that parents attended school:

	Father	Mother
0–6 years	□	□
7–9 years	□	□
10–12 years	□	□
more than 12 years	□	□

Father's occupation: _____
Mother's occupation: _____

PLEASE READ THE INSTRUCTIONS CAREFULLY

In the following questionnaire, the same statement refers to 9 persons, members of the family and relatives (father, mother, 10-year-old boy, 10-year-old girl, 20-year old male, 20-year-old female, grandfather, grandmother, uncle/aunt). Please respond separately for each member of the family. In responding to the members of the family, think of the members of YOUR family.

Some questions refer to *wife*. This always refers to the *mother* of the family (YOUR MOTHER). The same applies to questions referring to *husband*. This concerns the *husband*, who is of course also the *father* of the family.

If some members of the family (e.g. *grandparents*) have passed away, we would ask you to answer as if they were alive.

If you have more than one *uncle* or *aunt*, choose the ones that are closer to you. If you do NOT have an *uncle* or *aunt*, answer in the manner you would most likely respond, if you had one.

The same applies to the *10-year-old boy, 10-year-old girl, 20-year-old male, 20-year-old female* – that is, refer to your self at those ages, or, if you do not have a brother or sister, answer in the manner you would most likely respond if you had one.

If you are a student, please answer the following questions as if you lived at your permanent place of residence with your family.

Please answer the question by using the following scale:

    6 = in the same house,
    5 = upstairs/downstairs/ next flat,
    4 = opposite house or building,
    3 = in the same neighborhood,
    2 = in the same town, city,
    1 = live far away.

How far do you live from the following persons?

father	mother	siblings	grandfather	grandmother	uncle/aunt

Please answer the following two questions by using the scale:

    6 = daily,
    5 = once or twice a week,
    4 = every two weeks,
    3 = once a month,
    2 = once or twice a year,
    1 = rarely.

How often do you meet and see the following persons?

father	mother	siblings	grandfather	grandmother	uncle/aunt

How often do you communicate by telephone with the following persons?

father	mother	siblings	grandfather	grandmother	uncle/aunt

For each statement mark your answers on the stated behavior using the following scale:
6 – very much, 5 – much , 4 – enough, 3 – a little, 2 – very little , 1 – not at all.

1. *Father* provides emotional support to *children*	
Mother provides emotional support to *children*	
Grandfather provides emotional support to *grandchildren*	
Grandmother provides emotional support to *grandchildren*	
Uncle/aunt provides emotional support to *nephews and nieces*	
Father provides emotional support to *grandparents*	
Mother provides emotional support to *grandparents*	
10-year-old boy provides emotional support to *grandparents*	
10-year-old girl provides emotional support to *grandparents*	
20-year-old male provides emotional support to *grandparents*	
20-year-old female provides emotional support to *grandparents*	
Father provides emotional support to his *wife*	
Mother provides emotional support to her *husband*	
Grandfather provides emotional support to *father/mother*	
Grandmother provides emotional support to *father/mother*	
Uncle/aunt provides emotional support to *father/mother*	
10-year-old boy provides emotional support to *younger siblings*	
10-year-old girl provides emotional support to *younger siblings*	
20-year-old male provides emotional support to younger *siblings*	
20-year-old female provides emotional support to younger *siblings*	

2. *Father* keeps the *family* united	
Mother keeps the *family* united	
Grandfather keeps the *family* united	
Grandmother keeps the *family* united	
Uncle/aunt keeps the *family* united	
10-year-old boy keeps the *family* united	
10-year-old girl keeps the *family* united	
20-year-old male keeps the *family* united	
20-year-old female keeps the *family* united	

3. *Father* tries to keep a pleasant environment in the family	
Mother tries to keep a pleasant environment in the family	
Grandfather tries to keep a pleasant environment in the family	
Grandmother tries to keep a pleasant environment in the family	
Uncle/aunt tries to keep a pleasant environment in the family	
10-year-old boy tries to keep a pleasant environment in the family	
10-year-old girl tries to keep a pleasant environment in the family	
20-year-old male tries to keep a pleasant environment in the family	
20-year-old female tries to keep a pleasant environment in the family	

4. *Father* conveys traditions, manners, and customs (e.g. reads, tells stories) to *children*	
Mother conveys traditions, manners, and customs (e.g. reads, tells stories) to *children*	
Grandfather conveys traditions, manners, and customs (e.g. reads, tells stories) to *grandchildren*	
Grandmother conveys traditions, manners, and customs (e.g. reads, tells stories) to *grandchildren*	
Uncle/aunt conveys traditions, manners, and customs (e.g. reads, tells stories) to *nephews and nieces*	
10-year-old boy conveys traditions, manners, and customs (e.g. reads, tells stories) to *younger siblings*	
10-year-old girl conveys traditions, manners, and customs (e.g. reads, tells stories) to *younger siblings*	
20-year-old male conveys traditions, manners, and customs (e.g. reads, tells stories) to *younger siblings*	
20-year-old female conveys traditions, manners, and customs (e.g. reads, tells stories) to *younger siblings*	

5. *Father* conveys the religious tradition to *children*	
Mother conveys the religious tradition to *children*	
Grandfather conveys the religious tradition to *grandchildren*	
Grandmother conveys the religious tradition to *grandchildren*	
Uncle/aunt conveys the religious tradition to *nephews and nieces*	
10-year-old boy conveys the religious tradition to *younger siblings*	
10-year-old girl conveys the religious tradition to *younger siblings*	
20-year-old male conveys the religious tradition to *younger siblings*	
20-year-old female conveys the religious tradition to *younger siblings*	

6. *Father* contributes to the preservation of family relations (e.g. family gatherings during the holidays, anniversaries)	
Mother contributes to the preservation of family relations (e.g. family gatherings during the holidays, anniversaries)	
Grandfather contributes to the preservation of family relations (e.g. family gatherings during the holidays, anniversaries)	
Grandmother contributes to the preservation of family relations (e.g. family gatherings during the holidays, anniversaries)	
Uncle/aunt contributes to the preservation of family relations (e.g. family gatherings during the holidays, anniversaries)	
10-year-old male contributes to the preservation of family relations (e.g. family gatherings during the holidays, anniversaries)	
10-year-old female contributes to the preservation of family relations (e.g. family gatherings during the holidays, anniversaries)	
20-year-old male contributes to the preservation of family relations (e.g. family gatherings during the holidays, anniversaries)	

7. *Father* supports *the grandparents* when in need (illness, financial problems, etc.)	
Mother supports *the grandparents* when in need (illness, financial problems, etc.)	
Grandfather supports *the grandchildren* when in need (illness, financial problems, etc.)	
Grandmother supports *the grandchildren* when in need (illness, financial problems, etc.)	
Uncle/aunt supports *the nephews and nieces* when in need (illness, financial problems, etc.)	

8. *Father* takes daily care (cooking, shopping) of *grandparents*	
Mother takes daily care (cooking, shopping) of *grandparents*	
Grandfather takes daily care (cooking, shopping) of *grandchildren*	
Grandmother takes daily care (cooking, shopping) of *grandchildren*	
Uncle/aunt takes daily care (cooking, shopping) of *nephews and nieces*	

9. *Father* is the protector of the family	
Mother is the protector of the family	
Grandfather is the protector of the family	
Grandmother is the protector of the family	
Uncle/aunt is the protector of the family	

10. When there are arguments or disputes, *father* makes the decision regarding the manner of solution	
When there are arguments or disputes, *mother* makes the decision regarding the manner of solution	
When there are arguments or disputes, *grandfather* makes the decision regarding the manner of solution	
When there are arguments or disputes, *grandmother* makes the decision regarding the manner of solution	
When there are arguments or disputes, *uncle/aunt* makes the decision regarding the manner of solution	

11. *Father* does housework (cleans, cooks, washes)	
Mother does housework (cleans, cooks, washes)	
Grandfather does housework (cleans, cooks, washes)	
Grandmother does housework (cleans, cooks, washes)	
Uncle/aunt does housework (cleans, cooks, washes)	
10-year-old boy does housework (cleans, cooks, washes)	
10-year-old girl does housework (cleans, cooks, washes)	
20-year-old male does housework (cleans, cooks, washes)	
20-year-old female does housework (cleans, cooks, washes)	

12. *Father* does the shopping, pays bills, etc.	
Mother does the shopping, pays bills, etc.	
Grandfather does the shopping, pays bills, etc.	
Grandmother does the shopping, pays bills, etc.	
Uncle/aunt does the shopping, pays bills, etc.	
10-year-old boy does the shopping, pays bills, etc.	
10-year-old girl does the shopping, pays bills, etc.	
20-year-old male does the shopping, pays bills, etc.	
20-year-old female does the shopping, pays bills, etc.	

13. *Father* takes the *children* to school	
Mother takes the *children* to school	
Grandfather takes the *grandchildren* to school	
Grandmother takes the *grandchildren* to school	
Uncle/aunt takes the *nephews and nieces* to school	
10-year-old boy takes the *younger siblings* to school	
10-year-old girl takes the *younger siblings* to school	
20-year-old male takes the *younger siblings* to school	
20-year-old female takes the *younger siblings* to school	

14. *Father* plays with the *children*	
Mother plays with the *children*	
Grandfather plays with the *grandchildren*	
Grandmother plays with the *grandchildren*	
Uncle/aunt plays with the *nephews and nieces*	
10-year-old boy plays with the *younger siblings*	
10-year-old girl plays with the *younger siblings*	
20-year-old male plays with the *younger siblings*	
20-year-old female plays with the *younger siblings*	

15. *Father* helps *children* with homework	
Mother helps *children* with homework	
Grandfather helps *grandchildren* with homework	
Grandmother helps *grandchildren* with homework	
Uncle/aunt helps *nephews and nieces* with homework	

16. *Father* teaches good behavior to *children*	
Mother teaches good behavior to *children*	
Grandfather teaches good behavior to *grandchildren*	
Grandmother teaches good behavior to *grandchildren*	
Uncle/aunt teaches good behavior to *nephews and nieces*	

17. *Father* contributes financially to the *family*	
Mother contributes financially to the *family*	
Grandfather contributes financially to the *family*	
Grandmother contributes financially to the *family*	
Uncle/aunt contributes financially to the *family*	
10-year-old boy contributes financially to the *family*	
10-year-old girl contributes financially to the *family*	
20-year-old male contributes financially to the *family*	
20-year-old female contributes financially to the *family*	

18. *Father* manages the family finances	
Mother manages the family finances	
Grandfather manages the family finances	
Grandmother manages the family finances	
Uncle/aunt manages the family finances	

19. *Father* gives pocket money to *children*	
Mother gives pocket money to *children*	
Grandfather gives pocket money to *grandchildren*	
Grandmother gives pocket money to *grandchildren*	
Uncle/aunt gives pocket money to *nephews and nieces*	

20. *Father* supports (at the beginning of their career) *the children*	
Mother supports (at the beginning of their career) *the children*	
Grandfather supports (at the beginning of their career) *the grandchildren*	
Grandmother supports (at the beginning of their career) *the grandchildren*	
Uncle/aunt supports (at the beginning of their career) *the nephews and nieces*	

21. When the parents are not home, *grandfather* babysits with *grandchildren*	
When the parents are not home, *grandmother* babysits with *grandchildren*	
When the parents are not home, *uncle/aunt* babysits with *nephews and nieces*	
When the parents are not home, *10-year-old boy* babysits with *younger siblings*	
When the parents are not home, *10-year-old girl* babysits with *younger siblings*	
When the parents are not home, *20-year-old male* babysits with *younger siblings*	
When the parents are not home, *20-year-old female* babysits with *younger siblings*	

22. *Grandfather* helps the *parents* with their work (fields, shop or family occupation)	
Grandmother helps the *parents* with their work (fields, shop or family occupation)	
Uncle/aunt helps the *parents* with their work (fields, shop or family occupation)	
10-year-old boy helps the *parents* with their work (fields, shop or family occupation)	
10-year-old girl helps the *parents* with their work (fields, shop or family occupation)	
20-year-old male helps the *parents* with their work (fields, shop or family occupation)	
20-year-old female helps the *parents* with their work (fields, shop or family occupation)	

FIVE-FACTOR PERSONALITY TRAITS

(Williams, Satterwhite, and Saiz, 1998)

EX-HI: EXTRAVERSION	EX-LO: EXTRAVERSION
AG-HI: AGREEABLENESS	AG-LO: AGREEABLENESS
CO-HI: CONSCIENTIOUSNESS	CO-LO: CONSCIENTIOUSNESS
ES-HI: EMOTIONAL STABILITY	ES-L0: EMOTIONAL STABILITY
OE-HI: OPENESS TO EXPERIENCE	OE-LO: OPENESS TO EXPERIENCE

Very much like me			Neither like me nor unlike me			Not like me at all
7	6	5	4	3	2	1

ES-HI	_____	1. Stable
ES-HI	_____	2. Optimistic
AG-HI	_____	3. Understanding
OE-LO	_____	4. Inhibited
EX-HI	_____	5. Sociable
OE-LO	_____	6. Conservative
EX-HI	_____	7. Active
OE-HI	_____	8. Spontaneous
CO-HI	_____	9. Responsible
AG-LO	_____	10. Quarrelsome
AG-LO	_____	11. Deceitful
CO-HI	_____	12. Organized
ES-L0	_____	13. Moody
CO-LO	_____	14. Careless
EX-LO	_____	15. Withdrawn
CO-HI	_____	16. Reliable
OE-HI	_____	17. Imaginative
CO-LO	_____	18. Lazy
EX-HI	_____	19. Outgoing
EX-LO	_____	20. Shy
AG-LO	_____	21. Rude
AG-HI	_____	22. Sympathetic
CO-LO	_____	23. Disorderly
OE-HI	_____	24. Adventurous
EX-LO	_____	25. Quiet
OE-LO	_____	26. Rigid
ES-LO	_____	27. Irritable

ES-LO	_____	28. Anxious
AG-HI	_____	29. Considerate
ES-HI	_____	30. Calm

VALUES

(Schwartz)

EM : Embeddedness	**IA: Intellectual autonomy**
CO: Conservatism	**AA: Affective autonomy**
HA: Harmony	**MA: Mastery**
EC: Egalitarian commitment	

As a guiding principle in my life, this value is:

Very import- ant	Important	Some- what important	Neither im- portant nor unimportant	Somewhat unimportant	Un- important	Not important at all
7	6	5	4	3	2	1

CO	_____	1. Family Security (safety for loved ones)
AA	_____	2. Pleasure (gratification of desires)
HA	_____	3. A World of Beauty (beauty of nature and the arts)
CO	_____	4. Respect for Tradition (preservation of time-honored customs)
IA	_____	5. Broadminded (tolerant of different ideals and beliefs)
CO	_____	6. Honoring of Parents and Elders (showing respect)
AA	_____	7. An Exciting Life (stimulating experiences)
MA	_____	8. Independent (self-reliant, self-sufficient)
MA	_____	9. Daring (seeking adventure, risk)
CO	_____	10. Social Order (stability of society)
EM	_____	11. Authority (the right to lead or command)
IA	_____	12. Creativity (uniqueness, imagination)
EM	_____	13. Wealth (material possessions, money)
IA	_____	14. Curious (interested in everything, exploring)
HA	_____	15. Unity with Nature (fitting into nature)
CO	_____	16. National Security (protection of my nation from enemies)
MA	_____	17. Choosing own Goals (selecting own purposes)
HA	_____	18. Protecting the Environment (preserving nature)
EM	_____	19. Social Power (control over other, dominance)
AA	_____	20. Enjoying Life (enjoying, food, sex, leisure, etc.)
CO	_____	21. Reciprocation of Favors (avoidance of indebtedness)

SELF-CONSTRUAL SCALE

(Singelis)

I: INDEPENDENT SELF	D: INTERDEPENDENT SELF

Strongly agree	Agree	Agree somewhat	Nether agree nor disagree	Disagree somewhat	Disagree	Strongly disagree
7	6	5	4	3	2	1

I _____   1. I enjoy being unique and different from others in many respects.

D _____   2. I respect people who are modest about themselves.

I _____   3. I feel it is important for me to act as an independent person.

D _____   4. I will sacrifice my self-interest for the benefit of the group I am in.

I _____   5. I prefer to be direct and forthright when dealing with people I've just met.

D _____   6. I feel good when I cooperate with others.

I _____   7. I am comfortable with being singled out for praise or rewards.

D _____   8. I often have the feeling that my relationships with others are more important than my own accomplishments.

I _____   9. Speaking up during a class (or a meeting) is not a problem for me.

I _____   10. I act the same way no matter who I am with.

D _____   11. My happiness depends on the happiness of those around me.

D _____   12. I will stay in a group if they need me, even when I am not happy with the group.

I _____   13. I try to do what is best for me, regardless of how that might affect others.

I _____   14. Being able to take care of myself is a primary concern for me.

D _____   15. It is important to me to respect decisions made by the group.

D _____   16. It is important for me to maintain harmony within my group.

I _____   17. I act the same way at home that I do at school.

D _____   18. I usually go along with what others want to do, even when I would rather do something different.

FAMILY VALUES

(Georgas)

HI: HIERARCHICAL ROLES OF MOTHER AND FATHER RE: RELATIONSHIPS WITH FAMILY AND KIN						
Strongly agree	Agree	Agree somewhat	Neither agree nor disagree	Disagree somewhat	Disagree	Strongly Disagree
7	6	5	4	3	2	1

HI _____ 1. The father should be the head of the family.

RE _____ 2. One should maintain good relationships with one's relatives.

HI _____ 3. The mother's place is in the home.

HI _____ 4. The mother should be the go-between the father and the children.

RE _____ 5. Parents should teach their children to behave properly.

HI _____ 6. The father should handle the money in the house.

_____ 7. Parents shouldn't get involved in the private lives of their married children.

RE _____ 8. The children have the obligation to care for their parents when they become old.

RE _____ 9. Children should help with the chores of the house.

RE _____ 10. The problems of the family should be solved within the family.

RE _____ 11. Children should obey their parents.

RE _____ 12. We should honor and protect our family's reputation.

RE _____ 13. Parents should help their children financially.

RE _____ 14. Children should respect their grandparents.

HI _____ 15. The mother should accept the decisions of the father.

RE _____ 16. The children should work in order to help the family.

_____ 17. The parents shouldn't argue in front of the children.

HI _____ 18. The father should be the breadwinner.

EMOTIONAL DISTANCE

(Georgas)

In this questionnaire you are requested to ask yourself: **"How close to these people or how distant from them do I feel?"** The list has a number next to each person from 1 to 22. Please write in the space a number, from 1 = Very far to 7 = Very close, which represents the **emotional distance** between you and this particular person – that is how close or distant from you do you feel this person.

In some cases you may find that you have never had any kind of contact with some of the persons on this list (e.g., son or daughter, grandmother is deceased, the President of your country). Think about how close to these people or how far from them you would feel if you came into contact with them and then place the respective numbers in the circle you chose. If you have more than one uncle or aunt, choose the ones that are closer to you. If you do NOT have an uncle or aunt, answer in the manner would would most likely respond, if you had one.

Place a number which corresponds to the emotional distance you feel from the person.

Very close	Close	Somewhat close	In the middle	Somewhat far	Far	Very far
7	6	5	4	3	2	1

_____ 1. Your mother
_____ 2. Your neighbors
_____ 3. Your friends
_____ 4. Your brothers or sisters
_____ 5. The journalist/reporters of the newspaper(s)
_____ 6. Your colleagues at work
_____ 7. Your acquaintances
_____ 8. The priest of the church (iman of the mosque, etc.) you attend
_____ 9. Your father
_____ 10. Your teachers at primary school
_____ 11. The prime minister/president of your country
_____ 12. Your grandparents
_____ 13. The shopkeepers in your local area/neighborhood (baker, grocer, etc.)
_____ 14. The writers you know
_____ 15. Your husband or your wife/your boyfriend or your girlfriend
_____ 16. Your fellow students
_____ 17. The members of the parliament of your constituency
_____ 18. Your cousins
_____ 19. Your teachers at high school
_____ 20. Your uncles or your aunts
_____ 21. The newscasters you know

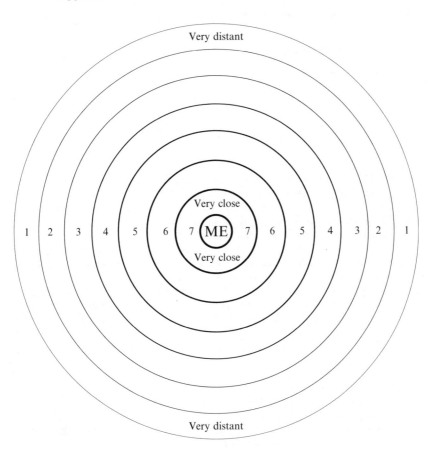

References

Aberle, D. F., Cohen, A. K., Davis, A., Levy, M., and Sutton, F. X. (1950). Functional prerequisites of society. *Ethics*, 60: 100–111.

Acar, F. (1991). Women in academic science careers in Turkey. In V. Stolte-Heiskanen, F. Acar, N. Ananieva and D. Gaudart (eds.), *Women in science: Token women or gender equality?*, pp. 147–171. Oxford: Berg.

Achoui, M. (1983). "The impact of ideology and organizational power on communication: A comparative perspective." Unpublished doctoral thesis, Rensselear Polytechnic Institute, Troy, New York.

Adeniyi, A. M. and Mivanyi, Y. J. (1999, August). Nutrition, child development and single parenthood in Kaduna metropolis, Kaduna, Nigeria. Paper presented at the IXth European Conference on Developmental Psychology, island of Spetses, Greece.

Aerts, E. (1993). Bringing the institution back in. In P. A. Cowan, D. Field, D. A. Hansen, A. Skonick and G. E. Swanson (eds.), *Family, self, and society*, pp. 3–41. Hillsdale, NJ: Erlbaum.

Ahmad, M. B. (1982). *The Muslim family laws*. Lahore: Kausar Brothers.

Ahnert, L., Krätzig, S., Meischner, T., and Schmidt, A. (1994). Sozialisationskonzepte für Kleinkinder: Wirkungen tradierter Erziehungsvorstellungen und staatssozialistischer Erziehungsdoktrinen im intra- und interkulturellen Ost–West-Vergleich [Socialization concepts of infants: Effects of traditional pedagogic concepts and governmental socialist pedagogic doctrines in an intra- and intercultural east–west comparison]. In G. Trommdsdorff (ed.), *Psychologische Aspekte des sozio-politischen Wandels in Ostdeutschland*, pp. 94–110. Berlin and New York: Walter de Gruyter.

Ahnert, L., Meischner, T., and Schmidt, A. (1995). Äquivalenzen in frühkindlichen Interaktionsmustern: Ein Vergleich von russischen und deutschen Mutter–Kind-Dyaden [Similarities in early interactional patterns: A comparison of Russian and German mother–child dyads]. In G. Trommsdorff (ed.), *Kindheit und Jugend in verschiedenen Kulturen*, pp. 65–81. Weinheim/Munich: Juventa Verlag.

Akande, A. (2000). School-related fears in children and their relationship to worries and anxiety in the twenty-first century Southern Africa. *Studia Psychologica*, 42: 303–360.

  (2002). "Lifeworlds in southern African states." Unpublished paper, University of Bath.

(2004). "Seek and ye shall find: Rethinking higher education in (South) Africa–Quo Vadis?" Unpublished paper, Institute of Research and Consultancy, South Africa.

Al-Badran, K. and Rwished, F. (1989). An empirical study for marriage contract in the eastern region of the Saudi Arabia Kingdom. *Studies and issues from the Arab Gulf society* [Arabic text] (Social and Labor Studies Series, N14, The Executive Bureau of the Ministry Council of Labor and Social Affairs of the Arab Gulf States Cooperation Counsel). Bahrain: Al-Manama.

Al-Khalifa, A. H. (1990). *Social factors impact on population distribution in Riyadh City neighborhoods: An empirical study* [Arabic text]. Riyadh: Center of Crime Research.

Al-Khariji, A. (1983). *Systems of the Muslim society with application on the Saudi society* [Arabic text]. Jeddah: Ramta.

Al-Masa'ad, A. (1995). "Social change and neighborhood relationship: An empirical study in Al-Malz area in Riyadh City" [Arabic text]. Unpublished master's thesis. College of Social Sciences, Al-Imam Saud University.

Al-Saif, M. I. (1997). *Introduction to the study of Saudi society* [Arabic text]. Riyadh: Al-Khariji.

Alberdi, I. (1995). *Informe sobre la situación de la familia en España* [Report on the situation of the family in Spain]. Madrid: Ministerio de Asuntos Sociales.

(1999). *La nueva familia española* [The new Spanish family]. Madrid: Taurus.

Albrow, M. and King, E. (1990). *Globalization, knowledge and society: Readings from international sociology*. London: Sage.

Alcock, J. (1998). *Animal behavior: An evolutionary approach*. Sunderland, MS: Sinauer.

Alexandrova, T. A. (1990). *Koe-chto o dedoushkah* [Something about grandparents]. Moscow: Znanie.

Allan, G. (1985). *Family life*. Oxford: Blackwell.

Allik, J. and McCrae, R. R. (2004). Towards a geography of personality traits: Patterns of profiles across 36 cultures. *Journal of Cross-Cultural Psychology*, 35: 13–28.

Amado, G. and Vinagre-Brasil, H. (1991). Organizational behaviors and cultural context: The Brazilian "jeitinho." *International Studies of Management and Organization*, 2: 38–61.

Amani, M. (2001). *General demography of Iran*. [In Farsi]. Tehran: Samt.

Anderson, M. (1971). *Family structure in XIXth century Lancashire*. Cambridge Studies in Sociology no. 5. Cambridge: Cambridge University Press.

Armstrong, P. (1990). Economic conditions and family structures. In M. Baker (ed.), *Families: Changing trends in Canada*, 2nd edn., pp. 67–92. Toronto: McGraw-Hill Ryerson.

Arriagada, I. (2002). Cambios y desigualdad en las familias latinoamericanas [Changes and inequality in the Latin American families]. *Revista de la CEPAL*, 77: 143–161.

Asante, M. K. (1993). *Malcom X as cultural hero and other Afrocentric essays*. New Jersey: Africa World Press.

Ataca, B. (1992). "An investigation of variance in fertility due to sex-related differentiation in child-rearing practices." Unpublished master's thesis, Bogazici University, Istanbul.

Ataca, B., Kağıtçıbaşı, Ç., and Diri, A. (2005). The Turkish family and the value of children: Trends over time. In G. Trommsdorff and B. Nauck, (eds.), *The value of children in cross-cultural perspectives*. Berlin: Pabst.

Ataca, B. and Sunar, D. (1999). Continuity and change in Turkish urban family life. *Psychology and Developing Societies*, 11: 77–90.

Attalides, M. (1981). *Social change and urbanization in Cyprus: A study of Nicosia*. Nicosia, Cyprus: Zavallis Press.

Attias-Donfut, C., Lapierre, N., and Segalen, M. (2002). *Le nouvel esprit de famille [The new family spirit]*. Paris: Odile Jacob.

Attias-Donfut, C. and Segalen, M. (1998). *Grands-parents: La famille à travers les generations* [Grandparents: The family across generations]. Paris: Odile Jacob.

Avort, A. van der, Cuyvers, P., and Hoog, K. de (1996). *Het Nederlandse gezinsleven aan het einde van de twintigste eeuw* [Family life in the Netherlands at the end of the twentieth century]. The Hague: Nederlandse Gezinsraad.

Aydin, B. and Oztutuncu, F. (2001). Examination of adolescents' negative thoughts, depressive mood, and family environment. *Adolescence*, 36: 77–83.

Azuma, H. (1986). Why study child development in Japan. In H. Stevenson, H. Azuma, and K. Hakuta (eds.), *Child development and education in Japan*, pp. 3–12. New York: W H. Freeman.

Badan Pusat Statistik, Indonesia (1996). *Survei penduduk antar sensus 1995*. Jakarta, Indonesia: BPS-Statistics Indonesia.

Bainame, K., Letamo, G., and Majelantle, R. G. (2002). "The effects of rural inequalities of fertility and migration in Botswana." Unpublished paper, Gaborone, Botswana.

Baker, M. and Dryden, J. (1993). *Families in Canadian society*. Toronto: McGraw-Hill Ryerson.

Baldi, S., Perie, M., Skidmore, D., Greenberg, E., and Hahn, C. (2001). Highlights of US results from the International IEA Civic Education Study (CivEd). Washington, DC: National Center for Education Statistics, USA. Retrieved from http://www.nces.ed.gov/timss.

Bales, R. F. (1950). *Interaction process analysis*. Cambridge, MA: Addison-Wesley.

Bales, R. F. and Slater, P. (1955). Roles differentiation in small decision-making groups. In T. Parsons and R. F. Bales (eds.), *Family, socialization and interaction process*, pp. 259–306. New York: Free Press.

Ballard, R. and Kalra, V. S. (1994). *The ethnic dimensions of the 1991 census: A preliminary report*. Manchester: Manchester Census Group, University of Manchester.

Bank of Botswana (2001). "Botswana." Unpublished report, Government Press, Gaborone, Botswana.

Barnett, R. C. and Shen, Y. (1997). Gender, high- and low-schedule control, housework tasks, and psychological distress: A study of dual-earner couples. *Journal of Family Issues*, 18: 403–438.

Barry, H., Child, I., and Bacon, M. (1959). Relations of child training to subsistence economy. *American Anthropologist*, 61: 51–63.

Basaran, F. A. (1974). *Psychosocial development: A study of children ages 7–11* [Turkish text]. Ankara, Turkey: Ankara University Press. (Reprint from Research VII, 1969).

Bastug, S. (2002). Household and family in Turkey: An historical perspective. In E. Ozdalga and R. Liljestrom (eds.), *Autonomy and dependence in family: Turkey and Sweden in critical perspective*, pp. 99–115. Istanbul: Swedish Research Institute.

Baumrind, D. (1980). New directions in socialization research. *American Psychologist*, 35: 639–652.

Bawin-Legros, B. (1988). *Familles, mariage, divorce: Une sociologie des comportements familiaux contemporains* [Families, marriage, divorce: Sociology of contemporary family behavior]. Liège, Belgium: Pierre Mardaga.

Beiser, M., Hou, F., Hyman, I., and Tousignant, M. (2002). Poverty, family process and the mental health of immigrant children in Canada. *American Journal of Public Health*, 92: 220–227.

Beishon, S., Modood, T., and Virdee, S. (1998). *Ethnic minority families*. London: Policy Studies Institute.

Bender, D. R. (1967). A refinement of the concept of household: Families, co-residence, and domestic functions. *American Anthropologist*, 69: 493–504.

Bendix, R. (1967). Tradition and modernity reconsidered. *Comparative Studies in Society and History*, 9: 292–346.

Bengtson, V. L. and Schrader, S. S. (1982). Parent–child relations. In D. J. Mangen and W. A. Peterson (eds.), *Research instruments in social gerontology*, vol. 2, pp. 115–128. Minneapolis: University of Minnesota Press.

Bennett, J. (1976). *The ecological transition*. London: Pergamon.

Beny, R., Nasr, S. M., and Bakhtiar, M. (1975). *Iran, the bridge of turquoise*. Toronto: McClelland and Stewart Ltd.

Berger, P. and Luckmann, T. (1999). *La construcción social de la realidad* [The social construction of reality]. Buenos Aires: Amorrortu.

Berghe, P. L. van de (1979). *Human family systems: An evolutionary view*. New York: Elsevier.

Berik, G. (1995). Towards an understanding of gender hierarchy in Turkey: A comparative analysis of carpet-weaving villages. In S. Tekeli (ed.), *Women in modern Turkish society: A reader*, pp. 112–127. London: Zed Books.

Berkner, L. K. (1975). The use and misuse of census data for the historical analysis of family structure. *Journal of Interdisciplinary History*, 5: 721–738.

Bernardes, J. (1997). *Family studies*. London: Routledge.

Berry, J. W. (1966). Temne and Eskimo perceptual skills. *International Journal of Psychology*, 1: 207–229.

(1967). Independence and conformity in subsistence-level societies. *Journal of Personality and Social Psychology*, 7: 415–418.

(1969). On cross-cultural comparability. *International Journal of Psychology*, 4: 119–128.

(1975). An ecological approach to cross-cultural psychology. *Nederlands Tijdschrift voor de Psychologie*, 30: 51–84.

(1976). *Human ecology and cognitive style: Comparative studies in cultural and psychological adaptation.* New York: Sage/Halsted.

(1979). A cultural ecology of social behavior. In L. Berkowitz (ed.), *Advances in experimental social psychology*, vol. 12, pp. 177–206. New York: Academic Press.

(1985). Cultural psychology and ethnic psychology. In I. Reyes Lagunes and Y. H. Poortinga (eds.), *From a different perspective*, pp. 3–15. Lisse, The Netherlands: Swets and Zeitlinger.

(1994a). Ecology of individualism and collectivism. In U. Kim, H. C. Triandis, Ç. Kağıtçıbaşı, S.-C. Choi, and G. Yoon (eds.), *Individualism and collectivism: Theory, method, and applications*, pp. 77–84. Thousand Oaks, CA: Sage.

(1994b). An ecological approach to cultural and ethnic psychology. In E. Trickett (ed.), *Human Diversity*, pp. 115–141. San Francisco, CA: Jossey-Bass.

(1995). The descendants of a model. *Culture and Psychology*, 1: 373–380.

(2000). Cross-cultural psychology: A symbiosis of cultural and comparative approaches. *Asian Journal of Social Psychology*, 3: 197–205.

Berry, J. W. Bennett, J. A., and Denny. P. (2000, July). *Ecology, culture and cognitive processing.* Paper presented at the fifteenth Congress of the International Association for Cross-Cultural Psychology, Pultusk, Poland.

Berry, J. W., Dasen, P. R., and Witkin, H. A. (1983). Developmental theories in cross-cultural perspective. In L. Alder (ed.), *Cross-cultural research at issue*, pp. 13–21. New York: Academic Press.

Berry, J. W. and Kalin, R. (2000). Multicultural policy and social psychology: The Canadian experience. In S. Renshon and J. Duckitt (eds.), *Political psychology: Cultural and cross-cultural foundations*, pp. 263–284. London: Macmillan.

Berry, J. W. and Kim, U. (1993). The way ahead: From indigenous psychologies to a universal psychology. In U. Kim and J. W. Berry (eds.), *Indigenous psychologies*, pp. 277–280. Newbury Park, CA: Sage.

Berry, J. W., Poortinga, Y. H., Pandey, J., Dasen, P. R., Saraswathi, T. S., Segall, M. H., and Kağıtçıbaşı, Ç., (eds.). (1997). *Handbook of cross-cultural psychology*, 2nd edn., vols. 1–3. Needham Heights, MA: Allyn and Bacon.

Berry, J. W., Poortinga, Y. H., Segall, M. H., and Dasen, P. R. (2002). *Cross-cultural psychology: Research and applications*, 2nd edn. New York: Cambridge University Press.

Berry, J. W., van de Koppel, J. M. H., Sénéchal, C., Annis, R. C., Bahuchet, S., Cavalli-Sforza, L. L., and Witkin, H. A. (1986). *On the edge of the forest: Cultural adaptation and cognitive development in Central Africa.* Lisse, The Netherlands: Swets and Zeitlinger.

Biasoli-Alves, Z. M. M. (1997). Famílias brasileiras do século XX: Os valores e as práticas de educação da criança [Brazilian families in the twentieth century: Child rearing values and practices]. *Temas em Psicologia*, 3: 33–49.

Blair, S. L., Blair, M., and Madamba, A. (1999). Racial/ethnic differences in High school students' academic performance: Understanding the interleave of social class and ethnicity in the family context. *Journal of Comparative Family Studies*, 30: 539–555.

Blood, R. O. and Wolfe, D. M. (1960). *Husbands and wives. The dynamics of married living.* New York: Free Press.

Blos, P. (1979). *The adolescent passage.* New York: International Universities Press.

Blumberg, R. L. and Winch, R. F. (1972). Societal complexity and familial complexity: Evidence for the curvilinear hypothesis. *American Journal of Sociology,* 77: 898–920.

Boesch, C. (1991). Teaching among wild chimpanzees. *Animal Behavior,* 41: 530–532.

Bogardus, E. S. (1925). Measuring social distance. *Journal of Applied Sociology,* 9: 299–308.

Bogenschneider, K. (2000). Has family policy come of age? A decade review of the state of US family policy in the 1990s. *Journal of Marriage and the Family,* 62: 1136–1159.

Bohannan, P. (1963). *Social anthropology.* New York: Holt, Rinehart and Winston.

Boiko, V. V. (1980). *Molodetnaya semya* [Families with small numbers of children]. Moscow: Statistic.

Bond, R. and Smith, P. (1996). Culture and conformity: A meta-analysis. *Psychological Bulletin,* 119: 111–137.

Bonke, J. (2004a). *Modern man: The slow move towards equality.* European Observatory on the Social Situation, Demography, and the Family. SDF Puzzle. Retrieved from http://www.oif.ac.at/sdf/sdf_05_2004.html.

(2004b). *The modern husband/father and wife/mother. How do they spend their time?* European Observatory on the Social Situation, Demography, and the Family. SDF Puzzle. Retrieved from http://www.oif.ac.at/sdf/sdf_05_2004.html.

Borisenko, B. K. (1998). *Vesylny zvuchai ta obriady na Ukraini* [Marriage customs in Ukraine]. Kiev: Naukova dumka.

Bott, E. (1971). *Family and social networks: Roles, norms, and external relationships in ordinary urban families.* New York: The Free Press.

Boutafnoushat, M. (1984). *The Algerian family* [Arabic text]. Algiers: University Publications National Office.

Boyd, R. and Richerson, P. (1983). Why is culture adaptive? *Quarterly Review of Biology,* 58: 209–214.

Brannon, L. (2002). *Gender: Psychological perspectives,* 3rd edn. Boston, MA: Allyn and Bacon.

Bravo, G. (1990). Imágenes de la vida cotidiana chilena, 1850–1930. Consideraciones sobre el matrimonio y la familia [Images of the Chilean daily life, 1850–1930. Considerations about marriage and family]. In S. Pinto (ed.), *Familia, matrimonio y mestizaje en Chile colonial,* pp. 85–102. Santiago: Universidad de Chile.

Bretschneider, P. (1995). *Polygyny: A cross-cultural study.* Uppsala, Sweden: Acta Universitatis Upsaliensis.

Brewster, K. L. and Padavic, I. (2000). Change in gender-ideology, 1977–1996: The contributions of intracohort change and population turnover. *Journal of Marriage and the Family,* 62: 477–487.

Bril, B. (1995). Les apports de la psychologie culturelle comparative à la compré-henson du développement de l'enfant [The relevance of comparative cultural psychology to the comprehension of child development]. In J. Lautrey (ed.), *Universel et différentiel en psychologie*, pp. 327–349. Paris: PUF.

Brink, G. van den (1996). *De grote overgang. Een lokaal onderzoek naar de modernisering van het bestaan. Woensel, 1670–1920* [The big transition. A local inquiry into the modernization of every day life. Woensel, 1670–1920]. Nijmegen: SUN.

Bronfenbrenner, U. (1979). *The ecology of human development.* Cambridge, MA: Harvard University Press.

Bronfenbrenner, U. and Weiss, H. B. (1983). Beyond policies without people: An ecological perspective on child and family policy. In E. Zigler, S. L. Kagan, and E. Klugman (eds.), *Children, families and government: Perspectives on American social policy*, pp. 393–414. New York: Cambridge University Press.

Brown, P. and Levinson, S. C. (1987). *Politeness: Some universals in language use.* Cambridge: Cambridge University Press.

Brune, N., Bulgutch, M., Fielding, J., Faulknor, A., Hawes, R., and O'Neill, M. (2003). *Defining Canada: History, identity, and culture.* Toronto: McGraw-Hill Ryerson.

Brunner, J. J. (1990). Tradicionalismo y modernidad en la cultura latinoamericana [Traditionalism and modernity in Latin American culture]. *Documentos de Trabajo, Serie Educación y Cultura, No. 4.* Santiago: FLACSO.

Buah, F. K. (1960). *Modern history since 1750.* Stella Marris College London: Macmillan.

Bulcroft, R. A. and Bulcroft, K. A. (1993). Race differences in attitudinal and motivational factors in the decision to marry. *Journal of Marriage and the Family*, 55: 338–355.

Burger, E. and Milardo, R. M. (1995). Manital independence and social networks. *Journal of Social and Personal Relationships*, 12: 403–415.

Burgess, E. W. (1926). The family as a unity of interacting personalities. *Family*, 7: 3–9.

Burton, M. L. (1996). Intergenerational patterns of providing care in African-American families with teenage childbearers: Emergent patterns in an ethnographic study. In V. L. Bengtson, K. W. Schaie, and L. M. Burton (eds.), *Adult intergenerational relations: Effects of social change*, pp. 79–96. New York: Springer.

Burton, M. L. and Jarrett, R. L. (2000). In the mix, yet on the margins: The place of families in urban neighborhood and child development research. *Journal of Marriage and the Family*, 62: 1114–1135.

Burton, M. L., Moore, C. C., Whiting, J. W. M., and Romney, A. K. (1996). Regions based on social structure. *Current Anthropology*, 37: 87–123.

Bussemaker, J. (1997). *Overheid, gezin en sekse: Naar een nieuwe consensus* [Government, family and gender: Towards a new consensus]. Jaarboek Gezinsbeleid. The Hague: Nederlandse Gezinsraad.

Cadolle, S. (2000). *La décomposition de la famille* [The disintegration of the family]. Paris: Odile Jacob.

Cândido, A. (1972). The Brazilian family. In T. L. Smith and A. Marchant (eds.), *Brasil: Portrait of half a continent*, pp. 291–312. Westport, CT: Greenwood Press.

Carlos, M. L. and Sellers, L. (1972). Family, kinship structure, and modernization in Latin America. *Latin American Research Review*, 7: 95–124.

Carter, B. and McGoldrick, M. (1999). *The expanded family life cycle: Individual, family, and social perspectives*. Needham Heights, MA: Allyn and Bacon.

Carvalho, M. C. B. (2000). O lugar da família na política social [The family within the social policy]. In M. C. B. Carvalho (ed.), *A família contemporânea em debate*, pp. 13–21. São Paulo, Brazil: EDUC/Cortez.

Cassia, P. S. and Bada, C. (1992). *The making of the modern Greek family*. Cambridge: Cambridge University Press.

Cavieres, E. (1990). Aspectos materiales y sentimentales de la familia tradicional colonial [Material and affective issues of the colonial traditional family]. In S. Pinto (ed.), *Familia, matrimonio y mestizaje en Chile colonial*, pp. 51–67. Santiago: Universidad de Chile.

(1997). Transgresiones al matrimonio en Chile tradicional: Las faltas a la ley y a la fe [Transgressions to marriage in traditional Chile: Faults to the law and to the faith]. In P. Gonzalbo (ed.), *Género, familia y mentalidades en América Latina*, pp. 39–60. San Juan: Editorial de la Universidad de Puerto Rico.

Census of Canada (2001, 1996, 1991, 1986). Ottawa: Statistics Canada.

Centro de Investigaciones Sociológicas, Ministerio de la Presidencia, Reino de España (1999). *Los jóvenes de hoy* [Today's youth]. Madrid: CIS.

(2002a, May–August). *Estudio no. 2443–Actitudes y creencias religiosas. Boletín Datos de Opinión no. 29* [Study no. 2443–Religious beliefs and attitudes. Opinion Data Bulletin no. 29]. Madrid: CIS. Retrieved from http://www.cis.es.

(2002b, December). *Estudio no. 2474 – Barómetro de opinión de diciembre. Expectativas 2003* [Study no. 2474 – December opinion barometer. 2003 Expectatives]. Madrid: CIS. Retrieved from http://www.cis.ess.

Cha, J. H. (1994). Changes in value, belief, attitude and behavior of the Koreans over the past 100 years. *Korean Journal of Psychology: Social*, 8: 40–58.

Chadwick, B. A. and Heaton, T. B. (1999). *Statistical handbook on the American family*. Phoenix, AZ: Orynx Press.

Cheal, D. (1993). Unity and the difference in postmodern families. *Journal of Family Issues*, 14: 5–19.

Chirkov, V., Kim, Y., Ryan, R., and Kaplan, U. (2003). Differentiating autonomy from individualism and independence: A self-determination theory perspective on internalization of cultural orientations and well-being. *Journal of Personality and Social Psychology*, 84: 97–110.

Chou, K.-L. (2000). Emotional autonomy and depression among Chinese adolescents. *Journal of Genetic Psychology*, 161: 161–169.

Christakopoulou, S. and Dawson, J. (2000). *Community well-being in West Humberstone*. Chester: Jon Dawson and Associates.

Chun, K., Balls-Organista, P., and Marin, G. (2003). *Acculturation: Advances in theory, measurement and applied research*. Washington: APA Books.

Cohen, J. (1988). *Statistical power analysis for the behavioral sciences*. Mawhaw, NJ: Erlbaum.

Cohler, B. and Geyer, S. (1982). Psychological autonomy and interdependence within the family. In F. Walsh (ed.), *Normal family processes*, pp. 196–227. New York: Guilford.

Cole, D. P. (1973). The enmeshment of nomads in Saudi Arabian society: The case of Murrah. In C. Nelson (ed.), *The desert and the sown: Nomads in wider society*, pp. 113–128. Research Series, N21. Berkeley: Institute of International Studies, University of California.

Collier, S. (1985). Chile from independence to the war of the Pacific. In L. Bethell (ed.), *The Cambridge history of Latin America*, vol. 3, pp. 583–613. Cambridge: Cambridge University Press.

Collier, J. and Yanagisako, S. I. (1987). *Gender and kinship: Essays toward a unified analysis*. Stanford, CA: Stanford University Press.

Comisión Económica para América Latina y el Caribe, Naciones Unidas (2000). *Las mujeres chilenas en los noventa: Hablan las cifras* [Chilean women in the nineties: Data's evidences]. Santiago: CEPAL/SERNAM.

Comisión Económica para América Latina y el Caribe, Naciones Unidas (2001). *Social panorama of Latin America 2000–2001*. Retrieved from http://www.eclac.cl.

Comisión Económica para América Latina y el Caribe, Naciones Unidas (2002). *Anuario estadístico de América Latina y el Caribe 2001* [2001 Statistical yearbook of Latin America and the Caribbean]. Retrieved from http://www.eclac.cl.

Comision Nacional de la Familia, Republica de Chile (1993). *Informe de la Comisión Nacional de la Familia* [Family National Commission Report]. Santiago: Servicio Nacional de la Mujer.

Contreras, J. (1991). Los grupos domésticos: Estrategias de producción y de reproducción [Domestic groups: strategies of production and reproduction]. In J. Prat, U. Martínez, J. Contreras and I. Moreno (eds.), *Antropología de los pueblos de España*, pp. 343–380. Madrid: Taurus.

Coontz, S. (2000). Historical perspectives on family studies. *Journal of Marriage and the Family*, 62: 283–297.

Cooper, D. (1971). *The death of the family*. Norwich: Penguin Press.

Cowan, P. A. (1993). The sky is falling, but Popenoe's analysis won't help us do anything about it. *Journal of Marriage and the Family*, 55: 548–553.

Cribier, F. (1981). Changing retirement patterns: The experience of a cohort of Parisian salaried workers. *Ageing and Society*, 1: 57–71.

Cruz, P. and Santiago, P. (1998). *Juventud y entorno familiar* [Youth and family environment]. Madrid: Instituto de la Juventud.

Curtis, G. E. (1992). *Bulgaria: A country study*. Sofia, Bulgaria: Federal Research Division, Library of Congress. Retrieved from http://lcweb2.loc.gov/frd/cs/bgtoc.html.

Cuyvers, P. (2000). You can't have it all – at least at the same time: Segmentation in the modern life course as a threat to intergenerational communication and solidarity. In S. Trnka (ed.). *Family issues between gender and generations*, pp. 30–43. Luxembourg: European Commission: Employment and Social Affairs.

Cuyvers, P. and Latten, J. (1999). *Alleen of samen? Alleen en samen!* [Single or together? Single and together!]. The Hague: CBS.

D'Cruz, P. and Bharat, S. (2001). Beyond joint and nuclear: The Indian family revisited. *Journal of Comparative Family Studies*, 32: 167–194.

Daguet, F. (1996). Mariage, divorce et union libre [Marriage, divorce and partners]. *INSEE Première*, 482: 1–4.

Dasen, P.R. (1975). Concrete operational development in three cultures. *Journal of Cross-Cultural Psychology*, 6: 156–172.

(1993). L'ethnocentrisme de la psychologie [The ethnocentrism of psychology]. In M. Rey (ed.), *Psychologie clinique et interrogations culturelles*, pp. 155–174. Paris: L'Hartmattan.

Dasen, P. R., Berry, J. W., and Witkin, H. A. (1979). The use of developmental theories cross-culturally. In L. Eckensberger, W. Lonner, and Y. H. Poortinga (eds.), *Cross-cultural contributions to psychology*, pp. 69–82. Lisse, The Netherlands: Swets and Zeitlinger.

De Raad, B. (1994). An expedition in search of a fifth universal factor: Key issues in the lexical approach. *European Journal of Personality*, 8: 229–250.

Dekovic, M. Pels, T., and Model, S. (in press). *Unity and diversity in child rearing: Family life in a multicultural society.*

Delaney, C. (1991). *The seed and the soil: Gender and cosmology in Turkish village society.* Berkeley: University of California Press.

Dench, G. (1996). *Transforming men.* London: Transaction Publishers.

Derlega, V. J., Cukur, C. S., Kuang, J. C., and Foryth, D. R. (2002). Interdependent construal of self and the endorsement of conflict resolution strategies in interpersonal, intergroup and international disputes *Journal of Cross-Cultural Psychology*, 33: 610–625.

Dessen, M. A. and Biasoli-Alves, Z. M. M. (2001). O estudo da família como base para a promoção da tolerância [Family studies as a base of promoting the tolerance]. In Z. M. M. Biasoli-Alves and R. Fischmann (eds.), *Crianças e adolescentes: Construindo uma cultura da tolerância*, pp. 183–193. São Paulo: EDUSP.

Dessen, M. A. and Braz, M. P. (2000). Rede social de apoio durante transições familiares decorrentes de nascimento de filhos [Social support network during family transitions to parenthood]. *Psicologia: Teoria e Pesquisa*, 16: 221–231.

Díaz-Guerrero, R. (1994). *La psicología del Mexicano* [The psychology of the Mexican]. Mexico: Editorial Trillas.

Doi, T. (1973). *The anatomy of dependence.* Tokyo: Kodansha International Press.

Donoso, J. (1989). *Casa de campo* [A house in the country]. Santiago: Editorial Antártica.

Droogers, A. (1988). Brazilian minimal religiosity. In G. Banck and K. Koonings (eds.), *Social change in contemporary Brazil*, pp. 165–175. Amsterdam: CEDLA.

Drouzhynin, V. (1996). *Psyhologia semyee* [Psychology of the family]. Moscow: KSP.

Duben, A. (1982). The significance of family and kinship in urban Turkey. In Ç. Kağıtçıbaşı (ed.), *Sex roles, family and community in Turkey*, pp. 73–99. Bloomington, IN: Indiana University Press.

Duncan, G. J. and Brooks-Gunn, J. (2000). Family poverty, welfare reform, and child development. *Child Development*, 71: 188–196.

Durkheim, E. (1888). Introduction a la sociologie de la famille [Introduction to the sociology of the family]. *Annales de la Faculté des Lettres de Bordeaux*, 10.

Durkheim, E. ([1892] 1921). La famille conjugale [The conjugal family]. *Revue Philosophique de la France et de l'Etranger*, 90: 1–14.

Edgell, S. (1980). *Middle-class couples*. London: Allen and Unwin.

Eibl-Eibesfeldt, I. (1989). *Human ethology*. New York: Aldine de Gruyter.

Ekstrand, L. H. and Ekstrand, G. (1987). Children's perceptions of norms and sanctions in two cultures. In Ç. Kağıtçıbaşı (ed.), *Growth and progress in cross-cultural psychology*, pp. 171–180. Berwyn, PA: Swets North America.

Eldering, L. and Leseman, P. P. M. (eds.). (1999). *Effective early education: Cross-cultural perspectives*. New York: Falmer.

Elovson, A. C. and Fleming, J. S. (1988). "Rationale for multidimentional self-esteem scale scoring and weighting." Unpublished manuscript, California State University.

Elzo, J. and Orizo, F. (1999). *Jóvenes españoles* [Spanish youth]. Madrid: Fundación Santamaria.

Ember, C. R. and Ember, M. (2002). *Cultural anthropology*, 10th edn. Upper Saddle River, NJ: Prentice Hall.

Encyclopédie Hachette Multimedia 99 (1999). (2 CD-ROMS). Paris: Hachette.

Encyclopédie Microsoft Encarta en ligne (2005). *France (population et société)*. Retrieved from http://fr.encarta.msn.com.

Engels, F. ([1884] 1942). *The origin of the family, private property and the state*. New York: International Publishers.

Enriquez, V. (ed.) (1990). *Indigenous psychologies*. Quezon City: Psychology Research and Training House.

Erkut, S. (1982). Dualism in values toward education of Turkish women. In Ç. Kağıtçıbaşı (ed.), *Sex roles, family and community in Turkey*, pp. 121–132. Bloomington, IN: Indiana University Press.

Eurostat (1995). *European community household panel*. Luxembourg: European Communities.

   (1996). *Demographic statistics*. Luxembourg: Commission of the European Communities.

   (2001). *The social situation in the European Union*. Brussels: European Commission, Directorate General for Employment and Social Affairs.

   (2002a). *Eurostat yearbook, 2002*. Luxembourg: Commission of the European Communities.

   (2002b). *First results of the demographic data collection for 2001 in Europe. Statistics in focus: Population and social conditions – Theme 3: Population and living conditions* (17/2002). Luxembourg: Commission of the European Communities. Retrieved from http://www.europa. eu.int/comm/eurostat.

Fallers, L. A., and Fallers, M. C. (1976). Sex roles in Edremit. In J. G. Peristiany (ed.), *Mediterranean family structures*. Cambridge: Cambridge University Press.

Farrell, B. (1999). *Family: The making of an idea, and institution, and a controversy in American culture*. Boulder, CO: Westview Press.

Fawcett, J. T. (1983). Perceptions of the value of children. In R. Bulatao, R. D. Lee, P. E. Hollerbach, and J. Bongaarts (eds.), *Determinants of fertility in the developing countries*, vol. 1, pp. 347–369. Washington, DC: National Academy Press.

Feldman (1975). The history of the relationship between environment and culture in ethnological thought. *Journal of the History of the Behavioral Sciences*, 110: 67–81.

Feldman, S. S. and Rosenthal, D. A. (1991). Age expectations of behavioural autonomy in Hong Kong, Australian and American youth: The influence of family variables and adolescents' values. *International Journal of Psychology*, 26: 1–23.

Feres, J. (2001). La pobreza en Chile en el año 2000 [Poverty in Chile in 2000]. *CEPAL, Serie estudios estadísticos y prospectivos*, No. 14. Santiago: EPAL/ MIDEPLAN.

Fernald, A. (1992). Meaningful melodies in mothers' speech to infants. In H. Papoušek, U. Jurgens, and M. Papoušek (eds.), *Nonverbal vocal communication: Comparative and developmental approaches*, pp. 263–281. Cambridge: Cambridge University Press.

Ferri, E. and Smith, K. (1996). *Parenting in the 1990s*. Report for the Joseph Rowntree Foundation, York, England.

Fields, J. (2003). Children's living arrangements and characteristics: March 2002. *Current Population Reports*, pp. 20–547. Washington, DC: US Census Bureau.

Finch, J. (1997). Individuality and adaptability in English kinship. In M. Gullestad and M. Segalen (eds.), *Family and kinship in Europe*, pp. 129–145. London: Pinter.

Finch, J. and Mason, J. (1993). *Negotiating family responsibilities*. London: Routledge.

Fisek, G. O. (1982). Psychopathology and the Turkish family: A family systems theory analysis. In Ç. Kağıtçıbaşı (ed.), *Sex roles, family and community in Turkey*, pp. 295–321. Bloomington, IN: Indiana University Press.

  (1993). Life in Turkey. In L. L. Adler (ed.), *International handbook of gender roles*, pp. 438–451. Westport, CT: Greenwood Press.

  (1995). Gender hierarchy: Is it a useful concept in describing family structure? In J. van Lawick and M. Sanders (eds.), *Family, gender and beyond*, pp. 63–72. Heemstede, The Netherlands: LS Books.

Fisek, G. O. and Sunar, D. (2003). Contemporary Turkish families. In J. Roopnarine and U. Gielen (eds.), *Families in Global Perspective*. Boston: Allyn and Bacon.

Flaquer, Ll. (2000). *Family policy and welfare state in southern Europe*. Barcelona: Institut de Ciènces Polítiques i Socials (Working Paper 185/00).

Flaquer, Ll. and Soler, J. (1990). *Permananecia y cambio en la familia española* [Continuity and change in the Spanish family] (Colección Estudios y Encuestas, no 18). Madrid: Centro de Investigaciones Sociológicas.

Forde, D. (1934). *Habitat, economy and society.* New York: Dutton.

Fortes, M. (1978). An anthropologist's apprenticeship. *Annual Review of Anthropology,* 7: 1–30.

Fourastié, J. (1983). Image de la population active en 1975 selon le niveau de qualification [Overview of the active working population according to level of qualification]. *Population,* 3: 489–498.

Franza, M. (1999). Les mineurs délinquants multirécidivistes: Une nouvelle forme de prise en charge; les Centres Éducatifs Renforcés [Recidivist delinquent minors: A new type of control; Special Educational Centers]. *Les Cahiers de l'Actif,* 282–283: 101–114.

Freedman, M. (1958). *Lineage organization in southeastern China:* London: Athlone.

Friedl, E. (1962). *Vassilika: A village in modern Greece.* New York: Holt Rinehart and Winston.

    (1967). The position of women: Appearance and reality. *Anthropological Quarterly,* 40: 97–108.

Fu, V. R., Hinkle, D. E., and Hanna, M. A. (1986). A three-generational study of the development of individual dependence and family interdependence. *Genetic, Social and General Psychology Monographs,* 112: 153–171.

Furstenberg, F. F., Jr. (1966). Industrialization and the American family: A look backward. *American Sociological Review,* 31: 326–337.

Furstenberg, F. F. and Nord, C. W. (1985). Parenting apart: Patterns of childrearing after marital disruption. *Journal of Marriage and the Family,* 47: 893–905.

Galbraith, J. K. (1996). *The good society: The humane agenda.* New York: Houghton Mifflin.

Galland, O. (1991). *Sociologie de la jeunesse: L'entrée dans la vie.* [Sociology of youth: Entrance into life] Paris: Armand Colin.

Gari, A. and Kalantzi-Azizi, A. (1998). The influence of traditional values of education on Greek students' real and ideal self-concepts. *The Journal of Social Psychology,* 138: 5–12.

Geertz, H. (1961). *The Javanese family. A study of kinship and socialization.* Glencoe, IL: The Free Press of Glencoe, Inc.

Georgas, J. (1986). Oikogeneiakes axies foititon [Family values of students]. *Greek Social Science Review,* 61: 3–29.

    (1988). An ecological and social cross-cultural model: The case of Greece. In J. W. Berry, S. H. Irvine, and E. B. Hunt (eds.), *Indigenous cognition: Functioning in cultural context,* pp. 105–123. Dordrecht, The Netherlands: Martinus Nijhoff.

    (1989). Changing family values in Greece: From collectivist to individualist. *Journal of Cross-Cultural Psychology,* 20: 80–91.

    (1991). Intrafamily acculturation of values in Greece. *Journal of Cross-Cultural Psychology,* 22: 445–457.

    (1993). An ecological-social model for indigenous psychology: The example of Greece. In U. Kim and J. W. Berry (eds.), *Indigenous psychologies: Theory, method and experience in cultural context,* pp. 56–78. Beverly Hills, CA: Sage.

(1999). Family as a context variable in cross-cultural psychology. In J. Adamopoulos and Y. Kashima (eds.), *Social psychology and cultural context*, pp. 163–175. Beverly Hills, CA: Sage.

(2000). E psychodynamiki tis oikogeneias stin Ellada: Omoiotites kai diafores me alles hores [The psychodynamics of the family in Greece: Similarities and differences with other countries]. In A. Kalantzi-Azizi and E. Besevegis (eds.), *Themata epimorphosis evaisthetopoisis stelehon psychikis hygeias paidion kai efevon*, pp. 231–251. Athens: Hellenika Grammata.

Georgas, J., Bafiti, T., Papademou, L., and Mylonas, K. (2004a). Families in Greece. In J. L. Roopnarine and U. P. Gielen (eds.), *Families in global perspective*, pp. 207–224. Boston, MA: Allyn and Bacon.

Georgas, J. and Berry, J. W. (1995). An ecocultural taxonomy for cross-cultural psychology. *Cross-Cultural Research*, 29: 121–157.

Georgas, J., Christakopoulou, S., Poortinga, Y., Goodwin, R., Angleitner, A., and Charalambous, N. (1997). The relationship of family bonds to family structure and function across cultures. *Journal of Cross-Cultural Psychology*, 28: 303–319.

Georgas, J., Gari, A., and Mylonas, K. (2004b). Relationships with kin in the Greek family [in Greek]. In L. Mousourou and M. Strategaki (eds.), *The issue of family policy: Theoretical perspectives and empirical investigations*, pp. 189–225. Athens: Gutenberg.

Georgas, J., Mylonas, K., Bafiti, T., Christakopoulou, S., Poortinga, Y. H., Kağıtçıbaşı, Ç., Orung, S., Sunar, D., Kwak, K., Ataca, B., Berry, J. W., Charalambous, N., Goodwin, R., Wang, W.-Z., Angleitner, A., Stepanikova, I., Pick, S., Givaudan, M., Zhuravliova-Gionis, I., Konantambigi, R., Gelfand, M. J., Velislava, M., McBride-Chang, M., and Kodiç, Y. (2001). Functional relationships in the nuclear and extended family: A 16 culture study. *International Journal of Psychology*, 36: 289–300.

Georgas, J., Vijver, F. J. R. van de, and Berry, J. W. (2004c). The Ecocultural Framework, ecosocial indicators and psychological variables in cross-cultural research. *Journal of Cross-Cultural Psychology*, 35: 74–96.

Gergen, H. (1991). The saturated family. *Networker*, September/October.

Gergen, M. M. and Gergen, K. J. (2000). Qualitative inquiry: Tensions and transformations. In N. K. Denzin and Y. Lincoln (eds.), *Handbook of qualitative research*, 2nd edn., pp. 1025–1046. Thousand Oaks, CA: Sage.

Ghana Statistical Service (1994). *Demographic and health survey*. Accra, Ghana: DHS/Macro International Inc.

(1998). *Demographic and health survey*. Accra, Ghana: DHS/Macro International Inc.

(2000). *2000 Population Census of Ghana*. Accra, Ghana: DHS/Macro International Inc.

Ghuman, P. A. S. (1994). *Coping with two cultures: A study of British Asian and Indo-Canadian adolescents*. Clevedon, UK: Multilingual Matters.

Ghraib, S. A. (1991). *Characteristics of agricultural societies in the Arab Gulf states* [Arabic text]. Riyadh: The Arabic Center for Security Studies and Training.

Giddens, A. (1991). *Modernity and self-identity*. Cambridge: Polity Press.

(1992). *The transformation of intimacy*. Cambridge: Polity Press.

Gilmore, D. D. (1987). *Honor and shame and the unity of the Mediterranean.* Washington, DC: American Anthropological Association.

Glenn, N. (1993). A plea for objective assessment of the notion of family decline. *Journal of Marriage and the Family,* 55: 542–544.

Gonzalbo, P. (1999). Introducción [Introduction]. In P. Gonzalbo (ed.), *Familia y educación en Iberoamérica,* [Family and education in Iberoamerica] pp. 9–20. México: Centro de Estudios Históricos, El Colegio de México.

Goode, W. J. (1963). *World revolution and family patterns.* Glencoe, IL: Free Press.

(1964). *The family,* 2nd edn. Englewood Cliffs, NJ: Prentice Hall.

Goodenough, W. H. (1970). *Description and comparison in cultural anthropology.* Chicago, IL: Aldine.

Goodwin, R., Adatia, K., Sinhal, H., Cramer, D., and Ellis, D. (1997). *Social support and marital well-being in an Asian community.* York, UK: York Publishing Ltd.

Goodwin, R. and Tang, C. S. K. (1996). Chinese personal relationships. In M. H. Bond (ed.), *The handbook of Chinese psychology,* pp. 294–308. Hong Kong: Oxford University Press.

Goody, J. (1983). *The oriental, the ancient, and the primitive: Systems of marriage and the family in the pre-industrial societies of Eurasia.* Cambridge: Cambridge University Press.

Gore, M. S. (1968). *Urbanization and family change.* Bombay: Popular Prakashan.

Gottfried, A. D., Gottfried, A. W., Bathurst, K., and Killian, C. (1999). Maternal and dual-earner employment. In M. E. Lamb (ed.), *Parenting and child development in "nontraditional" families,* pp. 15–38. Mahwah, NJ: Erlbaum.

Government of Botswana and United Nations Development Report (1997). *Botswana Human Development Report: Challenges for sustainable human development.* Gaborone, Botswana: UNDP.

Government of Georgia and United Nations Development Report (1996). *Human development report Georgia 1996.* Tbilisi, Georgia: UNDP.

Government of Pakistan (2001, 2002). *Economic survey, statistical supplement 2001–2002.* Islamabad, Pakistan: Ministry of Finance.

Grotevant, H. D. and Cooper, C. R. (1986). Individuation in family relationships. *Human Development,* 29: 82–100.

Gusfield, J. R. (1967). Tradition and modernity: Misplaced polarities in the study of social change. *American Journal of Sociology,* 73: 351–362.

Hadjiiski, I. (1995). *Portret na balgarina* [Portrait of the Bulgarian]. Sofia, Bulgaria: BAN.

Hagestad, G. (1986). The family: Women and grandparents as kinkeepers. In A. Pifer and L. Bronte (eds.), *Our aging society,* pp. 141–160. New York: Norton.

Hammel, E. A. (1972). The zadruga as process. In P. Laslett and R. Wall (eds.), *Household and family in past time,* pp. 335–374. Cambridge, UK: Cambridge University Press.

Harkness, J. A., Vijver, F. J. R. van de, and Mohler, P. Ph. (2003). *Cross-cultural survey methods.* New York: Wiley.

Harrison, L. E. (2000). Why culture matters. In L. E. Harrison and S. P. Huntington (eds.), *Culture matters: How values shape human progress*, pp. xvii–xxxiv. New York: Basic Books.

Haub, C. and Rogers, M. (2002). *Kids count. International data sheet*. Washington, DC: Population Reference Bureau.

Heise, J. (1979). *150 años de evolución institucional* [150 years of institutional evolution]. Santiago: Editorial Andrés Bello.

Hemert, D. A. van, Vijver, F. J. R. van de, Poortinga, Y. H., and Georgas, J. (2002). Structural and functional equivalence of the Eysenck Personality Questionnaire within and between countries. *Personality and Individual Differences*, 33: 1229–1249.

Hendrick, S. and Hendrick, C. (2001). *Liking, loving and relating*. Pacific Groove, CA: Brooks/Cole Publishing Company.

Hentschel, U., Sumbadze, N., and Schoon, I. (2001). Looking at families from a cross-cultural perspective. In U. Hentschel and L. Burlatchuk (eds.), *Focus Eastern Europe: Psychological and social determinants of behaviour in the transition countries*, pp.155–172. Innsbruck: StudienVerlag.

Herbst, P. G. (1952). The measurement of family relationships. *Human Relations*, 5: 3–35.

Herk, H. V. and Poortinga, Y. H. (2004). Evidence of method bias in data from six EU Countries. *Journal of Cross-Cultural Psychology*, 35: 346–360.

Hoffman, L. W. (1987). The value of children to parents and childrearing parents. In Ç. Kağıtçıbaşı (ed.), *Growth and progress in cross-cultural psychology*, pp. 159–170. Lisse, The Netherlands: Swetz and Zeitlinger.

Herk, H. van, Poortinga, Y. H., and Verhallen, T. M. M. (2004). Response styles in rating scales. *Journal of Cross-Cultural Psychology*, 35: 346–360.

Hoffman, L. W. (1988). Cross-cultural differences in childrearing goals. *New Directions for Child Development*, 40: 99–122.

Hofstede, G. ([1980] 2001). *Culture's consequences, Comparing values, behaviors institution, and Organization across nations*. Thousand Oaks, CA: Sage.

Holland P. W. and Wainer, H. (1993). *Differential item functioning*. Hillsdale, NJ: Erlbaum.

Hollos, M. and Leis, P. E. (1989). *Adolescents in a changing world*. New Brunswick, NJ: Rutgers University Press.

Hortacsu, N. (1989). Targets of communication during adolescence. *Journal of Adolescence*, 12: 253–263.

Hortacsu, N., Gencoz, T., and Oral, A. (1995). Perceived functions of family and friends during childhood, adolescence, and youth: Developmental theories of two Turkish groups. *International Journal of Psychology*, 30: 591–606.

Hortulanus, W. (1983). De ontwikkeling van de welvaartsstaat. In P. Idenburg (ed.), *De nadagen van de verzorgingsstaat* [The development of the welfare state]. Amsterdam: Meulenhof.

Houchard, B. (2000). *La famille: Une idée neuve en Europe*. Paris: Fondation Robert Schuman.

Howard, G. E. (1904). *A history of matrimonial institutions*. Chicago, IL. (repr. New York, 1964).

Hsu, F. L. K. (1971). Psychosocial homeostasis and jen: Conceptual tools for advancing psychological anthropology. *American Anthropologist*, 73: 23–44.

Hudson, R. A. (ed.). (1994). *Chile: A country study.* Washington, DC: Federal Research Division, Library of Congress. Retrieved from http://www.memory.loc.gov/frd/cs/cltoc.html.

Hundey, I., Magarrey, M., Evans, R., and O'Sullivan, B. (2003). *Canadian history: Patterns and transformations.* Toronto: Irwin Publishing.

Huntington, E. (1945). *Mainsprings of civilization.* New York: John Wiley and Sons.

Huntington, S. P. (1996). *The clash of civilizations and the remaking of world order.* New York: Simon and Schuster.

Hüwelmeier, G. (1997). Kirmesgesellschaften und Männergesangvereine [Amusement societies and mens' chores]. *Zeitschrift für Sozialisationsforschung und Erziehungssoziologie*, 17: 30–41.

Iachkova, M. (1997). *Semeistvoto I podgotovkata za nego* [Family and preparation for it]. Sofia, Bulgaria: ASSA-M.

Iglesias de Ussel, J. (1990). La familia y el cambio político en España [The family and political change in Spain]. *Revista de Estudios Politicos*, 67: 235–259.

  (1995). Trabajo y familia en España [Work and family in Spain]. *Revista Internacional de Sociología*, 11: 171–198.

Imamoglu, E. O. (1987). An interdependence model of human development. In Ç. Kağıtçıbaşı (ed.), *Growth and progress in cross-cultural psychology*, pp. 138–145. Lisse, The Netherlands: Swetz and Zeitlinger.

  (1991). "Changing intra-family roles in a changing world." Paper presented at the Seminar on the Individual, the Family and the Society in a Changing World, Istanbul, Turkey.

  (1994). A model of gender relations in the Turkish family. *Bogazici Journal: Review of Social, Economic and Admininstrative Studies*, 8: 165–176.

Indonesia Human Development Report (2001). *Towards a new consensus: Democracy and human development in Indonesia.* Jakarta, Indonesia: BPS, BAPPENAS, UNDP.

Information Services Department of Hong Kong SAR, People's Republic of China (2002a). *Hong Kong annual report 2001.* Hong Kong: HKSAR Government.

  (2002b). *Hong Kong 2001 population census summary results.* Hong Kong: HKSAR Government.

Inglehart, R. (1991). Changing human goals and values: A proposal for a study of global change. In K. Pawlik (ed.), *Perception and assessment of global environmental conditions and change.* Barcelona, Spain: International Social Sciences Council.

  (1997). *Modernization and postmodernization: Changing values and political styles in advanced industrial society.* Princeton, NJ: Princeton University Press.

Inglehart, R. and Baker, W. E. (2000). Modernization, cultural change, and the persistence of traditional values. *American Sociological Review*, 65: 19–51.

Ingoldsby, B. (1995). Family origin and universality In B. Ingoldsby and S. Smith (eds.), *Families in multicultural perspective*, pp. 83–96. New York: The Guilford Press.

Ingoldsby, B. and Smith, S. (eds.). (1995). *Families in multicultural perspective*. New York: Guilford.

Inkeles, A. (1998). *One world emerging?: Convergence and divergence in industrial societies*. Boulder, CO: Westview Press.

Inoue, T. (1977). *"Sekentei" no kozo: Shakaishinrishi heno kokoromi* [Structure of "sekentei": An attempt at the socio-psychological history]. Tokyo: NHK Books.

Institut National de la Statistique et des Etudes Economiques, République de France (1999). *Recensement de la population*. Paris: INSEE.

Instituto de la Juventud, Reino de España (2000). *Informe juventud en España* [Report on youth in Spain]. Madrid: INJUVE.

Instituto Nacional de Estadística, Reino de España (2002). *Cifras INE. Boletín informativo del Instituto Nacional de Estadística, 7/2002* [Figures INE. Informative bulletin of the National Institute of Statistics, 7/2002]. Madrid: INE. Retrieved from http://www.ine.es.

(2003). *Cifras INE. Boletin Informativo del Instituto Nacional de Estadística, 2/2003* [Figures INE. Informative Bulletin of the National Institute of Statistics, 2/2003]. Madrid: INE. Retrieved from http://www.ine.es.

Instituto Nacional de Estadística, Republica de Chile (1999). *Estadísticas de Chile en el siglo XX* [Chile's statistical data during the 20th century]. Santiago: INE. Retrieved from http://www.ine.cl.

(2003). *Censo 2002: Síntesis de resultados* [2002 census: A resume]. Santiago: INE. Retrieved from http://www.ine.cl.

Instituto Nacional de Estadistica Geografia e Informática, Estados Unidos Mexicanos (2001). *XII censo general de población y vivienda, 2000. Tabulados Básicos*. Aguascalientes, Ags., Mexico: INEGI.

Jahoda, G. (1995). The ancestry of a model. *Culture and Psychology*, 1: 11–24.

Jansen, H. A. M. (1987). The development of communal living in the Netherlands. In L. Shangar-Handelman and R. Palomba (eds.), *Alternative patterns of family life in modern societies*. Rome: Collana Monografie.

Jayakody, R., Chatters, L. M., and Taylor, R. J. (1993). Family support to single and married African American mothers: The provision of financial, emotional and child care assistance. *Journal of Marriage and the Family*, 55: 261–276.

Johnson, C. L. (2000). Perspectives on American kinship in the later 1990s. *Journal of Marriage and the Family*, 62: 623–639.

Jose, P. E., Huntsinger, C. S., Huntsinger, P. R., and Liaw, F-R. (2000). Parental values and practices relevant to young children's social development in Taiwan and the United States. *Journal of Cross-Cultural Psychology*, 31: 677–702.

Kabloukov, V. A. (1989). *Problemy studencheskoi semiee [Problems of student's family]*. Moscow: Znanie.

Kağıtçıbaşı, Ç. (ed.). (1982a). *Sex roles, family and community in Turkey*. Bloomington, IN: Indiana University Press.

Kağıtçıbaşı, Ç. (1982b). *The changing value of children in Turkey*. Honolulu, Hawaii: East-West Center, Publ. No. 60-E.

(1985). Culture of separateness–culture of relatedness. In C. Klopp (ed.), *1984 Vision and reality. Papers in Comparative Studies*, vol. 4, pp. 91–99. Columbus, OH: Ohio State University.

(1986). Status of women in Turkey: Cross-cultural perspectives. *International Journal of Middle East Studies*, 18: 485–499.

(1990). Family and socialization in cross-cultural perspective: A model of change. In J. Berman (ed.), *Cross-cultural perspectives: Nebraska symposium on motivation, 1989*, pp. 135–200. Lincoln, NE: Nebraska University Press.

(1996a). *Family and human development across cultures: A view from the other side*. Hillsdale, NJ: Lawrence Erlbaum.

(1996b). The autonomous-relational self: A new synthesis. *European Psychologist*, 1: 180–186.

(2002). A Model of Family Change in cultural context. In W. J. Lonner, D. L. Dinnel, S. A. Hayes, and D. N. Sattler (eds.), Online readings in psychology and culture (Unit 13, Chapter 1). Retrieved from http://www.wwu.edu/culture.

Kağıtçıbaşı, Ç. and Ataca, B. (2005) Value of children, family and say: A three decade portrait from Turkey. *Applied Psychology: An International Review*, 54 (3): 317–337.

Kağıtçıbaşı, Ç. and Sunar, D. (1992). Family and socialization in Turkey. In J. P. Roopnarine and D. B. Carter (eds.), *Parent–child relations in diverse cultural settings: Socialization for instrumental competency*, pp. 75–88. New Jersey: Ablex Publishing Corp.

Kağıtçıbaşı, Ç., Sunar, D., and Bekman, S. (1988). *Comprehensive preschool educational project: Final report* (Manuscript Report 209e). Ottawa: International Development Research Center.

(2001). Long-term effects of early intervention: Turkish low-income mothers and children. *Applied Developmental Psychology*, 22: 333–361.

Kain, E. (1990). *The myth of family decline: Understanding families in a world of rapid social change*. Lexington, MA: Lexington Books.

Kandiyoti, D. (1974). Some social psychological dimensions of social change in a Turkish village. *British Journal of Sociology*, 15: 47–62.

(1977). Sex roles and social change: A comparative appraisal of Turkish women. *Signs: Journal of Women in Culture and Society*, 3: 57–73.

(1982). Urban change and women's roles in Turkey: An overview and evaluation. In Ç. Kağıtçıbaşı (ed.), *Sex roles, family and community in Turkey*, pp. 101–120. Bloomington, IN: Indiana University Press.

(1988). Bargaining with patriarchy. *Gender and Society*, 2: 274–290.

Kapadia, K. M. (1956). Rural family patterns. *Sociological Bulletin*, 5: 111–126.

Kasto, H. S. (1982). *Perkawinan dan perceraian pada masyarakat Jawa: Suatu studi kasus di desa Harjobinangun, Yogyakarta*. [Marriage and divorce in a Javanese community: A case study in Harjobinangum village, Yogyakarta] Jakarta, Indonesia: Pusat Penelitian dan Studi Kependudukan, University of Gadjah Mada.

Kauffman, J.-C. (1993). *Sociologie du couple* [Sociology of the couple]. Paris: PUF.

Kazemi-Mortazavi, S. (1978). "Kulturspezifische Aspekte in der Beziehung zwischen Verhalten und raumlicher Umgebung" [Culture-specific aspects of the relationship between behavior and environment]. Unpublished doctoral thesis, Tübingen University, Germany.

Keller, H. (1997). Evolutionary approaches. In J. W. Berry, Y. H. Poortinga, and J. Pandey (eds.), *Handbook of cross-cultural psychology*, Vol. 1 *Theory and method*, 2nd edn., pp. 215–255. Boston, MA: Allyn and Bacon.

(2002). Development as the interface between biology and culture: A conceptualization of early ontogenetic experiences. In H. Keller, Y. H. Poortinga, and A. Schoelmerich (eds.), *Biology, culture and development: Integrating diverse perspectives*, pp. 215–240. Cambridge: Cambridge University Press.

Keller, H., Zach, U., and Abels, M. (2005). The German family. Families in Germany. In J. Roopnarine and U. P. Gielen (eds.), *Families in global perspective*, pp. 242–258. Boston, MA: Allison and Bacon.

Keniston, K. (1985). The myth of family independence. In J. M. Henslin (ed.), *Marriage and family in a changing society*, 2nd edn., pp. 27–33. New York: Free Press.

Kermode, J. (1999). Sentiment and survival: Family and friends in late medieval English towns. *Journal of Family History*, 24: 5–18.

Khatri, A. A. (1970). Personality and mental health of Indians (Hindus) in the context of their changing family organization. In E. J. Anthony and C. Koupernik (eds.), *The child in his family*. New York: Wiley.

(1975). The adaptive extended family in India today. *Journal of Marriage and the Family*, 37: 633–647.

Kiechel, W. (1987, April 13). When the boss wants you to move. *Fortune Magazine*, pp. 125–128.

Kim, M.-H. (1996). Changing relationships between daughters-in-law and mothers-in-law in urban South Korea. *Anthropological Quarterly*, 4: 179–191.

Kim, U. (1994). Individualism, collectivism, and child development: A Korean perspective. In P. M. Greenfield and R. R. Cocking (eds.), *Socialization of minority children: Cultural continuities and discontinuities*, pp. 227–257. Hillsdale, NJ: Lawrence Erlbaum.

(1995). *Individualism and collectivism: Psychological, cultural and ecological analysis*. Copenhagen: Nordic Institute of Asian Studies.

(2001). Culture, science and indigenous psychologies: An integrated analysis. In D. Matsumoto (ed.), *Handbook of culture and psychology*, pp. 51–76. Oxford: Oxford University Press.

Kim, U. and Berry, J. W. (eds.). (1993). *Indigenous psychologies*. Newbury Park, CA: Sage.

Kim, U., Park, Y. S., Kim, M. U., Lee, K. W., and Yu, S. H. (2000). Intergenerational differences and life-satisfaction: Comparative analysis of adolescents, adults, and the elderly. *Korean Journal of Health Psychology*, 5: 119–145.

Kim, Y., Butzel, J. S., and Ryan, R. M. (1998, June). *Interdependence and well-being: A function of culture and relatedness needs.* Paper presented at The International Society for the Study of Personal Relationships, Saratoga Spring, NY.

King, A. Y. C. and Bond, M. H. (1985). The Confucian paradigm of man: A sociological view. In W. S. Tseng and D. Y. H. Wu (eds.), *Chinese culture and mental health*, pp. 29–45. Orlando, FL: Academic Press.

Kiray, M. (1976). The new role of mothers: Changing intra-familial relationships in a small town in Turkey. In J. G. Peristiany (ed.), *Mediterranean family structures*. Cambridge: Cambridge University Press.

Kitayama, S. and Markus, H. R. (1994). Introduction to cultural psychology and emotion research. In S. Kitayama and H. R. Markus (eds.), *Emotion and culture: Empirical studies of mutual influence*, pp. 1–22. Washington, DC: American Psychological Association.

Klinger, A. (1990). *Integration of population policy and socioeconomic policy.* Paper presented at ECE First Informal Working Group Meeting on Integration of Population Policies and Socioeconomic Policies, Varna, Bulgaria.

Kluckhohn, C. and Murray, H. A. (1950). *Personality in nature, society, and culture.* New York: Alfred A. Knopf.

Kochetov, A. I. (1987). *Nachala semeinoi zhizni* [Beginning of married life]. Minsk, Belarus: Polymia.

Kojuharov, I. (1992). *National analysis of the situation of Bulgarian children and families.* Sofia, Bulgaria: Bulgarian National Committee for UNICEF.

Kon, I. S. (1988). Rebenok i obschestvo [Child and society]. Moscow: Mir.

Kooy, G. (1992). De ontwikkeling van partnerschap en ouderschap in de modern-westerse wereld [Development of partnership and parenthood in the modern western world]. In H. Moerland (ed.), *De menselijke Maat.* Arnhem, The Netherlands: Gouda Quint.

Korea National Statistics Office (2003). *Annual statistics.* Seoul: Government of Korea.

Kotzamanis, V. and Maratou-Alibrante, L. (1994). *Oi demographikes exelixis sti metapolemiki Ellada* [Greek demographics after World War II]. Athens: Livanis, Nea Synora.

Koutrelakos, J. (2004). Acculturation of Greek Americans: Change and continuity in cognitive schemas guiding intimate relationships. *International Journal of Psychology*, 39: 95–105.

Kravets, O. M. (1966). *Simeiny pobut i zvuchai ukrainskogo narodou* [Family lifestyle and traditions of Ukrainian people]. Kiev, Ukraine: Naukova Dumka.

Kroeber, A. L. (1909). Classificatory systems of relationship. *Journal of the Royal Anthropological Institute of Great Britain and Ireland*, 39: 77–84.

Kroeber, A. (1939). *Cultural and natural areas of native North America.* Berkeley, CA: University of California Press.

Kroger, J. (1998). Adolescence as a second separation–individuation process: Critical review of an object relations approach. In E. E. A. Skoe and A. L. von der Lippe (eds.), *Personality development in adolescence: A cross-national and life span perspective. Adolescence and society*, pp. 172–192. New York: Routledge.

Kwak, K. (2003). Adolescents and their parents: A review of intergenerational family relations for immigrant and non-immigrant families. *Human Development*, 46: 115–136.

Kwak, K. and Berry, J. W. (2001). Generational differences in acculturation among Asian families in Canada: A comparison of Vietnamese, Korean, and East-Indian groups. *International Journal of Psychology*, 36: 152–162.

Laing, R. D. (1969). *The divided self.* New York: Pantheon.

Lambiri-Dimaki, I. (1972). Dowry in modern Greece: An institution at the crossroads between persistence and decline. In C. Safilios-Rothschild (ed.), *Toward a sociology of women*, pp. 74–75. Lexington, MA: Xerox College Publishing.

Lappo, G. M. (1984). *Stranee i narodee* [Countries and peoples]. Moscow: Mysl.

Lasch, C. (1979). *The culture of narcissism.* New York: Warner.

Laslett, P. (1971). *The world we have lost*, 2nd edn. London: Methuen.

(1972). Introduction: The history of the family. In P. Laslett and R. Wall (eds.), *Household and family in past time*, pp. 1–89. Cambridge: Cambridge University Press.

Lau, S. (1981). Chinese familism in an urban-industrial setting: The case of Hong Kong. *Journal of Marriage and the Family*, 43: 977–992.

Le Play, F. (1855). Les ouvriers européens [The European Workers]. *Études sur les travaux, la vie domestique et la condition morale des populations ouvrières de l'Europe, précédées d'un exposé de la méthode d'observation.* Paris: Imprimerie impériale.

(1871). *L'organisation de la famille* [The organisation of the family]. Paris: Tegui.

Lebra, T. S. (1976). *Japanese patterns of behavior.* Honolulu: University of Hawaii Press.

Leburu-Sianga, F. and Molobe, E. (2000). *ADEA prospective stocktaking capacity building study: A focus on human resource development for the Ministry of Education.* Gaborone, Botswana: ADEA Publications.

LeGoff, J. (1985). *L'imaginaire médiéval.* Paris: Gallimard.

Leñero, O. L. (1982). *El niño y la familia* [The child and the family]. Ciudad de México: SCPEIN.

Lesthaeghe, R. (1980). On the social control of human reproduction. *Population and Development Review*, 6: 527–548.

Lesthaeghe, R. and Surkyn, J. (1988). Cultural dynamics and economic theories of fertility change. *Population and Development Review*, 14(1): 1–47.

Letamo, G. and Majelantle, R. G. (2001). Factors influencing low birth weight and prematurity in Botswana. *Journal of Bioscience*, 33: 391–403.

Lévi-Strauss, C. ([1949] 1969). *Les structures élémentaires de la parenté.* [The elementary structures of kinship]. Boston, MA: Beacon.

(1969). *The elementary structures of kinship.* London: Eyre and Spottiswoode.

Levinson, D. and Malone, M. J. (1980). *Toward explaining human culture.* New Haven, CT: HRAF Press.

Levitt, M. J., Weber, R. A., and Guacci, N. (1993). Convoys of social support: An intergenerational analysis. *Psychology and Aging*, 8: 323–326.

Levy, M. (1949). *The family revolution in modern China*. Cambridge, MA: Harvard University Press.

Lewis, C. (2000). *A man's place in the home: Fathers and families in the UK*. York: Joseph Rowntree Foundation.

Liljestrom, R. (2002). The strongest bond on trial. In Liljestrom and Ozdalga (eds.), *Autonomy and dependence in the family*, pp. 59–79. Istanbul: Swedish Research Institute.

Lin, C-Y. C. and Fu, V. R. (1990). A comparison of child-rearing practices among Chinese, immigrant Chinese, and Caucasian-American parents. *Child Development*, 61: 429–433.

Linton, R. (1936). *The study of man*. New York: Appleton-Century-Crofts.

(1945). *The cultural background of personality*. New York: Appleton-Century-Crofts.

Lomax, A. and Berkowitz, W. (1972). The evolutionary taxonomy of culture. *Science*, 177: 228–239.

Lovell-Troy, L. (1980). Clan structure and economic activity: The case of Greeks in small business enterprise. In S. Cummings (ed.), *Self-help in urban America*, pp. 58–85. Washington, NY: Kennikat Press.

Lynn Bolles, A. (1996). *Sister Jamaica: A study of women, work, and households in Kingston*. Lanham, MD: University Press of America.

Maccoby, E. M. and Jacklin, C. N. (1975). *The psychology of sex differences*. Stanford, CA: Stanford University Press.

MacFarlane, A. (1978). *The origins of English individualism*. Oxford: Blackwell.

(1986). *Marriage and love in England: Modes of reproduction 1300–1840*. Oxford: Blackwell.

Magnis-Suseno, F. (1984). *Etika Jawa. Sebuah Analisis Falsafi tentang Kebijaksanaan Hidup Jawa*. [Javanese ethics. A philosophical analysis of Javanese living wisdom.] Jakarta, Indonesia: Penerbit PT Gramedia.

Main reasons for divorce [Arabic text]. (2000, December 30). *Al-Youm. A daily newspaper*, p. 583. Algiers, Algeria.

Makaveeva, L. (1991). *Balgarskoto semistvo* [The Bulgarian family]. Sofia, Bulgaria: Balgarska Akademia na Naukite, Etnografski Institut s Muzei.

Makgoba, M. W. (1997). *The Makgoba affair: A reflection on transformation*. Pretoria, South Africa: Vivla Publishers and Book Sellers.

Makgoba, M. W. and Seepe, S. (2004). Knowledge and identity: An African vision of higher education transformation. In S. Seepe (ed.), *Towards an African identity of higher education*, pp. 13–58. Pretoria, South Africa: Vista University and Skotaville Media.

Malinowski, B. (1927). *Sex and repression in savage society*. London: Routledge and Kegan Paul.

Mandela, N. (1994, May 11). A time for healing the wounds. *The Star*.

Mansfield, P. and Collard, J. (1988). *The beginning of the rest of your life?* Basingstoke: Macmillan.

Maratou-Alibrante, L. (1995). *H oikogenia stin Ellada: Oikogeniaka protypa kai syzigikes praktikes* [Family in Greece: Family norms and spouse functions]. Athens: National Social Sciences Center.

(1999). Diageneakes sxeseis sti synchrone epoche [Intergenerational relationships in modern epoch]. *Greek Review of Social Research*, 49–76: 98–99.

Marks, N. F. and McLanahan, S. S. (1993). Gender, family structure, and social support among parents. *Journal of Marriage and the Family*, 55: 481–493.

Marx, K. ([1867] 1936). *Capital*. New York: Modern Library.

Matsumoto, D. (1999). Culture and self: An empirical assessment of Markus and Kitayama's theory of independent and interdependent self-construals. *Asian Journal of Social Psychology*, 2: 289–310.

Mbeki, T. (2002). *Presidential speech at the graveyard of Sarah Bartman*. Pretoria, South Africa: Government Press.

McCrae, R. E. and Terraciano, A. (2005). Universal features of personality traits from the observer's perspective: Data from 50 cultures. *Journal of Personality and Social Psychology*, 88: 547–561.

McGlone, F., Park, A., and Smith, K. (1998). *Families and kinship*. London: Family Policy Studies Centre.

McKenzie, D. J. (1995). *The new Germany: Social, political and cultural challenges of unification*. Exeter: University of Exeter Press.

McLanahan, S. and Teitler, J. (1999). The consequences of father absence. In M. E. Lamb (ed.), *Parenting and child development in "nontraditional" families*, pp. 83–102. Mahwah, NJ: Erlbaum.

Mead, G. H. (1934). *Mind, self, and society*. Chicago, IL: University of Chicago Press.

Meeker, M. (1976). Meaning and society in the Near East: Examples from the Black Sea Turks and the Levantine Arabs (Parts I and II). *International Journal of Middle East Studies*, 7: 243–270 and 383–423.

Mendras, H. (1997). *L'Europe des Européens: Sociologie de l'Europe occidentale*. Paris: Gallimard.

Menon, T., Morris, M. W., Chiu, C., and Hong, Y. (2000). Culture and the construal of agency: Attribution to individual versus group dispositions. *Journal of Personality and Social Psychology*, 76: 701–717.

Mermet, J. (1999). *Francoscopie: Comment vivent les Français?* [Francoscopie: How do the French live?] Paris: Larousse.

Metz, C. H. (1993). *Algeria: A country study*. Washington, DC: Federal Research Division, Library of Congress.

Milardo, R. M. (1997). Social networks and marital relationships. In S. Duck (ed.), *Handbook of personal relationships*, pp. 505–522, Chichester: John Wiley & Sons.

Millar, J. and Warman, A. (1996). *Family obligations in Europe*. London: Family Policy Studies Centre.

Miller, J. G. (1997). Theoretical issues in cultural psychology. In J. W. Berry, Y. H. Poortinga, and J. Pandey (eds.), *Handbook of cross-cultural psychology*, Vol. 1. *Theory and method*, 2nd edn., pp. 85–128. Boston, MA: Allyn & Bacon.

Ministerio de Educación, Cultura y Deportes, Reino de España (2000). *Sistema educativo español* [Spanish educational system]. Madrid: MECD. Retrieved from http://www.mecd.es.

Mishra, R. C., Sinha, D., and Berry, J. W. (1996a). Cognitive functioning of tribal groups in Bihar. In H. Grad, A. Blanco, and J. Georgas (eds.), *Key issues in cross-cultural psychology*, pp. 89–101. Amsterdam: Swets & Zeitlinger.

(1996b). *Ecology, acculturation and psychological adaptation: A study of Advasi in Bihar*. Delhi: Sage Publications.

Mitteraurer, M. and Seider, R. (1982). *The European family: Patriarchy to partnership from the middle ages to the present*. Oxford: Blackwell.

Mivanyi, Y. J. (1988). "The extended family system and learning styles of Junior Secondary School (JSS) III Adamawa and Taraba States of Nigeria." Preliminary investigation to a doctoral thesis, University of Jos, Jos, Nigeria.

(2002). *National census on water rehabilitations and supply–Kano State: A report*. Nigeria.

Modood, T., Berthoud, R., Lakey, J., Nazroo, J., Smith, P., Virdee, S., and Beishon, S. (1997). *Ethnic minorities in Britain: Diversity and disadvantage*. London: Policy Studies Institute.

Mogey, J. (1991). Families: Intergenerational and generational connections–conceptual approaches to kinship and culture. *Marriage and Family Review*, 16: 47–66.

Montecino, S. (1993). *Madres y huachos. Alegorías del mestizaje chileno* [Mothers and bastards. Allegories of Chilean half-caste]. Santiago: Editorial Cuarto Propio-Ediciones CEDEM.

Moore, C. A. (1974). Introduction: The humanistic Chinese mind. In C. A. Moore (ed.), *The Chinese mind: Essentials of Chinese philosophy and culture*, pp. 1–10. Honolulu: University Press of Hawaii.

Moran, E. (1982). *Human adaptability: An introduction to ecological anthropology*. Boulder: Westview Press.

(1990). *The ecosystem approach in anthropology*. Ann Arbor, MI: University of Michigan Press.

Morgan, L. H. (1870). *Systems of consanguinity and affinity of the human family*. Washington, DC: Smithsonian Institution.

Mortazavi, S. (1996). *Iranian school spaces* [In Farsi]. Tehran: Iranian Ministry of Education.

(2000). *Attitudes of feminine rural high-school pupils towards immigration* [In Farsi]. Tehran: Pajuheschnameh University of Shahid Beheshti.

Mortazavi, S. and Karimi, E. (1992). Cultural dimensions of paternalistic behavior: A cross-cultural research in 5 countries. In S. Iwawaki, Y. Kashima and K. Leung (eds.), *Innovations in cross-cultural psychology*, pp. 147–151. Amsterdam: Swetz & Zeitlinger.

Mousourou, L. M. (1985). *Oikogeneia kai paidi stin Athena* [Family and child in Athens]. Athens: Estia.

Mthembu, T. (2004). Creating a niche in internationalization for (South) African higher education institutions. In S. Seepe (ed.), *Towards an African identity of higher education*, pp. 77–82. Pretoria, South Africa: Vista University and Skotaville Media.

Muncie, J. and Sapsford, R. (1995). Issues in the study of "the family." In J. Muncie, M. Wetherell, R. Dallos, and A. Cochrane (eds.). *Understanding the family*, pp. 7–37. London: Sage

Muñoz, M. and Reyes, E. (1997). *Una mirada al interior de la familia* [A glance inside the family]. Santiago: Ediciones Universidad Católica de Chile.

Munroe, R. L. and Munroe, R. H. (1997). A comparative anthropological perspective. In J. W. Berry, Y. H. Poortinga, and J. Pandey (eds.), *Handbook of cross-cultural psychology*, Vol. 1. *Theory and method*, 2nd edn., pp. 171–213. Boston, MA: Allyn & Bacon.

Muramoto, Y. (2003). An indirect self-enhancement in relationship among Japanese. *Journal of Cross-Cultural Psychology*, 34: 552–566.

Muramoto, Y. and Yamaguchi, S. (2003). *"Jikohige" ga kietu toki: Naishudan no kankeisei ni oujita jiko to shudan no seikou no katarikata* [When "self-effacement" disappears: Narratives of personal and ingroup successes depending on an ingroup relationship]. *Japanese Journal of Psychology*, 43: 253–262.

Murdock, G. P. (1949). *Social structure*. New York: Free Press.

  (1957). World ethnographic sample. *American Anthropologist*, 59: 664–687.

  (1967): *Ethnographic Atlas*. Pittsburgh, PA: HRAF Press.

  (1969). Correlations of exploitative and settlement patterns. In D. Damas (ed.), *Contributions to anthropology: Ecological essays* (Bulletin no. 230, Anthropological Series no. 86). Ottawa: National Museum of Canada.

  (1975). *Outline of cultural materials*. New Haven, CT: Human Relations Area Files.

Murray, M. (1994). *The revolution deferred: The painful birth of post-apartheid South Africa*. London: City Press.

Mylona, L. (1986). *Cypriot woman*. Nicosia, Cyprus.

Nakane, C. (1970). *Japanese society*. Berkeley, CA: University of California Press.

Naroll, R., Michik, G. L., and Naroll, F. (1974). Hologeistic theory testing. In J. G. Jurgensen (ed.), *Comparative studies by Harold E. Driver and essays in his honor*. New Haven, CT: HRAN.

Neder, G. (1998). Ajustando o foco das lentes: Um novo olhar sobre a organizaCão das famílias no Brasil [Adjusting the focal point: A new glance at the family organization in Brazil]. In S. M. Kaloustian (ed.), *Família brasileira: A base de tudo*, pp. 26–46. São Paulo and Brasilia: Cortez and UNICEF.

Nederlandse Gezinsraad (2001). *Gezin: Beeld en werkelijkheid* [Family: Image and reality]. The Hague, The Netherlands: Nederlandse Gezinsraad.

Needham, R. (1974). *Remarks and inventions: Skeptical essays about kinship*. London: Tavistock.

Nhlapo, T. (1992). *Marriage and divorce in Swazi law and custom*. Mbabane, Swaziland: Swazi Press.

Nimkoff, M. F. and Middleton, R. (1960). Types of family and types of economy. *American Journal of Sociology*, 66: 215–225.

Nogueira, A. H. (2001). "Padrões culturais e normas para comportamentos de lideranca: Um estudo comparativo entre empregados de empresas de previdência privada do Brasil e dos EUA" [Cultural patterns and norms for leadership behaviors: A comparative study among employees of private social security agencies in Brazil and the US]. Unpublished master's thesis, University of Brasilia, Brazil.

Norval, A. L. (2001). "Deconstructing apartheid." Unpublished paper, University of Essex, UK.

Nsamenang, B. (1992). *Human development in cultural context*. Newbury Park, CA: Sage.

Nukunya, G. K. (1969). *Kinship and marriage among the Anlo Ewe-speaking people of Ghana* (London School of Economics, Monographs on Social Anthropology, 37). London: Athlone Press.

(1992). *Tradition and change in Ghana: An introduction to sociology*. Accra, Ghana: Ghana Universities Press.

Nurhaena (1995). "Keterlibatan Ayah dalam Pengasuhan Bayi dan Anak Kecil." [Father's involvement in rearing babies and toddlers]. Unpublished research report, Faculty of psychology, University of Indonesia, Depok, Indonesia.

Oboladze, U. (1990). *Women's issue in writings of Ilia Chavchavadze*. Tbilisi, Georgia: Tbilisi State University Publishing House.

Office Nationale des Statistiques, République Algérienne Démocratique et Populaire (2005). *L'annuaire statistique de l'Algérie No 20: Résultats 1999–2001*. Algiers: ONS.

Office of National Statistics, UK (2000). *Social trends 2000*. London: The Stationery Office.

Office of National Statistics, UK (2001). *Britain 2001*. London: The Stationery Office.

Office of National Statistics, UK (2002). *UK 2002, Official yearbook of the UK*. London: The Stationery Office.

Olson, D. H., McCubbin, H. I., Barnes, H. L., Muxen, M. J., Larsen, A. S., and Wilson, M. A. (1989). *Families: What makes them work*, updated edn. Newbury Park, CA: Sage.

Olson, E. A. (1982). Duofocal family structure and an alternative model of husband–wife relationship. In Ç. Kağıtçıbaşı (ed.), *Sex roles, family and community in Turkey*, pp. 33–72. Bloomington, IN: Indiana University Press.

Omolara, P. A. (1995). "A study of the effects of parental separation on the academic performance and personality traits of children." Unpublished paper, Department of Education (Technical), Kaduna Polytechnic, Kaduna, Nigeria.

Organization for Economic Co-operation and Development, Program for International Students Assessment (2004). *Messages from PISA 2000*. Retrieved from http://www.pisa.oecd.org.

Orlove, B. S. (1980). Ecological anthropology. *Annual Review of Anthropology*, 9: 235–273.

Orrego-Luco, L. (1983). *Casa grande* [Great house]. Santiago: Editorial Andrés Bello.

Owen, D. W. (1996). The Other–Asians: The salad bowl. In C. Peach (ed.), *Ethnicity in the 1991 Census*. London: HMSO

Owens, R. (1971). Industrialization and the Indian joint family. *Ethnology*, 10: 223–250.

Ozgur, S. and Sunar, D. (1982). Social psychological patterns of homicide in Turkey: A comparison of male and female convicted murders. In Ç. Kağıtçıbaşı (ed.), *Sex roles, family and community in Turkey*, pp. 349–381. Bloomington, IN: Indiana University Press.

Panayotopoulos, B. (1985). Dimension et composition de la famille péloponnélsienne aux environs de 1700: Quelques remarques [Dimensions and Composition of the Peloponnesian family around 1700: some comments]. In C. Piault (ed.), *Famillies et biens en Gréce et à Chypre*, pp. 29–44. Paris: Editions L'Harmattan.

Papademou, L. (1999). Koinonike kai psychologike analyse tis oikogeneias [Social and psychological analysis of the family]. *Psychologia*, 6: 165–173.

Papadopoulos, T. (1998). Greek family policy from a comparative perspective. In E. Drew, R. Emerek, and E. Mahon (eds.), *Women, work and the family in Europe*, pp. 47–57. London and New York: Routledge.

Park, A., Curtice, J., Thomson, K., Jarvis, L., and Bromley, C. (2001). *British social attitudes: The 18th report*. London: Sage.

Park, Y. S. and Kim, U., (2004). *Parent–child relationship in Korea: Indigenous psychological analysis of self-concept and family role*. Seoul: Kyoyook Kwahaksa.

Parsons, T. (1943). The kinship system of the contemporary United States. *American Anthropologist*, 45: 22–38.

(1949). The social structure of the family. In R. N. Anshen (ed.), *The family: Its functions and destiny*, pp. 33–58. New York: Harper.

(1965). The normal American family. In S. M. Farber (ed.), *Man and civilization: The family's search for survival*, pp. 34–36. New York: McGraw-Hill

Pasternak, B. E., Ember, C. R., and Ember, M. (1976). On the conditions favoring extended family households. *Journal of Anthropological Research*, 32: 109–123.

(1997). *Sex, gender and kinship: A cross-cultural perspective*. Upper Saddle River, NJ: Prentice Hall.

Pavliouk, S. P., Goryn, G. U., and Kyrchiv, R. F. (1997). *Ukrainske narodoznavstvo* [Ukrainian folklore]. Lviv, Ukraine: Fenix.

Pearson, V. M. and Stephan, W. G. (1998). Preferences for styles of negotiation: A comparison of Brasil and the US. *International Journal of Intercultural Relations*, 22: 67–83.

Peletz, M. (1995). Kinship studies in late twentieth-century anthropology. *Annual Review of Anthropology*, 24: 343–357.

Pelto, P. (1968). The difference between "tight" and "loose" societies. *Transaction*, 5: 37–40.

Peristiany, J. G. (1965). *Honor and shame: The values of Mediterranean society*. London: Weidenfeld and Nicolson.

Peters, J. (1990). Cultural variations: Past and present. In M. Baker (ed.), *Families: Changing trends in Canada*, 2nd edn., pp. 166–191. Toronto: McGraw-Hill Ryerson.

Phalet, K. and Schönpflug, U. (2001). Intergenerational transmission of collect-
ivism and achievement values in two acculturation contexts: The case of
Turkish families in Germany and Turkish and Moroccan families in the
Netherlands. *Journal of Cross-Cultural Psychology*, 32: 186–201.

Pithon, G., Ho Can Sung, A., and Brochain, E. (2003, April). "Les parents des
familles vulnérables et traditionnelles, vivant en France métropolitaine et en
Martinique, préconisent-ils les mêmes modèles de bien traitance que ceux
véhiculés par un programme en éducation parentale?" [Is it recommended
that parents of vulnerable families in metropolitan France and Martinique
use the same treatment models as those delivered by a programme
of parental education?]. Paper presented at the International Congress
AIFREF- EUSARF "In the best interests of the child: Cross-cultural
perspectives", University of Leuven, Leuven, Belgium.

Pithon, G., Terrisse, B., Gordon, D., Prévôt, O., and Vallerand, S. (2004). La
résolution de problèmes éducatifs: Entraînement interactif à la communication parents–enfants au moyen d'un programme de formation sur
cédérom [The resolution of educational problems: Developing interactive
communication between parents and children using a CD Rom teaching
program]. In E. Palacio-Quintin, J. M. Bouchard, and B. Terrisse (eds.),
Questions d'éducation familliale, pp. 443–454. Brussels: Laval.

Poortinga, Y. H. and Vijver, F. J. R. van de (2000). How different are personality
traits cross-culturally and how are they different? *Contemporary Psychology*,
45: 89–91.

    (2004). Culture and cognition: Performance differences and invariant struc-
tures. In R. J. Sternberg and E. Grigorenko (eds.), *Culture and competence:
Context of life success*, pp. 139–162. Washington, DC: American Psychological Association.

Popenoe, D. (1988). *Disturbing the nest: Family change and decline in modern
societies*. Chicago, IL: Aldine.

    (1993). American family decline, 1960–1990: A review and appraisal. *Journal
of Marriage and the Family*, 55: 527–555.

Popular Bank of Cyprus (2002). *Kyprovarometro* [Cyprusbarometer]. Nicosia,
Cyprus: PBC.

Programa de las Naciones Unidas para el Desarrollo (2002a). *Informe sobre
desarrollo humano 2002* [2002 human development report]. Ciudad de
México: Ediciones Mundi-Prensa.

    (2002b). *Nosotros los chilenos: Un desafío cultural. Informe de desarrollo humano en
Chile en 2002* [We, the Chileans: A cultural challenge. 2002 human development report for Chile]. Santiago: PNUD.

Psychogios, D. (1987). *Prikes, fori, stafida kai psomi* [Dowries, taxes, raisin and
bread]. Athens, Greece: National Social Sciences Center.

Razi, Z. (1993). The myth of the immutable English family. *Past and Present:
A Journal of Historical Studies*, 140: 3–44.

Reca, I., Pérez, E., and Espíndola, E. (1996). Familias y hogares en situaciones
críticas en Chile según censo 1992 [Families and households under critical
conditions in Chile, according to 1992 census]. *Documentos de Trabajo No.
46*. Santiago: Servicio Nacional de la Mujer.

Reitz, J. G. (2001). Immigrant success in the knowledge economy: Institutional change and the immigrant experience in Canada, 1970–1995. *Journal of Social Issues*, 5: 579–613.

Religion Statistics Geography (2002). *Religion by location index.* Retrieved September, 2002, from http://adherents.com.

Requena, F. (1994). Redes de amistad, felicidad y familia [Networks of friendship, happiness, and family]. *Revista Española de Investigaciones Sociológicas*, 66: 73–89.

Ribeiro, D. (1997). *O povo brasileiro: A formação e sentido do Brasil* [Brazilian people: The formation and meaning of Brazil]. São Paulo, Brazil: Companhia das Letras.

Ribeiro, R. M., Sabóia, A. L., Branco, H. C., and Bregman, S. (1998). Estrutura familiar, trabalho e renda [Family structure, work, and income]. In S. M. Kaloustian (ed.), *Família brasileira: a base de tudo*, pp. 135–158. São Paulo, Brazil: Cortez and UNICEF.

Richard, L. L. (1980). *Algeria*. World Bibliographical Series, vol. 19. Oxford: Clio Press.

Roberts, R. E. L., Richards, L. N., and Bengtson, V. L. (1991). Intergenerational solidarity in families: Untangling the ties that bind. *Marriage and Family Review*, 16: 11–46.

Robinson, G. (1997). Families, generations, and self. *Ethos*, 25: 303–322.

Rodriguez Mosquera, P. M., Manstead, A. S. R., and Fischer, A. H. (2002). Honor in the Mediterranean and northern Europe. *Journal of Cross-Cultural Psychology*, 33: 16–36.

Romanelli, G. (1997). Famílias de classes populares: Socialização e identidade masculina [Families of working classes: Socialization and masculine identity]. *Cadernos de Pesquisa-NEP*, 1–2: 25–34.

 (1998). O relacionamento entre pais e filhos em famílias de camadas médias [Parent–child relationships in middle-class families]. *Cadernos de Psicologia e Educação Paidéia*, 8: 123–136.

 (2000). Autoridade e poder na família [Authority and power in the family]. In M. C. B. Carvalho (ed.), *A família contemporânea em debate*, pp. 73–88. São Paulo, Brazil: EDUC/Cortez.

Rossi, A. S. (1993). Intergenerational relations: Gender, norms, and behavior. In V. L. Bengtson and W. A. Achenbaum (eds.), *The changing contract across generations*, pp. 191–212. Hawthorne, NY: Aldine de Gruyter.

Roussel, L. and Bourguignon, O. (1976). *La famille après le marriage des enfants* [The family after marriage of the children] (Travaux et documents, no. 78). Paris: INED/PUF.

Ruble, D. N., Costanzo, P. R., and Oliveri, M. E. (1992). *The social psychology of mental health*. New York: Guilford.

Ryan, R. M. and Deci, E. L. (2000). Self-determination theory and the facilitation of intrinsic motivation, social development, and well-being. *American Psychologist*, 55: 68–78.

Ryan, R. M. and Lynch, J. H. (1989). Emotional autonomy versus detachment: Revisiting the vicissitudes of adolescence and young adulthood. *Child Development*, 60: 340–356.

Ryan, R. M., Stiller, J., and Lynch, J. H. (1994). Representations of relationships to teachers, parents, and friends as predictors of academic motivation and self-esteem. *Journal of Early Adolescence*, 14: 226–249.

Saal, C. D. (1987). Alternative forms of living and housing. In L. Shangar-Handelman and R. Palomba (eds.), *Alternative patterns of family life in modern societies*. Rome: Collana Monografie.

Sachs, A. (1992). There's a constitution about. *South Africa International*, 22: 187–8.

Safilios-Rothschild, K. (1967). A comparison of power structure and marital satisfaction in urban Greek and French families. *Journal of Marriage and the Family*, 29: 345–349.

(1971). A cross-cultural examination of women's marital, educational and occupational options. *Acta Sociologica*, 14: 96–113.

Salazar, G. (1990). Ser niño "huacho" en la historia de Chile (siglo XIX) [Being a bastard child in the history of Chile (nineteenth century)]. In *Proposiciones, No. 19: Chile. Historia y "bajo pueblo,"* pp. 55–83. Santiago: SUR Ediciones.

Salinas, R. (1994). Uniones ilegítimas y desuniones legítimas. El matrimonio y la formación de la pareja en Chile colonial [Illegitimate unions and legitimate splits. Marriage and partnership in colonial Chile]. In P. Gonzalbo and C. Rabell (eds.), *La familia en el mundo iberoamericano*, pp. 173–192. Ciudad de México: National Autonomous University of Mexico.

Sam D. L. and Berry, J. W. (2006), (eds.) *Cambridge handbook of acculturation psychology*. Cambridge: Cambridge University Press.

Samara, E. M. (1992). Novas imagens da família "à brasileira" [New images of the Brazilian family]. *Psicologia-USP*, 3: 59–66.

Santos, N. R. (1998). Governo corta na saúde e educação para pagar uma dívida impagável [Government cuts on health and education to pay an invaluable debt]. *Jornal da Ciência*, 401: 7–8.

Sarvestani, K. K. (1998). *The land of Mehr and Mah*. Shiraz, Iran: Daneshnameh Pars Publishing.

Sass, J. and Ashford, L. (2002). *Women of our world*. Washington, DC: Population Reference Bureau.

Schmitt, E. (2001, May 15). For the first time, nuclear families drop below 25% of households. *New York Times*, 1.

Schneider, D. M. (1968). *American kinship: A cultural account*. Chicago, IL: University of Chicago Press.

Schwartz, S. H. (1992). Universals in the content and structure of values: Theoretical advances and empirical tests in twenty countries. In M. P. Zanna (ed.), *Advances in experimental social psychology*, Vol. 25, pp. 1–65. San Diego, CA: Academic Press.

(1994a). Are there universal aspects in the structure and content of human values? *Journal of Social Issues*, 50: 19–45.

(1994b). Beyond individualism-collectivism: New cultural dimensions of values. In U. Kim, H. C. Triandis, Ç. Kağıtçıbaşı, S.-C. Choi, and G. Yoon (eds.), *Individualism and collectivism: Theory, method, and applications*, pp. 85–119. Thousand Oaks, CA: Sage.

Seepe, S. (2004). *Speaking truth to power.* Pretoria, South Africa: Vista University and Skotaville Media.

Segalen, M. (1986). *Historical anthropology of the family.* Cambridge: Cambridge University Press.

Segalen, M. (1996). *Sociologie de la famille* [Sociology of the family] (4th edn. 2000). Paris: Armand Colin.

Segall, M. H., Dasen, P. R., Berry, J. W., and Poortinga, Y. H. (1999). *Human behavior in global perspective: An introduction to cross-cultural psychology,* 2nd edn. Boston, MA: Allyn and Bacon.

Serrano, S. (1999). Quién quiere la educación? Estado y familia en Chile a mediados del siglo XIX [Who wants education? State and family in Chile by the middle of the twientieth century]. In P. Gonzalbo (ed.), *Familia y educación en Iberoamérica,* pp.153–171. Ciudad de México: Centro de Estudios Históricos, El Colegio de México.

Servicio Nacional de la Mujer, Republica de Chile (2001). *Mujeres chilenas: Estadísticas para un nuevo siglo* [Chilean women: Statistical data for a new century]. Santiago: SERNAM.

Setiloane, G. M. (1975). *The ideal of God among the Sotho-Tswana.* Leiden, The Netherlands: Balkema.

Seymour, D. C. (1999). *Women, family, and child care in India: A world in transition.* Cambridge: Cambridge University Press.

Shablia, O. (1995). *Sotsiologia, ikonomika, geografia Ukrainee* [Sociology, economy and geography of Ukraine]. Lviv, Ukraine: Zvit.

Shah, A. M. (1968). Changes in the Indian family. *Economic and Political Weekly,* 3: 127–135.

(1996). Is the joint household disintegrating? *Economic and Political Weekly,* 31: 537–542.

Shojaii, M. (2004). Iranian women are still waiting and hopeful [in Farsi]. *Journal of Zanan,* 110: 16–22.

Shweder, R. A. and Sullivan, M. A. (1993). Cultural psychology: Who needs it? *Annual Review of Psychology,* 44: 497–527.

Silitshena, P. M. A. (1982). *The regrouping policy: The north-east district of Botswana.* Ibadan, Nigeria: Heineman.

Silverstein, M. and Bengtson, V. L. (1997). Intergenerational solidarity and the structure of adult child–parent relationships in American families. *American Journal of Sociology,* 2: 429–460.

Singelis, T. M. (1994). The measurement of independent and interdependent self-construals. *Personality and Social Psychology Bulletin,* 20: 580–591.

Singelis, T. M. and Brown, W. P. (1995). Culture, self, and collectivist communication: Linking culture to individual behavior. *Human Communication Research,* 21: 354–389.

Singelis, T. M. and Sharkey, W. F. (1995). Culture, self-construal, and embarrassability. *Journal of Cross-Cultural Psychology,* 26: 622–644.

Singelis, T. M., Triandis, H. C., Bhawuk, D. P. S., and Gelfand, M. J. (1995). Horizontal and vertical dimensions of individualism and collectivism: A theoretical and measurement refinement. *Cross-Cultural Research,* 29: 240–275.

Sinha, D. (1988). The family scenario in a developing country and its implications for mental health: The case of India. In P. R. Dasen, J. W. Berry, and N. Sartorius (eds.), *Health and cross-cultural psychology: Toward applications*, pp. 48–70. Newbury Park, CA: Sage.

(1991). Rise in the population of the elderly, familial changes and their psychosocial implications: The scenario of the developing countries. *International Journal of Psychology*, 26: 633–647.

(1997). Indigenizing psychology. In J. W. Berry, Y. H. Poortinga, and J. Pandey (eds.), *Handbook of cross-cultural psychology*, Vol. 1. *Theory and method*, 2nd edn., pp. 129–169. Boston, MA: Allyn and Bacon.

Sinha, S. R. (1985). Maternal strategies for regulating children's behavior. *Journal of Cross-Cultural Psychology*, 16: 27–40.

Skolnick, A. (1993). Change of heart: Family dynamics in historical perspective. In P. A. Cowan, D. Field, D. A. Hansen, A. Skolnick, and G. E. Swanson, (eds.), *Family, self, and society*, pp. 43–68. Hillsdale, NJ: Erlbaum.

Slaughter, D. T. (ed.) (1988). *Black children and poverty: A developmental perspective*. San Francisco, CA: Jossey-Brass.

Smith, S. (1995). Family theory and multicultural family studies. In B. Ingoldsby and S. Smith (eds.), *Families in multicultural perspective*, pp. 5–35. New York: The Guilford Press.

Smith, P. B. and Bond, M. H. (1999). *Social psychology across cultures*, 2nd edn. Boston, MA: Allyn and Bacon.

Smith, P. B., Peterson, M. F., Ayestaran. S., Jesuíno, J. C., and Ferdman, B. M. (in press). Cultural values and decision behaviour in work organisations. In M. Ros and V. V. Gouveia (eds.), *Social psychology of human values: Theoretical, methodological, and applied developments*. La Coruña, Spain: Biblioteca Nueva.

Sociaal en Cultureel Planbureau, Nederland (1995). *Tijdopnamen* [Time recordings]. The Hague, The Netherlands: SCP.

Song, M. (1997). Children's labour in ethnic family businesses: The case of Chinese take-away businesses in Britain. *Ethnic and Racial Studies*, 20: 690–716.

Spasovska, L. (1985a). *Pokolenia i semeistvo (sotsialni aspecti)* [Generations and family (social aspects)]. Sofia, Bulgaria: Otechestven Front.

(1985b). *Semeistvoto: Sociologicheski ocherk* [The family: Sociological depiction]. Sofia, Bulgaria: BAN.

Spencer, H. (1876). *Principles of sociology*, vol. 1. London: Appleton.

Sperry, L. and Carlson, J. (1991). *Marital therapy: Integrating theory and technique*. Denver, CO: Love Publishing Company.

Spielmann, K. A. and Eder, J. F. (1994). Hunters and farmers: Then and now. *Annual Review of Anthropology*, 23: 303–323.

Stacey, J. (1993). Good riddance to "the family": A response to David Popenoe. *Journal of Marriage and the Family*, 55: 545–547.

Standley, K. (1993). *Family law*. Houndmills and London: Macmillan.

Starr, J. (1989). The role of Turkish secular law in changing the lives of rural Muslim women, 1950–1970. *Law and Society Review*, 23: 497–523.

State Department of Statistics for Georgia (2000). *Statistical Yearbook of Georgia – 2000*. Tbilisi, Georgia: SDS.

(2001). *Households in Georgia – 2000*. Tbilisi, Georgia: SDS.

State Institute of Statistics, Republic of Turkey (1991). *Statistical Indicators, 1923–90*. Ankara, Turkey: SIS. Retrieved from http://www.die.gov.tr.

(2001). *Women's indicators and statistics*. Ankara, Turkey: SIS. Retrieved from http://www.die.gov.tr.

Statistical Service of the Republic of Cyprus (2003). *Demographic report 2000*. Nicosia, Cyprus: Government Printing Office.

Statistisches Bundesamt, Bundesrepublik Deutschland (1999). *Datenreport. Zahlen und Fakten über die Bundesrepublik Deutschland* (Schriftenreihe der Bundeszentrale für politische Bildung, Band 365) [Data report. Numbers and facts about the Federal Republic of Germany (Paper series of the Federal Office for Political Education, vol. 365)]. Bonn: Germany.

Steil, J. M. (2001). Family forms and member well-being: A research agenda for the decade of behavior. *Psychology of Women Quarterly*, 25: 344–363.

Steinberg, L. and Silverberg, S. B. (1986). The vicissitudes of autonomy in early adolescence. *Child Development*, 57: 841–851.

Steward, J. (1955). *The concept and method of cultural ecology: Theory of culture change*. Urbana, IL: University of Illinois Press.

Stewart, S. M., Bond, M. H., Chan, W. Zaman, R. M., Dar, R., and Anwar, M. (2003). Autonomy from parents and psychological adjustment in an interdependent culture. *Psychology in developing societies*, 15: 31–49.

Stewart, S. M., Bond, M. H., Deeds, O., and Chung, S. F. (1999). Intergenerational patterns of values and autonomy expectations in cultures of relatedness and separateness. *Journal of Cross-Cultural Psychology*, 30: 575–593.

Stewart, S. M., Bond, M. H., Ho, L. M., Zaman, R. M., Dar, R., and Anwar M. (2000). Perceptions of parents and adolescent outcomes in Pakistan. *British Journal of Developmental Psychology*, 18: 335–352.

Stewart, S. M., Bond, M. H., Zaman, R. M., McBride-Chang, C., Rao, N., and Fielding, R. (1999). Functional parenting in Pakistan. *International Journal of Behavioral Development*, 23: 747–770.

Stewart, S. M., Zaman, R. M., and Dar, R. (in press). *Pakistani mothers perceptions of autonomy as a psychological need. Psychology and Developing Societies*.

Sugareva, M. (1996). *Balgarskoto semeistvo v prehoda kam pazarna ikonomika* [The Bulgarian family in the transition period]. Sofia, Bulgaria: Fondation "Svobodna Initsiativa."

Sumbadze, N. (1999). *Social web: Friendships of adult men and women*. Leiden, The Netherlands: DSWO Press.

Sunar, D. (1988). Attitudes of Turkish students toward elderly relatives. *Journal of Cross Cultural Gerontology*, 3: 41–52.

(2002). Change and continuity in the Turkish middle-class family. In Ozdalga, E. and Liljestrom, R. (eds.), *Autonomy and dependence in family: Turkey and Sweden in critical perspective*, pp. 217–237. Istanbul, Turkey: Swedish Research Institute.

Sunar, D. and Fisek, G. (2004). Contemporary Turkish families. In U. Gielen and J. Roopnarine (eds.), *Families in global perspective*. Boston, MA: Allyn and Bacon.

Swaan, A. de (1988). *In care of the state: Health care, education and welfare in Europe and the USA in the modern era.* Cambridge: Polity Press.

Swatridge, L. A., Wright, I. A., Hildebrand, W., Oliver, C. A., and Pyzer, G. D. (2000). *Canada: Exploring new directions,* 4th edn. Ottawa: Fitzhenry and Whiteside Ltd.

Sybstelniy, O. (1991). *Ukraina istoria* [History of Ukraine]. Kiev, Ukraine: Lubid.

Takano, Y. and Osaka, E. (1999). An unsupported common view: Comparing Japan and the US on individualism/collectivism. *Asian Journal of Social Psychology,* 2: 311–341.

Talmon-Garber, Y. (1970). Social change and kinship ties. In R. Hill and R. Konig (eds.), *Families in east and west: Socialization process and kinship,* pp. 504–524. The Hague: Mouton.

Taylor, R. D. and Wang, M. C. (eds.) (2000). *Resilience across contexts.* Cambridge: Cambridge University Press.

Telbizov, K. (1946). *Zemedelskoto semeistvo* [The agrarian family]. Varna, Bulgaria: Fond Nauchni Izledrania.

Ten Berge, J. M. F. (1986). Rotatie naar perfecte congruentie en de Multipele Groep Methode [Rotation to pefect congruence and the Multiple Group Method]. *Nederlands Tijdschrift voor de Psychologie,* 41: 218–225.

Thiersch, F. (1833). *De l'état actuel de la Grece* [On the contemporary situation of Greece]. Leipzig.

Thorton, A. (1984). Modernization and family change. In *Social Change and Family Policies. Proceedings of the twentieth International CFR Seminar.* Melbourne: Australian Institute of Family Studies.

Thorton, A. and Fricke, T. E. (1987). Social change and the family: Comparative perspectives from the west. *Sociological Forum,* 2: 746–779.

Timur, S. (1972). *Türkiye'de Aile Yapisi* [Family structure in Turkey]. Ankara: Hacettepe Üniversitesi Yayinlari.

Tinbergen, N. (1963). On aims and methods of ethology. *Zeitschrift für Tierpsychologie,* 20: 410–433.

Tomasello, M., Kruger, A., and Ratner, H. (1993). Culture learning. *Behavioral and Brain Sciences,* 16: 495–552.

Tooby, J. and Cosmides, L. (1992). The psychological foundations of culture. In J. Barkow, L. Cosmides, and J. Tooby (eds.), *The adapted mind: Evolutionary psychology and the generation of culture,* pp. 19–136. New York: Oxford University Press.

Torres, C. V. (1999). "Leadership style norms among Americans and Brazilians: Assessing differences using Jackson's return potential model." Unpublished doctoral dissertation, California School of Professional Psychology, San Diego, CA, USA.

Torres, C. V. and Dessen, M. A. (2004). Brazilian culture, family, and its ethnic-cultural variety. Manuscript submitted for publication.

Triandis, H. C. (1987). Collectivism vs. individualism: A reconceptualization of a basic concept in cross-cultural psychology. In C. Bagley and G. K. Verma (eds.), *Personality, cognition, and values: Cross-cultural perspectives on childhood and adolescence,* pp. 2–42. London: Macmillan.

(1994). *Culture and social behavior.* New York: McGraw-Hill.

(1995). *Individualism and collectivism*. Boulder, CO: West view.

Triandis, H. C., Bontempo, R., Villareal, M. J., Asai, M., and Lucca, N. (1988). Individualism and collectivism: Cross-cultural perspectives on self-group relationships. *Journal of Personality and Social Psychology*, 54: 323–338.

Triandis, H. C. and Vassiliou, V. (1972). An analysis of subjective culture. In H. C. Triandis (ed.), *The analysis of subjective culture*, pp. 299–335. New York: Wiley.

Troadec, B. (2001). Le modèle écoculturel: Un cadre pour la psychologie culturelle comparative [The ecocultural model: A framework for comparative cultural psychology]. *International Journal of Psychology*, 36: 53–64.

Tseng, W. S., Lin, T. Y., and Yeh, E. K. (1995). Chinese societies and mental health. In T. Y. Lin, W. S. Tseng, and E. K. Yeh (eds.), *Chinese societies and mental health*, pp. 3–18. Hong Kong: Oxford University Press.

Tsoukalas, K. (1982). *Exartisi kai anaparagogi. O koinonikos rolos ton ekpadeftikon micharismon stin Ellada (1830–1922)* [Dependence and reproduction. The social role of educational procedures in Greece (1830–1922)]. Athens: Themelio.

Tucker, L. R. (1951). *A method for synthesis of factor analytic studies* (Personnel Research Section Report No. 984). Washington, DC: Department of the Army.

Tuijl, C. van, Leseman, P. P. M., and Rispens, J. (2001). Efficacy of an intensive home based educational intervention programme for 4- to 6-year-old ethnic minority children in the Netherlands. *International Journal of Behavioral Development*, 25(2): 148–159.

Tylor, E. B. (1889). On a method of investigation the development of institutions: Applied to laws of marriage and descent. *Journal of the Royal Anthropological Institute of Great Britain and Ireland*, 18: 245–272.

UNICEF (2000). *Children and women in Georgia: A situational analysis*. Tbilisi, Georgia.

UNICEF/National Planning Commission (1998). *Child survival, protection and development in Nigeria: Key social statistics*. Abuja, Nigeria.

United Nations Statistics Division (2002a). *Demographic, Social and Housing Statistics*. Retrieved September, 2002, from http://unstats.un.org/unsd.

(2002b). *Energy Statistics*. Retrieved September, 2002, from http://unstats.un.org/unsd.

United States Census Bureau (2000). *Statistical abstract of the United States: 2000*. Washington, DC: US Government Printing Office.

Uzoka, A. F. (1979). The myth of the nuclear family. *American Psychologist*, 34: 1095–1106.

Valdés, X. (1995). Familia, matrimonio e ilegitimidad en la hacienda del siglo XX [Family, marriage and illegitimate children in the twentieth century estate]. *Proposiciones*, 26, *Aproximaciones a la Familia*: 150–165. Santiago: Ediciones SUR.

Valero A. (1995). El sistema familiar español: Recorrido a través del último cuarto de siglo [The Spanish family system: journey through the last quarter of the century]. *Revista Española de Investigaciones Sociológicas*, 70: 91–105.

Vaskovics, L. A., Garhammer, M., Schneider, N. F., and Job, O. (1994). *Familien und Haushaltsstrukturen in der ehemaligen DDR und in der Bundesrepublik Deutschland von 1980–1989: Ein Vergleich* [Family and household structures in the former GDR and the Federal Republic of Germany, 1980–1989: A comparison]. Materialien zur Bevölkerungswissenschaft, special issue 24. Wiesbaden: Bundesinstitut für Bevölkerungsforschung.

Vassiliou, G. (1966). *Dierevnisis metavliton ypiserchomenon is tin psychodynamikin tis Ellinikis oikogenias* [An exploration of psychodynamic variables of Greek family]. Athens: Athenian Institute of Anthropos.

Vassiliou, V. and Vassiliou, G. (1973). The implicative meaning of the Greek concept of philotimo. *Journal of Cross-Cultural Psychology*, 4: 326–341.

Vayda, A. P. and McKay, B. (1975). New directions in ecology and ecological anthropology. *Annual Review of Anthropology*, 4: 293–306.

Vayda, A. P. and Rappoport, R. (1968). Ecology, cultural and non-cultural. In J. Clifton (ed.), *Cultural anthropology*, pp. 477–497. Boston, MA: Houghton Mifflin.

Vijver, F. J. R. van de (2006). *Culture and psychology: A SWOT analysis of cross-cultural psychology*. In Q. Jing, H. Zhang, and K. Zhang (eds.), *Psychological science around the world*, vol. 2, pp. 279–298. London: Psychology Press.

Vijver, F. J. R. van de and Leung. K. (1997). *Methods and data analyses for cross-cultural research*. Newbury Park, CA: Sage.

Vijver, F. J. R. van de and Poortinga, Y. H. (2002). Structural equivalence in multilevel research. *Journal of Cross-Cultural Psychology*, 33: 141–156.

Wadia, D. N. (1966). *The geology of India*, 3rd edn. London: Macmillan.

Wagstaff, M. (2001). Family size in the Peloponnese (southern Greece) in 1700. *Journal of Family History*, 26: 337–349.

Waite, J. and Heydari, J. (1995). *Iran. Earth, wind and water.* Tehran, Iran: Yassavoli Press.

Warrin, J., Solomon, Y., Lewis, C., and Langford, W. (1999). *Fathers, work and family life*. London: Family Policy Studies Centre.

Watkins, D., Mortazavi, S., and Trofimova, I. (2000). Independent and interdependent conceptions of self: An investigation of age, gender and culture differences in importance and satisfaction ratings. *Cross Cultural Research*, 34: 113–134.

Weber, M. ([1904] 1958). *The Protestant ethic and the spirit of capitalism*. Translated by T. Parsons. New York: Charles Scribner's Sons.

Weisner, T. S., Bradley, C., and Kilbride, P. L. (1997). *African families and the crisis of social change*. Westport, CT: Bergin and Garvey.

Weiss, J. (2000). *To have and to hold: Marriage, the baby boom, and social change*. Chicago, IL: University of Chicago Press.

Werner, C., Brown, B., and Altman, I. (1997). Environmental psychology. In J. W. Berry, M. H. Segall, and Ç. Kağıtçıbaşı (eds.), *Handbook of cross-cultural Psychology*, vol. 3 *Social behavior and applications*, pp. 253–290. Boston, MA: Allyn and Bacon.

Westen, D. (1985). *Self and society*. Cambridge: Cambridge University Press.

Westermarck, E. A. (1894–1901). *History of human marriage*.

White, L. and Rogers, S., (2000). Economic circumstances and family outcomes: A review of the 1990s. *Journal of Marriage and the Family*, 62: 1035–1051.

Whitehead, B. D. and Popenoe, D. (2003). *The state of our unions: The social health of marriage in America. The National Marriage Project*. Retrieved from http://marriage.rutgers. edu/Publications.

Whiten, A., Goodall, J., McGrew, W. C., Nishida, T., Reynolds, V., Sugiyama, Y., Tutin, C. E. G., Wrangham, R. W., and Boesch, C. (1999). Cultures in chimpanzees. *Nature*, 399: 682–685.

Whiting, J. W. M. (1974). *A model for psychocultural research*. Annual Report, Washington, DC: American Anthropological Association.

(1981). Environmental constraints on infant care practices. In R. H. Munroe, R. L. Munroe, and B. B. Whiting (eds.), *Handbook of cross-cultural development*, pp. 155-179. New York: Garland

Whiting, J. W. M. and Child, I. L. (1953). *Child training and personality*. New Haven, CT: Yale University Press.

Wilke, J. R. (1993). Changes in US mens' attitudes toward the family provider role, 1972–1989. *Gender and Society*, 2: 261–279.

Williams, J. E. and Best, D. L. (1982). *Measuring sex stereotypes: A thirty nation study*. Beverly Hills, CA: Sage.

(1990). *Measuring sex stereotypes: A multination study*. Beverly Hills, CA: Sage.

Williams, J. E., Satterwhite, R. C., and Saiz, J. L. (1998). *The importance of psychological traits: A cross-cultural study*. New York: Plenum.

Williamson, J., Softas-Nall, B., and Miller, J. (2003). Experiences and emotions of grandparents raising grandchildren: Their experiences and emotions. *The Family Journal*, 11: 23–32.

Witkin, H. and Berry, J. W. (1975). Psychological differentiation in cross-cultural perspective. *Journal of Cross-Cultural Psychology*, 6: 4–87.

World Bank (2000). *Living standards measurement study*. Washington, DC: DECRG-LSMS section.

(2002). *World development report 2002*. New York: Oxford University Press.

Wu, D. Y. H. and Tseng, W. S. (1985). Introduction: The characteristics of Chinese culture. In W. S. Tseng and D. Y. H. Wu (eds.), *Chinese culture and mental health*, pp. 3–13. Orlando, FL: Academic Press.

Yanagisako, S. J. (1979). Family and household: The analysis of domestic groups. *Annual Review of Anthropology*, 8: 161–205.

Yang, C. F. (1988). Familism and development: An examination of the role of family in contemporary China Mainland, Hong Kong, and Taiwan. In D. Sinha and H. S. R. Kao (eds.), *Social values and development: Asian perspectives*, pp. 93–123. London: Sage.

Yang, K.-S. (1986). Chinese personality and its change. In M. H. Bond (ed.), *The psychology of Chinese people*, pp. 106–170. New York: Oxford University Press.

(1995). Chinese social orientation: An integrative analysis. In T. Y. Lin, W. S. Tseng, and E. K. Yeh (eds.), *Chinese societies and mental health*, pp. 19–39. Hong Kong: Oxford University Press.

(1996). The psychological transformation of the Chinese people as a result of societal modernization. In M. H. Bond (ed.), *The handbook of Chinese psychology*, pp. 479–498. Hong Kong: Oxford University Press.

Yeh, M. H. (1990). "Chinese familism and its change" [In Chinese]. Unpublished manuscript.

Young, M. and Willmott, P. (1957). *Family and kinship in East London*. Glencoe, IL: The Free Press.

Zach, U. (2003). Familien im Kulturvergleich [Families across cultures]. In H. Keller (ed.), *Handbuch der Kleinkindforschung*, 3rd edn., pp. 321–352. Bern, Germany: Huber.

Zadoenko, L. (1999). *Shlioybi i rozlutsenia v Ukraini* [Marriage and divorce in Ukraine]. Retrieved November 20, 2002, from http://www.ukrstat.gov.ua.

Zaman, R. M. (1992). Psychotherapy in the Third World: Some impressions from Pakistan. In U. P. Gielen, L. L. Adler, and N. A. Milgram (eds.), *Psychology in international perspective*, pp. 314–321. Amsterdam: Swets and Zeitlinger.

Zatsepin, V. I. (1991). *Molodaya semya* [Young family]. Kiev, Ukraine.

Zill, N., and Rogers, C. (1988). Recent trends in the well-being of children in the United States and their implications for public policy. In A. J. Cherlin, (ed.), *The changing American family and public policy*, pp. 31–115. Washington, DC: Urban Institute Press.

Zinkewych, O. and Hula, V. (1993) *Ukraine*. Ellicott City, MD: Smoloskyp.

Index